"A fantastic compendium of great Hollywood stories"
—PHYLLIS DILLER

"*Hollywood Anecdotes* shares a world of beautiful memories and touches my heart."
—MARY MARTIN

"This should be extremely fascinating to the public interested in the history of motion pictures brought to the present."
—JANET LEIGH

"A grand and glorious aggregation of glimpses at filmdom's Golden Age—and then some"
—JOAN BENNETT

"Terrific! For those who love Hollywood trivia"
—TIPPI HEDREN

"A fine job...brought back many memories of the people I have known throughout my career."
—GENE AUTRY

"This is a delightful collection. Even Plutarch would have been amused if he'd lived in this century."
—ROSEMARY DeCAMP

Books by Paul F. Boller, Jr.

George Washington and Religion (1963)
Quotemanship (1967)
American Thought in Transition, 1865–1900 (1967)
American Transcendentalism, 1830–1860 (1974)
Freedom and Fate in American Thought (1978)
Presidential Anecdotes (1981)
Presidential Campaigns (1984)
A More Perfect Union, with Ronald Story (1984)

Books by Ronald L. Davis

A History of Opera in the American West (1965)
Opera in Chicago: A Social and Cultural History (1966)
The Social and Cultural Life of the 1920s (1972)
A History of Music in American Life (3 volumes) (1980–82)

HOLLYWOOD ANECDOTES

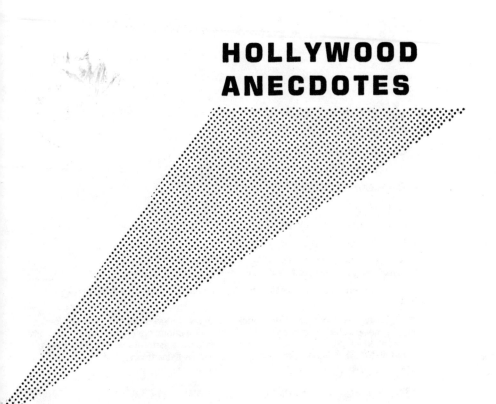

PAUL F. BOLLER, JR.
RONALD L. DAVIS

WILLIAM MORROW
AND COMPANY, INC.
NEW YORK

Library of Congress Cataloging-in-Publication Data

Boller, Paul F.
  Hollywood anecdotes.
  Bibliography: p.
  Includes index.
  1. Moving-picture industry—California—Los Angeles—
Anecdotes, facetiae, satire, etc. 2. Hollywood (Los
Angeles, Calif.)—Social life and customs—Anecdotes,
facetiae, satire, etc. I. Davis, Ronald L. II. Title.
PN1993.5.U65B65   1987   384'.8'0979494   87-11287
ISBN 0-688-05875-2

Printed in the United States of America

First Edition

1 2 3 4 5 6 7 8 9 10

BOOK DESIGN BY PANDORA SPELIOS

EKA 2

Permissions

A screenwriter wrote to tell a producer he was dedicating his first novel to him and soon after received a telegram: PLEASE ADVISE DATE OF CEREMONY AND WHAT I SHOULD WEAR.

Wear whatever you like, Jeff Barnard and Joe B. Frantz, to whom we dedicate this book. We won't stand on ceremony.

Preface

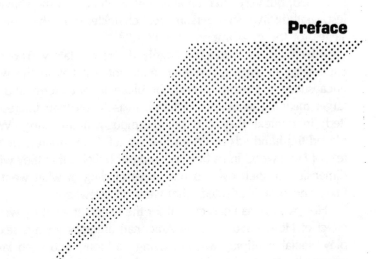

There's a story among movie people that when Gertrude Stein returned to New York after visiting Hollywood in the 1930s, someone asked her: "What is it like—out there?" "There *is* no 'there'—there," Stein is reported to have exclaimed. She was being facetious. There was plenty out there (though perhaps too helter-skelter for her taste), and what was out there has fascinated people, high and low, for decades. When John F. Kennedy invited writer-director Billy Wilder to dinner at the White House, the latter was all set to discuss world affairs, but found the President interested only in movie gossip. "When in the world," he asked Wilder right off, "are they going to finish *Mutiny on the Bounty?*" JFK always relished stories about Hollywood.[1]

Tales of Hollywood, authentic and apocryphal, exist in abundance. In *Hollywood Anecdotes,* we have recounted some of the best of them for the enlightenment, edification, and, we hope, enjoyment of both film-lover and general reader, and we have tried our best to distinguish fact from factoid in the telling. Some of the stories we tell strike us as highly dramatic; others, as hilarious; and still others, as rather poignant. But all of them, we believe, cast light on some aspect of filmmaking in Hollywood, from its beginning in the Silent Era before World War I until its present status as largely a purveyor of R-rated movies for teenagers. "In a drop of dew," British historian Lewis Namier pointed out years ago, "can be seen the colors of the sun." But Plutarch said it first: "Nor is it always in the most distinguished achievements that men's virtues or vices may be best discerned; but very often an action of small note, a short saying, or a jest, shall distinguish a person's real character more than the greatest sieges, or the most important battles."[2]

Anecdotes, as Plutarch recognized, are revelatory. Though often captivating in themselves, their main interest lies in the way they encapsulate a person, period, or place in brief form and convey larger meaning to us in shorthand. In isolation their interest is limited; in context they can be enormously illuminating. We have placed the hundreds of stories that we tell here squarely in the context of Hollywood in its heyday, and our belief is that they will add a dimension of their own to our understanding of what went on out there and how it affected what went on elsewhere.

Hollywood has been crucial for the twentieth-century world. The effect of Hollywood films on American attitudes toward sex, work, play, social relations, ways of living, fashions, and even language, especially during its Golden Era in the thirties and forties, has been prodigious. American movies have also been tremendously influential abroad. As Allied forces liberated one European country after another from Nazi rule during World War II, it was said that the first request of the people was for food, and the second for an American movie. And in Japan, the emperor had barely decreed surrender in August 1945 before Tokyo's leading movie house was showing an old prewar (and somewhat moth-eaten) American film, *The Call of the Yukon,* to a standing-room-only audience, and Japanese youths dressed like Charlie Chaplin's Little Tramp were traipsing up and down the streets to the unconcealed delight of pedestrians. When Dublin-born Mashey M. Bernstein decided to become an American citizen in May 1985, he gave major credit for his decision to American movies. "The America I love and believe in is one of stark individuality, bold adventure and honest iconoclasm," he wrote in *Newsweek.* "It is an America comprised of Shane's defense of the innocent, Dorothy's sense of wonder, Dirty Harry's cockiness, Scarlett O'Hara's determination, Mr. Smith's sense of right and wrong, and Tom Joad's honesty in *The Grapes of Wrath.*"[3]

Hollywood has been lavish as well as intrusive. At its height in the 1930s and 1940s it was producing enough films, grade A's and B's, to fill up every day of the year with a new movie—and leap year too, for that matter. Some of the best productions were very good indeed; and even some of the B's were not without merit. Though American film critics have tended to disparage Hollywood's offerings, European filmmakers, from Russia's Sergei Eisenstein in the 1920s to France's Jean-Luc Godard in the 1960s, have been appreciative. "To see a film by Griffith, Hawks, Cukor, Hitchcock, Mankiewicz," wrote French director Eric Rohmer in 1955, "or even a comedy, a thriller or a Western by a lesser-known signatory, has always been enough to reassure me and convince me that for the talented and dedicated filmmaker the California coast is not that den of iniquity that some would have us believe. It is rather that chosen land, that haven which Florence was for painters of the Quattrocentro or Vienna for musicians in the nineteenth century."[4] Moviemaking has been the one art, historian Arthur Schlesinger, Jr., insists, in which the United States has excelled. "Delete the American contribution from music, dance, painting, sculpture, even perhaps from poetry and the novel, even more doubtfully, from architecture," he once wrote, "and the world's achievement is only marginally diminished." But, he added, "Movies without the American contribution are inconceivable."[5]

Schlesinger was struck by the zest, creativity, and excitement Hollywood filmmakers brought to their work in the 1930s. Making movies in those days was clearly a labor of love and loyalty for most Hollywoodians. When Orson Welles first visited a Hollywood studio in the mid-thirties he could barely conceal his boyish glee. "This," he cried, "is the biggest electric train any boy ever had!" There was, to be sure, the celebrated "Hollywood Lament"—"This is a dirty business. It ruins your digestion; it undermines your self-respect; it drives you nuts"—but it was invariably capped by the Hollywood Exultation: "I wouldn't be doing anything else for the world!"[6] The old-time moguls were "monsters and pirates and bastards right down to the bottom of their feet," director Richard Brooks reflected in 1970, "but they *loved* movies. They loved *making* movies, they loved *seeing* movies. . . ."[7] At the 1948 preview of *Key Largo*, starring Humphrey Bogart and Lauren Bacall, Jack Warner stood gleefully in the lobby afterward, greeting people as they came out of the auditorium. "Great picture!" he exclaimed. "How do you like it, little lady, it's a powerful picture, don't you think?"[8]

In *Hollywood Anecdotes* we have tried to recapture the zest, energy, verve, and sheer fun involved in moviemaking in America. We have written essays about various aspects of Hollywood life and work to go with the stories we tell about it; and while our book is not a comprehensive history of the American film industry, it is no mere book of gossip about film stars either. There is history: essays and stories dealing with Hollywood's evolution from a tiny business turning out crude little silent films for penny arcades and nickelodeons into one of America's leading industries, producing highly sophisticated sound films, garbed in color and enhanced by technical effects that would have stupefied the earliest filmmakers. There is also analysis: stories and essays describing the work of the different kinds of craftsmen (for filmmaking is a collective art) who put the films together—producers, directors, writers, editors, crew members, and musicians. We have said something here, too, about the role of censorship in guiding filmmakers (for censorship had a stimulating as well as a restricting effect) during Hollywood's Periclean Age, and what difference Supreme Court decisions in the 1960s ending censorship made. And there is a discussion of the movie industry's response to the challenge of television in the 1950s, with appropriate tales chronicling that response.

The bulk of the book, of course, has to do with the film stars themselves (the sex queens, the macho guys, the comics, the supporting actors and actresses), for it was they who, for good or ill, penetrated most deeply into the American consciousness and shaped foreign perceptions of American thought and civilization. Many of Hollywood's celebrities were typecast, but most of them appeared in a variety of film genres: dramas, comedies, musicals, Westerns, epics, horror and suspense pictures, biopics, and classics based on literary masterpieces. And to understand what Hollywood was doing it has been necessary to say something about each of the different kinds of films in which the stars were featured. There are chapters, too, on the sexual images appearing on the screen, on films containing social significance, on the lowly but popular B pictures, and on the behavior of film folk on set and off. Our main emphasis has been on the good old Golden Days of Hollywood picture-making.

The day after the Japanese attack on Pearl Harbor in December 1941 and President Roosevelt's call for a declaration of war by Congress, MGM mogul Louis B. Mayer held a luncheon for studio executives and reminded the somber group of the dangerous times in which they lived, expressed the studio's determination to do all it could to support the war effort, and then lifted his wineglass and declared: "Gentlemen, I think it fitting at this time that we drink a toast to our President. . . ." He paused for everyone to lift his glass and then said solemnly: "To our President . . . Nicholas M. Schenck."[9] If Mayer's toast is deliciously revealing, so is the exchange between stage stars Alfred Lunt and Lynne Fontanne, who made a film, *The Guardsman*, for MGM in 1931. Fontanne was the first to see the film's rushes and she was devastated. "Alfred," she wailed, "we're ruined. You photograph without lips and I come out old and haggard and ugly and I lisp and I walk like an elephant. I look like I forgot my lines, my feet are big, I look and sound terrible." But as she started weeping, Lunt murmured: "No lips, eh?"[10]

But Hollywood wasn't Vanity Fair for all its denizens. "Ah, stardom," actor Lee Marvin once told *The Hollywood Reporter*. "They put your name on a star in the sidewalk on Hollywood Boulevard and you walk down and find a pile of dog manure on it. That tells the whole story, baby!" James Cagney once refused to do an interview after retiring from movies because he regarded his—and most films—as "sculpture in snow." His point is arguable, his modesty refreshing. More common is the story told (and retold) about the movie star who, meeting an old hometown friend at a party, discoursed at length on her movie appearances and then paused suddenly and exclaimed: "But tell me something about yourself, dear . . . How did you like my last movie?"[11]

Sources for stories like these are varied: autobiographies, memoirs, and biographies of the filmmakers and performers; news stories about what was going on in the film capital; and magazine articles about Hollywood and its doings. But one of the major sources for our book has been the records of the Oral History Program on the Performing Arts at Southern Methodist University in Dallas, Texas. Founded in 1973 and headed by Ronald L. Davis, professor of history at SMU, the Oral History Collection there has accumulated over 450 taped interviews with performers in films, on the stage, and in the concert hall, ranging all the way from the character actor Ralph Bellamy (who played second man in dozens of Columbia run-of-the-mill programmers), to the highly gifted and versatile Lillian Gish, who started making silent films in 1912 and was still appearing in movies in the 1980s.

In Hollywood, as in the academic world, there is a great deal of foolishness, but there is a lot of creative enterprise as well. In *Hollywood Anecdotes* we have tried to show what America's film center was like, especially during its Golden Days, with its grievous shortcomings as well as its glorious achievements.

Contents

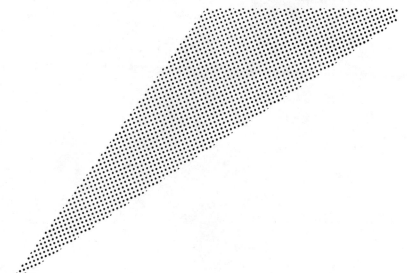

I. THE
BEGINNING

Penny Arcades
and
Nickelodeons

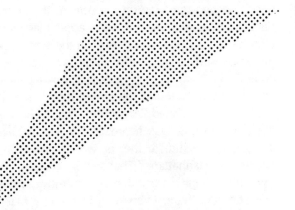

To see the first movies cost only a penny: about what it took to buy an apple, some nails, a roll, or a piece of candy. But they didn't appear on a silver screen; they were run off in Kinetoscopes, that is, battery-operated peep-boxes, which were available, along with phonographs, marble games, and strength machines, in penny arcades in the main part of town. For a time they were almost as popular as video games today.

The Kinetoscope, invented in 1889, was easy to operate. You simply put a penny in the coin slot, turned a crank, and then, as the film rolled, you saw a little show lasting about a minute: Fatima doing her belly dance, horses galloping along a road, trains headed down the track toward you. The first Kinetoscopes began appearing in the early 1890s and went over big with people looking for low-priced entertainment. Soon there were penny arcades in the business sections of most cities, containing rows of Kinetoscopes lined up for the delectation of the masses.

Thomas A. Edison designed the Kinetoscope, but he didn't think much of it. He regarded it as a mere toy, though he enjoyed the profits it was making. When his associates suggested devising ways of projecting the film's image on the screen, he balked. "No," he said, "if we make this screen machine that you are asking for, it will spoil everything. Let's not kill the goose that lays the golden egg."[1]

Without projection, though, the goose would probably have died, and Edison finally came around. On April 23, 1896, he unveiled his Vitascope, a primitive projection machine, at Koster & Bial's Music Hall in New York City.

Edison's Vitascope show was a sensation. When a white screen descended from above, the lights went down, and some "living pictures" began appearing on the screen, the audience was stunned at first, then spellbound. People applauded loudly as two young blondes did an umbrella dance on the screen, screamed in fright as the angry surf rolled toward them, and laughed heartily when two comedians engaged in a burlesque boxing match. "So enthusiastic was the appreciation of the crowd long before the extraordinary exhibition was finished," reported The New York Times, "that vociferous cheering was heard."[2] Theater manager Charles Frohman thought the legitimate theater would never be the same after that evening in Manhattan. "That settles scenery," he told a reporter resignedly. "Painted trees that do not move, waves that get up a few feet and stay there, everything in scenery that we simulate on our stage will have to go. Now that art can make us believe that we see actual, living nature, the dead things of the stage must go."[3]

The stage, of course, stayed, but movies moved on. Soon after Edison's New York show, vaudeville theaters began acquiring Vitascopes and making the new moving pictures an integral part of their daily bills. Train and surf scenes, comedy routines, dances, and episodes from stage plays dominated their programs, but there were efforts to present current events as well: President William McKinley at his home in Canton, Ohio, the sinking of the Maine in 1898 (simulated in a bathtub), and the fighting in Cuba (also simulated) during the Spanish-American War. But the novelty of the Vitascope eventually wore off and vaudeville's middle-class patrons started getting bored with the little piecemeal shows it projected. At length, movies ended up as "chasers" at the end of vaudeville shows, to be run off as people were leaving. It looked as though the goose were cooked after all.

At this point the proprietors of the penny arcades revived the dying bird. Though still featuring Kinetoscopes, they decided to acquire the Vitascopes that the vaudeville theaters were discarding and see if they could attract people to their stores with pictures on the screen. They also began taking films out of the Kinetoscopes, splicing them together to produce shows lasting ten or more minutes, and then setting aside a room in back or upstairs in which to run them off on the Vitascope. To their surprise and joy, the immigrant masses in the big cities took to the screen shows at once and began flocking in large numbers to see them.

In 1902, a Los Angeles enterpriser threw out all the Kinetoscopes, turned his whole arcade into a place for projecting pictures on a screen, called it "The Electric Theater," and began offering "Up-to-Date High-Class Motion Picture Entertainment Especially for Ladies and Children."[4] Three years later two exhibitors in McKeesport, Pennsylvania, near Pittsburgh, converted their store into a fancy theater with a colorful front and an elegant interior and began advertising a twenty-minute film show, accompanied by piano and phonograph music, for only five cents. They also coined a name for their theater: "nickelodeon." The price was modest but the name fancy.

The McKeesport nickelodeon was a huge success. From morning until midnight its ninety-odd seats were always filled, and some people even paid to stand in back to watch the screen. The lure of profits—more than a thousand dollars a week—soon led enterprisers in other cities to follow suit, and they began renting vacant stores everywhere and converting them into movie theaters. Within a year Pittsburgh had one hundred nickelodeons; within three years the United States had close to ten thousand. "If the nickel delirium continues to maintain its present hold," wrote one observer, "there will be in a few years more of these cheap amusements than saloons."[5]

The "nickel delirium" would doubtless have subsided had filmmakers continued to grind out the same old stuff: comic bits, chases, scenes from popular stage plays, news events, dances, and acrobatic acts. In France, though, Georges Méliès, and in the United States, cameraman Edwin S. Porter, an admirer of Méliès, began experimenting with something new: the film narrative. Porter's first important film with a story, *The Life of an American Fireman* (1903), showing fire fighters going to the rescue of a woman and child in a burning building, was skillfully edited although it seems primitive today. But one of his next narrative films, *The Great Train Robbery* (1903), which he planned as a "spectacular," is still fun to watch. Lasting about twelve minutes, it tells the story of a mail train held up by armed bandits, the organization of a posse to pursue them, and the capture and destruction of the gunmen at the end. To titillate audiences Porter included a big close-up of one of the cowboys firing his pistol directly at the camera. "This scene," exhibitors were told, "can be used to begin or end the picture."[6]

Porter's *The Great Train Robbery*, the first real American movie, was a "smasheroo," as Hollywood would later put it, and gave the movie industry a big boost. When it unrolled on the screen for the first time, people in the audience shouted, "Catch 'em" and "Get 'em," roared their approval at the picture's end, and insisted on seeing it over again. Most nickel theaters chose the Porter picture as their initial offering when they opened their doors and they revived it frequently in the years that followed. Porter went on to film more stories for the nickelodeons, and scores of other moviemakers did the same. By 1909, *American Magazine*'s drama critic reported, with some astonishment, "almost one hundred and ninety miles of film are unrolled on the screens of America's seven thousand canned theaters every day in the year."[7]

America's first narrative films were short (one reel), lasting only twelve to fourteen minutes, and many of them dealt with realistic issues of interest to the nickelodeon's working-class audiences: strikes, economic exploitation, poverty, and graft. But respectable people turned up their noses at them as "cheap shows for cheap people," and complained about some of the titles: *Capital vs. Labor, The Long Strike, The Girl Strike Leader, From the Submerged, Lily of the Tenements*.[8] The *Chicago Tribune* thought the influence of films was "wholly vicious" and the *Christian Leader* excoriated moviemakers as a "set of revolutionaries training for the overthrow of government."[9] Before long, middle-class reformers were organizing boards of censorship at both the state and national levels and commencing the long struggle to keep filmmaking within the bounds of social and economic propriety.

Some observers took a benign but pedagogic view of the new mass medium. Novelist William Dean Howells, for one, liked movies but wanted them used mainly in the public schools for educational purposes. Britain's George Bernard Shaw saw things more clearly: A movie, he pointed out in an interview, "is educating you far more effectively when you think it is only amusing you."[10] Movies, as Shaw foresaw, did become a powerful educational force, but not in the classroom, for moviegoers wanted entertainment, not erudition. But they learned plenty from the screen too. "I enjoy these shows," said a Harlem store clerk in 1907, "for they continually introduce me to new places and new people. If I ever go to Berlin or Paris I will know what the places look like. . . . I know what a fight in an alley in Stamboul looks like; have seen a paper-mill in full operation, from the cutting of the timber to the stamping of the pulp;

have seen gold mined by hydraulic sprays in Alaska, and diamonds dug in South Africa. I know a lot of the pictures are fake, but what of that? It costs only five cents."[11]

A Kiss Is But a Kiss
The first movie kiss—between stage stars May Irwin and John C. Rice—came in 1896 and produced a storm. Though *The Kiss,* as the film was called, lasted only fifty feet, it roused the wrath of a prim publisher in Chicago named Herbert S. Stone. "Neither participant is physically attractive," he exclaimed, "and the spectacle of their prolonged pasturing on each other's lips was hard to bear." Pronouncing the film "absolutely disgusting," he called for "police interference." But the *New Orleans Daily Item* leaped to the defense. "Kissing," observed the editor, "has been a custom time out of mind." American filmmakers perpetuated the custom.[12]

Apple-Tree Girl
A filmmaker once requested information about the daily receipts of the Kinetoscopes in one penny arcade and received the following breakdown: *U.S. Battleship at Sea,* 25 cents; Joseph Jefferson in *Rip's Sleep,* 43 cents; *Ballet Dancer,* $1.05; *Girl Climbing Apple Tree,* $3.65. "I think," he mused, "we had better have some more of the 'Girl-Climbing-Apple-Tree kind.'"[13]

Films vs. Theater
Sigmund "Pop" Lubin prospered with the films he made for the nickelodeons at his Philadelphia studio, but he was never convinced he was in the right business. "I was a fool to go into making movies instead of producing plays," he once told a friend. "In the theater an actor can rush on stage and yell, 'The ship has sunk with all on board!' In the movies you have to spend five thousand dollars to show the ship sinking. And actors can get drowned . . . and sue you!"[14]

From Stage to Screen
After seeing a film version of one of his performances on the stage, an actor told a dramatic critic that it "was the most extraordinary experience I ever went through—actually to see myself acting." "Now," sighed the critic, "you understand what we have to put up with."[15]

Sound Effects

In Burlington, New Jersey, a projectionist seized a bare electric wire rather than the switch in his projector and shrieked for help as a current of 1,000 volts shot through his body. But the audience thought it was a phonographic accompaniment to the blood-and-thunder picture on the screen and applauded loudly. Finally the piano player saw what was happening and turned off the current.[16]

Auto Race

One nickelodeon was showing a film of a great French auto race and suddenly, in the most exciting part, the film broke and the projectionist stopped the show in order to splice. "Oh hell!" cried a rough-looking lumberman in the audience. "The race'll be over before he gits the dern machine fixed!"[17]

Audience Participation

In a Pittsburgh nickelodeon a man in the audience got so worked up over seeing some men push a woman around in the film he was watching that he suddenly jumped up, pulled out a gun, and fired five shots at the figures on the screen, thus precipitating a panic. As the police hauled him off to jail, he muttered that it was "a shame to let those men ill-treat a woman" that way.[18]

Hard of Hearing

A couple of slightly befuddled New Yorkers entered a nickelodeon when the pianist was taking a break. "What are those fellows in that pictur' saying, Mike?" asked the first. "Shure, I can't hear a word," wheezed his companion. "Let's get a seat further up front."[19]

CHAPTER 2

Silent Features

The Nickelodeon Era was short-lived. After 1908 the price of admission to movies began climbing: to a dime and then a quarter and even to thirty-five cents in some theaters.

The double-digit inflation produced few complaints. Moving pictures, after all, were becoming longer, more expensive to produce, and better in quality. What came to be called "feature pictures," several reels long, began replacing the old one-reelers and attracting middle-class audiences to the movie houses in large numbers for the first time. As early as 1912 a writer for the *Moving Picture World* was looking forward to the production of "feature plays" that would "help us understand those problems of human nature which only Genius can purposely and patiently unravel, which tend to develop our ever-increasing capacity for knowledge and happiness."[1] (Solemnity, the gift of the Puritans to the nation, shaped much film commentary from the outset.)

The appearance of feature pictures transformed the film industry. With features came the "star system," accompanied by floods of publicity about leading performers, torrents of fan mail from all over the world, and the appearances of dozens of idolatrous fan magazines, chock-full of fact, fiction, and fantasy, circulating widely. To show the new feature pictures, moreover, posh new movie palaces began springing up and replacing the dingy old storefront nickelodeons in all the nation's big cities. And to make the new pictures, filmmakers were moving to California just before World War I to take advantage of the pleasant climate and varied terrain there, and centering their activities on the little town of Hollywood, a suburb of Los Angeles. Gradually, as movie production developed into a big business during and after World War I, Hollywood became the film capital of the world. It also became a magical name, connoting luxury, glamour, adventure, and sexual excitement for millions of film-lovers around the globe.

It's hard to believe: There was considerable resistance at first to making pictures longer than one reel. Grinding out one-reelers for the nickelodeons was extremely profitable, and the businessmen running things saw no reason to change their ways. Moviegoers, they were convinced, couldn't or wouldn't sit still long enough to watch pictures more than ten or twelve minutes long. The Motion Picture Patents Company, a powerful organization made up of the nation's largest producers and distributors, decreed one reel as the length for all its films; and the Film Service Association, a group of exhibitors, meeting in New York on January 30, 1910, went on record as being strongly opposed to any reel over nine hundred feet in length. When David Wark Griffith made a two-reel picture, *Enoch Arden,* in 1911, Biograph Company released the two reels separately. Only after audiences protested did exhibitors begin showing both reels on the same program.

In Europe, to Griffith's envy and dismay, filmmakers were producing movies even longer than *Enoch Arden.* In France, actress Sarah Bernhardt made a four-reel version of the play *Queen Elizabeth* (1912), which, brought to this country by nickelodeon proprietor Adolph Zukor, did nicely in his theaters and confirmed his belief that moviegoers wanted longer pictures. Italy's eight-reeler, *Quo Vadis?* (1912), did even better when presented as a "special attraction" at hiked prices in legitimate theaters in New York City and elsewhere. Chafing at the restrictions his employers at Biograph placed on him, Griffith sneaked out to California with his crew in 1913 and produced *Judith of Bethulia* in four reels, which Biograph reluctantly released after keeping it on the shelf for a year or so. Meanwhile Zukor organized the Famous Players Company to film popular Broadway plays, with the stars playing their stage roles in the film. But the future of movies, as Zukor himself came to realize, did not lie with filmed stage plays or with the extremely static kind of features being imported from Europe. The future lay with directors like Griffith, who early realized that moving pictures had to develop their own special ways of presenting things if they were to be of any lasting interest.

Griffith was a remarkable innovator. With considerable justification he has been called the "father of film technique," the "king of directors," and the "father of the film art." He was an indefatigable experimenter in the new medium—in choosing stories and themes, in making use of the camera, in directing his players, and in cutting and editing the completed film—and his influence on moviemakers in his own day and for years afterward has been prodigious. "The task I'm trying to achieve," he once said, "is above all to make you see."[2] He did just that: with close-ups, long shots, vistas and vignettes, iris effects, fade-ins and fade-outs. He filmed Shakespeare, Tolstoy, Poe, Maupassant, Cooper, and Tennyson for the working-class people who crowded the nickelodeons. His cinematic adaptation of Robert Browning's *Pippa Passes*, said a writer for *The New York Times*, surprised and pleased, "is being given in the nickelodeons and Browning is being presented to the average motion picture audiences, who have received it with applause and are asking for more."[3] When, at long last, movie executives approved longer pictures for the masses, Griffith went to work in 1914 on what was to be one of the most famous films of all times: *The Birth of a Nation*.

Based on Thomas Dixon's novel and play *The Clansman*, a strident glorification of the Ku Klux Klan, and centered on life in the South during the Civil War and Reconstruction, *The Birth of a Nation* (1915) was a thoroughly racist film. The nation whose birth it celebrated at the end of Reconstruction was based squarely on white supremacy and a paternalistic view of blacks. Griffith arranged a special screening for his twelve-reel movie in the East Room of the White House and was elated when Woodrow Wilson, a Southerner like Griffith himself, exclaimed afterward that it was "like writing history with lightning" and "all so terribly true."[4] But Griffith was surprised and hurt when civil rights leaders in the North vehemently denounced the film and White House spokesmen discreetly disavowed the President's remarks. The celebrated director, for his part, insisted he loved black people and went on to issue a pamphlet calling for "freedom of the screen."

Griffith's racial views were in fact unexceptionable in 1915; most professional historians in those days took a thoroughly Griffithian view of Reconstruction. But Griffith's film was far more than a racial view of the nation; it was an exciting and thoroughly cinematic drama that transcended its parochial outlook and held audiences ev·

erywhere spellbound for more than three hours. Because of its epic scope, narrative sweep, and technical virtuosities, *The Birth of a Nation* was a major turning point in film history and it had the effect of transforming filmmaking, both here and abroad. All subsequent films have been shaped to some extent by Griffith's monumental masterpiece (as well as by his magnificent failure, *Intolerance*, a year later). After Griffith, movies were no longer frivolous diversions for the poor and uneducated; they were taken seriously by people with schooling and status. Nor were they any longer mere imitations of stage plays; they took on an independent life of their own. Griffith's 1915 film, according to film historian Arthur Knight, "established once for all that the film was an art in its own right—and Griffith was its master."[5]

Of course Hollywood continued to turn out carloads of inconsequential films, long and short, after *The Birth of a Nation*. There were countless potboilers during and after World War I whose titillating titles were probably the most novel thing about them: *Sinners in Silk, God Gave Me Twenty Cents, The Golden Bed,* and *The Mad Whirl.* There were also crudely melodramatic cliff-hanging serials, in ten or more chapters, like *The Perils of Pauline,* starring Pearl White, which brought millions of people (not all of them kids) back to the movie houses week after week to see how Pauline had surmounted her newest and truest peril in the previous episode. Even producer-director Cecil B. De Mille's pictures, though full of striking scenes, could scarcely be taken seriously as lasting contributions to the art of films. De Mille featured bathtub and bedroom scenes; he also developed a surefire formula for luring crowds into theaters: religious pictures (like *The Ten Commandments*) in which people who sinned went down to their implacable doom, but had a lot of fun fooling around until doomsday arrived. Even America's favorites—the golden-haired Mary Pickford ("America's Sweetheart"), the exuberant and acrobatic Douglas Fairbanks, the glamorous Gloria Swanson, the darkly handsome Latin lover Rudolph Valentino, and the enigmatic Greta Garbo ("the woman nobody knows, the woman everybody wants to know")—all made films that seem mostly quaint and even comical when viewed today.[6] But Ernst Lubitsch, who came over from Germany in 1922, brought sparkling wit, irony, and sophistication ("the Lubitsch touch") to films like *Forbidden Paradise* (1924) and *So This Is Paris* (1926); and Austrian-born Erich von Stroheim's passion for realistic details and psychological probings make films like *Foolish Wives* (1922), *Greed* (1924), and *The Wedding March* (1928) seem impressive even today. D. W. Griffith himself continued producing films, good and bad, after *The Birth of a Nation*. When *Broken Blossoms*, with Lillian Gish and Richard Barthelmess, was released in 1919, *The New York Times* hailed it as a "masterpiece" and the *Literary Digest* thought it proved once more that, with Griffith, films were becoming a "new art . . . as important as music and poetry."[7]

Hollywood was probably at its best with comedy during the Silent Era. Certainly serious cineasts in Europe thought this was the case, and highbrow critics in the United States for the most part agreed. Writing in 1924, Gilbert Seldes said of America's movies: "The drama film is almost always wrong; the slap-stick almost always right. . . ."[8] Hollywood's serious offerings tended to be slick, pretentious, self-conscious, and overstated. But its comedies were fresh, forthright, breezy, irreverent, and strewn with novelties. Mack Sennett, the "King of Comedy," studied Griffith's techniques when working for him at Biograph and then went off on his own in 1912 as a producer at Keystone Company. From Sennett came scores of one-reelers featuring trouble-prone Bathing Beauties, zany Keystone Kops, careening tin lizzies, frenetic chases, pratfalls for the pompous, and skillfully aimed custard pies for just about everyone. "It's got to *move!*" Sennett insisted, and so his pictures did, from idiocy to absurdity and then back again.[9] Sennett gathered around him an engaging group of inspired clowns to help him make up comedies as they went along: pretty Mabel Normand, cross-eyed Ben Turpin, Roscoe "Fatty" Arbuckle, and talented young women destined for fame like Gloria Swanson and Carole Lombard.

Sennett's greatest discovery was Charlie Chaplin. Chaplin, a pantomimist with a British troupe touring the country, went to work for Keystone in 1913, when he was twenty-four. His experience there was at first disappointing; Sennett's predilection for knockabout antics and breakneck speed just wasn't Chaplin's style. One day Sennett said, "We need some gags here," and told Chaplin, "Put on a comedy make-up. Anything will do." Chaplin improvised: put on big shoes, baggy pants, a tight little coat, a small derby hat, and a false moustache, which he cut down to a dark blur under his nose. With the addition of a cane, he was ready for his "screen test." When he began strutting around in front of Sennett, swinging his cane and tipping his hat when bumping into things, the latter started laughing and, thus assured, Chaplin began explaining what he had in mind. "You know this fellow is many-sided," he said, "a tramp, a gentleman, a poet, a dreamer, a lonely fellow, always hopeful of romance and adventure. He would have you believe he is a scientist, a musician, a duke, a polo player. However he is not above picking up cigarette butts or robbing a baby of its candy. And, of course, if the occasion warrants it, he will kick a lady in the rear—but only in extreme anger!" "All right," cried Sennett in great glee when Chaplin had finished, "get on the set and see what you can do there."[10] What Chaplin did there had everyone, including stagehands and carpenters, howling with laughter. And the Little Tramp, born at Keystone that day, went on to worldwide fame, first in one-reel and two-reel comedies, and then in feature pictures that movie fans loved and intellectuals adored.

Chaplin wasn't Hollywood's only outstanding comedian. Buster Keaton, the Great Stoneface, who, like Chaplin, began with comedy shorts and proceeded to feature-length films, was as good as Chaplin in some respects and in some ways even better. Harold Lloyd, the bespectacled but brash young "gofer," also did skillful work in both two-reelers and features. Chaplin's The Gold Rush (1925) and The Circus (1928) continue to captivate audiences today in a way that most of Hollywood's ponderous silent dramas can never do. But Keaton's Sherlock Jr. (1924) and The General (1927), and Harold Lloyd's Safety Last (1923) are, like Chaplin's masterworks, as fresh and funny for audiences in the late twentieth century as they were for moviegoers early in the century.

By the 1920s Hollywood was one of the most famous cities on earth. For millions of people, young and old, it was a Heavenly City, peopled by unutterably dazzling stars, whose doings on- and off-screen, meticulously chronicled in the daily and weekly press, made it seem to be the real center of creation. It was also an Emerald City to which thousands of aspiring young men and women flocked every year, seeking fame and fortune, and to which millions of tourists trekked to see the lavish mansions of their idols, visit their studios, and perhaps even glimpse them from afar in restaurants and night-clubs. Hollywood was Fashion City, too, introducing designs and setting styles for both men and women here and abroad. Rudolph Valentino made sideburns the vogue for a while; Clara Bow, the "It" girl ("It" equaled sex appeal), popularized the bobbed-hair, short-skirted flapper look. Cecil B. De Mille employed fashion experts to design dresses, hats, shoes, and lingerie for his leading ladies, and the costumes they wore on the screen were zealously copied by women throughout the country.

For old-fashioned Americans, however, Hollywood was Sin City, the sybaritic site for easy sex, drink, and drugs, on-screen and off. By 1922, criticism of Hollywood's manners and morals by the querulous had become so vehement that the major studios organized the Motion Picture Producers and Distributors of America to formulate a "code" that would set limits and bounds to the films they were turning out. But the Production Code, as administered by "Czar" Will Hays, former Postmaster General in President Warren Harding's cabinet, was easily circumvented if one followed De Mille's method: Good always overcomes evil and vice is always punished at the film's end. That way, six reels of sinning and one reel of sobbing became commonplace.

For performers (and other film people as well) Hollywood was really two cities: a city of glamour if one made it to the top, but a city of hard work, too, involving long hours on the set, fierce competition with other players, and the ever-present danger of losing favor with the public. Studio executives had one firm rule, "the customer is always right," and the execution of the rule could be cruel indeed. As public tastes shifted from year to year, there were wild fluctuations in the fortunes of film people. The "It" girl could become the "Ain't" girl overnight; a performer might earn $300,000 one year and be out of work the next. Clara Bow, once famous, lost her box-office appeal and ended by spending long nights at home playing poker in the kitchen with her maid and cook; Richard Arlen, once a movie big shot, descended into B pictures and then into obscurity.

Economic insecurity was pervasive in movietown. And it dogged the studios as well as the stars. Moviemaking was an unending process of trial and error. Each new picture was an experiment; it might make or break a producer, director, or performer. In the late 1920s the Emerald City was clearly in a crisis. Movie attendance was declining rapidly in the United States. The American people seemed to be losing interest in moving pictures and having more fun with their cars and radios. By 1926 the situation was so bad that one major studio, Warner Bros., was headed for bankruptcy. To stave off disaster Warners decided to try out the Vitaphone, a new device for producing sound as well as sight in the movie house. The experiment with sound worked wonderfully; the short "talkies" that Warners released went over even bigger with the public than producers had anticipated, and the studio was soon making feature-length sound films as well. Both *The Jazz Singer* (1927), part talkie, and *Lights of New York* (1928), an all-talking picture, were enormous successes. The public, it was clear, wanted pictures to talk as well as move.

And as other studios began shifting to sound too, people began flocking back into the movie theaters in great numbers. The crisis was over; sound pictures saved Hollywood. By 1929 the Silent Era was suddenly over.

Jerky

D. W. Griffith started out in movies as an extra, but tradition has it that he was no great success at first; on the screen it looked as if he had four arms. It turned out, though, that he deliberately made jerky movements at first because movies jerked on the screen in the early days and he thought that was the way he was supposed to act.[11]

Gish's Ring

As a director, Griffith always made it clear what he expected from performers. Directing Dorothy Gish, Lillian's sister, in a light comedy one day, he told her: "Now, honey, when you open that telegram and learn that [your boyfriend's] coming back to you, you get so excited that you pee a ring around yourself."[12]

Director

The dignified D. W. Griffith sometimes had his "off" moments. "Move these ten thousand horses a trifle to the right," he ordered an assistant one day as his thumb probed one of his large nostrils. "And that mob out there three feet forward," he added, thumb still in nose. While his orders were being carried out, he looked down at a little boy who was watching him in fascination. "Young man," he said, "when you grow up would you like to be a director?" "Naw," drawled the youngster, "my father doesn't let me pick my nose."[13]

Flickers

One day, during a break, one of the girls happened to say something about working in "flickers," and Griffith lost his temper. "Never let me hear that word again in this studio," he cried. "Just remember, you're no longer working in some second-rate theatrical company. What we do here today will be seen tomorrow by people all over America—people all over the world! Just remember that the next time you go before the camera!" After Griffith left the set, Lionel Barrymore told Lillian Gish: "It wasn't so long ago that D.W. himself used to talk scathingly of 'flickers' and 'galloping tintypes.' But now he has a vision. He really believes we're pioneering in a new art—a medium that can cross over barriers of language and culture. That's why he drives himself so hard." Then he added: "And you know, Lillian, I'm beginning to believe he's right."[14]

Selznick and the Czar

Shortly after the overthrow of the Russian czar in 1917, Lewis J. Selznick, a film mogul who had suffered persecution as a Jew when he was a boy growing up in czarist Russia, sent a cable to Nicholas II: WHEN I WAS A POOR BOY IN KIEV SOME OF YOUR POLICEMEN WERE NOT KIND TO ME AND MY PEOPLE STOP I CAME TO AMERICA AND PROSPERED STOP NOW HEAR WITH REGRET YOU ARE OUT OF A JOB OVER THERE STOP FEEL NO ILL WILL WHAT YOUR POLICEMEN DID SO IF YOU WILL COME NEW YORK CAN GIVE YOU FINE POSITION ACTING IN PICTURES STOP SALARY NO OBJECT STOP REPLY MY EXPENSE STOP REGARDS YOU AND FAMILY.[15]

Subtitles

The best silent features used as few title cards as possible, but they all depended on them to some extent for dialogue and for moving the story along. Many of them seem amusing today. WHY ARE YOU SO GOOD TO ME, CHINKY? Lillian Gish asks Richard Barthelmess, who plays a Chinese man, in Broken Blossoms (1919). AFTER TEA AND NOODLES, announces another title card as Barthelmess, the "Yellow Man," trots down the street. Sometimes subtitles were brief and to the point: NEXT MORNING; CAME THE DAWN. Too often, though, they were flowery: PASSION, THAT FURIOUS TASKMASTER, STRIKES WITHOUT WARNING AND LEAVES THE MARK OF ITS LASH ACROSS THE SOUL. In one movie, as screen lover Ramon Novarro clasped his sweetheart to his breast and sailed his canoe down the raging rapids, the title card read DOWN THE VIRGIN FALLS. Occasionally when a dramatic film was previewed, people laughed in the wrong places and producers would hastily insert comedy titles and convert it into a comic film. There were even some comedies transmuted into dramas after previews by the adroit use of captions and title cards. "There was a man named Ralph Spence who did all the titling in those days," according to director Mervyn LeRoy, "and made himself a fortune because he could make a drama comedy or a comedy a drama."[16]

Gish on Ice

Lillian Gish was a remarkable performer. The nicknames were all complimentary: "The World's Darling"; "Queen of the Silent

Drama"; "Lillian the Incomparable"; "The First Lady of the Screen." Her dedication to her work led writer Edward Wagenknecht to call her the "artist's artist" in 1921. "Words, especially prose, seem horribly wooden in discussing her. . . ," he exclaimed. "Hers is a personality which can be adequately described only in terms of music or poetry. . . . In her presence one wants instinctively to talk blank verse. . . ." Declared drama critic George Jean Nathan in the pages of *Vanity Fair:* "That she is one of the few real actresses that the films have brought forth, either here or abroad, is pretty well agreed upon by the majority of critics."

Gish's performance in D. W. Griffith's famous melodrama *Way Down East* (1920) dazzled filmgoers. There were two great outdoor scenes in the picture to which she gave all she had to make them convincing. The first shows her lost in a blizzard, and the second shows her floating down the river on an ice floe toward a towering waterfall. Gish trained hard for the two scenes: did exercises, went on walks in freezing weather, and took cold baths. When a blizzard hit Long Island in March, Griffith was ready to start shooting at Orient Point. It took three men to hold the camera while Gish braved the blizzard, and at one point her face was caked with ice and snow and there were icicles on her eyelashes. Yelled Griffith to cameraman Billy Bitzer above the howling storm: "Billy, move in! That face!— get that face!" "I will," Billy shouted back, "if the oil doesn't freeze in the camera!" Griffith's face froze during the shooting and several men in the crew got pneumonia. But Gish survived it all to do the celebrated ice-floe sequence a week or two later.

The ice-floe scene was shot at White River Junction in Vermont, where the ice was twelve to sixteen inches thick and frozen solid when the *Way Down East* company arrived. Griffith had the ice sawed and dynamited to get pieces for the floating scene, and Gish conceived the idea of letting her hand and hair drag in the water when she was on the ice cake. After a few rehearsals, Gish's hair froze and she felt as if her hand were in a flame. "Not once, but twenty times a day," according to Richard Barthelmess, the male lead, "Lillian floated down on a cake of ice, and I made my way to her, stepping from one cake to another, to rescue her. I had on a heavy fur coat, and if I had slipped, or if one of the cakes had cracked and let me through, my chances would not have been good. As for Lillian, why she did not get pneumonia, I still can't understand. She has a wonderful constitution. . . . No accidents happened. The story that I missed a signal and did not reach Lillian in time, and that she came near going over the falls, would indicate that she made the float on the ice-cake but once. As I say, she made it numberless times, and there were *no falls*. Lillian was never nervous, and never afraid. I don't think either of us thought of anything serious happening, though when I was carrying her, stepping from ice-cake to another, we might easily have slipped in."

At the very end of the rescue scene, there is an instant when the ice cake seems to start over the falls, just as Barthelmess, carrying Lillian, steps onto another cake, and then another, and half-slips into the water before reaching the shore. But the critical moment at the brink of the waterfall was actually made later on in the summer, on a Connecticut farm, and the ice cakes were painted blocks of wood attached to piano wire. There was a real waterfall, fifteen feet high, at this place, and once a carpenter in the crew went over it and hurt himself badly. But in the film Niagara Falls was blended into the Connecticut falls with a startling effect. Years afterward, Barthelmess said to Gish, "I wonder why we went through with it. We could have been killed. There isn't enough money in the world to pay me to do it today." Gish added: "But we weren't doing it for money."

In the 1980s, film critic Michael Wood saw a revival of *Way Down East* in a New York theater filled with giggling and scoffing young people. But when they saw Lillian Gish get herself stranded on the ice floe and head straight for the vast waterfall, they all became suddenly still. And when she was finally rescued, one youngster, previously scornful, cried out in great relief: "Christ Almighty!"[17]

Lip Readers
In Elinor Glyn's *Three Weeks* (1924), silent star Aileen Pringle turned in a nice performance as a queen who runs off to spend three weeks with a young British aristocrat. But the Deaf and Dumb Society reprimanded her severely. In one scene, when Conrad Nagel picks her up with a tender look on his face, her lips are saying: "If you drop me, you———, you———, I'll break your neck!"[18]

Death Scene
When Lillian Gish was preparing for Mimi's tragic end in *La Bohème* (1926), she visited a hospital to study lung disease, lost weight, and finally arrived at the studio so pale and emaciated that director King Vidor feared she might perish if he didn't film the famous death scene at once. But when he came to shoot the scene, Gish played it so

realistically that everyone on the set thought she had actually passed away. She had "completely stopped breathing," Vidor recalled, "and the movement of her eyes and eyelids was absolutely suspended." When the cameras stopped rolling and she remained motionless, Vidor went fearfully over to her and touched her gently on the arm. To his—and everyone else's—immense relief she turned her head slowly and smiled faintly. Gish's performance, Vidor said later, was "the most realistic" he had ever seen. "I hope," he added, "I shall never see a similar one quite so well done."[19]

Fairbanks and Chaplin

One day Charlie Chaplin passed a Hollywood movie house and stopped to look at the posters advertising the Douglas Fairbanks comedy being shown there. Suddenly he noticed a young man watching him. "Have you seen this show?" Chaplin asked him. "Sure," replied the young man. "Any good?" Chaplin wanted to know. "Why, he's the best in the business," cried the young man. "He's a scream! Never laughed so much at anyone in all my life." "Is he as good as Chaplin?" "As good as Chaplin!" cried the young man. "Why, this Fairbanks person has got that Chaplin person looking like a gloom. They're not in the same class. Fairbanks is funny. I'm sorry you asked me, I feel so strongly about it." Announced Chaplin coldly: "I'm Chaplin." "I know you are," laughed the young man. "I'm Fairbanks." It was the beginning of a beautiful friendship.[20]

Difficult

Famous for his acrobatics, Fairbanks was asked once what was the most difficult thing he ever did before a camera and he answered: "Make love."[21]

Goin' Home

In the summer of 1925 Greta Garbo left Europe to make films in Hollywood. Because of her reserve she was called the "Swedish Sphinx" and was quoted as having made two succinct statements: "I want to be alone" and "I t'ank I go home." She probably never said the former, and, as to the latter, there are a couple of theories about its provenance.

According to one story, while making her first American film, *The Torrent*, in 1926, Garbo had to plunge into an icy pool of water for one scene. She emerged, trembling with the cold. "Fine," said the director, "now let's do it again." Once more she plunged into the icy water and came out shivering and shaking. "That's great," beamed the director. "Now let's do it again." At this point Garbo walked around the pool of water, gazed into its clear, cold depths a moment, then picked up her cloak from a chair, and strolled away, saying, "I t'ank I go home."

Another story has it that in 1927 Garbo went to see MGM head Louis B. Mayer to demand more money. "Greta," said Mayer, "haven't I done everything to make you happy here?" "No," she said. "What more can I do?" asked Mayer. "Give me more money," said Garbo. "Why?" cried Mayer. "Think how much better you are since [leaving] Berlin. What kind of money were you making then? Was it anywhere near the six hundred dollars a week we pay you now?" "You are paying Jack Gilbert ten thousand a week," Garbo reminded him. "I see what you mean," said Mayer. "I agree with you; I will make a new arrangement. How much will make you happy?" "Five thousand dollars a week," said Garbo. "I'll give you twenty-five hundred," Mayer told her. "I t'ank I go home," she said. Mayer then caved in; he agreed to $5,000.

Who knows? Perhaps an MGM publicity man, not the Swedish Sphinx, first came up with the famous valedictory. Hollywood thrives on apocryphal aphorisms.[22]

Garbo's Heat
When the script of Tolstoy's *Anna Karenina* was being prepared for Greta Garbo, the producers decided to change the title because they thought a foreign name might confuse audiences. After considering various one-word titles, they finally settled on *Heat*. But screenwriter Frances Marion balked. "I think that would be a good ad for Dante's *Inferno*," she cried, "but I'd hate to see on the billboards—Greta Garbo in *Heat!*" In the end the film was called *Love* (1927).[23]

The Sheik
Rudolph Valentino, the great Latin lover, became a model for many young men in the 1920s. They began calling themselves "sheiks," after Valentino appeared in *The Sheik* (1921). And after he appeared in *Blood and Sand* (1922), playing a Spanish bullfighter, they began cultivating sideburns, sleek hair, and wide-bottomed trousers in the Valentino fashion.

Some people resented the Valentino influence; they thought there was something decadent about it. In 1925, the *Chicago Tribune* ran an unsigned article entitled PINK POWDER PUFFS, calling attention to the fact that the men's room in one of the city's new ballrooms contained a powder machine as well as a soap dispenser.

"A powder dispensing machine!" exclaimed the writer. "In a men's washroom? *Homo Americanus.* Why didn't someone quietly drown Rudolph Guglielmo [sic], alias Valentino, years ago? We personally saw two 'men' . . . insert coins, hold kerchiefs beneath the spout, pull the lever, then take the pretty pink stuff and put it on their cheeks in front of the mirror. . . . Hollywood is the national school of masculinity. Rudy, the beautiful gardener's boy, is the prototype of the American male. Hell's bells. Oh, sugar."

When Valentino saw the *Tribune* article he was outraged. "I'll get his name from the *Tribune,*" he told George Ullman, his agent. "I'll challenge him to a fight in any way he wishes." On July 19, 1926, he wrote a lengthy letter TO THE MAN (?) WHO WROTE THE EDITORIAL HEADED 'PINK POWDER PUFFS' IN SUNDAY'S *TRIBUNE,* in which he said: "You slur my Italian ancestry; you cast ridicule upon my Italian name; you cast a doubt upon my manhood. I call you, in return, a contemptible coward, and to prove which of us is a better man I challenge you to a personal test." Dueling, he went on to say, was illegal, but boxing and wrestling weren't, so he challenged the anonymous writer to meet him "in the boxing or wrestling arena to prove in typically American fashion (for I am an American citizen) which of us is more a man." When there was no response, he sent off another letter to the "Powder Puff Editorialist," saying it was "evident you cannot make a coward fight any more than you can draw blood out of a turnip. . . . I feel I have been vindicated because I consider his silence as a tacit retraction. . . ."

Valentino never heard from the *Tribune* writer. But he did hear from Frank "Buck" O'Neil, boxing writer for the *New York Evening Journal.* O'Neil said Jack Dempsey had told him Valentino packed a he-man punch, but he didn't believe it. "I don't believe Valentino can really fight," O'Neil phoned to tell Ullman, "and I'd like to take him on in a friendly bout myself to prove it. If Valentino is willing to meet me, I'll guarantee not to hurt him." When Valentino heard this, he insisted on having a match as soon as it could be arranged. The two men finally met on the roof garden of New York's Ambassador Hotel for the fight. They sparred lightly for a while and then exchanged sharp blows to the chin. O'Neil followed this up by aiming a punch at the actor's jaw, but he missed. Valentino countered with a blow to the side of O'Neil's head and O'Neil went sprawling to the floor. Valentino helped him up and they went at it again for two more rounds and finally called it quits. "I was wrong about Rudy," O'Neil admitted afterward; and he shook Valentino's hand and said, "You're all man! That punch of yours that knocked me down had the power of a mule's kick. Next time Jack Dempsey tells me something I'm going to believe him."

The following day *The Son of the Sheik* (1926) opened at the Strand theater in New York. Crowds began gathering there at eight in the morning and soon the lines stretched for blocks. When the theater finally opened, the crowd rushed in like a herd of elephants. But Valentino's fans continued to mill about in the streets outside and it took a whole squad of policemen to get the great lover safely past them and into the theater. After the picture was over Valentino made an informal speech, and then tried to leave. Thousands of people were waiting outside, and when he came out, some of his fans broke police lines, rushed up to him, ripped off his tie, tore buttons off his coat, knocked off his hat, and snatched his cuff links as souvenirs. The policemen finally managed to get him into his car. As it pulled away, he told Ullman in disbelief: "Whew! Those New Yorkers almost loved me to death!"

Death came soon after. Valentino had been suffering pains in the abdomen for some time, but he refused to see a doctor. Despite increasing discomfort, he went down to Atlantic City to make an appearance. Not long after, he was stricken with appendicitis, taken to the hospital, and died on August 23, 1926, at thirty-one. His body was laid in state at a funeral home in Manhattan, with the announcement that the public would be allowed to view it. Immediately a crowd of thirty thousand people, mainly women, gathered outside.[24]

Did Good
Cecil B. De Mille once met a breathtakingly beautiful woman at a party and decided to cast her in one of his pictures. But he changed his mind when he discussed acting with her and she announced: "Whatever I have did, I have did good."[25]

Rembrandt
Like D. W. Griffith, Cecil B. De Mille enjoyed experimenting with the camera in order to achieve unusual effects on the screen. Once, when he was directing pictures for the Jesse L. Lasky Feature Play

Company, he borrowed a large lamp from an opera company and placed it in such a way on the set that only half of the hero's face was visible while the other half was in shadow. Pleased by the striking effect he had achieved, he sent the picture to Sam Goldwyn, sales manager for the company in New York, expecting high praise. Instead came a frantic wire: CECIL, YOU'VE RUINED US. YOU'VE LIGHTED ONE-HALF THE ACTOR'S FACE AND THE EXHIBITORS WILL PAY ONLY HALF PRICE. De Mille thought this over for a while and then wired back: IF YOU AND THE EXHIBITORS DON'T KNOW REMBRANDT LIGHTING IT IS NO FAULT OF MINE. Shortly after that came another wire from Goldwyn: CECIL, YOU ARE WONDERFUL, REMBRANDT LIGHTING. THE EXHIBITORS WILL PAY DOUBLE.[26]

De Mille's Fire Stuff

When William De Mille, Cecil's brother, first wrote the screenplay for *We Can't Have Everything* (1918), he included a spectacular fire in the plot that destroys a motion-picture studio and reduces the leading lady to poverty. But studio executives ordered him to keep expenses down, so he reluctantly eliminated the big fire and had the movie company go bankrupt instead. Cecil, who was directing the picture, was disappointed by the change. "You may be right from the story standpoint," he told his brother, "but somehow, to me, a blazing studio with lots of people running around and plenty of physical danger for our heroine is a lot more interesting, on the screen, than the sight of business ledgers full of red ink."

About a month later Cecil started filming the picture on location in Griffith Park in Los Angeles. When he finished the day's work and the crew headed back to the studio, they noticed smoke rising from the sky somewhere off to the southwest. "That looks as though it might be close to the studio," cried De Mille, and he ordered the driver to get there as fast as he could so they could get some footage out of it. It turned out that it was their own studio that was going up in flames. Brother Bill was already on the scene, and he and Cecil had the same idea: They would get their "fire stuff" after all. So cameras were set up, players leaped into their costumes, and the shooting commenced. The firemen were astonished when they arrived; they had never seen the victims of a conflagration enjoying it so much. After they had put out the fire and left, Cecil told his brother: "I always felt we needed that fire stuff, but you were quite right—it's damned expensive!"[27]

Lonesome Redwood

Novelists are usually disappointed by the film versions of their novels; but Cecil B. De Mille insisted that films must say things in their own way and this necessitated crucial departures from the original. In 1916 he did a filming of *The Trail of the Lonesome Pine,* based on the popular novel by John Fox, Jr., and the play by Eugene Walter. When Fox and Walter saw the De Mille movie, they were stunned by the changes made. "Well," sighed Walter, as they left the theater, "at least De Mille kept the pine tree." "No," said Fox disconsolately, "it was a redwood."[28]

Golden Bed

When Cecil B. De Mille was making *The Greatest Show on Earth* in 1951, a dignified middle-aged woman walked up to him on the set one day and announced: "Mr. De Mille, you probably don't remember me, but I was a harlot in your golden bed." De Mille was taken by surprise, looked around in great embarrassment as the crew started laughing, and then remembered: She had been in a film of his entitled *The Golden Bed* in 1925.[29]

CHAPTER 3

The Coming
of Sound

Photoplay editor James R. Quirk thought silence was golden. When there was talk of adding sound to films in the early 1920s, he registered a strong protest. The "greatest processes of the universe are those of silence," he announced in May 1921. "The 'talking picture' will be made practical, but it will never supersede the motion picture without sound." Why not? Because, he said, it "will lack the subtlety and suggestion of vision—that vision which, deprived of voice to ears of flesh, intones undisturbed the symphonies of the soul."[1] But the American public heartily disagreed. Six years after Quirk's paean to silence it went crazy over *The Jazz Singer*, a film containing a bit of dialogue, when it opened on Broadway in October 1927. Within a year, talking pictures had become the rage. The movie actor's new slogan, said a wag, was now: "Eat, drink, and be merry, for tomorrow we dialogue!"[2]

The Jazz Singer was by no means the first talking picture. Talkies, in fact, are about as old as movies. When Thomas A. Edison invented the Kinetoscope, he wanted to combine it with his phonograph to produce pictures that talked as well as moved. And W.K.L. Dickson, his assistant, claimed to have done just that. When Edison returned from a trip to Paris in 1889, Dickson reported years later, he took the great inventor into a darkened room and projected a picture onto a screen that showed Dickson entering a room, saying, "Welcome home again," and then counting from one to ten. But Edison soon lost interest in the project and silent pictures went on to triumph in the marketplace.[3]

Nevertheless, the idea of "talkies" persisted. While Edison remained uninterested, other inventors continued to experiment with devices for synchronizing sound and sight; and by the early 1920s they had developed two major ways of making talking pictures: Movietone, which put a soundtrack on the movie film, and Vitaphone, which synchronized the film with talking-machine discs. But Hollywood executives remained largely indifferent to these developments. Films that talked, they contended, were a mere novelty and could never be more than a passing fad. Then, Warner Bros., a minor studio struggling to get out of the red, became interested. Late in 1925 the Bell Telephone engineers gave Sam Warner a demonstration of its sound-on-disc Vitaphone. "It's far from perfect," Sam told his brother Harry afterward, "but it's farther along now than films were when they first swept the country. It can be improved rapidly, and it will sweep the world." He convinced Harry, and Albert and Jack as well. The brothers Warner decided to take a chance on Vitaphone.[4]

In the spring of 1926 Warners began making short Vitaphone comedies with music and sound effects that went over well in theaters possessing sound equipment. About the same time Fox Film Corporation began turning out Movietone shorts, which included newsreels (shots of President Coolidge) as well as comedies. Warners then proceeded to release its first Vitaphone feature: *Don Juan,* starring John Barrymore. The Barrymore film, which opened at the Warner theater in New York on August 6, was essentially a silent film with a musical accompaniment added, but it did contain an introductory sequence in which Will Hays, president of the Motion Picture Producers and Distributors Association, appeared on the screen and talked about the virtues of Vitaphone. Hays overlooked the drawbacks: the poor quality of the sound and the fact that sometimes disc and film got out of sync. "One night," recalled the engineer who monitored the showing, "when we had been running for a couple of weeks, Will Hays opened his mouth and out came the tones of a banjo."[5] But the audience seemed to like the show (though *New Republic* reviewer Stark Young thought it was "A Terrible Thing"), and Warners decided to make a feature starring Al Jolson, famous Mammy singer, that included songs as well as a musical score.[6]

For Jolson's film appearance Warners selected a sentimental play,

The Jazz Singer, about a Jewish boy who defies his father, a cantor, and sings popular songs in a bar. There was to be no dialogue in the film, only sound effects, music accompanying the narrative, and Jolson singing a few songs. But during the shooting, right after Jolson sang his first song, "Dirty Hands, Dirty Face," everyone on the set looked so pleased that the singer suddenly began ad-libbing, as was his wont. "Wait a minute, wait a minute, you ain't heard nothin' yet!" he cried. "Wait a minute, I tell ya, you ain't heard nothin'!" Then he asked the band to play another song and began singing it with gusto. Director Alan Crosland and the sound technicians were thunderstruck; they were sure Jolson had ruined the scene. That night, when they were looking at the rushes, Crosland wanted to cut out the part where Jolson had departed from the script. But co-producer Darryl F. Zanuck insisted on leaving it in, at least for the time being, for he thought it might work; and before the shooting was over he decided to keep it in and add several more scenes to the film in which Jolson spoke. Jack Warner was upset when he heard what Zanuck was doing. He urged him to cut out these "talking tricks." Brother Harry was worried too. "What if they laugh when they hear that guy talking?" he cried. "God, we'll be ruined." But Zanuck's instincts were right. When *The Jazz Singer* opened in New York the night of October 6, 1927, the audience was thrilled by the sound of Jolson's voice. In the scene where the singer suddenly shouted, "Wait a minute, you ain't heard nothin' yet," people gasped in surprise and then started clapping. And when, at the end, Jolson sang to his mother and then fell on one knee, faced the camera, and cried, "Mammy!" there were shouts of approval.[7]

The Jazz Singer was a smash hit. "Mr. Jolson's persuasive vocal efforts were received with rousing applause," reported *New York Times* reviewer Mordaunt Hall the next day. "In fact, not since the first presentation of Vitaphone features more than a year ago at this same playhouse, has anything like the ovation been heard in a motion-picture theater."[8] And as long lines formed day after day at the Warner theater in New York, exhibitors in other cities began hastily installing sound equipment in their theaters so they could take advantage of the Jolson film's popularity. *Photoplay,* though, was unfriendly. Not only did it relegate a review of the film to its back pages, it also gave the review an unfriendly title: "Al Jolson with Vitaphone Noises."[9]

Photoplay wasn't all wrong. Vitaphone did produce squeaks and squawks at times (leading smart-alecks to define a parrot as "a canary that's taken up Vitaphone") and there was still a sync problem. Before long, however, Warners shifted from sound-on-disc to sound-on-film (which became standard), and there was a steady improvement in the quality of the sound. By the time Warners released *Lights of New York,* its first full-length, all-talking picture, in July 1928, it was clear that talkies had won the day. All the major studios started converting to sound, adding talking scenes to their silents and rushing all-talking pictures into production. At the same time exhibitors everywhere began installing sound equipment in their theaters. And, to the delight of Hollywood producers, as more and more theaters went over to sound, movie attendance began soaring. "In Hollywood," *Time* reported, "people talk of a revolution in the cinema industry. . . . Searches are underway to find actors and actresses who make pleasant noises as well as pleasant faces. Old-time favorites have been tested, classified, told to practice talking before their bedroom mirrors. . . ."[10]

Time was right about the revolution. Panic hit Hollywood as sound took over. Foreign stars with heavy accents like Emil Jannings, Vilma Banky, and Pola Negri worked on their English for a while and then decided to return to Europe. Home-grown celebrities like Marie Prevost, who couldn't remember lines, were reduced to supporting roles and then went into retirement. Other stars stuck it out with talkies a year or two and then left the screen: Norma Talmadge (who had a "Vitagraph accent"), Corrine Griffith (who, said *Time,* "talks through her nose"), and May McAvoy (whose line in one film, "I am thick of thutth thilly antickth," brought unintended laughter).[11] Nor did America's famous screen lover John Gilbert fare well in the new films. Gilbert had a nice tenor voice, but recordings in the early talkie days had a way of raising voices a bit and Gilbert's came out high-pitched and a little silly during torrid love scenes. "It is getting so that reviewing a John Gilbert picture is embarrassing," wrote one critic. "It isn't that Mr. Gilbert's voice is insufficient; it's that his use of it robs him of magnetism, individuality, and, strangest of all, skill. He becomes an uninteresting and inexpert performer whose work could be bettered by hundreds of lesser-known players."[12] In January 1929 *Photoplay* celebrated in verse the new consternation among old performers:

I cannot talk—I cannot sing
Nor screech nor moan nor anything.

Possessing all these fatal strictures
What chance have I in motion pictures?[13]

Stage people flocked to Hollywood; the studios were eager to hire experienced talkers.

Despite the crisis, many of Hollywood's silent players made the transition to sound quite comfortably. Gloria Swanson, Bebe Daniels, and Gary Cooper had no real problems; nor did Richard Dix, Fay Wray, Adolphe Menjou, or Paul Lukas. Jean Arthur listened to her first playback and cried out in horror: "A foghorn!" But the "foghorn" quality in her voice probably helped make her one of America's favorite performers during the 1930s and 1940s. When William Powell heard his voice for the first time, he rushed out of the room and said he was going into hiding; in short order, though, he became a hit in sound films. But what about Greta Garbo? Could she survive the change to sound? There was much speculation. MGM executives were so afraid her husky voice would work against her that they continued starring her in silents during 1929. But Garbo worked hard on her accent and the following year she made her first talkie, Anna Christie, a film version of Eugene O'Neill's well-known play. Theater marquees hailed the event: GARBO TALKS! And when the Swedish actress appeared on the screen in an early scene and said, "Gif me a visky, ginger ale on the side—and don't be stingy, baby," MGM executives—and Garbo's fans—breathed a sigh of relief. Her voice meshed perfectly with her screen personality.[14]

Garbo's triumph, in a way, symbolized the triumph of talking pictures. For Garbo was even more intriguing in talkies than she had been in silents. Movies could be better than ever, it seemed, if filmmakers made deft use of the new sound without sacrificing all the achievements of the silent-film makers. Not everyone thought this was possible. There were regrets for a time about the new day. Photoplay refused to take talkies seriously at first and predicted people would soon tire of them. United Artists executive Joseph Schenck also thought talkies were a fad and would soon die out; and gossip columnist Louella Parsons made fun of "scraping, screeching, rasping sound films" and looked confidently forward to a return to silence.[15] Charlie Chaplin sniffed that "motion pictures need dialogue as much as Beethoven symphonies need lyrics," and continued making silent pictures.[16] And then, in 1940, with The Great Dictator, he, too, capitulated and, like Garbo, talked with great success.

Having acquired a voice, the Hollywood film tended at first to garrulousness. "It is talking at the top of its voice," complained critic Gilbert Seldes, "talking to itself, talking in its sleep."[17] Drawing-room comedies in which people did little but talk and drink tea poured out of the studios until moviegoers finally got sick of pictures that were little more than filmed stage plays. Musicals were popular, too, for a time: "all-talking, all-singing, all-dancing" pictures, sometimes in color, featuring stars of Broadway musicals as well as ballerinas and vaudeville performers. And then, as the public got over its passion for musical numbers, Hollywood began experimenting with a variety of genres that eventually became permanent staples for the industry: horror films like *Dracula* (1931) and *Frankenstein* (1931); gangster films like *Little Caesar* (1930), *Public Enemy* (1931), and *Scarface* (1932); confession films like *Possessed* (1931) and *Back Street* (1932); and then topical films like *I Am a Fugitive from a Chain Gang* (1932) that dealt realistically with America's problems during the Great Depression. And before long, though no one realized it at the time, Hollywood entered what some people in retrospect regard as its "Golden Era."

Sound and Fury

"It was the night of the *Titanic* all over again," recalled one MGM performer when sound began to take over in Hollywood, "with women grabbing the wrong children and Louis B. [Mayer] singing 'Nearer My God to Thee.'" But many people doubted talkies were here to stay. "Without improvements," said Thomas A. Edison, "people will tire of talkers. Talking is no substitute for the good acting we had in silent pictures." Stage star Ethel Barrymore agreed. "The theater-going public," she declared, "won't put up with the talkies. It won't stand having its ears hurt and its intelligence insulted." Her brother John (the "Great Profile") insisted it took cigarettes to make talking pictures tolerable. "Why, I can light a cigarette in twenty different ways," he bragged, "and smoke it in sixteen positions. Frankly, for me, it has saved many a lousy picture, where the tobacco was better than the dialogue." *Variety* called sound pictures "chirping tintypes."[18]

Photoplay, the best of the fan magazines, was a determined holdout. Reviewing a short sound film in January 1929, the magazine had this to say: "We hope that they make a lot more talkies like this one, and then—goody, goody!—maybe they won't make any more. Now wouldn't that be just dandy! It is all very crude and unreal. The characters, as usual, seem to speak from their vest pockets. There is but one real consolation—it is only a two-reel picture."

Lillian Gish shared *Photoplay*'s disdain for the new medium. When she returned from Europe in the spring of 1929 and was asked her opinion of talkies, she told reporters: "The public has a newer and better toy. Give a little girl a doll that walks and she's delighted. But give her one that also says, 'Mama,' and she is entranced. The talkies say 'Mama.'" Playwright and film critic Robert Sherwood went to Shakespeare to find an appropriate quote with which to describe a sound picture: "It is a tale told by an idiot, full of sound and fury, signifying nothing." When some observers suggested that in time talking pictures would replace the legitimate theater, drama critic George Jean Nathan snorted: "The day that sees men waiting at the stage door for an electric phonograph to come out, will see the day that talkies will triumph over the theater."[19]

By the end of 1928, though, as studios and theaters rushed to acquire sound equipment, it was clear that silence was no longer golden in the film world. "Well, boys," said Cecil B. De Mille with finality, "it looks as though we're all going to work for the telephone company." Even *Photoplay* editor Quirk finally threw in the towel. President Calvin Coolidge's pronouncement seemed to be definitive: "The silent picture is dead. We have come into an entirely new era in motion picture development. The talking picture is one of the greatest forces for good and for civilization." Early in 1929, *Photoplay* offered a prize of $500 for the best new name for talking pictures, which were then being called *soundies, speakies, squawkies,* and *talkies.* Some of the suggestions: *pictovox, photophone, phonies, cinophone, vocafilm, photovoice, audies, audifilm.* But *talkies,* fortunately, persisted with the public. And then, as sound became universal, people started talking about the *movies* again.[20]

Punkest Gags

Comedian Harold Lloyd's *Welcome Danger* (1929), a feature picture, was originally shot as a silent, but at the preview there was a one-reel sound comedy on the bill that attracted all the attention. "And they howled at this comedy," said Lloyd ruefully after the preview. "They had the punkest gags in it, but they were laughing at the pouring of water, the frying of eggs—it didn't matter—the clinking of ice in a glass." Lloyd was devastated. "My God," he cried, "we worked our hearts out to get laughs with thought-out gags, and look here: just because they've got some sound to it, they're roaring at these things. . . ." In the end he gave way and began converting *Welcome Danger* into a talkie, adding dialogue here and there and dubbing in sound effects elsewhere. And the revamped picture had a good reception.[21]

Thound Filmth

During the days when talkies were taking over, *Photoplay* continued to regale its readers with little verses about the crisis confronting silent performers when called upon to speak. In November 1928 came these lines:

> If you can speak, and not call 'birdie' boidie'—
> If you can laugh, and make it sound like fun—
> If you will not refer to 'poifect loidy'—
> Hey, hey! You'll be in talkies yet, my son!

In March 1929 there were more lines:

> For yearth and yearth I thstarred in pictureth
> And never notithed any thrictureth,
> But now, with talkieth, what a meth!
> They say I cannot thspeak an eth!

And in December 1929, when talkies had triumphed, came *Photoplay*'s final verses:

> Little Miss Starlet, in ermine and scarlet,
> Getting a thousand a day,
> Along came the talkies, revealing her squawkies—
> And put poor Miss Starlet away![22]

Four Little Words

The changeover to sound came so quickly that it caught Gary Cooper and Nancy Carroll just as they were finishing a silent picture called *The Shopworn Angel* (1928). But a bit of dialogue was added before its release. For fifty-nine minutes and forty-five seconds of the hour-long film, Cooper and Carroll played it in silence. Then came the dialogue. "I studied my script containing this new thing called dialogue," Cooper told an interviewer in 1956, "until I was letter perfect." Then, in the film's final scene—a wedding—came the dialogue:

COOPER: "I do."
CARROLL: "I do."

"On those four words," recalled Cooper, "the picture was released as a talkie."[23]

Poignant Scene

When sound came to films, Paramount hired Randolph Scott, young actor from Virginia, as Gary Cooper's dialogue coach. But Cooper was intimidated at first by the demands of the sound crew. In one scene for *The Virginian* (1929), he froze as soon as the clapsticks announcing the take were clacked in front of his face. The scene was to be a poignant one. In it, Cooper, the Virginian, has caught his old friend Steve (Richard Arlen) rustling, both know the posse will have to hang him, and the two sit on the ground and talk mournfully to one another.

But Cooper couldn't do the scene. Flustered by the noise of the clapstick, his mind went blank in one take after another. Finally the director called it a day. The following morning Arlen came up with a solution: Since he sat with his back to Cooper during the shot, perhaps they could tape Cooper's lines to Arlen's shirt out of sight of the camera and then Cooper could read them. Arlen's suggestion worked perfectly. With Cooper reading his lines from Arlen's back, the director was able to get the shot in one take. And when the film was completed, this particular scene came off remarkably well on the screen. In it, Cooper's eyes are downcast (so he can read his lines) and he speaks haltingly (as he strains to read), as if overcome with emotion over Arlen's plight.[24]

Damn Postcards

Clive Brook's first talkie, *Interference* (1929), used records, and when his proud mother went to see it, sound and sight got out of sync a couple of times. In one scene, Brook receives an anonymous postcard, tears it up with the remark, "Another one of those damn postcards," and starts kissing his wife. But the needle got stuck in the groove at this point. The result: As Brook fervently embraced his wife, he kept saying, "Another one of those damn postcards, another one of those damn postcards!"[25]

Act of God

When sound came, one actress, frightened at the thought of having to learn dialogue, invoked the act of God clause to obtain release from her contract. When her producer protested, she told him: "A New York millionaire wants to marry me, and if that ain't an act of God, you tell me what is!"[26]

Is It Cricket?

In silent-film days, directors didn't have to worry about noise on the set. At times, in fact, they had musicians play while shooting a scene in order to put the performers in a proper mood. With the coming of sound, however, extraneous noises could ruin a scene and necessitate costly retakes. One day, an extra who was hired for a day's work on an early sound film purposely brought a pocketful of crickets with him and turned them loose on the set when no one was looking. As a result, sound technicians spent three days trying to track down the source of the strange chirping that kept ruining their recordings. But the mischievous extra—and all the other extras—pocketed three-day pay checks instead of one when the sequence was finally finished.[27]

Color-blind

Talkies eliminated the ringing telephone on studio sound sets; a flashing red light was now the way to let the director know that there was a call for him. But one day, toward the end of 1929, when First National studios was shooting *Spring Is Here*, no one on the set noticed the operator's flash for some time. Suddenly actress Louise Fazenda spied the light from a far corner of the set where rehearsals were in progress and called out: "The phone is ringing! Is everybody color-blind?"[28]

Sinkem

In the new jargon for talkies, the word *sinkem* meant "begin synchronization." But in a boating scene for a Paramount picture being made in 1929, when the director yelled, "Sinkem!" one of the extras sitting in a boat on a lake wailed: "Oh, wait, for heaven's sake! I'm no stunt woman. I can't swim a stroke!"[29]

Sing, Not Act

Rudy Vallee was considered a good radio singer, but not much good as an actor in his early Hollywood days. In his first talkie, *The Vaga-*

bond *Lover* (1929), every time he tried to act, according to one tale, director Marshall Neilan shouted: "Hey, you—sing!"[30]

All Talking
On the marquee of the Hollywood theater late in 1929: PAUL MUNI IN SEVEN FACES—ALL TALKING.[31]

II. PRODUCTION

CHAPTER 4

Moguls

By 1929 the structure of the American film industry was evident. Five studios dominated: Paramount, Metro-Goldwyn-Mayer, Fox, Warner Bros., and RKO. Following the big five closely were Universal, Columbia, and United Artists, known in the business as the "little three."[1]

The moguls heading these studios were latter-day buccaneers who boldly navigated uncharted seas, risked millions, and demonstrated a visceral instinct for what audiences would pay to see. They ruled their studios like tyrants, imposing their unique personalities upon underlings and overseeing the production of every picture. Short on formal education, they nevertheless knew what should go on film, and most of them had charisma and style frequently bordering on taste. Above all they were showmen who created stars and built the Hollywood tradition. "They did it with their guts," actor Gregory Peck observed. "They got personally involved—Zanuck, Jack Warner, Sam Goldwyn, Harry Cohn, all those fellows. I liked them because they had zest and red blood in them."[2]

Most of these studio heads were immigrants. They came from varied backgrounds, but nearly all had been poor and practically all were Jewish, willing to enter an industry not yet respectable. Carl Laemmle, the tenth of thirteen children, emigrated from Germany and had been in the clothing business. Adolph Zukor, orphaned as a boy in Hungary, became a furrier's apprentice shortly after coming to America. Samuel Goldfish (later Goldwyn) had been an office boy in Poland, then a blacksmith's assistant, and eventually went into the glove business in America. Louis B. Mayer came from Russia and worked in scrap metal before setting up his own junk business. Later Mayer claimed he could remember nothing of his Russian boyhood except hunger. The father of the Warner brothers was a cobbler from the Polish village of Kraznashiltz, who traveled as a peddler before settling with his family in Youngstown, Ohio, where son Jack worked in a meat market.

Like the late nineteenth-century robber barons, the Hollywood moguls created personal empires, reaped fortunes, and wielded vast power. Along the way they learned to recognize talent and acquired the skills necessary to make creative decisions. Part czar and part Big Daddy, the studio mogul ran every aspect of his studio—calling meetings, watching rushes, visiting sets, determining everything that went on. Their approach was neither cultivated nor highbrow. Instead they skillfully balanced what mass audiences wanted with discretion and a tough sense of business.

Adolph Zukor, one of the pioneers, was a modest man with an extraordinary mind who remained in the background, yet his position as president and later chairman of the board at Paramount Pictures was powerful. Although he was consulted on every project before it went into production, Zukor's participation was characteristically quiet. Despite his customary politeness, few doubted his iron hand. Film publicist Arthur Mayer remembered a telegram he once received from Zukor that blended firmness and gallantry. YOU'RE HERE-WITH DISCHARGED, the telegram read. BEST REGARDS. REMEMBER ME TO MRS. MAYER.[3] Choreographer LeRoy Prinz, on the other hand, recalled Zukor in his later years—he lived to be 103—toddling onto the set of a musical number and asking, "Do you mind if I watch, LeRoy?" Prinz sent for a chair, and Zukor sat and watched the rehearsal. Frequently he would remark as he left, "Now you're getting too rough with those girls, Mr. Prinz."[4]

With foreign distribution in mind, Zukor was concerned about the success of Paramount's product abroad as well as in the United States. His interest transcended the commercial aspect of filmmaking, for he felt deeply the responsibility of sending pictures abroad in which the lives of Americans would be viewed by foreigners, in many cases for the first time. "He not only had to think in terms of American dollars," Zukor's son, Eugene, explained, "but he had to think within the world of diplomacy."[5] He traveled to foreign countries, made a diplomatic entree, and either opened an office or sold Paramount films for distribution. To test his product he often invited his young son and daughter to sit in the theater. "For many years he did that," Eugene Zukor claimed, "even after we were eighteen or nineteen. If it stood that test, then he knew he was on the right track."[6]

Carl Laemmle, another devoted family man, was as shrewd a trader as any of his rivals. His paternal attitude earned him the affectionate title "Uncle Carl." Laemmle more than anyone else blatantly defied the Trust (as Edison's monopolistic Motion Picture Patents Company was called) and kept open the neighborhood theaters in the ghettos. He formed a production company, the Independent Motion Picture Company of America, known as IMP, and in 1909 launched the star system by hiring Florence Lawrence and billing her by name in IMP films. Heretofore Lawrence had been known simply as "The Biograph Girl," since Biograph never listed players. In March 1914, just before hearings in the government's antitrust suit ended in the Trust's demise, Laemmle bought 230 acres in the San Fernando Valley north of the Hollywood hills. Ground was broken in October, and the following March, Universal City opened.

Perhaps the greatest titan of them all, Louis B. Mayer, organized a company in 1924 out of three failures: the Goldwyn, Metro, and Mayer enterprises. As if by magic, Metro-Goldwyn-Mayer became the Tiffany's of Hollywood studios, boasting more stars than there are in the heavens. Relying heavily on Irving Thalberg, the boy genius of production, Mayer built the biggest, most sumptuous stable of them all, with emphasis on glamorous stars. "Think big," Mayer instructed Thalberg, confident that his boy wonder was a man of taste as well as a perfectionist, and Thalberg's feeling for story value soon won him respect throughout the industry. Mayer also ordered his cameramen to emphasize his stars' beauty, for MGM was selling elegance.

At the same time Mayer wanted the studio to have a family atmosphere that didn't exist elsewhere. He insisted on "homemade" apple pie in the commissary, while chicken soup, prepared from Mayer's own recipe, became obligatory for studio employees. A great sentimentalist, Mayer believed fervently in motherhood, God, and country. Whereas Darryl Zanuck favored "dishy" sorts of girls like Alice Faye and Betty Grable, Mayer went in for grand ladies, women's stories, and historical romances that made Greer Garson queen of the lot. Still, Mayer, like most of the moguls, had an eye for party girls and often flirted with them or showered them with gifts. Rarely did he sleep with them. It became a standing industry joke that "L. B. Mayer couldn't catch a piece of tail in a cathouse."[7]

On the lot Mayer was a commanding figure, almost awesome, with deep-brown eyes that projected a sense of enormous power. From behind a huge white desk surrounded by all kinds of buttons and trophies, this consummate ham cajoled his stars into doing his bidding—sometimes sternly, sometimes tearfully. Unlike Zanuck or Harry Cohn, he rarely saw a film until it was completed. From time to time he visited sets, however, followed by his entourage and hustling from one place to another. "He was the great God of the sky," contract player Marshall Thompson remembered.[8] But others were less generous. "I'd rather have TB than L.B.," an MGM writer once put it.[9]

At Warner Bros. the reputation of Jack Warner was even worse. A real martinet, Jack fought with practically everyone on the lot— Humphrey Bogart, Bette Davis, Olivia de Havilland, James Cagney, an endless list. "Working for Warner Bros.," screenwriter Mel Shavelson remarked, "was like making love to a porcupine. A thousand pricks against one."[10] Yet Warner hid his crusty shrewdness behind a clown's mask and became known as a notorious jokester. Jack Benny once said that Warner "would rather tell a bad joke than make a good picture."[11] Certainly he seldom missed a chance to inflict a poor quip. "What's new?" director Mervyn LeRoy asked his boss one morning. Jack paused a moment, then answered, "New York, New Jersey, New Hampshire, pneumonia!"[12]

Despite Jack Warner's crude slogan that "uneasy lies the head that wears the toilet seat,"[13] Warner Bros. emerged as the number-one studio for hard-action, realistic drama. If Metro was Tiffany's, Warners was Macy's. In his strange way, though, Warner also demonstrated taste. Never the gifted filmmaker Darryl Zanuck was, he wisely delegated production to more creative minds while concentrating on the business side of moviemaking.

Originally there were four Warner brothers. Albert was in charge of distribution. Sam was the force behind sound until shortly before his death. Harry, the eldest and a money wizard, was in charge of finances. Following in their father's footsteps, Harry had learned the cobbler's trade as a youth. Even at the height of the family's fortune, Harry could be seen walking down studio streets picking up nails and popping them in his mouth. But it was Jack who ran the Burbank studio with a gambler's instinct, confident the public would prove him right. "Don't pay attention to bad reviews," he would say in secure moments. "Today's newspaper is tomorrow's toilet paper."[14]

When it came to coarseness, Harry Cohn at Columbia surely wrote the book. Emerging from the immigrant herd crammed into Manhattan's Lower East Side, Cohn quit school in his early teens to become a Tin Pan Alley song plugger. Like his competitors he had a marvelous sense of what the public wanted. "Screw the critics," Cohn advised. "They're like eunuchs. They can tell yo how to do it, but they can't do it themselves."[15] Harry claimed he had a foolproof method for judging whether audiences would like a picture or not. "If my fanny squirms, it's bad. If my fanny doesn't squirm, it's good. It's as simple as that." Writer Herman Mankiewicz was present when Cohn made this revelation and, after thinking it over, remarked: "Imagine—the whole world wired to Harry Cohn's backside!"[16]

No Hollywood mogul controlled a studio more loudly or completely than Cohn did. He was a "bastard's bastard," it was said, and the atmosphere at Columbia was always tense; employees claimed they could sense whether "His Crudeness" was in the studio or not. He had an opinion on everything, made decisions instantly, and insisted on knowing what was going on in each department. He was everywhere, too, dashing up stairs two or three at a time. If a designer left a light burning in her office, Harry Cohn was there to turn it off. If a writer spent too much time away from his typewriter, Cohn ordered him from across the courtyard to get back to work. Someone once asked Harry why he was so rough on the people who worked for him. His answer was direct: "I am the king here. Whoever eats my bread sings my song."[17]

Yet many Columbia veterans admitted that they were in that small group who actually liked Harry Cohn. They respected his knowledge, his eye for talent, his shrewdness, his basic honesty. Stars knew where they stood with Harry, and if they talked his language, more often than not they gained his respect. On occasion he could be charming, then turn around and shout something demeaning to an actor who was down on his luck. But Cohn was not afraid to take chances, and beyond question he was the one who built Columbia, a small studio, into the success it became. "Columbia, the Germ of the Ocean," carpers called it, but Cohn brought in Frank Capra and Rita Hayworth and turned his studio into the pride of Poverty Row. Although he seldom spoke of his early years, he never forgot the hardships he had suffered as a boy. Later, after Columbia's position was assured, he explained why he drove himself so hard: "So *my* sons won't have to sleep with their grandmother."[18]

Cohn never advertised the fact that he was Jewish, any more than the others did. "Around this studio," he stated plainly, "the only Jews we put into pictures play Indians."[19] Curiously, the first of the moguls to film a strong condemnation of anti-Semitism (*Gentleman's Agreement*, 1947) was Darryl Zanuck, the only Gentile in this early generation of tycoons. Hailing from the tiny farming community of Wahoo, Nebraska, Zanuck had headed production at Warner Bros. before forming Twentieth Century Pictures with Joseph Schenck, and later merging with the Fox Film Corporation. Like Harry Cohn, but on a bigger scale, Zanuck put his heart and soul into every picture made. More than a solid administrator, Zanuck was an extraordinary filmmaker. He had an amazing knack for analyzing a script and pinpointing its weaknesses while strutting around the conference room with a polo mallet in hand. A little man with enormous energy, Zanuck possessed an insatiable appetite for sports and women, especially the latter.

To Zanuck motion pictures were supposed to do just that—*move*. He felt they should never be static. In addition to higher-echelon intellectuals who surrounded him, Zanuck brought in a group of more physical types such as Sam the barber. A good horseman and a strong man physically, Sam became a kind of general factotum around Twentieth Century-Fox. There was also Nick the Greek, who ran the commissary, and John the Frog, Zanuck's French coach. Most evenings after dinner, usually around eleven-thirty, Zanuck sat in the screening room with his henchmen. After the film was shown, he asked what Sam or Nick or the Frog thought of it, trusting them for honest opinions. Together they constituted his straw vote of the public at large, and he valued their views. Sometimes the discussions dragged on until three or four in the morning.

While Zanuck often deleted motivation from scripts, leaving mostly action, once he approved a script, the writer's word was law at Twentieth Century-Fox. Zanuck was recognized as a brilliant film editor, particularly when it came to construction. Whereas Mayer favored great ladies and old-fashioned romance, Zanuck preferred tougher pictures—Westerns, gangster stories, screen biographies, and films based on current events in which men were the major protagonists. He ruled with the air of an emperor, but he had insight, decisiveness, and the ability to measure up to challenges.

At RKO lack of continuity in management proved a constant problem. RKO changed heads almost yearly. Producer Pandro Berman claimed that he worked for seventeen different administrations there in as many years. Not coincidentally, RKO was frequently in and out of receivership and bankruptcy, depending on whoever was taking over. Howard Hughes finally bought the studio in 1948, but his leadership was always on the ethereal side. Everybody on the lot talked about him, yet few ever saw him. Right after Hughes acquired the studio, it was claimed, he went there in the middle of the night to look it over. He was driven over the lot, got out and walked around, and finally gave signs that he was ready to leave. A lesser executive said to him, "Well, you've seen it now. What do you have to say?" Hughes replied, "Paint it."[20] Some maintained he never set foot in the studio again, preferring to operate out of his bungalow at the Beverly Hills Hotel.

Another millionaire-turned-film-entrepreneur was Herbert J. Yates, who formed Republic Pictures in 1935, a lesser studio specializing in budget Westerns, serials, and adventure yarns. A former executive of the American Tobacco Company, Yates took over the old Mack Sennett studio on Ventura Boulevard, consolidating Mascot Pictures and several independent outfits into Republic. Yates himself knew little about making movies, but he was a tough businessman and a pleasure to know socially. After succeeding with a string of "singing cowboy" features starring Gene Autry and Roy Rogers, "Papa" Yates, as he was known to studio employees, fell in love with Czech skater Vera Hruba Ralston, lavished money on her productions, and eventually married her. No box-office attraction, Ralston was one of the major factors in Republic's undoing. By 1957 Yates's studio had abandoned movie production to focus on television, which by then was eating at the core of the big studio system.

Despite all the complaints about the autocratic, disreputable tactics of the Hollywood moguls, in retrospect they are revered with a devotion transcending nostalgia. "Those old-timers had something about them," director Vincent Sherman concluded in what appears an industry consensus. "They couldn't intellectualize about a subject or the fine points of characterization, but they had a feel for the overall piece—whether it was something good, whether it was real, whether it was honest, whether the public would like it."[21] No sooner had the actors, directors, and agents taken over film production than the genius of the old moguls was sorely missed. Even as early as 1919, when Mary Pickford, Douglas Fairbanks, Charlie

Chaplin, and D. W. Griffith formed United Artists as a distribution company for independent producers, Metro-Goldwyn-Mayer's Richard Rowland had expressed contempt for the new approach. "The lunatics have taken over the asylum," he fumed.[22] But the craziness had just begun.

Mayer and Son

Louis B. Mayer loved to view himself as the patriarch of the Metro lot, surrounded by his working children. After romantic lead Robert Taylor had been at MGM long enough to deserve a raise, he made an appointment to see the boss. "Mr. Mayer," the actor began, "you know I've been here for some time now. I'm doing bigger parts, but I haven't gotten any more money." Mayer looked shocked. "My boy," L.B. said, "you know you're like my son. God never saw fit to give me the blessing of a son; He gave me two beautiful daughters instead. But if He *had* given me a son, Bob, I would have wanted him to be exactly like you. We've such big plans for you. You can't imagine what we have in store for you." By this time Mayer was practically sobbing. "It hurts me deeply that you've come to me and asked for money at a time like this." Taylor wound up consoling the mogul over the injury he had unintentionally caused. When he came out of Mayer's office, a friend asked, "Well, Bob, did you get your raise?" Taylor replied, "No, but I gained a father."[23]

Weightlifting

Jack Warner was an impatient reader. He admitted that he'd rather take a fifty-mile hike than plow through a book; he much preferred getting a synopsis from his story department. But while director Mervyn LeRoy was crossing the Atlantic one summer by steamer, he noticed dozens of passengers reading Hervey Allen's massive best-selling novel *Anthony Adverse* (1933). Never one to pass up a good story idea, LeRoy sent off a radiogram to Warner saying: PLEASE READ ANTHONY ADVERSE. WOULD MAKE GREAT PICTURE FOR US. Jack cabled back: READ IT? I CAN'T EVEN LIFT IT.[24]

Immediate Recognition

For a film about big business, a Columbia Pictures screenwriter needed a grandiloquent speech for a tycoon to make to his board of directors and decided to use the ancient Roman hero Spartacus's oration to his gladiators. "What the hell is this?" yelled Harry Cohn, when he came across the speech in the script. When the writer tried to explain the historical background of the oration, Cohn became impatient. "I don't want any of that crap," he exclaimed. "I want a speech that every person in the audience will recognize immediately." "You mean like Hamlet's soliloquy?" ventured the writer. "No! No!" screamed Cohn. "I mean something like 'To be or not to be.'"[25]

Don't Tell

Harry Cohn brought Broadway actor Ralph Bellamy to Columbia for Frank Capra's *Forbidden* (1932). But before doing the Capra film, Harry insisted he make a sea picture the studio filmed every few years with minor changes. Since shooting on the sea story ended the day before the Capra one began, Bellamy decided he had to have a stand-in. No sooner had he informed the studio manager of this than word came down that Harry Cohn wanted to see him. Bellamy went into Cohn's office to find Harry irate. "What the hell is this? You New York actors, wanting a stand-in!" The actor tried to explain that to do justice to either part, a stand-in would be essential. The two pursued the matter hotly, with four-letter words spewing from both. After considerable yelling, Cohn calmed down. "All right," he said, "you can have a stand-in—on one condition. Don't tell Jack Holt!" (Jack Holt was under contract to the studio, and he made scores of pictures on tight schedules.)

A year later Bellamy found himself under contract at Columbia, working in film after film. There was no Screen Actors Guild then, but some of his associates arbitrarily had taken to quitting at six o'clock. Bellamy decided if anyone had a right to do that, he did. Within days Harry Cohn sent word that he wanted to see the actor after work. "What the hell is this?" Cohn shouted. "You New York actors, walking off a set!" Again, they went at it furiously. Finally Bellamy said, "Harry, if that's the way it is, tear up the contract." With that Cohn quieted down. "All right," he said, "you can quit at six o'clock—on one condition. Don't tell Jack Holt!" Bellamy stayed on the lot for five years and never even *met* Jack Holt.[26]

Relativity

The studio heads adored royalty and celebrities from all walks of life and always made a fuss over them whenever they had the chance. At one time or another Hollywood feted Queen Marie of Romania, Lady Mountbatten, George Bernard Shaw, and eventually Nikita Khrushchev. When Albert Einstein was given a tour of Warner Bros. all the brass turned out to greet him. "This is the great Professor Einstein," an executive said as he introduced the distinguished guest to Jack Warner. "He invented the theory of relativity." Jack's ears perked up. "Well, Professor, I have proved a theory of relatives, too." Einstein seemed interested. "Really?" he said. "Yes," Jack answered. "Don't hire 'em."[27]

In Your Pocket

When Louis B. Mayer went to the White House and was introduced to Franklin D. Roosevelt, he put his watch on the desk and said, "Mr. President, I'm told that when anyone spends eighteen minutes with you, you have them in your pocket." Exactly seventeen minutes later Mayer got up, said good-bye, and left.[28]

Jack Forgets

Shortly after the United States entered World War II, Madame Chiang Kai-shek came to the United States on a fund-raising mission to aid China. When she visited Hollywood, the studios, with Jack Warner at the helm, threw a banquet in her honor. Jack also decided to invite the lady to lunch at his studio, making sure all the department heads and an appropriate number of his stars were on hand to greet her. In a gracious speech Madame Chiang thanked Warner for his hospitality and praised the company's stars for their contributions both to the war effort and to her people. She sat down to prolonged applause, as Warner stood up to reply. Jack thanked his guest for her generous words, then paused. Company regulars grew nervous, fearing what might come next. Looking straight into Madame Chiang's eyes, Jack said, "Holy cow, that reminds me. I forgot to pick up my laundry."[29]

Homer

Harry Cohn heard there was a good story, *The Iliad,* written by somebody named Homer, and thought it might have picture possibilities. He called his writers together and said, "Now, boys, I want a one-page treatment of it by tomorrow." So a team of Columbia writers worked all night, and the next morning, blurry-eyed, they handed

Harry a one-page synopsis. Cohn read it, but looked doubtful: "There are an awful lot of Greeks in it!"[30]

What They Want

At Harry Cohn's funeral (or was it L. B. Mayer's?) someone asked Red Skelton, "How come so many people are here?" Said Skelton: "Give the people what they want, they'll all show up."[31]

CHAPTER 5

Studio Life

In the Golden Age each studio was like a complete little city, with its own stars, directors, writers, cinematographers, composers, and designers. It also had its own police department and a school for underage contract players, and in most cases its own barber shop, dentist's office, hospital, and commissary. In those days theaters booked pictures before they had even been shot, for each studio turned out forty to fifty pictures a year. Yet each had its own particular atmosphere, flavor, and style, evident in the types of stories it shot, the lighting used, and the texture of its musical scores.

The largest was Metro, the Cadillac of studios, where the lavish musicals were made, boasting three huge lots. It made the biggest pictures, had the biggest talent roster, the biggest soundstages, and it was the richest. Everything there was deluxe, making it the queen of the industry. Stars were driven from their dressing rooms to sets by limousine. "To me it was fairyland," actress Janet Leigh recalled.[1] While outsiders found Metro the most pretentious, it was for studio regulars like a big family in which workers in the various departments developed their talents and spent their careers. Songwriter Harry Warren, who came to Metro from Warner Bros. by way of Twentieth Century-Fox, thought he had found paradise at last. "The birds sing all day at Metro," he used to kid.[2]

Paramount, on the other hand, home of the Bing Crosby–Bob

Hope *Road* pictures, was far more relaxed, more happy-go-lucky, sometimes called the country club of studios. Physically it reminded actress Carolyn Jones of a New England village, and she remembered Y. Frank Freeman's boxer dogs playing with film cans like Frisbees in the evenings after the gates were closed. Not only was Paramount less structured than Metro, but it was also run in a more democratic fashion, not dominated by the egos that prevailed elsewhere. Sultry Lizabeth Scott, who was under personal contract to Hal Wallis at Paramount, described life there as "a huge ball, full of color—pinks and lavenders and purples and blues and white. There was happiness and gaiety—it was unreal in a sense. And yet I couldn't wait to go to work."[3]

Warner Bros. was more like a factory, specializing in down-to-earth, nitty-gritty pictures—gangster films with Bogart and Cagney, melodramas with Bette Davis. Newcomers often complained of a concentration-camp atmosphere, claiming the place was full of spies, politics, and fear. "We at Warners were the peasants," actor Pat O'Brien maintained. "At Metro they were the aristocracy."[4] Yet there were advantages to knowing who owned the studio, and a familial attitude did develop at Warners, even though everybody beefed about the front office. "It was like a family feud in the Democratic Party," director Irving Rapper said. "We were always fighting, getting suspensions. But I must say, it was a family."[5]

The most beautifully landscaped studio was Twentieth Century-Fox, which boasted a park copied after one in Paris and a huge backlot where Century City now stands. At Fox, where Shirley Temple and later Betty Grable reigned supreme, the buildings were artistically designed, the atmosphere friendly. RKO, back to back with Paramount, was a smaller lot and fairly informal, although budgetary restrictions were obvious, except possibly on the Fred Astaire–Ginger Rogers musicals. Universal, which had developed into a top studio during the Silent Era, declined in prestige after sound came in, for years specializing in adventure yarns and what the industry called "tits and sand" pictures, exhibiting Maria Montez or Yvonne De Carlo in exotic costumes. Out in the San Fernando Valley, Universal was almost like a ranch, a happy, sleepy place, though it made about fifty films a year. Once Columbia started its upward climb, it acquired an almost sweatshop reputation, known to some as the Black Hole of Calcutta. Columbia's big pictures—the Capra films and the Rita Hayworth musicals—were expensive, but the studio turned out hundreds of B movies, and there was an aura of cheapness around.

Physically Columbia was a rat maze of cubbyhole offices, and workers insisted the stages were bugged. When Charles Walters directed a film there, after being at Metro for years, he was ready to leave five times a day. "That was a junkyard compared to MGM," he complained.[6] Republic, on the threshold of Poverty Row, was originally in a field almost by itself. Specializing in low-budget Westerns, Republic was a well-run, folksy operation with its own backlot and adequate soundstages. Dale Evans, queen of the cowgirls, felt at Republic that she was back home in Texas; Gene Autry, the studio's most popular singing cowboy, compared its atmosphere to "a great big country picnic" in which actors and crew worked happily together.[7]

Each studio had its stock company in which everybody knew everybody else, and a sense of collegiality prevailed. Directors, choreographers, and songwriters helped one another on assignments, while old-timers felt an obligation to assist newcomers, introducing them to all the departments. Of course there were studio politics and intrigue, but with three thousand to five thousand people working on the major lots, that could be expected. Yet a spirit of cooperation predominated—to a point where the tight family atmosphere often caused newcomers to feel shut out. The company assembled to make each film, on the other hand, became a unit unto itself, sharing in-jokes and problems, so that even actors borrowed from other lots were quickly absorbed into the group.

Above the artists and technicians was a kind of feudal hierarchy; contract players did not feel free to approach the studio potentates, and they frequently viewed stars as too lofty for simple exchanges. Young actors and actresses found the atmosphere exciting—watching the stars they had read so much about and seeing the great names on offices and dressing rooms. It was a magical experience for them, filled with glamour and beautiful people. Even an actress of Helen Hayes's stature was not immune to the magic, for the Broadway legend was thrilled to find herself at MGM during the early 1930s. "There were all these gods and goddesses that I had been worshiping on the screen," she remembered. "There they all were in the flesh. I was just agog the whole time I was there."[8]

Despite the pecking order, most Hollywood celebrities were craftsmen who knew that their business was to create a superior product with integrity and style that would also do well at the box office. Although there were any number of pretty girls around for the amusement of producers, executives, and visiting dignitaries, the bulk of a studio's personnel consisted of professionals who had come up through an apprenticeship system. Most lots had a drama coach who worked with young players and prepared them for picture assignments. Lillian Burns headed the talent department at MGM, whereas Lela Rogers, Ginger's mother, occupied that position at RKO. In addition there were singing, dancing, fencing, and horseback lessons, and instruction in how to take care of the body, how to present oneself in interviews, how to put on makeup, and anything else useful to budding stars. Contract players with potential were nurtured into stardom. Appropriate material was found for them, publicity planned, and ways charted to present their fresh talent advantageously to producers, directors, and executives. While a regular paycheck provided security, there was always the fear of a dropped option, since beginners' contracts were normally renewed every six months.

Before the formation of the professional guilds, Hollywood crews worked a six-day week. Actors arrived at the studio each morning about seven o'clock; actresses were already there, studying their lines while sitting under dryers. Directors came around eight, stopped at the makeup department to say hello to their stars and have doughnuts and coffee, and then reported to the set. Shooting usually started at nine o'clock. Young players not working on a movie showed up around nine for lessons or to walk from set to set and talk to producers and directors, learning by watching and listening to the pros. Saturday was normally a half day, although location shooting or unusual circumstances might extend work "until the leading lady fainted Sunday noon."[9]

Lunch in the studio commissary was an opportunity to relax and a time for interviews, table hopping, and socializing. Warners had its Green Room, Fox its Café de Paris, and Paramount its sea of tables with commissary head Pauline Kessinger on hand to greet everybody. Generally there was a writers' table, a cameramen's table, an editors' table, a special-effects department table, and so on, although the crew of a picture in production might sit together. At Paramount young contract players sat at a large circular table in the center, known as the "Golden Circle," so that they could be seen by those involved with casting. There were tables reserved for special interviews, too, but most stars simply took whatever seat they chose, often in costume. Prices were reasonable. The menu at Paramount included Turkey and Eggs à la Crosby, a Bob Hope Cocktail, Strawberries Heston, a Dorothy Lamour Salad, and others named after current stars. No liquor was served in the commissaries; the drinking crowd at Warners frequently went across the street to the Lakeside Country Club, while the RKO bunch gathered at Lucey's.

Along with the laughter and hilarity was a fair share of bitching. Workers at every studio griped constantly, and contract players in practically all instances felt exploited. It was difficult to find a steady stream of challenging assignments for every talent on the lot. Most performers thought that if they drew one exciting role in two they were faring well. Often the dry spell proved longer, causing some individuals to feel the front office was indifferent to their professional advancement. "Keep them working" seemed to be the slogan, no matter how vapid the story. But budgets had to be balanced, scripts had to be written, roles had to be cast. If family members proved obstinate, the studio exercised its right to suspend them, denying salary until the recalcitrant turned more cooperative. Insiders at Twentieth complained they had been sentenced to Penitentiary Fox, while those elsewhere fussed about a workhouse system in which all were at the mercy of the overlords in charge.

But the good moments and warm relationships lingered in memory long after the servitude was over. Dating situations developed, as couples fell in and out of love. A character actress might at last be handed a part so right for her there was no way she could go wrong. Gossips in the makeup department passed word around that old Jack Warner himself had gone to the backlot to console a technician whose wife had died. After a beginning player lost a dream part, the cop on the gate suddenly called him by name. Those were the times that made studio life memorable—even more than getting a bigger dressing room, the Christmas parties, or the tinsel and glamour that went with being part of a Hollywood studio. What counted most and sustained morale was the camaraderie and the knowledge that the finest talent in the industry was contributing to a team effort.

From the vantage point of a star, the experience was both exhilarating and unnerving. "I thought I was in another world," said Argentine actor Fernando Lamas of his Metro days. "Everybody was so helpful; it was an extraordinary experience. Everything was done for you. They treated you like you were a mixture of jewel and retarded child, because they kept you in cotton. If you had a headache, three doctors came on the set with three pills and three shots. If you needed a driver's license, some inspector from the Department of

Motor Vehicles came to the studio. This pampering confused a lot of people in my business, and they got into trouble emotionally many times."[10]

By the 1960s the big studios were beginning their decline. Even Metro-Goldwyn-Mayer around 1956 reminded Carolyn Jones "of an ancient dowager that was divesting herself of her jewels before going to bed at night, and she was about halfway through."[11] Twenty years later all the studios had become real estate operations, generally part of a vast conglomerate, run by businessmen who leased space to independent producers and television. The halcyon days were long over. When Jayne Meadows returned to Metro in the early 1970s for a television series, there was no makeup department, and dark sheets hung over everything. "You never saw anybody walking down the streets," recalled Meadows. "Occasionally a bicycle, with some grip or engineer. It was a ghost town." But in her mind she could still hear Esther Williams and June Allyson and Elizabeth Taylor and Deborah Kerr and Greer Garson laughing and talking as they had their hair done before going off to various sets. And she could remember all the stage doors opening on the dot of twelve as everybody rushed out on the way to the commissary.[12] "I was happy to have been at MGM from 1947 to 1951 to see the Golden Era of Hollywood in its full bloom," agreed actress Arlene Dahl. "I came in on the tail end, but I'm very happy I was there at all."[13]

Protectress

Ego-centered though Hollywood might be, genuine relationships did grow out of working situations. When Joan Lorring arrived at Warner Bros. to play in the Bette Davis version of *The Corn Is Green* (1945), she was still a teenager. Until that time she had roller-skated to work, mainly radio jobs, but John Dall, who played the Welsh boy in the Davis film, offered to drive her over to Burbank, since he lived nearby. Hollywood casting offices had told Lorring she was not pretty enough for movies, to the point that she developed a serious complex. The situation did not go unnoticed by Bette Davis.

The cast gathered to watch rushes one day, and in the footage shown were close-ups of Joan playing a young seductress, looking much older than she actually was. Convinced she was a real clock stopper, the young actress was embarrassed at seeing herself on the screen. By the time her first close-up was over, she was practically under the seat in front of her. Suddenly she heard a voice from the row behind her, whispering softly so nobody else would hear. Lorring knew immediately the whisperer was Bette Davis. "When I first came to this studio," the voice said, "there was a very beautiful actress on the lot. When we would come to rushes, her mother would say every time there was a close-up of her, 'There's my beautiful darling now.' . . . But," added Davis, "*I'm* still here!"[14]

Sound Advice

Although actress Jayne Meadows later came to realize that her best feature was her smile, she had been told after her initial tests at Metro that her teeth were too white. Following instructions, she spent the next several months careful not to expose her snowy teeth, and developed a complex about it. During a makeup test for *Undercurrent* (1946) with Katharine Hepburn, the director said, "Smile, Jayne, smile." Meadows dutifully explained, "Oh, they told me not to smile. My teeth are too white." Hepburn overheard the remark and stepped forward. "My dear, they told me not to smile because it made me look like a horse," she said. "I've made it pay for years. Smile."[15]

Bellyful

Cecil B. De Mille was too busy to look at menus and decide what he wanted for lunch, so he asked commissary head Pauline Kessinger to make his selection. She decided that the director liked pea soup, and every Monday she saw to it that he had a bowl of split-pea soup, a piece of custard pie, and a glass of milk. One day the kitchen ran out of peas. When De Mille came in with his entourage, Pauline grew panicky. She went over to their table and said, "I'm very sorry, Mr. De Mille, but I'll have to give you something else today. I think I'm going to have to fire the chef because we ran out of peas." De Mille smiled and put both arms around her. "Honey, may I tell you something?" the Hollywood legend asked. "I hate split-pea soup." Kessinger was aghast. "But Mr. De Mille," she cried, "why have you let me serve it to you for twenty years?" "You seemed to be so pleased with that choice," said De Mille fondly, "I didn't want to hurt your feelings."[16]

No Shadowboxing

Late in her career Ethel Barrymore was under contract to MGM. By that time she was far more interested in baseball and boxing than she was in discussing the finer points of acting. One afternoon Barrymore was sitting in her wheelchair listening to a baseball game on the radio, when young Esther Williams, full of enthusiasm, rushed up to her dressing room. "Oh, Miss B," the swimmer-turned-actress asked, "are you going to see the dailies?" Barrymore replied in her mellifluous voice, "No, my dear, no. Never see dailies—never." Undaunted, Williams inquired perkily, "But Miss B, doesn't it help your performance to see dailies?"

Barrymore looked at her with turquoise eyes, her face still vibrant and alive. "My dear," she said imperiously, "I *never* saw myself on the stage."[17]

Clerical Garb

During World War II Metro made a film about the French resistance movement called *The Cross of Lorraine,* in which Sir Cedric Hardwicke, an accomplished British actor, played a provincial priest. One noon Sir Cedric, still in priestly attire, started for the commissary with director Tay Garnett. On the way they passed a stage where Tommy Dorsey's band was rehearsing for a musical. A group had gathered before the open doors to listen to Dorsey's music, so Hardwicke and Garnett joined them. After some minutes the director reminded his actor that they had only an hour for lunch and should move on. As they turned to go, Sir Cedric bumped full force into Greer Garson, who at the time was working on *Mrs. Miniver.* Garson, observing the clerical robe, lowered her eyes and murmured, "I'm *so* sorry, Father." Hardwicke, deadpan, blessed the actress with the sign of the cross, then—inspired by Dorsey's jazz—executed an outrageous bump and grind. Garson, at last recognizing the actor, burst into laughter. For months afterward, whenever Sir Cedric met the red-haired actress, he solemnly muttered, "Bless you, my daughter."[18]

No Pearl Harbor

After the surprise attack on Pearl Harbor in December 1941, West Coast residents were ready to believe that Japanese bombers or even an invasion force might strike the mainland any day. Blackouts and air-raid drills were ordered to prepare the area for the worst. The Lockheed aircraft plant in Burbank was only a few blocks from Warner Bros., and someone pointed out that from the air Japanese bombardiers might not be able to tell the difference. Jack Warner decided to take the matter in hand. He went to the studio's paint shop and ordered an enormous sign made for the roof of one of his soundstages. It was a twenty-foot arrow pointing toward Burbank, with the words: LOCKHEED—THAT-A-WAY.[19]

The Lion Meows

When director Marshall Neilan was under contract to MGM and a new contract was brewing, he told some people at the studio that "an empty taxicab drove up this morning and out stepped Louis B. Mayer." He didn't help himself with Mayer later on when, at a big MGM preview, attended by all the studio big shots, he arranged it so that when Leo the Lion, MGM's trademark, appeared on the screen at the beginning of the picture it didn't give the usual growl but came out with a kitten's meow instead.[20]

Son Jimmy

When character actress Ann Doran learned that James Dean had been killed in a car crash, she was more grieved than surprised. Doran had played the actor's mother in *Rebel Without a Cause* (1955), released just weeks after his untimely death. During the making of the film she had come to know him well; she also became aware of his obsession with fast vehicles. Dean had bought a motorcycle during the shooting of *Rebel* and was eager to show it off. "Let me take you for a ride," he said to his screen mother. "No way," replied Doran. But he begged until she finally agreed. Dean had gone through the Warner Bros. lot, learned every soundstage, and knew which ones had both front and back doors open. He took Doran at breakneck speed all over the lot, roaring through soundstages, alternating from sunshine to darkness, with the actress screaming her head off. When they finally stopped, Doran was a wreck, needing a complete makeup job and a hairdo.

But the rebellious Dean and his screen mother grew close, far closer than their relationship in the film itself. After the movie was finished Doran was awakened at her home one morning around three o'clock by someone in her front yard yelling, "Mom! Mom!" The actress stuck her head out a window and asked, "Who is it? You're going to wake the neighbors." From out in the yard she heard a drunken voice say, "It's your son Jimmy." Doran invited Dean in and took him to the kitchen. She brewed some coffee, and the two of them sat on the kitchen floor while the young actor poured out his loneliness. They talked until dawn, and it was the first of several such visits. "He was not the self-assured person everybody believed he was," the actress declared. "He was kind of in limbo. He had great doubts about himself and where he was going. He was *that* lost."[21]

CHAPTER 6

Producers

The concept of the film producer grew out of the industry's need to make the fifty-two films that distributors wanted annually from each studio during Hollywood's heyday. It was the producer's job to find stories, develop screenplays, cast them, select directors, and oversee the making, scoring, and editing of films. The producers didn't finance pictures until the independents emerged, since most of them worked for companies that put up their own money. But strong producers were more than packagers, for they also had a part in the actual construction of films. They collaborated with writers, especially playwrights or novelists who were unsure of cinematic techniques.

Relations between producers and directors of films were frequently stormy; they were often more a test of strength than teamwork. Ultimately one or the other prevailed by force of personality, talent, or temperament. A strong director, once the picture was in his hands, insisted on complete control. But a forceful producer like David O. Selznick, who wanted to run things, clashed with directors and often forced their resignation. In other cases, however, producers viewed their role as simply a catalyst in putting the elements together, and then, content to be organizer rather than creator, stood aside once filming began. Those involved in the creative aspects of filmmaking usually viewed producers with suspicion, and clashes between the two were legion. Samuel Goldwyn fought bitterly with Rouben Mamoulian and ultimately fired him from *Porgy and Bess* (1959), which Mamoulian had directed on the stage as both play and opera. Even more notorious was Selznick's dismissal of George Cukor from *Gone With the Wind* (1939), after the director had made all the tests and started actual shooting, because Clark Gable was uncomfortable with Cukor's reputation as "a woman's director." Yielding to pressure, Selznick replaced Cukor with Gable's friend Victor Fleming. John Huston was fired from a remake of *A Farewell to Arms* (1957). And King Vidor walked off *Duel in the Sun* (1946) because he was unwilling to tolerate Selznick's interference and determination to turn a small Western into a spectacle equal to his triumph with *Gone With the Wind*.

John Ford, perhaps the greatest of all action directors, wouldn't allow scriptwriter or producer on his set. If either violated this rule, Ford coldly asked, "Don't you have an office?"[1] Once a producer scolded Ford for falling behind schedule. Ford then tore ten pages from the script, it was said, and remarked, "Now, we're three days ahead of schedule," and never shot the missing pages.[2] Even mild-mannered George Cukor ordered Metro producer Arthur Hornblow, Jr., to stay off his stage. Whenever Hornblow wanted to speak with Cukor, he had to phone him and make an appointment to see him in his office.[3]

Thalberg, Goldwyn, and Selznick were probably the three most forceful producers of the Golden Era, although Hal B. Wallis ranked only a step below. Irving Thalberg worked for Carl Laemmle at Universal, then became L. B. Mayer's head of production while still in his early twenties, quickly establishing Metro as the most glamorous film factory in Hollywood. Thalberg personally supervised many of the company's top productions, often reshooting entire sequences before giving his final approval. Eventually Goldwyn and Selznick both organized their own studios and were the first great independents. Goldwyn had been a glove salesman, in business with a man named Archie Selwyn. After they separated and Goldwyn had changed his name from Goldfish, Selwyn supposedly said, "Not only did he steal a large part of my money, he also stole half of my name." An often-told industry joke was that the producer stole the wrong half—he should have changed his name to "Selfish."[4]

A man of taste and a perfectionist, Goldwyn demanded the best, whatever the cost. He believed in lengthy preparations and in financing his pictures mainly with his own money, and he once junked $600,000 worth of film because it didn't measure up to his standards. As long as one agreed with Sam it was easy to get along with him; otherwise he could be impossible. A clever man without formal education, Sam's mangling of the English language was legendary, giving rise to a multitude of oft-quoted Goldwynisms. "A verbal contract," Sam insisted, "isn't worth the paper it's written on!"[5] In the heat of discussion he once said, "I can answer you in two words— *im* possible."[6] But Sam could also appear magnanimous: "I don't care if my pictures don't make a dime, so long as everyone comes to see them." Although many of these malaprops were undoubtedly manufactured by publicists, Goldwyn's wife Frances admitted that she had actually heard him utter about half of the famous sayings attributed to him.[7]

In addition to his determination to make successful pictures, Goldwyn was genuinely devoted to quality. Because he was proud of his reputation and wanted his name associated with the best product possible, he courted talent. He brought in writers like Lillian Hellman and Robert Sherwood as well as directors like William Wyler, and he was willing to spend whatever it cost to produce the finest in entertainment. His studio usually made only one film at a time so that he could give full attention to it. His comedies with Danny Kaye were lavish, for as Sam put it, "Our comedies are not to be laughed at."[8] But while Goldwyn respected talent in others, he had even greater esteem for his own gifts. Once in an interview a reporter made the mistake of saying, "When Willy Wyler made *Wuthering Heights* . . ." Goldwyn stopped him. "*I* made *Wuthering Heights*," he said icily. "Wyler only directed it."[9]

Equally anxious to make good movies, David O. Selznick also played a dynamic role in every step of filmmaking. A perfectionist with a mind for detail, Selznick was a man of exceptional energy, part of it induced by pills, and worked hour after hour, totally absorbed in his current project. According to actress Joan Fontaine, "Selznick was incapable of ordering a dinner in a restaurant without paying tremendous attention to it, and telling everybody what to have, and then going out and telling the chef how to do it."[10] Called "the great dictator" because he often dictated to his secretary until eleven o'clock at night, he wrote endless memos on every conceivable aspect of production. And he might ask a writer to dine with him, then keep him talking about the script until five in the morning.

"I'll be in about midday tomorrow," he often remarked as they broke up. "Do you think you could have what we've discussed on paper by then?"[11]

Difficult as Selznick might have been to work for, his vitality and enthusiasm were infectious. Tough businessman though he was, he could also be warm and charming, and his talent was unmistakable. His shortcomings, particularly toward the end, stemmed from his unbridled ambition to surpass even his own successes. As a result he tried to turn ordinary stories into epics, became increasingly meddlesome in scriptwriting, built bigger and grander sets, used great actors in small roles, and insisted on more of everything until his excessive zeal got the best of him. But Selznick believed in the romance of Hollywood, lived it in his life and work, and emerged as a godlike, fanatical figure, because of his drive for greatness and perfection.

Hal Wallis, on the other hand, had a far more practical point of view and was decidedly less egotistical than Selznick. His judgment was excellent, for he not only knew what would sell at the box office but also what had quality and taste as well. "Wallis could be a tyrant," recalled director Irving Rapper, but he was an expert and knowledgeable producer who "could tell you a budget while you were talking to him. He knew value immediately."[12] After succeeding Darryl Zanuck as production head of Warner Bros., Wallis moved to Paramount, where he was granted complete autonomy. There he headed his own production company and had his own contract players, but used the studio's facilities and released his pictures under the Paramount emblem. "Wallis took cinema out of the trite world and made it more intellectual," Lizabeth Scott maintained, "but not ponderously so. He knew just where to stop to keep it entertaining."[13]

In addition to the independents, each studio had its own roster of producers who worked under a company production head. At Metro, where producers enjoyed tremendous power, they were meticulously structured. At the top were men like Pandro Berman, Arthur Freed, and Sam Zimbalist, who got the choice properties and their pick of talent. Below them was a lesser group, and under them a third group that encompassed the producers of B pictures. In musicals alone, MGM boasted three major producers—Arthur Freed, Joe Pasternak, and Jack Cummings—each with a different style. Freed had been a Tin Pan Alley songwriter, and his pictures (An American in Paris, 1951) reflected the sophistication he had acquired through his years of associating with Irving Berlin, Cole Porter, George Gershwin, and Jerome Kern. Pasternak preferred sweeter stories, fables and fairy tales, often rooted in Europe and reflecting an operatic and concert tradition. In Pasternak Land mothers and fathers were respected, the flag was honored, and there were no terrible people. His films (*The Student Prince*, 1954) exhibited a fey sense, with everything turning out happily. Cummings was more adventuresome and willing to attempt the unusual, which he did most notably in *Seven Brides for Seven Brothers* (1954).

Henry Blanke of Warners was an excellent producer and highly sympathetic to directors. Jerry Wald, another Warners dynamo, was full of ideas and suggestions. At Twentieth Century-Fox, production was dominated by Darryl Zanuck, but company stalwarts included William Perlberg and Lamar Trotti, a writer turned producer. Universal had Aaron Rosenberg and later Ross Hunter, who succeeded in restoring glamour to filmmaking. Occasionally stage producers with great prestige made their way to Hollywood, among them John Houseman, a man of impeccable taste who worked at Paramount, RKO, and for five years at Metro.

Producer Pandro Berman observed that someone had to have his individual stamp on every picture. "It could be the writer," he said, "it could be the director, it could be the producer, it could even in some cases be the star, if he were a man like Doug Fairbanks, Sr. But all pictures should contain some person's drive and some person's point of view." Berman felt his own stamp was probably on about half of the 115 pictures he produced. It was always necessary to strike a balance between quality and a product the public wanted to see. Part of a producer's job, as Berman saw it, was "to fight like hell to have something above the average."[14] He himself produced many above average, notably the Rogers and Astaire musicals at RKO and *Father of the Bride* (1950) at Metro.

By the late 1940s the independent producers were making greater inroads into the industry, releasing their films through one of the major studios, especially RKO and United Artists. While the profits were bigger, so were risks. Frederick Brisson learned on his first project, *The Velvet Touch* (1948), featuring his wife, Rosalind Russell, how nerve-racking the problems facing independents could be. In his office Brisson installed a sign: BE KIND TO THE PRODUCER. TOMORROW HE COULD BE THE GATE MAN AND MAY NOT LET YOU IN THE STUDIO.[15]

Nothing Like Success

Writer Sidney Howard was working for Samuel Goldwyn when Sinclair Lewis's *Dodsworth* was published. "It would make a good picture," Howard told Goldwyn. "You can buy it for twenty thousand dollars." Sam looked into it, but decided he wasn't interested. "If you don't make this picture," Howard warned, "I'm going to do a play from it." That suited Goldwyn, so Howard wrote the play and it was a huge success. Goldwyn then decided he must buy the play and paid $165,000 for it, a big price in those days. "See, I told you," Howard told Goldwyn. "You could have bought it for twenty thousand dollars." Goldwyn was unperturbed. "I'd rather pay a hundred and sixty-five thousand for a successful play," he replied, "than twenty thousand for a novel that I don't know what it's going to be like."[16]

Great Dictator

When Alfred Hitchcock received the Milestone Award of the Screen Producers Guild in 1965, he reminisced, "When I came to America twenty-five years ago to direct *Rebecca*," Hitchcock said, "David Selznick sent me a memorandum." He paused for dramatic effect. "I've just finished reading it." There was laughter, followed by another pause. "I think I may make it into a motion picture," Hitchcock continued. "I plan to call it *The Longest Story Ever Told*."[17]

Desperation

Producer Sam Spiegel was a prototype of the rotund, cigar-chomping, tough-as-nails wheeler-dealer. One story goes that his reputation as a taskmaster almost drove writer Irwin Shaw to desperate measures. Shaw's wife awoke one morning at 3 A.M. to find her husband in the bathroom shaving. "Why?" she asked. "I'm going out to kill Sam Spiegel," Shaw is said to have replied.[18]

Goldwynisms

Sam Goldwyn always hired the hottest publicists in town, telling them he didn't care what they wrote about him so long as it was clean and that his name was spelled *Goldwyn*, not *Goldfish*. Since the press preferred colorful copy, columnists zeroed in on Sam's mixed metaphors and malaprops. "Include me out" became among the more famous, but the list is endless:

"You've got to take the bull by the teeth."

"Anyone who would go to a psychiatrist ought to have his head examined."

"I read part of it all the way through."

"It rolls off my back like a duck."

"I had a monumental idea this morning, but I didn't like it."

"I want to make a picture about the Russian Secret Police—the G.O.P."[19]

No Originality
When Sam Goldwyn learned that producer Jesse Lasky's second son would be named William, he was incensed. "Why would you name him Bill?" he snapped. "Every Tom, Dick, and Harry is named Bill."[20]

Alive and Well
When Goldwyn invited Henry Koster, director of Deanna Durbin's biggest hits, to take over The Bishop's Wife (1947), he asked Koster how he'd like to work with Laurette Taylor. "I'd love to," Koster said. "She's a great actress. But she's dead." Sam protested vigorously: "Two hours ago she was sitting where you are sitting now, and I talked to her!" Goldwyn called in his secretary and asked, "What was that lady's name who was just sitting here two hours ago? The actress." "Loretta Young," the secretary told him. "See!" Sam gloated. "What did I tell you? She's not dead!"[21]

Smell of Success
Jack Warner was outraged when Hal Wallis decided to leave Warner Bros. and form his own production unit at Paramount. Wallis gave a month's notice, and Jack vowed to make that month intolerable. He started by locking Wallis out of his office. Wallis set up a desk on the lawn, determined to continue performing his duties. When Warner heard what had happened, he ordered a truckload of horse manure emptied alongside Wallis's improvised office.[22]

Too Negative
Once Sam Goldwyn tentatively selected Yes, Yes as the title of an Eddie Cantor comedy. But his friend Abe Lehr, who had worked with Goldwyn in a glove factory as a young man, opposed the idea. "I don't like it," he told Goldwyn. "Give me one reason why Yes, Yes is

not a good title," said Goldwyn. "It's too negative," said Lehr. Exclaimed Goldwyn: "And they claim I say funny things!" But he changed the title.[23]

Ban

In April 1939, about the time that Mussolini invaded Albania, a producer's friend came running up and cried, "Have you heard the latest news?" "No, what happened?" asked the producer. "Italy," exclaimed the friend, "just banned *Marie Antoinette!*"

Nothing to It

When Edmund Grainger was producing *The Fabulous Texan* (1947) for Republic, he hired some reservation Indians to serve as experts to make sure the smoke signals called for in the script were authentic. After the picture was completed, Grainger congratulated them on their careful supervision. "It was easy," one of the Indians explained. "We learned how to do it from the movies."[25]

CHAPTER 7

Directors

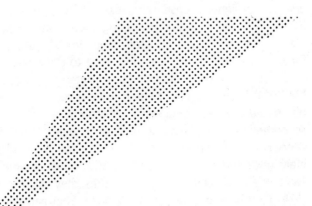

"Every picture has a certain rhythm which only one man can give it," maintained director Fritz Lang. "That man is the director. He has to be like the captain of a ship."[1] The stage is primarily a writer's and actor's medium, while a film usually belongs to the director, since he is the one who above everyone else shapes a work and places his stamp on it. The French *auteur* theory regards the director as the major creator—and thus the author—of a film. The director, according to this theory, is the force that blends the component arts and techniques into a harmonious whole. "He must know how to use the various members of the production company," Edward Dmytryk wrote, "to play them as a composer plays the keys of a piano."[2] He must make the actors feel secure. He must create an atmosphere on the set conducive to good work, easing tensions, yet stimulating his performers' emotional juices since there is no immediate audience to do that for him, only the camera.

"It is miserable to make a picture," director Dmytryk insisted. "You suffer tremendously. It's a horrible business because there's no business in the world that's as tough, that's as intense, that occupies your mind, your heart, everything, twenty-four hours a day. After a while you dream about it, you have nightmares about it. It never leaves you. It's amazing that this is a business of shadows, of making believe, and yet it's more real than any reality."[3] A director must develop inordinate concentration, until he is aware of every sound and mike shadow, details nobody else would notice. "You get to the point that every nerve in your body is related to what's happening on that set," declared Vincent Sherman.[4]

At least half of a director's working time is devoted to preparation, planning what the camera will photograph. He works with writers, set designers, costumers, cameramen, and technicians, and assists his actors in understanding their characters. Actress Signe Hasso, for one, hated directors who drifted, simply following performers with a camera, allowing them to do whatever they wished. "You have to have a pattern," Hasso stated. "You have to have some kind of rules, some craft behind the whole thing."[5] Yet the director has to stay within budgetary limitations and keep on a shooting schedule, knowing that his next assignment could depend on the success of his current picture. During the big-studio era directors were under contract just as stars and producers were. Even the best were often coerced into making films they disliked or knew were inferior. A veteran director told Vincent Sherman when he first went to Warner Bros., "If you get one movie you like out of six, that's really a good average."[6] Great directors, like King Vidor or John Ford, might expect one in two. To improve the ratio, some of the most powerful became their own producers, in an attempt to select better material and tighten their control over production. Still, the studio front office was always there to oversee budgets, forcing compromises. "Like all artists," executive Eugene Zukor observed, directors will "work on the biggest canvas you can give them."[7] A production manager was therefore responsible for expenses and making sure they didn't exceed the budget.

Cecil B. De Mille established the Hollywood director in archetypal form, although D. W. Griffith and Erich von Stroheim made more significant movies. Wearing riding breeches and boots, with a crop he struck against them for emphasis, De Mille was every inch a showman, living the legend for the sake of publicity. In late 1913 De Mille, an athletic, balding man of thirty-two, set out from New York with Dustin Farnum and a few others for Flagstaff, Arizona, to film *The Squaw Man*. Either their train arrived in bad weather or they decided the terrain was wrong, and they continued on to Los Angeles. They rented a barn, converted the horse stalls into dressing rooms, built an outside stage, hired some Indians and cowhands, and on December 29 began shooting the first important feature film made in California.

De Mille quickly emerged as the image of Hollywood. His pictures were made for the public, not the critics, and were lavish in every detail. He swept onto the set with an entourage trained to anticipate his every need. From his director's chair he spoke through a megaphone or bullhorn, even when the setup was small. While De Mille could be charming and good-natured, he could also be cruel, barking at extras through his megaphone, calling them names, abusing his assistants, never letting anyone forget he was king. "He looked like Caesar at all times," remembered choreographer LeRoy Prinz. "Everything was dramatic."[8]

De Mille was a visualist; his forte was handling effects and crowd scenes. Intimate shots he normally left to a dialogue director, while he concentrated on spectacle, always thinking of the big screen. He was shrewd enough to show more sex than practically anyone in the business, taking his stories from the Bible and thereby making them acceptable to the censorship office. Yet De Mille's conviction that he was filming something significant carried across to audiences, bringing them back time and again. Yul Brynner, who made an early film appearance in De Mille's remake of *The Ten Commandments* (1956), became a lifelong admirer. "There are some monstrous performances," Brynner acknowledged of this last De Mille film. "There are some monstrous mistakes, and yet it has this extraordinary drive of De Mille to do something important and something truly beautiful, which shines and drives that movie through to a conclusion."[9]

Most of the old silent-film directors continued to believe, even after the advent of sound, that the more they could tell with the camera the better. Allan Dwan, a former Notre Dame football star, went to work for the Essanay studios in 1909, directing over 250 one-reelers before undertaking his first feature film in 1914. Dwan was a tough codger who had stood up to the Trust when hired gunmen appeared on his set to prevent the shooting of an independent picture. Later he directed *Robin Hood* (1922) and *The Iron Mask* (1929) for Douglas Fairbanks, then carried his visual approach into the making of sound films. Raoul Walsh, Henry King, and William Wellman all learned their craft during the Silent Era and remained visual storytellers, direct and down-to-earth. Jack Warner once said, "To Raoul Walsh a tender love scene is burning down a whorehouse."[10] Certainly Walsh was happiest when photographing action; dialogue only became important when it was essential to furthering the story.

King Vidor advanced the silent technique to a more creative level than most of the other directors did, and his films, particularly *The*

Big Parade (1927) and *The Crowd* (1928), are filled with visual imagery; he has been compared with metaphoric realists like Andrew Wyeth and Robert Frost. He did excellent work in sound too. But Capra and McCarey were equally good with sound, especially when it came to comedy. Frank Capra, a Sicilian immigrant, fell in love with America and emerged during the Great Depression as Hollywood's strongest spokesman for democracy and the common man. Capra dared to make patriotism fashionable, reviving a nation's faith in the ideals of Jefferson and Lincoln through such folk heroes as Jeff Smith, Longfellow Deeds, and John Doe. While Capra tempered his populism with humor, comedy was Leo McCarey's paramount strength, reflecting the director's own easygoing personality. With *Going My Way* (1944), McCarey won an Academy Award for best direction. Another of the old silent directors, he was never comfortable with the written word, and in rehearsing a scene would suddenly say, "Now forget the script and just talk it through." After his actors ad-libbed the scene, McCarey would often remark, "You know something? That sounds better than what we have written down here."[11]

Orson Welles was once asked to name the three best directors in the history of Hollywood. "I like the old masters," Welles answered, "by which I mean John Ford, John Ford, and John Ford."[12] Unquestionably, Ford was the supreme camera director, who knew composition and how to capture terrain better than anyone in the trade. He directed *The Iron Horse* (1924), one of the first Western spectacles, immediately establishing himself in that genre. A tender man with a gruff exterior, Ford surrounded himself with his own stock company, bullying the people he loved most, frightening those who didn't understand him. He wore a black patch over one eye and habitually chewed on the corner of a handkerchief. To achieve the proper mood, he had an accordian player, Danny Borzage, on the set at all times, rendering tunes like "Red River Valley" and "Bringing in the Sheaves." He was seldom comfortable directing women, and preferred to do a scene in one take, rarely bound to the written word, concentrating on atmosphere. "Pappy" Ford, as he was called, loved people who drank and was himself a hard boozer when not working. "His hands and eyes were so gentle," said Ford regular Harry Carey, Jr., "and yet somehow there was a part of him that John Wayne physically exemplified, something he always wanted to be. So he created that on the screen. He wanted to be a two-fisted, brawling, heavy-drinking Irishman that could do what Wayne did. He was a unique, complex man."[13]

With the advent of sound, Hollywood studios raided the Broadway stage for directors as well as stars, frequently hiring them to coach dialogue. George Cukor, one of the finest directors from the theater, took great pains with actors, had an eye sensitive to decor and beauty, but never became proficient in camera technique. He took for granted that the cameraman knew his business and he believed that a director's foremost obligation was to the script. "The text tells you where the camera should be," Cukor declared, "what the emphasis should be. I don't think that's a question of your judgment. . . . If the story is good, the director is halfway there."[14] Rouben Mamoulian, who alternated between stage and screen, proved more experimental, insisting he'd had "enough dialogue to last me a long time" in the theater. "What fascinated me was the camera and the things we could do with camera."[15]

With troubled times in Europe, Hollywood saw an influx of foreign directors. Ernst Lubitsch arrived from Berlin during the Silent Era to make *Rosita* (1923) with Mary Pickford, perfecting his light, sophisticated touch with films like *The Merry Widow* (1934) and *Ninotchka* (1939). Lubitsch died during the making of *That Lady in Ermine* (1948) and was buried in a glass-covered coffin with a cigarette in his hand. After the funeral fellow directors William Wyler and Billy Wilder were walking silently toward their parked cars. "Pity. No more Lubitsch," Wyler finally said. "Worse," Wilder answered. "No more Lubitsch pictures."[16]

William Dieterle came to Hollywood to make German versions of American pictures. A pleasant man socially, who always wore white gloves, Dieterle could be demanding, even insulting on the set. So could Fritz Lang and Otto Preminger, both from Vienna. Lang, an exacting martinet, knew precisely what he wanted in each sequence and explained it so fully he drew incredible performances from actors. With the crew his methods were so rough that stagehands threatened to drop sand bags on him.[17] Preminger was perhaps the most tyrannical of all. He might start by sarcastically criticizing actors and end up screaming at them, as he worked himself into a state of "Otto-intoxication."[18]

From Russia came Lewis Milestone, who specialized in hard-hitting films about war, most notably *All Quiet on the Western Front* (1930). His technique was essentially motivating actors and allowing them to fill in the details. That particular approach broke down on the remake of *Mutiny on the Bounty* (1962), mainly because of Marlon Brando's power to interfere and constant rewrites. Finding the situation impossible, Milestone picked up a copy of *The Hollywood Reporter* and was leafing through it when the producer appeared on the set to watch a scene being shot. "Aren't you going to watch the scene?" the producer asked. "What for?" Milestone said. "When the picture is finished, I'll buy a ticket and see the whole bloody mess in a theater."[19]

Michael Curtiz, a versatile Hungarian director, rivaled Sam Goldwyn as a wrecker of the English language. Flamboyant, talented, a bundle of nervous energy, Curtiz had the reputation of eating actors for breakfast. He once described Bette Davis as "the flea in the ointment and a no good sexless son-of-a-bitch."[20] Patience was never Mike's long suit. "The next time I send a damn fool for something," he once said, "I go myself."[21] Curtiz had a Packard that he drove in second gear for a year before he realized there was a third gear.[22] He was nevertheless a man of taste, and on the set no detail was too small for his eye to catch. He worked fast, had great expertise with the camera, was particularly skillful at mass movement of people, and proved best on panoramic pictures like *The Charge of the Light Brigade* (1936).

England's Alfred Hitchcock, the master of suspense, was a highly technical director, meticulous in planning every move for his actors, sketching each scene in advance for camera angles. "When the screenplay is finished," Hitchcock often said, "the picture is finished. Because from then on it's merely a matter of putting it on the screen."[23] He shot a film so sparingly that it couldn't be edited except the way he shot it. Part of his genius was that he forced viewers to use their imaginations; audiences were never sure what they saw. Personally Hitchcock was enigmatic, ranging from sadist to sweet, gentle fat man. "Emotionally," actress Tippi Hedren claimed, "he had all kinds of frustrations and neuroses. . . . He thought of himself as looking like Cary Grant. That's tough, to think of yourself one way and look another."[24] Time and again he put his heroines through trials that bordered on cruelty, taking a self-assured actress and deliberately breaking her down.

Whereas Hitchcock saw actors as little more than bodies for him to manipulate, William Wyler's method was practically the opposite. Wyler found explaining what he wanted extremely difficult. Born in Alsace, he came to California in 1921 to work for "Uncle" Carl Laemmle at Universal. Gradually he matured into one of Hollywood's most respected directors, winning three Academy Awards: *Mrs. Miniver* (1942), *The Best Years of Our Lives* (1946), and *Ben-*

Hur (1959). Yet Wyler firmly believed that his first duty was to entertain. "A passion for your subject and a knowledge of your craft,"
Wyler said, "are the two essential things."[25] Although vitally concerned with characterization, Wyler didn't believe in directing actors, preferring to let them shape their own performances. He sat
directly under the camera, seldom saying much, watching his actors'
movements. Careful about every line, look, and thought, he filmed
take after take, sometimes thirty or forty, striving for perfection.
When actors began to go stale or impatiently demanded to know
what their director wanted, Wyler's typical response was, "I want it
better."[26] Eventually some new insight, a new interpretation of a line
or word, came into the scene. Wyler would yell, "Great! That's it,"
at last seeing what he wanted.

The bulk of Hollywood's directorial talent in the Golden Age had
grown up with the industry. Victor Fleming, a native Californian who
directed both *Gone With the Wind* and *The Wizard of Oz* (1939),
began his career as an assistant cameraman for Allan Dwan. Henry
Hathaway, another Californian, started in films as a child actor,
worked as a messenger boy at Universal and propman for Frank
Lloyd, then became an assistant director. Later Hathaway was noted
for Westerns like *The Sons of Katie Elder* (1965) and *True Grit* (1969)
and semidocumentaries like *The House on 92nd Street* (1945).
George Stevens (*Shane,* 1953; *Giant,* 1956) had been a cameraman
during the Silent Era, whereas Edward Dmytryk (*Raintree County,*
1957; *The Carpetbaggers,* 1964) and Robert Wise (*The Sound of Music,* 1965) had both been film cutters. George Seaton (*Airport,* 1970),
Joe Mankiewicz (*All About Eve,* 1950), Billy Wilder (*Sunset Blvd.,*
1950) and John Huston (*The Maltese Falcon,* 1941; *The African
Queen,* 1951) all established themselves as writers in Hollywood before turning director.

Musicals lured another group of directors from Broadway. Busby
Berkeley joined Warner Bros. as a choreographer in 1930, directing
his first picture three years later. More concerned with cinematic
effects than with dance itself, Berkeley choreographed for *42nd Street*
(1933) and revolutionized the faltering screen musical. Vincente
Minnelli had been a Broadway art director before coming to MGM,
where he quickly established himself as a visual artist without peer,
working in Technicolor much as a painter would. Minnelli spent so
much time lining up details and framing every shot that his crew
referred to him as "the gargoyle director." On *Yolanda and the Thief*
(1945) he kept Lucille Bremer in a bubble bath from eight in the

morning until eleven, fussing over background decorations seen through the crook of her arm as she answered a telephone.[27]

Each studio had its formula directors, solid craftsmen who brought pictures in on schedule and within budget, but contributed little special value to the scripts assigned them. They did their job, sometimes making three or four movies a year—some good, some bad, others mediocre. Most company directors were efficient, businesslike, willing to cut corners whenever the studio demanded. Actors seldom faulted them, yet weren't particularly excited about working with them. James Cagney, however, remembered them more critically. Although he acknowledged those with talent, "many directors are just pedestrian workmen," he claimed, some of whom "couldn't direct you to a cheap delicatessen."[28] Big stars in such instances might usurp most of the directorial power themselves, but when a cast included two headstrong stars, chaos could develop. Asked how he enjoyed directing Bette Davis and Miriam Hopkins in *Old Acquaintance* (1943), Vincent Sherman replied, "I didn't direct them. I refereed."[29]

In the 1950s stage directors like Arthur Penn, Elia Kazan, and George Roy Hill, as well as television directors like Delbert Mann and Sam Peckinpah, made their mark in feature films. A new breed later appeared with Stanley Kubrick, Peter Bogdanovich, Francis Ford Coppola, Michael Cimino, and Woody Allen. Like their predecessors, each of these directors infused films with their individual personalities, shaping materials in unique ways. Curiously, the most successful director in recent years, Steven Spielberg, was philosophically rooted in old Hollywood. "Each of us would like to do to the industry what Irving Thalberg did to it fifty years ago," Spielberg said in 1982,[30] admitting that he dreamed for a living. "I love the work the way Patton loved the stink of battle. But when I grow up, I still want to be a director."[31]

C.B. Gets Message

De Mille loved to talk to his extras and insisted on their complete attention. Every day before breaking for lunch, he'd give the assemblage a lecture: "Now this morning," he'd begin, "I want everybody to listen to me," and then he'd go on and on and on. One day he looked down from his perch and saw two women talking. "Hold it just a minute," he cried. "Ladies, you and you come up here please." The two women dutifully mounted the platform. "Now," the director ordered, "if what you have to say is so important, please tell everybody over the microphone. Go ahead, tell them." One of the delinquents took the mike and sheepishly explained, "Well, I was just asking my friend when was that old, bald-headed son-of-a-bitch gonna let us have lunch!" De Mille turned purple, grabbed the microphone and yelled, "Lunch!"[32]

Deadlines

W. S. (Woody) Van Dyke, an old director of silents who did the original *Tarzan* picture, almost invariably finished assignments ahead of schedule. Early in the sound period he was making one of the *Thin Man* movies at MGM with William Powell and Myrna Loy. For a trucking shot down a long refectory table, he had seated most of the Metro stock company, character actors audiences knew on sight. At the head of the table was the group's boss, played by a bespectacled veteran who always wore a black moustache. The old actor had a long speech to deliver as the camera trucked down the table, photographing the reactions of all the other characters. As the camera got to the end, the actor said, "And that's all I've got to say." He sat down and actually *died*. Realizing what had happened, an assistant said, "You'd better get Doc Jones." So they called the studio doctor, and he said, "Yes, he's dead. Better get him out of here." They started to remove the body, when Woody Van Dyke yelled, "Hold it! Hold it!" He took out his viewfinder and got down in back of the actor's body, looking for an over-the-shoulder shot. "All right," Van Dyke finally said, "take him out, but leave the coat." And he kept on working.[33]

Wheelchair

Directing could be dangerous, especially if the director acted in a picture too, as Orson Welles did when making *Citizen Kane* (1940). To show Kane's face aging, Welles wore special lenses in his eyes, along with makeup that made it hard for him to see. In one scene, he cut his hand badly on some furniture and in another he fell down a flight of stairs and injured one of his ankles. For the next two weeks he directed from a wheelchair.[34]

Believe in You

When Jesse Lasky, Jr., went to work for De Mille on *The Buccaneer* (1958), De Mille asked, "Do you believe in God, Jesse?" "Yes sir, I think so." "Think so?" De Mille said. "But you don't know." "I believe in you, sir," the writer replied. "Not a bad beginning," De Mille allowed, thumbing some of Lasky's pages.[35]

For Art
"Wild Bill" Wellman had a reputation for being tough. In the last scene of *Battleground* (1949), a platoon of soldiers, having just fought the Battle of the Bulge, was supposed to march up out of a ravine looking tired but proudly determined. The scene was shot on a hot day, and the men were all sweltering under their overcoats and heavy equipment. One soldier in the group, Tommy Breen, was a real war hero, having lost a leg when an American tank ran over him in the South Pacific. So Wellman put him in front as the *Battleground* platoon started walking out of the ravine. Suddenly he shouted, "Breen, you're out of step. Let's do it again." The men went back and started marching out again. "Breen, goddamn it, get in step!" Wellman barked again and demanded another take. But as he continued to yell at Breen, with his one leg, and ordered more takes, the veteran's fellow performers became indignant and then furious. In the end Wellman got exactly what he wanted on film and he embraced Breen and apologized. Not until then did the actors realize the method behind Wild Bill's madness.[36]

Interference
John Ford resented studio interference with his work on the set. Once, when he was out on a prairie shooting a Western, a man came riding up on horseback with an urgent message: a wire from producer Sol Wurtzel complaining that Ford was behind schedule. Ford scanned it and then looked over at a cowboy who helped out on his pictures. "Ed," he yelled, "I have a message here from Wurtzel. I'm going to fold it up and I want you to shoot a hole straight through the name." He held the wire up in his right hand and stood there calmly as the cowboy put a rifle to his shoulder and fired. Ford then unfolded the wire and held it up for everyone to see. The bullet had gone right through Wurtzel's name. There was applause and everyone went back to work.[37]

Knuckles
While on a six-day week in Italy filming *Cleopatra* (1963), director Joseph Mankiewicz spent his days shooting and his nights and Sun-

days writing and rewriting to keep things moving. On the set one day Elizabeth Taylor, playing Cleopatra, saw him biting his nails. "Joe," she cried, "don't bite your fingernails." "I'm not," he told her. "I'm biting my knuckles. I finished the fingernails months ago." Eventually he began wearing gloves while writing to preserve what was left of his nails.[38]

Fish Pond
John Farrow, Mia's father, had a reputation for being arrogant and sadistic, causing more than one actress to rush to her dressing room in tears. During the 1940s Farrow worked mainly at Paramount, where there was a fish pond in the courtyard between the administration building, the actors' dressing rooms, the producers' building, and the production offices. The pond was stocked with large goldfish. Repeatedly Farrow was seen standing beside the pond, a silver-handled cane in his hand, hitting goldfish over the head. It seemed to be his favorite pastime.[39]

Language Like That
In the early sound days, Cecil B. De Mille was directing a scene in which a cowboy was to fall off his horse after a rifle shot. "No matter what happens," De Mille told the cameraman, "I want you to keep grinding. Understand? Don't stop for anything." The scene went off as planned; it was so realistic, in fact, that a substitute studio doctor, on the movie set for the first time, thought the cowboy had really been injured, and rushed up to administer first aid. De Mille exploded in wrath when he saw what was happening. He jumped out of his chair and rushed toward the doctor, shaking his fist and hurling expletives at him. Frightened half to death by De Mille's rage, the doctor fled in panic from the set, and the director returned, huffing and puffing, to his chair.

The next day De Mille ran off the previous day's rushes in the projection room. He seemed surprised as he saw the doctor suddenly rush across the screen, pursued by a bald-headed man showering a torrent of abuse at him. "Who in the world is that?" De Mille asked, puzzled. "That's the studio doctor," an assistant told him. "I know that," said De Mille impatiently. "I mean the man using that frightful language." "That, sir, is you," said the assistant. "Young man," said the pious De Mille frostily, "that may *appear* to be me, but I assure you it is not. I never use language like that."[40]

Rough on Clergy

Hardboiled Mike Curtiz was explaining a scene while a little guy playing a minister was walking in back of him. "You watch," said Mike. "You watch how the camera moves here. You watch now." Right behind the minister was a huge excavation about twelve feet deep. "Then we come back," Mike explained, "we move with the camera." As he stepped back, the fellow playing the minister fell right into the pit. Curtiz looked down and, without missing a beat, said, "Get another minister!"[41]

Best Show

When young Mary Anderson played in *Lifeboat* (1944), she was eager to please director Alfred Hitchcock and his cameraman and to learn as much as she could about profile photography. "Mr. Hitchcock," she said one day, "what do you think is my best side?" "My dear," he replied without looking up at her, "you're sitting on it."[42]

Disagreements

Lewis Milestone and producer Sam Goldwyn had more confrontations than usual making *The North Star* (1943). One afternoon Goldwyn called the director into his office, intending to embarrass him in front of a studio employee. Sam began by accusing Milestone of tampering with the Lillian Hellman script, and when the director tried to explain, Goldwyn yelled louder and pounded his desk. Milestone controlled himself for several minutes, but finally asked, "If my work is so terrible, why don't you fire me?" Goldwyn shouted, "No! I won't fire you!" By then exasperated, the director insisted, "Go ahead! Fire me! I'm sick and tired of this!" But Goldwyn held firm: *"No! I won't, and that's final!"* Furious, Milestone turned and stormed out. As the shaken studio employee got up to leave, Goldwyn said, grinning with satisfaction, "I told him, didn't I?"[43]

Demonstration

While directing *The Shock* (1923) on the set of a New York street, Lambert Hillyer jumped from a second-story window during a rehearsal and broke his arm. "I told you to hire a double for this stunt," raged Irving Thalberg. "I did," groaned Hillyer, "but I had to show him how to do it."[44]

Major Wyler Wins Oscar

Shortly after completing *Mrs. Miniver,* William Wyler enlisted in the air force and was stationed with the Ninety-first Bomber Group near Oxford. One day he received a call from the editor of *Stars and Stripes* in London, inquiring if Major Wyler had a photograph of himself. Wyler said he didn't. "Do you know where I can get one?" the editor persisted. Wyler asked why he needed it. "You won the Academy Award," the man informed him. "Don't you know that?" Wyler said, "No! When?" The editor answered, "Last night in Hollywood at the Academy Awards." Wyler had to chuckle. For five consecutive years he had gone to the Academy Awards ceremony, having been nominated for best director. "I went in with a suitcase to bring home the Oscars and got nothing," the director explained. "Now I get one and I'm not there!" His wife accepted for him.[45]

Spik English

Russian-born director Gregory Ratoff spoke with an accent so thick he was almost unintelligible, especially to anyone not fluent in English. During the making of *Intermezzo* (1939) Ratoff frequently shouted at the Swedish-born Ingrid Bergman, "Vy don' you spik English? Say it like I do!"[46]

Final Word

John Ford had little tolerance for meddlesome producers, including Sam Goldwyn. During the shooting of *The Hurricane* (1937), Sam managed to sneak a look at the rushes, only to find fewer close-ups of Dorothy Lamour and Jon Hall than he thought necessary. The next day Goldwyn appeared on the set and suggested tentatively to Ford that perhaps he was not shooting enough close-ups. The director replied pugnaciously, "Now, I'll tell you, Mr. Goldwyn, *I'm* making this picture the way *I* feel it should go. If I want a close-up this big," and hit Goldwyn in the stomach with the back of his hand, "I'll make 'em that big. Or if I want 'em *this* big," and he struck Sam in the chest, "they'll be this big." Then, clenching his fist, he said, "I might want them even bigger!" Intimidated, Goldwyn left the set with a companion at his side. As they walked across the lot, Sam felt compelled to have the final say. "Well, anyway," he muttered, "I put it in his mind."[47]

CHAPTER 8

Writers

Most filmmakers agree that the success of any project begins with the script. Even Cecil B. De Mille conceded that writers were more important than stars, producers, cameramen, or directors, including himself. "You can do nothing unless you have it on paper first," director Mervyn LeRoy pointed out.[1] Even in musicals the writing supported all else. "The script is everything," echoed director Edward Buzzell, who had once been a Broadway song-and-dance man. "If you get a good script, you'll get a good picture."[2] Actors work hardest and suffer most when the script is bad. "You struggle, you claw, and you scratch trying to camouflage a bad script," Gregory Peck declared. "When the script is sound and the structure is there, you just sort of sail through. It's work, but it's fun at the same time."[3]

Despite their acknowledged importance, writers in the big-studio system consistently complained about poor working conditions and their low status in the Hollywood pecking order. Novelist Charles Marquis Warren, under contract to Paramount during the late 1940s, claimed the only way he could get on a set to watch his pictures being shot was to pay fifty cents and join a studio tour. Writers at Warner Bros. agreed that work there was a grind, for Jack Warner insisted that they keep a nine-to-five-thirty schedule, take only half an hour for lunch, and wear their pencils down to a certain length by the end of the day. Warners' writers used to put their pencils into a sharpener to grind them down to half an inch. When any of their pictures received a bad review, their response was often, "Well, we don't know why, because we were there at nine o'clock, we took a half hour for lunch, and our pencils were down to here. So it couldn't be our fault."[4]

Well paid though they were, screenwriters suffered the frustration of sharing a script with several other writers and never knowing what would come out in the end. Screenplays went through numerous revisions by one team after another, so that it was sometimes difficult to determine who contributed what. Producer Walter Wanger had two writers under contract for $2,500 a week named Towne and Baker, both good idea men who understood film. Towne was practically illiterate, saying things like, "Bring that dame in here and she'll do this. . . . Then the punk comes in. . . ." The more dignified Baker put their material on paper after the two had worked out the action. "Oh, this stinks," Towne would say. "Nobody will ever stand for that." Wanger claimed they wrote every sequence on toilet paper, which they hung on the wall. When they were ready, the producer would go in and comment, "That seems a little too long. There might be a dead spot there." If the writers agreed, they'd simply tear off a couple of sheets of toilet paper. Once the blueprint of the action was completed, Wanger would bring in Dorothy Parker to rewrite their material and insert the dialogue.[5]

Studios hired a bevy of junior writers, starting them at $75 a week. Most had published short stories; all welcomed a steady income. Since each studio had to keep its stars busy, the production office was constantly searching for suitable vehicles for them. "OK," writers might be told, "we're looking for a picture for Cary Grant." Usually writers were teamed up, and a dozen or more teams might be working on stories for Cary Grant. After the writers turned them in, perhaps two or three would stand out as possibilities. The story outlines of these would then be given to the studio's top contract writers for development.[6] If junior writers came up with enough good ideas, they soon received more money and found themselves in the top echelon. If they failed, their option was not picked up and they were dropped.

Scripts frequently were written with a particular star in mind and tailored to suit that star's salient characteristics. In scenes for Gary Cooper the dialogue needed to be kept short, so that whatever Cooper said seemed important. Often scenes didn't work as they were written once the director started shooting. They had to be changed by last-minute revisions, generally a collaboration between the writers and the director, who toiled until the situation rang true. Directors trained in motion-picture technique generally preferred a fluid attitude toward the script. "You keep yourself open until the very last possible second in which you finally record a scene," Edward Dmytryk said.[7]

Scripts were thrown together within days when the studio had a pressing commitment. A previous film might be reworked or an old story the studio had owned for years dusted off, or two earlier scripts merged. In these cases the whole locale might change for better effect or to disguise the repetition. When the director sensed he didn't have much of a script to work with, he knew the struggle ahead. Often he had to introduce physical action or contrive situations to take attention away from the spoken word. Directors and writers did the best they could under such circumstances, attempting at least to present their material in good taste.

Contract writers developed something of a double philosophy— writing scripts they believed in but turning out others strictly to earn a living. MGM offered the pleasantest atmosphere for writers, who were seldom as pressed there as elsewhere to come up with something in a short time. Still, Metro writers enjoyed little independence, for what they wrote was determined by individual producers. Stature was usually linked to a writer's pay and office location. In the MGM writers' building there were two floors. Those with offices on the second floor were well paid and respected; those on the first floor were neither well paid nor respected. Most envied of all were those not totally dependent on motion pictures—novelists, playwrights, and other published authors.[8]

At Paramount the writers' building was almost a fraternity. All of the comedy writers were on the fourth floor, where they gathered around the coffeepot by the switchboard and exchanged ideas. "If anybody was stuck, everybody would pitch in and try to help them out," Melville Shavelson remembered.[9] Writers at Warner Bros. and Columbia were expected to keep office hours, including a half day on Saturday, and turn out a minimum number of pages a week.

Nunnally Johnson, one of old Hollywood's top screenwriters, considered himself "a businessman's writer, strictly a nine-to-five fellow." Even on his honeymoon he spent at least a portion of every day at the typewriter.[10] He was one of Twentieth Century-Fox's most creative writers and worked closely with Darryl Zanuck on film classics like *Jesse James* (1939) and *The Grapes of Wrath* (1940). Thoroughly aware of the visual side of moviemaking, Johnson turned out scripts that were skillfully constructed and literate. In the projection room, watching a day's rushes, he frequently said to the director, "You look; I'll listen."[11]

There were always serious writers—Robert Sherwood, Elmer Rice, F. Scott Fitzgerald, William Faulkner, Clifford Odets, Gore Vidal—who worked for Hollywood, especially when they needed money. From Broadway came Howard Lindsay, Maxwell Anderson, Ben Hecht and Charles MacArthur, Moss Hart, Lillian Hellman, Garson Kanin, Betty Comden and Adolph Green. Most of them soon learned that in screenwriting the fewer words the better. John Steinbeck, who knew his limitations as a pictorial dramatist, expressed relief that Nunnally Johnson was to construct a screenplay from his novel *The Moon Is Down*, and told him, "Tamper with it."[12]

Screenwriting as a craft probably reached a peak when Herman J. Mankiewicz collaborated with Orson Welles on *Citizen Kane* (1941), often regarded as the finest American film ever made. Mankiewicz was a self-destructive genius who, as a regular at the Algonquin Round Table in New York, had been highly regarded for his intelligence and wit. His brother, writer-director Joseph L. Mankiewicz, was also superb with verbal touches as well as marvelous little darts and innuendos. But each major studio had its share of writing talent, beginning with Anita Loos and Frances Marion, who in the Silent Era fashioned scenarios of unusual wit and effectiveness. Later, after sound was introduced, Metro had John Lee Mahin, Donald Ogden Stewart, Frances Goodrich, and Albert Hackett; Twentieth Century-Fox had Philip Dunne and Ring Lardner, Jr.; Paramount had Charles Brackett and Billy Wilder; Columbia had Jo Swerling; while Warners had Howard Koch and the Epstein twins.

But when the House Un-American Activities Committee launched its purge in 1947, studio heads grew frightened, because many of their writers showed left-wing tendencies and some were even members of the Communist party. Seven of the famous Hollywood Ten, who served prison sentences for contempt of Congress, were writers. Scores more were eventually blacklisted as a result of the "Waldorf-Astoria decree," in which producers, nervous about negative publicity, agreed not to employ anyone thought to have Communist affiliations. The entire industry was suddenly paralyzed with fear. Top writers fled to more tolerant climates in New York and Europe, leaving Hollywood with a vacuum where talent had once abounded.

Leftists who stayed worked at reduced fees and muted their criticism, even cloaking their identities in pseudonyms.

By 1952 Carl Foreman, working for liberal producer Stanley Kramer, was able to comment on public cowardice in recent events, wrapping his allegory in a traditional Western format. In his acclaimed *High Noon*, starring Gary Cooper, Foreman used "Hadleyville" to suggest Hollywood. He admitted that Marshal Kane's choice between conscience and conformity to community pressures was similar to his order to appear before the House investigating committee, which to many was a violation of his civil liberties.[13] In 1956 Dalton Trumbo, a member of the Hollywood Ten, won an Academy Award for *The Brave One* (1956), which he wrote under the pseudonym of Robert Rich. Gradually the hysteria subsided. Four years later Trumbo received full credit on *Exodus* and *Spartacus*, but the damage to Hollywood's morale had been done.

Great Idea

In 1942 Cecil B. De Mille was working on *Reap the Wild Wind*, a sea epic starring John Wayne and Ray Milland. His scriptwriters were Charles Bennett, Alan LeMay, and Jesse Lasky, Jr., none of whom could come up with a satisfactory ending. "We've got to find an end to this movie," De Mille told them one evening, but all remained stumped. The next morning Charles Bennett was taking his bath when he suddenly thought, "Giant squid!" When the director and his team settled down to discuss the end of the film a few hours later, De Mille reiterated, "We still haven't got it." "Giant squid!" Bennett exclaimed. He then got up and acted out the whole sequence as he had invented it in the bathtub. He played all the parts: John Wayne, Ray Milland, the squid—acting out their life-and-death struggle in front of De Mille. When he finished, the director sat back with an ecstatic look on his face. "Yes, Charles," he said, "and in Technicolor."[14]

Pola Negri and Lardner

When the temperamental Polish star Pola Negri was making *Bella Donna* (1923), she insisted that only those connected with the picture be permitted on the set. But one day, writer Ring Lardner was visiting the studio and was allowed to go on the stage despite the "no visitors" sign. When Pola saw him she blew up and cried, "Who ees that funny-looking man? R-re-remove him or I weel not go on weeth thees picture!" "Quiet, Pola," whispered the director. "That's Ring Lardner." "Who ees thees Ring Lordner?" she cried. "A very important author," said the director. "So?" breathed Pola. She rolled her eyes seductively toward Lardner and murmured: "Introdooce me, plizz. I weel eenspire heem to write a beautiful sonnet!"[15]

Best Effort
Joan Crawford met F. Scott Fitzgerald at a party. When the author humbly announced he would be writing her next screenplay, the actress looked at him with burning eyes. "Write hard, Mr. Fitzgerald," Crawford said, "write hard!"[16]

Racing Scenes
When screenwriter John Gregory Dunne learned that a friend of his was doing a screenplay for a racing picture, he was surprised. "I didn't know you were interested in auto racing," he said. "I'm not," said his friend. "Bores me stiff." "Then how do you handle the racing scenes?" Dunne asked. "With the magic of stage direction," he answered. "SEQUENCE TO BE STAGED BY DIRECTOR."[17]

Faulkner and Gable
In 1932 novelist William Faulkner went to Hollywood to do some screenwriting for MGM. One day he joined his friend producer-director Howard Hawks and Metro star Clark Gable for some dove hunting in the Imperial Valley. En route he and Hawks got to talking about books, and Gable listened quietly for a few minutes and then decided to get in on the conversation. "Mr. Faulkner," he said, "what do you think somebody should read if he wants to read the best modern books? Who would you say are the best living writers?" "Ernest Hemingway," replied Faulkner, "Willa Cather, Thomas Mann, John Dos Passos, and William Faulkner." Surprised by the answer, Gable was silent for a moment and then asked: "Do you write?" "Yes, Mr. Gable," said Faulkner calmly. "What do you do?"[18]

After Hours
Writer Norman Krasna clashed with Jack Warner toward the end of his work on *Princess O'Rourke* (1943), which starred Olivia de Havilland. Jack insisted Warner Bros. writers put in a full day's work

and, impatient at the delay, accused Krasna of quitting early. "God-dam it," Warner said, "we have to have an ending. We have Olivia on salary at fifteen thousand dollars a week." Looking at his watch, Krasna announced, "I have the problem solved. I have the perfect ending." Warner grew excited, as everyone at the conference table could plainly see. "Well," he said expectantly, "what is it?" Krasna replied, "I can't tell you." Warner demanded to know why. "Because," Krasna explained, glancing again at his watch, "I thought of the answer after five-thirty."[19]

Sure Thing

F. Scott Fitzgerald claimed he liked Sam Goldwyn because "You always knew where you stood with him: nowhere."[20]

Saving Warner Bros.

Warners featured Dennis Morgan in a series of popular *Two Guys* comedies directed by veteran David Butler. Finally the studio threw Morgan a *Two Guys* script he refused. Three weeks before shooting was to begin, Jack Warner called writer Mel Shavelson into his office. "We have to write a script from scratch," he explained, emphasizing the need for haste and that there was no time to build sets. In two days Shavelson and Jack Rose came up with a story called *It's a Great Feeling* (1949), in which Morgan didn't want to make a movie and the studio couldn't find a girl star.

Butler and producer Bill Jacobs liked the idea. "There's only one problem," said Butler. "We have to tell the story to Dennis Morgan and get his approval." Shavelson suggested the star come in. "No," the director interrupted. "Dennis won't come into the studio." Shavelson saw no problem; the writers would go to him. "No, you're a writer," Butler reminded. "You can't leave the studio until five-thirty." Shavelson still saw no problem; they'd simply see the star after work. "You can't do that either," Butler insisted. "After five o'clock Dennis can't hear. He's been bending his elbow since noon and by five o'clock he's on the floor." Shavelson agreed that was a problem.

Butler had a solution. "I've got a convertible," he said. "Lie down in back." So Shavelson stretched out in the back of the car, and Butler threw a blanket over him before they drove out of the gate. They went over to Lakeside Country Club, where Dennis Morgan was finishing his fourth martini. The writer told Morgan the story, and the star loved it. Butler again threw the blanket over Shavelson, and they drove back into the studio with no problem.[21]

Put Everything In

Writers often felt that directors destroyed their scripts. While Fritz Lang was shooting *The Woman in the Window* (1944), screenwriter Nunnally Johnson grew furious watching the rushes. When Joan Bennett appeared in her role as vamp, Nunnally said, "Oh, my God, I forgot to write that she did *not* carry a two-foot cigarette holder!"[22]

Mystery Man

The Treasure of the Sierra Madre was written by B. Traven, a mysterious man who avoided photographs and publicity, living alone in Mexico. When Warner Bros. bought the *Sierra Madre* story rights, no one in Hollywood had ever seen the author, although director John Huston did exchange letters with him. Huston informed the novelist that a shooting schedule had been set, with Humphrey Bogart in the lead, and requested a personal interview. "I can guarantee nothing," Traven replied, "but if you will come to the Hotel Reforma in Mexico City, early in January, I will try and meet you there."

Huston flew to Mexico on the specified date. He waited patiently, but the mysterious author didn't show up. As Huston was preparing to leave, a thin, gray-haired man walked up and handed him a card reading: H. CROVES—TRANSLATOR—ACAPULCO. He showed Huston a note from Traven that said, "This man knows my work better than I do." Croves appeared so knowledgeable that Huston hired him as technical adviser on the film during the months of location shooting.

From the outset Croves took an interest in every detail of production, but Huston noted his refusal to allow his picture to be taken. When the director told him that Traven was not answering his letters, Croves offered no comment. Once the crew was back in California, Huston showed Bogart a rare photograph he had uncovered of B. Traven. "Do you recognize this guy?" the director asked Bogie, smiling. "Sure," the actor replied. "That's old Croves. I'd know him anywhere."[23]

Time

Sam Goldwyn hired excellent writers and expected them to devote all their creative energies to making Goldwyn pictures. If they worked for him long enough, they learned to expect calls any time of day or night. When Robert Sherwood was engaged to write a Goldwyn script, he returned to the quiet of his Long Island home to work. At three o'clock in the morning, his telephone rang. Goldwyn was calling from the West Coast, where it was only midnight. "Do you know what time it is?" Sherwood sleepily asked. There was a brief pause before he heard Sam ask his wife, "Frances, Bob wants to know what time it is."[24]

Homebody

When William Faulkner went to work for him, Jack Warner promised the writer a sumptuous office and two secretaries. "Thank you, Mr. Warner," Faulkner said, "but if it's all the same to you, I'd rather work at home." Warner assured him he wouldn't have to punch a clock; considering the prestige his name would bring to the studio, he could come and go as he pleased. "I would prefer not to work in an office," Faulkner insisted. Jack decided for once he could relax his rules, assuming the writer had leased a house in Beverly Hills.

Plans went ahead for *The Big Sleep* (1946), and some weeks later an emergency arose. Warner asked his secretary to phone Faulkner. "You know he works at home," the secretary reminded. "Of course," Warner said. "Call him at home." A few minutes later a voice spoke from the intercom on Jack's desk: "This is long distance. We're ready on your call to Mr. Faulkner." Warner looked startled. "Long distance," he yelled. "Yes, sir," the operator answered. "He's in Oxford, Mississippi." Warner grabbed the receiver. "Mr. Faulkner, how could you leave town without letting me know?" Jack asked impatiently. "You said you'd be working at home." Faulkner sounded relaxed. "This is my home," he explained. "I live in Mississippi."[25]

Capone, Not Scarface

While Ben Hecht was working on the script for *Scarface* (1932), word leaked out that it was a biographical study of Al Capone. Late one night two Capone henchmen appeared at Hecht's hotel room to make certain nothing derogatory about the gangster appeared on the screen. "Is this stuff about Al Capone?" they asked, guns bulging their coats. "God, no," Hecht replied. "I don't even know Al." The writer pointed out that he had left Chicago about the time Capone was coming to power. "I knew Jim Colisimo pretty well," he said.

"I also knew Mossy Enright and Pete Gentleman." "Did you know Deanie?" one of the gunmen asked. "Deanie O'Banion?" the writer said. "Sure. I used to ride around with him in his flivver." "Okay," the gangsters agreed. "We'll tell Al this stuff you wrote is about them other guys." They started out, but halted at the doorway. "If this stuff ain't about Al Capone, why are you callin' it *Scarface*?" one asked. "Everybody'll think it's him." "That's the reason," Hecht answered. "Al is one of the most famous and fascinating men of our time. If we call the movie *Scarface*, everybody will want to see it, figuring it's about Al. That's part of the racket we call showmanship." His visitors left satisfied.[26]

Biblical Language

Harry Cohn stormed into a story conference one morning, obviously in a foul mood. "God damn it!" he shouted. "Do I have to do everything around here?" "What's the trouble, Harry?" asked Clifford Odets, who happened to be present. "I may not be a college man," said Cohn, "but I know Goddam well that in Biblical times people did not go around saying, 'yes, siree' and 'no, siree.'" The writers unanimously agreed. "Well, then, what's it doing in the script?" Harry fumed. "Where?" asked Odets. Cohn slapped the open script down and pointed to a page. Odets nodded as he read, "'yes, sire' and 'no, sire.'" The others moved over to peer at the page. "We'll fix it, Harry," one of them finally said.[27]

Practical Joke

When Charles MacArthur and Ben Hecht agreed to prepare a script of *Wuthering Heights* for Sam Goldwyn, the distinguished critic Alexander Woollcott invited them to his island in Lake Champlain to write, fearing his friends would ruin one of his favorite novels unless he supervised. Knowing what a snoop Woollcott could be, the writers left phony pages lying around where he was sure to find them, describing what happened to Heathcliff during the interim between his leaving Cathy as a poor Gypsy boy and his return as a man of means. Their twist on Emily Brontë's story had Heathcliff going to America and fighting Indians and cattle thieves with blazing six-guns. Woollcott read the pages and shrieked, "You vandals! You have raped Emily Brontë!" Smiling, MacArthur replied, "She's been waiting for it for years."[28]

It Pays to Listen

Carolyn Jones, who later played Morticia in television's *The Addams Family*, won an Academy Award nomination for her portrayal of an existentialist girl in Paddy Chayefsky's *The Bachelor Party* (1957). Originally Chayefsky had written a New York character the Texas actress didn't understand. Jones went to the writer and said, "I know I'm going to do this part badly. I just can't do it." Chayefsky took her criticism seriously and said, "Please stick with this; when we get to New York, I promise I'll rewrite it."

The evening before shooting was to begin, Chayefsky came to Jones's hotel room and said, "Read this," as he handed her some typewritten pages. Carolyn started reading and got to where the girl says, "Just say you love me, you don't have to mean it." "*That* girl I know," she told the author. "*That* girl I understand." Later she explained, "That's the line everybody remembers. When she said that, she became a character. And that's what won the Academy Award nomination—not me. It was the writing."[29]

CHAPTER 9

Discovery
and
Casting

"Hollywood always changed and never changed," observed historian Robert Sklar. "Even at the height of its world-wide popularity, prestige and influence, it never lost the character of a gold-rush boom town."[1] Hundreds trekked in monthly, hoping for discovery and success at the end of the rainbow. The twentieth-century forty-niners came by bus, car, and railroad, filled with ambition and grand illusions. Like their nineteenth-century counterparts, most were destined for disappointment. Hollywood was bursting with handsome young men and beautiful women, many of whom were talented as well as determined. But when so many competed for the few roles available, beauty and talent weren't enough; it was necessary to be seen by the right person at the right time, and this was often a matter of chance. Many of the unknowns who rose to stardom owed their success to one lucky moment that gave them their golden opportunity.

Every six months the major studios brought in a new group of hopefuls, used them in crowd scenes, perhaps giving one or another a line or two to observe the impact they made on preview audiences. At the end of the option period one or two might be retained, while the rest were let go. A few of the rejects might have better luck at another studio, but most of them packed their shattered dreams and returned home. For those who aspired to stardom, there was fulfillment for few, heartbreak for many.

Even for the fortunate, trying times were ahead. Jayne Meadows remembered sitting in makeup artist Jack Dawn's chair for two and a half hours while the entire Metro makeup department critically studied her face, walking around her and talking about her as if she weren't human. "The nose points too much. We'll have to put a little dark on the nose," someone insisted. "Oh, she has very deep sunken eyes. A lot of white under the eyes . . ." said someone else. "Yes, well, the eyes are very dark and very high eyebrows, so not much shading behind the eye, and very little false eyelashes, just half." For Meadows it was a devastating experience.[2] Red-haired Arlene Dahl, among the true beauties, had been a highly successful model before entering films. At MGM they put a black wig on her and made her look like Hedy Lamarr for an early photo session. Then they discovered she had one Eurasian eye, so the makeup department made her up to look like Madame Butterfly, even shaving off part of her eyebrows in the process.[3]

After the makeup came the selection of suitable names. Spangler Arlington Brugh became Robert Taylor, Archibald Leach became Cary Grant, Lucille Le Sueur was renamed Joan Crawford, while Ruby Stevens became Barbara Stanwyck. Studio publicity releases made even the lowliest contract player sound like a rising star, despite internal reservations about her or a dearth of suitable roles. Every attractive girl on the lot was a "starlet," whether she had spoken a line of dialogue or not. Writer Ben Hecht once said that in Hollywood "starlet is the name for any woman under thirty not actively employed in a brothel."[4]

After the coming of sound the most reliable source of fresh talent was the Broadway stage. Several times a year studio heads and producers visited New York, saw all the new shows, and went backstage to talk with promising performers. If their potential seemed sufficient, screen tests were arranged in New York or Los Angeles. The studio paid all expenses to California, greeting the prospective stars at the train station in Pasadena with photographers, limousines, and much folderol, putting them up at the Garden of Allah or the Beverly Hills Hotel. The introductory visit was as much a vacation as it was an arduous business session.

Studio scouts also combed the country in search of new faces, even though more acting talent probably came out of the Pasadena Playhouse than any other single theater, in part because of its proximity to Hollywood. The scouts held contests, visited college campuses, scanned little theater groups, and looked at thousands of pictures of beauty contenders, often more as publicity stunts than real quests for future stars. MGM's Search for Talent contests shot screen tests onstage at major movie theaters across the country, while Jesse Lasky's Gateway to Hollywood competition, sponsored by RKO, culminated in a national radio show.

Radio itself produced a number of top stars, especially singers and comics. Broadcast drama emphasized voice over glamour, and turned up strong supporting actresses like Mercedes McCambridge, Audrey Totter, Joan Lorring, and Betty Garde. Twentieth Century-Fox talent scout Ivan Kahn discovered Linda Darnell on a visit to Dallas, Dorris Bowdon at Louisiana State University, and Mary Healy at the Roosevelt Hotel in New Orleans, all on the same trip. Dorothy Lamour had been bandleader Herbie Kaye's vocalist before wearing a sarong at Paramount, whereas Diana Lynn was a child prodigy on the piano prior to turning actress. Ronald Reagan had been a sports announcer, Judy Garland (then known as Baby Gumm) part of a sister act in vaudeville. Ava Gardner had trained as a secretary; John Wayne had been a college football player. Audie Murphy was a war hero, George Murphy a dancer, Vanessa Brown a quiz kid, Esther Williams a swimmer, and Sonja Henie, Vera Ralston, and Belita were all skaters. Nor was Hollywood's search limited to the United States. Louis B. Mayer made a trip to Europe in 1938 and signed both Greer Garson and Hedy Lamarr there.

Once under contract, a young hopeful needed to be cast in a series of parts that would show his or her talent to best advantage. For younger, less established players particularly, securing meaty parts was difficult, since there were always countless others coveting the same roles. Eagerness to learn did have its, rewards, and studio dramatic coaches—Lillian Burns at Metro, Phyllis Loughton at Paramount, Sophie Rosenstein at Universal—could push young people they found promising, preparing them adequately and bringing them to the attention of producers. The most ambitious newcomers sought out the list of pictures about to be made, found ways of seeing producers, and kept their ears open for inside leaks about roles that were coming up. Rarely did the casting couch prove an effective route to stardom, although most studios kept a certain number of stock girls around for the pleasure of visiting dignitaries and exhibitors.

Even stars often had to test for roles, while young players and aspiring directors gained much of their early experience making tests.

After a part was assigned, newcomers worked with either the studio coach or a drama teacher off the lot, like the respected Florence Enright, who advised players on how to handle roles and helped them prepare their scenes. Performers with little previous acting experience might continue receiving such guidance long after they had achieved stardom.

Lest their stars grow too demanding, studios made sure there was always an adequate replacement available. MGM brought Deborah Kerr from England in part to make certain Greer Garson remembered there were other porcelain-skinned redheads of ladylike demeanor. Twentieth Century-Fox kept June Haver, a blond dancer of fair ability, as a backup for Betty Grable. Warners had Ida Lupino, Faye Emerson, and later Martha Vickers as possible replacements for Bette Davis, while Dane Clark was viewed as an emergency substitute for John Garfield. Imitating success was a favorite Hollywood custom; Swedish actress Marta Toren represented one of many attempts to produce another Garbo. Yet looking too much like an established star could work against a young actress. If the resemblance was too strong, the star might even insist her young rival be let go. Similar talent could also pose problems. Singer Allan Jones quickly realized he had no future at MGM, where he was in the shadow of Nelson Eddy.[5]

Typecasting was a complaint actors frequently leveled at the old Hollywood system. If a performer played a certain type successfully, that's the kind of role that would probably be offered until the image faded. After Martha Hyer was nominated for an Academy Award for her work in *Some Came Running* (1958), she played nothing but repressed schoolteachers and society women for two years. Even worse, after she played Jenny Denton in *The Carpetbaggers* (1964), she received script after script in which she was asked to play a whore with a heart of gold.[6] On the other hand, casting against type sometimes offered advantages. Donna Reed, who built a career on sweet parts, won an Oscar for playing a prostitute in *From Here to Eternity* (1953); Shirley Jones made much the same reversal in *Elmer Gantry* (1960) and also won an Academy Award. Dick Powell, the boyish tenor of numerous Warner Bros. musicals during the 1930s, became an unexpected sensation as detective Phillip Marlowe in *Murder, My Sweet* (1945); according to author Raymond Chandler, he was the best Phillip Marlowe in films.[7]

New Star

Einstein visited Hollywood and attended the Los Angeles opening of
City Lights (1931) with Chaplin. There's a story that while he was in
Hollywood he tried to explain his theories to a studio executive. "For
instance, consider Betelgeuse," he said by way of illustration. "Betelgeuse, one of the greatest stars in the whole system, can be photographed merely by means of one ray of light. . . ." "Uh-huh," said
the executive. After the great physicist left, the executive grabbed the
phone and called his casting director. "Say, you," he shouted, "I
want you should go out and sign up this feller Betelgeuse, and I want
you should sign him up quick. Einstein, who knows everything, says
he's one of the greatest stars in the business."[8]

Hot Spot

When Michael Curtiz was testing actors for *The Charge of the Light
Brigade* (1936), starring Errol Flynn, David Niven tested for the part
of Flynn's friend in the movie. He had to play the test scene with
Olivia de Havilland. When he arrived for the test, wearing riding
boots and carrying a fly whisk, he found a dozen other hopeful
young actors all dressed in exactly the same uniform as his. By the
time the scene had been played a dozen times and six actors curtly
dismissed by Curtiz, everything Niven had hoped to do had already
been done. His mind was a blank when Curtiz, with heavy accent,
called out, "Next man." Niven was led out of the shadows by an
assistant and introduced to de Havilland and Curtiz. She smiled a
tired smile and shook hands. Curtiz said, "Where's your script?"
"You mean the four pages I was given for the scene, Mr. Curtiz?"
"Yes," said Curtiz, "where is it?" "Well," said Niven, "I've learned
it, Mr. Curtiz. I don't have it with me." "I asked you *where* it is!"
cried Curtiz. "Well," said Niven, "it's in my dressing room at the
other end of the studio." "Run and get it," shouted Curtiz. Niven
hesitated; it was 100 degrees in the shade and the soundstage was
not air-conditioned, and after witnessing the efforts of the other performers, Niven reckoned he had no chance of getting the part. "You
———," he finally told Curtiz, "you run and get it." Curtiz's reaction was instantaneous. "Dismiss the others," he cried, "this man
gets the part."[9]

Sheridan Takes the Prize

When Paramount was preparing the release of *Search for Beauty* (1934) featuring Buster Crabbe and other musclemen, studio publicists decided to invite theater owners across the country to advertise for the most beautiful girl in their community. Jack Benny, Mary Livingstone, George Burns, Gracie Allen, and choreographer LeRoy Prinz headed a committee of judges to select the most beautiful of the local winners, and the lucky girl would receive a Paramount contract. The celebrities named were strictly for publicity; the actual choice was left to LeRoy Prinz and his assistant. Boxes of photographs poured in from every state. Stunned by the numbers involved, Prinz told his assistant, "Just throw the pictures up in the air and when they land face down, eliminate them. When you get down to the last ten, let me know."

The assistant did as he was told, and Prinz was called in to judge the final ten. The choreographer looked over the finalists, read a bit of information on each one, but simply grew confused. Finally he said, "Well, I'm not going to go through all this." So he threw the ten pictures up in the air, rejecting the ones that landed face down. Finally only one picture landed on its back. The girl came from Texas; the studio changed her name from Clara Lou to Ann Sheridan.

Years later Prinz and Sheridan happened to be at the same cocktail party. "Annie," the choreographer asked, "do you know how you got into this business?" Sheridan, a down-to-earth lady with a marvelous sense of humor, replied: "Well, I know you had a lot to do with it, because my first job was as one of your chorus girls." Prinz laughed and told her the story. "Your picture was the last to land on its back," he concluded. "And, you S.O.B.," Sheridan returned, enjoying her own wit, "I've been on my back ever since!"[10]

Cagney's Complaint

Zanuck hired James Cagney after seeing him perform on Broadway, and gave him a small role in George Arliss's *The Millionaire* (1931), but he was shocked when he saw the rushes. Cagney was obviously uncomfortable in his role. Then suddenly, in one of the loops of film that hadn't yet been cut, Cagney was seen turning toward the camera. Assuming the scene was over, he curled his lip in anger, and from him came the words: "For God's sake, who wrote this crappy dialogue anyway?" Zanuck knew at once he had his man, the tough young punk he was looking for. Soon after came Cagney's first big film, *The Public Enemy* (1931).[11]

Noble Head

Henry Wilcoxon was playing the lead in *Eight Bells* in London when Cecil B. De Mille was casting the part of Mark Antony in *Cleopatra* (1934). Since sound had recently come in, any broad-shouldered young actor who could speak effectively was a candidate, but producer Benjamin Glazer thought Wilcoxon had unusual possibilities and arranged for him to visit Hollywood. When the British actor arrived at the Paramount studio, he was at once escorted in to see the great man himself, who happened to be with his costume designer, Natalie Visart. After looking Wilcoxon over, De Mille said, "Well, Nat, what do you think of him?" Absorbed in her craft, Visart answered, "My God, C.B., what a head for a helmet!"[12]

Some Aria!

Mary Martin tested for every studio in Hollywood without success; then she went to New York and became an overnight sensation singing Cole Porter's "My Heart Belongs to Daddy" in the Broadway musical *Leave It to Me*. While singing the number she performed a modest striptease that stopped the show. Paramount immediately set up a test for her and specifically requested to hear her high voice. Mary arrived at the studio wearing her "Daddy" costume and, to show off her high soprano, proceeded to sing "Caro Nome" from *Rigoletto*. Not knowing the right movements, she began slipping off her clothes as she sang the aria, just as she did eight times a week in *Leave It to Me*. On the high C she was down to her teddy. Paramount signed her to star in *The Great Victor Herbert* (1939), giving her all high songs.[13]

Plain John

Studio heads insisted on the marquee value of stars' names. At the Group Theater in New York, John Garfield had been known as Jules, but that wouldn't go in Hollywood. Jack Warner almost vetoed the surname, saying: "What kind of name is Garfield anyway? It doesn't sound American." Garfield pointed out that it was American enough for a president of the United States. Warner decided *Garfield* could stay, but *Jules* had to go. Why not call him James Garfield? "But that was the President's name!" Julie exclaimed. "You wouldn't name a goddam actor Abraham Lincoln, would you?" Warner thought it over. "No, kid, we wouldn't, because Abe is a name most people would say is Jewish, and we don't want people to get the wrong idea." Exasperated, Garfield shouted, "But I *am* Jewish!" They finally settled on John.[14]

Wayne, Too

The producers at Fox liked John Wayne's screen tests, but didn't care for his name, which was Marion Morrison. "What is he, a fairy or something?" complained Winfield Sheehan, head of production. "That's no name for a leading man." The others agreed they had to come up with a good American name. Raoul Walsh had studied the American Revolution and knew his generals, including "Mad" Anthony Wayne. "How about Anthony Wayne?" the director suggested. "Nah, too Italian," someone objected. "Okay, we'll Americanize it. Tony Wayne," said Walsh. "Now he sounds like a fairy again," was the consensus. "Well, what's the matter with just plain John?" So John Wayne it was.[15]

Elephant Girl

Lucille Ball was eager to leave Columbia and had only one picture left on her contract, for which Harry Cohn owed her $85,000. Since Harry had no picture for her, he was willing to let her go and sent her a rotten script he knew she'd turn down, thereby negating their contract. When her agent explained Cohn's ploy, Lucy vowed not to let him get away with it, insisting she'd stay and earn her $85,000.

When Cohn heard she had accepted the picture, he was stunned. Even Sam Katzman, the producer, tried to talk her out of it. "I'm sorry, Mr. Katzman," Lucy told him. "I think it's a wonderful part. I never turn anything down." Cohn was furious, but had to start *The Magic Carpet* (1951), knowing Lucy's fee would eat up most of the budget.

In the meantime Cecil B. De Mille had called from Paramount and invited her to play the Elephant Girl in *The Greatest Show on Earth* (1952), a plum role in an all-star production. Lucy was thrilled. She started fittings for the costumes Edith Head was designing for her, working on *The Magic Carpet* at the same time. One day the wardrobe girl at Paramount asked if she was gaining weight. Lucy didn't understand, but upon further thought went straight to her doctor, and there she learned she was pregnant.

The good news, however, raised problems. If she told Harry Cohn, he'd fire her for natural causes and scrap the picture. If she told De Mille, word would leak back to Cohn; either way she'd lose the $85,000. Since the shooting schedule on *The Magic Carpet* was only about ten days, Lucy decided to finish the picture and then see De Mille. She completed Cohn's film, collected her money, and immediately called her agent. "I have to tell Mr. De Mille that I can't do his picture," she said. With her agent and her husband, Desi Arnaz, Lucy went to De Mille's office. "Mr. De Mille, if there's anything I ever wanted in my life," she began, "it's to be directed by a great director like yourself and have a part like this." De Mille looked puzzled. "You've got it," he assured her. "But I can't do it," said Lucy. "I'm pregnant." She explained the situation, and De Mille slowly accepted the fact that he'd lost his Elephant Girl. "I must say, Lucille," he said, smiling at last, "you're the only woman I know who's ever screwed Desi Arnaz, Harry Cohn, Paramount Pictures, and C. B. De Mille all at the same time!"[16]

Older
In the early sixties, when Jane Fonda was still a young starlet, she rather naïvely told Marilyn Monroe, then in her thirties, "Just think of all the wonderful parts you can play when you're older." "No, no," Monroe quickly responded, "*you* play them!"[17]

Nothing Obvious
Dina Merrill discovered to her chagrin that the old studio heads thought in formula terms. The luscious actress met Buddy Adler some months before signing her Twentieth Century-Fox contract. Impressed, the new Fox production head set up a photographic test for her. Dina looked surprised and wanted to know why. Adler couldn't believe her naïveté: "Obviously to see whether you photograph, Miss Merrill." "Mr. Adler, I was a model when I was eighteen," Dina rejoined. "Clearly I do quite well in that department. Aren't you interested in whether I can act?" When Adler said, "No," Merrill was shocked. "Why do we study?" she asked. "That's your problem, honey," Adler replied. "Set up the test." Dina took the test. The Fox makeup department made her up to look like a combination of Joan Crawford and Betty Grable, and she flunked. But in time she became a leading lady in films.[18]

C.B. and Yul
The King and I was in its seventh month on Broadway when the stage-door man announced to Yul Brynner at intermission: "There's

an elderly gentleman here who says he's Cecil B. De Mille and that he *must* see you immediately." Brynner was standing in his dressing room, drenched with perspiration. "Well, if he insists," said Brynner, "let him in." De Mille walked in and asked, "Mr. Brynner, how would you like to play a leading role in a movie that your great grandchildren will see?" "I'd like that very much, Mr. De Mille," Brynner replied. "Then would you please accept to play Ramses in *The Ten Commandments?*" said C.B. They shook hands and that settled it, although their lawyers spent three years working out details.

The Ten Commandments (1956) was De Mille's last picture. During the filming he and Brynner became fast friends. The actor completed his part months before the final shooting, but flew back for the last day, which coincided with De Mille's birthday. "I could see he just didn't want to get off that boom," Brynner remembered. "His one regret, I think, was that he didn't die as he finished the film. He was so sad. He kept trying to think of another shot when it was really over."[19]

CHAPTER 10

Actors
and
Actresses

When movies first became popular, acting in films brought little public recognition; film producers purposely kept their actors and actresses as anonymous as possible. Building up stars the way the theater did, they agreed, would surely force salaries to rise astronomically and was therefore to be avoided. In the early years, furthermore, the public regarded Hollywood actors with suspicion; they were denied admission to exclusive clubs and rarely invited into fashionable homes. Apartment houses in Los Angeles frequently posted signs announcing, NO DOGS, CHILDREN, OR ACTORS.[1] Around 1910, however, movie performers began emerging from obscurity and some of them became stars. And by the time of World War I the movie stars had become America's untitled aristocracy.

The trend toward stardom began with Florence Lawrence, who had earned $15 a week at Biograph before fans started calling her "the Biograph Girl." When Carl Laemmle hired her as "the IMP Girl" and immediately publicized her name, Florence became the first movie star. In 1910, perhaps as an experiment, "Uncle Carl" arranged a personal appearance for her in St. Louis, where crowds of enthusiastic admirers went wild, tearing at her clothes and snatching buttons for souvenirs.[2] The brief era of the anonymous actor was over; the day of the glamorous movie queen had dawned.

While Florence Lawrence was emerging as a screen personality,

Mary Pickford was rising at Biograph and becoming known as "Little Mary." And Douglas Fairbanks was winning popularity in romantic comedies at Triangle, enough so that in 1916 he formed his own production company. Pickford and Fairbanks, who got married in 1920, were key factors in the trend toward enthroning movie stars. They lived in regal splendor and held court at Pickfair, their baronial Hollywood Hills estate. Off the screen as well as on they set a style and tone that hundreds of young Americans burned to emulate. The movie industry was never the same again, for stars quickly became the most important elements in successful movies and vital to a studio's prosperity. Thereafter the silent-film makers sought photogenic young men and women for their acting coaches and publicity departments to mold into screen stars.

Young actors and actresses who aspired to stardom were expected to retain a youthful, attractive appearance on the screen and off, and their conduct had to be within the bounds of accepted morality. Hollywood's Golden Era was a period in which millions of people lined up at movie box offices throughout the land to watch and admire the beautiful people on the screen. Moviegoers copied their idols' dress, hairstyles, values, behavior, and mannerisms; no monarchs in history had ever been so slavishly imitated by adoring subjects.

By the 1920s the ballyhoo had reached epidemic proportions, as fan magazines deluged readers with an endless stream of news poured out by imaginative studio publicity experts. Stars were kept away from the public but exhibited just enough to make them enticing, until an aura was built around them. The mystique of Garbo, the lusty exoticism of Pola Negri, the mystery of Valentino, were all carefully orchestrated by publicists who understood public yearnings. In 1925 Gloria Swanson became the first Hollywood beauty to marry an authentic European noble, the French marquis Henri de la Falaise de la Coudraye, thereby giving the industry an aristocratic linkage, to the delight of filmmakers and fans alike.

Although the public joyfully swallowed the hoopla, privately Hollywood was never sure how seriously to take itself. While its stars were lionized and developed egos to match their salaries, there was always a haunting uncertainty that "the flickers" were even respectable, much less serious, art. De Mille loved to say, "An actress is something more than a woman, but an actor is something less than a man."[3] And many stars did develop problems trying to evaluate their worth as human beings apart from the larger-than-life images overshadowing them. Even within the acting profession, making faces for movies was for years considered far inferior to performing before footlights. Stage actress Ina Claire made a classic remark reflecting this attitude shortly after her marriage to John Gilbert. "How does it feel to be married to a great star?" a reporter asked her. "I don't know," she replied. "Why don't you ask Mr. Gilbert?"[4]

Screen acting developed rapidly into a different craft from stage acting. Performers constantly had to be aware of hitting marks to stay in focus, yet in certain respects acting for the screen was more honest. Since the camera picks up every tiny nuance, film acting must be realistic, more a matter of *being* than behaving. Reactions are magnified on the screen, so it is easy for actors to be too expressive. Actors from the stage especially find this a problem and must constantly bear in mind they are not playing to the second balcony. Shortly after arriving in Hollywood, character actor Walter Abel went to his friend James Cagney in bewilderment. "What the hell is this, Jim?" Abel asked. "I'm at a loss." Cagney, who had been around awhile, answered, "Walter, don't act into that lens. It will come to you. You don't do anything." Abel later explained, "So I learned how to think. And that's it in the movies, because that glass eye, the camera, will go right inside your brain."[5] After more than forty years of successful filmmaking, Gregory Peck concluded that it is "intimacy and the total revealment of self that makes for a good screen actor."[6]

Hollywood's raid on Broadway following the advent of sound produced a new kind of star, which was personified by Spencer Tracy, Pat O'Brien, Katharine Hepburn, Joan Bennett, Bette Davis, and Fredric March. All were trained for the theater, and all successfully made the transition to film. Others with stage experience, like Clark Gable, Tyrone Power, and Robert Taylor, turned themselves into effective screen performers by hard work. Still others had almost no acting experience at all, yet grew into popular film personalities. Lew Ayres had played banjo and guitar with a jazz band; Fred MacMurray had been a saxophone player. Lucille Ball, Susan Hayward, and scores of others had been models, Virginia Mayo a showgirl, Betty Grable a big-band singer, Lana Turner a local high school student. "I don't believe in acting schools," director Mervyn LeRoy insisted. "People are born to be actors and actresses. Anybody that's got heart I can make act, anybody."[7]

Spencer Tracy, almost unanimously regarded as the greatest screen actor of them all, shunned heavy discussions on professional techniques. "Memorize your lines," he said, "and don't bump into the furniture." He always came to the set thoroughly prepared, low-keyed, and completely natural. He worked with great economy, never using two words if he could substitute a nod. He made each take different by altering his timing or phrasing, or by slightly rearranging a prop. And Tracy knew how to listen. His great open face responded with such natural expression and his voice remained so calm and conversational that he appeared not to be acting at all. Someone once accused Tracy of always playing himself. "What the hell am I supposed to do," the actor replied, "play Bogart?"[8]

Ronald Colman, another master of acting before the camera, was known for his mellifluous voice, superb phrasing, and mobile face. Colman seemed to have great movement without any flurry. "He economized," George Cukor explained, "and very often your eyes couldn't see it, but you saw it on the screen."[9] Much the same could be said of Gary Cooper, who didn't pretend to act, but knew more about the close-up than practically anyone in the trade. "If you were on a set and watched Cooper doing a scene," character actor Lloyd Nolan recalled, "you'd wonder what they were paying him for. But when you saw the rushes, you knew. Picture acting is all in the eyes."[10] Jimmy Stewart learned that early in his career, and invented an irresistible character. Time and again he played Jimmy Stewart, deferring to the character in the screenplay only enough to satisfy the demands of the writer and director.

Golden Age audiences didn't expect to see a different person in every picture; they wanted to see Jimmy Stewart or Spencer Tracy play *that* part. The characters screen actors created for themselves were often so fascinating that watching them regularly in different roles kept moviegoers coming back for more. Director King Vidor claimed he used to think in terms of 50 percent the way an author wrote the character and 50 percent the actor's individual personality. "I had learned that working on *Billy the Kid* (1930) with Wallace Beery, who was playing Pat Garrett," said Vidor. "I decided it would come out better to let Wallace Beery play Wallace Beery, with a little bit of Pat Garrett. . . . That was these fellas' power. That's why they were big stars; they had something of their own."[11]

Charismatic stars like Clark Gable and John Wayne may not have been great actors in the classic sense, but they were serious craftsmen who exhibited an unmistakable presence that captivated audiences. Gable, perhaps the all-time star of stars, was a far better actor than most critics acknowledged, and always brought to any character his own unique power. By sheer force of personality he captured the viewer's attention and held it. On the set he was charming, easy to work with, sensitive to direction, a thorough professional. Gable was king, and those who worked with him conceded that he was in a class by himself.

Tyrone Power, darkly handsome and a matinee idol, was from a distinguished theater family and wanted desperately to become a fine actor himself. A warm person who was plagued by self-doubts about his work, Power loved the adulation that went with stardom. But he also longed to expand his talents, and eventually achieved that goal on the stage. Robert Taylor, among the handsomest stars ever to grace the silver screen, actually developed a complex over his good looks. Shy and uncertain of his abilities, Taylor grew into a better performer than even he realized—never a genius, but a personality that audiences found enchanting.

Humphrey Bogart, who created one of the strongest screen personas, remains a major cult figure thirty years after his death. An intelligent and solid professional, Bogart was a skillful rather than great actor who always seemed crusty and annoyed. He spent a lot of time grousing, smoking incessantly, and playing Bogie. Hollywood restaurateur Dave Chasen once said, "The trouble with Bogart is that he thinks he is Bogart."[12] To his private circle of friends Bogart often claimed that he hated acting. "I'd like to be anything but an actor," he told Lizabeth Scott during the making of Dead Reckoning (1947). "It's such a foolish life."[13] But he worked at developing his craft.

Of all the screen actresses, Greta Garbo emerges as perhaps the most fascinating. Disciplined and intelligent, Garbo exuded an ethereal quality that crew members and audiences alike found spellbinding. Even on the set she held herself aloof, projecting the regal air that made her queen of the MGM lot. Others tried to emulate Garbo's queenly role, and none tried harder than Joan Crawford. Shortly after Crawford came to Metro, her friend William Haines gave her some advice. "You've got to draw attention to yourself," Haines told her. "There are fifty other girls trying to get roles in pictures, and the producers don't know one pretty face from another. You've got to make yourself known."[14] Crawford never forgot and turned herself into the consummate star. She learned every trick of the trade, knew lighting, always knew where the camera was, knew cutting, and recognized what she could and couldn't do well. With Crawford there was no kidding around; being a movie star was for her more than appearing as one before the camera—she was one in her private life as well. Dressed elegantly, she arrived on the lot accompanied by a French maid and a uniformed chauffeur. Having risen from poverty, she was determined to conduct herself the way she imagined the upper crust lived.

Other film actresses had their own eccentricities. Claudette Colbert, one of the queens of the Paramount lot, was a pleasant person and genial to work with, but she always insisted on being photographed from one side. The studio had to build special sets for her so her entrances could be made from the side she preferred. Loretta Young ordered a large mirror stationed beside the camera, allowing her to act out each scene before shooting it to make sure the lighting was what she wanted. Marlene Dietrich, who was plump and not terribly chic when she came from Germany, was made into a great fashion image by Paramount designer Travis Banton. She became one of the most irresistible figures in the world, certainly among the most exciting in Hollywood. Barbara Stanwyck appeared less glamorous, but she was a versatile actress and a director's pet. Known to friends and colleagues as "Missy," Stanwyck showed little pretense, worked as a member of the team, and turned out pictures good and bad on the assumption that it was visibility that counted.

It is doubtful that any woman in Hollywood came on as strong as Bette Davis, who on occasion could be considerate but was always demanding. She fought with directors constantly, a real "ball breaker," as one of them called her. Irving Rapper, who directed Davis in three major pictures, admitted: "She was a rebellious hellion, and she was very, very difficult."[15] Still, the results were such that Davis became Warners' biggest star, sometimes referred to as "the fifth Warner brother."

At RKO ambitious Ginger Rogers may have been queen of the lot but she was such a good sport and such a regular person that lesser figures never viewed her position as dynastic. Irene Dunne, at RKO and Columbia, was a pleasure to work with, friendly and professional, yet cautious about her lighting and appearance. Lucille Ball, who worked for Sam Goldwyn, then RKO, Columbia, and Metro, claimed her career was built on roles Ann Sothern couldn't or wouldn't do. Gradually Ball developed into one of the top comediennes on the screen, and she bought the old RKO studio at the height of her fame on television.

Katharine Hepburn's stardom came far more from strength of character and dramatic ability than glamour. Because of her long neck, cameramen had to shadow from her chin down, yet her prominent cheekbones became an asset. Columnist Art Buchwald once called them "the greatest calcium deposit since the White Cliffs of Dover."[16] In the early 1940s, when film actresses all had their eyebrows plucked and wore false lashes and noticeable cheek rouge, David Selznick introduced a more natural school of cosmetics for Ingrid Bergman, Joan Fontaine, and Dorothy McGuire. Ingrid Bergman, tall and impatient with Hollywood phoniness, often went out in flats and lisle stockings, shunning the glamorous makeup and wardrobe expected of stars at that time.

Stage actors generally arrived in Hollywood with fairly snobbish attitudes, and many complained of the difficulty in building a character, since films are shot out of sequence, often beginning with the end or middle. Most theater actors, however, came to appreciate the opportunities to display talent in screen acting and even found they enjoyed movie work once they had adjusted. George Arliss, whose career began in the London theater, became the prestige actor for a time at Warner Bros., winning an Academy Award in 1929 for his sound remake of *Disraeli*. Arliss was succeeded by Paul Muni, a dedicated stage actor from the Yiddish theater and a wizard at makeup. Muni, who possessed a powerful voice, used a recording device to prepare scenes, but began with an external approximation of the role; he was the acme of perfection at all times. An assistant director once called Muni to work on a day he wasn't scheduled. "How long will it take you to get ready, Mr. Muni?" the assistant wanted to know. The actor answered, "Four hours." The assistant didn't understand, since his makeup shouldn't have required very long. Muni explained, "Two hours for the outer man, two hours for the inner man."[17] His wife, Bella, was always on the set with him signaling whether or not a take had been good, although Muni himself seldom got out of character for a moment.

Helen Hayes, despite two Academy Awards, never felt at home in front of a camera, missing the invisible bond she found in the theater between the audience and the performers. In making films with "that mechanical thing" in front of her, "that eye" glaring at her, she was uncomfortable.[18] Others insisted that in Hollywood, making successful films was more important than developing a craft or nurturing an artist's soul, and that film work was destructive to a serious career. When dedicated actors and performers from other media were thrust together on the same assignment, tension could, and sometimes did, result. Singer Gordon MacRae recalled doing a dramatic scene lying on a hospital bed with a cast on. He was ready for the camera to start rolling, while his co-star, Swedish "method" actress Viveca Lindfors, was standing in a corner getting mentally prepared for their scene together. "Nobody understood what the hell she was doing," said MacRae.[19]

Probably there were more personalities in old Hollywood than actors, but most were hardworking, considerate professionals who did their best to deliver what was expected of them. Eventually vaudevillians, singers, burlesque comedians, dancers, models, a circus acrobat, former stunt men, as well as trained actors, won Academy Awards for acting. Even those who seemed casual and far removed from what they were doing—Robert Mitchum, for example—were serious about their work, and generally developed into competent performers. For the most part there was a spirit of give and take and friendly understanding between the assorted types. "It's a brotherly profession," Gregory Peck maintained. "We understand what the other fellows go through. I don't think anyone else can know what it is to stand up in front of the camera under the lights eight or nine hours a day and maintain a level of intensity. I love actors. They're good, open-hearted, amusing, talented people in a very dangerous profession, with a lot of risk taking, a lot of self-exposure, putting emotions to work, and calling on themselves to be at a high pitch all the time, onstage or in front of the camera. It takes mental and physical stamina, and then the whole thing is to make it look easy. But you do a hard day's work on a movie set."[20]

As with any profession, there were delinquents who failed to prepare or refused to rehearse. Ray Milland, who earned an Academy Award in 1945 for *The Lost Weekend,* was notorious for letting his stand-in rehearse in his place, then going to the script girl the next morning and asking, "What are we going to shoot today?"[21] Fortunately, Milland was a quick study and picked up instantly what his director wanted. Young Ava Gardner made a practice of staying out and dancing most of the night, arriving for work in the morning exhausted and with rings under her eyes.[22] Betty Grable was far more interested in playing the horses than she was in learning her lines or rehearsing. For a scene in *Call Me Mister* (1951), she and Benay Venuta were supposed to enter an office. The scene, as usual, was shot out of sequence, and just before they started shooting, Venuta asked Grable, "Betty, have we met this guy before?" Grable turned on her charm and said, "Who knows, Benay? Let's just hit the marks."[23]

But the most flagrant renegade of all was handsome, fun-loving Errol Flynn. Flynn was a wildcat—fighting with men, bedding beautiful women, and according to recent accounts, occasionally scrambling the two. He took his acting casually at best, arriving on the set late in the morning, drinking during the afternoon, cutting up unmercifully. But few actors wore costumes the way he did, making them seem part of him, and he could handle a sword and make it look real. The first draft for Flynn's *Adventures of Don Juan* (1949) was a delicate script that the writer modestly compared to a piece of Venetian glass. Jack Warner screamed, "The hell with that—this is Flynn. He's either going to be fighting or fucking. Get some guts into the thing!"[24]

Few actors in life, of course, were what they appeared on the screen. Valentino, the great lover, was in reality a rather retiring man, uncertain of his sexuality, far from the dashing romantic hero the public adored. Carole Lombard, who looked like an angel but swore like a sailor, was so shy she wouldn't walk through the Paramount commissary without her secretary or somebody else at her side. Alice Faye, a vital performer, was nervous and insecure enough about her work that she quit appearing in films, insisting it took too much out of her. Wise-talking Jean Arthur approached scenes with such trepidation that she sometimes threw up before a take. Blond, athletically built Alan Ladd, whose specialty was macho types, stood less than five feet nine inches tall. A competent rather than good actor, Ladd possessed a resonant voice and a natural demeanor audiences found believable. If his leading lady was tall, the studio either ordered trenches dug for her to stand in during love scenes or built a platform for Ladd.

Stars of the first magnitude felt a personal responsibility for a picture's success, knowing they would receive the blame if it failed. By the time Greer Garson replaced Norma Shearer as queen of the Metro lot, a Greer Garson picture was a prestige assignment for contract players and crew, although success or failure depended on Garson herself. An actress of rare generosity, she seldom threw her weight around and viewed the production from an overall point of view. While L. B. Mayer preferred to see her as a grande dame, she showed a delightful sense of humor, was quick to laugh, and adored her rare opportunities to play comedy. Garson had the perfect style for her time—a gorgeous redhead, bigger than life. There were always two or three wardrobe people on the set to adjust her makeup and make sure every hair was in place. If Garson got mud on her face in a scene, she was quickly made up again, so that the next time audiences saw her the mud had vanished. Even with mud on her face she looked dignified and glamorous, every inch the diva Mayer intended her to be.

Studio contracts for actors were normally for forty weeks, with twelve weeks off scattered throughout the year. There would be other weeks when stars were paid but not working. If they weren't making pictures, they might spend hours in the portrait gallery or engaged in some form of publicity. The big studios closely protected their stars, partly on the assumption that they needed to preserve the larger-than-life images they projected on the screen. On personal-appearance tours stars traveled with all sorts of publicity and security people around them to keep clamoring fans at a safe distance. Fernando Lamas remembered attending the preview of his first American movie in Westwood when he was unknown and unrecognized. Nobody spoke to him when he entered the theater with some Metro officials. Coming out he was mobbed.

Yet most stars, at least most of the ones who survived, viewed stardom as a business—an interesting business that paid well and provided fun and a creative outlet. As Robert Mitchum once said, "It's better than working in a bank."[25] While Hollywood suffered more than its share of casualties, the scores who became confused or lost, most actors and actresses kept their perspective and worked hard at developing their art. Edward G. Robinson told young Florence Henderson on the set of *Song of Norway* (1970), "My dear, stars are in heaven. Just do your job and be professional. That's what it's all about."[26] The most successful realized they gave up much by living in the public eye, and the weight of celebrity sometimes magnified personal problems beyond resolution. William Powell, who enjoyed a long career in Hollywood, once remarked, "Money is the aphrodisiac which fate brings you to cloak the pain of living."[27] Most stars were painfully aware there would be a time when it all must end or when their careers would slow down, but many who experienced a premature decline felt deeply wronged. When John Gilbert arrived to pick up his check on his final morning at MGM, he found workmen were already converting his dressing room into David O. Selznick's office. "Please, gentlemen," Gilbert said, "the corpse isn't even cold yet."[28]

Most stars were wise enough to realize that moviemaking was a cooperative effort and that their success depended upon the skills of a team. Certainly no serious actor was unmindful of the contribution his supporting players made. All the major studios maintained stock companies that allowed for casting dimension. The featured players in these companies, though not stars, were giants in their own right, often called "picture savers" within the business, since the performances of character actors could add immeasurably to the entertainment value of mediocre scripts. Metro had the longest roster of featured players, consisting of titans like Frank Morgan, Lewis Stone, Agnes Moorehead, Leon Ames, Dame Gladys Cooper, Jimmy Durante, Marjorie Main, Louis Calhern, Mary Astor, and Dame May Whitty. Warners boasted Sydney Greenstreet, Peter Lorre, Glenda Farrell, Alan Hale, Claude Rains, Eve Arden, Frank McHugh, Gale Sondergaard, Guy Kibbee, and S. Z. Sakall. All of these actors and actresses were well known to the moviegoing public, fairly well paid, and could count on continuous employment; sometimes they worked on two or three pictures at the same time. Cesar Romero recalled shooting scenes for three different films in one day at Twentieth Century-Fox—beginning one, finishing another, doing retakes on a third.[29]

Below the character actors were the stock players, mostly beginners who hoped to be elevated to the featured or star sections. The bigger studios had upward of thirty or forty young women (fewer young men) under stock contracts, grooming them with classes, occasionally giving them a line as a receptionist or allowed to say, "Hello, how are you?" Many were let go after six months and replaced by others who looked more promising.

Although featured players were well respected and generally knew all the angles to filmmaking, they also understood the problems. Long waits on the set proved among the most wearisome aspects of filming. Matching up movements in long shots, medium shots, and close-ups was a process they needed to bear in mind constantly. Character actors might occasionally be assigned the lead in B pictures, but most were destined to remain in supporting roles. For younger, more ambitious performers this could be frustrating. Keenan Wynn claimed he made seventy pictures at MGM and acted nine times. His father, comedian Ed Wynn, once said, "For those of you who don't know who Keenan Wynn is—when Esther Williams dives in the pool, he's the fellow who gets splashed."[30] Keenan himself claimed his billing was always "with," "and," or "also." "That's okay with me," he said. "Let the stars take the blame."[31]

Looking Ahead

Hollywood, as someone said once, is the world's biggest crap game—nothing's certain. Clark Gable received his MGM contract on the strength of his performance in *The Secret Six* (1931), which featured Jean Harlow, Wallace Beery, and Ralph Bellamy. One evening Bellamy was eating alone in a Hollywood restaurant when Gable walked in and asked to join him. "What do you think of this thing out here?" Gable finally asked. "I don't know," Bellamy replied. "I've just come out, and this is the first thing I've done." "I just got out here myself," Gable said. "I just got paid eleven thousand dollars for playing a heavy in a Bill Boyd Western. Eleven thousand dollars—no actor's worth that!" He paused thoughtfully, then added, "I've got myself a room at the Castle Argyle up at the head of Vine Street; I've bought a secondhand Ford. But I'm not buying anything you can't put on the Santa Fe Chief because this isn't going to last."[32]

Mob Scene
Van Johnson was the heartthrob of the bobby-soxers during World War II; in fact, when he married, a standing joke was that teenage girls across the nation were wearing their bobby socks at half-mast. Van made *The Romance of Rosy Ridge* (1947) at the height of his popularity. During location shooting the cast discovered an amusement park near their hotel. Van desperately wanted to ride the roller coaster, but knew he couldn't without being accosted by fans. Finally he and actor Marshall Thompson decided to try disguising Johnson. They put a stocking cap on him to cover his red hair, penciled on a moustache, and found a heavy coat for him. The two friends then walked to the park and made their way to the roller coaster, with only an occasional stare. About halfway through the ride the roller coaster had to stop, because word had spread that Van Johnson was on it. Hysterical fans began swarming over the tracks and scaffolding. A cordon of firemen and policemen were called to the scene to prevent people from getting killed. It took a firemen's ladder to rescue the two actors from the scaffolding and a police escort to hustle them into a local fire station. Even then the determined mob broke a glass door in the station before a police car managed to convoy the teenagers' idol safely back to his hotel.[33]

One in Ten
Once Lee Marvin and Gary Cooper stopped for gas and Cooper gave the attendant a $10 check to pay for it. "I'm going to frame this!" exclaimed the attendant. Afterward Marvin asked Cooper: "How

many of your checks ever come back to the bank?" "About one in ten," said Cooper.[34]

Crawford's Diamond

Joan Crawford was a star at all times, off the set as well as on it. At producer Jerry Wald's house one evening she wore a diamond pasted on her forehead over her left eye. Guests assumed Crawford was launching a new fad in jewelry. Finally director Jean Negulesco couldn't conceal his curiosity any longer and asked Joan why. "Johnny, don't you see?" Crawford replied. "Nobody has noticed the bags under my eyes."[35]

Wayne at Harvard

In 1974, John Wayne, in exchange for publicity for one of his new films, agreed to submit to a roasting by the *Harvard Lampoon*. He arrived in Cambridge on an armored personnel carrier for a press conference. One student in the Harvard Square Theatre audience where he appeared a little later asked him, "Do you look at yourself as an American legend?" "Well," drawled Wayne, "not being a *Harvard* man, I don't look at myself any more than necessary."[36]

Beginning to Get It

Jack Lemmon recalled his early days under director George Cukor: "Every time I'd deliver my lines, he'd say, 'Less.' After several times of hearing him say 'Less' after I'd finished, I said, 'Mr. Cukor, if you keep it up, I won't be acting at all.' And Cukor said, 'You're beginning to get it, my boy.'"[37]

Wrong Russell

After a successful career in films Rosalind Russell returned to the stage and was a hit on Broadway with shows like *Wonderful Town* and *Auntie Mame*. (She went on to do a film version of the latter in 1958.) She was amused, though, when she came out of the stage door one night after performing in *Wonderful Town* and, while signing autographs, was rejected by a woman who looked at her signature and said, "That's isn't what I wanted." "Why not?" asked Roz in some surprise. "I wanted *Jane* Russell," grumbled the woman, "the one with the big . . ." She didn't need to finish; Roz knew the movie star with the thirty-eight-inch bustline.[38]

Schwartz Mob

Shortly after appearing in the gangster movie *Scarface* (1932), Paul Muni boarded the S.S. *Pennsylvania* for a trip through the Panama Canal to California. He soon discovered that Bugsy Siegel, a West Coast hood, was also aboard. Siegel walked the deck every day with his bodyguard and glared at Muni every time he saw him, almost as though he thought *Scarface* had slandered gangsters. One night one of Siegel's bodyguards cornered Muni in the dining salon. "Bugsy and us went to that Strand The-ay-ter to see that new picture," he grunted. "Hey, that-there was no actor. He was the real goods. Tell me, Mister, what mob was you with?" "The Schwartz mob," said Muni, a New Yorker, promptly. "Lower East Side."[39]

Hepburn Hits Her Mark

Montgomery Clift was ill at the time *Suddenly Last Summer* (1959) was filmed. Elizabeth Taylor remained supportive, but Monty was consistently late and had trouble remembering lines. Producer Sam Spiegel wanted to fire him after viewing early rushes, while director Joe Mankiewicz grew short-tempered and badgered the actor mercilessly. Katharine Hepburn became increasingly disenchanted with Mankiewicz, in part because she felt the director had been unkind to Clift, but also for personal reasons. On the last day of shooting, as Hepburn was about to leave, she went to Mankiewicz and said, "Are you finished with me?" The director indicated he was. "You're quite sure you won't need me for retakes or dubbing or additional close-ups?" Hepburn asked. "I've got it all, Kate," assured Mankiewicz, "and it's great. *You're* great." Hepburn persisted, "You're sure that I'm absolutely through with this picture?" The director grinned and repeated, "Absolutely." Furious, Hepburn said, "I just want to leave you with this." Whereupon she threw back her head and spat in his face. Then, marching into Sam Spiegel's office, she spat on his floor. (Exactly where she spat varies, but there seems to be no disagreement that she spat.) Hepburn never worked with either Mankiewicz or Spiegel again.[40]

Life at Forty-five

At a luncheon party an actress noted for her sarcasm looked at Rosalind Russell and said, "I dread to think of life at forty-five." "Why?" asked the quick-witted Russell. "What happened then?"[41]

Dissipation

When the thirty-three-year-old Lionel Barrymore saw one of his first films, *Friends* (1912), unroll on the screen, he was astonished by his appearance. "Am I really that fat?" he asked co-star Mary Pickford. "I want you to tell me the truth, little girl. Am I that fat?" "I'm sorry, Mr. Barrymore," said Pickford diffidently, "but you are." "That does it," said Barrymore resolutely. "No more beer for me." After that, he went on a diet, ran in Central Park wearing four sweaters, and gradually slimmed down for his subsequent pictures. Several years later he happened to pass a Broadway movie theater with a poster, LIONEL BARRYMORE INSIDE, out in front, and went in out of curiosity to see one of his early pictures. "That's Lionel Barrymore?" he heard a woman cry indignantly when he appeared on the screen. "Why, I saw him week before last and he was as thin as the number eleven on a door. How could he get so fat so soon?" "Dissipation!" cried her companion disgustedly.[42]

Age of Stars

To find the age of an actress, it was once claimed, a Hollywood press agent takes the year of her birth, subtracts it from itself, then burns the paper the figures were written on. The publicist next adds last week's fan mail to the box-office receipts from the star's last picture, subtracts her salary, divides the remainder by the number of press agents assigned to her, subtracts the number of her marriages, adds three months for every child she has had, and knocks off ten years for gallantry. If the age is still higher than the one the boss ordered, he works in slight mathematical errors until the result comes out right.[43]

Till Then

Producer Joe Pasternak was so crazy about Marlene Dietrich he kept begging her to go to bed with him. "I'll go to bed with you when Hitler is dead," the actress finally told him. So one day in 1945, he called Dietrich, announced that Hitler had been reported dead, and said that he was ready to collect. Marlene replied, "Hitler is alive and well and living in Argentina!"[44]

Putdown

When the celebrated British actress Mrs. Patrick Campbell came to Hollywood to do some movies, she couldn't help condescending to the young stars whom she encountered. At a George Cukor party she told Colleen Moore, "You're such a pretty little thing. You should be in the movies." "I am," said Colleen quietly. A little later, when Mrs. Campbell pretended not to recognize Douglas Fairbanks, he sighed, "If you don't know who I am, I'd better fire my press agent." But when she told Bebe Daniels, "You are so beautiful, you should be in movies," Bebe said sharply, "And what did you say your name is?" Boomed Mrs. Campbell angrily, "I am Mrs. Patrick Campbell." "Oh," said Bebe, "of the Campbell soup family?"[45]

Out of Debt

In the early 1960s, Judy Garland was out of debt for the first time in her adult career. She told Freddie Fields, her manager, and his associate, David Begelman, that with all the millions she had made in films, she had never really seen any of it. So after one of her concerts they came to her suite with a big brown paper bag filled with greenbacks—fives, tens, twenties—and let her run her hands through them and throw them gleefully up into the air.[46]

How You?

One of the few fake stories told about Cary Grant that he didn't mind was the one about his exchange with a magazine editor in the early 1960s. When the editor sent a telegram demanding to know, HOW OLD CARY GRANT? he is supposed to have replied: OLD CARY GRANT FINE, HOW YOU?[47]

Alias Harriet Brown

When English playwright Ivor Novello came to Hollywood during the 1930s, George Cukor inquired if there were some special treat he might arrange for him. "I have only one desire," replied Novello. "To meet Garbo." "Done," said Cukor. "But I must tell you that at the moment she does not want to be known as Garbo. You must live with the fiction that she is Harriet Brown." Novello did as he was instructed, and he and "Miss Brown" got along famously, chatting about the several acquaintances they had in common. After a second and third meeting at Cukor's, Novello took the liberty of asking, "Miss Brown, now that we know each other so well, do you think I might call you Harriet?"[48]

Marlene Looks Her Best

Marlene Dietrich never underestimated the importance of clothes. She dressed with the same professionalism with which she approached every other aspect of the picture business. Audiences paid to see her well dressed, and Marlene was not one to let them down. Madame Ginette Spanier, director of a Paris fashion house, discovered to her exasperation that when Marlene tried on a garment and said, "I'll take it," the trouble had just begun. Once, after remaking the lining of a jacket for Dietrich six times, the clothier couldn't control herself any longer. "Look," she said, "the film public is going to look at you and your legs. They're not going to notice a pleat on the right side of your bust. And if they do, the film will be a flop anyway." "Ah," Marlene said, "but if in twenty years' time my daughter should supervise a reshowing of my films, she would notice the pleat and think Mother had lost her touch." Madame Spanier had no answer for that and remade the lining a seventh time.[49]

Enough Faces

"Why *did* you give up the movies?" David Niven once asked Greta Garbo, knowing her last picture, *Two-Faced Woman,* had been made in 1941. Garbo thought for a moment and then said quietly: "I had made enough faces."[50]

On and Off

"Off-screen," a fellow at Warners once told James Cagney, "you're very quiet and unassuming, but when you get on there, you're a pretty boisterous fella." Cagney admitted this was so. "Now," the fellow went on, "when are you acting—on-screen, or off?"[51]

Walks Again

When Marlon Brando was making his first film, *The Men* (1950), a movie about World War II veterans who had lost their legs in combat, he lived in a wheelchair for a time with some army-hospital paraplegics in order to learn all about them. One day he went to a tavern with some of them for a few beers, and a Salvation Army lady came in to collect some wastepaper. Shocked when she saw the legless veterans in wheelchairs, she raised her arms and cried: "Oh, Lord, grant that these men may be able to walk again!" Whereupon Brando got up and walked and she nearly passed out. The paraplegics all roared with laughter.[52]

Coop's Nose

In one of his earliest pictures Gary Cooper played a location scene so well it was shot in a single take. But that night Coop went to the director's tent. "If you don't mind," he said, "I'd like to do that scene over again in the morning. I seem to remember at one point I picked my nose I was so nervous." "Listen," said the director, "you were so damn nervous you were great. You keep acting that way and you can pick your nose into a fortune." Coop never forgot what the director told him. Years later, after he had flopped trying to take acting "seriously" in pictures like *Saratoga Trunk* (1945), he told his old director: "Guess I'll have to go back to my nose."[53]

Final Turn

Early in 1974 Susan Hayward received an invitation to present the best-actress award at the annual Academy Awards ceremony on April 2. Hayward had been gravely ill for months. A tumor had formed on the left side of her brain and was spreading rapidly to the right side. Brain seizures occurred almost hourly, lasting from five to ten minutes. Because of her condition, nobody at the Academy expected her to appear, but since it was customary for former Oscar winners to serve as presenters, it was decided to extend Hayward a courtesy invitation. Much to everyone's surprise she accepted.

Determined to look spectacular, she called her friend Nolan Miller, who designed a high-necked, full-length gown of black sequins for the occasion. Her paralyzed right hand he concealed beneath points of black lace. Hayward picked out a diamond necklace, bracelet, and earrings, and asked Frank Westmore if he would come to her house on the afternoon of the telecast to do her makeup. Although the illness had done slight damage to her face, Westmore was shocked by her appearance. Cobalt treatments had destroyed her beautiful red hair, eyebrows, even her eyelashes, so that Westmore had to reconstruct the look of thirty years before, covering her bald head with "the goddamnedest Susan Hayward wig they ever made." He worked feverishly for hours, until at last it was time for her to leave for the Dorothy Chandler Pavilion.

Moments before Hayward walked onstage, a doctor gave her a massive dose of Dilantin to ward off seizures. She heard David Niven announce her name and started shaking badly. Charlton Heston, her co-star in *The President's Lady*, took her arm and murmured, "Easy, girl." Together they walked slowly to the podium as the crowd rose for a standing ovation. Hayward wavered a bit but managed to read the names of the five nominees and to announce that the winner was Glenda Jackson. Regally she made her way backstage again, completely drained. "Well," she said, "that's the last time I pull that off." She collapsed in a seizure later that evening. By summer she was confined to a wheelchair and she died in less than a year.[54]

Kate and Spence

Spencer Tracy hadn't worked in four years when producer-director Stanley Kramer got the idea of reuniting Tracy and Hepburn in *Guess Who's Coming to Dinner?* (1967). The actor had been sick for months, and Kramer felt involving him in work might be therapeutic. Katharine Hepburn had not been seen professionally for nearly five years; she had chosen to devote herself to the ailing Tracy, with whom she had had a long and loving relationship. But Tracy and Hepburn liked the interracial theme of Kramer's picture and agreed to do it.

From the outset the task proved strenuous for everyone concerned. Tracy could work only for short periods, so shooting had to be scheduled around him. Four days before work on the film was completed, Tracy told Stanley Kramer, "I read the script again last night, and if I were to die on the way home tonight, you can still release the picture with what you've got." But the final scenes were shot. Resting at home, Tracy phoned his friend Garson Kanin. "Did you hear me, Jasper?" he shouted into the receiver. "I finished the picture!" Twelve days later he was dead.

At the 1967 Academy Awards presentation, both Tracy and Hepburn were nominated for their performances. But while Katharine Hepburn won for best actress, Rod Steiger was announced winner in the best-actor category for *In the Heat of the Night*. Hepburn was in France at the time, filming *The Lion in Winter*. When she was telephoned from Hollywood and told of her victory, she asked, "Did Mr. Tracy win too?" "No," she was told, "Rod Steiger did." For a moment there was silence. "Oh, well," she said, "I'm sure mine is for the two of us."[55]

CHAPTER 11

Child Stars

"Asked how he liked children, W. C. Fields used to growl, "Parboiled." For months he engaged in a seriocomic feud, on-screen and off, with Baby LeRoy, a little scene-stealer who appeared in several films with him. When a nurse brought orange juice for the three-year-old during a break between scenes on one picture, Fields told her, "I'll give the little nipper his juice," and sneaked gin into the drink. A little later, when the shooting was resumed and Baby LeRoy was too groggy to perform, Fields advised, "Walk him around, walk him around," and added sorrowfully: "He's no trouper. The kid's no trouper. Send him home!" But the kid stayed, and in the end added to the fun of the great comedian's newest film.[1]

Child stars may have irked Fields, but the great American public adored them. Many of the earliest movies, including *The Great Train Robbery* (1903), featured little girls performing kindly, even heroic, deeds to ringing applause in the nation's nickelodeons. Teenaged Mary Pickford became so popular as America's—and the world's—"Sweetheart" that she continued playing youthful roles into maturity. But with the appearance of *The Kid* (1921), Charlie Chaplin's first feature, which teamed seven-year-old Jackie Coogan with Chaplin's Tramp, child stars became a big thing for the first time in Hollywood. The rage for child actors like Jackie (and Mary) wasn't new with movies. Little Cordelia Howard won love and acclaim in the 1850s for her role as Little Eva in the stage version of *Uncle Tom's Cabin*. And in the 1880s and 1890s youthful players like Elsie Leslie (admired by Mark Twain), Lotta Crabtree, and Elsie Janis won a devoted following among America's theatergoers. But where thousands of people flocked to see gifted young child stars on the stage, millions crowded the nation's movie houses to watch "those endearing young charmers" on the screen. Motion pictures democratized the child-star cult just as they did everything else in the entertainment world.

The vogue of child performers was at its height in this country from the early 1920s until the late 1930s. There was Baby Jane—and Baby Sandy, Baby Peggy, and Baby Rose Marie—as well as Baby LeRoy. But Jackie Coogan was undoubtedly the nation's most popular movie child for a decade or so after *The Kid*. When Jackie caught cold, the news pushed the President off the front page; and when Jackie visited Europe, people in London, Paris, and Rome jammed the streets to get a sight of him, and the pope granted him an audience. Unfortunately, "senility finally got him at thirteen," as one wit put it, and he lost his following. But by then he had made more than a dozen well-received pictures about homeless orphans and had earned millions in Hollywood. When he came of age, though, he discovered his family had consumed most of his fortune. Out of Jackie's plight came the "Coogan Act," designed to safeguard a child star's hard-won earnings.[2]

About the time Jackie Coogan started on the yellow-brick road to fame, producer Hal Roach decided to start making kid movies. He looked out of his office window one day and saw some youngsters engaged in a heated argument over pieces of wood in a lumberyard. "All of a sudden," he recalled, "I realized I'd been watching this silly argument over the sticks for fifteen minutes. I'd spent fifteen minutes because these are *real* kids. I mean they're on the square. They're just kids being kids. So I thought if I could find some clever street kids to just play themselves in films and show life from a kid's angle, maybe I could make a dozen of these things before I wear out the idea."[3] He made far more than a dozen. The first few two-reelers he made of, by, and for kids in 1922—*Our Gang, Fire Fighters, Young Sherlocks*—were a hit with adults as well as children, and before he got through he had turned out 221 *Our Gang* comedies, silent and sound, featuring such "Little Rascals" as "Spanky" McFarland, Mary Kornman, "Alfalfa" Switzer, Dickie Moore, and Jackie Cooper. Reviewers as well as exhibitors took to them with enthusiasm; *The New*

York Times called them "wonderful, great fun, a half hour's delight for young and old."[4]

At Roach's studio there was a revolving door for gang members. When performers reached eleven or twelve, they had to retire and be replaced by new youngsters. In all, some 176 small fry, averaging about seven years of age, appeared in the *Our Gang* comedies between 1922 and 1944. But thousands of youngsters took screen tests for the series and never made it. Among the rejects: Shirley Temple and Mickey Rooney. But Shirley went into another series, *Baby Burlesks*, parodies of adult films and stars, and Mickey became the featured player in a series of shorts about a tough little guy named Mickey McGuire. Then both youngsters graduated to feature films and soon moved to top place at the box office.

Shirley Temple, who entered movies in 1931 at three, was "Little Miss Miracle." Her bright, lively, no-nonsense performance in *Stand Up and Cheer* (1934) made her a star overnight; and by 1935, when she was only seven, she had become the nation's number-one box-office attraction. In film after film the lovable little celebri-tyke smiled, sang, danced, and quipped, and she also set grown-ups straight on the problems of life. Her fame was almost unbelievable. She appeared on *Time*'s cover in 1936, received more lines in *Who's Who* than Cary Grant, and was sought out on the set by such notables as H. G. Wells, Noël Coward, Eleanor Roosevelt, and Thomas Mann. She was well liked abroad, too, especially in Japan, and came to be called America's Greatest Unofficial Ambassador. "She's the world's eighth wonder. . . ," exclaimed Twentieth Century-Fox's Darryl Zanuck, whose studio she helped put into the black. "There is no one in the world to compare her with—why, she's a wonder."[5] One day, when John Steinbeck was discussing plans to film *The Grapes of Wrath* with Zanuck, the secretary suddenly rushed into the room. "Mr. Zanuck," she cried, "there's been an accident on one of our sets. Shirley Temple has lost her tooth!" "Her *front* tooth?" exclaimed Zanuck. "Her front tooth," nodded the secretary. "For God's sake, tell 'em to do something," cried Zanuck, and as he headed for the door Steinbeck said quietly: "Don't bother about me. *The Grapes of Wrath* is unimportant compared to Shirley Temple's tooth."[6]

Shirley Temple stayed at the top of the box office from 1935 until 1938 and then yielded first place to Mickey Rooney, an energetic and versatile teenage actor, in 1939. "The Mick," as he was called, had been in movies ever since he was five, but it wasn't until 1935, when he gave a striking performance as Puck in Warners' *A Midsummer Night's Dream,* that producers began giving him prominent parts in major films: *Ah, Wilderness!* (1935), *Little Lord Fauntleroy* (1936), and *Captains Courageous* (1937). It was a B picture, though, that took him to the top. In a low-budget programmer for MGM called *A Family Affair* (1937), Rooney's portrayal of Andy Hardy, the clean-cut but cocky son of a small-town judge, went over so big with moviegoers that exhibitors began clamoring for more films about the lad. MGM was glad to oblige; Rooney appeared in a series of Hardy films after that, was number one at the box office from 1939 until 1941, and remained among the top ten stars in Hollywood until he went into the army in 1944. "I am Andy Hardy," he once announced, with considerable exaggeration. "I feel right playing Andy."[7] About this time *Variety* suggested that people in rural communities disliked movies about small towns: STIX NIX HIX PIX. But *Variety* was wrong: The sticks as well as the hicks liked the Hardy pix. In one town a stranger approached the Mick and asked if he remembered him. "To be honest," said Mickey, "I'm afraid I don't. Where did we meet?" "Why, I saw you in *Love Finds Andy Hardy,*" said the man angrily and stormed off.[8]

Mickey Rooney wasn't the only teenage star during Hollywood's Golden Era. Judy Garland, who appeared in several musicals (and in Hardy pictures as well) with Rooney, suddenly became famous at eighteen with her performance as little Dorothy in *The Wizard of Oz,* and won a special Oscar as "the best juvenile performer of the year" in 1939. Both Garland and Rooney, despite their ups and downs, went on to successful careers on stage and screen after their juvenile years were over. But Deanna Durbin, another teenage idol, deliberately retired to private life after a dozen dazzling years of stardom. A singer, like Garland, Durbin saved Universal Pictures from bankruptcy with her first feature, *Three Smart Girls* (1936), when she was sixteen. She went on to appear in one musical hit after another for Universal, and in 1938 shared with Mickey Rooney a special Academy Award for "bringing to the screen the spirit and personification of youth."[9] Other youthful spirits of the era: the bee-stung, lower-lipped Jackie Cooper, genteel little Freddie Bartholomew, impish Jane Withers, spunky Virginia Weidler. Being a child star during Hollywood's great days was tougher than most movie fans realized. "Dear child," went a fan letter in the late thirties, "we have only one prayer to offer . . . *don't grow up.*"[10] Some film kids never did. The descent from celebrity to obscurity with advancing age was too much for them and they ended in despair.

How does one account for America's love affair with film kids—babies, preadolescents, teenagers—in the period between the two World Wars? Was it simply an expression of the love of children found in all cultures, with the United States, the world's film center, simply better at putting kids on the screen than moviemakers elsewhere? Or was it a symptom of the nation's obsession with youth: its reluctance to grow up, as European critics charged, and abandon the simplicities of childhood for the ambiguities of maturity? Or was it largely a *faute de mieux:* a retreat into the supposedly innocent world of children during the years when the Hays Office was circumscribing adult themes so narrowly? One thing is clear. During the grim years of the Great Depression the breezy optimism and spunky self-assurance of performers like Shirley Temple meant much to the nation's moviegoers. President Franklin Roosevelt paid tribute to the likable little lass in 1936. "When the spirit of the people is lower than at any other time, during this Depression," he declared, "it is a splendid thing that for just fifteen cents an American can go to a movie and look at the smiling face of a baby and forget his troubles."[11]

World War II killed the child-star fad. Shirley Temple's merry moppets and Mickey Rooney's hick-town Hardy boy seemed out of place in a war-torn world. Moviegoers still sought entertainment and escape during and after the war, but they would no longer sit still for the sugary sentimentalities of the prewar kid pictures. In the 1950s came "rebels without a cause," like James Dean, who were bewildered and unsure of themselves, and in the 1960s and 1970s came "rebels with a cause," who calmly took on the establishment and flouted its conventions. By the 1980s, however, filmmakers had come up with a new genre with which to delight their now largely teenage audiences: movies about adolescents coming of age sexually. "The teenage avalanche may have helped sweep the Western from the screen," observed film critic Stanley Kauffmann in April 1985. "The adolescent energy that once went into applauding men who leap onto horses, who handle and fire pistols, now goes into applause for non-metaphoric riding and firing."[12] Some adults liked the new high school soft porn too. But not *New York Times* columnist Russell Baker. "I do not want to see a teener," he said of the new genre. "I do not want to watch incredibly beautiful adolescents wrestle with primitive instincts." What he wanted, he said, was an old-fashioned "oater" of the kind that kids used to crowd theaters in the old days to applaud.[13]

Imagination
In one scene in *Oliver Twist* (1922), Jackie Coogan is supposed to start crying when one of the boys in the orphanage asks him, "Where's your muvver?" and he replies, "My mother is dead, sir." But Jackie just couldn't make the tears come. "Just try to imagine that your mother really is dead," director Frank Lloyd told him. But though they tried it again there were still no tears. "Mr. Lloyd," Jackie finally said, "would it be all right if I imagine that my dog is dead?"[14]

Not Celebrity Enough
When Jackie Coogan toured Europe in 1924 to support Near East Relief (a campaign to help orphans in Palestine, Syria, Greece, and Armenia), he was greeted by huge crowds everywhere and welcomed in person by high officials in every country he visited. In France, however, the famous former premier Georges Clemenceau, irked by all the to-do made over a little boy, sent a telegram to Jackie's father, turning down an invitation to meet the young star. I DO NOT SCREEN WELL ENOUGH, he explained, NOR AM I CELEBRITY ENOUGH TO MEET YOUR ILLUSTRIOUS SON.[15]

Tears
In *Skippy* (1931), Jackie Cooper had three crying scenes and it was difficult for him to produce tears each time. The first time, his grandmother, who was with him on the set, said, "Be a good boy and cry," but though he tried, he failed miserably. Director Norman Taurog yelled and hollered at him and called him a lousy actor, but that produced anger, not tears, and things soon reached an impasse. Then Taurog arranged for a boy wearing the Skippy costume to appear on the set. That did it. Overwhelmed by the thought of another boy taking over his part, Jackie started crying. Taurog quickly shot the scene, called him a good actor, and gave him an ice cream cone.

The second crying scene was just as hard for Jackie as the first. This was partly because he had a dog in the scene with him and liked the dog so much he felt too happy to cry. After Taurog had worked on him for a while without success, he instructed the security guard to take the dog away. "The policeman's got your dog," he told

Jackie. "He's taken your dog and he's going to kill it." "Why?" wailed Jackie. "What did I do?" "You won't cry," said Taurog. So Jackie tried again, but still no tears came. Then he heard a pistol shot in the distance. "The policeman has shot your dog," Taurog told him solemnly. "He shot him because the dog distracts you. You're more interested in the dog than you are in your work." At this point Jackie burst into tears and Taurog got his scene. After it was over the security guard brought the dog back and Taurog gave Jackie some ice cream again for his "realistic" acting job.

Jackie knew he had one more crying scene to do, and since he knew he couldn't produce tears on demand, he began worrying about the terrible things the director would do this time to induce him to cry. When the time came to shoot the scene, however, his mother (who was with him on the set this time) did something that apparently hadn't occurred to anyone before: She took her little boy aside, discussed the scene with him, went over the lines with him, and explained how grief-stricken Skippy was in the scene over the loss of a close friend. As Jackie talked about Skippy and his friend, he began weeping. Still crying, he took his place on the set and did the scene in one take. It was probably his best scene in the picture.[16]

Ends Happier
Some parents in New York took their little boy to see Jackie Cooper in *Skippy* (1931) and then, later on, to see the sequel, *Sooky* (1931). After seeing the latter, the boy was ecstatic. "Better'n *Skippy*, even," he remarked. "It ends happier." "But it doesn't end happier, James," said the mother. "Doesn't Sooky's mother die?" "Oh, sure," said James, "but in *Skippy* the dog died."[17]

Holiday
At first Shirley Temple's parents didn't realize how famous their little girl had become around the world. They continued to live in a small house in Santa Monica and avoided showering her with luxuries. Once, when they decided to take her on a holiday to Hawaii, they told Harry Brand, chief publicity man at Fox, that they didn't know anybody there and would appreciate being put in touch with people who could show them the sights. Brand promised to help them out. And when they arrived in Honolulu, they were astonished to find 100,000 people waiting to greet them. Honolulu's schoolchildren had been given the day off to see Shirley.[18]

Propositions

One day Shirley Temple's father, a bank teller in Santa Monica, sought out Darryl Zanuck. "I've had some letters," he said hesitantly. "They're all from women." He stopped in some embarrassment and then went on: "They make propositions. They want me to father a child for them." Zanuck started grinning. "Can you guarantee you'll give them a girl?" he asked. "Or even another Shirley?" "Nope," said Temple. "Then don't be unfaithful to your wife," Zanuck advised. Zanuck's breeziness shocked Temple. "I've certainly no intention of doing any such thing," he exclaimed. "I just thought you ought to know that there are women around like that." "Terrible, isn't it?" said Zanuck in mock horror. "Don't tell Mrs. Temple," said Temple as he left. "She'd be ashamed of her sex."[19]

All Their Assets

When Fox merged with Twentieth Century in 1935, there was a big party in the Beverly Hills Hotel to celebrate the event, attended by Wall Street bankers as well as studio executives, stars, directors, and writers. Shirley Temple, who had saved Fox from bankruptcy, was the star of the evening. When she entered the ballroom, just before the speeches, and passed the table of screenwriter Sam Hellman, the latter impulsively reached out, took her hand, spun her around, and then stood up, lifted her high over his head, and told her what a wonderful little performer she was. "Suddenly," he recalled, "a horrible silence fell on the room, and I looked toward the head table. There all the bankers from New York had turned white and were mopping big drops of sweat from their brows. I realized then what I was doing. Here I was holding practically all the assets of Twentieth Century-Fox in my hands. It scared me so I nearly dropped her. But I managed to set her on the floor, and when I looked at the head table again the bankers were sighing big sighs of relief and the color was creeping back into their faces."[20]

Ignorance

One day Shirley Temple's studio arranged for her to meet John J. Pershing, the famous World War I general, then nearly eighty years of age. After introductions, Shirley proudly showed him her autograph book filled with the signatures of scores of famous stars. When she asked him if he knew any of them, he admitted he hadn't even heard of most of them. Afterward, appalled by his ignorance, Shirley exclaimed to a studio aide: "How did he ever get to be a general!"[21]

Not Real

Shirley Temple stopped believing in Santa Claus after visiting a Los Angeles department store with her mother just before Christmas and lining up with a group of youngsters waiting to meet Santa. When her turn came and the man playing Santa took her on his lap and began whispering to her, she indignantly pulled herself away, went back to her mother, and told her he couldn't possibly be a real Santa. "He asked for my autograph," she explained, "and said he saw all my movies."[22]

Badge of Honor

For the fun of it, director Allan Dwan organized a Shirley Temple police force, with Shirley as chief, had badges made with the words SHIRLEY TEMPLE POLICE on them, and distributed them to everyone on the set. To his surprise, wearing the badges off the set brought special favors: prompt attention in department stores and good tables in restaurants and nightclubs. One morning Dwan was late for work, started speeding, and was stopped by a traffic officer. When he told the officer he was a movie director and anxious to get to the studio where a famous star was waiting for him, the latter snorted his disbelief and got out his ticket book. Suddenly Dwan pulled out his SHIRLEY TEMPLE POLICE badge. "Holy cow!" cried the policeman. "My kid would give her right arm for this!" "Here, take it," said Dwan, "give it to her with Shirley's compliments." He then pinned it on the policeman's coat and the latter happily waved him on.[23]

Most Important Man

Just after meeting H. G. Wells, Shirley Temple was told that the popular British writer was the most important person in the world. "Oh, no he's not!" she chirped. "God is the most important and the governor of California is second." When the egotistic Darryl Zanuck, head of her studio, heard what she had said, he cried: "Didn't you ask her who was the third?"[24]

Dirty Trick

In the 1930s Mickey Rooney's great idol was Clark Gable. When Gable wore loose wool sport coats and vest sweaters, so did Rooney; and when Gable took to wearing a felt hat with the brim turned back, Rooney soon acquired one too. He also adopted the Gable swagger, the Gable pipe, and the Gable way of addressing waitresses as

"Honey" and "Toots." "Someday I'll play a dirty trick on that kid," cried Gable when he saw Rooney driving a smart green roadster like his own. "I'll start wearing a sarong and driving around in a hearse!"[25]

Mickey and the President

When he paid a call on the White House, young Mickey Rooney, then top at the box office, took President Roosevelt's teasing remark with the utmost seriousness. "Well, Mickey, my boy," said FDR, "someday I hope you'll be able to spare enough time so we can have a man-to-man talk." "Yes, sir," said Mickey, matter-of-factly, "I can get time off from the studio any day for that."[26]

All Your Life

Dickie Moore was only eleven when he played a small part in *The Story of Louis Pasteur* (1936), and he frequently found life on the set tiresome. "Ma," he wailed one day, "why can't I go out and play like the rest of the kids? Why do I have to be an actor?" "But, Dickie," said his mother firmly, "it's what you've wanted *all your life*!"[27]

Cutest Baby

In the 1930s, thousands of American mothers took their kids to Hollywood hoping to get them into the movies, and they succeeded in making life miserable for casting directors like Warners' Solly Baiano. One day when Baiano was at work in his office, his secretary buzzed him. "Some lady's on the phone from the Good Samaritan Hospital," she told him. "She won't tell me what she wants, but she says it's urgent." Baiano took the receiver. "Mr. Baiano?" said the voice on the other end. "I hope you don't think I'm just another one of those proud parents—but this morning I gave birth to the cutest blue-eyed baby you've ever seen. I know you must hear this from a lot of mothers, but I'm sure my child is very unusual. So won't you please remember us the next time you need a baby for a picture?"[28]

Hair Dyed Yellow

One Saturday, as Norman Taurog (who received an Oscar for his direction of *Skippy*) was leaving for a football game, an aggressive woman forced her way into his office and pushed her seven-year-old boy in front of him. "I want you to hear my son recite *The Raven*," she cried. "He's simply bursting with talent, and you just have to give him a part in a picture." Taurog told her he wasn't doing any casting, and tried to leave, but she grabbed his arm and held on to it until he agreed to listen. The mother then gave the signal and her boy, nervous and embarrassed, began reciting the Poe poem in a rapid, mechanical fashion. "Well, what do you think *now*, Mr. Taurog?" she cried, when the recitation was over. Taurog turned to the boy and asked him whether he wanted to be an actor. "Johnny, don't answer that," interceded the mother. But Taurog repeated the question and finally Johnny blurted out: "I hate acting—I want to be playing. Besides, I don't like having my hair dyed yellow!"[29]

Too Young
For the premiere of *Babes in Arms* (1939), in which she starred with Mickey Rooney, Judy Garland, once a child star but now eighteen, hoped for her first Adrian. "Too young," ruled MGM's Louis B. Mayer. Snapped gossip columnist Hedda Hopper: "Not too young to make ten million dollars for your company!" Judy got the dress.[30]

So Much Velvet
In the fall of 1943, MGM producer Pandro S. Berman decided he wanted the eleven-year-old Elizabeth Taylor for the lead in *National Velvet*, a film about Velvet Brown, a little girl who disguises herself as a boy, palms herself off as a jockey, and rides her horse to victory in the Grand National Sweepstakes in Britain. But Berman thought she was too small at the time and decided to wait until she grew a little. He wanted her to be tall enough to play opposite Mickey Rooney before he started shooting. "Considering that Mickey was only titty-high," he said, "she really didn't have to grow that much."

After she made the picture, however, the MGM publicity department concocted a dramatic account of how she came to play the part. She read the best-seller on which the movie was based, according to the MGM story, and went to Berman seeking the part. She was going on twelve, she told him, was a good rider, and had a good English accent, since she had been born in London. "Sorry, honey," Berman is supposed to have said, "but you're too short." He then stood her in the doorway and put a pencil mark on the wall to indicate her height. "You need at least three more inches," he said. "Well, I'll grow," she supposedly told him. After that, the story goes, she began eating voraciously, exercising vigorously, and taking long rides every day, and when the three months were up, went back to Berman's office, stood proudly by the mark on the wall, showed off her three inches, and got the part. Berman was so impressed by her pluck, the story has it, that he left the mark on the wall in his office until he left MGM twenty years later. It is a pleasant but tall tale. Though Elizabeth Taylor enjoyed telling it herself, it has no basis in fact. Taylor didn't need spurious stories in any case to prove she was a plucky person.[31]

Giggles and Tears

In *National Velvet* (1944) Elizabeth Taylor, then twelve, cried on the screen for the first time. In the film, her horse was supposed to have colic, and when the jockey, played by Mickey Rooney, tells her he doesn't think the horse will live, she starts crying. Just before the take, Mickey, trying to be helpful, told her: "Honey, you know in this scene you have to cry." "Yes, Mickey, I know." "Well," he said, "you should think that your father is dying and your mother has to wash clothes for a living, and your little brother is out selling newspapers on the street and he doesn't have shoes and he's cold and shivering and your little dog was run over." To Mickey's surprise his harrowing tale of woe produced girlish giggles instead of tears and it was a long time before Elizabeth could get serious again. But when she came to do the scene, she forgot everything Mickey had said. Instead, "all I thought about," she recalled, "was the horse being very sick and that I was the little girl who owned him." And the tears came.[32]

Oh, No!

When Shirley Temple became a teenager, her fans were reluctant to face the fact that she was no longer a little girl. At the sneak preview of *That Hagen Girl* (1947), when Ronald Reagan said to Shirley, then nineteen, in one scene, "I love you, will you marry me?" people in the audience shouted, "Oh, no!" The producers deleted the line before releasing the film for general distribution.[33]

Hold My Breath

When Shirley Temple ran for office in California in the late 1960s, her supporters put up posters containing a big picture of her when she was a child star with the words IF YOU DON'T VOTE FOR ME, I'LL HOLD MY BREATH!

CHAPTER 12

On the Set

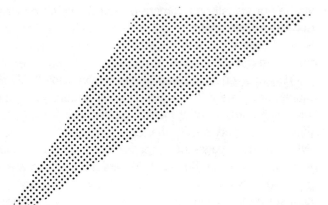

Once the script was approved and the cast chosen, the real work of filmmaking began, and it was like no other activity. Most Hollywood directors quickly recognized that an essential part of their job was creating conditions on the set that were conducive to good work. "I wanted to make people want to come to work the next morning," Mervyn LeRoy said. "I was tough at times, because you don't get [excellence] by being sweet all the time. But you can't scare actors."[1] Henry Koster produced a relaxed atmosphere by joking, while John Ford kept Danny Borzage playing folk tunes on the accordion. With no audience there to applaud, fellow workers tended to bolster the confidence of each other by commenting on how great the rushes were the day before. "There's a euphoric feeling that has to envelop the set," observed actor Tom Ewell, "because if they didn't have that everybody would be walking around with such glum faces and depressed spirits."[2]

"Film," Ernst Lubitsch used to say, "is a foreign word that means *wait*."[3] Certainly the interminable waiting, while the cameras are set up, lighting arranged, and the set prepared can prove an emotional drain and a bore to performers. "You get ready to do a scene," singer Mel Tormé recalled, "and it never lasts more than a minute and a half or at most two minutes. It's the waiting around that's maddening."[4] Actress Ann B. Davis, who achieved fame with *The Bob Cum-*

mings Show and *The Brady Bunch* on television, hated making films for that reason. She arrived for a screen test, costumed and made up at eight-thirty in the morning, her adrenaline flowing as if she had just stepped off a stage. They were ready to shoot her test at five that afternoon. "All of the sawdust had run out of me and I was really beat," she remembered. "But one thing I learned from that; when you're not actually on camera or rehearsing, sit down and shut up, because you've got to be just as perky at eight o'clock at night as you were at eight o'clock in the morning. You just have to force yourself into a kind of artificial excitement to keep your energy up."[5]

This was especially true during Hollywood's Golden Age, when money and time didn't impose the restrictions they would later on. The big studios wanted their A productions filmed beautifully, and they encouraged taking the time necessary to make them right. Whereas thirty pages of script might be shot in a single day for a television series, in the old studio era three or less was considered a good· day's work on major feature films. Director George Cukor claimed he developed the habit of talking to his actors about anything and everything to keep their creative juices flowing until the next take. The more spectacular the production, the longer preparations were likely to take. Cornel Wilde remembered shooting the London fire sequence in *Forever Amber* (1947) and standing around indefinitely, eventually going to his dressing room and lying down. "You're half asleep," Wilde recalled, "and they knock on the door and say, 'Ready for a take,' at three in the morning. You get up and start being sharp and bright. It's hard."[6]

Then there was the problem of hitting marks, being in the exact spot so the camera would be in focus, which limited a performer's freedom of movement to a constricted area. Since all the scenes on a given location or using the same set would likely be shot before moving on, scripts rarely were filmed in sequence. A master shot was taken to establish the locale, then a medium shot, and finally close-ups of the players involved. Technical considerations even meant filming everything taking place on one side of a room before moving to the other. An actor might say, "I love you," in the morning, then wait until afternoon for the actress to say "You do?" As Rosemary DeCamp explained, "There's a terrible lag. Most people with enough concentration could remember their attitude when that person on the other side of the room talked to them. But that was the trick—to remember in your close-ups exactly the emotion and recapture the feeling."[7]

The reactions of players to the camera varied widely, but stage actors in particular found it terribly mechanical. "It was dreadful," said Jayne Meadows, "the minute the crew was all around me, and the camera was close, and I had to talk to the actors as if that great big thing didn't exist. Frightening, just frightening."[8] Some found it difficult to repeat a scene time and again without losing spontaneity, while others seemed not to catch fire until several repetitions. Performers with only a little stage experience often preferred the freshness of film work, which long rehearsals and nightly performances in the theater could erode. Lizabeth Scott, a model before she became understudy to Tallulah Bankhead in *The Skin of Our Teeth* on Broadway, fell in love with the camera. "There was just something about it," she said. "Nothing made me happier than to do things for it, the camera. It was as if I were mesmerized by that lens. In actuality I was performing for it. I was interested in pleasing it to the ultimate."[9]

In movie work actors normally learn their lines the night before, then rehearse before each take. During the big-studio era the average day shooting A pictures was nine to six, with a half-day on Saturdays. On B pictures work could continue past midnight, although the Screen Actors Guild did insist on twelve hours off between calls. To fill up time between takes, performers might play gin rummy, talk shop, swap stories, or listen to records in their dressing rooms. Birthdays generally called for a celebration, with a cake and appropriate gifts. Practical jokes served as frequent diversions, ranging from Susan Hayward's taking the light bulbs out of Robert Montgomery's dressing-room mirror to Laraine Day's stand-in sewing the bottoms of Kirk Douglas's pants together. Bob Hope and Red Skelton were two notorious pranksters, ad-libbing and having a grand time even during actual takes. Arlene Dahl opened her dressing-room door early in the shooting of *A Southern Yankee* (1948) to discover a stinkbomb Red had placed there.

Not that all the work was fun, nor all the relationships congenial. Directors could be vicious, performers sometimes difficult or unpredictable. Occasionally alliances developed, splitting a company into warring camps. If the producer or director fell in love with the leading lady, colleagues complained that she got all the close-ups. If the director was weak and the star strong, a battle royal might ensue, with the director taking out his frustrations on those he knew couldn't fight back. On the other hand, personal attitudes frequently carried over and affected work on the set. Robert Stack, for instance, had known Carole Lombard since he was a boy; he had taught her to shoot when he was about thirteen. "She was an idealization of everything a young boy thinks of in a woman," said Stack. "She was beautiful and sexy-looking and kind. And she treated me as a man when I was only about thirteen. She never condescended. So the sun rose and set on her as far as I was concerned." Suddenly in *To Be or Not to Be* (1942) for Ernst Lubitsch, when Stack was twenty-three, he was expected to play a love scene with the thirty-four-year-old Lombard, posing for him at least a strange situation.[10]

On most sets the atmosphere was one of friendly helpfulness, even when the project wasn't anybody's favorite. Rosemary DeCamp fondly recalled Ann Sheridan's buying her a cup of coffee on the first day of shooting *Nora Prentiss* (1947), while Ann Doran later voiced amazement at walking into a makeup room one morning and finding Barbara Stanwyck on hands and knees cleaning up the mess. De Mille insisted that he wanted no extras on his set; everyone was an actor with a unique contribution to make, and those who showed something special were rewarded. Lucille Ball maintained she owed her start to doing things nobody else would, little things that appeared unimportant. "To me they seemed like an invitation to waltz," Ball declared. "I could scream, I could run, and I could certainly wear a mud pack." Before long directors began to say, "Get that girl, she gets it done."[11]

Like most artists, film people loved their work and thrived on it, despite the most exasperating circumstances. They accepted the fact that they were making pictures for a mass audience and struggled to create something of quality within a commercial system. Fuss and fume though they might, most performers looked forward to their next assignment, hoping it would be the one to make the rest seem worthwhile. Gregory Peck recalled working on *The Yearling* (1946) at MGM in the morning, then driving down the street about half a mile in Culver City to work on *Duel in the Sun* (1947) for Selznick in the afternoon. "I may have gotten my Florida cracker accent and my Texas cowpoke accent confused at times," the actor said. "But I was a bear for work in those days. I thought it was fun."[12]

For those involved, each picture had a life of its own—its own start, its own finish, a closed little world with a particular group of people working together intimately. Once the film was over, that feeling could never quite be recaptured. "Nothing in Hollywood is permanent," David O. Selznick commented. "Once photographed, life here is ended. It is almost symbolic of Hollywood that Tara had no rooms inside. It was just a facade."[13] When a picture was finished, it was like an amputation or a divorce; all the feelings and affection that had built up on the set over several weeks were abruptly terminated, leaving an empty feeling. "You live so closely together," Joan Fontaine remarked, "it's rather traumatic. Suddenly you are ousted from the nest. You go back to collect your things in your makeup room and decide to visit the set. All those gaffers and electricians and everybody else who were your chums yesterday are now busy on something else, and you feel that you're in the way, a fifth wheel."[14]

Barrymore Initiates Hepburn

When Katharine Hepburn made her first film, A Bill of Divorcement (1932), there were stories about her quarrels with leading man John Barrymore. After a particular scene had been repeated several times, according to one account, Hepburn turned to Barrymore and screamed: "I'll never play another scene with you!" Barrymore answered, "My dear, you never have."[15]

Razzing Claudette

During the making of Midnight (1939), Don Ameche and director Mitch Leisen pulled one of the oldest gags on Claudette Colbert. They picked out the most ancient extra on the set and sent him to Claudette's dressing room. When she opened her door, the extra said, "Miss Colbert, I've adored you ever since I was a little boy." Guessing at once who was behind this, she chased Ameche all over the lot.[16]

Bogie's Nod

Filming on Casablanca (1943) started without a finished script. It wasn't even known whether Ingrid Bergman would wind up with Humphrey Bogart or with Paul Henreid. Scenes were shot on a day-to-day basis, with director Michael Curtiz scanning pages of script as they came from the typewriters. The actors, not knowing where they were headed, grew upset and jittery. Whenever they approached Curtiz for information, he'd simply snarl, "Actors! Actors! They want to know everything!"

One morning Curtiz told Bogart, "You've got an easy day today. Go on that balcony, look down and to the right, and nod. Then you can go home." Bogie asked, "What am I nodding at? What's my attitude?" Curtiz snapped, "Don't ask so many questions. Get up there and nod, and then go home." So Bogie followed instructions. Not until long afterward did he realize that his nod had triggered the famous "Marseillaise" scene, where the nightclub orchestra drowns out some Germans singing "Die Wacht am Rhein," one of the classic moments in the picture.[17]

Hello, Dolly

When Henry Fonda went from Broadway to Hollywood, he soon learned that movie scripts were quite different from stage scripts. Stage scripts contained the character's name on a page in capital letters with the appropriate dialogue under it; movie scripts put the character's name and the dialogue on the left side of the page and the camera movements on the right side. In one of the first scenes for *The Farmer Takes a Wife* (1935), which Fonda had done on Broadway, a woman named Molly is in a hotel lobby, a man named Dan (played by Fonda) enters, and they have some dialogue. But as they go into the dining room, the script read, "DOLLY with them," and when they left, the script said, "DOLLY with them." "I like this script," Fonda told director Victor Fleming, after looking it over. "It's very good, but who's Dolly? She's always there, but she never says anything." Fleming laughed, explained, and Fonda learned his first lesson as a film performer.[18]

Ermine Exchange

Douglas Fairbanks, Jr., had a birthday during the making of *That Lady in Ermine* (1948), and Lubitsch made an occasion of it. About five o'clock in the afternoon, champagne and a cake were brought out and, in keeping with their picture title, Betty Grable presented her co-star with an ermine-lined jock strap. Later in the filming, Grable had a birthday, and Fairbanks gave her an ermine-lined chastity belt.[19]

Loretta's Swear Cup

Ethereal Loretta Young and rough-and-ready Robert Mitchum had their differences on the set of *Rachel and the Stranger* (1948). When making films Loretta always brought a collection cup to which company members were expected to contribute if they swore. A "hell" cost twenty-five cents, "goddamn" fifty cents, and so on, and the money was donated to a home for unwed mothers. Annoyed during a scene, Mitchum rammed a $5 bill into the cup before letting loose a blast of expletives.[20]

The Real Item

Producer Hal Wallis grew impatient with an incompetent actor playing one of gangster Eduardo Ciannelli's henchmen in Marked Woman (1937). "Who is that monkey?" Wallis demanded of director Lloyd Bacon. "Why the hell didn't you get a menacing-looking character? He looks like some five-dollar extra. Couldn't you see he wasn't right for the part of a gangster?" Bacon's reply broke up Bette Davis and the others on the set. "I'm sorry to tell you," said Bacon, "that he is one of Lucky Luciano's favorite gang members. We put him in the picture for realism!"[21]

Siblings

In Ethel Barrymore's first talkie, Rasputin and the Empress (1932), there was much talk about how the three Barrymores would vie with each other to dominate the film. When a reporter asked Ethel whether she would be nervous doing a talkie with her brothers, John interposed, "You need not worry about Miss Barrymore getting nervous," he said. "She'll be standing right in front of the camera—in front of us." Producer Irving Thalberg was amused by the situation. "You know, Jack," he said, grinning, to John Barrymore, "you have to kill Lionel in the last reel. You don't mind, do you?" "I don't mind," said John, "but the way he's going to steal this picture from his brother and sister, I ought to kill him in the first reel."[22]

The Lion's Roar

Queen of the Amazons (1947) was a terrible jungle picture, which was filmed at a studio on Western Avenue as an independent production and had good actors and practically no money. In it was the original MGM lion, but by then the poor thing was so decrepit he had no teeth. The producer had a false set made for him. The film was shot during the summer, and one exceptionally hot day the lion was supposed to attack the hero (really his trainer dressed like the hero). It was so hot that every time the director was ready to start the scene, the lion would lie down. After several tries without success, someone opened the big doors of the soundstage to let in some air. The lion revived, and while no one was looking, got up and walked out. He wandered down Western Avenue all by himself, still proudly sporting his false teeth and frightening pedestrians needlessly.[23]

Five-day Test
Paul Muni had a theory he called the "Five-Day Test," which he had learned from an old stage-door man and which he thought ought to govern behavior on the set during the shooting of a film. "The first day of a rehearsal," he said, "everybody in a company always falls in love with somebody else. Boys fall in love with girls; girls fall in love with boys; boys fall in love with boys. The oldest character man in the company always falls for the prettiest ingenue. If you're lucky, sometimes it works the other way around, and the young ones fall for the old ones. This happens to anybody who still has his eyesight and a few glands left. But take my advice, kid. Always wait five days. At the end of that time, if you still want it, *then* do something about it. But you usually don't."[24]

What Counts
Harold Russell, a double amputee who had lost both his hands in the service during World War II, not only won an Academy Award in 1946 for best supporting actor for his role in Sam Goldwyn's *The Best Years of Our Lives*, but a special Oscar voted by the Academy's board of governors as well—the only time any actor ever won two Oscars for the same part. Despite his handicap, Russell had learned to use his "hooks" adeptly and had emerged remarkably well adjusted, firmly believing "it's what's left that counts." The cast of *Best Years* enjoyed an exceptional rapport, although at first Myrna Loy, one of the film's stars, seemed self-conscious and uneasy with Russell's disability. Sensing her discomfort, the young veteran walked over to her on the set, took her hand with one hook, and patted it with the other. The actress immediately relaxed, and their relationship from then on was a warm one.[25]

Slap-happy
In *The Wizard of Oz* (1939), Dorothy learns that the ferocious lion she encounters on the yellow-brick road is a coward when she slaps him and he starts crying. Filming the scene, though, produced a crisis. When Judy Garland (Dorothy) slapped Bert Lahr (the Cowardly Lion), the latter's reaction was so comical that Judy burst into screams of laughter instead of continuing with her lines. Director

Victor Fleming ordered another take, but again Lahr's facial expressions reduced Judy to laughter. Judy then went behind a tree and said, "I will not laugh. I will not laugh." But in the next take she was again convulsed with laughter. After a few more takes she became hysterical; she simply couldn't stop laughing. At this point Fleming went over and slapped her hard on the face. "All right now," he said, "go back to your dressing room." Judy did as he instructed. And when she returned a few minutes later she said, "O.K.?" and then performed the scene perfectly.[26]

Dried up

In *The Mudlark* (1950), Irene Dunne played the part of Queen Victoria, and Alec Guinness played the famous British prime minister Benjamin Disraeli. The high point of the film was a moving speech Disraeli made in Parliament, punctuated by a long and dramatic pause halfway through. Darryl Zanuck regarded it as one of the most effective moments of silence in film history, and, since the script hadn't called for it, he asked Guinness later on how he came to think of it. "I didn't," said Guinness frankly. "In the middle of my speech, I forgot my lines—dried up."[27]

Counting

Years after the film was made, caricaturist Al Hirschfeld and his wife, actress Dolly Haas, went with Marlene Dietrich to see *Morocco* (1930) at the Museum of Modern Art. Fascinated with Dietrich's performance, Hirschfeld asked her, "Marlene, how did you get that wonderful expression at the end when you kick your shoes off and make your way into the desert to follow Gary Cooper?" Remembering how the scene was shot, Dietrich replied, "I did what Joe von Sternberg asked me. I counted from twenty-five backwards!"[28]

Unusual Virus

Among the stand-ins on *The Private Lives of Elizabeth and Essex* (1939) was a young lady of easy virtue. Practically every male on the set had enjoyed an afternoon with her, and toward the end of shooting, director Mike Curtiz himself had gone off to lunch with her. When Curtiz returned alone, Errol Flynn and the crew were standing around waiting. "Mike," said Flynn innocently, "a terrible thing happened to Ken, the electrician, while you were out." Curtiz looked concerned. "He became very ill," Flynn explained coolly. "We called the doctor. He said Ken had this unusual disease—kind of a V.D. It can hit a man without a moment's warning." Curtiz was unsympathetic: "Well it serves him right. Who was the damn fool playing around with?" Flynn flashed a boyish grin. "I'm afraid it was one of the girls in our own family, one of the stand-ins," and he casually dropped the girl's name. Curtiz turned white and ran off the set, headed for the studio's first aid station. He never found out it was just one of Errol's practical jokes.[29]

On Camera
In *Julia Misbehaves* (1948), Elizabeth Taylor had Peter Lawford as her fiancé, but she also had a big crush on him off-camera and everyone on the set knew it. At one point the script called for them to kiss passionately and then for Elizabeth to say, "Oh, Ritchie, what are we going to do?" The two went into a clinch and Elizabeth delivered her line and then sighed, "Oh, Peter, what am I going to do?" She turned deep red as she heard a burst of laughter on the set.[30]

No Way
On *Mrs. Miniver* (1942) Dame May Whitty had a "two-shot" with young Richard Ney. The titled English actress asked the handsome newcomer to react in a certain way so the next line would make more sense. "Of course, Dame May," said Ney, "I shall do as you say, but I think my way is better." "Young man," said Dame May, looking down her nose at him, "you haven't *got* a way!"[31]

Time Out
Filming on *Yankee Doodle Dandy* (1942), a musical about George M. Cohan, began the morning after the Japanese attack on Pearl Harbor. The cast was in costume, sitting on a soundstage, and some of the members were crying. Everyone listened quietly to President Roosevelt's speech to Congress calling for a declaration of war, and when it was over, director Michael Curtiz turned the radio off and was ready to start shooting. But James Cagney, star of the film, interrupted him. "It seems to me," he said, "this is the time for a prayer." For a minute or two all was quiet and then Curtiz said, "All right now, let's go to work and make a really wonderful picture."[32]

Private Collection
When Elia Kazan was directing *Pinky* (1949), Ethel Barrymore worked well with him despite his exhausting insistence on perfection. "That's wonderful," he'd say after a take. "Now let's do it once more." "And what's this one for," Ethel once snapped, "your private collection?"[33]

Welles Enough
Orson Welles directed *The Lady from Shanghai* (1948) for Harry Cohn, stretching a sixty-day schedule into ninety. As costs soared, production manager Jack Fier was assigned the task of curbing Welles's excesses, and the two locked in combat. As the picture was nearing completion, Welles erected a sign reading: THE ONLY THING WE HAVE TO FIER IS FIER ITSELF. Fier retaliated with his own sign: ALL'S WELL THAT ENDS WELLES.[34]

All Kinds
De Mille often used LeRoy Prinz to choreograph the crowd scenes for which his spectacles became famous. On *The Crusades* (1935) LeRoy encountered more than his share of trouble, turning the epic into a comedy so far as Prinz was concerned. For the sequence in which the Christians storm the Moslem fortress, the studio had gone out on the streets to recruit the number of extras necessary for the battle, bringing in anyone who needed work. Since the second assistant was plastered, Prinz stood over on the side of a field holding back the crusaders until De Mille called "Action." Finally the director gave the signal, and the soldiers in their heavy armor began scaling the fortress walls, using ladders slanted over a moat. Others were shooting blazing arrows or hurling rocks at the enemy, actually huge sponges big enough to knock a man over. The Moslems were pushing some of the ladders over, causing Christian soldiers to fall into the moat, armor and all.

In the midst of this De Mille yelled, "Cut, cut!" A guy raced past LeRoy Prinz screaming for dear life; someone had shot him in the rear with a flaming arrow. Crew members waded through the moat, pulling up warriors who were actually drowning. Although the water was less than three feet deep, the armor was so heavy they couldn't get their heads up. "They looked like sardine cans coming up," recalled Prinz, "the way water was pouring out of those armored suits."

From atop his tower De Mille said, "No good! Get ready. We'll do it again." Prinz lined up his soldiers again over on the side, awaiting the director's go-ahead. For two days they worked on the scene, until everyone was exhausted. From out of a suit of armor on the second afternoon, Prinz heard an effeminate voice mutter to a friend, "Well, I'll be damned if I come back here tomorrow!"[35]

Skywriting

Toward the end of his life John Barrymore depended on blackboards with his lines on them during shooting, even though he usually knew the lines anyway. "The blackboard is to me what a net is to a circus trapeze artist," he said. "He can do his quadruple somersaults with confidence as long as he knows that the net is there to catch him just in case." But when he contemplated playing *Macbeth* in the Hollywood Bowl, someone wondered how he'd manage without blackboards. "I'll have them use skywriting," he said.[36]

Small Package

Mickey Rooney and Carolyn Jones became good friends on *Baby Face Nelson* (1957). She realized what a brilliant performer he was, but liked to tease him. After an especially fine scene she'd say, "Mickey, if you'd been a head and a half taller, you'd be dangerous." One afternoon they were shooting a scene with antique cars. Since the setups took longer than usual, the two of them spent a lot of time talking. Mickey got to telling Carolyn about his string of ex-wives—nothing too private, just how he had married women taller than he. He became poetic and eventually pensive, sitting in an old 1930s car with a cap over his eyes. "Yeah," he finally said, "I put shoes on them, and they walk away from me."[37]

Can't Do It Any Other Way

In *The Private Lives of Elizabeth and Essex* (1939), there is a scene in which Errol Flynn, playing young Lord Essex, Queen Elizabeth's lover, appears at court, walks down the aisle toward the queen (Bette Davis), and gets a cold reception because he didn't visit her right after returning from Ireland. "Well, m'lord Essex," says Davis, "what have you to say for yourself?" "I have much to say for myself—," says Flynn, "but little for you!" At these words Davis hauls off and whacks him in the face before the whole court.

At the rehearsal for the scene, Davis (who had wanted Laurence Olivier, not Flynn, to play Essex) hit Flynn so hard he almost passed out, and he went in some agitation afterward to see her in her dressing room. "Bette," he said, "I want to talk to you about something." "Oh, I know perfectly well what you are going to say," said Davis haughtily, "but if you can't take a little slap, that is just too bad! . . . I can't do it any other way. . . . That's the kind of actress I am—and I *stress* actress!" Flynn left with his mind made up; if she slugged him again he would hit her back. To his surprise, however, when they shot the scene, she merely simulated the blow; her hand came close to the side of his nose and missed it by a fraction of an inch.

Flynn was gratified by Davis's restraint, but still irked by the supercilious way she had treated him. A few days later, when they were rehearsing a scene in which he was called on to give her a playful slap on the back, he decided to escalate the gesture. "I held my hand way out there. . . ," he said later, "and it went sailing right through her Elizabethan dresses, slappo, smack on her Academy Award behind." As Davis looked on him with fury, he said genially: "I'm awful sorry. I don't know how to do it any other way. . . ." She never spoke to him again off the set.[38]

Wyman's Gift

Magnificent Obsession (1954) was Rock Hudson's first solid dramatic role, and he was nervous—especially because his co-star, Jane Wyman, had recently won an Oscar. He frequently blew lines, so that thirty or forty takes became necessary, but Wyman never complained. After the picture was over Hudson said to her, "You really went out of your way, Jane, to be nice to me when you didn't have to. I want you to know that I do know that. I appreciate it, and I love you for it." Wyman smiled. "Let me tell you something," she said. "It was handed to me by somebody, and I handed it to you. Now it's your turn to hand it to somebody else."[39]

President of What?

Ronald Reagan, the only movie star ever to become president, appeared in fifty-three films, beginning with *Love Is on the Air* in 1937 and including *Knute Rockne—All American* (1940) and *King's Row* (1942), in which he gave his best performances. While making the

CHAPTER 13

The Crew

When a film is widely acclaimed for its excellence the leading actors and the director receive most of the praise, although actors in supporting roles are often recognized. Most moviegoers may not be aware of it, but filmmaking is above all a cooperative effort, a triumph of teamwork on the part of a number of gifted and dedicated individuals, not simply a director and a star or two. Without capable assistants to look after details, skilled and imaginative cameramen to do the shooting, and talented art directors, costume designers, and makeup people, high-quality films could not be produced. If any one of these fails to perform his or her duties to the fullest, the quality of the film will be impaired. It takes the best efforts of everyone involved to make an outstanding film.

As a result Hollywood sets are usually crowded with crews of forty to sixty people, each an expert in a particular craft. A common denominator among the old studios was the quality of the various departments, for all of them were excellent. Since filmmaking is a concert of talents, harmony and cooperation are essential to efficiency. This might not be a problem if every craft did not contain its prima donnas. Astute producers and directors quickly learn the advantages of knowing crew members on a first-name basis, while stars are often judged by their peers on how well they get along with technicians. Respect is frequently earned by little courtesies such as asking about a gaffer's little boy who just had a tonsil operation or about the new home a grip recently bought.

A key figure in keeping things moving is the assistant director, whose duty is not to assist in directing, but to serve as a foreman, making sure the director has everything he needs and that actors are on the set when scheduled to be there. An assistant director in the old days normally worked with the same director time and again. De Mille's first assistant was a man named Cullen Tate; over the years C.B. affectionately called him Hesy Tate.

A second assistant also works in tandem with the first, taking care of all the details and paper work and keeping track of the footage shot. In the big-studio era it was the second assistant who informed the casting office as to the types of extras needed on a given day. Gerd Oswald recalled working as second assistant on several Alan Ladd pictures and screening the extras in the morning to make certain none of them towered above the diminutive star.[1] The third assistant in those days was primarily a herder who supervised logistics. When Otto Lang worked as third assistant to William Wellman on *The Ox-Bow Incident* (1943), his initial job was to see that the horses were properly placed and facing the right direction, and making sure the number of horses and colors matched the shots taken the day before. When asked what he was doing, Lang replied: "I'm counting horses' asses. That's my job."[2]

While the cinematographer works closely with the director, he also has his own operator and crew. The cameraman himself rarely sits behind a camera, but like the director, is an artist, searching for ways to capture the mood of every scene. Lighting is the key to a unique style, and each of the great cinematographers had his own techniques for using light. Joseph Ruttenberg, tops among the thirteen cameramen under contract to MGM, was distinguished by his skillful play with shadows. His dramatic use of shadows in *Gaslight* (1944) earned him one of his ten Oscar nominations. Ruttenberg used a soft focus on women, sometimes with the sheerest stocking as a diffusion disc, and preferred working in black-and-white to color, since halftones offered greater dramatic possibilities.[3]

The experienced director talks over angles with his cameraman and specifies setups, which may be modified later. An established director generally has his own method for achieving a distinctive quality that characterizes his work. François Truffaut observed that Hitchcock filmed murder scenes as if they were love scenes and love scenes as if they were murder scenes.[4] Whenever Joe Ruttenberg worked with Mervyn LeRoy or Vincente Minnelli, he knew each would want a moving camera, which created additional lighting problems. One day LeRoy said to Ruttenberg, "Joe, I just want a close-up of putting a key into the lock of that door over there," but he wondered how such a tight shot could be lighted. The resourceful Ruttenberg walked over to the door, struck two matches, and said, "Let's go."[5]

Gregg Toland is often considered the finest cinematographer Hollywood ever produced, and his contribution to the look and feel of Citizen Kane (1941) still stands as a revolutionary achievement. A small, wiry man, Toland was an exceptional innovator, able to keep the foreground, middle ground, and background all sharp by using a wide-angle lens and increased light. His deep focus gave audiences more to look at, allowing them to see both action and reaction, letting them do their own cutting, as it were. "This influenced my direction to some extent," said William Wyler,[6] who worked with Toland on both The Little Foxes (1941) and The Best Years of Our Lives (1946). Since the wide-angle lens distorts, it was essential to know how to use the distortion to advantage. One sequence of a film might be hard and harsh, another soft and diffused, depending on the dramatic texture.

Like all artists, cinematographers usually work best when given some leeway, and some of them are as temperamental as any star. Leon Shamroy, who was outstanding in his field, was a cryptic, arrogant, opinionated man and difficult to work with. Because he would yell and was downright rude even to stars, crews called him "Grumble Guts." Yet Shamroy had a warm side, and his team of workmen realized that underneath his rough exterior was a heart of gold. "Shamy," as friends called him, had a passion for horse races, and whenever he wasn't on the set he was likely on the telephone, checking out the day's winners at various racetracks.

A director also has lengthy discussions with the art director, always with the script, his sense of place, and feelings about characterization firmly in mind. Ultimately it will be the director who approves every set, but talented art directors make their creative impact. Harry Horner's contribution to the turn-of-the-century look in The Heiress (1949) added immeasurably to the atmosphere William Wyler and his cast achieved dramatically. Richard Day's sets similarly underscored the mood of Elia Kazan's direction on A Streetcar Named Desire (1951), along with Lucinda Ballard's costumes and Alex North's musical score. Each of the big studios had superlative art directors: Cedric Gibbons at Metro, Lyle Wheeler at Twentieth Century-Fox, and Hans Dreier at Paramount. Each, of course, functioned as part of a team. William Cameron Menzies, often considered the best ever on production design, made charcoal drawings of every setup. While Menzies usually worked on big productions like *Gone With the Wind* (1939) and *For Whom the Bell Tolls* (1943), he once employed his talents to make the small film *Reign of Terror* (1949) appear important.

Costume designers are also vital to the overall effect, providing sketches for final selection by producers, directors, and stars. Adrian at Metro, Orry-Kelly at Warners, Robert Kalloch at Columbia, and Howard Greer and Travis Banton at Paramount were gifted designers who made fashion an integral part of motion pictures. Appropriate costumes contributed to the telling of a story, and the big-studio era was a time of glamour, when stars were expected to look like stars. Actresses wore real jewelry because it made them feel better, even though it meant paying insurance and having an armed guard on the set. Each studio had its huge store of costly fabrics from Switzerland, Paris, and Rome—rich brocades, cut velvets, hammered satins—everything a designer might need. Most studios had women who sat at looms, and beaders who made jeweled dresses, often working six to eight months on a single garment.

Edith Head, who apprenticed under Banton and Greer at Paramount, received thirty-four Academy Award nominations for costume design. Head noted that her ideas came from the script. "A script," she said, "tells you exactly the kind of persons, their status, their social background, their locale. When you read a script, it tells you pretty much how the people should look."[7] During her early days Head created the Veronica Lake look, the Dorothy Lamour look, and the "Latin American look" with Barbara Stanwyck, often setting fashion trends the public emulated. But for the most part her designs remained simple and classic for both period and contemporary films.

Makeup was another area that produced Hollywood legends. The six Westmore brothers became the most famous by following in their father's footsteps. Each of them eventually headed the makeup department of a major studio. There was also Charles Dudley at Fox and Jack Dawn and William Tuttle at Metro, all talented makeup artists. In hairstyling Sydney Guilaroff at MGM was probably the best known, although every studio had a department head with several staff members, each assigned to specific stars.

There were also sound technicians and special-effects experts like Gordon Jennings and John P. Fulton at Paramount. Willis O'Brien was responsible for the animation in *The Lost World* (1925) and *King Kong* (1933). Each set had its script girl, who kept a record of every shot, describing the camera movement, the clothes worn, and details like the length of an actor's cigarette. When required, an animal trainer was present, and like a stage mother, eagerly demonstrated for directors the talents of his charges. Yet intimate as these various relationships might be during the making of a picture, the closeness generally ended with the last day's shooting. "That seems to be the tragedy of a Hollywood friendship," Henry Koster observed, "it dies after working together finishes."[8]

Established

Once an actor has been introduced in a film, the director has to use him, no matter how temperamental he may become. He's been established. The same is true of sets. Once a set has been established, it can't be changed without giving the audience an explanation. Once Michael Curtiz was shooting a football picture at Warner Bros. His assistant director was a former All-American, while Mike's brother (who spoke less English even than Mike did) was in charge of the second unit. The brother asked the football player, "What's the next action?" The former All-American answered, "When the play starts, the right tackle comes over and takes out the opposing guard." Mike's brother said, "You can't take him out, he's been established."[9]

Real Talent

The entire action of Alfred Hitchcock's *Lifeboat* (1944) was confined to a floating raft, filmed in a large studio tank. The actors were subjected to enormous wind fans and water-spraying machines, and several of them fell ill with chills and fever, among them Tallulah Bankhead. But the indomitable Tallulah stood up under the heat of the lights, the submersions, and even being doused by 5,400 gallons of water, for which she received a round of applause from crew members. Bankhead also won applause for her bawdiness, which Hitchcock admired almost as much as her professionalism. But there was criticism when the actress stopped wearing underwear, a fact that became apparent every time she climbed the ladder to enter the tank. Yet the director refused to reprimand her. "You might consider this is a matter for the wardrobe department," said Hitchcock, "or perhaps for the makeup people—or perhaps it's even for hairdressing!"[10]

The Light That Failed

For years Joe Ruttenberg was Greer Garson's favorite cameraman at MGM, for she was convinced he showed her to better advantage than any other cameraman. Ruttenberg employed an array of mysterious screens, discs, and gobos to shade the light and bring out her best features, and when Adolphe Menjou worked with Garson, he had to thread his way through all kinds of stanchions and gadgets to appear in a scene with her. Ruttenberg had Greer's face so bathed in light that it became a luminous moon, while Menjou stood in the shadows, actually feeling chilly. Finally the actor said, "Put a little light on me, Joe, I'm going to catch a cold."[11]

Several years after her days of glory, it is said, Garson returned to Metro for a film and, of course, asked for Joe Ruttenberg, who was still there. "You know, Joe," she said, disappointed after they photographed the wardrobe tests, "you're not photographing me as well as you used to." "I'm sorry, Greer," said Ruttenberg, smiling, "I'm ten years older."[12] It's a cute story and it was also told of Marlene Dietrich and Norma Shearer.

Which Nose?

On Cyrano de Bergerac (1950), actor José Ferrer, director Michael Gordon, and the makeup team realized that Cyrano's nose would have to withstand the scrutiny of close-ups. What might have been effective on the stage would not be suitable before the camera. So they worked on the nose with the greatest care, enlarging the nostrils and giving it a bit of an upward tilt for panache. An artist drew various possibilities for them to consider and eventually made a plaster-of-Paris mask as a model. In the throes of working out the details, Mike Gordon and his wife went to dinner with the Robert Prestons. Over drinks Mike went on and on about the nose, eventually becoming pretty boring to the rest. Finally Preston said, "Well, so which nose got the part?" And Gordon's wife, well aware of producers' predilections, cried merrily: "The one with the big tits, of course!"[13]

A Matter of Time

Veteran director Andrew Stone appreciated skillful photography but felt cameramen took unreasonable time to light sets, mainly to justify huge salaries. In Stone's view Leon Shamroy was a great cinematographer and a fantastic actor. During the making of *Stormy Weather* (1943), the two clashed when the cameraman wanted a whole day to light a large set. Finally they compromised. Shamroy would sit in the sun, reading a paper, until the gaffer appeared and tapped him on the shoulder. Then the cameraman would strut onto the stage and point to various lights. The gaffer would nod—all dramatically done, without a word. Shamroy would return to his sunny spot and continue reading. Half an hour later the gaffer would return, and the procedure would begin again. "All done in silence, for dramatic effect," recalled Stone. "Just an absolute act." The director agreed Shamroy got fabulous results, but had his suspicions confirmed when they were called back for additional footage. Since Stone was then involved with another film, he was scheduled to work with Shamroy early one Saturday. The cameraman was outraged because he was supposed to go by private plane to the Stanford game with friends and it appeared he would miss his flight. "Look," Stone told him, "you're not fooling me; I'm onto the charade. Nobody is here, it's Saturday. I'm not going to tell anybody. So why don't you just light the set in ten minutes and get your plane?" Within fifteen minutes they had the scene shot, and "Shamy" caught his plane.[14]

Intimacy

For a brief time Edmund North, later a major screenwriter, worked as a production assistant for Samuel Goldwyn, eager to learn about the physical side of filmmaking. Since Goldwyn put up his own money, he was mindful of costs, even on big, splashy pictures like *The Real Glory* (1939), which starred Gary Cooper and dealt with the Philippine insurrection. When the budget came through, North's boss said, "Look, I'm going to be busy on the set. Take this budget in to the old man and get his okay." So North went in, Goldwyn looked quickly at the bottom line, and proceeded to throw a fit. "You're ruining me!" shouted Sam. "What are you doing?" When he finally stopped ranting, North said, "Mr. Goldwyn, from the beginning of this project you said you wanted a spectacle." "Yes," screamed Goldwyn, "but, goddamit, I wanted an *intimate* spectacle!"[15]

Step Aside

Howard Hawks, who produced and directed the screwball comedy *Bringing Up Baby* (1938), got along fine with Katharine Hepburn, who starred in it with Cary Grant, but at times she tried his patience. One day, he recalled, she got to "talking and talking and *talking*," and when the assistant director consulted Hawks about something, she went on talking anyway. "Quiet on the set," Hawks called, but Hepburn kept going on. Finally Hawks told his assistant to tell everybody to sit down and just look at Hepburn. In a moment or two Hepburn realized what was happening. "What are we waiting for?" she wanted to know. "I was just wondering when the parrot was going to stop talking," Hawks told her. "I want to have a word with you," said Hepburn angrily, and took him aside. "Howard," she said, "these people are friends of mine, and if you say things like that to me, you're liable to get yourself into trouble." Hawks looked up and saw an electrician in the flies above them with a big lamp. "Eddie," he called up, "if you had a choice of dropping that lamp on Miss Hepburn or me, which would you choose?" And the electrician yelled back: "Step aside, Mr. Hawks!"[16]

Foreign Picture Award

During the shooting of *Sunset Boulevard* (1950) cinematographer John Seitz had questions about the camera setup for the scene where Gloria Swanson is lying in bed after attempting suicide. "Johnny," director Billy Wilder told him, "it's the usual slashed-wrist shot."[17] A little later Wilder told the cameraman: "Keep it out of focus. I want to win the foreign picture award."[18]

Who's Wong?

When the great Chinese cinematographer James Wong Howe opened a restaurant in Hollywood, the local press sent a photographer to take pictures of the celebrated cameraman and his staff outside the new café. The newspaper photographer knew nothing of Howe's acclaim; to him it was just another assignment. He proceeded to line up the fledgling restaurateur and his staff, only to find he couldn't fit them all into his picture. So he backed into the street, with traffic whizzing by on either side. Not wanting to see the man hit by a passing car, Howe suggested he use a wide-angle lens. "Just stick to your chop suey," said the surly photographer, "and let me take the pictures."[19]

Going Hollywood

Seven Wonders of the World (1956) was a Cinerama travelogue, held together by the barest plot. In one sequence an earnest fellow is determined to reach St. Peter's Square with his wife and five children in time to be blessed by the pope on Easter Sunday. Director Ted Tetzlaff filmed the sequence in Rome and, to get a good close shot, had his technicians build a platform facing the balcony where His Holiness, Pius XII, would appear. The pontiff proved charming and interested in the technique that would capture his blessing for millions of theatergoers as well as the throng gathered outside the Vatican. He was instructed on how to hit marks and became enchanted with the preparation and equipment. His gracious ways and gentle humor completely won over Tetzlaff's crew, so that their work turned into a labor of love. After the director was satisfied with his tower close-up of His Holiness, he told his cameraman, "Cut and print it." But the pope was not so easily satisfied. "If you don't mind, could we do it over again?" he asked Tetzlaff. "I'm sure I can do it better."[20]

CHAPTER 14

On Location

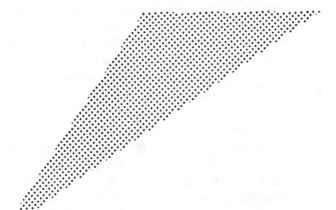

"A rock is a rock, a tree is a tree. Shoot it in Griffith Park," old-time movie moguls used to say.[1] It was not until after World War II that studios adopted the practice of sending production companies to do the filming where the story action took place. The old studios had enormous back lots or ranches out in the Valley for outdoor shooting. Character actor William Le Massena recalled roaming fascinated through the Twentieth Century-Fox back lot during the mid-1950s, before it was dismantled to build Century City. "It just seemed like miles of old sets and jungles and seaports and city streets and tanks where they had sea battles," the actor said. "It was all in a semistate of decay and rot and disintegration. But it was so beautiful, and I'd be there all by myself with all those ghosts of a thousand *Bountys*. It was terrific."[2]

If scenes from India or Africa were needed and none was available in stock footage, the studio sent camera units to those places to photograph background shots. Actors then performed in front of a screen with the location projected behind them. Gregory Peck remembered the artificiality of making *The Snows of Kilimanjaro* (1952): "Someone had gone to Africa and shot a rhino for the benefit of Twentieth Century-Fox. They had that on film, and I pointed my rifle at the charging rhino, and when the red light blinked off camera-range, I pulled the trigger and down went the rhino."[3]

Actual location work was for years restricted largely to Westerns, when the whole crew would travel to Utah or Arizona or New Mexico. A second unit might also be sent to make shots for the studio to use as process plates. Location shooting was most likely on big-production Westerns, because producers wanted those pictures to appear important. Filming on location was usually more expensive and more complicated technically. Recording sound outdoors and keeping out extraneous noises always proved difficult, with frequent dubbing necessary to achieve the quality desired. If there was much action, the costume department provided duplicates, in case something happened to any of the costumes while the company was away from the studio. Stormy weather could also cause serious problems.

If conditions were bad, nerves frequently became so frayed that serious bickering occurred. Because work had to end at sundown, actors were obliged to rise before dawn and be made up and in costume, ready to start shooting with the first light. Sometimes extreme heat or cold added to the discomfort. Arlene Dahl burned badly from the sun on her first location near Kanab, Utah, and her red hair bleached until it was almost blond. During the filming of *Roughshod* (1949), Martha Hyer suffered a ruptured appendix and had to be operated on in a first aid shack up in the mountains.

John Ford, a veteran at working on location, particularly in Monument Valley, knew that morale was essential to keep a picture on schedule. He banned film talk in the evenings, but encouraged singing and playing games, from dominoes to poker. Practical jokes were interminable; the butt of them was usually burly Ward Bond, a Ford regular who was quite opinionated and reactionary. Morale was no problem for performers who enjoyed being outdoors and who liked location work. "The elements were all around you," said Virginia Mayo. "It made you feel good. I loved working in those Westerns. Of course the great Southwest is my favorite part of the country."[4]

Other than for Westerns, almost all filming was done in California until the late 1940s. *Treasure Island* (1934) was shot mainly on Catalina Island, where the biggest problem was keeping yachts, airplanes, and water-skiers out of the picture. The trench warfare in *All Quiet on the Western Front* (1930) was filmed on a hill near Newport Beach. *The Good Earth* (1937), a film about China, was photographed entirely in California, while the dueling sequences in *The Three Musketeers* (1948) were shot in Pasadena parks, with Gene Kelly stressing the balletic in part to keep attention off the backgrounds. *Waterloo Bridge* (1940) was filmed on an MGM sound-stage, not in London. For *The Robe* (1953), Twentieth Century-Fox built Jerusalem on the back lot, shooting some exteriors in the Valley.

Around 1949 Hollywood discovered Europe. At that time the studios had a great deal of money frozen in foreign countries; the only way to get it out was to make pictures there. Americans enjoyed a tax advantage by living and working abroad for two-year periods, and this appealed to the stars. Because Hollywood unions were pricing themselves out of popularity, filmmakers quickly took advantage of cheaper labor costs abroad. Soon actual locations were used anywhere in the world, adding an artistic aura as well as authenticity by shooting in London, Paris, Tokyo, Madrid, or Rome. Eventually it became easier to sell scripts to be filmed in Europe than those that could be shot in Hollywood.

Producer Pandro Berman recalled his first experience in making an entire picture at MGM's studio in England. He was filming *Ivanhoe* (1952) with Robert Taylor, and the studio was empty except for his company. Berman estimated that he had saved $650,000 by making the film at the British studio, and he had been spared the usual interference by the Culver City hierarchy, allowing him to concentrate on his assignment. He found infinitely better casting possibilities for the project among English character actors, while having the British countryside as background added immeasurably to the picture's attractiveness.[5]

When William Wyler made *Roman Holiday* (1953), his was one of the first American companies to make a film in Rome. Since most Italians then rode motor scooters, traffic was light and filming could be done right in the streets. The company was in Rome for six months and found the experience delightful. When the director returned to Rome in 1958 and filmed *Ben-Hur*, however, the situation was quite different. Metro's financial condition was unstable and the size of the production made Wyler's life a nightmare. For eight months he had practically no social life, working six days a week and reserving Sundays for script problems. In the end he left Italy exhausted.[6]

Negotiations with foreign governments often prove troublesome on location work, particularly where large numbers of extras are involved, and current diplomatic relations are almost invariably reflected in how a foreign movie company is treated by both citizens and officials. Billy Wilder's *A Foreign Affair* (1948) was shot in Berlin at a time when animosities aroused by the war were still strong enough to cause friction. Some of the local population were convinced the Americans had come to make an anti-German propaganda film, and their resentment led to fisticuffs.[7]

Timing sometimes poses problems for natural reasons. On *Lust for Life* (1956), Vincente Minnelli's crew had to race to capture the ripening wheat fields in France on film so they would match van Gogh's color palette. The effort proved worthwhile, for the results brought critical raves.

Gradually Hollywood cameras truly became eyes to the world, as more and more production moved out of Los Angeles. Actors and directors even started selecting the projects that offered the most unusual travel opportunities, especially later in their careers. Edward Dmytryk claimed he knew *Soldier of Fortune* (1955) was a potboiler when he agreed to direct it, but he was eager to work with Gable and he wanted to visit Hong Kong. And director Delbert Mann maintained, "I love location shooting. Most of filmmaking today is that. I enjoy the problems, the coping with weather and the physical problems, trying to retain the focus on people and their relationships in front of different settings which have freshness and newness to them."[8]

Acrobat

Most actors coming to Hollywood from the stage avoided "rough stuff" when making films. Falling off cliffs, diving from burning buildings, riding spirited horses, and getting punched in the nose they left to doubles. Douglas Fairbanks was always an exception, for he never used a double. Fairbanks was a superb athlete—a fine swimmer, splendid boxer, skillful polo player, remarkable acrobat, fast runner, and fearless horseman. Often he performed physical feats on the spur of the moment while a movie was being shot. In one picture he was supposed to enter a house through the door, but when he noticed his sweetheart beckoning from an upper window he impulsively scaled the walls instead. In another he was trapped on the roof of a country home, and rather than retreat (the way the scenario suggested) he leaped into a nearby tree, caught a limb, and landed on the ground. When *The Half-Breed* (1916) was being filmed, one scene took place beside a fallen redwood whose giant roots rose twenty feet into the air. "Climb up on top of those roots, Doug," director Allan Dwan shouted. Instead, Fairbanks walked over to a young sapling near the base of the tree, bent it over, and with a sudden spring let the sapling catapult him to the uppermost root. "What do you want me to do now?" asked Fairbanks, grinning. "Come back the same way," the director laughed.[9]

Staggering

When Lewis Milestone was directing *The Captain Hates the Sea* (1934) for Columbia, he had trouble with John Gilbert, who drank excessively. "It's too goddamn bad," said studio head Harry Cohn, "but if a man wants to go to hell, I can't stop him. Shoot around him as much as you can. But keep the picture moving!" Milestone tried to do so. When the company went to San Pedro harbor on location, he persuaded the maritime union to allow the ship used in the film to sail despite a shipping strike. The director thought Gilbert could be controlled more easily at sea, where liquor was less available. He failed to consider the rest of the cast, including other confirmed imbibers such as Victor McLaglen, Walter Catlett, and Leon Errol, who supplied Gilbert with drinks out of their private reserves. Production on the film became even slower, for the actors were often too drunk for their dialogue to be understood. Finally Cohn fired off a cable to Milestone: HURRY UP. THE COST IS STAGGERING. The director cabled back: SO IS THE CAST.[10]

Launching Lunch

Director Michael Curtiz's lack of enthusiasm for lunch was well known. "What do you need lunch for?" Mike would storm. "A glass of milk's enough. Breakfast, that's it, when you get up. No lunch. Work, work!" Once Curtiz was shooting a scene at Malibu beach with about 350 extras, preparing for a motor launch to come up to the dock. It was just a little after eleven when Mike got on the loudspeaker and said, "Send for the launch!" Whereupon 350 extras, misunderstanding his accent, broke for lunch. So at ten minutes after eleven, box lunches had to be passed out, while Curtiz stood fuming.[11]

Cold

Most of *The Commandos Strike at Dawn* (1943) was filmed in Canada. Before the first of British actress Anna Lee's love scenes with Paul Muni, director John Farrow said to her, "There's something I have to tell you. Paul doesn't like any kind of physical contact with his leading ladies. He doesn't like you to put your hands on him."

Lee wasn't sure how to play a love scene with no physical contact, but kept her hands behind her back as she kissed Muni gingerly.

Later she learned that it wasn't Muni who objected to such contact, but his wife, Bella, who watched him like a hawk on location. After the company returned to Hollywood, Muni and his leading lady were scheduled for publicity stills. They went up on the roof at Columbia, where the cameraman was waiting to photograph them. Again Anna Lee was demure, keeping her hands to herself. But this time Muni said, "Now we must do something like Vilma Banky and Rudolph Valentino." He pulled Lee over in a mad embrace, which surprised her so that she couldn't respond very passionately. "Oh," Muni said, releasing her, "you English women are so cold!"[12]

What Next?

Location work was not only long and exhausting; sometimes it was also dangerous. One day, when director Ken Annakin was shooting *Swiss Family Robinson* (1960) for Walt Disney, he took stunt man Freddie Clarke aside and gave him his instructions for the following day. "On Thursday," he said, "I'm going to shoot the big scene with the pirates. I want you to do a fall from the edge of those cliffs, missing the rocks below, and then hit the sea." Clarke studied the eighty-foot drop, the sharp rocks, and the shark-infested waters for a moment or two and then asked quietly, "What do I do Friday?"[13]

Boredom

The company of *This Man's Navy* (1945) went to Asbury Park, where the picture was shot. During location filming director William Wellman's mother, a proper Bostonian, visited him and he gave a dinner party for her. Wellman sat at one end of the table, his mother at the other, with Wallace Beery, Tom Drake, and the rest of the cast seated between them. As the evening wore on, Wellman grew increasingly drunk, obnoxiously so. At one point he barely pulled himself up, and with his glass raised, said: "Ladies and gentlemen, there she is, that dear little old lady—my mother, who bore me." Mrs. Wellman, a charming woman all of four feet tall, lifted her glass and replied: "Yes, son, and now you bore me."[14]

Blow the Smoke

When Warner Brothers filmed *Dive Bomber* in June 1941, the U.S. Navy wasn't at all happy about having the film company at sea on the *Enterprise* for a week, but the studio secured permission in Washington over the heads of navy brass. To make matters worse, Michael Curtiz, with his Shubert musical-comedy accent, was directing. "Be good fellow," Curtiz would say to the ship's commanding officer and then pull him by the sleeve over to wherever he wanted him to stand. "Be good fellow," Mike would then repeat, indicating that the commander should stay put. After a few days the naval officers were so furious at Curtiz and his imperious orders over the speaker all day that they retaliated by holding battle practice every night, making it impossible for the Hollywood people to get any sleep. Mornings the performers had such bags under their eyes that Curtiz decided to save their close-ups until later. Coming back into San Diego harbor after a horrible week, the director decided to shoot the needed close-ups against the ship's superstructure rather than toward the sea, and positioned his cast accordingly. As the *Enterprise* neared shore, however, black smoke suddenly started pouring into camera range. "Art," Curtiz yelled to his assistant over the speaker, "tell the captain to blow the smoke the other way"[15]

Upstaged

Character actor Walter Huston showed up on the first day of shooting in Mexico for *The Treasure of the Sierra Madre* (1948) with his teeth out. Humphrey Bogart took one look at him and ripped off his toupee. "I'll be damned if I'm going to let that old bum upstage me," Bogie said in disgust. "I'm not going to show up with a toupee if he's going to have his teeth out." But the studio hit the ceiling: "No, you have an image and you must wear the toupee."[16]

Laundered Money

Financing film production was often a problem, forcing directors at times to be resourceful fund-raisers. Most of *A Walk in the Sun* (1945) was shot near Malibu Lake, but money ran out just as they started shooting. For the first two weeks director Lewis Milestone met the payroll out of his own pocket, while he scurried around trying to locate additional funds. He finally obtained them from the underworld, securing Las Vegas money that gamblers were trying to launder. The movie dealt with a platoon of young soldiers marching inland from a beach in Italy. From the day Milestone got the fresh money, the composition of the platoon changed. The principals stayed the same, but the extras suddenly included several heavily bearded men around thirty-five years old who were there to protect the gamblers' investment. The location became one of the greatest gambling sets in Hollywood history, for there was a crap game going from morning till night.[17]

Just a Few

When a film called for certain weather conditions, directors could only hope to be lucky. Unwilling to take chances, John Ford hired an Indian called Old Fat to keep the weather right during the making of *She Wore a Yellow Ribbon* (1949). One day at lunch, when everyone was seated on benches at a long table, Ford called Old Fat over and said, "Now this afternoon I want just a few little clouds, not too many, just a few." Some of the cast snickered, and Ford gave them a sharp look as Old Fat walked away. The Indian went up on a hillside and began a ritual apparently aimed at producing the right sky. Sure enough, to the amusement of skeptics in the company, that afternoon there were just a few tiny clouds.[18]

Deaf Ones

Filming on location could be perilous for performers. On *The African Queen* (1951) Katharine Hepburn had a scene at the foot of Murchison Falls in which she had to get into the water to release the boat, which was stuck in some reeds. "Oh!" Kate exclaimed when John Huston asked her to do it. "The river's full of crocodiles!" She was absolutely right, but Huston said, "Don't worry. I'll have my prop men fire a few rounds of ammunition into the water. You'll find the crocodiles get scared by the noise, and they'll vanish." Hepburn thought that over and answered, "Yes, but what about the deaf ones?" She went in anyway.[19]

Adrift

Gregory Peck once had a terrifying experience on location. During the shooting of *Moby Dick* (1956), Peck was riding an eighty-foot rubber whale ten miles off the coast of Wales in the Irish Sea. The weather was bad and the sea was already choppy when a strong gale suddenly blew up. Waves were soon twelve to sixteen feet high, with Peck scrambling to stay on the back of the slippery whale. He had Ahab's wooden leg strapped on, and there were ropes and harpoons sticking out of the synthetic beast that he had to hang on to. The camera was in a motor launch alongside, while the whale was towed by another motorboat with an underwater towline. A fog bank suddenly blew in, the wind rose, and as the whale tossed and pitched, the towline snapped. In a matter of seconds the actor was out of sight, shrouded by dense fog.

Peck yelled to signal his whereabouts; the crew also began yelling, but the little motor launch was having a tough time in the turbulent sea. After what seemed like hours, the whale loomed up through the fog. The crew bumped the bow of the boat up against the rubber beast, and Peck slid down its side to safety. Peck had been in serious danger, and during those tense moments he had experienced extreme fear. "I was frightened," he admitted later. "Bad writers always say, 'Fear clutched at his stomach.' Well, fear clutched at my stomach."[20]

Nasser and King Richard

When the second Ten Commandments (1956) was being filmed in Egypt, Cecil B. De Mille and his associate producer, actor Henry Wilcoxon, were invited to meet the new Egyptian president, Gamal Nasser. A limousine drove them to his palace, where the filmmakers were escorted into a reception room. There were four chairs arranged in two groups, facing each other but slightly staggered. After shaking hands Nasser and De Mille were seated in the front chairs, while Wilcoxon and Nasser's aide, General Amer, were seated just a little behind their respective chieftains. Nasser proved an excellent conversationalist and quite charismatic, but he talked directly to Wilcoxon, almost ignoring De Mille. The director would ask a question, and Nasser would answer looking straight at Wilcoxon, to the point that it became embarrassing. Wilcoxon kept trying to shift the focus, saying, "Well, Mr. De Mille, of course, is the producer, and he'd be able to answer that better than I." But still Nasser's attention remained fixed on Wilcoxon.

Eventually General Amer realized the actor's discomfort and with a sort of chuckle proceeded to explain: "As you know, Mr. Wilcoxon and Mr. De Mille, you both made a picture called The Crusades." The filmmakers nodded. "Mr. De Mille was the producer and director, and Mr. Wilcoxon, you played King Richard. When President Nasser and I were boys in military school together, that was one of our favorite pictures. President Nasser said then that if he ever became head of his country, he would like to be like Richard. He wanted to be like King Richard so much that we gave him a nickname. At school we used to call him Henry Wilcoxon."[21]

Research

On location in Japan for *My Geisha* (1962), Frank Westmore faced the problem of making Shirley MacLaine up to look Oriental without the eye tabs he had forgotten. When he informed the star that he had found a satisfactory substitute, she insisted on knowing what it was. Westmore showed her an enormous condom, from which he began cutting small pieces for eye tabs. MacLaine laughed and said, "You bastard, that can't be yours." Westmore acted insulted and affirmed that the giant rubber had indeed been custom-made to accommodate his extraordinary anatomy.

The improvised tabs worked, and after several hours of filming, Westmore left the set to visit the men's room. As he walked down the corridor, he heard footsteps behind him. Whenever he stopped, so did the footsteps. He continued on to the bathroom and stepped up to a urinal, with the footsteps following him all the way. He glanced around to see Shirley MacLaine standing at his shoulder, looking downward. "I knew that rubber wasn't yours," she said, turning on her heel and stalking out.[22]

Pushover

George Sanders was a private man with a reputation for hating children and animals. On the set of *Dark Purpose* in Italy (1964), he spent hours with his glasses on his nose reading Italian comic books. Shirley Jones, also on the picture, had brought along her two children—Shaun Cassidy was then three, Patrick just a toddler. Occasionally Shirley brought Shaun on the set, and for some reason the child couldn't leave Sanders alone. He'd pull his little chair up and just sit and stare as the reserved actor read his comics in Italian. This went on for hours. The child never pushed; he just sat and watched Sanders read. After about four days Shirley discovered Sanders holding Shaun on his lap. George was reading to the boy in Italian from the comic books, while Shaun sat with his big eyes looking as if he understood every word.[23]

The Painted Desert

When *Lawrence of Arabia* (1962) was being made, some scenes were filmed in Spain, at Seville, where the Moorish-Arabic architecture gave the required effect. Akaba was completely re-created in Spain, with a Turkish camp alongside it. Heavily involved in the structural side of the filming was Vic Simpson, who told an interviewer, "I spent two years on *Lawrence* as Master Painter, covering the whole scenic side of the picture. You may not believe this but there were several sequences for which we had to spray the desert with paint to get the desired colour effect."[24]

Crisis

The Strategic Air Command wanted *A Gathering of Eagles* (1963) made to counterbalance *Fail-Safe* (1964), an antiwar picture being made at the same time. But director Delbert Mann and his crew had to sit down six months in advance and list in detail every piece of military equipment needed and schedule to the minute every necessary flight takeoff, knowing they could film it only once. They were to shoot in the SAC underground headquarters at Omaha, with the *real* red phone that was connected to every SAC base in the world. The production crew visited the Omaha headquarters, prepared the picture months in advance, specified everything they needed, and received full cooperation throughout. When they returned in the fall of 1962 to shoot the scene where Rock Hudson picks up the red phone, however, the air was filled with tension. Map boards that had previously been visible were covered, SAC personnel was scurrying about, and military guards were everywhere. Delbert Mann and his crew were granted permission to shoot rather reluctantly, but it was made clear they had two days and no more. The filmmakers were mystified, not knowing what had gone wrong. They shot their scene and left. Two days later the Cuban missile crisis was made public [25]

CHAPTER 15

Editing
and
Scoring

Touring Paramount one time in the early thirties, Baron Rothschild visited the cutting room, where Edward Dmytryk was busily at work. After listening to Dmytryk explain the job of a cutter for about twenty minutes, the baron suddenly interrupted. "It would appear," he exclaimed, "that film editing *is* the art of film-making!" Dmytryk was delighted by the observation; he thought it right on the mark. Even after he moved from editing to directing films, he continued to insist on how crucial the former was to motion pictures. Without the development of editing, he liked to point out, movies would have been little more than photographed stage plays.[1]

The earliest films were unedited and, after the novelty wore off, unexciting. They consisted largely of "moving snapshots" of actual events—people walking, ships sailing, trains chugging away—taken from a distance and lasting no longer than the events being filmed. Even when a filming was planned in advance—two people bumping into each other and getting into a fight—the camera recorded the scene in one continuous shot from the front view, and the effect was stagey and static. It wasn't until 1902, when Edwin S. Porter began piecing together several strips of film containing different scenes so he could tell a little story, that movies began coming to life. Before Porter, audiences saw exactly what filmmakers saw; after Porter, audiences began seeing what filmmakers wanted them to see. But Porter's editing was rudimentary. He didn't begin to envisage the possibilities open to filmmakers who were willing to experiment with cutting and splicing and joining different shots together to create a unity of their own in a moving picture.

D. W. Griffith was the great experimenter. In editing, as in other aspects of filmmaking, his contribution to motion pictures was prodigious. He quit filming scenes from a fixed position in one long take and began breaking them up into shots—long, medium, and close— in order to call the viewer's attention to various details he wished to emphasize in telling his story. He also made use of flashbacks, close-ups, and dissolves, placed cameras on trucks to get shots of moving trains, and by cross-cutting (showing two pieces of related action in quick alternation) developed the famous "Griffith last-minute rescue" sequences that roused audiences everywhere to a high pitch of excitement. Until Griffith, movies had been the legitimate theater's poor relation; with Griffith, they achieved autonomy and status as an art form in their own right. In an editorial on April 5, 1915, the *Independent*, a New York weekly, pointed out that with the new developments in editing, film plays had become in some respects superior to stage plays. Filmmakers like Griffith, the *Independent* noted, "can change the scene oftener than the Elizabethan dramatist. He can dip into the future or the past as tho [sic] he were in Wells's time-machine. . . . He can reveal the mind of his characters in two ways, neither of them possible on the stage, first, by bringing the actor so close that the spectator can read his facial expression, and, second, by visualizing his memories or imaginings. He can, if he so desires, wreck a train, burn a house, sink a ship or blow up a fort, since he does not have to repeat the expense every night."[2]

Griffith's techniques soon became the stock in trade of filmmaking everywhere, and by the 1920s the film editor (who now had the Moviola, an editing machine, to facilitate his work) had taken his place beside the director, the cameraman, and the performers as a major contributor to the art of motion pictures. Some directors entrusted the work of putting films into final shape entirely to the cutter; others worked closely with the editor or did most of the editing themselves. But even if the editor did the lion's share of the work, he remained largely an anonymous figure. Editing, after all, to be successful, had to be unobtrusive. It would never do if audiences became aware of the cutting process. Good editing produced natural, logical, and illuminating movement on the screen. Its job was to call attention to the details of the film narrative, not to itself.

Insiders, though, appreciated the work of the editor. When Darryl F. Zanuck began working for Warner Bros. in the 1930s, he spent most of his time at first in the cutting room, learning the craft. He was impressed by the way skillful editors could turn a turkey into a triumph by judicious cutting and rearranging of shots. "I realized that all isn't lost," he recalled years later, "when the script is a dud, the director is a deadhead, and the actors don't know their asses from their elbows. Unless it is a complete and utter disaster, there is no single film that can't be rescued and turned into a seeable movie. . . ."3 Zanuck put himself in solid with Jack Warner when he turned a potential flop entitled *Tiger Rose* into an acceptable film after two days of careful editing. Years later, as head of Twentieth Century-Fox, he was still rescuing films from disaster by his last-minute editing.

With sound films, dialogue as well as visual images became part of the editor's responsibility. If players "blew their lines," editing rather than retakes might set things aright. Or if changes in the direction of a film made words uttered in early scenes outmoded, an editor could fix things up by alterations on the soundtrack. And if the rough cut of a film seemed talky and slow-paced, eliminating unnecessary dialogue could get things moving again. Sometimes, in fact, editors put together the best parts of speeches delivered several times by a performer in order to produce the effect sought by the director. When Leo McCarey was filming *Ruggles of Red Gap* (1935), he had a problem for a time with a scene in which Charles Laughton, playing an English butler, recites the Gettysburg Address in a Western saloon. The trouble was that Laughton was so overcome with emotion as he recited the address that the effect was a bit ludicrous. McCarey shot the scene forty or fifty times without getting what he wanted, and finally Laughton begged for mercy and McCarey agreed to postpone further shooting. At this point cutter Edward Dmytryk proposed putting together a complete soundtrack of the speech by using the best parts of the various takes, and McCarey decided to try his suggestion. Dmytryk then went to work on the soundtrack, using a line here, a phrase there, and sometimes only a word or two elsewhere, and finally pieced together a complete version of the speech. And after eliminating the first cut (Laughton with tears streaming down his cheeks as he spoke), which brought laughter at the first preview, he produced an excellent scene. Laughton's performance, in fact, was the high point of the film. For years afterward, radio networks asked him to recite the Gettysburg Address whenever Lincoln's birthday rolled around.[4]

If editing saved many a picture, so did music. "There never was a *silent* film," producer Irving Thalberg once said frankly. "We'd finish a picture, show it in one of our projection rooms, and come out shattered. It would be awful. We'd have high hopes for the picture, work our hands off on it, and the result was always the same. Then we'd show it in a theatre, with a girl down in the pit, pounding away at a piano, and there would be all the difference in the world. Without that music, there wouldn't have been a movie industry at all."[5] The music wasn't always good. Sometimes the local pianist (or organist) missed the point of a picture and played an *adagio lamentoso* where a *sinister misterioso* was called for. Some accompanists, too, used Rossini's "William Tell Overture" so often for chases that audiences groaned when they heard it again. In time the much overworked "Hearts and Flowers" for "blighted love" scenes produced laughter rather than tears. But "cue sheets"—containing suggestions for music, classical and popular, for specific films—helped a great deal. Even better were the piano scores for feature pictures that became customary after D. W. Griffith commissioned composer Joseph Carl Breil to prepare an original score to accompany *The Birth of a Nation*. In film music, as in everything else, Griffith was a pioneer.[6]

When pictures started to talk, producers at first took a dim view of background music in films that were not plainly labeled "musicals." They were afraid that if people heard incidental music in dramatic films they would ask, "Where's the music coming from?" But sound pictures seemed cold and lifeless without music of some kind, and filmmakers began permitting a little music; if something seemed desirable to support a love scene or a long silent sequence, they arranged for a violinist or a shepherd with a flute to wander across the screen to explain the presence of music. At RKO, however, the head of the music department, Max Steiner, with the encouragement of producer David Selznick, began adding background music to film dramas without visual explanations of any kind, and the response of audiences and critics was extremely favorable. By 1932, RKO producers had gotten into the habit of handing all of their major films to Steiner to score; his music, they discovered, not only added enormously to the effectiveness of films like *Symphony of Six Million* (1932); it also probably saved films like *The Most Dangerous Game*

(1932) from failure. Steiner's music for *King Kong* (1933) was a *tour de force;* it was so integral to the impact of the film as a whole that composer-pianist Oscar Levant said he thought the movie should have been advertised as a concert, with pictures on the screen accompanying Steiner's music.[7]

In 1936, Warner Bros. engaged Steiner's services, gave him separate "main title" credits, started using his Warners logo fanfare music at the beginning of all its pictures and began entrusting its most ambitious productions to his care. For the next three decades Steiner shared the trials and tribulations of Bette Davis ("He got in bed with me," she joked), participated with verve in the derring-do of Errol Flynn, assisted Jimmy Cagney and Humphrey Bogart in prison breaks (Levant considered Steiner especially good in prison-break fogs), and periodically went west with Gary Cooper, Randolph Scott, and others who looked tall in the saddle. But he was only one of several composers who put a major imprint on American films during Hollywood's Golden Age. Erich Wolfgang Korngold, who had composed operas and symphonies before coming to Hollywood from Vienna in 1935 to score films, painted on a vaster canvas than did Steiner; and, working for Warners, he produced rousing scores for epic films like *The Adventures of Robin Hood* (1938) that still seem impressive. Twentieth Century-Fox had Alfred Newman; Paramount, Miklos Rozsa; and Columbia, Dimitri Tiomkin. And later on, gifted composers like Bernard Herrmann, Alex North, Elmer Bernstein, and Henry Mancini appeared on the scene.

On occasion, serious composers like Aaron Copland and George Antheil did scores for Hollywood movies. But Antheil himself was inclined to think that specialists in film music ought to do the job. Writing in *Modern Music* in 1938, he pronounced Steiner a "veritable genius" when it came to movie music, who by his work made even so silly a film as *Green Light* (1937) of some interest. Steiner's "artisanship," Antheil declared, "amounts practically to artistry. Many of his recent scores show daring advances and startling newnesses, all of which indicate that Hollywood music, such as it is, definitely 'goes forward.' Tendencies from such a source as Max Steiner are 'authentic' since they are truly Hollywood in scope and reason."[8]

In recent years tastes in film music have changed drastically. Only a few of Hollywood's scores from the Golden Age hold much interest for movie-lovers today. The majority seem sentimental, over-orchestrated, and obtrusive in films they were supposed to assist, not dominate. The old-fashioned symphonic score has now become the exception. Since the late sixties, rock music has become almost mandatory for Hollywood's offerings; so have musical scores that could be put on records and marketed simultaneously with a picture's release. In the 1980s the majority of Hollywood movies have had soundtrack album spinoffs containing title songs and a half-dozen cuts performed by popular rock singers.

There have been changes in editing as well as in music. The traditional way of editing a film, with its emphasis on smooth continuity, also came to seem old-fashioned to filmmakers in the sixties and seventies. Experiments with "jump cuts"—taking characters from one location to another without any transitional shots—became common; so did "flash cuts"—quick flashbacks, representing the sudden welling up of memories in the mind of a character. For A Thousand Clowns (1965), editor Ralph Rosenblum prepared one sequence in such a way that the dialogue between two of the film's leading characters occurs over a visual montage that shows them successively at a junk dealer's, walking with a parade, at Lincoln Center, on a dock, at a fishing pier, on a ferry, at Liberty Island, on Park Avenue, and in Central Park.

Innovators like Rosenblum did not approve of the more flamboyant editing that became a fad for a time. But they did favor efforts to free editing from the rigidities of the past. The best editors, Rosenblum insisted, "do not cut according to formulas or habits of mind, but face each new assignment with trepidation because they know routine solutions do not exist."[9] But whatever the solutions, editing is as crucial to the success of a film today as it was when Dmytryk was explaining it to Baron Rothschild. "The only moment that really counts," said director Sydney Pollack in 1985, "is when the actors are gone, when everyone's gone, when you're alone in the editing room and . . . have the new material you need to put the film together."[10]

Jumping Around

When it came to editing, D. W. Griffith was an indefatigable experimenter. He broke scenes up into separate shots, showing one actor's face, another actor's reaction, and then perhaps an object to give the scene depth and dimension. He experimented with sudden changes of time and space, too, driving some producers to distraction with his innovations.

In the scene in *Enoch Arden* (1911) in which the shipwrecked husband, finally rescued, returns home to find his once-grieving wife has remarried, Griffith ordered the camera to close in on the woman's face, and then, to make sure the audience knew what she was thinking, switch to a shot of the husband on the desert island. When one of Griffith's associates saw the rushes, he thought D.W. had lost his mind. "You can't jump around like that," he remonstrated. "It doesn't make sense. The audience will never understand it." "Of course they will," insisted Griffith. He was right. In the end his technique (not entirely new with him) became common in filmmaking.[11]

Suspenders

When brilliant but nonconformist Erich von Stroheim was assigned to direct *The Merry Widow* (1925), Irving Thalberg kept a careful eye on him, for his celluloid was at times pretty sizzling. In one fiery seduction scene, Stroheim had John Gilbert making love to Mae Murray while his suspenders dangled on the floor. Thalberg had given Stroheim specific orders not to have any dangling suspenders in the scene, so afterward he had them blotted out in the lab, using a trick traveling matte shot in an optical printer, this at a cost of $15,000.[12]

Bancroft and the Bang

In the late 1920s George Bancroft became a star overnight because of his performance as a gangster in *Underworld* (1927), and he was hard to work with after that. When playing the lead in *The Dragnet* (1928), he continually clashed with the director, Josef von Sternberg. "Now, George," said von Sternberg before one take, "this is a very simple scene. We should be able to get it in one take. All you have to do is walk up that flight of stairs. You think you've thrown your pursuers off the track so you are relatively relaxed. But they've been tailing you. Now, the camera is going to be on your back. But when I say 'Bang,' that's when you get it. You grab the banister and twist around, until you're facing the camera. As you slip down the steps you try to reach for your gun. But I'll say 'Bang!—Bang!' again, and that's it. I don't think we even have to rehearse it. Just give it to me as real as you can. Now, George, are you sure you understand what I'm saying?" "Yes, Joe," said Bancroft quietly. So von Sternberg cried, "Action!" and the "King of the Underworld," as he had come to be .alled, started up the creaky stairs of an old boarding house. At the third step, von Sternberg yelled, "Bang!" But Bancroft kept going up the stairs. "God damn it, George!" von Sternberg screamed. "What's the matter with you—are you deaf?" Again he yelled, "Bang!—Bang!" But Bancroft refused to fall. "Don't shout at me, Joe," he said. "Of course I heard you. But just remember this. One shot can't stop Bancroft." Not until he had been fired at several times did he consent to fall.

By the time of the picture's preview, though, von Sternberg had edited things to suit himself. In his cutting, he established Bancroft on the stairs, cut away for a moment, and then cut back to him on the final "Bang!" that made him grab the banister and twist forward. Judicious editing succeeded in bringing the mighty Bancroft down in one shot after all.[13]

Six More Yards
In 1930, Max Steiner complained that he was asked to be a tailor as well as a musician. When the theme song in one picture ran out before the actors finished their lines, the producer asked for more musical footage: "Six more yards, something we can chop off anything to make it fit."[14]

Monroe Recordings
Marilyn Monroe was not a professional singer but always sounded good whenever she sang in films. Some people thought her voice was dubbed, although it wasn't. But the studio's sound technicians helped out. They made twenty-five recordings of her songs, and then Ken Darby, one of her singing coaches, took the twenty-five pieces of tape home, cut them up, and put them together so she had the proper phrasing in each part of the song. The next day Monroe listened to the paste-up and tried to recreate it. The results were invariably excellent.[15]

Where's the Music Coming From?
When Morrie Ryskind completed the script for *The Cocoanuts* (1929), a Marx Brothers musical, co-director Joseph Santley told him he hadn't shown where the music under the dialogue in some of the scenes was coming from. "What do you mean, where does the music come from?" cried Ryskind. "Where does the music *ever* come from? The guy says to the girl, 'Something is on my mind,' and the girl says, 'Really, what is it?' and somebody in the orchestra hits a

note and they sing. That's where the music comes from." "No, no," said Santley, "motion picture audiences won't accept that." So he hired sixty men to sit in a bandstand and pretend to be playing instruments in scenes where music starts up under the dialogue. Somehow, though, in the course of shooting the film, the cameramen neglected to take any pictures of the fake band. The result was that audiences never did find out "where the music came from" in certain scenes in *The Cocoanuts*. But, as Ryskind said, "Nobody gave a damn, of course."[16]

Bomb

When *Thanks a Million* (1935), the story of a crooner (Dick Powell) who runs for governor, was sneak-previewed in Santa Monica, it was a disaster. Preview cards called the picture "awful," "bilge," "crap." "My God," thought producer Darryl Zanuck afterward, "I must have been so close to it, I lost all viewpoint. Jesus, it was a bomb!" So he took the film back to the studio and went to work on it. "I ran it reel by reel," he recalled, "stopping after each reel, making notes. Suddenly I found the weakness. I cut twelve minutes, that's all, and rearranged the rest." When he previewed the edited version in Santa Barbara, it received a big ovation and went on to become a big hit everywhere. "More than anything else," Zanuck later reflected, "the success of that movie saved my first year at Fox from disaster."[17]

Curbstone Autopsies

When Darryl Zanuck was satisfied with a cut, he got his staff together and took the movie off to be previewed somewhere. Then, right after the preview, he went into a huddle with his assistants—one producer called them "curbstone autopsies"—to see if the film needed further editing. Once, after a preview, Zanuck and his staff gathered to discuss the film in front of a nearby candy store, and a bystander who had seen the film came up and told them what he thought. Everyone figured he was from the studio and listened carefully to his comments. As the man left, Zanuck asked what department he was in. When he learned that the man didn't work for him, he sent one of his assistants after him and hired him on the spot.[18]

Big Bees

One film musician consulted the great composer Arnold Schönberg, then living in Hollywood, about music he had been assigned to do for an airplane sequence. "Airplane music?" said Schönberg thoughtfully. "Just like music for big bees, only louder." After that, airplane music was called "big bee music" among film composers.

After hearing Schönberg's "Verklärte Nacht" over the radio, MGM's Irving Thalberg sent a man to invite him to do music for *The Good Earth* (1937). The emissary found Schönberg uninterested, so he launched into a long discourse on the possibilities for music in the film, especially in its "big scene" toward the end. "Think of it!" he cried. "There's a terrific storm going on, the wheat field is swaying in the wind, and suddenly the earth begins to tremble. In the midst of the earthquake Oo-Lan gives birth to a baby. What an opportunity for music!" "With so much going on," said Schönberg mildly, "what do you need music for?"

Schönberg never did music for a Hollywood film. Possibly it was because he told one producer who asked what his method of work would be: "I will write the music, and then you will make motion pictures to correspond to it."[19]

Fooled Again

One producer (who had the final say-so on music for films he made) attended a Hollywood Bowl concert that featured Beethoven's C-minor symphony. He suffered in silence until the coda of the final movement, which repeats the tonic and dominant chords, with flourishes, several times. At each recurrence of the tonic, the producer got up to leave and then fell back in his seat as the music went on. About the third time the tonic and dominant chords sounded, he turned and muttered, "The rat fooled me again!" As for the two-piano concerto by Mozart on the same program, he told a friend: "It never got anywhere."[20]

Musical Fitting

In 1935 Warner Bros. hired Erich Wolfgang Korngold to do the music for *A Midsummer Night's Dream*. His job involved reorchestrating Mendelssohn's score and adding some new material of his own. Korngold liked to begin work while a film was in production, and sometimes he visited the set and even read the script before composing his music. One day, while *A Midsummer Night's Dream* was being shot, he ran into James Cagney, who was playing Bottom in the film, on the way to his office. "Hold still, Mr. Cagney," he cried. "Hold still a minute." Then he began walking slowly around the actor, looking him over carefully from head to toe, and humming quietly to himself. At length he seemed satisfied, thanked Cagney, and left. Afterward Cagney said he almost felt like asking Korngold when he should come in and try on his new theme.[21]

French Horns

When Darryl Zanuck headed Twentieth Century-Fox, he had something to say about everything that went into the making of a film, including the music. For *Under Two Flags* (1936), he insisted the score should include Cui's "Orientale" and Tchaikovsky's "Chanson Arabe," which, he said, was "something they could whistle." In one picture taking place in Paris, he listened to some music on the soundtrack designed to accompany the main character taking a stroll in the city and cried: "Not bad. Not bad. But it's not French enough." Then he thought for a moment and suddenly snapped his fingers and exclaimed: "I've got it! Put in a few more French horns!"[22]

Shorter Horizon

At the preview of *Lost Horizon* (1937), an elegant film about Shangri-La, a peaceful utopia in the Himalayas, the audience sat quietly through the first ten minutes and then began tittering. Director Frank Capra, visibly upset, ran to the foyer for a drink of water. "People who made that picture," a man at the fountain remarked, "should be shot." The preview cards afterward were devastating. After three days of thinking it over, Capra went to the cutting room and ordered his cutting editor to take the main title from the beginning of the first reel of the picture and splice it onto the beginning of the third reel. That was the only change he asked for; it would shorten the picture by twenty minutes and, by eliminating the lengthy preliminaries, get to the point at once.

"What makes you so damn sure throwing away the first two reels will work?" Capra's boss Henry Cohn asked him. "I'm not *sure* it'll work," said Capra. "But it's the only change I could think of in three days without sleep. Let's preview it again." So they arranged a showing in San Pedro without the first two reels. There wasn't a laugh or titter in the wrong place. The audience was spellbound. A simple change had made the picture a success. But times—and tastes—change. Years later film specialists restored the first two reels and pronounced Capra's original version better than the edited film.[23]

Goldwyn Music

Sam Goldwyn knew everything about films—costumes, settings, characters, dialogue, plot construction—except music, and he was able to put the "Goldwyn touch" on every aspect of the films he produced except the musical score. When he made his first musical, he heard one-step time described as two-four time and thereafter referred to it as "two-by-four time." He wanted the Easter music for a Greek orthodox service in *We Live Again* (1934), a film based on Tolstoy's novel *Resurrection,* to be just right, but when the recording of the music was accidentally played backward for him he pronounced it superb. Once he told a composer that his music for a film wouldn't do. "What's the matter with it?" asked the composer. "There's not enough sarcasm in it," said Goldwyn. In 1937 he became enthusiastic about Cole Porter's famous song "Night and Day," and during the production of a new musical picture he told everyone: "We must have something like 'Night and Day' for our new show." One evening one of Goldwyn's associates had dinner with him and played the Porter number on the phonograph. "What tune is that?" asked Goldwyn.[24]

Showman

Herbert Stothart, leading composer and musical director for MGM for many years, was as famous for his showmanship as for his musicianship. "Maybe he doesn't know music that well," said studio executives, "but he is a showman."

Once, MGM's William Axt was assigned to do music for a film called *At the Balalaika,* and the producers told him: "We need a song. Something like 'Volga Boatman.' Will you find it?" Axt said he would; a week later he played his song for them. "Very nice," they told him, "but it's no 'Volga Boatman.'" So he tried again, and they were still not satisfied with his music. After the third try, they called in Stothart to get his advice. "Why don't you use 'Volga Boatman'?" he said. "Sure," they nodded, "why don't we use 'Volga Boatman'?" And they did. "See," one of them said afterward of Stothart, "we got a showman."[25]

Making Beethoven

After using music from the Pastorale Symphony in one part of *Fantasia* (1940), producer Walt Disney exclaimed: "Gee! This'll make Beethoven!"[26]

Can't Be Wrong

Late one afternoon, when Max Steiner was conducting his score for Warners' *Now, Voyager* (1942), his friend Victor Young, composer for Paramount, dropped by to pick him up and take him home for the weekly card game with other film musicians. While waiting, he listened carefully to the love music Steiner had written for the picture and jotted it down on a piece of paper. The following day, when he went to his studio to do some work, he had one of his arrangers there orchestrate the Steiner theme and then made a recording of the Paramount orchestra playing it. That night he took the recording home and cut it into a recording he had already made of a local news program.

A few days later Steiner arrived at Young's house for the usual card game. Toward the end of the evening one of the players suggested turning on the radio to hear the news. First came the voice of the local announcer, next came Young's recording of the *Now, Voyager* theme. "Listen to that!" cried Steiner, jumping to his feet. "That's my theme!" "Oh, don't be silly," said Young, "deal the cards." "Listen to them—they've stolen my music!" wailed Steiner. "How could they steal your music?" scoffed Young. "That's a program that's been on five times a week, fifty-two weeks a year, for years and years, and they've used that signature ever since they first went on radio." "It can't be!" screamed Steiner. "*I just wrote it!*" He was so upset that Young hastened to reveal the little trick he had played on him. Steiner's theme, with words added ("It Can't Be Wrong") and sung by Frank Sinatra, made the hit parade after the picture's release.[27]

Sing It, Sam

In *Casablanca* (1942), black musician Dooley Wilson played the part of Sam, the pianist-singer in Humphrey Bogart's café who reluctantly did as Ingrid Bergman requested: "Play it, Sam. Play 'As Time Goes By.'" After the film became a hit, Wilson received a contract to appear as a nightclub star. But on opening night the manager of the club asked Wilson why there was no piano on the stage. To his surprise Wilson told him he didn't know how to play the piano; he could only sing. It turned out that the piano music in the famous *Casablanca* scene had been dubbed in.[28]

Where They Came From

When Alfred Hitchcock was filming *Lifeboat* (1944), he announced he wanted no background music because the story took place in a boat out in the middle of the ocean, and if there was music people would wonder where it was coming from. "Just ask Mr. Hitchcock," said the studio's music department head, "where the camera comes from, and I'll tell him where the music comes from!"[29]

The Major and the Minor

A producer once instructed composer Victor Young to have his music in the major for the leading actress whenever she was on the screen and in the minor for the male star. And when the two were on the screen at the same time, he said, the music should be both major and minor.[30]

Happy Ending

When Darryl Zanuck and Otto Preminger ran off *Laura* (1944) in the projection room, they both realized it was seriously flawed. "We certainly missed the boat on this one," sighed Zanuck. So he went to work editing the film and before long had eliminated most of the picture's weaknesses. But Zanuck and Preminger disagreed strongly about the film's ending. Preminger (who had replaced Rouben Mamoulian as director) was convinced that the ending he had devised for the picture was just right, but Zanuck didn't like it. Over Preminger's protests, he had a scriptwriter prepare a new ending and had the cast reassembled to shoot it. "Mine was better," Preminger said later. "I just knew it. But how could I convince him now, when it was so late in the day?"

But luck was with Preminger. When Zanuck ran off the revised *Laura* in the projection room, Broadway columnist Walter Winchell was his guest that evening, and he enjoyed the film thoroughly. "Darryl, that was big time, big time!" he said when the film ended. "A great film, great, great, great!" But then he went on: "But are you going to change the ending? What's happening at the end? I didn't understand." Zanuck looked over at Preminger, who was trying to conceal a smile, and then broke into a grin. "Do you want to have your old ending back?" he asked the director. "Yes, sure," said Preminger, still trying to conceal his excitement. "Okay," said Zanuck and then left for supper with Winchell. So Preminger's ending was restored and *Laura* went on to win high praise from the public. Preminger never forgot Zanuck's flexibility on this occasion.[31]

Wozzeck

One day a bright new director had a conference with composer David Raksin and told him he didn't want "any of that Hollywood music" in his picture. What he wanted, he said, was "something different, really powerful—like *Wozzeck*." Raksin was overjoyed; to hear the name of Alban Berg's operatic masterpiece invoked by the man with whom he would be working was exciting. Indeed, it was almost too good to be true. After years of struggling with people who knew so little about music, it looked as if he was now to work with a director who was sophisticated musically. In a state of euphoria, Raksin invited the director out to his farm for dinner so they could discuss the film away from the distractions of the studio.

In Raksin's living room, the two men, drinks in hand, phonograph playing, began talking about the picture. Raksin remembered thinking that this was the way things ought to be; he liked the script, admired the director, and couldn't wait to begin discussing music for the new film. But the director suddenly turned irritable. "What's that crap you're playing?" he growled. "That crap," said Raksin quietly, "is *Wozzeck*." He realized at once that he had another tough job ahead of him.[32]

Orgasm Theme

When David Selznick engaged Dimitri Tiomkin to do the music for *Duel in the Sun* (1946), he told him he intended to approve all the musical themes for the picture. "Dot I understand," said Tiomkin. Not long after, he received a long memorandum from Selznick instructing him to compose eleven themes for the picture, including a Spanish theme, a ranch theme, a love theme, a desire theme, and an orgasm theme. "Love themes I can write," Tiomkin said. "Desire too. But orgasm! How do you score an orgasm?" "Try!" Selznick exclaimed. "I want a really good *shtump*."

Tiomkin spent the next few weeks working hard on his themes, and for the orgasm theme he developed a dramatic crescendo that he thought Selznick would like. After Selznick heard what Tiomkin had done, he gave his tentative approval and let Tiomkin get to work on the orchestration. When Tiomkin completed the score and was ready to begin recording it, Selznick dropped by for a conference. "Dimmy," he said, "I'll tell you a secret. We ran the picture at a preview in New Jersey and it didn't go so well. Then we added canned music for a preview in New York, and that didn't help, either. So you can see that the music will need to contribute a great deal to the picture. Can you let me hear that love theme again? Just whistle it." Tiomkin at once obliged. "I love it," said Selznick. "Now would you please whistle the desire theme?" Again Tiomkin whistled. "Fine! Fine!" cried Selznick. "Now the orgasm theme." Tiomkin whistled once more. But this time Selznick shook his head. "No, that isn't it," he said firmly. "That's just not an orgasm." At his request Tiomkin went to work on the music again.

Finally Tiomkin was ready with his revised score. "Play the orgasm theme," Selznick told him when they met again, "and put the film on the screen so I can get the full effect." This time, as Tiomkin played the piano, a passionate love scene with Gregory Peck and Jennifer Jones appeared on the screen. "I like it," said Selznick, when it was over, "play it again." The second time Tiomkin added some jazz beats as he played. "Play it again," instructed Selznick, when he finished, and Tiomkin performed for the third time. "Dimmy," said Selznick finally, "you're going to hate me for this, but it won't do. It's too beautiful." Tiomkin could hardly keep his temper. "Meesair Selznick," he cried, "vot is troubling you? Vot don't you like about it?" "I like it," said Selznick, "but it isn't orgasm music. It's not the way I ———!" "Meesair Selznick," exclaimed Tiomkin, "You ——— your way, I ——— my way. To me, *that* is ———ing music!" Selznick collapsed in laughter at Tiomkin's outburst and finally let the composer have his way.[33]

Actually Does Play

In 1947, when Katharine Hepburn played Clara Schumann in *Song of Love*, a film based on the lives of Robert Schumann and Johannes Brahms, she impressed everyone with her versatility. Director Clarence Brown had arranged for her to fake Clara Schumann's playing at a wooden piano, with Arthur Rubinstein supplying the real playing for the soundtrack. "Nonsense!" cried Hepburn, when she heard of the arrangement. "What's nonsense?" Brown asked her. "The idea that I'm going to pound at some goddamned keyboard," snorted Hepburn. "I'm going to play a real piano. Rubinstein can carry the bulk of the works, but I'm going to lead in with the first few bars, and I'll bet nobody knows the difference!"

Hepburn lived up to her promise. She worked hard with a professional pianist for weeks and finally produced a first-rate bit of playing for *Song of Love.* "If I hadn't seen it and heard it with my own eyes and ears," said Rubinstein after viewing the sequence, "I wouldn't have believed it. That woman is incredible! She actually does play almost as well as I do! And when she ends and I begin, only I in the whole world could tell the difference!"[34]

Helps the Music
Once, Cecil B. De Mille, disappointed with a scene in one of his pictures, turned to composer Elmer Bernstein and said: "You'll have to help it with music, Elmer." "You know, Mr. De Mille," Bernstein replied, "I would much rather work on a scene which helps the music."[35]

CHAPTER 16

Censorship

Censorship is ubiquitous. No time or place is without it. Even in a society as free as America's there are always limits to what people may say and do in public. But times—and places—change, and with changes in social arrangements come modifications in styles and standards. The impermissibles of one age frequently become the conventionalities of another, and one era's allowables may well become another's intolerables. The history of films in the United States is a fascinating story of clashing opinions about what is to be regarded as right, fitting, and proper to project on the screen for the masses. From almost the beginning American movies have both reflected and helped shape the nation's ever-changing folkways and mores.

Censorship came early. Not long after nickelodeons became popular with the public, the *Chicago Tribune* denounced "The Five-Cent Theatre" as intolerably vicious, and an Illinois judge charged that movies were responsible for "more juvenile crime coming into my court than all other causes combined."[1] The appearance of films like *Cupid's Barometer*, *An Old Man's Darling*, *Gaieties of Divorce*, *Beware*, *My Husband Comes*, and *The Bigamist* led Chicago to empower the police department to preview and license all films. And in New York the mayor closed down all movie shows for a time because of their perceived wickedness. As the clamor against nickelodeons spread to other cities, the film producers were finally stirred to action. In 1909 they organized the National Board of Censorship (renamed the National Board of Review of Films in 1921) to screen all the films they made and delete scenes regarded as unsuitable for the public. Self-censorship, in short, was the answer to threats of government censorship. The action of the filmmakers succeeded in muting criticism to some extent, but many communities (and some states too) went on to establish censorship boards anyway. Furthermore, the Supreme Court ruled in 1915 that movies were "a business pure and simple" and lacked the constitutional protection of free speech that books, magazines, and newspapers possessed. Despite the censors, though, the moviemakers continued to turn out films that pleased the public. There was a steady increase in moviegoing during and after World War I.

In the 1920s the purifiers of films were again roused to wrath. Hollywood, they charged, was largely responsible for the relaxation in manners and morals that followed World War I. They were shocked by some of the Jazz Age's movies: *Why Be Good?*, *Sinners in Silk*, *Women Who Give*, *A Shocking Night*, *Luring Lips*, *Red Hot Romance*, *Scrambled Wives*, *The Truant Husband*, *Her Purchase Price*. They were even more upset by the promotional material being circulated. DOES IT PAY TO LOVE WITHOUT QUESTION? queried one movie poster. IF YOU ARE IN DOUBT, LOVE WITHOUT QUESTION. STOP, LOOK, LOVE WITHOUT QUESTION. ALL WOMEN LOVE WITHOUT QUESTION. IT HAUNTS YOU TO LOVE WITHOUT QUESTION. IT IS PASSION THAT MAKES ONE LOVE WITHOUT QUESTION. Another poster proclaimed: HER HUSBAND DREW THE GIRL TO HIM AND—A LONG, LONG KISS, A KISS OF YOUTH AND LOVE AND BEAUTY, ALL CONCENTRATING LIKE RAYS INTO ONE FOCUS, KINDLED FROM ABOVE; SUCH KISSES AS BELONG TO EARLY DAYS. WHERE HEART, AND SOUL, AND SENSE IN CONCERT MOVE, AND THE BLOOD IS LAVA, AND THE PULSE IS ABLAZE![2]

The new freedom of the Roaring Twenties coincided with a series of scandals involving some of America's best-known stars, and before long the censorious were calling Hollywood "Sodom by the sea" and demanding intervention. Thundered Montana senator Henry L. Myers in an impassioned speech to Congress in June 1922: "At Hollywood, Calif., is a colony of these people, where debauchery, riotous living, drunkenness, ribaldry, dissipation, free love, seem to be conspicuous. . . . These are . . . the characters from whom young people of today are deriving a large part of their education, views of life, and character-forming habits. From these sources our young people gain much of their view of life, inspiration, and education. Rather a poor source, is it not? Looks like there is some need for censorship, does it not?"[3]

Film mogul Adolph Zukor tried to reassure the public. Interviewed in Paris, he told reporters that Hollywood was a peaceful place: "No drinking—very little smoking. And as for the evenings—they're just as quiet! Why, they're practically inaudible. No sound at all but the popping of the California poppies."[4] But he failed to convince the querulous. Clergymen, educators, and club women continued their assault on the "studio sewers" in California, and some of them even called for action by the federal government to clean up the place. At length, movie executives moved once more to take defensive measures. In December 1921 they formed the Motion Picture Producers and Distributors of America (MPPDA) and invited Will H. Hays, President Harding's Postmaster General and an elder in the Presbyterian Church, to become head of the organization. The MPPDA's objective was to establish and maintain "the highest possible moral and artistic standards in motion picture production," and Hays, as president (at $100,000 a year) was to see that it did so.

Hays was reluctant at first to leave Washington, and he has left a touching account of how and why he finally decided to accept the MPPDA job. Shortly after talking to the movie people and just before Christmas, he went home to Indiana to think things over. On Christmas morning, as he was at breakfast, he overheard his little boy Bill and Bill's two cousins Charles and John arguing in the next room. "I'm going to be Bill Hart," said Bill, Jr. "No, you're not," said Charles, "I am." "Neither of you is," said John, the eldest, "I am." Hays put down his newspaper and thought: "Out of the mouth of babes and sucklings Thou has perfected praise." For the first time, he recalled, he realized that movie stars like William S. Hart were real, close, and important to his son and nephews, and that movies were important to millions of other children, and to grown-ups as well. With this sudden insight, he stood up and in the shadow of the Christmas tree silently repeated the vow of St. Paul: "And this I do."[5]

What did Hays do? Mainly encourage moviemakers to tone down their offerings. He also called on moviegoers to demand better pictures, and tried to convince the skeptical that Hollywood wasn't really so wicked a place after all. At the very outset he made a Lockean statement of aims: "We must have toward that sacred thing, the mind of a child, toward that clean and virgin thing, that unmarked slate—we must have toward that the same sense of responsibility, the same care about the impressions made upon it, that the best teacher or the best clergyman, the most inspired teacher of youth would have."[6] In 1927, the Hays Office, as the MPPDA came to be called, listed eleven Don'ts and twenty-five Be Carefuls for filmmakers. The Don'ts banned profanity, nudity, drugs, perversion, and willful offense to any nation, race, and creed; the Be Carefuls cautioned filmmakers to avoid bad taste when dealing with sex and crime. ("What a marvelous scenario!" cried a foreign director when he read the list.)[7]

Under Hays's prodding, Hollywood tried to be more careful, and for a time criticism of its morals subsided and calls for federal censorship died down. But some filmmakers chafed under the Hays restrictions. When Ben Hecht went to Hollywood in 1925 to write scripts, screenwriter Herman Mankiewicz warned him: "I want to point out to you that in a novel a hero can lay ten girls and marry a virgin for a finish. In a movie this is not allowed. The hero, as well as the heroine, has to be a virgin. The villain can lay anybody he wants, have as much fun as he wants cheating and stealing, getting rich and whipping the servants. But you have to shoot him in the end. When he falls with a bullet in his forehead, it is advisable that he clutch at the Gobelin tapestry on the library wall and bring it down over his head like a symbolic shroud."[8] Appalled, Hecht wrote his first original film story, Underworld (1927), entirely around the villain.

But Hollywood did not continue to Be Careful long enough to appease the censorious. In the late twenties, when the screen began to talk, the purifiers leaped into action again. They didn't like the language (borrowed from the stage) used in some of the new talking pictures, and they were bothered by the vogue of gangster and confession films during the early days of sound. In 1930 the Hays Office tried to placate critics by coming up with the Motion Picture Production Code, which not only set forth basic moral principles to guide the studios but also presented a list of specific prohibitions having to do mainly with sex and violence. But there was no way of enforcing the new code, and although Hays kept nudging the studios, there was far more evasion than compliance by the filmmakers. In a series of studies sponsored by the Payne Fund, investigators reported that the emphasis on sex and crime in movies was encouraging antisocial behavior among young moviegoers.

For the guardians of morals the arrival of Broadway comedienne Mae West in Hollywood in 1932 may well have been the last straw.

Mae West kidded sex, but she took it seriously, too, as an indubita- ble—and all-pervasive—fact of life. And with her insinuating smile, sensuous swagger, sultry singing, and suggestive one-liners, she seemed to symbolize everything the moralists thought was wrong with the movies. In *She Done Him Wrong* (1933), her first starring picture, she tells Cary Grant upon their first meeting: "Why don't you come up sometime 'n' see me?" And as he stares at her, she adds confidently: "Aw, you can be had." Elsewhere she remarks: "When women go wrong, men go right after them." And when someone calls her a "fine woman," she heartily agrees: "One of the finest women who ever walked the streets." At one point in the picture she sings "A Guy What Takes His Time," and at another, "I Wonder Where My Easy Rider's Gone." Puritanical Americans may not have known that "easy rider" meant "pimp," but they certainly knew that Mae West meant easy sex. They decided they had had quite enough. Shortly after the release of *She Done Him Wrong,* Episcopalians formed the Committee of Motion Pictures to combat immorality in the movies, and the Catholic Church began throwing picket lines around theaters showing movies deemed offensive.

In 1934 strict censorship became a reality in Hollywood for the first time. Early that year a committee of Roman Catholic bishops organized the National Legion of Decency to review all new films, rate them as to their morality, and see to it that the faithful boycotted "morally objectionable" films and the theaters that exhibited them. The Legion quickly won a national following. Many Protestant and Jewish leaders endorsed its aims, and millions of Catholics signed the Legion's pledge: "I condemn indecent and immoral pictures . . . and promise to stay away altogether from places of amusement which show them as a matter of policy."[9] And stay away they surely did; movie attendance began dropping rapidly in big cities with large Catholic populations. Frightened by the loss of revenue, Hollywood executives looked to Will Hays ("Where there's a Will there's a way") for help, and "Czar" Hays, as he was called, promised to take immediate action to meet the crisis. First, he had the old Production Code of 1930 rewritten and expanded, with Catholic advice, and then he entrusted its enforcement to a Production Code Administra- tion, headed by Joseph I. Breen, a young Catholic newspaperman, with headquarters in Hollywood. Breen's office soon became Holly- wood's chief censor: It supervised the making of every film produced there, from initial idea to final product, and issued (or withheld) a seal of approval ("Purity Seal") before its general release. Violation of the Code meant a $25,000 fine, and, worse still, Legion condemnation and consequent boycott by Catholics.

With the Breen office in business, Hollywood entered a new era. From the mid-thirties until the early sixties the Production Code Administration diligently policed the industry—saw to it that sexual passion was kept within bounds on the screen, that virtue was always rewarded and vice punished, and that no vulgarity was ever uttered by the performers. Mae West's new film, *It Ain't No Sin*, was changed to *I'm No Angel* (1933), and toned down so much that she was reported to have burst into tears over the carnage wrought on her script. "Blonde Bombshell" Jean Harlow's *Born to Be Kissed* was retitled *100% Pure* for a time and finally ended up as *The Girl from Missouri* (1934).

But it wasn't only the titles that became tamer—so did the subject matter. Producers turned increasingly to what they regarded as safe subjects during the thirties: family pictures (*Judge Hardy's Children*, 1938), classics (*A Tale of Two Cities*, 1935), operatic musicals (*Rose Marie*, 1936), biographies (*The Story of Louis Pasteur*, 1936), and screwball comedies (*My Man Godfrey*, 1936). Under the code, words like *floozy* were forbidden, Robin Hood was barred from kicking a sheriff in the stomach, and a scene in which a woman sprayed perfume behind her ears was deleted. One producer protested vehemently when Breen asked him to cut the popular expression "Nuts to you," out of his film. "But, Joe," he wailed, "everybody says 'nuts to you.' It's accepted." "Not by the code," said Breen. "Nuts to the code," cried the producer. "Nuts to you," retorted Breen.[10]

The Hays Office wasn't Hollywood's only censor. Foreign governments also had considerable say-so when it came to American movies, for they could boycott a studio if they didn't like its offerings. Before World War II Hollywood producers were so anxious to preserve their profitable markets abroad that they carefully avoided or soft-pedaled anti-Fascist themes in order not to offend foreign dictators. Paramount's *Blockade* (1938) started out as an anti-Fascist film about the Spanish civil war, but was so watered down during production that when it was finally completed it was practically a-political.

Local censors added restrictions of their own to those of the Hays Office. Kansas cut drinking scenes out of films; Chicago banned scenes of bootlegging and the carrying of firearms; the Ohio censor reduced the number of punches exchanged in fistfights; and

Memphis deleted scenes in which black performers like Lena Horne and Cab Calloway appeared and banned *Our Gang* comedies showing black and white kids together in school.

During the 1940s the chairman of the Memphis board of censors, octogenarian Lloyd T. Binford, was particularly censorious. Not only did he ban a picture featuring an actress who had been divorced several times; he also banned a picture about a Texan's struggle to wrest a living from the soil, because he thought it reflected on the South. And of *Duel in the Sun* (1946), David Selznick's steamy super–horse opera starring Gregory Peck and Jennifer Jones, he exclaimed: "It is a barbaric symphony of passion and hatred! It is mental and physical putrefaction! It is stark murder! It is stark horror! It is stark depravity! God help America!" Once a reporter for *Variety* asked him why he banned *Lost Boundaries* (1949), a film about interracial brotherhood, and he said: "For no particular reason."[11]

Local censorship was perforce piecemeal and partial. The main censor during Hollywood's heyday was the Production Code Administration, and its officials went about their work with zeal and industry. Some observers thought the Code reduced American films to the level of goody-goody characters like Elsie Dinsmore and Little Lord Fauntleroy and made them "emasculated, empty, and meaningless" for serious people.[12] But other observers pointed out that resourceful filmmakers often succeeded in getting around the censors and that the Code's proscriptions actually put a premium on creative imagination and subtlety in producing pictures. *The Maltese Falcon*, for example, received the Purity Seal in 1941, and yet, in its realistic portrayal of greed, betrayal, cynicism, and sexual unconventionality, it was about as far from Elsie Dinsmore as it is possible to be. The heyday of the Code was, in fact, the period sometimes called Hollywood's Golden Age. From this period came such classics as *Modern Times* (1936), *Gone With the Wind* (1939), *The Letter* (1940), *Citizen Kane* (1941), and *The Little Foxes* (1941). Despite the Code, Bette Davis never played Elsie Dinsmore on the screen, nor did Katharine Hepburn. And neither Clark Gable nor Humphrey Bogart ever resembled Little Lord Fauntleroy in any of their films, despite all the prohibitions.

The Code was short-lived; it lasted only a couple of decades. In the 1950s there was a steady drift away from its mandates. After World War II, as after World War I, there was an easing of manners and morals in the nation, and Hollywood, in the fifties, as in the twenties, both reflected and reinforced the new trends. The rise of television, too, impelled movie producers to seek new themes (like drugs and homosexuality) in an effort to persuade people to leave the tube and come into the movie houses. A series of Supreme Court decisions commencing in 1952, moreover, reversed the old 1915 ruling and began extending the guarantees of free speech to movies. Meanwhile, the Production Code Administration itself came down off its high horse; responding to the new atmosphere, it began concentrating on the quality and taste of films as a whole rather than on specific words, lines, and scenes. Soon it was approving one film after another that it once would have condemned.

Back in 1932, before the days of the Purity Seal, Greta Garbo had played a whore in the movie version of Eugene O'Neill's *Anna Christie*. But when MGM wanted to remake the film in the 1940s, the Production Code Administration ordered the deletion of the prostitute from the picture, and the studio ended by shelving the project. In 1962, though, when MGM decided to reissue the Garbo film, the PCA gave it a seal of approval without a murmur. "Times have changed," mused one of the PCA officials.[13] They certainly had. In the late 1960s American film morals turned a complete somersault. Soon most of the old Production Code's prohibitions were becoming commonplace occurrences on the nation's screens. The impermissibles of the old days, in fact, had practically become *de rigueur* for American films in the new liberated era. "Producers today are free to make films about virtually anything they want, in any way they want," observed *New York Times* film critic Vincent Canby in March 1986. "It's a bad joke that they're manacled to an audience even more restrictive in its way, than were those arbiters of taste who ruled Hollywood no less whimsically from 1930 until 1968." The new arbiters of taste: action fans, adventure addicts, and, above all, teenage audiences who turned up their noses at the old-fashioned "family pictures" of the Code days.[14]

Griffith and the Censors

D. W. Griffith developed an ingenious way of dealing with the censors. He invited them to lunch, discovered what their special interests were, and then, at appropriate moments during screenings, would get them talking about their pet subjects. He even got by with a realistic childbearing scene in *Way Down East* (1920) at a time when Pennsylvania didn't even permit scenes of women knitting baby garments.[15]

Forsaken

After completing *Joan the Woman* (1917), his first epic, Cecil B. De Mille took it to New York for approval by the censors there. When the screening was over, a clergyman who was present said he didn't see anything offensive in the picture. But a woman on the censor board disagreed. "Yes," she said, "there is one thing that has to come out. It's the line where Joan says, 'My God, my God, why has Thou forsaken me?'" De Mille asked her whether she knew who had first spoken that line. "It doesn't make any difference who spoke it," persisted the woman. "It means that God would forsake someone, and it has to come out." "My dear lady," intervened the clergyman at this point, "I wonder whether you are aware that those words were said by Jesus on the cross." De Mille won his point.[16]

Stopwatch

When Paramount decided to make *Beyond the Rocks* (1922), studio executives thought they had a real sizzler: a steamy love story by British writer Elinor Glyn, the sultry glamour of Gloria Swanson, and the romantic magic of Rudolph Valentino. The trouble was that the Hays Office had decreed that kisses on the screen could last only ten feet. In the end, the director shot each Swanson-Valentino clinch twice: once for the foreign version and once for American release. This meant that only Europeans and Latin Americans got to see the passionate Swanson-Valentino kisses in the movie. In the United States, Valentino hardly got his nostrils flaring before the scene ended. American fevers, said Swanson ruefully, were now "controlled by a stopwatch."[17]

Violating the Code

One day Will Hays called a meeting of the publicity directors of the various studios to criticize the sexy advertisements they were using for some of their pictures. Suddenly, as he was giving examples of the kind of promotion material he thought violated the spirit of the Production Code, a pair of amorous pigeons lit on the ledge of one of the windows outside and began to go to work. "What's going on out there?" cried Hays as all eyes turned toward the window. "They're violating the Production Code, sir," explained MGM's advertising manager just as Hays spied the pigeons.[18]

Ping!

One of the punch lines at the end of *The Front Page,* the hard-boiled Broadway comedy about the newspaper world, was, "The son of a bitch stole my watch!" It always brought down the house. "Gee," said Adolphe Menjou, who was to speak the line in the 1931 film version of the play, "wouldn't it be great if we could say that line?" "You're going to say it," director Lewis Milestone assured him. "We'll get run out of Hollywood," warned Menjou. "No," said Milestone, "I'll tell you what to do when the time comes."

Milestone didn't actually decide how to handle the line until the last minute. While rehearsing the scene, which takes place in a newsroom, he suddenly noticed that a bell sounded on the typewriter whenever the carrier reached the side of a page. "This is it!" he cried, and gave Menjou his instructions: He was to sit down at the desk as one of the reporters was typing, pick up the phone, and start talking. And just as he got to the S.O.B. line, the typewriter bell would sound, *ping,* at the right moment. Milestone did thirty-six takes before getting it right, but in the end Menjou got to say the line: "The son of a—*ping!*—stole my watch!" "My God," said Milestone's associates, struck by the way he had outwitted the Hays Office, "the man is a genius!"[19]

Replacement

Censorship restrained the Marx Brothers as well as everyone else. In one scene in *Duck Soup* (1933), Harpo proudly displays the tattoo of an outhouse on his chest, and when Groucho slaps him on the back, the outhouse door swings open and a little hand reaches out and closes it. Because of the Hays Office, however, the producers decided to replace the outhouse with a doghouse and have a live dog come out barking when Groucho claps Harpo on the back.[20]

Von Sternberg and the Censors

One day the proud, crotchety, and independent-minded director Josef von Sternberg was told that there were three lines in one of his scripts that would rouse the censors in Ohio to wrath. Infuriated by the thought of shallow Philistines dictating artistic endeavor, von Sternberg exclaimed, "Tell the Ohio board of censors that I will not approve the script until they reject every word!"[21]

Sooner or Later

In a scene in one of the Bob Hope–Bing Crosby movies of the 1940s
Dorothy Lamour slips out of her famous sarong and goes for a swim
in the lagoon. But at precisely the moment when she drops the
sarong, the film makes a quick cut to the shot of a train whizzing by
a crossing, and then returns to Lamour, who is now swimming gracefully in the water. "I've been to see the picture eight times now and
I'm going again," Bob Hope tells the audience from the screen.
"Sooner or later that train is bound to be late. . . ."[22]

Wonderful Idea

There may have been a Production Code, but filmmakers knew how
to get around it. Writer Ben Hecht was amused by the clever ways
producers hinted at fornication in their films without violating the
Code; he got the impression, in fact, that every couple behaving decorously on the screen began making passionate love as soon as the
scene dissolved.

One day Hecht got a call from Bernie Hyman, MGM production
head, asking for help on a movie about to be shot. "I won't tell you
the plot," Hyman said. "I'll just give you what we're up against. The
hero and heroine fall madly in love with each other—as soon as they
meet. What we need is some gimmick that keeps them from going to
bed right away. Not a physical gimmick like arrest or getting run over
or having to go to the hospital. But a purely psychological one. Now
what reasons do you know that would keep a healthy pair of lovers
from hitting the hay in Reel Two?" Hecht told him that frequently a
girl had values that kept her virtuous until she got married and that
there were also men who preferred to wait for coitus until they had
married the girl they adored. Hyman could hardly believe his ears.
"Wonderful!" he cried, struck by the novelty of the idea. "We'll try
it."[23]

Fine Word

Producer David O. Selznick felt it was absolutely necessary to end
Gone With the Wind (1939) with a strong statement by Rhett Butler
(Clark Gable) when he leaves Scarlett O'Hara (Vivien Leigh):
"Frankly, I don't give a damn." To have Gable say, "Frankly, I don't
care," he insisted, would ruin the impact of the movie's final scene.
But the Hays Office stubbornly refused to let Selznick use the word
damn, and Selznick finally wrote a long letter to Hays pleading his

case. "The word as used in the picture," he said, "is not an oath or a curse. . . . The worst that could be said for it is that it is a vulgarism, and it is so described in the Oxford English dictionary. . . . Nor do I feel that in asking you to make an exception in this case . . . this one sentence will open up the floodgates [of profanity]. I do believe, however, that if you were to permit our using this dramatic word in its rightfully dramatic place, it would establish a helpful precedent . . . giving your office discretionary powers to allow the use of certain harmless oaths and ejaculations whenever they are . . . not prejudicial to public morals. The omission of this line spoils the punch at the very end of the picture and on our very fade-out gives an impression of unfaithfulness after three hours and forty-five minutes of extreme fidelity to Miss Mitchell's work which has become . . . an American Bible." Hays finally overruled his board of advisers and let Gable utter the accursed word. But he fined Selznick $5,000 for having violated the Production Code.[24]

Nothing

"Geoff," director Preston Sturges told censor Geoffrey Shurlock one day, "I've got a problem. I've got a scene with my leading lady sitting at a dressing table making up for the evening. She's dressed in a half-slip and a brassiere. You think that'd be all right?" "Is there some special reason you can't use a full slip?" Shurlock wanted to know. "Yes," said Sturges. "You see, Geoff, the girl's preparing to put on a midriff formal. My costume designer tells me that every woman in the audience would know that you don't wear a full slip under a midriff formal. They'd laugh, you know." "Then have her sitting at the dressing table in a negligee," suggested Shurlock. "I can, Geoff, if it's really necessary," said Sturges. "But, for goodness' sake, is a half slip and brassiere really so exposing as all that? It's certainly more covering than you'd see at the beach. . . ." "I think you have something there," admitted Shurlock, and he agreed to discuss it with his colleagues. A few days later he delivered the bad news. "Preston—I'm sorry!" he told the director. "The boys all say, it's a full slip, or nothing!" "It's a deal!" chortled Sturges. "I'll take nothing!"[25]

New Testament

In *They Knew What They Wanted* (1940), Charles Laughton played the part of Tony, an Italian wine maker who marries a mail-order bride, discovers she is cheating on him, and then forgives her in the end. But the Production Code specified that adultery must always be punished on the screen, and the screenplay ran into immediate trouble with the censors. Laughton went with producer Erich Pommer, director Garson Kanin, and writer Robert Ardrey to see Joseph Breen, head of the Production Code office, to discuss the matter. Breen liked the screenplay but refused to relax the rules. "The sinner," he told them, "must be punished!" Even when Kanin and Ardrey said there was no point in making the picture unless there was forgiveness at the end, Breen stood firm. Suddenly Laughton spoke. "Do I understand, Mr. Breen," he said, "that the Code *does not recognize the New Testament?*" Breen, a good Catholic, looked up in astonishment. "Christ forgave the adultress, didn't he, Mr. Breen?" continued Laughton. Breen was quiet for a minute or two and then said slowly, "Well, Mr. Laughton, you may have a point there." And to the delight of everyone concerned he let the forgiveness scene stay in the picture.[26]

Alcoholics

When Katharine Hepburn became interested in filming *Happy Birthday*, the Broadway comedy of the 1940s written by Anita Loos and starring Helen Hayes, she was surprised to learn that the censors vehemently objected to the idea. The play deals with a prim librarian who gets tipsy on her birthday and wakes up the next morning with a husband instead of a hangover. "What's objectionable about the story?" Loos asked Hepburn. "I don't know," Hepburn answered, "but come out here and we'll find out." The two women had a meeting with Eric Johnston, then head of the MPPDA, and he told them the play was pro-alcoholism. "The message," he said, "seems to be to get drunk, lose your inhibitions, win a man, and forget your troubles." Hepburn and Loos were astonished; they couldn't understand how a comedy like *Happy Birthday* could be considered a plug for booze. "We argued, but it did no good," Loos recalled. "Johnson was convinced we wanted to turn all the spinsters in America into alcoholics."[27]

Psychiatrist

In *Beyond the Forest* (1949), Bette Davis visits an abortion clinic at one point to get rid of an unwanted baby. But upon instructions from the censors, the producers replaced the clinic sign in the scene with a sign containing the word PSYCHIATRIST on it. Both Davis and her director, King Vidor, were disgusted by the change. "I don't think that fooled anybody," said Vidor. "It was still obvious that she was trying to get rid of her baby."[28]

Long Kiss

Alfred Hitchcock enjoyed outwitting the censors. In making *Notorious* (1946), he arranged for Cary Grant and Ingrid Bergman to engage in a kissing scene that lasted far longer than the three seconds permitted by the Production Code Administration. In the film, Bergman and Grant begin kissing, talk briefly, resume kissing, lean away for a moment and kiss again, nibble on each other's ears, and get back to kissing again. For audiences, the scene was one prolonged sensational kiss. But the two stars never at any one point kissed for more than three seconds, so it got by censors.[29]

Religious Grounds

When Rex Harrison and Lilli Palmer, then married, were making the film version of the play *The Four Poster* in 1952, the censors forbade them to appear in a double bed together, with or without wedding rings, insisted that if one of them was in bed, the other had to have "one foot on the floor," and cut out several lines that had been famous in the play. One deletion infuriated the two stars, for it had gone over big with audiences. It involved the exchange between the young bride and her husband on their wedding night, after she had climbed into bed and he was sitting on a stool taking off his slippers. "You know," says the young woman nervously, "I've never seen a man . . . uh, completely . . ." "Well," says the bridegroom calmly, "you haven't missed much." When the censors deleted these lines from the script, Harrison and Palmer went angrily to see Eric Johnston, MPAA head, to protest. "There's nothing immoral about that," they exclaimed. "You're right," admitted Johnston. "On moral grounds we wouldn't have touched it. But we had to cut it on religious grounds, because man is made in the Lord's image, you understand?"[30]

Inspection

For one scene in *The Last Time I Saw Paris* (1954), Elizabeth Taylor showed up displaying more cleavage than usual, and the assistant director called in MGM's "bust inspector"—an earnest young woman with horn-rimmed glasses—to evaluate the situation. The woman took one look at Taylor, demanded a ladder, and when it was brought to the set, climbed to the top rung and peered intently down into Taylor's bosom. Then she announced the dress would have to be replaced. When the director, Richard Brooks, exploded in wrath, the bust inspector burst into tears and fled the set. Soon after filing her report she quit her job.[31]

Standing Up

In Let's Make Love (1960), one scene, showing Marilyn Monroe rolling around on a bed with Yves Montand, was so suggestive that Frank McCarthy, censorship expert for Twentieth Century-Fox, was called in for advice. McCarthy assured director George Cukor the scene would never be approved. But Cukor disagreed. He decided to invite Harold Shurlock, official in the Breen office, to visit the set and watch the scene as it was being shot.

As soon as Shurlock arrived, Marilyn Monroe began turning on the charm. "So you're Shurlock," she purred. "This is the first time I've ever met a censor." She chatted pleasantly with him for a while and then joined Yves Montand to do the scene. Afterward, when Shurlock began objecting to it, she turned to him, as if surprised, and asked what was wrong with it. Shurlock told her that her wriggling and rolling was in a horizontal position. "I don't understand," said Monroe. "What's wrong?" "Well—it's horizontal," repeated Shurlock. "It's as though you were getting ready for the sex act." "Oh, that," said Monroe with a bright smile, "you can do that standing up. So what?" And she won her point.[32]

Drama

Comedy

Musicals

Westerns

Spectacles

Horror
and
Suspense

Classics
and
Biopics

Message Movies

B Pictures

III. THE
PLAYBILL

CHAPTER 17

Drama

All screen drama, whether based on classic literature, plays, novels, short stories, or original scripts, presents the viewer with an artistic experience unlike that of any other medium. In Hollywood the play was no longer the thing, since words were ultimately less important than imagery. Next to images, movement emerged as the most vital element in motion-picture technique.[1] Filmmakers quickly discovered the possibilities for achieving dramatic effects by shifting the camera's position during the playing of a scene, keeping the most significant action near screen center. Even with the addition of sound, movies remained an art form distinctly different from the theater.

A frequent criticism of filmed stage plays is that the transferral process has not eliminated staginess or excessive dialogue, thereby denying the film the sensuous excitement that better screen adaptations offer. "Movies—which arouse special, private, hidden feelings—have always had an erotic potential that was stronger than that of the live theater," Pauline Kael maintained. "Movies can overwhelm us, as no other art form, except, perhaps, opera does. . . ."[2] Exceptional acting can assist a talky drama, but static stage methods are inappropriate for filmmaking. When The Petrified Forest was screened in 1936, the movie made Humphrey Bogart a star, even though the picture itself was judged a pedestrian piece of work, since every move in it seemed rehearsed and director Archie Mayo gave "the feeling that he has even retained the stage blocking."[3]

A number of techniques have been employed to make filmed plays more attractive to movie audiences. Opening a play up by filming some of the action outdoors is a frequent device to increase movement. Robert Bolt's *A Man for All Seasons* (1966) was turned into an elegant, handsome film with breathtaking photography of its English locales, while James Goldman's *The Lion in Winter* (1968), besides boasting stellar performances, did an excellent job of portraying life in the twelfth century. Other successful screen adaptations stay close to the theater piece but achieve their visual quality by concentrating on atmosphere and lighting, moving the camera naturally through interiors or focusing on details in ways not possible on the stage. Elia Kazan's film treatment of *A Streetcar Named Desire* (1951) is a remarkable screen version that, apart from an occasional widening of the action, follows the Tennessee Williams play faithfully (not counting cuts demanded by the censorship office). The film's cinematic quality was achieved by moving the camera through the rooms of Stella and Stanley's New Orleans apartment and onto the porches and balconies, and making close-ups of Blanche's restless movements and fanciful gestures, as well as of facial expressions and exchanges of looks between characters.[4]

Camille, which had served opera, the dramatic stage, and previous screen versions, proved to be Garbo's finest role. The Metro film (1936) was made visually compelling by the beauty of Cedric Gibbons's set designs.[5] Overelaborate sets and costumes, on the other hand, can dwarf a simple story, as happened with the screen adaptation of Broadway's wartime hit *Life with Father* (1947). Hollywood casting can also ruin a successful play, for the old star system frequently necessitated rewriting an important character part to accommodate a major star, usually with disastrous results. If the leading role was left intact and the Broadway actor played it, subordinate casting generally had to ensure a movie's appeal for screen audiences. When Shirley Booth was brought to Paramount to recreate her role in William Inge's *Come Back, Little Sheba* (1952), Booth won an Academy Award for her sensitive portrayal, but producer Hal Wallis took care to cast Hollywood's Burt Lancaster against type as her alcoholic husband to protect the project against box-office disaster.

Novels and even short stories by nature are more cinematic than stage dramas, simply because the theater does not lend itself to constant changes of focus. Still, when a novel or short story is turned into a movie, a metamorphosis occurs. Philosophical fiction, in which the writer is deeply concerned with the projection of ideas, is the most difficult material to translate to the screen. While novelists like Theodore Dreiser realized early that "motion pictures offer great possibilities as a medium of art,"[6] most of them recognized their own inability to write for movies. "The moving picture work of my own which seemed best to me," said William Faulkner, "was done by the actors and the writer throwing the script away and inventing the scene in actual rehearsal just before the camera turned." Faulkner acknowledged that he would never be a good motion-picture writer, freely admitting that film work did not have the urgency for him that novels and short stories did.[7]

A few classic novels have been made into successful films that in their own way are also works of art. *Wuthering Heights* (1939), one of the great love stories of all time, was brought to the screen by William Wyler and Sam Goldwyn in a production of haunting beauty, with sterling values in all categories. Henry Fielding's *Tom Jones* (1963) became a lusty, rollicking masterpiece on the screen, remarkably true to the spirit of the book, yet full of such cinematic touches as offscreen narration, accelerated action, and even silent-film titles. MGM romanticized Flaubert's *Madame Bovary* (1949), making it a child's fantasy of adultery, but the film works on its own terms. In one sequence, for example, Vincente Minnelli ingeniously devised a scene in which Emma looks into an oval mirror and sees herself at a majestic ball, surrounded by officers and gentlemen in evening clothes, the only time in her life that reality matches her dreams.[8]

More often the classics have been reduced to mere action. *Billy Budd* (1962) contained little of Melville's metaphysical thrust, but Pauline Kael felt the film's tense, straightforward narrative was probably the right approach, resulting in "not a great motion picture, but . . . a very good one."[9] Most of Hemingway's novel *To Have and Have Not* was scrapped when Warners bought the title, reducing the film (1944) to the kind of romantic melodrama audiences had been clamoring for since *Casablanca*.[10] Still, the Bogart-Bacall movie in its own right is a classic. *Elmer Gantry* (1960) dilutes the issues probed by Sinclair Lewis's novel, is overloaded with crowds, fires, and human stampedes, but the film makes a strong statement about demagoguery anyway.[11]

The Heiress (1949), taken from a play based on Henry James's *Washington Square*, follows the novel closely and doesn't reject confinement. In fact, the camera utilizes the interior of the Washington Square mansion to suggest the claustrophobia that Catherine Sloper (Olivia de Havilland) feels in her cloistered life,[12] and the approach works. Stanley Kubrick's *Barry Lyndon* (1975), on the other hand, drawn from Thackeray's *The Memoirs of Barry Lyndon, Esq.*, while a stunning recreation of life in mid-eighteenth-century Europe and filled with pastel landscapes, is slow-moving and dramatically hopeless.[13]

During Hollywood's Golden Age, contemporary fiction was a more frequent source for movie dramas than the classics, with bestsellers by Edna Ferber, Fanny Hurst, and Herman Wouk particularly attractive to commercial filmmakers. James M. Cain also became popular with Hollywood. While Cain was never a successful screenwriter himself, his novels and short stories provided the basis for several of Hollywood's most popular pictures during the 1940s: *Double Indemnity* (1944), *Mildred Pierce* (1945), and *The Postman Always Rings Twice* (1946). *Postman* has inspired three different films, although the author did not see the original Lana Turner–John Garfield version (made in 1946) until 1976—thirty years after its release. His reaction was: "I was surprised that it was no worse than it was."[14]

Best-selling novels have continued to be a favorite source for dramatic films. Arthur Hailey's 1968 novel, *Airport,* became a glossy, $10 million blockbuster on the screen (1970), combining human drama with taut action, and managed to win favorable critical notices as well as an Academy Award nomination for best picture of the year. Producer Ross Hunter considered the movie "a good old-fashioned *Grand Hotel* of the air" and the crowning achievement of his highly successful career.[15] *The Godfather* (1972), from the Mario Puzo best-seller of 1969, had its roots in the gangster films of the 1930s but presented a realistic portrait of a Mafia dynasty, in which organized crime becomes a nightmare image of American capitalism. The picture not only benefited from an excellent script but was an extraordinary achievement cinematically.[16]

Other sources of film stories are radio and television. Radio provided the screen with an occasional drama, among the finest of which was *Sorry, Wrong Number* (1948). The problem in making the film centered around how to open up Lucille Fletcher's radio play about an invalid named Leona confined to her bed and talking on the telephone. The solution lay in allowing the camera to roam her room and the first floor below and letting it escape Leona's sickroom during a series of flashbacks. Paddy Chayefsky's *Marty* (1955) became the first television drama transformed into a major motion picture, winning the Academy Award for best picture of that year. The film legitimized television for the public and critics alike, retaining the simple intimacy of the home medium yet capturing the flavor of the Bronx through outdoor location shooting.

Original screenplays like *Sunset Boulevard* and *All About Eve* (both 1950) freely use the flashback, voice-overs, cross-cutting, and other techniques uniquely suited to film. Perhaps the best example is still Orson Welles's *Citizen Kane* (1941), widely revered as one of the best motion pictures ever made. *Kane* is a symphony of cinematic innovation, utilizing sound, lighting, and shadows as never before. Harmonizing a complex story with expert acting, *Citizen Kane* emerges as a visual masterpiece both in its overall design and in the richness and imagination of its myriad detail.

Interestingly, most Hollywood stars—singers, dancers, and comedians alike—never seemed to feel they had arrived until they appeared in a successful dramatic picture. Bing Crosby won his Academy Award for best acting playing a Catholic priest in *Going My Way* (1944), although he was nominated later for *The Bells of St. Mary's* (1945) and *The Country Girl* (1954). Frank Sinatra, after a major career slump, reestablished his reputation by winning the Oscar for best supporting actor, playing Maggio in *From Here to Eternity* (1953). Singer Shirley Jones surprised everybody, including her director, Richard Brooks, by turning in an award-winning performance as a prostitute in *Elmer Gantry*. Shirley MacLaine, brought to Hollywood as a dancer, reached her pinnacle with a multifaceted portrayal of the self-centered mother in *Terms of Endearment* (1983), justly rewarded with an Oscar after sporadic nominations. Not only has the Motion Picture Academy been sympathetic to such skillful offbeat casting, but it has definitely preferred drama in its choice of outstanding pictures. Of the forty-two films so honored since 1945, all but twelve have been dramas; six have been musicals, four spectacles, and only two (*The Sting* and *Annie Hall*) out-and-out comedies.

Happy Ending

During the making of his grim antiwar film *All Quiet on the Western Front* (1930), Lewis Milestone was pressured by Universal producers, who wanted the drama to end happily. The director resisted, preferring to remain true to Erich Maria Remarque's novel, based on the author's experiences in the German army during World War I. But at one point he called one of the producers on the telephone and said, "I've got your happy ending. We'll let the Germans win the war."[17]

Reluctant Gunman

Edward G. Robinson didn't really enjoy playing a gangster and hated the sound of gunfire. That posed problems for director Mervyn LeRoy during the shooting of *Little Caesar* (1930). "Every time he squeezed the trigger," LeRoy said, "he would screw up his eyes." Take after take the actor did the same thing. "In the end," the director insisted, "we had to tape up his eyelids to make sure it wouldn't show."[18]

Time After Time

Many Hollywood dramatic films were mediocre because they repeated the same old formulas over and over again. When Edward Buzzell was directing at Warner Bros., he grew dismayed that the studio kept making the same stories repeatedly. Finally he went to Hal Wallis, then head of production, and said: "Hal, why do you do these goddamn pictures so many times?" Wallis answered, "As long as they buy them, we'll make them." Later, when Eddie went to Metro, he found the same thing. Given a story to film that had been reworked time and again, Buzzell protested to Louis B. Mayer. "Let's steal from ourselves before somebody else does," Mayer told him.[19]

Last Resort

William Wyler had to ram *Wuthering Heights* (1939) down Sam Goldwyn's throat. Sam didn't like people dying, and it took Wyler a year or more to convince him otherwise. The script had been written by Ben Hecht and Charles MacArthur for Walter Wanger, who hoped to produce the film with Sylvia Sidney and Charles Boyer. Sidney brought the property to Wyler's attention when the director was making *Dead End* (1937). Wyler immediately thought it was great, but Goldwyn refused to have anything to do with the classic until he found out Bette Davis wanted Jack Warner to buy it for her. "Can Merle Oberon play the role?" Sam asked Wyler. When the director assured him she could, Goldwyn agreed to purchase the *Wuthering Heights* script, because he had Oberon under contract and needed a picture for her.[20]

A Night at the Oscars

After *Lady for a Day* (1933), a dramatic film about Apple Annie's twelve hours as a lady, went over so big with the public and critics, director Frank Capra began hoping for four Academy Awards. The film had been nominated for best picture, best writing, best direction, and best actress, and no picture had ever won four major Oscars. It would set a record. At the Academy Awards banquet Capra's old friend Will Rogers was to hand out the Oscars. During the technical awards the eager director applauded and grinned, his excitement mounting. Then came the first of the major awards—best screenplay, the first of the four Capra expected to sweep. He looked over at Bob Riskin's table, where Bob was smoking furiously. Then Will Rogers announced the award: to Victor Heerman and Sarah Mason for *Little Women*. Capra was stunned but not overcome. "Guess I'll have to settle for three," he told his friends at the table. Then came the award for best direction. Will Rogers read the nominations, Capra sneaked a last quick look under the tablecloth at his wrinkled acceptance speech, and listened. Rogers made a few nice remarks about directors and then: ". . . and the best director of the year is . . . the envelope please . . ." He opened it and laughed. "Well, well, well, what do you know? I've watched this young man for a long time. . . . Saw him come up from the bottom, and I *mean* the bottom. It couldn't happen to a nicer guy. COME UP AND GET IT, FRANK!" Capra's table exploded into cheers. The jubilant director began wedging through crowded tables up to Rogers, while the spotlight searched around trying to find him. "Over here!" he waved. Then suddenly the spotlight swept away from him and picked up a flustered man standing on the other side of the dance floor—Frank Lloyd. The applause was deafening, as the spotlight escorted Lloyd (who had directed *Cavalcade*) onto the dance floor and up to the dais, where Will Rogers greeted him with a big hug and a hearty handshake. Capra stood in utter disbelief until someone shouted, "Down in front!" His walk back to his table was the longest and saddest of his life. He felt like crawling under a rug. The rest of the evening deepened the wound. For best actress not May Robson but Katharine Hepburn for *Morning Glory*; for best picture not *Lady for a Day* but *Cavalcade*.[21] Capra later won Oscars for *It Happened One Night* (1934), *Mr. Deeds Goes to Town* (1936), and *You Can't Take It With You* (1938).

All American

Lillian Hellman's *The Children's Hour* opened to rave notices on Broadway and became one of the long-running plays of the pre–World War II era. After reading the smash reviews, Sam Goldwyn told his associate producer Merritt Hulburd, "Maybe we ought to buy it." "Forget it, Mr. Goldwyn," Hulburd said. "It's about lesbians." "Don't worry," replied Sam, "we'll make them Americans." Revised by Hellman herself and retitled *These Three*, the picture was one of Hollywood's best dramas in 1936.[22]

Marlene's English

Making the English version of *The Blue Angel* (1930) proved a harrowing experience for Hollywood newcomer Marlene Dietrich, whose English was none too good at the time. Playing Lola-Lola, the humiliating cabaret singer who destroys a professor (Emil Jannings), Marlene sang "Falling in Love Again," but had trouble with the line "Men cluster to me, like moths around a flame." The word *moths* kept coming out *moss*. Director Josef von Sternberg had her repeat the scene 235 times over two days of shooting, until everyone was ready to collapse. Finally von Sternberg gave up. "All right!" he said to one of the musicians in the band accompanying Marlene. "When she comes to the word 'moths' I want you to shout, 'Bring me a beer, bring me a beer!'" The musician obeyed; consequently nobody heard Dietrich mispronounce the word.[23]

Lend an Ear

Joe Mankiewicz was responsible for taking Marlon Brando out of a T-shirt and putting him in a toga, casting him as Marc Antony in *Julius Caesar* (1953). Many felt Brando wasn't up to the role, and his "Friends, Romans, countrymen" speech supplied material for stand-up comics throughout the English-speaking world. Before shooting started, the actor listened to recordings of all the great Shakespearean actors right up through Michael Redgrave and John Gielgud, and then played a tape he had made of the "Friends, Romans, countrymen" speech for Mankiewicz. "Marlon," sighed Mankiewicz, "you sound exactly like June Allyson. We've got a lot of work to do."

Eventually, Brando, discovering nuances during rehearsals, turned in a performance that captured not only Marc Antony's caginess but the animal anger of a warrior as well. Mankiewicz was sitting on a ladder and Brando was in rehearsal clothes when the breakthrough came. Marc Antony, entering with Caesar's body, began his speech: "Friends, Romans, countrymen, lend me your ears." A crowd of three hundred Hollywood extras were milling about and mumbling, so his words were barely audible. Suddenly Mankiewicz got an idea. "Marlon, get mad," he suggested. With that Brando said, "Friends, Romans, countrymen, LEND me your ears." The director later recalled the effect of that moment: "I swear to you that's the only time in my entire career I ever felt a chill go up my spine. . . . I'd never heard it read that way before."[24]

Dirty Talk

When Columbia bought the screen rights to From Here to Eternity, James Jones's best-selling novel about G.I.'s in World War II, several people wondered why in the world Harry Cohn would buy a dirty book like that. One wag answered, "He thinks everybody talks that way."[25]

Capital Punishment

Some directors went to great lengths to capture the real-life drama of the stories they were filming. Director Robert Wise's realistic depiction of Barbara Graham's gas-chamber execution in I Want to Live! (1958) remains one of the strongest indictments of capital punishment ever put on film. Wise became emotionally involved in the story, interviewing many of the actual people in the case. He talked with the nurse who spent the last night with Barbara at San Quentin and also with the priest who heard her final confession. Wise got permission from the warden to be taken through every step in preparing to take a person's life.

"Everything that I showed in the film," Wise, said, "is exactly what they do—fixing this, getting the telephone ready, all that detail is exactly what they do to prepare for an execution." He even witnessed an execution. "I felt like a ghoul asking for it," the director confessed, "but I did feel very strongly that I wanted to show as honestly as I could what the whole experience was like."

Wise stood beside the assistant warden and a doctor while a young black man was brought in. He had been given a couple of reprieves, had been in San Quentin over two years, and finally this was it. The director didn't know what to expect and wondered whether he'd be able to watch the execution without becoming ill. "I forced myself to do it," Wise said, "because I felt it was important to the picture. Fortunately it was not hysterical or anything, so I found I was able to watch." He tried to duplicate the whole atmosphere with Susan Hayward in *I Want to Live!* "Of course, the whole actual death went on for eight or nine minutes," said Wise. "There was much more writing of hands and things like that than I wanted to show. But everything in the picture was as direct and honest a reproduction of the drama as I could possibly do."[26]

CHAPTER 18

Comedy

For most people, silent drama today is practically un-
viewable. Even the D. W. Griffith classics are mainly of interest to
specialists in film history. In pictures like *America* (1924), Griffith's
epic about the American Revolution, the pacing seems slow, the acting mannered, and the subtitles grandiloquent. With silent comedy,
however, it is quite otherwise. Many of the old-time comedies still
seem fresh and lively. And the great comedians of the Silent Era—
Chaplin, Keaton, Lloyd, Laurel and Hardy—are still as wonderful in
their various ways as they were decades ago. Even the Keystone Kops
are fun to watch for a while.

The Kops came first. In moviedom's salad days Mack Sennett was
the "King of Comedy" and the Kops his specialty. So were pratfalls,
pies in the face, and parodies of the pompous. In 1913 Sennett went
to work for the Keystone Studio, turned it into a "fun factory," and
began flooding movie houses with short comedies in which funny-
looking people bumped into each other, tripped over things, fell off
cliffs, and in general made fools of themselves and anybody else who
happened to be around. There was usually a grand chase, too, at the
end of Sennett comedies: frenetic policemen rushing out of sta-
tionhouses, jumping into tin lizzies, and hurtling down the street in
what James Agee called "a majestic trajectory of pure anarchic motion" that drew bathing beauties (another Sennett specialty), dogs,

cats, babies, automobiles, locomotives, and innocent bystanders into their wake "like dry leaves following an express train."[1] Years later a smart aleck asked Sennett, "What exactly did you have to know to be a good Keystone Kop?" "You had to understand comic motion," Sennett told him. "You mean," smirked the wise guy, "make funny faces?" At that point Sennett pushed the man into a nearby pool and, when he came up, explained: "That's comic motion."[2]

Sennett did more than turn out slapstick. At Keystone he provided basic training, so to speak, for one of America's greatest film comedians: Charlie Chaplin. Chaplin joined Sennett in 1913 and after several weeks of trial and error finally created the Tramp—the little fellow with the derby, cane, sad smile, and soulful eyes—and in a series of two-reelers began developing him into a full-bodied character who was both dignified and funny. The Tramp went over big with movie audiences—and with critics too—and Chaplin was soon writing and directing his own films and at times even composing music for them. By the time he came to concentrate on feature pictures— The Kid (1921), The Gold Rush (1925), The Circus (1928)—he was famous around the world and the darling of intellectuals who otherwise looked down on movies. Chaplin's fans disagreed violently over which was Chaplin's—and thus filmdom's—greatest picture. "Oh well," Sennett once remarked, "he's just the greatest artist who ever lived."[3]

Buster Keaton, though, rivaled Chaplin in the affections of movie-lovers. Some critics, indeed, rate him higher today because, unlike Chaplin, he had no cutesy moments in his films; nor did he ever lapse into sentimentalism. Keaton's creation—the Great Stone Face—had no time for pathos. His predicaments were astonishing and his ability to survive adversity almost unbelievable. With impassive face and horizontal hat, he responded to "die Tücke des Objekts" (the malice of things), as German writer Theodor Vischer called it, with infinite patience and determination: wind, rain, hail, mechanical obduracy. And, unlike the Tramp, who frequently ended up with nothing, he always managed to win out against great odds and take the girl home with him in the end. In making his films, Keaton liked to stage ingenious mechanical gags and, eschewing doubles, insisted on acting as his own stunt man. In Steamboat Bill, Jr. (1928), he arranged for the front of a house, weighing two tons, to fall on him, with only a small window opening in the upper story saving him, both in film and in fact, from destruction. His best film, The General (1927), a dramatic comedy about a Southern engineer who rescues his beloved locomotive, *The General,* from Union raiders during the Civil War, takes its place beside Chaplin's *The Gold Rush* at the top of any list of America's greatest silent comedies.

Harold Lloyd, the third of the great silent clowns, was not as good as Chaplin and Keaton, but at his best he was very good indeed. Like Chaplin and Keaton, he stressed character as well as comic situations. He called his creation "the glasses character": a young man with horn-rimmed spectacles, neatly dressed, innocent but ambitious, who was never at a loss for thinking up ways out of dreadful dilemmas and startling situations. Lloyd wasn't the stuntman Keaton was. In *Safety Last* (1923), an amazingly fast-paced picture featuring his perilous ascent up the side of a twelve-story building, he used a double in long shots and for close-ups worked on sets only two or three stories high. When he was in Chicago promoting the picture, city officials wanted to have him lowered from the top of the Wrigley Tower so he could break a bottle of champagne over the building's clock, but he politely declined. To the people who had gathered to see him perform a stunt similar to the one he did in *Safety Last,* he announced that he had no intention of committing suicide, and they accepted his refusal good-naturedly. Still, he was called "the King of Daredevil Comedy," became enormously popular in the 1920s, and did better at the box office at times than either Chaplin or Keaton.

Popular, too, from the beginning, was the most famous comedy team in film history: Laurel and Hardy. Stanley Laurel and Oliver Hardy had both acted in scores of films before joining forces, but it was not until they came together toward the end of the Silent Era that they began generating film magic. It was Hal Roach, another comedy maker like Sennett, who brought the two together in 1926. Their first efforts were tentative and groping, but they soon developed the two characters that made them beloved around the world: the thin, innocent-looking Laurel, with a penchant for mischief, and the fat, pompous Hardy, with the cherubic face and short temper. Very early, the "boys" (as their wives called them) developed their trademarks— Laurel's bewildered hair-scratching, panoramic smile, and descent into tears in sudden panic; and Hardy's embarrassed tie-fiddling, dumbfounded double takes, grandiose gestures, and resigned stare at the camera in disbelief at "another fine mess" his pal had gotten him into. In Laurel-and-Hardy films, the *dummkopf* duo faithfully observed the code duello: In a quarrel, each person takes his turn at hitting his opponent and then courteously waits for the latter to respond in kind. On occasion, too, the little quarrel gradually escalates into a battle royal, involving everybody in the vicinity. In *The Battle of the Century* (1927), which writer Henry Miller called "the greatest comic film ever made," Laurel and Hardy staged the biggest pie-throwing sequence ever to appear on the screen; *Two Tars* (1928) reaches its climax in a big car-wrecking fight that turns a highway into a junkyard; and *Big Business* (1929), one of the funniest comedy shorts ever made, ends in the "reciprocal destruction" of an entire house (belonging to old Scotchman James Finlayson) and scores of Christmas trees (which Laurel and Hardy are trying to peddle one summer day).[4] Reviewing movies for *The Spectator* in the 1930s, British writer Graham Greene ventured the heresy that Laurel-and-Hardy films were "more agreeable than Chaplin's."[5]

Laurel and Hardy made the transition to sound without difficulty and so did Harold Lloyd. Keaton, though, went into a quick decline with his sound pictures and the same fate befell Harry Langdon, a baby-faced comic who had promised much toward the end of the Silent Era. Chaplin, for his part, refused to give the Tramp a voice, but managed to survive gloriously anyway; *City Lights* (1931) and *Modern Times* (1936), masterpieces both, had music on the sound-track but no dialogue. When Chaplin finally capitulated to sound in *The Great Dictator* (1940), the Little Tramp was no more. By that time, a new group of comedians, for whom sound was crucial, had come to the fore and joined the American pantheon of comic greats: the Marx Brothers, Mae West, and W. C. Fields.

The new comedians stressed character as well as comic situations; they also went much further than the silent funnymen had gone in their assaults on middle-class respectability in all its forms. Beginning with *The Cocoanuts* (1929), the Marx Brothers—fast-talking Groucho, punster Chico, and pantomimist Harpo—brought anarchy to the screen, and by their feverish activity and breezy irreverence reduced one American sacred cow after another to absurdity: politics, war, democracy, government, education, opera, law, medicine, college sports. The Marx Brothers were masters of lateral logic. "Do you want to be wage slaves?" Groucho asks some bellboys in *The Cocoanuts* who are striking for higher wages. "Of course not. Well, what makes wage slaves? Wages. I want you to be free. Remember, there's nothing like *Liberty*, except *Collier's*, and *The Saturday Evening Post*. Be free, my friends. One for all and all for me—me for you and three for five and six for a quarter." In *Animal Crackers* (1930), Groucho and Chico sit down halfway through the picture to discuss the disappearance of a valuable painting belonging to

Groucho's high-society friend Margaret Dumont (whose baffled hauteur in Marx Brothers films surely deserved a special Oscar of some kind). "We'll search every room in the house," says Groucho. "What if it ain't in this house?" Chico asks. "Then we'll search the house next door," says Groucho. "What if there ain't no house next door?" Chico wants to know. "Then we'll build one," says Groucho. At that point the two start drawing up plans for building a house next door. "Cheerful maniacs" was what humorist Robert Benchley called them.[6]

The Marx Brothers kidded about everything. Mae West, another popular fun-maker in the thirties, concentrated on sex. "Sex," she once pointed out, "was out in the open" in her pictures.[7] La West looked sexy: an hourglass figure, wavy blond hair, a sensual face. She behaved sexy: swaggered and swayed, even in repose, with one arm akimbo. Above all, she talked sexy: Her sultry Brooklynese transformed the most innocent remarks into sexual statements. "It's not what I do, but the way I do it," she declared. "It's not what I say, but the way I say it." F. Scott Fitzgerald called her "the only Hollywood actress with an ironic edge and a comic spark." Her films abounded in worldly wisecracks: "it's better to be looked over than overlooked"; "it's not the men in my life that count; it's the life in my men"; "I'm a girl who lost her reputation and never missed it"; "good women are no fun; the only good woman I can recall in history was Betsy Ross; all she ever made was a flag."[8]

There were almost as many men as wisecracks in Mae West's films, and she always got the one she wanted in the end, and not by waiting for him to take the initiative either. Some people were offended by the open sexuality of films like She Done Him Wrong and I'm No Angel (both 1933). "Isn't it about time Congress did something about Mae West?" William Randolph Hearst once asked in an editorial in one of his newspapers.[9] Congress never got around to Mae West, but the Hays Office did; her later films, toned down by self-censorship, lacked the spice of her first pictures. By then, though, she had become as American as apple pie. "She is an institution," wrote New York Times reporter Steven V. Roberts, "a living legend, as much a part of American folklore as Paul Bunyan or Tom Sawyer or Babe Ruth."[10]

The greatest funnyman of the Depression era (and perhaps of any era) was the raspy-voiced W. C. Fields. Some of his admirers took to calling him "the Great Man," and The New Republic's acidulous Otis Ferguson thought his presence made even his inferior films worth seeing. Fields's appeal was in some ways puzzling. The roles he played were disreputable: card sharps, charlatans, cheapskates, deadbeats, boozers. His hatreds (on- and offscreen), moreover, were seemingly endless: children, dogs, bankers, doctors, cops, land-ladies. He muttered a great deal, too, in his pictures, and it takes more than one screening to catch all the acerbic asides. But he looked funny, with his bulbous nose, straw hat, and cigar, moved with grace (he had started out as a juggler), and was good at physical comedy: pratfalls, pantomime, mugging, double-takes. Above all, he loved the English language. Largely self-educated, he developed a passion for amusing-sounding words and high-falutin' ways of putting things, and he made wonderful use of them for comic purposes. "What a euphonious appellation," he tells Mae West in *My Little Chickadee* (1940), when she says her name is Flowerbelle; he goes on to ask if he can kiss her "symmetrical digits" ("Sure, help your-self," is the reply). Other favorites of Fields: taradiddle, peregrina-tions, effulgency, comquat, cognomen, nomenclature, amanuensis. The name Cuthbert, though, turned his stomach, at least if it was the name of his film daughter's seemingly wimpish boyfriend. Fields wrote most of his own screenplays and picked his noms de plume (and names for the characters he portrayed on the screen) with ten-der-loving care: Otis J. Cribblecoblis, Mahatma Kane Jeeves, Egbert Sousé, Cuthbert J. Twillie, Larson E. Whipsnade. Most of his best work—like that of the Marx Brothers and Mae West—was in the early thirties. But his later work is also rewarding, and *The Bank Dick* (1940) may well be his best picture.

By the late thirties the golden age of comedy was rapidly coming to an end. The Marx Brothers were running out of steam, a sanitized Mae West was no longer packing them in, and even W. C. Fields was not always in top form anymore. With Walt Disney's animated cartoons (Mickey Mouse) and Warner Bros.' Bugs Bunny replacing two-reel comedies in popularity, moreover, Laurel and Hardy were losing out, too, and they turned to making feature pictures, with mostly disappointing results. For a time, "screwball comedies," cen-tering on cornball heroes, scatterbrained heroines, nutty families, daffy dialogue, and madcap story lines, seized the public's fancy; and while most of them seem dated today, the best ones are still delightful: *It Happened One Night* (1934), *My Man Godfrey* (1936), *Bringing Up Baby* (1938). In the forties and fifties a new group of talented comedians appeared on the screen—Bob Hope, Red Skel-ton, Danny Kaye, Jerry Lewis—but they lacked the bite of Hollywood's greatest comic figures and, except to aficionados, their films are mostly forgettable. In the sixties and seventies came new faces: Mel Brooks, Gene Wilder, Goldie Hawn, and, above all, the bespectacled and self-deprecating schnook Woody Allen, who combined silliness with sophistication and thrilled highbrow moviegoers with his references to Freud and Kierkegaard. A sizzling young black talent, Eddie Murphy, with a fast-talking jive mouth, began taking the country by storm in the eighties and has shown signs of becoming this decade's leading comedian on the screen.[11]

Mark Twain thought the world's ills came mainly from hypocrisy and humbug, particularly in high places, and he was convinced that humanity's last, best hope lay in laughter. Unfortunately, he observed, most people saw the comic side of only "low-grade and trivial things" and overlooked the "high-grade comicalities" that permeated society and government.[12] Had Twain lived into Hollywood's Golden Age, he would undoubtedly have enjoyed the fun its comedians had with "low-grade and trivial things"; but he would have adored the way the best of them went after "high-grade comicalities" too. The world is still ailing, despite their fun-making, but who is to say it wouldn't be worse off without their comedy? Laughter's work, as Twain realized, is never done. A good horselaugh, H. L. Mencken used to say, is worth ten thousand syllogisms.

Keystone Pies

One day back in 1913 a director was trying to get the cross-eyed Ben Turpin to laugh, but Turpin didn't feel like laughing. Then Mabel Normand noticed on a bench a lemon meringue pie that some workmen had brought to lunch, and she picked it up and hurled it smack into Turpin's face. Turpin laughed good-naturedly and wiped the pie from his face. Afterward, when Mack Sennett saw the pie scene in the projection room, he almost fell over with delight. So did audiences when the film was released. Pie throwing at once joined pratfalls and mad chases as stock in trade for the Keystone comedies. The studio bought so many pies from a nearby grocery store that the proprietor began specializing in custard pies. "Those were a special kind of pie," Sennett once explained. "They were full of a sort of paste and sticky stuff so that when they hit they didn't splatter too much, but dripped nice and gooey."[13]

Keaton on Comics

Buster Keaton learned early that audiences don't like it when a comic is smarter than they are. In one of his pictures, he recalled, "a guy goes by eating a banana and drops the banana peel. Then I come on the other way, turn the corner and walk into the camera. Everyone knows that I'm going to slip on the banana peel—only I don't. I walk right over the peel and give the high sign into the camera. Okay, so we preview the picture. The scene doesn't get a titter. Not a titter and nobody can figure out why. Finally I get the idea and we go back and shoot the scene over again. We do it exactly the same, only this time, after I walk over the banana peel and into the camera, giving the high sign, the camera follows me and I slip on another banana peel that I haven't seen and down I go. Yaks. The audience wants his comic to be human, not clever."[14]

Getting Down

In 1925 Buster Keaton hired Robert E. Sherwood to write an original screenplay for him in order to give the film a touch of class. Sherwood went to work and soon came up with a story about a young couple who are at the top of a sixty-story building under construction in New York when they discover the elevator has stopped working for the night. The trouble was that Sherwood couldn't devise an interesting way of getting the couple down from the building and so nothing ever came of the idea. Thirty years later Keaton ran into Sherwood in the lobby of the Savoy Hotel in London. "Don't worry, Buster," cried Sherwood as soon as he saw the stone-faced comedian. "I'll get you down from there yet!"[15]

New Suit

When Charlie Chaplin's mother came from England to the United States and saw her son for the first time in his screen costume, she cried: "Charlie, I have to get you a new suit!"[16]

Charlot

One afternoon when Charlie Chaplin was in Paris, he slipped away from his hotel to take a walk on the Left Bank. But as he was strolling along the streets he received an urgent call of nature. He stopped to ask a porter where he could find a men's room, but since he couldn't speak French and the porter knew no English, he couldn't get his message across. He then decided to convey his plight by pantomime;

he grunted and groaned and wriggled and rolled his eyes to heaven. But he only succeeded in frightening the porter away. He then tried his pantomime on a cab driver, but only managed to amuse him by his antics.

While Chaplin was working on the cabbie, people began stopping to watch him and soon they were breaking into applause. But just as he was about to lose hope, a shopkeeper who knew some English came out of his store and said, "Do you want a job? You could draw in the customers, my amiable citizen." "Not a job," gasped Chaplin, "a toilet!" Suddenly the shopkeeper recognized him. "Charlot!" he screamed in ecstasy. "Charlot!" At this point Chaplin rushed into the store, found a restroom in back, ran in, slammed the door, and locked it. But the crowd followed him in, shouting his name in French, and began tearing the place apart. First they got the door down and then the walls, and then they began fighting over souvenirs of the occasion. Chaplin managed to escape before they started in on his clothes and by the time he got back to his hotel his peristalsis was gone. After that he was always careful about his casual strolls about town.[17]

Fortuitous Trick

When he began making The Great Dictator (1940), Charlie Chaplin had some doubts about a picture satirizing Adolf Hitler. "What do you think?" he asked friends. "Truly. Should I make it? What if something happens? To Hitler. Or the situation. I could be stuck with nothing. What do you think?" "Charlie," his friend Douglas Fairbanks told him firmly, "you don't have a choice! This is one of the most fortuitous tricks in the history of civilization—that the greatest living villain in the world and the greatest comedian should look alike. Now stop asking 'if' and get on with it."[18]

Tying One On

Not long before he began directing Laurel-and-Hardy comedies, Leo McCarey was in New York with Mabel Normand, Hal Roach, and Charley Chase, and one evening they decided to go off to a nightclub. But McCarey had never learned how to tie a bow tie and he asked for help. "Let's nobody tie his tie," said Normand mischievously. So they all left McCarey with his black tie hanging down and told him to join them as soon as he finished dressing. McCarey sat in the hotel room cursing his luck for a while and then recalled that his friend Lee Garmes, a Paramount cameraman, had told him that he, too, had trouble handling bow ties and that his wife, a professional skater, was good at it. So McCarey called Hollywood, learned that Garmes was in New York, too, and finally managed to track him down. "You're in luck," Garmes told him. "My wife's about to go out to work but she'll stop by on her way and tie your tie." A little later Mrs. Garmes came by and made a beautiful bow knot for McCarey.

With a look of triumph McCarey arrived in the nightclub and told his friends what had happened. No sooner had he finished than Normand reached over and pulled the bow out of his tie. "You little son-of-a-bitch!" exclaimed McCarey, as everyone laughed, and then Hal Roach pulled out his own tie, to general applause. The tie pulling quickly became contagious. "It began to spread to other tables," McCarey later reported, "and everybody started pulling each other's ties and, running out of ties to pull—it was too much fun to stop—they started ripping collars off—rrrriip—until everybody's collar was off. Then somebody got an idea that if you took a knife you could start up the seam of a tuxedo, then grab ahold and tear it, and this was very effective." Before long the nightclub was in shambles. "Well," McCarey liked to tell people, "*that* was the basis for at least a dozen Laurel and Hardy pictures."[19]

Applause
Asked why he left the stage for films, humorist Will Rogers (who made both silent and sound movies) drawled: "Pictures are the only business where you can sit out front and applaud yourself."[20]

Writing for the Marx Brothers
George S. Kaufman wrote the script for *The Cocoanuts,* a smash hit on Broadway, which became the Marx Brothers' first movie. But he didn't like writing for the comedy team because there was so much ad-libbing. Once, while he was watching *The Cocoanuts* backstage, a friend came up to chat. "Shush!" cried Kaufman. "I think I heard one of my lines!" Asked to write another show for the Marxes, he reportedly exclaimed: "Are you crazy? *Write* a show for the Marx Brothers? I'd rather write for the Barbary pirates." He once asked: "How can you write for Harpo? What do you put down on paper? All you can say is 'Harpo enters,' and then he's on his own." But Kauf-

man worked on the scripts for *Animal Crackers* (1930) and *A Night at the Opera* (1935), among the Marx Brothers' best.[21]

Pursuit

Harpo's problem was that since he didn't speak, he had to keep thinking up things to do if he wasn't to be overshadowed by Groucho and Chico. Once, to throw Groucho off balance, he paid a chorus girl in *The Cocoanuts* to run suddenly across the stage so he could run after her, leering and honking his horn. Groucho took it calmly; he simply looked up, said, "The nine-twenty's right on time," and went on with his scene. Harpo's chase brought a big laugh and it became part of his routine on stage and in films. After the show he learned that the chorus girl was a friend of gangster Legs Diamond; he quickly found a new girl for the show.[22]

Late for the Show

Harpo Marx liked to tell the story of how he was late for a matinee because he was stopped by a cop for speeding. He told the officer he was playing downtown in a show and was already late for the performance. "I'm one of the Marx Brothers," he said, "and if you'll let me go, I'll give you two free seats." "I hate the Marx Brothers," said the cop, taking out his ticket book. "Well," said Harpo, "would your wife like to go? I'll give her the seats." "My wife hates the Marx Brothers," said the cop. "Well," said Harpo, "is there anyone in your family who does like us?" "Yeah," said the cop, "I think Aunt Sophie does." "Great," said Harpo, "how about two free seats for Aunt Sophie?" "Not on your life," said the cop. "We hate Aunt Sophie." Harpo gave up at this point. "So he wrote out the ticket," he reported afterward, "and that's how I was late for the show." Chico's daughter, though, claimed this was rightfully Chico's, not Harpo's, story.[23]

Testing

Groucho said the only sure way to test a gag was to try it out on Zeppo, the fourth brother, who played romantic leads in the first few Marx Brothers movies. If he liked it, said Groucho, they threw it out.[24]

Guy in Pittsburgh

"Making a film with Garbo," said Robert Montgomery, "does not constitute an introduction." Garbo was extremely reserved and became coldly indignant if someone sought to intrude on her privacy. Once Groucho Marx saw her approaching in slacks and a floppy hat, and he stopped, bent down in his famous crouch, and peeked up under the brim. When he met her icy look, he quickly backed away, muttering: "Pardon me, ma'am, I thought you were a guy I knew in Pittsburgh."[25]

Half-Jewish

Once Groucho Marx phoned a Beverly Hills swimming club from which his tearful son Arthur had just been barred. "My son is only half-Jewish," said Groucho, "so could he go in up to his bellybutton?"[26]

Hamlet

"Mr. Marx," a *Los Angeles Times* reporter asked Groucho soon after he arrived in Hollywood for his latest picture, "do you want to play Hamlet?" Groucho gave him the eye and replied: "Not unless he gives me a stroke a hole!"[27]

Conferences with Thalberg

In 1935, the Marx Brothers moved from Paramount to MGM, and their first conference with Irving Thalberg was set for ten o'clock in the morning. The Marxes arrived on time, waited four hours for Thalberg, and finally left. The next day the appointment was for two o'clock, but they didn't get to see Thalberg until three. "Now, look, Mr. Thalberg," said Groucho angrily, "we've been stars in three Broadway shows, in vaudeville and in motion pictures. When we have an appointment, we are accustomed to having it kept. Yesterday we waited four hours and finally left. Today we were kept waiting an hour. In the future, don't ever call us unless we can see you at the appointed hour."

Thalberg apologized and promised to be punctual from then on. At the Marx Brothers' next appointment, he had them ushered into his office right on time. But after they had been conferring for about twenty minutes, he was called away on an urgent matter. "Okay, let's show him," said Harpo. So the brothers pushed filing cabinets against the door, climbed out of the window, and left. The next time they met, Thalberg was on time, but, again, in the middle of the meeting, was called away on urgent business. This time Harpo got some potatoes from the commissary kitchen, Chico and Groucho built a big fire in the office fireplace, and all three took off their clothes. When Thalberg returned, he found the Marx Brothers sitting stark naked in front of the fire roasting potatoes. "Wait a minute, boys!" he said gamely, and then phoned the commissary to send butter for the potatoes. He never walked out on them again.[28]

Clay and Wood

Sam Wood directed two Marx Brothers movies, but the brothers Marx frequently clashed with him because he insisted on so many takes to shoot a scene. They felt that by the tenth take all the spontaneity was gone. One day, while shooting *A Day at the Races* (1937), the Marx Brothers made such mincemeat out of Wood's direction that he finally lost his temper. "You can't make an actor out of clay!" he exploded. "Nor a director out of Wood!" shot back Groucho.[29]

Getting Paid

In the summer of 1936, the Marx Brothers took their new show, *A Day at the Races*, on a road tour to try out some new scenes before filming them. In San Francisco one night, when the house was packed and the audience enthusiastic, the show went over its schedule of one hour. To speed things up, the director sent Groucho onstage while Chico was playing the piano. Groucho went into his routine, but the audience wanted Chico to keep playing and began booing Groucho. Groucho waited calmly until the audience quieted down and then said: "I have to stay here—I'm getting paid. But nobody's keeping you." That brought the house down and the show was able to go on.[30]

Fredonia

When the Marx Brothers made *Duck Soup* (1933), a satiric comedy about a zany utopia called Freedonia, they didn't realize there was a little town in New York pronounced the same way. To their surprise, shortly after the picture's release, the mayor of the New York town wrote an angry letter to Paramount to complain. "The name of Fredonia has been without a blot since 1817," he declared. "I feel it is my duty as Mayor to question your intentions in using the name of our city in your picture." Groucho took it upon himself to write back. "Your Excellency," he said, "our advice is that you change the name of your town. It is hurting our picture. Anyhow, what makes you think you're Mayor of Fredonia? Do you wear a black moustache, play a harp, speak with an Italian accent, or chase girls like Harpo? We are certain you do not. Therefore, we must be Mayor of Fredonia, not you. The old gray Mayor ain't what he used to be."[31]

Casablanca

When the Marx Brothers began working on *A Night in Casablanca* (1946), Warner Bros., citing the famous Humphrey Bogart–Ingrid Bergman film *Casablanca* (1942), threatened a lawsuit. "I had no idea that the city of Casablanca belonged exclusively to Warner Bros. . . . ," Groucho wrote the studio. He was sure, though, he went on to say, that the average movie fan could learn in time to distinguish between Ingrid Bergman and Harpo. "I don't know whether I could," he added, "but I certainly would like to try." Then he got to the point. "You claim you own Casablanca and that no one else can use that name without your permission," he wrote. "You probably have the right to use the name Warner, but what about Brothers? Professionally, we were brothers long before you were. . . . Now, Jack, how about you? Do you maintain that yours is an original name? Well, it's not. It was used long before you were born. Offhand, I can think of two Jacks—there was Jack of 'Jack and the Beanstalk' and Jack the Ripper, who cut quite a figure in his day. . . . As for you, Harry, you probably sign your checks, sure in the belief that you are the first Harry of all time and that all other Harrys are imposters. I can think of two Harrys that preceded you. There was Lighthouse Harry of Revolutionary fame and a Harry Applebaum who lived on the corner of 93rd and Lexington Avenue."

Groucho's letter puzzled people at Warners. They wrote again asking him if he could give them some idea of what *A Night in Casablanca* was about. "There isn't much I can tell you about the story," Groucho wrote back. "In it, I play a Doctor of Divinity who ministers to the natives and, as a sideline, hawks can openers and pea jackets to the savages along the Gold Coast of Africa. . . . When I first meet Chico, he is working in a saloon, selling sponges to barflies who are unable to carry their liquor. Harpo is an Arabian caddie who lives in a small Grecian urn on the outskirts of the city. . . . As the picture opens, Porridge, a mealy-mouthed native girl, is sharpening some arrows for the hunt. Paul Hangover, our hero, is constantly lighting two cigarettes simultaneously. He apparently is unaware of the cigarette shortage."

Groucho's second letter seems to have puzzled the Warners people even more than the first one. They wrote back to say they still didn't understand the story line and would appreciate more details. Groucho at once wrote to say there had been some plot changes. "In the new version, I play Bordello, the sweetheart of Humphrey Bogart," he told them. "Harpo and Chico are itinerant rug peddlers who are weary of laying rugs and enter a monastery just for a lark. This is a good joke on them, as there hasn't been a lark in the place for fifteen years. . . . Across from this monastery, hard by a jetty, is a waterfront hotel, chock-full of apple-cheeked damsels, most of whom have been banned by the Hays Office for soliciting. . . . Harpo marries a hotel detective; Chico operates an ostrich farm. Humphrey Bogart's girl, Bordello, spends her last years in a Bacall house."

Warners dropped the subject at this point. But not Groucho. When Warners announced production of *Night and Day* (1946), a Cole Porter biopic, Groucho wrote the studio to complain that the title was stolen from the Marx Brothers' *A Night at the Opera* (1935) and *A Day at the Races* (1937).[32]

All the Joy
Once, when he was in Montreal, Groucho was getting out of an elevator and a priest came up to him. "Groucho," he said, putting out his hand, "I want to thank you for all the joy you've put in the world." "Thank you, Father," said Groucho, shaking his hand. "And I want to thank you for all the joy you've taken out of it."[33]

Quitting Time
After the Marx Brothers moved from New York to Hollywood to do movies, Chico had a way of arriving late on the set in the morning and then trying to leave early on the pretext that "it's after quitting time in New York."[34]

Big Question
Groucho was just as irreverent offscreen as on. Once he attended a spiritualists' meeting and when the medium got in contact with the

Great Spirit and asked for questions from the audience, he got up and asked: "What's the capital of North Dakota?"[35]

Helpful

One day a local newshen called on Mae West for an interview. "Miss West," she said, "do you think you would like to be a mother and would you be a good mother if you were a mother?" Somewhat surprised, West said, "Are you a mother yourself?" "I am not," said the reporter firmly, "nor am I even married." "Neither am I," said West. "This ought to be a real helpful conversation."[36]

Secret

One day Mae West and Alison Skipworth were ready to play a scene, but the latter was on edge, because she was afraid West was going to steal it. She told the director that West's timing was ruining the characterization she was creating and to West she said haughtily: "You forget I've been an actress for forty years." "Don't worry, dear," said West with a little smile. "I'll keep your secret."[37]

Night School

Hedda Hopper once asked Mae West how she came to know so much about men. "Baby," said West, "I went to night school!"[38]

Playwright

"I always thought Mae West was the most famous figure in drama," Tennessee Williams once said, "and she had the figure to prove it." When the comedienne heard of Williams's remark, she said, matter-of-factly, "It's true. When you think about it, what other playwrights are there besides O'Neill, Tennessee and me?"[39]

The West Way

Discussing a script with Mae West, director Ernst Lubitsch criticized her for taking all the good lines and giving none to the other performers. "I'm writin' the story and I'm the star," she said firmly. "But in every story there must be two characters," persisted Lubitsch. "Look at *Romeo and Juliet*." "Let Shakespeare do it his way," said West huffily, "I'll do it mine. We'll see who comes out better."[40]

Not Easy

At a dinner at Roddy McDowall's, opera star Beverly Sills spoke graciously to Mae West about the opera scene in *Goin' To Town* (1935) and asked: "Who dubbed 'My Heart at Thy Sweet Voice' for you?" "What do y'mean, who dubbed it?" cried West. "I sang it myself. After all, I've got a trained voice." "I wasn't aware," said Sills nervously, hoping to drop the subject, "how wonderful." "Do you know that aria?" West asked. "Oh, I think I used to," stammered Sills. "I don't anymore." "Well, I'll tell you one thing about it," West told the Metropolitan Opera diva, "it isn't easy."[41]

Good Line

When he was making *Tillie and Gus* (1933), W. C. Fields did some ad-libbing in one scene that cost Paramount plenty. In this particular scene, which was shot after eleven o'clock at night, he was working in a diver's costume, something was supposed to have gone wrong, and he was hauled up, presumably half drowned, and the script called for him to gasp, "Is there a doctor in the house?" This was a good line, everybody thought, and the reaction of audiences later proved they were right. But instead of speaking the line, Fields pointed at his gigantic diving footgear and, referring to a famous prizefighter, exclaimed: "Primo Carnera's carpet slippers." When reproved for changing the line, he said, "Why, that's funny. Everybody knows about Carnera's big feet." But it was necessary to redo the scene and it was now approaching midnight. On coming up a second time, Fields pointed to his massive diving shoes again and said: "Charlie Frobisher's bedroom slippers." He was again scolded for changing the line. "What's the matter with you?" said Fields. "Don't you know the name, Charlie Frobisher, always gets a laugh? People will howl at it." The director had never heard Fields do such bad ad-libbing, and he began wondering whether the old master was losing his touch. It was now past midnight. Fields was sent into the tank again and this time, on coming up, he spoke the proper line. But it soon became clear that Fields had by no means lost his touch; his contract, it turned out, gave him $800 extra every time he worked past midnight.[42]

Transfusion

When one of W. C. Fields's favorite directors became ill, he offered himself for a blood transfusion, but the doctor said firmly, "On the contrary, we're trying to get the alcohol out of him!" And when Fields himself got injured, Wilson Mizner sent him a telegram: SORRY YOU ARE HURT. MY BLOOD IS TWO-THIRDS FORMALDEHYDE FROM DRINKING HOLLYWOOD GIN. HOWEVER IF YOU NEED BLOOD TRANSFUSION CAN LET YOU HAVE TWO QUARTS.[43]

Inflation

Whenever the federal excise tax on liquor went up, W. C. Fields would lament: "The cost of living has gone up another dollar a quart."[44]

Might Come Back

Harpo Marx visited W. C. Fields once and the latter showed him his attic. It was filled with hundreds of cases of liquor. "Bill," said Harpo, "what's with all the booze?" "Never can be sure Prohibition won't come back, my boy," explained Fields.[45]

Looking Better

W. C. Fields once hired a doctor to stop him from drinking, but at the same he did everything he could to outwit the doctor. Gradually, though, the doctor gained the upper hand; he tracked down nearly all of Fields's hiding places and blocked off nearly all of his private suppliers. Then one day Fields offered to teach the doctor how to play golf. "That's fine," said the doctor. "Both of us should be more in the open air."

Fields's golfing attire was a baggy suit of tweed. His chief instruction to his pupil was to tell him the main point about golf was to stare intently at the ball before swinging at it. "You can't stare at it too long," Fields said. "Before you take a cut at it, count to ten slowly." So Fields carefully arranged the doctor in a golfing stance and then stepped directly behind him. "Now count," he ordered. "One . . . two. . . ," began the doctor. "Much slower," cried Fields. "One . . . two. . . ." "Still slower," said Fields. "Now, don't take your eye off the ball." As the doctor stared and counted slowly, Fields took a small bottle from his voluminous tweeds and drained it. And every time the doctor concentrated on the ball thereafter, Fields followed the same procedure, for he had loaded his suit with little bottles of whiskey. For eight days Fields gave the doctor golf lessons this way. "Now you have been eight days without a drink," said the doctor finally, "and you're looking better already!"[46]

Blackout

For a time W. C. Fields lived in a large house a level or two below
Cecil B. De Mille's place. One night during World War II there was a
blackout, and since Fields didn't seem to be aware of it, De Mille
went down to his place and rang the bell. "I'm Cecil De Mille," he
announced, when Fields, slightly under the weather, opened the
door. "There's a blackout going on." "A what?" cried Fields. "Don't
you know we're having a blackout?" snorted De Mille. "A blackout!" repeated Fields uncertainly. "Yes, Mr. Fields, a blackout," said
De Mille impatiently. "Turn off your lights and fill your bathtub."
The reference to emergency storing of drinking water missed Fields
completely; all he could think of was the elaborate bathing sequences in De Mille pictures. "My God, cease!" he shouted. "Can't
we have a blackout without one of your bathtub scenes?"[47]

Loopholes

There is a story that when W. C. Fields was on his death bed, he
suddenly reared up and told his cronies: "You know, I've . . . been
thinking about . . . those poor little newsies out . . . there. Peddling
their papers in cold . . . and rain . . . sole support of . . . their mothers. I want . . . to do something for them." "Wonderful!" exclaimed
his friends. "That's wonderful, Bill." Fields lapsed into silence for a
moment and then murmured: "On second thought,———'em!" A
little later, a friend dropped by and found him reading the Bible. He
was astonished. "Bill," he exclaimed, "what in the world are you
doing reading the Bible?" "Looking for loopholes," explained
Fields.[48]

What Happened

Frank Capra thought a film about the making of It Happened One
Night (1934) might have been funnier than the prize-winning film
itself. He happened to pick up Cosmopolitan in a barbershop one
day, he recalled, came across Samuel Hopkins Adams's short story
"Night Bus," liked it, and decided to film it. "Forget bus pictures,"
Columbia's Harry Cohn told him. "People don't want 'em. MGM
and Universal just made two bus operas and they both stink."

But Capra went ahead anyway. In the fall of 1933 he went into a
huddle with Robert Riskin and they came up with a screenplay they
called It Happened One Night to show Cohn. "Well," said Cohn,
"I'm glad you took that lousy 'bus' outta the title." But Columbia

executives were hostile; they said it was "nothing but a bus picture," without any "oomph," and insisted the title was too long. "Well, Frank," said Cohn at the next story conference, "let's get off the pot. What about this bus picture?" "Harry," said Capra, "I've listened to all the comments. . . . But I don't agree with them. I like the script, and I want to *make* it—as is." "All right," Cohn finally said. "We've screwed around enough with this bus thing. If Capra wants to make it, that's good enough for me."

Casting was the next problem. Myrna Loy turned down the part of the girl and so did Margaret Sullavan, Miriam Hopkins, and Constance Bennett. Gradually it dawned on Capra that the leading characters—the girl, a spoiled young rich girl, and the guy, a long-haired Greenwich Village painter—were not very appealing. So Capra and Robert Riskin rewrote the parts and made the heroine a feisty young woman who was bored with being rich and the guy a tough, crusading reporter. "Now, Harry," Capra told Cohn, "if we can cast a good man star first, it'll be easier to get a girl."

Capra finally cast the leads, but both were reluctant players at first. MGM loaned Clark Gable to Columbia (which lacked MGM's prestige) to punish him for demanding more money, and Gable was miffed at being sent "to a little independent on Poverty Row—Siberia for me." Next came the leading lady. "I gotta brainstorm—" Cohn suddenly told Capra at the next conference. "Claudette Colbert." "Colbert?" cried Capra. "She's under contract to Paramount." "Yeah, yeah," said Cohn, "but she's taking a four-week vacation. And I hear that French broad likes money. Why don't you and Riskin go to see her personal?" Capra did just that. "Paramount pays me twenty-five thousand per picture," Colbert told him. "You *double* that, and finish with me four weeks from today—which you can't—so please leave me alone." To her surprise, Capra agreed to her terms. "Oh, for God's sake!" she cried. "I'll do the picture." But she said she was leaving for Sun Valley on December 23; it was now November 21.

Shooting the film got off to a bad start. Gable was still sore at being exiled to Columbia, and it took a couple of days before he began enjoying his part in the picture. As for Colbert, she argued a lot with Capra about her part at first. In the famous hitchhiking scene in which she proves that her leg is more persuasive than Gable's thumb, she refused to lift her dress. But when Capra hired a chorus girl with shapely legs to double for her, Colbert cried: "Get her out of here! I'll do it. That's not *my* leg." The "walls of Jericho" scene—in which Colbert and Gable separate the twin beds in a motel room by a blanket draped over a clothesline—also gave trouble for a time. Colbert refused to undress in front of the camera because she wanted to feature her acting, not her figure. But this produced an even sexier scene: Gable watching her drape her underthings one by one on the "walls of Jericho." When shooting was completed in record time and Colbert joined her friends in Sun Valley, she was quoted as saying, "Am I glad to get here! I've just finished the worst picture of the year."

At the preview the audience liked *It Happened One Night,* but some of the Columbia people were critical; they thought it too long (two hours) and urged cuts. "Whatta ya say, Frank?" asked Cohn. "I'm sick of it, Harry," sighed Capra. "Ship it!" So Cohn gave the order: "Ship it!" To everyone's astonishment, Capra's new film was a big hit with both critics and the public. And in February 1935 it won five Oscars: best picture, best actress, best actor, best screenplay, and best director. Columbia was no longer a Poverty Row Studio.[49]

Finding and Losing

When Gregory La Cava was directing the cockamamie comedy *My Man Godfrey* (1936), he and William Powell, who played the butler, Godfrey, disagreed on how Powell's part should be played. "You haven't found Godfrey yet!" La Cava told Powell. So the two of them sat down one evening over some Scotch to discuss the character. Hours (and a bottle or two of Scotch) later, they finally reached perfect agreement on the character Powell was playing. The next morning La Cava arrived at the studio with a terrible headache but determined to get in a good day's work on the picture. But Powell failed to show up. Finally a telegram signed by Powell was delivered to La Cava. It read: WE MAY HAVE FOUND GODFREY LAST NIGHT BUT WE LOST POWELL. SEE YOU TOMORROW.[50]

Hillside

During the filming of *Bringing Up Baby* (1938), director Howard Hawks was impressed by Katharine Hepburn's gift for improvisation. "In one scene she broke the heel of a shoe," he recalled. "She was right on camera, and without fluffing a line, she said, as she limped, 'I was born on the side of a hill!'"[51]

Little Bee

Walt Disney, famous the world over for his animated cartoons, admitted he was not a great draftsman and that after 1926 he didn't even do any of the drawing for the pictures coming from his studio. His strength lay in his ability to think up ideas for engaging characters—Mickey Mouse, Donald Duck, Goofy, Pluto—developing plots, and making imaginative use of technical resources available to filmmakers. "Do you draw Mickey Mouse?" a little boy asked him one day. Disney admitted he didn't draw anymore. "Then you think up all the jokes and ideas?" persisted the lad. "No," said Disney, "I don't do that." "Mr. Disney," said the boy, puzzled, "just what do you do?" "Well," Disney later said he told the boy, "sometimes I think of myself as a little bee. I go from one area of the studio to another and gather pollen and sort of stimulate everybody."[52]

Triplets

In May 1933, Walt Disney's animated cartoon *Three Little Pigs*, about three little pigs and a hungry wolf, opened at Radio City Music Hall. Since it was an innovative cartoon short, in color and with special music, Disney expected a good response, but to his disappointment, critics and audiences were lukewarm about it. Then the cartoon comedy was shown in other movie theaters in New York and suddenly caught on. The next thing Disney knew, radio stations and band leaders were asking for permission to play one of the songs featured in the film: "Who's Afraid of the Big Bad Wolf?" Disney hadn't even arranged to publish the music, and to meet demands for sheet music he had to send musicians with flashlights into darkened theaters to copy down words and music from the screen. The song soon swept the country; the Big Bad Wolf became a kind of symbol of the Great Depression against which Americans were fighting. President Roosevelt let it be known it was one of his favorite films. And in December, when Mrs. Disney gave birth to a baby girl, she almost said she wished she had given her husband a son and then corrected herself. It should have been triplets![53]

Mickey's Tail

Perhaps the best sequence in Walt Disney's *Fantasia* (1940) is the one featuring Mickey Mouse as the Sorcerer's Apprentice, to the accompaniment of Paul Dukas's music. When Disney was supervising this part of the film, he began acting out scenes the way he wanted the animators to portray Mickey and got so caught up in what he was doing he practically became Mickey on the set. He walked like Mickey, rolled his eyes like Mickey, grinned like Mickey, and even ate like Mickey. One day, when he was Mickey-Mousing his way past some animators, he suddenly looked around after dodging a passing truck. "What's with the boss?" one of the animators asked. "He's looking around to see if that truck ran over his tail!" came the answer.[54]

Anti-Nazi

When Ernst Lubitsch's anti-Nazi comedy *To Be or Not To Be* (1942), starring Jack Benny and Carole Lombard, opened in Miami, Jack's father went to see it, and when he saw Jack appear on the screen wearing a Nazi uniform, he left the theater in a fury. Late that night Jack, who heard what had happened, called to explain, but his father let loose a flood of abuse. Finally Jack interrupted, told him the movie was a satire, and explained that in the film he was only pretending to be a Nazi in order to rescue some people from the Nazis. The following day Jack's father went to see the movie again, loved it, and went to see it every day after that as long as it played in Miami. And he usually cried at the end too.[55]

Big Kick

One afternoon in 1943 Eleanor Roosevelt, the first lady, entertained Bob Hope, Groucho Marx, Jimmy Cagney, and several other Hollywood stars on the White House lawn to thank them for the work they were doing entertaining U.S. troops. As she passed down the line and greeted each of the performers rather formally, she came to comedienne Charlotte Greenwood, famous for her comic dances and for her ability to kick her long legs high over her head. As Mrs. Roosevelt approached, Greenwood suddenly did one of her big kicks, and Groucho Marx leaned over and told Mrs. Roosevelt, "That's what you could do, if you just put your mind to it." The first lady moved quickly on without comment.[56]

Blond

When the script for *Up in Arms* (1944) was finished and comedian Danny Kaye arrived in Hollywood to do his scenes, Sam Goldwyn looked at the first test and was horrified. "He looks too—too—" Goldwyn sputtered, unable to bring himself to say "Jewish." "Well," said his wife, "he *is* Jewish." But Goldwyn summoned Kaye to his office and ordered: "Do something about your nose." But Kaye refused, and Goldwyn continued to growl about the way he looked in new tests.

One night Goldwyn sat up all night discussing the picture with his wife, and the next morning they went to the studio to look at Kaye's screen tests again. Suddenly Goldwyn jumped to his feet and cried: "I've got it! I've got it!" He grabbed the telephone and called the hairdressing department. "Expect Danny Kaye in ten minutes," he shouted. "He'll be having his hair dyed blond." A little later Kaye's reddish brown hair was transformed into a wavy mane of blond hair, and after the release of *Up in Arms* it became his trademark. He became so famous that he began receiving letters from all over the world, some of them addressed simply to "Danny Kaye, U.S.A." And people cited Goldwyn's brainstorm about Kaye's hair as another example of his genius as a filmmaker.[57]

Playing Comedy
When character actor Edmund Gwenn was on his death bed in the hospital in 1959, George Seaton, who had directed him in his Oscar-winning role as Santa Claus in *Miracle on 34th Street* (1947), dropped by for a visit one day and was so distressed to see how ill he was that he sighed: "It's tough, isn't it?" "Yes it is," Gwenn is said to have murmured. "But it's not as tough as playing comedy."[58]

Poifect Gent
When MGM's dignified leading lady Greer Garson appeared on long-nosed comedian Jimmy ("Schnozzola") Durante's TV show, the latter was anxious for everyone to behave properly. "Miss Garson is a perfect lady," he said, "so watch yourselves." That afternoon he went over a routine with Garson. "You say dis and den dere's a laugh," he explained. "Den I say dis and den dere's a laugh." "But what if they don't laugh?" she asked. "Den we both go down the terlet," said Durante.[59]

Aunt Minnie
Billy Wilder was a patient director, but when he was working on the comedy *Some Like It Hot* (1959), he almost lost his mind coping with Marilyn Monroe's lateness on the set and her insistence on going over the dialogue dozens of times before shooting. Finally he simply resigned himself to the inevitable. "My Aunt Minnie would always be punctual and never hold up production," he told columnist Sheilah Graham, "but who would pay to see my Aunt Minnie?"[60]

CHAPTER 19

Musicals

With the coming of soundtracks for movies, musicals were spectacular successes as well as failures for nearly half a century. A number of singing or dancing performers attained stardom and worldwide popularity before studio financial limitations curtailed production of the costly musical. In the interim, innovators had exercised their talents to make the era of musicals one of the most memorable in Hollywood history.

The first talkie, *The Jazz Singer* (1927), was also a musical, and its success transformed Warner Bros. into a major studio. By 1929 the more tune-filled the movies were, the better. "All singing! All dancing! All talking!" became an industry motto. Musicals were literally ground out by the score, while even dramatic pictures celebrated the coming of sound with a song or two. The saturation point was quickly reached, and three years later the screen musical was virtually dead. The singing actors who had recently made moviegoers giddy with delight had suddenly become a drug on the market. Exhibitors were assuring customers on theater displays that their latest attraction was *not* a musical.

Although the early-style musicals seemed dead, production head Darryl F. Zanuck at Warners sensed that the time was ripe for fantasy involving song and dance. With the Depression at its lowest ebb, the country yearned for escape, and, Zanuck concluded, audiences would welcome a make-believe world where chorus lines replaced breadlines and success could be won for a song. With Lloyd Bacon directing and Busby Berkeley supervising choreography, Zanuck began a new era in musical films with *42nd Street* (1933), starring Ruby Keeler and Dick Powell. Jack Warner didn't know until the picture was screened that *42nd Street* was a musical, or he would have protested.[1] Harry Warren, who was working for Remick Music Company when Warners bought the music-publishing firm and moved him to California, collaborated with Al Dubin in writing the score. The songs were an immediate success, for people came out of theaters whistling the title tune, "Lullaby of Broadway," and "Shuffle Off to Buffalo," advertising the show more effectively than any team of publicists.

Most of the credit for *42nd Street*'s success, however, went to Busby Berkeley, whose cinematic choreography dazzled audiences. Feisty and sometimes abrasive, Berkeley was skilled in camera art, depending on cinematic tricks like top shots to make his work interesting, and creating a kaleidoscope of musical hallucinations. In *Footlight Parade* (1933) Berkeley closed his "By a Waterfall" number with a human fountain, while *Gold Diggers of 1933* found Ginger Rogers leading a group of girls wearing coin-covered costumes in a campy routine called "We're in the Money," while audiences wished that it were so.

Berkeley's revolution in musicals didn't go unnoticed by the other studios. *Flying Down to Rio* (1933) launched the peerless team of Fred Astaire and Ginger Rogers at RKO. Romantic and stylish, Rogers and Astaire demonstrated that stage dancing could be captured on film and made exciting. A dedicated worker and chronic perfectionist, Astaire conceived and rehearsed his numbers weeks in advance, most often with choreographer Hermes Pan. While Rogers was not his most talented partner, her forte lay in her ability to sell a number effectively. Together they were dynamite. Unlike Busby Berkeley, who specialized in ensembles, Astaire preferred not to move the camera in any conspicuous way, achieving his action by keeping the camera still and panning across the performers. Pandro Berman, their producer at RKO, wisely secured top songwriters—George Gershwin, Jerome Kern, Irving Berlin, and Cole Porter—so that each show boasted a superior score. Depression audiences came to identify with Astaire's unique style, in part because he infused his élan with touches of raffishness. It was said that Rogers gave Astaire sex appeal while he gave her class, but whatever the explanation, their chemistry was magic.

At Universal, teenager Deanna Durbin made a string of inexpensive pictures that saved the studio from bankruptcy. Beginning with *Three Smart Girls* (1936), she sang her way into the hearts of moviegoers around the world, introducing thousands to serious music in the process. Durbin possessed an excellent voice, which could have been trained for opera, but she was uncomfortable before the camera and disliked making movies. Henry Koster, who directed the first half-dozen of her pictures, went to her house nights to teach her the fundamentals of acting. He said, "The mouth goes up in the corners when you smile and goes down when you cry." That's where they started, but her first picture was a tremendous hit that made millions.[2]

Fox had its box-office darling in Shirley Temple, who sang and danced like a doll, whereas Paramount secured the leading crooner from radio, Bing Crosby. Crosby's melodious voice, together with his casual air and folksy personality, made him an immediate favorite. At the height of his popularity, he teamed with Bob Hope and Dorothy Lamour in *The Road to Singapore* (1940), which initiated a series that, by combining comedy and song, made the trio among the screen's top money-makers. By then all the major studios had songwriters under contract and had established high-quality music departments. Rather than try to work with an orchestra off to the side of a huge soundstage, Hollywood learned to prerecord musical numbers, with performers singing and dancing to a playback. Although there were problems synchronizing lips, the technical quality of sound was greatly enhanced.

Metro hit upon the winning combination of Jeanette MacDonald and Nelson Eddy in *Naughty Marietta* (1935), the first of a series of successful screen versions of popular operettas. *The Wizard of Oz* (1939) with Judy Garland, filmed in the new three-color process, was a musical version of L. Frank Baum's famous book and became a movie classic. Although it was a difficult picture to make because of the intense light then required for Technicolor, MGM established its reputation for producing top-quality original musicals, with no detail too small for close attention. In *The Wizard,* Ray Bolger, playing the Scarecrow, waited every morning while someone in wardrobe counted the pieces of straw sticking out of his arms before going on the set. "Detail was the thing Metro was known for," said Bolger.

"That's where they achieved their perfection. Every period piece was thought out—every clock on the mantelpiece, every cloisonné, or whatever."[3]

Throughout the 1940s and 1950s Metro remained the leading studio for musicals, attracting the cream of the Broadway musical world, putting together the best staff, and spending money lavishly. Producer Arthur Freed had been a songwriter himself and understood music. He also had an eye for talent, and headed his unit with brilliant, creative musicians capable of tastefully addressing a mass audience. Roger Edens, Lennie Hayton, Kay Thompson, and young André Previn all became part of the most spectacular production team in film history. Freed brought Van Johnson, June Allyson, Betty Garrett, and Nancy Walker from Broadway and showcased Gene Kelly. His choreographers were Robert Alton and Charles Walters; his composer-conductor was John Green. He wisely gave Vincente Minnelli the chance to direct instead of keeping him as art director. While Joe Pasternak and Jack Cummings produced their share of fine musicals at MGM, Freed's work represented the Hollywood musical at its best.

Once Freed hired his talented staff, he gave them the freedom to do their job as they saw fit, allowing them ample time for preparation. David O. Selznick had brought Gene Kelly to Hollywood after he won acclaim on Broadway in *Pal Joey*. Kelly made his first film, *For Me and My Gal* (1942), starring Judy Garland and directed by Busby Berkeley, on a loan-out to MGM. Freed quickly recognized that Kelly was a young man with fresh ideas about converting dance to the screen. Rather than the kind of numbers Berkeley had become famous for (forty pianos lighted with neon, a hundred girls playing violins), Kelly wanted to make dance interesting on a two-dimensional screen. A more athletic performer than Fred Astaire, Gene Kelly transferred much of his dance outdoors, giving the illusion of movement and space rather than the appearance of stage dancing. Freed made Kelly a choreographer and encouraged him to experiment with color, helping him create an American style of dance that eventually was uniquely cinematic.[4]

While Kelly's innovations started on *Cover Girl* (1944) with Rita Hayworth at Columbia, Metro remained his home base. *On the Town* (1949) broke new ground and altered the whole concept of screen musicals, most of it shot on location in New York. *An American in Paris* (1951), ending with a seventeen-minute ballet, won an

Academy Award for best picture. Irving Berlin, who had written scores for several MGM musicals, was dubious about the ballet and remarked to Vincente Minnelli, "I hope you boys know what you're doing."[5] The ballet, with Gershwin's music and in dazzling color, grew increasingly popular with audiences with the passage of time. But of all his work, Gene Kelly believed *Singin' in the Rain* (1952) would probably last the longest, not just for the thrilling title number alone, but also because of its statement on Hollywood and American society. "The way I look at a musical," Kelly explained, "you are commenting on the human condition no matter what you do. A musical may be light and frivolous, but by its very nature, it makes some kind of social comment."[6]

Fred Astaire, who had temporarily retired after making *Blue Skies* (1946) at Paramount, returned to MGM for *Easter Parade* (1948), when Gene Kelly broke an ankle. Astaire went on to achieve some of his biggest successes with the Freed unit, including *The Barkleys of Broadway* (1949) with Ginger Rogers, who was brought in after Judy Garland fell ill. For *Royal Wedding* (1951) he devised a classic number in which he danced on the walls and ceiling, a technique made possible by having the room revolve. Astaire loved trick numbers and practiced energetically until he got all the pieces right. "People stop me on the street to this day," the dancer said years later, "asking me how I got around that room. For a while I had to carry a little diagram to show them. But it was all done in one piece. We didn't cut anything to get me up there."[7]

Like producers for the Broadway stage after *Oklahoma!*, Freed's production staff integrated musical numbers into the story by having songs flow naturally out of the dialogue. Jerome Kern had begun the trend in the theater with *Show Boat* in 1927, and the concept was continued by Rodgers and Hart, Kurt Weill, and others. *Meet Me in St. Louis* (1944), with a score by Hugh Martin and Ralph Blane, was a masterpiece in musical cinema that captured the mood of turn-of-the-century American family life beautifully. Judy Garland's ballad "The Boy Next Door" reflects Esther Smith's character, while "Have Yourself a Merry Little Christmas" is wedded to plot development. *Summer Holiday* (1948), based on Eugene O'Neill's *Ah, Wilderness!*, carried the technique still further. All the songs were written expressly for the script, and one of them, "Spring Isn't Everything," was taken right out of O'Neill's text. The barroom scene where Mickey Rooney gets drunk with a tart was all done to music. "Everybody cried when we were recording that," composer Harry Warren re-membered. "That was one of the best musicals I ever did, although it wasn't a box-office success."[8]

Joe Pasternak had produced the early Deanna Durbin pictures at Universal, and at Metro he continued to favor girl sopranos such as Kathryn Grayson and Jane Powell. But the studio also brought in great names from serious music: Wagnerian tenor Lauritz Melchior, German soprano Lotte Lehmann, pianist José Iturbi, and choreo-graphers Eugene Loring, David Lichine, and Michael Kidd. Kidd made the barn-raising sequence in Jack Cummings's Seven Brides for Seven Brothers (1954) one of the most exciting dances ever con-ceived for film. The young performers rehearsed for five weeks before shooting began, since movement was the pivotal element, breathtak-ing in its display of energy.[9]

With the Hollywood musical a major box-office draw during the late Depression and World War II years, all the studios attempted to emulate Metro's success. Twentieth Century-Fox brought in Alice Faye and Betty Grable, who became the favorite pinup girl of the armed forces. Grable was never a great dancer and knew her limita-tions, but she could tap well, fake the rest, and sing a song effec-tively. She was vivacious and had a beautiful body and magnificent legs. "She invented the word barrelhouse," said choreographer Charles Walters, who worked with Grable in DuBarry Was a Lady on Broadway, "the dirtiest-mouth dame I've ever known. But on her it was adorable." Songwriters struggled to come up with something fresh for the blond pinup queen, material that would lend itself to interesting photography and her special talents. For Billy Rose's Dia-mond Horseshoe (1945) Harry Warren and Mack Gordon concocted a tune called "In Acapulco." "We had to get something for the cho-reographer to do," said Warren, "something for him to produce that had color."[10]

Director Walter Lang tried to turn the Fox musicals into an art form, but he never equaled Metro's quality, coming closest with State Fair (1945) and its original Rodgers and Hammerstein score. Dan Dailey won the lead opposite Grable in Mother Wore Tights (1947), launching a partnership that extended over four pictures. If Fred As-taire was the breezy, white-tie-and-tails dancer and Gene Kelly the athletic ballet dancer, Dailey was the happy hoofer inspired by bur-lesque and vaudeville. "In those days with Technicolor," Dailey re-membered, "you had a thousand lights pouring down on you. So when you were doing a dance number, it was hot work. You'd melt.

They'd run in and keep mopping you off with ice-cold shammies between takes."[11]

Columbia made impressive musicals, with Rita Hayworth as Harry Cohn's star attraction. Hayworth, a talented dancer, made two pictures with Fred Astaire and looked stunning in Technicolor extravaganzas like *Down to Earth* (1947). Columbia also enjoyed great success with *The Jolson Story* (1946) and *Jolson Sings Again* (1949), in which Larry Parks mouthed convincingly to Jolson's soundtrack, and later brought in Frank Sinatra for *Pal Joey* (1957). Cohn considered these his prestige productions and spent enough money on them to give Columbia's top pictures a lavish look. Costuming in musicals was always important, providing appropriate color to enhance the choreography.

Getting a song from screen musicals onto the *Hit Parade* on radio or television was a constant goal, for it greatly improved a picture's chances for success. Rita Hayworth's fiery rendition of "Put the Blame on Mame" from *Gilda* (1946) is probably remembered even more than the movie itself, while Jerome Kern's "Long Ago and Far Away" from *Cover Girl* (1944) and Gershwin's "Love Walked In" from *The Goldwyn Follies* (1938) became popular standards.

Studios were quick to capitalize on the successes of other studios. If Fred Astaire made *Flying Down to Rio* at RKO, some other studio was likely to make *Flying Down to Buenos Aires* with whatever dancer they could find to do similar routines. Warner Brothers reentered the field of musicals during the late 1940s with Doris Day as their biggest property, supported by Gordon MacRae, Gene Nelson, and occasionally Virginia Mayo. But by then Warners was not particularly progressive in its approach, generally using songs already in the studio library and formula choreography. Creative performers had to fight to get in anything original. "The whole imaginative and creative thrust was kind of missing," said dancer Gene Nelson, "because Warners was making a product, whereas MGM was making something artistic."[12]

By the mid-1950s the original screen musical was coming to an end. *Seven Brides for Seven Brothers, High Society* (1956), *Les Girls* (1957) and *Gigi* (1958) were Metro's last giant efforts. *There's No Business Like Show Business* (1954) was the last big original musical at Twentieth Century-Fox until *Star!* (1968). Costs were soaring, and musicals required much rehearsal time and lengthy preproduction work, making those pictures tremendously expensive at a time when studios were beginning to retrench. Screen versions of successful

Broadway productions were still made on the assumption that only blockbuster musicals with an established reputation could lure audiences away from their television sets. *West Side Story* (1961), *The Music Man* (1962), *My Fair Lady* (1964), *The Sound of Music* (1965), *Oliver!* (1968), and *Cabaret* (1972) all enjoyed solid acclaim but were reminders that the film musical was merely an occasional echo of what it once had been.

No entirely original screen musical appeared until 1975, when *Funny Lady* was made as a sequel to Barbra Streisand's earlier portrayal of Fanny Brice in *Funny Girl* (1968). Peter Bogdanovich's *At Long Last Love* (1975), despite the popularity of Burt Reynolds, was a notorious box-office disaster, and *New York, New York* (1977), with stunning work by Liza Minnelli in a big-band setting, became a cult film without ever gaining general popularity. *The Rose* (1979), *Xanadu* (1980), and *Pennies From Heaven* (1981) were pale efforts at reviving the genre, while *All That Jazz* (1979) stood in a class by itself as the most cinematic musical since the Metro heyday. Certainly *The Wiz* (1978), *A Little Night Music* (1978), *Annie* (1982), and *A Chorus Line* (1985) have done little in their recent screen adaptations to cause optimism about a renaissance in movie musicals, whereas continuing inflation makes MGM's former opulence and leisurely schedules seem like a luxurious empire out of some distant fairyland.

Chevalier and Louise

Innocents of Paris (1929) was Paramount's first big musical, so the entire studio was tense about it. The night they shot the song "Louise," every executive on the lot was present. Around two in the morning Maurice Chevalier began singing the number to a girl sitting on a garden wall, with an orchestra playing off to one side. Chevalier stood right in front of the girl as he sang, "Every little breeze seems to whisper 'Louise.'" And his hand fluttered in the air like a breeze. "Birds in the trees," and he pointed to birds up in the trees. "Whispers each little rose," and he cupped his hands like a rose. "Tells me it knows I love you, love you. Every little beat that I feel in my heart," and he felt his heart and so on. Chevalier finished the chorus, and when the orchestra started again, he sang the second refrain with the same gestures.

"Dick," lyricist Leo Robin told his collaborator, composer Richard Whiting, "he's doing it all wrong." "Don't tell me he's doing our song wrong," said Whiting, noting that Chevalier was a great international performer. "He's doing it wrong," Robin persisted. So Whiting suggested Robin talk to director Richard Wallace. "Are you out of your mind?" said Wallace when Robin approached him. "This is Chevalier. Don't tell me he's doing the song wrong." Robin stood his ground: "He's doing it wrong. And I don't want him to ruin our song. It's important that it be a hit. It's our first song for Paramount, and our future depends on it." "Well," said Wallace, "look, if you feel that strongly about it, go over and tell him."

So Robin walked up to the star and said, "Mr. Chevalier, you've made a worldwide reputation for your style of singing, and I'm just a beginner in this business. But maybe I can give you a suggestion. Here in this country when we sing a song to a girl, we just stand there and look at her and just sing the words. That way you establish the song first, and the audience gets to know the words. Then in the second chorus, you do those wonderful gestures of yours. That builds to a climax, and it becomes wonderful." "Ro-ban," cried Chevalier angrily, "you are wrong!" Robin slunk off the set and went down to the end of the stage, hiding behind a piece of scenery, mortified and scared. "Well, it looks like I'll be on the next train back to New York," he thought.

The orchestra struck up the introduction again, and Leo Robin heard Chevalier sing the first chorus of his song and begin the second. All of a sudden the singer stopped the orchestra and started calling, "Ro-ban." The frightened lyricist didn't answer, not wanting to be fired in front of everyone. "Ro-ban," Chevalier called again. Eventually the director joined in. "Leo, come up here. You're needed." Finally Wallace sent a prop boy to fetch him. Fearing the worst, Robin approached the great Chevalier, aware everyone was watching. "Ro-ban," Chevalier said looking down at him, "you are right!"[13]

One Good Song

Jack Warner hated the thought of wasting time and money. He once asked composer Harry Warren how long it took to write a song. "About three weeks," Warren told him. Warner was horrified. "Three weeks!" he yelped. "Three weeks to write one lousy song!" Warren shook his head. "No," he answered. "Three weeks to write one good song."[14]

Golfer

There was no greater perfectionist in films than Fred Astaire, who rehearsed tirelessly for weeks on end before shooting began on his pictures. He was also an accomplished golfer, finding the sport great relaxation. In *Carefree* (1938) he did one of the numbers he did fairly often, dancing over tables and furniture, up and down halls, out on the terrace, and winding up on a golf course. Director Mark Sandrich took his crew over to Pasadena for the golf-course portion of the routine, which was shot as a continuous scene. There were a dozen or more golf balls lined up, which Astaire was to hit with a club—all in rhythm. A loudspeaker had been rigged outdoors to play the pre-recorded soundtrack, so he could keep his rhythm exact. He was dancing all the time, and everything had to be done on cue. Astaire hit the golf balls, and when the crew went to retrieve them, they found the dozen balls all lying on the green within eight feet of one another! Fred obviously had done some serious practicing.[15]

Gershwin

Choreographer Hermes Pan had George Gershwin's score for the Astaire-Rogers movie *Shall We Dance?* (1937) and was about to start rehearsals. He walked onto an assigned stage to find a pianist already there. "Look," he said, "would you mind playing this for me? I'm going to start rehearsing tomorrow, and I haven't heard it yet." So the pianist started playing the title song. Pan asked if he couldn't play it a little faster. "It has such a strange tempo," he said. "It's almost like a march." The pianist played the number for him different ways, but the choreographer still wasn't satisfied. "Gershwin or no Gershwin, this isn't for me," he concluded. "This is not my type of dance feeling. I don't know what to do with it." Then he went off to a meeting with Astaire, producer Pandro Berman, and Sandrich to discuss his problem with the music. A few minutes later the pianist walked into the room, and it turned out he was the great Gershwin himself. Pan nearly went through the floor. "I'm sorry," he cried, "I didn't know who you were." "Well," said Gershwin, "you know, you're probably right." The encounter gave Pan a lesson in humility he never forgot. "I've never met a genius who wasn't humble," he said. "The people who have talent are always the easiest to work with and the most natural."[16]

100 Musicians
The 1936 musical *Three Smart Girls* rescued Universal from bankruptcy, made Deanna Durbin a star, and gave a big boost to the career of director Henry Koster, who had come over from Germany to make his first picture. But Koster was worried about his next assignment; he had no ideas for a new picture and the story department couldn't seem to find anything suitable for Deanna. Then, one day, an old fiddle player he had known in Vienna came looking for a job and Koster obligingly called up a friend who was a musical director to see if he needed a good fiddle player. "There are hundreds of musicians in Hollywood who are out of work," replied the friend. Koster was appalled. "Something should be done about a situation like that," he exclaimed. "Of course," said the musical director, "but what can I do? I have all the musicians I need." Suddenly Koster had a brilliant idea: The next Deanna Durbin movie would be a movie about musicians and it would require the hiring of scores of professionals, including fiddle players. The upshot: *One Hundred Men and a Girl* (1937), another musical hit starring Durbin.[17]

Bargain
Even though *Billion Dollar Baby*, a musical by Betty Comden and Adolph Green, had been a flop on Broadway, Sam Goldwyn acquired the screen rights. "I got a great bargain today," Sam boasted. "I bought a *Billion Dollar Baby* for only a hundred thousand dollars."[18]

Turn-of-the-Century Garland
Songwriters Hugh Martin and Ralph Blane wanted their songs for *Meet Me in St. Louis* (1944) as integrated into the plot as possible, although in the first version of "Have Yourself a Merry Little Christmas" they went overboard. The original lyric, sung in the movie by Judy Garland to little Margaret O'Brien, who's crying over their family's impending move, was simply too negative: "Have yourself a merry little Christmas, this may be our last, next year we will all be living in the past. Have yourself a merry little Christmas, pop that champagne cork, next year we will all be living in New York." "God, that's so sad," Garland told Blane. "Can't you make a more positive, happy lyric? I can be sad, but if I'm sad and the lyrics are sad, it's too sad. It's too much of one thing." Blane understood and came up with the version that's still sung every December: "Have

yourself a merry little Christmas, let your heart be light. From now on our troubles will be out of sight."

For "The Trolley Song" the songwriters wanted to capture the historic flavor of 1903, so Ralph Blane drove over to the public library in Beverly Hills and got out old periodicals and newspapers. On one page he found a picture of a double-decker trolley with a caption under it reading CLANG, CLANG, HERE COMES THE TROLLEY. He closed the book and went back to the studio. "Hugh," he told his partner, "I've got it! 'Clang, clang, clang went the trolley.'" They finished the song in ten minutes, and both Judy Garland and producer Arthur Freed loved it.

Garland was an instant study, but in the rush to record "The Trolley Song" she got the lyrics wrong. She sang "buzz, buzz, buzz" instead of "bump, bump, bump," on the first take. It was so exciting and had such spirit, Roger Edens said, "God! That's it, print it." "But, Roger, she sang the lyrics wrong," the songwriters protested. "She went 'buzz, buzz, buzz' instead of 'bump, bump, bump.'" "Who'll know?" said Edens. "She'll just have to learn it wrong and sing it that way when we shoot, so she'll be in sync." And, of course, nobody noticed—except forever after, Garland had to sing the lyrics wrong.[19]

Reagan's Career in Show Business

In 1943, Warner Bros. sponsored *This Is the Army*, a musical comedy written by Irving Berlin, in which First Lieutenant Ronald Reagan, on leave from the army, played the lead opposite Joan Leslie, with the profits going to army relief. At one point in the picture Irving Berlin sings his own World War I song, "Oh, How I Hate to Get Up in the Morning," but his voice was so poor that one of the crew members standing next to Reagan whispered to him: "If the fellow who wrote this song could hear this guy sing it he'd roll over in his grave." During the first week of shooting, Reagan was introduced to Berlin five times and each time the latter said he was glad to meet the thirty-two-year-old actor. "Young man," he told him one day, after seeing some of the rushes, "I just saw some of your work. You've got a few things to correct—for example, a huskiness of the voice—but you really should give this business some serious consideration when the war is over. It's very possible that you could have a career in show business." Reagan thanked him for his kindness and refrained from telling him he had been making movies since 1937.[20]

Rhythm

Twentieth Century-Fox musicals were frequently entertaining, but Darryl Zanuck rarely permitted the innovations Gene Kelly achieved in musical numbers at Metro. Dan Dailey once came up with a great idea for a picture: His character is drunk and walking past the loading doors of the old Metropolitan Opera House in New York, where the orchestra is playing Stravinsky's *Firebird*. The music is coming through the loading doors, so the character starts to dance down the street. The musicians have reached the fourth part of *Firebird*, which is quite rhythmic. Dailey worked hard on his concept for a couple of months, perfecting it into something he knew was special. When he demonstrated the idea for Zanuck and his entourage, everyone thought it was a remarkable dance. "And it was!" Dailey agreed. "Because it was all rhythm." Finally he got word from the producer's office: "Gee, we like the dance so much, but could you do it to 'Birth of the Blues'?" So Dailey ended up doing part of the dance to "Birth of the Blues."[21]

Behind the Desk

One day Lew Brown was summoned to the office of a musically illiterate producer and told how to rewrite his songs. Brown said he had written fifteen Broadway shows, but the producer told him he was wrong about the songs. "How do you know I'm wrong?" cried Brown. "Because you're standing in front of this desk and I'm sitting behind it," said the producer.[22]

Blue Heaven

Songwriters Harold Arlen and Ralph Blane had written what they thought was a perfect score for Fox's *My Blue Heaven* (1950) and resented the fact that the title of one of their songs wasn't used as the title of the picture instead of that old chestnut "My Blue Heaven," a hit tune years before. So they made an appointment to see Darryl Zanuck. "Yes, Harold," said Zanuck when they arrived at his office, "you wanted to see me?" "Yes," said Arlen, sitting down at the piano in Zanuck's office, "we feel like the songs we wrote for *My Blue Heaven* are lovely, and the title of the picture is one we didn't have anything to do with. Considering our reputation as songwriters, we feel you could use one of our songs as the name of the picture." "Boys," sighed Zanuck, "you can change the name of Twentieth Century-Fox faster than you can change the title of *My Blue*

Heaven." Just at that point the self-ejecting cigarette holder Arlen had in his mouth went click, sending his cigarette across the room, where it fell in front of Zanuck's desk, with sparks flying everywhere. Arlen quickly went down on his hands and knees, beating out sparks, while Blane stood by the piano, nearly hysterical with laughter. Zanuck was vastly amused, but the picture was called *My Blue Heaven* anyway.[23]

Mucus?

Everyone involved with making it seemed enchanted with *The Sound of Music* (1965), except actor Christopher Plummer, who played Captain von Trapp. Plummer hated the picture so much he referred to it as *The Sound of Mucus.* Then the rushes started coming in and the cast was invited down to a little theater in Salzburg to watch them after the day's shooting. "We suddenly realized what a gloriously beautiful picture this was," actress Anna Lee remembered. Even Plummer changed his attitude overnight.[24]

Worried

Even the great songwriters could demonstrate concern over how their material would be treated on the screen. During the making of *White Christmas* (1954) Irving Berlin paced up and down nervously before each prerecording session. As Bing Crosby was preparing to record the title song, Berlin looked unusually worried, even though Bing's version of the number had been a yuletide favorite for years. Finally Crosby said to him, "Irving, you know we have a hit in this song. Why don't you go back to your office and relax? You have nothing to worry about. Believe me, we'll do it fine." The film has since become an annual tradition on television.[25]

Feathers

Ginger Rogers and Fred Astaire were preparing to shoot the "Cheek to Cheek" number in *Top Hat* (1935), when Ginger arrived in a dress covered completely with ostrich feathers. They began to dance and feathers flew everywhere, blinding Astaire and making him sneeze. After an hour he gave up. A meeting was held with the dress designer who assured them everything would be OK. But the next day the feathers kept flying, and by afternoon Astaire threw up his hands, white with anger. Ginger burst into tears, and angry words were exchanged. Finally, the designer agreed to spend the night sewing each feather into place. The next day, a few feathers flew, but they were able to shoot the dance. From then on, Astaire insisted on inspecting his partners' costumes before filming. Despite all the commotion, the "Cheek to Cheek" number proved one of the highlights of the Astaire-Rogers partnership.[26]

CHAPTER 20

Westerns

Movies about the Old West are quintessentially American. "The Western," James Stewart once declared, "is an original. An American feels 'this is ours.'" William S. Hart, one of the first cowboy stars, thought Westerns captured "the very essence of national life" and were inextricably "bound up in American citizenship." The French regard the Western as *le cinéma américain par excellence.*"[1]

From almost the beginning Hollywood thought of American history largely in terms of life on the frontier. For heroes, filmmakers turned to cowboys rather than to explorers, settlers, and Constitution makers; and for legends about national origins they looked to the taming of the West rather than to the winning of independence and the framing of the Constitution. The Founding Fathers were apparently too aristocratic for the popular taste; cowpunchers seemed to have the democratic, individualistic, and freewheeling ways that Americans liked to think were peculiarly their own and thus worth celebrating in cinema. But even before the development of movies the American people had become fascinated with the West. They read huge quantities of dime novels and pulp-magazine tales about it and flocked in droves to Wild West shows. And when the movies came, they took a big shine to the "horse operas" that began appearing on the nation's screens. Sagebrush sagas quickly became favorites with the moviegoing public.

The West portrayed in films was largely the trans-Mississippi West: the land of cowboys and Indians from about 1860 to 1890. Edwin S. Porter's famous little movie *The Great Train Robbery* (1903) was one of the first Westerns, and though it was filmed in New Jersey, it pictured the Far West, where train robberies were still taking place. The popularity of the Porter picture encouraged other filmmakers to produce movies about the West, and they were soon turning out hundreds each year, short pictures at first and then features.

With Western features came Western stars: first, "Broncho Billy" Anderson, and then William S. Hart and Tom Mix. Hart, who knew the Old West well, insisted on realistic details; Mix, who was anxious to show Americans what the Western pioneer had done for his country, took a more romantic approach. So did Mix's imitators in the 1920s: Hoot Gibson, Ken Maynard, Buck Jones, and Tim McCoy. And when the public got tired of cliché-ridden "action oaters" about good guys, bad guys, and sweet dames, Hollywood turned to massive epics about the frontier. *The Covered Wagon* (1923), the first Western spectacular ("an American *Odyssey*"), celebrated the dauntless pioneers who crossed mountains, prairies, and rivers, and survived Indian attacks on their long trek to California and Oregon in 1848 and 1849. Old-timer Hart complained that the film contained errors "that would make a western man refuse to speak to his own brother," but the public loved it and it was a big grosser for years.[2] The following year came another, even better, spectacular, *The Iron Horse*, John Ford's stirring film about the building of the first transcontinental railroad in the late 1860s.

The coming of sound in the late twenties seemed to doom Westerns. The camera lost its mobility for a time and it was difficult to film outdoor scenes. But with improved recording techniques, Westerns took hold again and became more popular than ever. Sound effects added enormously to the thrill of seeing stampeding cattle, cavalry charges, fistfights, gun duels, and barroom brawls on the screen. In 1929 came *In Old Arizona,* "the first 100% all-talking drama filmed outdoors," which won an Academy Award for its leading man, Warner Baxter; and *The Virginian,* a much-filmed Owen Wister story, which, this time around, gave a big boost to the fortunes of Gary Cooper (who gets to tell villain Walter Huston: "When you call me that, *smile!*"). Two years later the great success of *Cimarron,* a film about the land rush to Oklahoma in 1889, made it clear that moviegoers liked epic Westerns in sound even better than they had the old silent spectaculars.

Most Westerns, though, were conspicuously unspectacular: B pictures, flocks of them, starring Ken Maynard, Hoot Gibson, Tim McCoy, and William Boyd (Hopalong Cassidy); serials like The Lone Ranger ("Hi-Yo, Silver!"); and "musical Westerns" with cowboys like Gene Autry and Roy Rogers taking time out to yodel a bit between action sequences. Since school kids were the most fervent fans of serials and B Westerns, youth groups, parents' associations, and church organizations were enormously pleased when singing cowpoke Gene Autry promulgated the "Ten Commandments of the Cowboy" in the late 1930s: 1. A cowboy never takes unfair advantage—even of an enemy; 2. A cowboy never betrays a trust; 3. A cowboy always tells the truth; 4. A cowboy is kind to small children, to old folks, and to animals; 5. A cowboy is free from racial and religious prejudice; 6. A cowboy is helpful and when anyone's in trouble he lends a hand; 7. A cowboy is a good worker; 8. A cowboy is clean about his person and in thought, word, and deed; 9. A cowboy respects womanhood, his parents, and the laws of his country; 10. A cowboy is a patriot.[3]

There were "adult Westerns," of course, as well as B pictures for the kids: John Ford's Stagecoach (1939), a sophisticated Western that rescued John Wayne from years of B's and started him on the road to becoming Hollywood's biggest cowboy hero; The Ox-Bow Incident (1943), a harrowing tale about the lynching of the innocent; and My Darling Clementine (1946), Ford's deftly told story about U.S. Marshal Wyatt Earp and his brothers. Hollywood's big-time Westerns didn't always observe Autry's Cowboy Commandments; there was a tendency, in fact, to glamorize homicidal outlaws like Jesse James and Billy the Kid and to sentimentalize about prostitutes with hearts of gold. After World War II, moreover, Westerns began placing more emphasis on sex than the traditional wild-and-woollies had done, and, in the greatest novelty of all, even presented some of the cowboy protagonists as aging and tired of it all and plagued with neuroses. There was an increasing effort, too, to portray the American Indian's side of the Western story, though some of the old silents had treated native Americans with sympathy and compassion.

Why the persistent popularity of films about the West? "Why," as a Western writer once put it, "do people want to spend so much time staring at the wrong end of a horse?"[4] Chiefly because Westerns moved the way a moving picture should. In the most successful Western films there was a maximum of action and a minimum of talk: cattle roundups, Indian encounters, saloon fights, buffalo stampedes, frantic chases, spectacular battles, and suspenseful gunfights. James Stewart, star of many a Western, once recalled that scripts for Western films usually weighed far less than scripts for any other kind of film because of the paucity of dialogue. Once he agreed to do a radio version of one of his Westerns and when he arrived at the station for rehearsals found the producers frantic. "It's just impossible for us to do this," they told him, "because no one says anything!"[5] In Westerns, one performer observed, "the story is usually so action-packed that they don't require that much of you. Sometimes the horses seem to have more talent than you do."[6] For John Ford, who directed scores of pictures, silent and sound, about the West, action was the primary appeal of Western films. "The Western is the *real* picture," he insisted. "It's full of action and character. You see the outdoors—nature, horses, rivers, valleys. The people move. The Western is truly a moving picture."[7]

Action, to be sure, wasn't the only attraction. There were other reasons for the vogue of Westerns: stunning locations, beautiful horses, melodramatic simplicities, moral clarities, and nostalgic (and patriotic) portrayals of an earlier America. Without resorting to pretentiousness (the pitfall of film analysis), it may even be said that the classical Western story had a mythic quality about it that appealed to Americans seeking certainties in the past that seemed lacking in the present. "The Western," declared *Time* in an essay on the genre in 1959, "is really the American morality play, in which Good and Evil, Spirit and Nature, Christian and Pagan, fight to the finish on the vast stage of the unbroken prairie. The hero is a Galahad with a six-gun, a Perseus of the purple sage. In his saddlebags he carries a new mythology, an American *Odyssey* that is waiting for its Homer. And the theme of the epic, hidden beneath the circus glitter of the perennial Wild West show, is the immortal theme of every hero myth: man's endless search for the meaning of life."[8]

But there was nothing immortal about the Western movie. The triumph of television in the 1950s struck a heavy blow at Hollywood's horse operas. For one thing, it killed off the B Western; studios began releasing their backlog of old B pictures to the new competitor and then stopped making that type of film completely. For another, as TV turned to Western shows itself (*Gunsmoke, The Rifleman, Bonanza*), Hollywood abandoned its experiment with relatively inexpensive Westerns in Technicolor, featuring second-string-ers like Randolph Scott, Audie Murphy, and Rory Calhoun. Filmmakers did continue to produce first-rate pictures about the West—like *High Noon* (1952), *Shane* (1953), and *The Searchers* (1956)—but the low-budget Western, once so popular and profit-able, was now a thing of the past.

In the 1960s there was a gradual change in mood in Hollywood's A Westerns; they became increasingly realistic (i.e., critical) in their depiction of life on the frontier and even cynical at times about life in general. In the new Westerns there were no longer any clear-cut he-roes and villains, nor did good necessarily win out in the end. The cowboy came off his high horse; he tended to be as seedy as the outlaws he was pursuing. "Our mythic heroes," observed one film critic in 1971, "were sick, dirty, violent, decadent, and otherwise far-from-perfect creatures. So that's why," he added, with a gleeful burst of insight, "the nation's values are screwed up." One critic even suggested that the unpopular Vietnam War had its roots "in the blood-drenched turf of the O.K. Corral." As James Coburn remarks at one point in *Pat Garrett and Billy the Kid* (1973): "It feels like times have changed."[9]

Perhaps the most striking feature of the new Western films was not their rejection of the ancient pieties but their emphasis on vio-lence and brutality. Sam Peckinpah led the way. His 1969 Western, *The Wild Bunch*, contained so much blood and gore that some critics were appalled. *Newsday's* Joseph Gelmis called it "the bloodiest movie I've ever seen, maybe the bloodiest movie ever made"; and Arthur Knight, writing in *Saturday Review*, observed that everyone in the film was "so thoroughly hateful and corrupt as to richly deserve the fate that Peckinpah has in store for him. . . ."[10] Peckinpah in-sisted he portrayed brutality in order to turn people against it, but Knight wasn't entirely convinced. "I would prefer to believe," he wrote, "that Sam Peckinpah was sincere when he stated that he wanted to make a picture so strong, so stomach-churning, so detailed in its catalogue of horrors that all the glamour, all the attraction of violence for its own sake would promptly disappear. I think he is wrong, but I very much doubt if anyone who was not totally honest in his wrongheadedness could ever come up with a picture as revolt-ing as this."[11]

But the public took to the new violence with aplomb. *The Wild Bunch* did well at the box office, and so did *The Getaway* (1972) and other violence-laden Peckinpah offerings. Some sophisticates thought

Peckinpah's brutal realism was far more artistic than the old kitsch; they insisted, too, that it skillfully unmasked the brutalities of the established order for all to see. But old-timers like Tim McCoy deplored the new Westerns. "It's the tough guy who's the hero, not the fine upstanding fellow," he lamented. "And then the sickness that's coming with them now. Gracious, films are filled with nothing but filth and pornography and profanity. . . . You can't get violent enough these days."[12]

In February 1974 *New Yorker* film critic Pauline Kael proclaimed the demise of the Western film. "A few more Westerns may still straggle in," she wrote, "but the Western is dead."[13] Not precisely. Though public interest shifted from Western movies to movies about outer space, Hollywood continued to produce Westerns—about Broncho Billy, frontier scouts, train robberies, horse thieves, the James gang—into the 1980s, if in considerably reduced quantities. And some of the nation's leading performers have appeared in the post-Kael Westerns: Kirk Douglas, Burt Lancaster, Marlon Brando, Clint Eastwood. But the tone of the newest Westerns was different. If the 1970s had emphasized the sleazy side of life on the frontier, the 1980s returned to the mythic West in which the Manichean struggle between the forces of good and evil was primary. In *Pale Rider* (1985), Clint Eastwood rides quietly into a tiny frontier settlement where some bad folks (a land baron and his mercenaries) are picking on some good folks (hardworking gold miners), coolly disposes of the bad men in a stunning showdown at the end of the picture, and then rides away again as silently as he had come. Whether he would return again remained an open question.

Reel Truth

Yakima Canutt, famous stuntman in Westerns, once overheard Tom Mix spin some yarns about the Old West for a group of tourists. "Tom," he said, after the people had left, "you kinda handle the truth a little bit reckless, don't you?" Mix shrugged his shoulders. "What the hell," he said. "They're here for entertainment. So I give them a reel out of one of my pictures."[14]

Snake Scene

Appearing in Westerns was sometimes hazardous. When he was shooting *The Virginian* in 1914, Cecil B. De Mille used a California rattlesnake that he had arranged to have defanged beforehand. When he let the snake loose, it headed for actor Monroe Salisbury, who was sitting on the ground with his knees drawn up, and it coiled between his calves and thighs. "It's all right," De Mille assured Salisbury. "He's been defanged. Don't worry." But the propman pulled De Mille's sleeve agitatedly; they were using the wrong snake. "He's not defanged, Mr. De Mille!" he cried. "The zoo man says they didn't defang him, and neither did I!" "Monroe," De Mille told the startled actor quietly, "don't move. Sit perfectly still. No one move— no one." For a minute or two everyone on the set was still as night and waited. Then the snake slithered away, one of the cowboys there shot it, and everyone breathed freely again.[15]

Kiss Me, Kate

William S. Hart's pinto horse Fritz formed a great attachment for a mare named Cactus Kate. "How proud Fritz was," Hart recalled, "when he and Cactus Kate . . . were loaded in trucks to go on location. The little rascal knew what it meant and he knew his ability to show off in front of his family." But for one picture Hart took Fritz to location without Kate. The scene was ready, but when he went to mount Fritz, the horse fought back. Hart talked to him, walked with him, unsaddled and saddled him up, and did all the little tricks he knew to get the horse off his grouch. But nothing worked; every time he tried to mount, Fritz resisted. "Well, old-timer," Hart finally exclaimed, "if you must fight and buck, let's go!" Then he caught the horse unawares and succeeded in mounting him. But Fritz was furious; he kicked, ran sideways, and finally charged the cameras. As the cameramen scattered in every direction, Hart jumped off, tried to calm the trembling horse, and decided on a new tactic. "Boys," he said, "I may be a damn fool, but let's try it. Send for Kate." And they did. "Kate came . . . Fritz rubbed noses with her," Hart wrote afterward, and then let Hart mount him and get the scene he wanted, with Kate watching. "Do horses understand?" Hart wondered.[16]

Big Fight

In one of William S. Hart's pictures there was to be a big free-for-all in a restaurant during the course of which Hart knocks out one of the extras hired for the scene. "Partner," Hart told the extra, a big bruiser who was obviously a professional boxer, just before shooting started, "of course you know your business, but as you and I have never fought before, I want to explain how we try and work it." He then told the man to pull his punches as much as he could, and he would do the same, but that the important thing was to make it look like a real fight, even if they hurt each other a bit. "Another thing, brother," Hart went on, as the extra remained silent, "when I judge we have enough for the scene, I'll take the first good opening I can get and land on you. Of course, I'll pull the punch as much as I can, but you'll feel it; also, just as the punch lands, I'll say, 'Go,' and you go down, just as you would in a knockdown." But the extra continued to be silent; he simply stared at Hart. So the latter elaborated the last point. "When I say 'Go,' the director will also holler, 'Go,'" he explained, "and you go down so we can't make any mistake."

Hoping the instructions were clear, the director yelled, "Camera!" and the fighting started. Hart quickly found the extra was taking the scene far more seriously than he wanted him to, but at least, he thought, they were getting a realistic scene out of it. Finally he decided they had had enough; he lunged at the fellow and yelled, "Go!" But instead of going down, the extra charged him like a mad bull. "Go!" Hart yelled again. "Go—Go!" But the extra simply redoubled his efforts. Furious, Hart fought back so hard he succeeded in flooring him and then leaped on him and began punching, kicking, and gouging him. When the other men on the set managed to separate the two, Hart stormed about the set excoriating the extra for disregarding his instructions. "Wait a minute, please, Mr. Hart," said the man who had hired the extra. "You're all wrong." Then he explained. "We forgot to tell you that this man is stone deaf," he said sadly. "He can't hear a thing." Somewhat mollified, Hart took the guy to the doctor for repairs and paid the bill. He never saw the man again.[17]

Phony Cowboys

Tom Mix did his own stunts in pictures and avoided camera tricks. But one day a loud-mouthed cowboy from Texas visited the studio, began making fun of movie cowboys, and said no real cowpuncher would waste his time making movies.

Somewhat amused, Mix asked the Texan for pointers on how to do things right. First he asked him how to rope properly and pointed out a peg on the stage that he said he had been unable to get a rope around. The Texan tried to rope the peg, failed, and said nobody could rope it from that distance. Mix then asked for a try and, to the man's chagrin, put his rope around the peg without any trouble. The visitor then challenged the "phony cowboys," as he called them, to a shooting match. Mix obligingly got a can and they both started shooting at it. The visitor did pretty well, but when he took his last shot he couldn't see the can anymore and missed it. Mix then found the can and sent it clear out of sight for good. At this point the visiting cowboy wanted to leave, but Mix asked him to demonstrate the Indian-grip hold for him. The Texan was a big guy, so he sat down at a table on the set opposite Mix with a big grin on his face and locked arms with him. A few minutes later, after a lot of straining back and forth, he found his arm flat on the table, where Mix had bent it. He decided to leave after that; he had had enough of "drugstore cowboys" for one day.[18]

Make It Ten

Hoot Gibson, who began as an extra in Westerns, was anxious for work. Once, when a director offered him an extra $5 if he allowed himself to be dragged by a running horse in one scene, he cried: "Make it ten and I'll let him kick me to death!"[19]

Good Material

One day, as screenwriter Frances Marion was headed for Sam Goldwyn's office for a conference about The Winning of Barbara Worth (1926), she noticed a tall, lanky fellow dressed like a cowboy leaning against the wall of the office building, talking through the window to Goldwyn's secretary. Impressed by his appearance, she took a couple of more looks at him as she went in the door. Inside, she found Goldwyn in a bad mood; he had assembled the cast for his new Western (including Ronald Colman and Vilma Banky), but still had no one to play the cowboy. "I can get you a young man who won't cost much," Marion told him. "He looks like good material to me." "Who?" asked Goldwyn skeptically. "Hold your horses, Sam," cried Marion. "I'll let you know in five minutes." She went out to Goldwyn's secretary. "Does that young man want to act?" she asked her. "He sure does," said the secretary. "Get him in here right away," Marion told her.

When the rugged young man entered Goldwyn's office, the producer looked him over and asked: "What experience have you had?" "None," drawled the cowboy. "I was an extra in one—two pictures." Goldwyn looked doubtfully at Marion, but she nodded her head approvingly, and he knew her advice had been good in the past. "All right, young man," he finally sighed. "I'll take a chance on you."

Goldwyn's decision turned out to be a wise one. The new young performer fit perfectly into *The Winning of Barbara Worth;* he seemed quite at home in the great outdoors, either on horseback or off. But his part was small and no one paid much attention to him when he wasn't before the camera. When the company went on location, he was bunked in a tent with a Chinese cook who threw knives at gophers, an old hack comedian, and a cardsharping bit player. And until the picture was released and became a big hit, no one even remembered his name: Gary Cooper.[20]

Good Thing

When Gary Cooper started making movies, his first name was Frank. But an agent suggested something a bit more unusual, and when Cooper asked her what she had in mind, she proposed the name of her hometown: Gary, Indiana. "It's a good thing," he said later, "she didn't come from Poughkeepsie!"[21]

Screen Test

One day in the early sound era, director Raoul Walsh, it is said, spotted an athletic-looking young man named Marion Michael Morrison working props on a Fox set, liked the cut of his jib, and decided to groom him for an acting job. "You're to stay on salary after this picture's over," he told him, "then I want you to learn how to throw tomahawks and knives and go to my dramatic teacher for coaching. I'm going to test you for the lead in *The Big Trail.*"

Morrison enjoyed learning how to throw knives and tomahawks, but taking dramatic lessons was something else again. The coach, he recalled, "was all very dramatic in his talk, all pseudo-Shake-spearean, and his idea of Western dialogue was 'Greetings, Great Bear, tell the Great White Mountain hello for me,' all in great round vowels." After two weeks of misery, he quit the lessons, and, when Walsh asked him why, he said: "If you want me to be that kind of actor, I can't cut the mustard." "That's just what the guy said!" laughed Walsh. "He said you'd never make an actor in a hundred years." "Well, it's been fun," said Morrison. "I'll go." "No, you won't," Walsh said firmly. "I'm testing you anyway."

It was a rough screen test. Morrison was teamed up with three experienced stage stars: Tyrone Power, Sr., Marguerite Churchill, and Ian Keith. "You're playing the leading scout of a wagon train heading West," Walsh told him beforehand. "There are no lines for you to learn. They'll just throw questions at you about the trip. Don't try to act. Just react naturally, as if it were happening in real life."

The trouble was that the other performers had read the script before the test, and, as the shooting began, they started hurling questions at Morrison: How long is the trip? Where will we eat? Will we see any buffalo? Will we encounter Indians? Morrison stuttered and stammered as he tried to improvise answers, and he began to feel like a fool. By the time Ian Keith started in on him, he had lost his temper. "Don't say any more!" he exploded. "Where are you from, mister? Why are you goin' West? Can you handle a rifle? You got pale hands, you sure as hell don't look the pioneering sort to me!" It was Keith's turn to become incoherent; he was startled by Morrison's sudden onslaught. Morrison was sure he had blown his chances at this point. But suddenly Walsh shouted: "Cut! He'll do!" And he gave young Morrison the role of leading man in *The Big Trail* (1930).

The Big Trail (made in a new 70mm Grandeur process) was no great shakes, and it did poorly at the box office. But it started the young man on the road to stardom. Under the name of John Wayne, he went on to make scores of Westerns, B's and A's, and in time became a symbol of gritty Americanism to thousands of people, even though he was neither a professional cowboy like Tom Mix nor a war hero like Audie Murphy. In July 1971 the Marine Corps League honored him as the man "who best exemplifies the word, 'American,'" and in 1979, just before his death, Congress voted him the Medal of Honor.[22]

Good Joke

Director W. S. Van Dyke was with Buck Jones on location and ready to begin work after lunch, but Buck was missing. Grumbling about the delay, Van Dyke got out the six-shooter he always carried and put bullets through a couple of cans. When Buck finally arrived, Van Dyke began dressing him down for holding up production, and the two got into a furious argument. Finally Van Dyke drew his gun, fired point-blank at Buck's stomach, and Buck dropped to the ground, groaning, "He's got me!" "You had it coming to you," yelled Van Dyke and fired twice more. At this point the other cowboys on the set jumped on Van Dyke and overpowered him. Meanwhile, one of the cowboys leaped on a horse and raced off for a doctor. Soon after, some of the crew members located a barn door, laid the moaning and groaning Buck on it, and carried him to a truck. Suddenly Buck stood up and started laughing. "You see," he told an interviewer afterward, "Van had put two or three loaded cartridges in his gun and the rest were blanks. He shot the cans to give the gang the idea that it was loaded all around. When he shot at me, of course, he'd reached the blanks and it didn't do me any harm except a few powder burns." "What if he had counted wrong?" gasped the interviewer. "Suppose he had got mixed up and put a bullet in your stomach?" "We thought of that—the next day," laughed Buck. "But he didn't. It sure was a good joke."[23]

End of Picture

John Ford's *Stagecoach* (1939) received high praise when it was released (Orson Welles reportedly saw it forty times before making *Citizen Kane*), but William S. Hart thought it was unrealistic. When the stagecoach made its run through hostile Indian country, he said, there wouldn't have been a prolonged chase culminating in rescue by the cavalry; in real life, the Indians would simply have shot the horses. "If they had," said Ford to critics like Hart, "it would have been the end of the picture, wouldn't it?" But he knew that the Apaches needed remounts and were more interested in the horses than in the passengers on the stagecoach.[24]

Sweatshirts

When Alabama manufacturer J. T. Flagg learned that singing cowboy Gene Autry received more fan mail than any other movie star and had an annual audience of more than 40 million people, he decided to add Gene Autry sweatshirts to his production of Babe Ruth sweatshirts. "I'm afraid you're too late," said Autry when Flagg tracked him down in Nashville. "I think they sold my sweatshirt rights to a chap in New York." Flagg at once got New York on the phone and was relieved to hear that the contract hadn't been signed. "I'll raise the New York man's bid!" he cried. Autry at once accepted his offer and the deal was concluded. "By the way," said Flagg afterward, "who was the New York chap?" "I don't know his name," said Autry, "but he was the representative of a firm called the Gardiner-Warring Company." "What!" cried Flagg. "That's my firm. That man is my agent." Then he added disgustedly: "And he didn't know enough to close a deal like that. Wait. I'll get him on the phone right now." But when he upbraided his New York agent, the latter defended himself. "Most people here," he said, "never heard of Gene Autry." The agent was right. The singing cowboy's films were never featured in big cities like New York; it was in the little towns and villages of the country that they went over big. "Some of 'em," said Autry in 1940, "play in towns so small even Mrs. Roosevelt hasn't been there."[25]

Walk the Horse

Jack Palance was enormously effective as the hired gunslinger in *Shane* (1953); he had a grimly determined expression on his face whenever he mounted or dismounted his horse. And the scene in which he dramatically walked his horse into town was one of the best in the picture.

But Palance's performance—which won him an Oscar nomination—was partly accidental. He was actually nervous around horses, had trouble mounting them, and when he finally succeeded after great effort in making a perfect dismount, director George Stevens used it for all the other scenes in the movie for both his dismounting and, run in reverse, for his mounting. As for the walking scene, Stevens had originally asked Palance to gallop into town, but he couldn't manage it. Then he asked him to try a canter, but this, too, failed. Finally Stevens told him simply to walk the horse, and he did it very nicely.[26]

Hammy Horses

When Marilyn Monroe was offered the lead as a saloon girl in *River of No Return* (1954), a friend warned her about co-star Robert Mitchum. "Watch him, Marilyn," she said. "Bob knows this business better than you do. He's all right if he likes you, but he's a scene-stealer if he doesn't." "Oh, I'm not scared of Bob stealing scenes," Marilyn replied. "It's those darned hammy horses that worry me." She was right to worry. The big, beautiful horses featured in Westerns were even greater scene-stealers than kids and dogs.[27]

If You Can

During one scene in *McLintock!* (1963), a Western comedy, John Wayne told Maureen O'Hara he didn't like the way she was playing it. "Come on, Maureen, get going," he urged. "This is your scene." O'Hara said she was trying to go fifty-fifty with him in the sequence.

"Fifty-fifty, hell!" scoffed Wayne. "It's *your* scene, so take it!" Then he added under his breath: "If you can!"[28]

Peckinpah Westerns

An interviewer once asked Sam Peckinpah whether he liked doing Westerns because the West was "almost the only mythology we have." "Hell, no," snorted Peckinpah. "I came by it naturally. My earliest memory is of being strapped into a saddle when I was two for a ride into the high country."

Peckinpah enjoyed making Westerns but he thought they were a prototype for other kinds of pictures. One evening writer John Gregory Dunne asked Peckinpah about his assignment to a new picture starring Paul Newman and Robert Redford, and he found it almost impossible to pin the director down. "Sam," he finally said, "what the hell is this picture all about?" "Write me a western," said Peckinpah. "Jesus, Sam," cried Dunne, "it's about two cops in New York City." "Every story," announced Peckinpah, "is a western." He went on to explain: "You put the hare in front of the hound and let the hound chase the hare." "Oh," said Dunne quietly. "Simple," smiled Peckinpah. But they never wrote the picture.[29]

CHAPTER 21

Spectacles

When Jesse Lasky was producing *The Covered Wagon* (1923), an ambitious picture about pioneers headed west in the 1840s, his boss, Adolph Zukor, began worrying about mounting expenses, and finally ordered him to suspend production. Exhibitors, he said, were complaining about the flood of Westerns pouring out of Hollywood and were clamoring for something different. "*Wagon* is not a Western," said Lasky loftily. "It's an epic." "An epic, eh?" cried Zukor excitedly. "Well, that's different. You go ahead. . . !"[1] *The Covered Wagon,* one of the big spectacles of the Silent Era, turned out to be a great success.

Spectacles were not new with *The Covered Wagon.* Here, as elsewhere, D. W. Griffith was the great pioneer before World War I. When Italy's *Quo Vadis?* (1913), a lavish but essentially static film about the early Christians, drew admiring crowds when shown in this country, Griffith was seized with a burning desire to do something just as ambitious, but more dynamic, on the screen. The result was America's first real epic film: *Judith of Bethulia* (1914), a four-reel biblical drama containing an elaborate set and some exciting battle scenes. But *Judith* was only a dress rehearsal for the most famous film of all: *The Birth of a Nation* (1915). With *Birth,* the importance of visual effects to motion pictures became obvious to everyone; and it became clear, too, that spectacles were excellent vehicles for showing movies off to best advantage. "What could the stage give to rival this?" cried one spellbound reviewer after seeing Griffith's Civil War epic. "What the novel? What the poem? Nothing—everything else, music, poetry, song, depreciate into nothing in comparison with such a marvelous portrayal of life and honor and patriotism."[2]

Not everyone was thrilled by The Birth of a Nation. The film's pervasive racism offended black leaders and their white friends, and some of them even called for censorship. Griffith deeply resented the criticism and decided that his next film would prove to the world that he was not a prejudiced person. There was only one way, in point of fact, in which he could have done this: produce a film about the courageous struggle of blacks like Harriet Tubman and Frederick Douglass for freedom. But it never occurred to him (or anyone else in those bigoted days) to make a film like that. Instead, he made a mighty movie entitled Intolerance (1916), centering on man's inhumanity to man through the ages and making a plea at the end for peace, toleration, brotherhood, and goodwill. Griffith's third epic was his greatest picture. Some film-lovers regard it as the greatest picture ever made.

Intolerance was unusually long and complicated. It told four stories: a modern one; one about the fall of Babylon to the Persian conqueror Cyrus the Great in 538 B.C.; one about the life of Jesus; and one about the massacre of French Huguenots on St. Bartholomew's Day in 1572. The last reel of the film brought characters from all four stories together into one of the most stupendous climaxes that ever appeared on the screen. But Griffith's themes were dwarfed by his sets. His reconstruction of ancient Babylon was particularly awesome; it covered several acres, towered three hundred feet high, and, for one scene, accommodated no fewer than five thousand people. The "new Griffith spectacle," wrote the reviewer for the New York Dramatic Mirror, "marks a milestone in the progress of the film. It reveals something of the future of the spectacle, something of its power to create pictures of tremendous and sweeping beauty, drama, and imagination."[3] Even Alexander Woollcott, who thought the story line fatuous, was bowled over by the grandeur of the sets. "Really," he wrote in The New York Times, "Mr. Griffith ranks with Cyrus. They both have taken Babylon."[4]

Most reviewers regarded Intolerance as an extraordinary experience, and because of favorable notices audience turnout was at first good. Then attendance dwindled and the film ended up a commercial failure. The interweaving of diverse stories seems to have puzzled some people and the high-keyed tone of the picture wearied others; its plea for peace, too, was out of tune with the mood of a nation about to plunge into World War I. But though it lost money, *Intolerance* was without doubt the most influential movie ever made. In it, Griffith showed moviemakers, once and for all, how to make great motion pictures. His film, Pauline Kael has observed, "is charged with visionary excitement about the power of movies to combine music, dance, narrative, drama, painting, and photography—to do alone what all the arts together had done."[5] All subsequent filmmakers, in Europe as well as the United States, have been in heavy debt to Griffith for the stunning visual techniques he developed while making his film.

Griffith went on to make two historical epics about the French and American revolutions—*Orphans of the Storm* (1922) and *America* (1924)—but they were only moderately successful. Western epics, like *The Covered Wagon,* featuring buffalo hunts, stampedes, prairie fires, and Indian fights, did much better at the box office than Griffith's films. Douglas Fairbanks's costume-and-adventure films, especially *Robin Hood* (1922) and *The Thief of Bagdad* (1924), also did well with the public. But Cecil B. De Mille's religious spectacles—*The Ten Commandments* (1923) and *The King of Kings* (1927)—did best of all.

De Mille based his religious spectacles on conscientious research and presented moviegoers with gorgeous sets, stirring action, and marvelous effects (like the parting of the Red Sea). Still, there was something meretricious about his pictures. As a spectacle maker he was far less driven than Griffith to convey ideas on the screen and far more willing to accommodate the public taste. For De Mille, too, a spectacle tended to be an end in itself. "I like spectacles," he told friends. "I like to paint on a large canvas."[6] He also liked to paint a great deal of sex onto the canvas in order to titillate his audiences. But he was a religious man, as he freely admitted. This meant that he saw to it that continence always triumphed over concupiscence in the final scenes of his dramas. De Mille was not alone in his approach. The enormously successful *Ben-Hur* (1926), MGM's lavish filming of the popular Lew Wallace novel about the time of Christ, also combined sex, spectacle, and spirituality in the De Mille fashion. It got to be a habit in Hollywood.

The conversion to sound in the late twenties made spectacles impossible to film for a time. By 1932, though, with improved recording techniques available, De Mille was at it again. First came *The*

Sign of the Cross (1932), a grandiose film about Emperor Nero and Christian martyrs; then *Cleopatra* (1934), featuring a gigantic barge with five hundred rowers, naval and land battles, and the biggest bath yet seen in a De Mille film; and finally *The Crusades* (1935), a somewhat ponderous picture filled with ornate sets, fancy costumes, and noisy battle sequences. By this time, though, De Mille baiting had become popular with critics. Reviewing *Cleopatra*, *Time* teased De Mille for abandoning realism by having the poison sac extracted from the live asp that Claudette Colbert used in the Cleopatra death scene. As for *The Crusades*, it was, wrote the *Time* reviewer, "a $1,000,000 sideshow which has at least three features which distinguish it from the long line of previous De Mille extravaganzas. It is the noisiest; it is the biggest; it contains no baths."[7] De Mille came to resent the joshing about the bathing scenes he featured in his epics. (In *The Sign of the Cross* Claudette Colbert takes a bath in a black marble pool filled with asses' milk.) Said he, solemnly: "My mind is not one that grasps the immorality of the bathroom."[8]

David O. Selznick did much better with critics than De Mille; he was called a *wunderkind*, not "the plumber's best friend." His famous Civil War spectacle *Gone With the Wind* (1939) won high praise from reviewers when it appeared and gathered more Oscars than all the De Mille pictures combined ever managed to win. De Mille felt the deprivation keenly; he thought his spectacles deserved more commendation by serious people than they ever received. But none of his showpieces has endured the way *Gone With the Wind* has. Writing about Selznick's masterwork three decades after it was first released, *The New York Times*'s Bosley Crowther declared: "There have been more ambitious, more expensive, and longer historical-spectacle films made in the years since this one. And there have been a few that have had more critical réclame. But there has never been one more effective than *Gone With the Wind*. There may never be."[9] No one ever said anything like that about a De Mille spectacle.

In the late thirties, W. C. Fields, who lived near De Mille, once snorted: "Some day, the———is going to be crushed under one of his epics!"[10] But De Mille remained uncrushable. In 1949, after World War II had killed interest in the spectacle film for a time, he led another revival of the genre with another Bible story, *Samson and Delilah*, starring Victor Mature and Hedy Lamarr, the plot of which he summed up for Paramount officials as follows: "Boy meets girl— and what a boy, and what a girl!"[11] The kidding predictably began at once. There was talk again of "run-of-De Mille pictures" and the "De Millennium" as well as jokes about De Mille's solemn mixing of piety and prurience. *Time* called the film's dialogue "Biblical ersatz with an Edgar Rice Burroughs flavor," and *The New Yorker* amusedly quoted De Mille's statement about his new "Scripturama": "My father studied for the ministry and read the Bible in our home, and this picture is near my heart. Furthermore, we have to take in $7,000,000 to break even." *The New Yorker's* heading: FURTHERMORE DEPARTMENT.[12] De Mille continued to be bothered by the teasing, but he went on making spectacles to the end. He filmed a circus story, *The Greatest Show on Earth,* in 1952, which won an Oscar, and did a remake of *The Ten Commandments* in 1956 that was technically even more impressive than the old silent version. By this time most of the other studios, impressed by De Mille's successes, were allotting huge budgets to film spectaculars that on occasion overtopped the work of the old spectacle-master himself.

In the fifties the big studios looked to film spectacles as a way of pulling people away from their television screens and back into movie theaters. They added new enticements, too, like 3-D and wide screens, but only the latter caught on. In 1953, Twentieth Century-Fox released a spectacular film, *The Robe,* based on Lloyd Douglas's best-selling novel about a garment belonging to Jesus, that had all the ingredients: religion, pageantry, magnificent sets, Technicolor, and CinemaScope. Hollywood's defiant slogan at this time, "movies are better than ever," meant mainly bigger and longer wide-screen spectacles about ancient Egypt, Greece, and Rome, and, of course, about Old and New Testament days.

Some of Hollywood's newest big-screen epics were silly: *Demetrius and the Gladiators* (1954), for example, and *Helen of Troy* (1955). Others succeeded in achieving the kind of dignity and grandeur that D. W. Griffith himself would probably have approved: *Spartacus* (1960), *El Cid* (1961), and *Lawrence of Arabia* (1962). But in the 1970s, when spectacles began losing their appeal for the increasingly youthful film audiences, producers lowered their sights and began churning out large-scale "disaster" films—*Airport* (1970), *Earthquake* (1974), *The Towering Inferno* (1974)—with impressive visuals but inane stories. In 1968, however, Stanley Kubrick came up with a marvelous science-fiction film, *2001: A Space Odyssey,* which impressed highbrows as well as middlebrows and went over big with the masses too. Within a few years sci-fi spectacles had become the big thing. In the seventies and eighties, films like *Star*

Wars, Superman (1978), Alien (1979), and their sequels broke all box-office records.

When movies turned to sound, dialogue was something of a problem for Hollywood's epic makers. What kind of voice did an ancient pharaoh have? How did Moses talk when he was laying down the law to his people? And what kind of English sounded convincing in the mouth of Nero? or Cleopatra? or Samson? or Noah? Some producers settled for mock-serious conversations in their films that were wonderful to hear. "It's strange to see you working," Cleopatra (Claudette Colbert) tells Caesar (Warren William) in De Mille's 1934 epic about the Queen of the Nile. "I've always figured you either fighting . . . or loving." "I've had experience with fighting," says Caesar coyly. "But not with loving, I suppose?" asks Cleopatra. "Not with pretty little queens," Caesar tells her. David and Bathsheba (1951) also had its cutesy confrontation. "David," says Bathsheba (Susan Hayward), "did you really kill Goliath? Was he as big as they say?" "I admit," confesses David (Gregory Peck), "he grows a little bigger every year." In Demetrius and the Gladiators (1954), a sequel to The Robe (1953), the talk is even campier. "To be a Christian is anything but dull these days," says Demetrius (Victor Mature). "Ooo!" cries Debra Paget, holding the robe, "I didn't know Christ was so tall. Was he as tall as you?" "Just about," says Victor Mature modestly. In The Ten Commandments (1956), Anne Baxter exclaims: "Oh, Moses, you splendid, stubborn, adorable fool!"[13]

Not all spectacle makers handled epic talk with tongue in cheek. Some of them took quite seriously the challenge of making heroic figures talk nobly but naturally in their films. They soon learned that British performers did better on the whole with hoity-toity talk than home-grown performers, though at times they handed them some pretty bland dialogue too. But America's Charlton Heston, star of many medieval and biblical spectacles, handled epic talk with ease and confidence. To some people he even looked like Michelangelo's Moses in The Ten Commandments (1956). But the trick was to keep conversation to a minimum in films about the ancient world. In movie epics it was the derring-do, not the dialogue, that counted.

All Out for Robin Hood!

Douglas Fairbanks was at first lukewarm about filming Robin Hood (1922). "I don't want to look like a heavy-footed Englishman tramping around in the woods," he moaned. Then he became excited about the acrobatic feats he could perform in the movie and decided to put his own money into the project. But he was stupefied when he returned from Europe to begin production and saw the gigantic set erected for the picture: a huge medieval castle, with turrets and battlements ninety feet high, spread along Santa Monica Boulevard. He took one look at it, according to director Allan Dwan, and pulled out of the project at once. "My pictures have always had the intimate touch," he explained. "We'd look like a bunch of Lilliputians in the halls of a giant if we used that set."

Dwan was deeply disappointed, but he assured Fairbanks he could use the expensive set in some other picture. A few days later he invited Fairbanks to visit the set to give him advice on another film he had in mind. As they walked around, they came to a wall where stone steps wound up outside a tower to reach a balcony hanging over a tremendous arch. "The hero," said Dwan, outlining the film he wanted to do, "would climb the stairs to confront his enemies on the balcony, then another group of adversaries would cut off his retreat by coming up the stairs." "End of hero," said Fairbanks, and turned to leave. "Not quite," said Dwan. "Look, I'll show you what I mean." Then he ran up the stairs, pretended to be dueling on the balcony, and then, to Fairbanks's astonishment, jumped on a long piece of drapery extending from the roof of the arch to the floor below, and slid gracefully all the way down to safety. "Say, Allan, that's terrific!" exclaimed Fairbanks, and after Dwan showed him the slide concealed beneath the drapes, he was eager to try it out himself. At this point he was eager, too, to begin production on *Robin Hood* after all. "Why didn't you show me the slide stunt before?" he asked. "As a matter of fact, it wasn't finished until yesterday," he was told.

Fairbanks was amused by the way Dwan had tricked him into changing his mind. But he was also grateful. For upon its release, *Robin Hood* broke box-office records all over the world. During its long run at Grauman's Egyptian Theatre, Hollywood Boulevard streetcar conductors no longer called out, "McCadden Place," the nearest stop, but simply announced: "All out for *Robin Hood*!"[14]

Fairbanks's Double
One scene in *Robin Hood* called for the hero to climb the chain of the big castle's drawbridge in order to get inside to confront the evil

Prince John. It was a dangerous feat, and Douglas Fairbanks's associates finally convinced him he should let a double do it. But the double performed clumsily, to Fairbanks's secret delight, and the director decided to try the scene again with another double. The following day, the new double his assistants had located appeared on the set wearing Robin Hood makeup and performed magnificently; he even looked like Fairbanks as he shot up the long chain while the cameras turned. But when he reached the top, he paused, flung out his hand in a sweeping gesture, and began grinning. At this point everyone realized what had happened: Fairbanks had decided to be his own double.[15]

Tablecloths and Beards

In 1922 Cecil B. De Mille offered $1,000 for the best idea for his next picture, received thousands of letters from all over the world containing suggestions, but liked best a short note that said simply: "You cannot break the Ten Commandments—they will break you." He settled on *The Ten Commandments* as the title of his new film.

When De Mille approached Paramount's Adolph Zukor with the idea, the latter was not impressed. "Old men wearing tablecloths and beards?" he snorted. "Cecil, a picture like that would ruin us." But De Mille persisted. "How much?" Zukor finally asked. "A million dollars," said De Mille. Zukor almost passed out at the thought. "Think of it," De Mille went on. "We'll be the first studio in history to open and close the Red Sea!" "Or maybe," wailed Zukor, "the first director to open and close Paramount!" But he gave in, and De Mille began work on the picture.

One day, as production dragged on, Zukor approached De Mille and said nervously: "Well, Cecil, the money piles up. What's the story?" "What do you want me to do," cried De Mille, "stop shooting and release it as *The Five Commandments*?" De Mille went on to make his *Ten Commandments,* and the picture did well at the box office when it was released in 1923. But after seeing it, humorist Will Rogers observed: "It's easy to see where God left off and Cecil De Mille began."[16]

In His Memory

In one of the most important scenes in *The Ten Commandments,* Moses descends from Mount Sinai with the sacred tablets and the Israelites gathered at the base of the mountain look at him with awe and reverence. De Mille shot the scene several times but was so disappointed with the expressions on the faces of the extras playing the part of Israelites that he finally called a break. Suddenly a bell in the town church nearby began tolling and De Mille called the cast together. With his voice breaking, he announced that one of the members of the cast had just died, leaving a widow and eight children behind. "Now, in his memory," he said solemnly, "I ask for two minutes of respectful silence." As everyone stood there, shocked and saddened by the news, the cameras began grinding away. It turned out that no one had died; it was just De Mille's way of getting what he wanted on film. The resulting scene was considered one of the best in the picture.[17]

Waiting for God
One day, during the filming of The Ten Commandments Theodore Roberts and James Neil, wearing their biblical costumes, stopped by to see director De Mille. After waiting outside his office for more than an hour, they finally told one of his underlings: "Tell God that Moses and Aaron are waiting without!"[18]

Adding Realism
The high point of Ben-Hur (1926) was the chariot race. To shoot the sequence, producer Irving Thalberg and unit manager Joe Cohn stationed forty-two cameras around the set: behind statues, in sandpits, on pillars, and among the hundreds of people filling the coliseum. Standing in the middle of the arena and looking over the crowd, Thalberg cried: "How many people do you have up there, Joe?" "Thirty-nine hundred," answered Cohn. "We need more," said Thalberg. Cohn asked him how he was going to find more extras at eight in the morning on Saturday. "Pull them in off the street, if necessary," Thalberg told him. Cohn did just that. He and his assistants plucked another four hundred people from streets, buses, trolleys, restaurants, all-night movies, and grocery stores, put them in togas, and placed them in the grandstand with the other extras. But just as they were ready to shoot the scene, a thick fog rolled in from the Pacific. There was nothing to do but wait until the fog lifted.

Two hours later the fog was gone and the cameras started turning. After a while Cohn went up to Thalberg and told him it would soon be time for a lunch break, but that there were only 3,900 box lunches for the 4,300 extras. Thalberg said there was no problem;

they would simply skip lunch and shoot straight through the afternoon. "But those people are hungry," protested Cohn. "They may riot." "Fine," said Thalberg calmly. "That'll add realism to the scene!"[19]

De Mille Decorum

The filming of The King of Kings (1927), De Mille's second big religious epic, began on August 24, 1926, amid much flourish. The clergy asked for a blessing—a Protestant bishop, Catholic priest, Jewish rabbi, Mohammedan teacher, Buddhist monk—and an organ played "Onward Christian Soldiers" as De Mille walked solemnly onto the set. His assistants handed out Bibles to the players and told them to use their biblical names during the shooting. They did: "Tell Caiaphas to get his makeup"; "We're ready for Jesus"; "Peter's wig is slipping, someone fix it." But one of De Mille's sidekicks offended the boss by asking, "Where in the hell is Judas?"

On the first day of shooting, when H. B. Warner, playing Jesus, arrived on the set in a flowing white robe, he looked the part so perfectly that some of the people there fell on their knees as he passed them. But Warner wasn't always so impressive. One day a newspaper photographer took a picture of him dressed as Jesus, draped on a chair, smoking a cigarette and reading the sports page. De Mille then issued strict orders about decorous behavior and told the cast it was important to keep frivolous stories about the project out of the papers. "They'll print anything to get a laugh," he warned. "I want to get through this picture without someone writing that she saw Caiaphas drunk at Ciro's last night, or Mary Magdalene sparking in a rumble seat on Mulholland Drive." At De Mille's request, Warner ate meals alone in his dressing room and wore a hood covering his face whenever he went outside. But De Mille himself didn't always observe the rules. When Warner performed badly in one scene, the director used such abusive language that Warner finally interrupted: "Mr. De Mille, do you realize to whom you are speaking?"

De Mille forbade wisecracks on the set. He also insisted that Warner and Dorothy Cummings, who was playing the Virgin Mary, sign a five-year contract promising not to accept future film roles that might lessen the dignity of the parts they were playing in The King of Kings. "It would never do," observed his brother and associate, William De Mille, "to have the Virgin Mary getting a divorce or Saint John cutting up in a nightclub. Therefore they all signed legal documents which underwrote their behavior and their chastity, it being clearly understood that, though breaking solemn vows taken at the altar was only human, breaking a contract with the Company was really important."

During the filming, De Mille sent out a questionnaire to find out what people knew about the Scriptures. Thousands of people responded. His favorite answer: *"The elders are a sort of bush from which you get berries to make wine."*

On Christmas Eve, 1926, De Mille finished filming the Crucifixion scene and called, "Cut!" But as the players started to leave, he cried, "Just a minute, if you please, ladies and gentlemen." Then he pointed out it was Christmas Eve and he suggested thinking about the birthday of the King of Kings for a few minutes. So the company stood silently as the organ played Christmas music. "That's all, ladies and gentlemen," De Mille finally cried. "Thank you. Good night, and happy Christmas."[20]

Plagiarism
When word reached Los Angeles that a plagiarism suit had been filed against *The King of Kings*, a newsman called De Mille for a statement. Forgetting that screenwriter Jeannie Macpherson had helped out on the script, De Mille said loftily: "I have always supposed that Matthew, Mark, Luke, and John were responsible for this story." Said the reporter: "Just how does it happen then that Jeannie Macpherson's name is plastered all over the billboards?"[21]

Super-Special
When one of the studios started in on a big biblical epic, the assistant director came to work the first day and found twelve disciples waiting to begin work. "Why only twelve disciples?" he yelled to his assistant. "Didn't you know this was to be a super-special? I want twenty-four." The next day, so the story goes, production was suspended.[22]

Big Production
During the shooting of one super-production, it was reported, the supervisor walked onto the set one day, glared, and saw small potted palms. "Stop!" he cried. "This is a BIG production. We've got to have BIG palms." And so the shooting was delayed for two hours at

the cost of $2,000 while the property man replaced the little palms with big ones.[23]

Epic Dilemma

Overheard in a studio the day after the preview of a film: "What's the verdict on the picture?" "Well, the producers don't know whether to shelve it or release it as an epic!"[24]

Cozy

For *The Sign of the Cross* (1932), Cecil B. De Mille arranged for the construction of a lavish set of ancient Rome and planned to make the burning of Rome a highlight of the picture. One morning he arrived on the set to find Charles Laughton, who played Nero, wearing toga and laurel wreaths and prancing about singing Latin verse to the accompaniment of a prop lyre. Afraid that Laughton wasn't taking the picture seriously enough, De Mille launched into a long harangue about the impermanence of man's mightiest works when compared to the divine power. "When I stand among the ruins of Ancient Rome—so perishable—" he concluded, "I cannot help but feel how much we need our faith. Faith is man's strength. With it I feel that God is in me, and I am in God.". "Really?" murmured Laughton. "How cozy!" It was his last job for De Mille.[25]

Cheesecake

In *The Sign of the Cross*, De Mille saw to it that Claudette Colbert, who played Nero's wife, Poppaea, had a huge marble pool full of real asses' milk in which to take a bath. But someone neglected to put fresh milk in the pool every day and soon the milk began turning into cheese and spreading an unpleasant smell through the studio. On the third day of shooting, when Colbert arrived for her bathing scene and found everyone complaining about the cheese smell, she started laughing. "Well," she said, "it's supposed to be a cheesecake shot, isn't it?"[26]

Elephants

Cecil B. De Mille had trouble with the elephants he hired from the circus to perform in *The Sign of the Cross*. In one scene, he wanted them to march by the cameras as part of a triumphal Roman procession; but when they heard all the clapping and shouting, they reacted by standing on their heads. A little later, the noise panicked some of them and in the end the whole herd stampeded. One of the actors was caught in the middle of the stampede, but the elephant carrying him in her trunk carefully put him on the ground and stood over his body to protect him until the elephant trainers brought things under control.[27]

De Mille's Lions
De Mille hired lions as well as elephants to use in The Sign of the Cross: twenty-five lions at $25 each. In one scene they were to run up some steps leading to the arena, where they were to attack the Christians kneeling in the sand. When it came time to film the scene, though, the lions lazily lay down near the steps instead of running up them.

"Listen," De Mille told one of the trainers, "this is costing a frightful lot of money. When are those lions going up?" "Oh," said the trainer, "lions don't know anything about that; they don't go up stairs." "Well," announced De Mille, "these lions are going up stairs!" He then grabbed a chair in one hand and an ax handle in the other, rushed toward the lions, shouting and lunging, and kept at it until the startled creatures sprang to their feet and rushed up the stairs. According to Peter Calvin, De Mille's grandson, De Mille's admonition on that occasion went onto the soundtrack. "If you listen closely," he insisted, "you can hear Grandfather in the background, yelling, 'Goddamn it, get going!'"

The lions got going all right, but they got even too. In the arena sequence, when the trainer was goading them into action, several young males let go on some of the players. "This is an outrage!" thundered De Mille. "Those god-damned lions of yours are urinating on my Christian martyrs!"[28]

De Mille Quake
After a severe earthquake hit the Los Angeles area in March 1933, actress Janet Gaynor, who was in one of the shaking studio buildings at the time, exclaimed: "I thought for a moment we'd got caught in one of Mr. De Mille's pictures!"[29]

Cleopatra's Snake
Before casting Claudette Colbert in the title role in Cleopatra (1934), Cecil B. De Mille thought he ought to have a little talk with her.

"You remember," he said, "how Cleopatra died. She committed suicide by putting an asp, which is a venomous snake, to her bare breast and letting it kill her." "Oh, Mr. De Mille," exclaimed Colbert, "I couldn't do that! A snake? I couldn't possibly—" "Wait, Claudette," he interrupted. "Don't say positively that you can't, or I cannot give you the part. You want to play it, don't you?" "Yes, but—" "No, now wait, please. I want you to play it. I don't want anyone but you for Cleopatra. We'll just not say any more about the snake until we come to it, and will you trust me if I tell you that you can play the scene?" Colbert reluctantly agreed, the shooting started, and De Mille was pleased with all the scenes she did for him.

Then came *Cleopatra*'s final big scene. In regal robes, Colbert was to mount the throne of Egypt for the last time and commit suicide. But before shooting the scene, De Mille borrowed a huge snake from the zoo, coiled it around him, and walked onto the set, pointing the snake's head straight at Colbert. "Oh, Mr. De Mille," she cried, as he approached the throne, "don't come near me with that!" But De Mille kept walking toward her. "I *cannot* touch it, Mr. De Mille!" she shuddered. "Well," said De Mille, "how about this?" And he brought out a tiny little snake in his other hand, just the size of an Egyptian asp. "Oh," cried Colbert thankfully, "that little thing? Give it to me!" So she played the death scene with the snake just as De Mille had planned for her to do all along.[30]

Earthquake

At MGM, Bob Hopkins was ingenious at thinking up ideas for blockbuster movies and then saying: "Okay—now put a word man on it." One day he cornered studio officials and shot out his latest brainstorm: "Earthquake—San Francisco—Gable and MacDonald—can't you see it . . . ? Clark's on one side of the street, Jeanette's on the other—goddamn street splits right between them—it's gotta be but terrific!" No sooner said than done. In short order MGM began shooting *San Francisco* (1936), featuring Clark Gable and Jeanette MacDonald, about the famous earthquake of 1906.[31]

No More Epics

One day in the late summer of 1936, Albert Lewin, Irving Thalberg's assistant, went to his boss with a fifty-page synopsis of Margaret Mitchell's best-selling novel *Gone With the Wind*. "You've got to read this," he cried. "It's long, but it's great. The role is made to order for Clark Gable, and the whole story is surefire." "All right, Al, I'll read it," said Thalberg. When he finally got around to reading the synopsis, Lewin asked him what he thought of it. "You're absolutely right," said Thalberg. "It's sensational. The role is great for Gable and it will make a terrific picture." Then he added: "Now get out of here with it." Lewin was bewildered. "Look," Thalberg explained, "I have just made *Mutiny on the Bounty* and *The Good Earth*. And now you're asking me to burn Atlanta? No! Absolutely not! No more epics for me now. Just give me a little drawing-room drama. I'm tired. I'm just too tired." A little later that year he died of pneumonia.[32]

Groucho Butler
When Hollywood became interested in *Gone With the Wind*, the author, Margaret Mitchell, stayed mostly aloof at first. She refused to go to California to help out on the script. And when the great game of picking stars to play the characters in her novel got under way, she made only one tongue-in-cheek suggestion: Groucho Marx (she was a fan) for the part of Rhett Butler.[33]

The Search for Scarlett
Shortly after purchasing the rights to *Gone With the Wind,* David Selznick directed Russell Birdwell, studio press chief, to launch an ambitious publicity campaign for the spectacular film he planned to make. "Why don't we put on a nationwide search for a girl to play Scarlett?" he exclaimed. Birdwell then sent talent scouts out to interview young hopefuls all over the country. He also called for applications for the part, and before long a torrent of mail was pouring into the studio. The "Scarlett Letters," as they were called, usually contained pictures; sometimes the would-be Scarletts wore antebellum gowns in them and sometimes nothing at all. On Christmas morning, a huge reproduction of the book *Gone With the Wind* appeared on Selznick's doorstep. As he opened the door, a girl in hoopskirts popped out of it. "I am your Scarlett O'Hara!" she announced merrily.

While interviewing unknowns, Selznick announced he would also consider professionals for the part of Scarlett. At once, some of Hollywood's biggest stars entered the contest: Bette Davis, Miriam Hopkins, Claudette Colbert, Joan Crawford, Margaret Sullavan, Carole Lombard, Paulette Goddard, Tallulah Bankhead. Katharine Hepburn was particularly insistent. "The part was practically written for me," she told Selznick. "I *am* Scarlett O'Hara!" But Selznick remained unconvinced; said he, bluntly: "I can't imagine Rhett Butler chasing you for ten years." "Well," she sniffed, "maybe other people's view of sex appeal is different from yours." For the fun of it, Selznick and his brother Myron, a talent agent, invited all of Hollywood's Scarlett contenders to a big party at the latter's elegant mountain home near Lake Arrowhead. The gathering was a flop. The stars resented being brought together this way for the amusement of the Selznicks.

Casting Rhett Butler was easy: Clark Gable was the obvious choice from the outset. Gable, though, had misgivings at first. "I was scared when I discovered that I had been cast by the public," he said later. "I felt that every reader would have a different idea as to how Rhett should be played on the screen, and I didn't see how I could please everybody." But he finally yielded and in August 1938 became a Gone With the Winder.

In December 1938, Selznick began production of the Civil War epic, even though he still had no Scarlett. He had some old sets assembled on the studio lot to look like Atlanta in 1864, and arranged to have them go up in flames, with doubles posing as Rhett Butler and Scarlett O'Hara, and with seven Technicolor cameras filming the scene from various angles. The date for the burning of Atlanta was set for December 11. That evening, Selznick took his friends and associates up to a special platform erected for the occasion and was ready to begin. "Where the hell is Myron?" he cried. "Goddammit, he's got to be here to see this!" But after waiting impatiently for an hour or so, he gave the signal to begin; the crew set fire to the buildings and the cameras began turning. While the fire was raging, Myron suddenly turned up on the set with some dinner guests, including his client Laurence Olivier and Olivier's girlfriend, a young British actress. "So there you are!" cried David angrily. "Where the hell have you been?" "Dave," said Myron, taking Vivien Leigh by the hand, "I want you to meet Scarlett O'Hara."[34]

Slept
According to Eleanor Roosevelt, President Roosevelt fell asleep when *Gone With the Wind* (1939) was run off for him in the White House. When it was over and he woke up, he cried: "No movie has a right to be that long!" But he was in a minority. Most people loved the film.[35]

De Mille and the Critics

Critics were rough on Cecil B. De Mille and his epics. They acknowledged that his biblical spectacles did famously at the box office, but they deplored the sexploitation and poor taste. Even *New York Times* critic Bosley Crowther, who was friendly to De Mille, couldn't help teasing about *Samson and Delilah* (1949), a "movie for DeMillions if there ever was one," containing "more chariots, more temples, more peacock plumes, more beards and more sex than ever before." Another critic called the film "the most expensive haircut in history."

Sometimes De Mille was candid. "We'll sell it as a story of faith, story of the power of prayer," he once said of *Samson and Delilah*. Then he went on: "That's for the censors and the women's organizations. For the public it's the hottest love story of all time." On other occasions he was disingenuous. Accused of making money out of nudity, especially in the biblical films, he would say: "I didn't write the Bible and I didn't create sin"; or, "If you condemn my Bible pictures, you condemn the Bible." At times, though, he tried to laugh off the criticism and pretend it redounded to his advantage. Once, when a writer who had helped on the script told him *Samson and Delilah* would receive good notices from the critics, he feigned disappointment. "Just a minute!" he cried. "I've got a lot of money tied up in this thing!"[36]

Not Just the Jaw

When the writers were conferring on the script for *Samson and Delilah*, they came to the scene in which Samson slays the Philistines with the jawbone of an ass. "Just a minute," interposed one of director De Mille's assistants. "The jawbone of an ass! Never! This is a De Mille picture and we gotta use the whole ass!"[37]

Bronx Prince

In his first scene for the Technicolor epic *The Prince Who Was a Thief* (1951), Tony Curtis, playing a handsome young Arab prince, takes Piper Laurie in his arms, looks up, and utters what have become classic words: "Yonder lies da castle of my fadder, de Prince." "Cut!" yelled director Rudolph Maté. "Tony," he wailed, in his heavy Hungarian accent, "is dat how you always talk?" "Sure," said Curtis, who grew up in the Bronx. "And you don't talk so hot yourself." At this point Curtis's friend Shelley Winters, who was visiting the set, got into the act. "Look around the set, Mr. Maté," she said.

"Everyone is laughing hysterically. If you do the picture straight, it'll turn out to be just another Cornel Wilde–Yvonne De Carlo Persian B picture. But if you let Tony talk like he does naturally, you'll have a hilarious comedy." "Well," said Maté, after thinking things over a moment or two, "this is only my sixth picture as a director, so if it doesn't turn out, I can always go back to being a cameraman. We'll shoot it like you suggest, and the bosses can decide tomorrow when they see the rushes." When Maté's bosses saw the rushes they decided to continue with what Winters called "the Bronx Prince," and the picture turned out to be a success as a comic epic.[38]

Kelp Is on the Way

For the scene in Cecil B. De Mille's remake of The Ten Commandments (1956) showing the Children of Israel crossing the Red Sea, it was necessary to construct posts and wires along the seashore to guide the players and keep them within the bounds the special-effects people had marked out. But to keep the fences from casting shadows that would show up on the film, it was necessary to shoot the scene at precisely high noon.

At 11:45 A.M., De Mille was on a platform with one of the cameras and the Children of Israel were ready to start moving. Then De Mille suddenly noticed that the sand over which they were to march simply didn't look like the bottom of a sea. In desperation, he offered a reward if anyone could come up with suggestions for saving the scene, but no one could think of anything. Then, as he looked over at the ocean a few hundred feet away, he noticed some kelp floating near the shore. He immediately jumped off the platform, told everyone to follow him, waded into the water, and returned with an armful of kelp, which he began strewing between the posts. Everyone followed suit, actors, actresses, cameramen, extras; and in a few minutes the long path between the fences looked like the bottom of a sea. Back on the platform again, De Mille blew his whistle and the Children of Israel began their march. It was exactly noon.[39]

Tablets

For the scene in which Moses comes down the mountain with the Ten Commandments in his arms, Charlton Heston, who played Moses in the 1956 version of De Mille's biblical epic, insisted on using tablets carved out of stone taken from the top of Mt. Sinai. "All right," cried De Mille, when it came time to film the crucial scene,

"Moses is coming!" But as Heston came down the mountain, the tablets were so heavy they had him practically on his knees. After that, he agreed to a retake in which he made his big entrance carrying wooden tablets.[40]

Party Pooper

When it came time to film the orgy around the golden calf for The Ten Commandments (1956), De Mille pulled out all the stops: He had half-naked girls writhing around in ecstatic passion and guys carrying gals off behind the rocks at the foot of Mount Sinai (reproduced in Paramount Studios). Then, suddenly, Charlton Heston appears as Moses with the tablets containing the Ten Commandments and cries, "Who is on the Lord's side?" At that point an assistant director called, "Lunch!" But as he left the set one of the girls in the suddenly suspended orgy scene yelled after him: "Party pooper!"[41]

The Man Who Played God

The big question during the production of The Ten Commandments (1956) was who should play God in the film. "Mr. De Mille," said one of the director's associates one day, "there is a question that's been bothering us." "Yes?" asked De Mille. "Well, sir," said the man, "who is going to be the Voice of God in the scene of the burning bush?" "Well," said De Mille, "who would you suggest?" "Well, sir," said the man, "there's only one real candidate for the Voice of God. You!" Everyone else agreed. De Mille thought it over for a moment and then said sadly: "Gentlemen, no. . . " "Oh," cried his associate, "but, why, sir?" "No," repeated De Mille. "You see," he explained, "my voice is too well known, and it would go round the world and everyone would say, 'That isn't God; that's Cecil B. De Mille.'" In the end Charlton Heston did the job; his voice, played back at low speed, was used for the sequence. But there was the inevitable De Mille joke about the psychiatrist who was needed in heaven because "God thought He was Cecil B. De Mille."[42]

De Mille History

The liberties Cecil B. De Mille took with history in his epics produced the following lines:

Cecil B. De Mille
Much against his will
Was persuaded to keep Moses
Out of the Wars of the Roses.[43]

Busy Army

In 1959 Samuel Bronston established a studio in Madrid and began producing a series of spectacular epics—*King of Kings, El Cid* (both 1961), *The Fall of the Roman Empire* (1964)—with the warm support of the Spanish government. For battle scenes he always recruited soldiers—sometimes as many as eight thousand—from the Spanish army. One day, it was reported, Spanish dictator General Franco said to his minister of war, "It has been a long time since I inspected the army. Fix a parade." "Sorry, Generalísimo," said the nervous minister, "it cannot be done. The army is making a movie for Samuel Bronston again."[44]

Cold Jordan

When Charlton Heston played John the Baptist in *The Greatest Story Ever Told* (1965), he stood in the Colorado River on a chilly November day for one scene and baptized scores of local people who had been hired to play the part of converts to Christianity. "It was lovely to see when it finally came to their turn," he recalled. "They'd step into the water and you'd see this expression of what I trust came across as ecstasy on their faces." But the water was so cold that some of them came up only semiconscious. "George," said Heston to director George Stevens after the scene was over, "if the Jordan had been as cold as the Colorado, Christianity would never have gotten off the ground."[45]

True Awe

In *The Greatest Story Ever Told*, John "Duke" Wayne played a cameo role as the Roman centurion who leads Jesus to his Crucifixion and has one line to deliver: "Truly, this was the Son of God." According to a popular, but apocryphal, story, when Wayne delivered his line for the first time, director George Stevens cut the action and told Wayne: "You're referring to the Son of God here, Duke. You've got to deliver the line with a little more awe." Whereupon

Wayne announced on the next take: "Aw, truly this was the Son of God."[46]

Terrible Time

Director John Huston found working on *The Bible* (1966) an exhilarating challenge—especially the Creation and the Ark sequences—but he also found it tough work. When people asked him how things were going, he said: "I don't know how God managed. I'm having a terrible time."[47]

Never Die

When filming *The Man Who Would Be King* (1975), an expensively produced historical drama, in Morocco, director John Huston came across an old man with a beard who was standing on one leg and leaning on a staff. He turned out to be one hundred years old, though he didn't look it, and Huston thought he would be just right for the part of Kafu Selim, the high priest, in the picture. With the help of an interpreter, he succeeded in persuading the old man to appear in the film, together with a patriarch in the local mosque and an ancient Berber from the high mountains. At the end of the shooting, Huston invited the three old men, who had never seen a movie before, into a projection room to watch themselves on the screen. After the lights came up, the three men began talking excitedly to each other and at length seemed to reach some kind of consensus. Huston turned to the interpreter and said: "Ask them what they think of what they saw." The answer came from Kafu Selim: "We will never die!"[48]

Horror

and

Suspense

Horror stories are as old as history. Ancient myths and legends tell of monsters and demons roaming the countryside, and folklore in all lands through the ages has peopled the world with witches, wizards, ghosts, and goblins. For the superstitious, tales of terror, even in modern times, contain explanations for life's oddities; for the enlightened, they provide good entertainments. It is not surprising that Hollywood took to horror films with enthusiasm in the 1930s; what is surprising is that it took American moviemakers so long to begin capitalizing on the public's fascination with the uncanny.

Three of Hollywood's favorite sources for "chillers" came from nineteenth-century British writers. And all three writers, appropriately enough, were inspired by nightmares. Mary Shelley had a scary dream one night about a monster created by a scientist with Faustian ambitions, and began writing *Frankenstein, or the Modern Prometheus* (1818). Robert Louis Stevenson had a dream too. He cried out in his sleep one night and when his wife woke him up he exclaimed: "Why did you wake me? I was dreaming a fine bogey tale." The bogey tale: *The Strange Case of Dr. Jekyll and Mr. Hyde* (1886).[1] Bram Stoker was another dreamer. After a late supper of crabmeat he dreamed about vampires, and soon after started work on *Dracula* (1897). The monster, the Jekyll-Hyde schizophrenic, and Count

Dracula all became familiar sights on Hollywood sets in the thirties and forties. So did werewolves, mummies, ghouls, and zombies. Stories about the latter, though, were largely the creation of Hollywood scriptwriters. British (and American) novelists never got around to writing noteworthy books about any of them.

In nickelodeon days came the first crude efforts at filming *Dr. Jekyll and Mr. Hyde* (1908) and *Frankenstein* (1908), but the public took to neither. D. W. Griffith did somewhat better with *The Avenging Conscience* (1914), based on the macabre tales and poems of Edgar Allan Poe. But the first notable horror movie in America was John Barrymore's *Dr. Jekyll and Mr. Hyde* (1920). Barrymore reveled in his double role as the respectable Jekyll and the repulsive Hyde. His transformation scene was a *tour de force;* he did the changeover without trick photography by gradually distorting the muscles of his face into grotesqueries before our very eyes. "One leaves the theater," said a New York reviewer, "with the belief that motion pictures are on the verge of a new era."[2] He spoke prematurely. For even Lon Chaney's famous shockers—*The Hunchback of Notre Dame* (1923) and *The Phantom of the Opera* (1925)—failed to generate a demand for more of the same. The passion for "horrifics" awaited the arrival of sound.

The first "horror talkie"—Warners' *The Terror* (1928)—was so mediocre that *Time* gave it only a short perfunctory review. Warners had hoped there was "gold in them thar chills," but it didn't turn out that way.[3] It took Universal's *Dracula* and *Frankenstein*, both appearing in 1931, to touch off the first cycle of horror films in the United States. Bela Lugosi, a Hungarian actor whose English was chillingly imperfect, made the part of the sinister Transylvanian vampire his very own from the moment he appeared early in the film and announced with a cruel smile: "I am—Dra-cu-la." And Boris Karloff, wearing sixty pounds of makeup and accessories, but inducing sympathy as well as revulsion by his performance, became identical with Dr. Frankenstein's monstrous creation for countless moviegoers. (James Whale, who directed *Frankenstein,* estimated that the seventy-one-minute picture gave people ninety-five chills, one chill every forty-five seconds.) Both *Dracula* and *Frankenstein* were smash hits and there were the inevitable sequels, since, as one producer remarked, "you can't keep a good monster down."[4] The vampire and the Monster, moviegoers soon learned, had brides and sons and daughters; and the two spooks were even to meet up with each other in due course. But the popularity of "chiller-diller-mellers," as

Variety called them, petered out with the appearance of *Dracula's Daughter* in 1936. Thus ended Hollywood's first horror cycle.

The second cycle began with the rerelease of the original Lugosi and Karloff films in 1938. Both pictures did so well at the box office that Universal realized it was back in the horror business again. There were more Dracula and Frankenstein films; there were also films (not all by Universal) about ghouls, zombies, mummies, and mad scientists. But a scary new creature of the night appeared on the scene and threatened to take over: the wolf man. Universal had produced *Werewolf of London,* with Henry Hull in the title role, in 1935, but it wasn't until Lon Chaney, Jr., appeared in *The Wolf Man* in 1941 that lycanthropes caught on with the public. "Whoever is bitten by a werewolf and lives becomes a werewolf himself," a Gypsy tells Chaney early in the film. He is bitten, of course, assumes a wolfish form when the moon is full, and wreaks plenty of havoc until he is finally killed by a silver bullet. (Gold won't do.) But not really killed. Somehow Hollywood's horrors had a way of surviving violent annihilation at the end of their films to reappear in new films and frighten new audiences.

Why the popularity of horror movies? Psychoanalysts, with Freud's study of ghost stories as a guide, stress sex appeal. *Dracula,* according to one psychiatrist, is "a kind of incestuous, necrophilous, oral-and-sadistic all-in wrestling match"; or, to put it somewhat differently, "a vast polymorph perverse bisexual oral-anal-genital sado-masochistic timeless orgy."[5] This seems a bit overwrought, even for a Freudian. Without denying the undoubted erotic content of vampire-monster-werewolf movies, it seems safe to say that the appeal of a good horror film, like that of any good scary tale, is in large part metaphysical: It speaks to our deep-seated fear of death and the unknown and to our efforts, largely on the subconscious level, to come to terms with life's inexplicabilities. In *Dracula,* Bela Lugosi fixes his eyes at one point on Professor Van Helsing (who is on to his tricks) and tries to place him under his spell, but the latter looks back without flinching, puts up a fierce resistance, and in the end forces Lugosi to give up. With Van Helsing (Edward Van Sloan) we moviegoers triumph, too, at least for the moment, over the universe's irrationalities.

Horror films also have a psychological appeal. They provide outlets for our inner hostilities and urges to violence. Asked why he liked horror movies, a New York truck driver put it simply: "Because I can always get such a good night's sleep afterwards!"[6] There is escape, too, in horror movies, as in all movies, but escape of a special kind. Anthropologist Margaret Mead saw fright films primarily as an escape from the actual horrors in modern life. "Today," she declared in an interview, "people are exposed to more actual crime and horror than ever before in history because of the tremendous advances in modern communication—on-the-spot radio and television, wirephotos, and so on. The monsters and mummies of the screen, which are always destroyed in the end just as the heroine is saved, are a relief from everyday horror."[7] But horror films are also a relief from everyday conventionalities. Boris Karloff himself may have gotten it just right when queried on the subject in 1957. "This genre of entertainment," said the Grand Old Man of Horror, "obviously fulfills a desire in people to experience something which is beyond the range of everyday human emotion. . . . [For] millions of filmgoers they relieve the humdrum life of the average individual better than any other kind of story, and that after all is what entertainment should always do."[8]

But what began in fear ended in farce. By the late 1940s Hollywood's fright flickers were losing their sting and producers were turning to burlesque. Vincent Price began hamming it up in Technicolor films based loosely on Poe stories, comedians Abbott and Costello introduced the Mummy, Frankenstein, and Dr. Jekyll and Mr. Hyde to wisecracks and slapstick, and a minor new genre, the teenage chiller (with youthful tongue in cheek), emerged: *I Was a Teenage Frankenstein*, *I was a Teen-age Werewolf* (both 1957), *Werewolf in a Girl's Dormitory* (1961). By this time even the old-time chillers seemed creaky and comical when shown on television. In the sixties, moviemakers turned serious again, but they were no longer interested in vampires, mummies, and werewolves; they centered most of their films on Satanism: *Rosemary's Baby* (1968), *The Exorcist* (1973), and *The Omen* (1976). And the effectiveness of the new horrifics came in part from the premise that had made the original *Dracula* so chilling: that the supernatural events taking place on the screen could and did actually happen. *The Exorcist* produced nausea, fainting, and hysteria in some theaters. "My janitors," reported one theater manager, "are going bananas wiping up the vomit."[9]

Chillers seem to be hardy perennials in the movie industry, but thrillers, that is, suspense films, have also been extremely popular with movie audiences. The earliest movies, indeed, were little more than brief cliff-hangers. But D. W. Griffith soon developed techniques—flashbacks, cross-cutting from scene to scene, the use of moving cameras mounted on automobiles and trains—that enabled filmmakers to heighten suspense on the screen and introduce it into feature-length productions. And although all drama contains suspense of some kind, Hollywood eventually developed a distinct genre of film in which suspense was the main ingredient: crime dramas, whodunits, spy pictures, disaster films, and psycho-thrillers. Alfred Hitchcock, the British director who began making films in America in 1939, was the acknowledged master of the art for many years. A specialist in suspense, he enjoyed giving audiences information that characters in his films didn't know in order to increase the suspense. "Knowing what to expect, the audience waits for it to happen," he once pointed out. "This conditioning of the viewer is essential to the build-up of suspense."[10]

In recent years psychological tension has come to be extremely important in American films, and some critics regard it as more sophisticated than conventional narrative suspense. But the old-time chases and cliff-hangers of moviedom's earliest years have by no means disappeared. With the extraordinary development of special effects during the past few years, in fact, suspense films have become more exciting than anything D. W. Griffith himself could ever have imagined. The cliff-per-minute sequences in *Indiana Jones and the Temple of Doom* (1984) would doubtless have dazzled—and delighted—America's film pioneers had they lived to see them.

Can't Sleep
When *Frankenstein* (1931) previewed in a Santa Barbara theater, it was said, women screamed, men trembled, and kids started crying. One man phoned the theater to say he was going to file suit because his nerves—and those of his wife and child—were shattered. Another man called the manager every five minutes after he saw the show to say, "I can't sleep because of that picture and you aren't going to either."[11]

Needed Watering
Charles Starrett, cowboy actor known as the "Durango Kid," lived near Boris Karloff off Coldwater Canyon and got to know the gentle Britisher well. One night, though, driving home from work, Starrett suddenly slammed on his brakes as he passed Karloff's house and almost had a wreck. "Boris, for God's sake," he yelled, running over to the garden where his friend, in full Monster regalia, stood, water-

ing can in hand, "what are you trying to do—scare me to death?" "Well, Charlie," said Karloff mildly, "we worked late tonight, and the rose garden needed watering. I didn't have time to wait around."[12]

Great Taste
Karloff enjoyed doing horror films, but he never pretended they were great art. "My wife is a woman of great taste," he once declared, "she has seen very, very few of my pictures."[13]

No Hits, No Runs, Just Terrors
During the Great Depression, Arthur Mayer, who ran the Rialto theater in New York, became a specialist in the "M product"—mystery, mayhem, and murder; he did his best "to glorify the American ghoul." When people called to find the name of the Rialto's latest horror picture, he had telephone operators start off by saying: "Help, murder, police! This is the Rialto, now playing Dracula, best thriller of the year!" Soon he became known as "the Merchant of Menace"; he was delighted when a gossip columnist quoted Sam Goldwyn as saying, "When I see the pictures they play in that theater it makes the hair stand on the edge of my seat!" He was equally pleased when The New York Times summed up one year at the Rialto with the words, "No hits, no runs, just terrors."

To advertise The Mummy (1932), Mayer stationed a huge dummy in front of the Rialto; it combined the most repulsive features of Frankenstein's Monster and Lugosi's Dracula and it grunted and growled as well. He nicknamed it Karloff. One day, Jack McManus, New York Times film reviewer, wrote that the show outside the Rialto was more entertaining than the one inside. Mayer was so pleased that he sent McManus the dummy as a gift. Unfortunately, it got stuck in the elevator on the way up to McManus's office and had to be chopped up and thrown away. For a month or two after that, Mayer noticed, the Times's notices were cool to the Rialto.[14]

Too Many Bodies
Toward the end of his life, Karloff had to wear a metal brace on one leg. "I can't breathe and I can't walk," he used to joke about his declining health. "Must be the result of carrying too many bodies upstairs!"[15]

Chariot Race

When producer Merian C. Cooper was planning *King Kong* (1933), the famous movie about a giant ape, he was anxious to include what moviemakers called a "chariot race" (a scene audiences would always remember, as they did the chariot race in *Ben-Hur*). Late one afternoon in February 1930, as he was leaving his office in midtown Manhattan, he heard the sound of an airplane, glanced out of the window, and saw a plane flying close to the New York Life Insurance Building, then the city's tallest building. At once it flashed into his mind: "If I can get that gorilla logically on top of the mightiest building in the world, and then have him shot down by the most modern of weapons, the airplane, then no matter how giant he was in size, and how fierce, that gorilla was doomed by civilization." And he reflected gleefully: "Well, if that isn't a chariot race, then I don't know what is." By the time RKO came to make the picture, Cooper had had to move Kong, first to the new Chrysler Building, and then, finally, to the Empire State Building, which, when completed in 1931, was the tallest structure in the world.

Kong's fight with the airplanes while perched on top of the Empire State Building thrilled the audience at the preview of *King Kong* in January 1933. But another scene upset the audience: the scene in which Kong shakes his pursuers off a log and into a chasm below, where they are attacked by huge slimy insects and snakes and eaten alive. When the log scene unrolled on the screen, some people began screaming, others got up and walked out of the theater, and still others began exchanging shocked comments. "It stopped the picture," Cooper recalled, "so the next day at the studio I took it out myself." Thus edited, the film had its world premiere in March 1933—at both the new Radio City Music Hall and the new RKO Roxy theater, with a combined seating capacity of 10,000—and was an immediate hit. By the end of the first week, close to 180,000 people had seen the film.[16]

Topping Them All

One horror writer who disliked juvenile stars exclaimed: "All I want to see is the horror picture to end all horror pictures. It should be called Frankenstein Meets Mickey Rooney. And I don't care how it comes out!"[17]

Tension

For one sequence in Alfred Hitchcock's thriller *Shadow of a Doubt* (1943), composer Dimitri Tiomkin had to rewrite "The Merry Widow" waltz, featured in the picture, giving it a sinister sound. At the preview, however, the audience giggled through Tiomkin's weird waltz harmonies and laughed loudly at other moments of terror on the screen. "Is calamity, Hitch," Tiomkin told the director afterward, "audience laughing." "Oh, that?" said Hitchcock calmly. "It was quite all right." "But, Hitch," persisted Tiomkin, "when should be fear, terror, they going ha-ha." "That was tension, Dimi," said Hitchcock. "The laughs were a sign the picture had them on edge." He went on to explain that American audiences always broke into nervous laughter when they were frightened and that it was a good sign for a suspense picture when they did. He was right. *Shadow of a Doubt* did splendidly when it was released and Hitchcock considered it his best film.[18]

Meltdown

While making *The Ghost of Frankenstein* (1942), Lon Chaney, Jr., suddenly turned to the director and cried: "Say, let's have the *Ghost* end with the monster melting right down before your eyes in the fire!" "Fine!" growled the director, "Great! And what do we start the next *Frankenstein* with? A grease spot?"[19]

Hitchcock's McGuffin

In spy pictures Alfred Hitchcock had to have what he called a "McGuffin," that is, something the spies were after (a secret formula, important papers, jewels, money), even though it played a peripheral role in the unfolding of the story. In *Notorious* (1946), which he started planning in 1944, Ingrid Bergman gets mixed up with German spies in Brazil, and it was necessary to get a McGuffin for them. "Let's make it uranium samples," Hitchcock told scriptwriter Ben Hecht, and the two of them called on Robert A. Milliken at the California Institute of Technology to learn something about the radioactive element. But when Hitchcock mentioned atom bombs, the Cal Tech physicist almost dropped his teeth, Hitchcock said later, for he was heavily involved at the time in the top-secret Manhattan Project for making the bombs. Milliken said it was absolutely impossible to make atom bombs, according to Hitchcock's tale afterward, and advised dropping the uranium McGuffin. But as they left Hitchcock told

Hecht: "I'm going ahead with the uranium McGuffin anyway." Hitchcock's story about Milliken, like his films, is very dramatic. The trouble with it is that by the time he got down to serious work on *Notorious* in the fall of 1945, the United States had dropped atom bombs on Japan and there was no longer anything secret about uranium.[20]

Terrific

In the 1950s producers and exhibitors fairly outdid themselves in promoting fright films. HORRENDOUS! MALIGNANT! proclaimed posters for *Macabre* (1958). THE MOST BLOOD-CHILLING HORROR SHOW EVER FILMED IN HOLLYWOOD! At *Macabre*'s screamiere, as it was called, some theaters offered life insurance: SO TERRIFYING WE INSURE YOUR LIFE FOR $1,000 IN CASE OF DEATH BY FRIGHT. . . . Other theaters had models dressed like nurses stand next to medicine chests in the lobby to offer "nerve-steadying pills" to the timorous. ATTENTION DOCTORS! screamed signs in some theater lobbies. PLEASE LET A THEATER ATTENDANT KNOW WHERE YOU ARE SEATED. YOU MAY BE NEEDED DURING THE SHOWING OF *MACABRE*. "Of course," said *Macabre*'s director and co-producer, William Castle, "it would be an awful thing if somebody actually did die in the theater," then adding, "the publicity would be terrific though!"[21]

Return of the Vampire

One night in 1956, comedian Joey Bishop was playing poker with some friends and one of the players said, "Did you hear that Bela Lugosi died today?" "He'll be back," said Bishop shortly without looking up from his cards.[22]

Really Terrifying

A fan once asked horror-film star Vincent Price what his nightmares were and Price, an avid art collector, told him they were ones in which he finds the *Mona Lisa* in a junk shop and somebody pokes a hole in it with an umbrella. "And that is really terrifying," he said.[23]

Pleasure

In one of the most frightening scenes in *Rosemary's Baby* (1968), Mia Farrow is stripped naked and raped by Satan. Director Roman Polanski did many takes before getting the sequence just as he wanted it and that meant that Farrow and the extra hired to portray the devil were in intimate proximity for hours. When the scene was finally completed to Polanski's satisfaction, the extra got up from the bed where he and Farrow had been lying, formally introduced himself, and said politely: "Miss Farrow, I want to tell you what a pleasure it's been working with you."[24]

CHAPTER 23

Classics
and
Biopics

Stories about the ignorance of movie moguls during Hollywood's Golden Age are legion: Sam Goldwyn's efforts to hire Washington Irving to do the screenplay for *The Legend of Sleepy Hollow;* Jack Warner's frank admission that he would "rather take a fifty-mile hike than crawl through a book"; Darryl Zanuck's remark, when visiting the Louvre, "We gotta be outa this joint in twenty minutes!"[1] The studio head, according to writer Ben Hecht, "is usually a man who has no taste to be violated or distorted. He admires with his whole soul the drivel his underlings produce in his factory."[2]

It wasn't all drivel. The movie tycoons sponsored "prestige pictures" as well as potboilers, and Hecht himself helped shape some splendid productions. Goldwyn, Warner, and Zanuck—and Harry Cohn, Irving Thalberg, and David O. Selznick—were all proud of their studios' serious offerings, even when they didn't make money, and they gloried in winning Oscars and having their films praised by serious critics. At times, too, they tried to engage the best writers and craftsmen they could find for their productions. In 1924 Goldwyn invited Freud to do a screenplay for him about psychoanalysis and was curtly rebuffed. A few years later he tried to persuade George Bernard Shaw to become a Goldwyn writer. "You know something, Mr. Shaw," he said earnestly, "if I had my choice, I would rather make a great artistic picture than—than eat a good meal." "Then we

can never get together, Mr. Goldwyn," returned Shaw, his eyes twin-
kling, "because your ideals are those of an artist and mine those of a
businessman."[3] Goldwyn never got around to doing a Shaw film, but
he did produce Charlotte Brontë's *Wuthering Heights* (1939) and
Lillian Hellman's *The Little Foxes* (1941). Thalberg filmed Shakespeare and Eugene O'Neill, Zanuck did John Steinbeck and Ernest
Hemingway, and Selznick, who specialized in bringing "classics" to
the screen, filmed Dickens, Tolstoy, and Mark Twain.

Selznick wasn't the first to film the classics. Even in the days of
nickel movies, filmmakers produced lots of crude one-reel versions
of the world's literary masterpieces. D. W. Griffith, of course, did
better with the classics than his predecessors. He had a firsthand
acquaintance with many of the great books and sought ideas for stories and characters in Tennyson, Browning, Tolstoy, de Maupassant,
and Stevenson during his early days as director. His favorite author
was Charles Dickens, and although he produced only one Dickens
film, he seemed to have found inspiration for his narrative film style
in the British writer's novels. Criticized for using a parallel "cut
back" in *Enoch Arden* (1911), he cried, "Well, doesn't Dickens write
that way?" "Yes, but that's Dickens," he was told, "that's novel writing; that's different." "Oh, not so much," insisted Griffith, "these are
picture stories, not so different."[4]

Griffith loved Shakespeare as well as Dickens, but filmed only
one of his plays, *The Taming of the Shrew* (1908), probably because
he thought subtitles were a poor substitute for Shakespeare's spoken
lines. But other moviemakers turned time and again to Shakespeare
in the film industry's salad days. The Great Bard was in the public
domain, for one thing, and he conferred respectability, for another.
Shakespeare "educates and improves the literary taste of the great
mass of people," declared the *Moving Picture World* in 1910. "Such
work is in the nature of an educational service."[5] But the little Shakespearean one-reelers (no fewer than ten in 1908) didn't always pass
muster with the fastidious. In Chicago, police censors called Vitagraph's *Macbeth* (1908) "worse than the bloodiest melodrama"
and ordered the deletion of several scenes deemed excessively violent.[6] Griffith himself opposed plans to film *Hamlet* in 1923. "There
are five murders in it," he observed. "What would the censors say
(and do)? Hamlet himself is a very morbid character, who commits
suicide, and I fear that not only the censors but the public would ban
it without the music of Shakespeare's words."[7] Griffith was right; it
was impossible to do justice to Shakespeare on the screen without

the music of his words. The takeoffs on Shakespeare—*A Ridin'
Romeo* (1921), *Love's Labour Won* (1922), *Bromo and Juliet* (1926)—
went over bigger with audiences in the silent days than the serious
ventures.

With sound, Hollywood did better by Shakespeare. First came
The Taming of the Shrew (1929), starring America's favorite film couple, Douglas Fairbanks and Mary Pickford. Neither player felt at ease
with Shakespeare, and Pickford thought the film damaged her career.
But *Time*, for one, liked the "vivid, hilarious farce" and praised Fairbanks's bravura style and Pickford's vixenish performance.[8] The film
credits produced considerable mirth: WRITTEN BY WILLIAM SHAKESPEARE
WITH ADDITIONAL DIALOGUE BY SAM TAYLOR.

Sam Taylor had nothing to do with Hollywood's next Shakespearean venture, a lavish production of *A Midsummer Night's
Dream* (1935), where the awkward performances of crooner Dick
Powell and beauty queen Anita Louise as the lovers spoiled an otherwise spirited filming of the Shakespeare comedy. The casting of the
clowns, though, was inspired. "As Bottom [James] Cagney is out of
character but still able to give it something," wrote Otis Ferguson in
The New Republic; "and his associates in earnest buffoonery—Joe E.
Brown, Hugh Herbert, etc.—are the best cast figures in the production. With their various interpolations and properties, they are made
into something that can be laughed at because it is real and funny,
rather than a classic thing to laugh at."[9] Ferguson also thought well
of Irving Thalberg's ambitious production of *Romeo and Juliet,* starring Leslie Howard and Norma Shearer, the following year, but he
regarded it as essentially "the framing of an old picture rather than
the execution of a new one."[10] No Sam Taylor this time: EVERY
WORD IS SHAKESPEARE'S, boasted MGM.[11] The film received friendly,
even glowing, reviews when first released, but seems a bit stodgy
today (as director George Cukor admitted some years later), and, like
A Midsummer Night's Dream, did poorly at the box office. Hollywood didn't try Shakespeare again until 1953, when it finally came
up with a splendid version of *Julius Caesar,* featuring Marlon Brando
as Mark Antony, that pleased critics and moviegoers alike.

Hollywood did more with classic British and Continental novelists
than with Shakespeare. With the founding of the Legion of Decency
in 1934, filming the classics seemed an expeditious way of placating
the censors. It was a labor of love, too, for producers like Selznick,
who had read and enjoyed the great novels as a boy. In the thirties
and forties came a series of stylish renditions of nineteenth-century

British and Continental masterpieces that received both popular and critical acclaim: *Anna Karenina* (1935), *David Copperfield* (1935), *A Tale of Two Cities* (1935), *Wuthering Heights* (1939), *Pride and Prej* *udice* (1940), and *Jane Eyre* (1944). Hollywood did pretty well by American writers, old and new, as well, during this period: *Babbitt* (1934), *Alice Adams* (1935), *The Adventures of Tom Sawyer* (1938), *Dodsworth* (1936), *The Wizard of Oz* (1939), *The Sea Wolf* (1941), *The Magnificent Ambersons* (1942). There was a tendency, it is true, to reduce the social complexities of the originals to individualistic simplicities and to add love interest and happy endings where they were lacking. But producers in Hollywood's Golden Age never did to Dickens, Tolstoy, and the Brontë sisters what they had done to Herman Melville's *Moby Dick* in the good old silent days: arrange in the last reel for Captain Ahab to kill the Great Whale, marry his girlfriend, and live happily ever after.

No doubt, the success of "classic" films rested in large part on stunning performances by Hollywood's most talented (and entrancing) stars: Katharine Hepburn in *Little Women* (1933) and *Alice Adams* (1935), for example, and the great Garbo in *Anna Karenina* (1935) and *Camille* (1937). But the supporting players also contributed mightily to the appeal of the "prestige pictures." Critics, indeed, frequently had kinder words for gifted performers like Basil Rathbone, Roland Young, and Edna May Oliver in secondary roles than for the principals in the industry's most celebrated productions. In the case of *David Copperfield* (1935), there is no question but that the casting of W. C. Fields as Micawber was little short of brilliant. Fields was reluctant to take the role at first, and then, after consenting, tried to convince David Selznick that he already had an English accent. "My father was an Englishman," he announced, "and I got this accent from him." In the beginning, though, he was a little apprehensive about his first assignment to a dramatic picture, and suggested inserting one of his juggling routines into the film. Told that Dickens had said nothing about Micawber's juggling, he muttered: "He probably forgot." Fields was drinking heavily at this time (a fifth of whiskey a day), and, as the day wore on, had to depend on off-camera cue cards for his lines. In the end, however, he made Micawber his own. *Time* praised all the performers in reviewing the film, but insisted that the best of the lot was Fields's "red-nosed, dazzled, grandiloquent and undespairing Micawber."[12]

For a time biographical films ("biopics") were almost as popular as classics. Like the latter, biopics were regarded as prestige pictures, and some of them did better at the box office than those based on the world's great literature. In the early thirties it looked as though British actor George Arliss was going to shape every moviegoer's view of some of the world's greatest movers and shakers: Alexander Hamilton, Benjamin Disraeli, Voltaire, Nathan Rothschild, Cardinal Richelieu, the Duke of Wellington. Then "Mr. Paul Muni," as Warners grandiloquently billed him, achieved renown for his portrayal of Louis Pasteur in 1936 and Emile Zola in 1937. Edward G. Robinson also did biopics for Warners; abandoning gangster films for the time being, he played Paul Ehrlich, the discoverer of Salvarsan, on the screen in 1940, and Paul Julius von Reuter, the founder of the famous news agency, in 1941. There were biopics about Abraham Lincoln, Thomas Edison, and Alexander Graham Bell as well. And there was also a flood of show-biz biopics—about popular composers, singers, dancers, and bandleaders—that were largely excuses for musical shows. "I don't think anybody cares about the *facts* of my life," says singer Al Jolson (Larry Parks) at one point in *Jolson Sings Again* (1949). "Names, dates, places—I'll give you a bunch of them and you can juggle 'em around any way you want. What really matters is the singing—and the story. . . ."[13]

In its approach to biography, Hollywood tended to hagiography. "Pasteur is too good and meek," complained Otis Ferguson of Muni's *The Story of Louis Pasteur* (1936). "His wife is too patient and sugary" and "the decent sentiment of the family scenes is so invariable as to get tiresome."[14] *Madame Curie* (1943) was if anything even more ethereal. So unworldly, even saintly, were Marie and Pierre Curie, as portrayed by Greer Garson and Walter Pidgeon, that one wondered where the sharp intelligence to do creative scientific work came from and whence came the gumption to persist in it against great odds. The biopics about political figures like Abraham Lincoln and Woodrow Wilson were similarly sentimental; they perpetuated rather than punctured the popular myths and ended by making their heroes smaller, not greater, than life. It seems never to have occurred to Hollywood's biopic makers that history's greatest achievers—like moviedom's great performers—may have been seriously flawed as human beings and that the shortcomings made the accomplishments all the more impressive.

Colonel

In 1927, when Jesse Lasky made plans to produce a picture about the feisty Theodore Roosevelt entitled *The Rough Riders,* he had trouble finding an actor who looked enough like the former president to play the lead. Finally his staff located a man named Frank Hopper, who, though not a professional actor, was a perfect double for T.R., and Lasky signed him up. But when director Victor Fleming began shooting the picture, he found Hopper so timid and unsure of himself that it was impossible to get any of the scenes right. Lasky contemplated abandoning the project. Then Production Code head Will H. Hays saved the day.

One afternoon, Hays, a dignified gentleman who had served as Postmaster General in President Harding's cabinet, visited Lasky, and the latter began moaning about his problem with the man he had hired to do T.R. Hays had an idea; perhaps, he told Lasky, he could bolster the man's confidence. So Lasky sent for Hopper, and as soon as the T.R. look-alike entered the room, said to Hays, "General, I have the honor of presenting Theodore Roosevelt." "Proud to make your acquaintance," said Hays, shaking Hopper's hand. "May I say, sir, the resemblance is perfect? But more than merely physical. I can see you have the same fearless nature, the same character and patriotism." Then he turned to Lasky and said: "Mr. Lasky, as former Postmaster General of the United States, I count this as a proud moment, and I thank you for the honor of meeting this man."

Hays's ploy worked beautifully. "The change in the man was as prompt as it was astounding," Hays wrote in his memoirs. "All at once he *became* the character he was to portray, and before the interview had ended he was talking and laughing, not really imitating Teddy consciously, but with his own confidence restored." Lasky gave orders that thenceforth all the people on the picture were to address Hopper as "Colonel" and show him the respect due the role he was playing, off the set as well as on. The man went on to give a creditable performance in the movie; and when he got back to his hometown he continued to strut around and lord it over his neighbors.[15]

Shows Promise

In the late 1920s, Samuel Goldwyn organized Eminent Authors Pictures, Inc., and hired Belgian poet and dramatist Maurice Maeterlinck to do a screenplay for him. "You'll get equal treatment with Rex Beach," he told him, and when Maeterlinck looked puzzled, Goldwyn asked his secretary to bring him all the contracts he had with "eminent authors" to show the Belgian what distinguished company he was in. "You're getting as much money as any of them," he announced, and handed him the Basil King contract. "You know Basil King?" he cried. "*Non,*" said Maeterlinck. Goldwyn then picked up another contract. "You know Rupert Hughes?" "*Non.*" "Mary Roberts Rinehart?" "*Non.*" And so it went, until Goldwyn finally whispered to his press agent, "What's the matter with this guy? Is he dumb?"

But Maeterlinck (who had published books on birds, bees, and flowers as well as plays and poems) went to work for Goldwyn anyway, and after a few weeks completed a lengthy script. When Goldwyn finished wading through it, though, the story goes, he ran out of his office yelling: "My God, the hero is a bee!" What Maeterlinck had done was to develop his own best-seller *The Life of a Bee* (1901) into a screenplay about a little boy. At this point both Goldwyn and Maeterlinck agreed it was a good idea for the latter to return to Belgium. "Don't worry, Maurice," Goldwyn told the Nobel Prize–winning writer as he saw him to the train, "you'll make good yet."[16]

Beeg Story
In 1928, one of the studios was considering the possibility of filming Emil Ludwig's best-selling biography *Napoleon* (1925). At a conference of studio officials, various actors were suggested for the role of the diminutive conqueror. Finally an exasperated magnate cried: "But dese are all little fellers dot you are suggesting. Dis is a beeg story so we got to haf a beeg actor for Napoleon."[17]

Riot of Fun
In one town, a theater advertised the Fairbanks-Pickford *Taming of the Shrew* (1929) as follows:

GLORIOUS FUN! CYCLONIC ACTION!
DOUG GIVES THIS LITTLE GIRL A HAND! SOCK!
RIGHT ON THE NOSE! 'CAUSE OUR MARY'S A MEAN
MAMA, AND DOUG'S TAMING HER! IT'S A RIOT OF FUN—
ENDING WITH A TENDER ROMANCE![18]

Wonderful Statue
When a young American touring England came upon a bronze figure of British statesman Benjamin Disraeli in Westminster Abbey, she

was tremendously excited. "My," she exclaimed, "what a wonderful statue of George Arliss!"[19]

Vanity Fair

Ignorance of the great classics was apparently widespread in Hollywood during its Golden Era and spawned many amusing (and possibly apocryphal) tales. One producer wanted to sign up Goethe as a screenwriter; another producer tried to set up an interview with Robert Louis Stevenson. An auditor at RKO reported that the cost budget for a projected screen version of *Hamlet* was incomplete; it included payment to the men who rewrote the play, but not the fee for the original author. About this time one Hollywood agent wrote William Makepeace Thackeray in care of the Modern Library, advising him there were screen possibilities in his novel *Henry Esmond,* and asking for authority to handle movie rights to the book. Publisher Bennett Cerf at once wrote back to say that the same author had an exciting thriller in preparation, which he planned to call *Vanity Fair.*[20]

Best Part

For a film version of Leo Tolstoy's novel *Resurrection,* retitled *We Live Again* (1934), Sam Goldwyn picked Fredric March and Anna Sten as the leads. But March thought his part was too small and complained to Goldwyn about it. "Freddie," said Goldwyn, patting him on the back, "you got the best part in the picture." Then, noticing Anna Sten frowning, he cried: "And, Anna, you got the best part too."[21]

Shakespeare Gift

When Warner Bros. decided to film *A Midsummer Night's Dream* in 1935, producer Hal Wallis wanted to have comedian Joe E. Brown play the part of Flute in it. But he told Ivan Kahn, Brown's agent (who received a fee of 10 percent for his services), that the Shakespeare picture was sure to lose money and all he could offer the performers was the great prestige and glory that would come to them from acting in the picture. "Do you mean," asked Kahn incredulously, "that you want Brown to work for nothing?" "Oh, no," said Wallis quickly, "we were thinking of making him a present. Say, a Packard car or a Cadillac." "And what does the agent get?" growled Kahn. "A bicycle?"[22]

Shakespearean Ad-lib

In one scene in *A Midsummer Night's Dream*, comic actor Brown, playing Flute, one of the clowns, was chased, tripped, pinched, bitten, and finally tossed into a lake by his fellow clowns. When he came to the surface he ad-libbed: "I won't play anymore." Brown's line produced a big laugh when the scene was run off in the projection room but there was a great deal of agonizing over whether to retain it. A Shakespearean scholar finally convinced the producers that Shakespeare himself, a hardworking actor-manager, enjoyed making audiences laugh. So Warners kept Brown's line in the film on the theory that Shakespeare would approve. American audiences did.[23]

Milkman

The Story of Louis Pasteur (1936), which dramatizes the development of "pasteurization" of milk, brought Warner Bros. much praise and Paul Muni, who played the title role, an Academy Award. But Jack Warner had predicted the picture would be a bust; it was just "the story of a milkman," he grumbled. His advisers, in fact, almost turned it into just that. They wanted to discard the original screenplay, which portrayed Pasteur's scientific dedication and integrity with verve and feeling, and substitute a simple love story that made the great French scientist a student in love with the medical-school dean's daughter. They also suggested a voice at the end of the film, intoning: "And to this day, housewives all over the world are grateful to this man, because he invented pasteurized milk." Fortunately Muni held out for the original script.[24]

How Long Is Good?

David Selznick read Charles Dickens's famous novel *David Copperfield* when he was a boy and was eager to make a film of it, even though Louis B. Mayer warned that classics were box-office poison. When Selznick went ahead with the project anyway, Mayer suggested featuring Jackie Cooper, MGM's popular child star, in the picture. But Selznick insisted on an English boy for the title role, sent director George Cukor to England on a recruiting job, and ended by engaging the likable young Freddie Bartholomew for the part. He then cast Lionel Barrymore as Peggotty, Edna May Oliver as Aunt Betsy, W. C. Fields as Micawber, Lewis Stone as Mr. Wickfield, Basil Rathbone as Mr. Murdstone, Roland Young as Uriah Heep, Herbert

Mundin as Barkis, Jessie Ralph as Nurse Peggotty, and Elsa Lan
chester as Clickett. It was an impressive cast.

When the picture was completed, it ran two and a half hours
much longer than most films in those days. The preview in
Bakersfield went badly, partly because an important prizefight was
going on in town the same night and the theater was two-thirds
empty. Mayer urged Selznick to cut the picture, and the latter finally
decided to drop two reels and eliminate the Lionel Barrymore part
completely.

At the next preview, in Santa Ana, the audience responded
favorably enough, but Selznick was still not sure about the picture.
Observing four women (who turned out to be schoolteachers) talking
animatedly in the lobby afterward, he went up and asked them what
they thought. "We loved the picture," said one of them, "except for
one thing; how could you possibly film David Copperfield and not
include Peggotty?" "Next time you see the picture," said Selznick,
his mind made up, "he'll be in it!"

Selznick did restore the Barrymore part to the film and made cuts
elsewhere. But in the end he still had a long picture on his hands:
two hours and thirteen minutes. MGM officials complained loudly
about its length. "How long can it be?" wailed Nick Schenck. "How
long is good?" Selznick shot back.

David Copperfield (1935) delighted critics and audiences alike.
No one complained about length. "As rich, uproarious, tragic and
astonishing as its original," according to Time, "it falls short in only
one department. Twice as long as an ordinary picture, it lasts only
two hours and ten minutes." Selznick later said he learned two things
from his experience with the picture: not to tamper with a classic and
not to worry about the length of a picture, so long as it was good.[25]

David's Trouble

For a time producer David O. Selznick specialized in movies like
David Copperfield and A Tale of Two Cities (both 1935), which were
based on classics that he had read and loved as a boy. But when he
decided to film Frances Hodgson Burnett's Victorian classic Little
Lord Fauntleroy (1936), about a little American boy ("Ceddie") who
becomes a British lord with long curls and a velvet suit, screenwriter
Ben Hecht sent him a telegram saying THE TROUBLE WITH YOU, DAVID,
IS THAT YOU DID ALL YOUR READING BEFORE YOU WERE TWELVE.[26]

Drawbacks

Darryl Zanuck once considered the idea of doing *Hamlet,* and when he met strong resistance from exhibitors he tried hard to win them over. The movie Hamlet, he said, wouldn't be a mope and a dreamer, but a man of action; the film, in fact, would be practically a gangster picture in costume, with public enemies and G-men pitted against each other in old Denmark. "It's all melodrama," he told the exhibitors. "Blood and thunder—seven murders—a fight with pirates—poisonings—swordplay—ghosts— all the excitement in the world." "Yes," said one theater owner, "but the greatest drawback would be the title." "And the next greatest drawback," said another exhibitor, "would be the author credit." At that point Zanuck decided not to do *Hamlet* after all.[27]

Blind Composer

For a time Jack Warner toyed with the idea of making a biopic about Beethoven with Paul Muni in the title role, and the latter went about preparing for the part with his usual zeal. He read up on Beethoven, experimented with makeup, and played Toscanini recordings of Beethoven symphonies at full volume hour after hour. One morning, deep in thought, he was strolling about his backyard, when Mrs. Mischa Auer, next-door neighbor, leaned across the fence and gave him a friendly greeting. But Muni completely ignored her and continued his walk. Later that day Mrs. Auer saw Muni's wife, Bella. "I hope I haven't offended Mr. Muni in any way," she told her. "I said good morning to your husband, and he just walked right by without answering." "Oh," laughed Mrs. Muni, "don't worry about that. He probably didn't even hear you. You see, today he's Beethoven, so naturally he's as deaf as a doorknob!"

After a few weeks Warner abandoned plans for a Beethoven movie and told producer Hal Wallis to "get some writers cooking" on a different biopic for Muni. "Anything but Beethoven," he said. "Nobody wants to see a movie about a blind composer."[28]

Only the Merchant

"Sam," Edward G. Robinson told Sam Goldwyn one day, "my studio is going to make *The Merchant of Venice.* They want me to play Shylock. Should I accept?" "Screw 'em," Goldwyn is said to have exclaimed. "Tell 'em you'll only play the merchant."[29]

Wizard's Coat

In *The Wizard of Oz* (1939), MGM's film version of L. Frank Baum's classic children's book, Frank Morgan plays the part of Professor Marvel in the first part of the film and the humbug Wizard later on. To locate an elegant but somewhat seedy coat that seemed to fit the part, MGM's wardrobe department bought up a rack of coats in a secondhand store in Los Angeles for Morgan to look over. He finally selected a Prince Albert coat of black broadcloth, with a splendid (but frayed) velvet collar, and it fit him perfectly. One day, after filming began, Morgan happened to turn out one of the coat's pockets and found the name L. Frank Baum inscribed inside. The *Wizard of Oz* company could hardly believe it. "We wired the tailor in Chicago," recalled Mary Mayer, unit publicist on the picture, "and sent pictures. And the tailor sent back a notarized letter saying that the coat had been made for L. Frank Baum. Baum's widow identified the coat, too, and after the picture was finished we presented it to her." But when the story was released to the press, skeptics dismissed it as a mere publicity stunt.[30]

Wuthering Sob

When filming the scene in *Wuthering Heights* (1939) in which Cathy (Merle Oberon) is lying dead in her bed with her family around her, David Niven (playing Edgar) glanced nervously at the instructions in his script: "Edgar breaks down at foot of bed and sobs." "Willy," he whispered to director William Wyler, "I can't do that." "Do what?" asked Wyler. "I don't know how to sob, Willy," said Niven. "Speak up. . . ," said Wyler, "louder." "I DON'T KNOW HOW TO SOB," yelled Niven. "Well," Wyler told the other performers, "you've all heard it—here's an actor who says he doesn't know how to act." Then he turned back to Niven and ordered: "Now . . . SOB!" Niven tried but couldn't bring it off. "Jesus," sighed Wyler, "can you make a crying face?" Niven tried again. "Oh, God," wailed Wyler, and then called propman Irving Sindler over. "Give him the blower," he told Sindler and the latter puffed menthol through a handkerchief into Niven's eyes. "Bend over the corpse," Wyler told Niven. "Now make your crying face . . . blink your eyes . . . squeeze a little . . . bend over the corpse . . . heave your shoulders." Niven carefully followed Wyler's instructions, but instead of tears coming out of his eyes, green slime began coming out of his nose. "Ooh!! How horrid!" screamed Merle Oberon in revulsion, jumped up from her deathbed, and fled to her dressing room.[31]

Diversion

In 1939, Fred Astaire and Ginger Rogers teamed up for the eighth time to do a biopic about the celebrated dancing couple Vernon and Irene Castle for RKO. When producer Pandro Berman bought the rights to the Castle story, he agreed to let Mrs. Castle, still living, have final approval over casting, script, and costumes, but almost immediately ran into trouble. Mrs. Castle approved of Astaire to play the part of her husband, but balked at having Rogers play opposite him. Berman finally won her over to Rogers but continued to be dogged by her interference. She wanted all her dancing costumes to be reproduced in exact detail, criticized Rogers's hairdo, complained about the script, and even insisted on having one of the scenes in the picture reshot. "Irene was driving me crazy until a very lucky thing happened," Berman said later. The lucky break: His secretary heard that the humane society was meeting to discuss an antivivisectionist bill going on the state ballot, mentioned it to Mrs. Castle, an ardent antivivisectionist, and, at Berman's suggestion, even took her to the meeting. "That was the last we saw of her," said Berman gratefully after the picture was completed. "Mrs. Castle took over the Southern California Humane Society and became so involved in the political campaign that she forgot about the movie."[32]

Wouldn't Pay Ten Cents

Darryl Zanuck's ambitious film about Woodrow Wilson and World War I had a premiere in Omaha, Nebraska, and the theater was packed. The next day, though, there were only a few people in the place. Zanuck, who had attended the premiere of *Wilson* (1944), was astonished, but one of the local doctors set him straight. "Why should they pay seventy-five cents to see Wilson on the screen," he said, "when they wouldn't pay ten cents to see him alive?"[33]

Shakespearean Gallop

While filming Shakespeare's *Henry V* (1944), Laurence Olivier, playing the king, taught his horse to gallop when he uttered the call to arms. "The horse seemed to know the lines as well as I did," Olivier recalled, "and would prick up his ears and go every time I got to 'St. George.'" When the film was completed, Olivier was given the horse and kept him at his country house. One day Noël Coward came to visit Olivier and the latter picked him up at the station in a trap pulled by this same horse. When Coward complained that they were moving too slowly, Olivier said, "Want more speed, do you?" Then he leaned toward the horse and began quoting Shakespeare: "Once more into the breach. . . ." To Coward's astonishment the horse galloped all the way home.[34]

Napoleon

One day, during the filming of Tolstoy's *War and Peace* (1956) in Italy, the first assistant director went up to Herbert Lom, who was playing Napoleon, and said: "Could you spare twenty minutes, Mr. Lom?" Then he pointed to a line of extras, all dressed in French uniforms of the Napoleonic era, and explained: "They all want to meet Napoleon." "You're joking," cried Lom. "No, no," said the director. "They're all officers, and they've expressed a desire to meet you and shake your hand." So Lom stood there in disbelief as the extras filed by, one by one, and solemnly shook hands with him. "They were clicking their heels," he said later, "and with great respect they all shook hands with Napoleon!"[35]

Not Real

"Gee, I can't say that," cried Henry Fonda, playing Pierre in *War and Peace,* when he came to one of the lines in the script. "It doesn't feel real." "Of course it isn't real," said director King Vidor. "It's a movie!"[36]

CHAPTER 24

Message
Movies

"If you have a message," Humphrey Bogart (or was it Samuel Goldwyn?) once told a reporter, "send it by Western Union." It was an old Hollywood quip. Movies provided entertainment, the studios insisted, not uplift. If they educated and enlightened the public, well and good, but they should never try to do so at the expense of entertainment. A preachy picture was bound to be ponderous; didacticism on the screen produced drowsiness, not devotion to a cause. The slogan "movies are better than ever" meant they were more fun, not more instructive.

Preston Sturges's *Sullivan's Travels* (1941) dramatized Bogart's point. In the Sturges comedy, filmmaker Sullivan (Joel McCrea) suddenly gets religion. "How can you talk about musicals at a time like this," he says impatiently to his associates, "with the world committing suicide, with corpses piling up in the streets, with grim death gargling at you from every corner, with people slaughtered like sheep. . . ?" Suggests one of his co-workers: "Maybe they'd like to forget that." He turns out to be right. Sullivan disguises himself as a hobo, mingles with the masses so he can learn how to make realistic pictures about the cold, hard world, and, to his chagrin, soon learns that the poor and downtrodden go to movies mainly to laugh and forget their troubles. "There's a lot to be said for making people laugh," he decides at the end of the picture. "Did you know that's all some people have? It isn't much, but it's better than nothing in this cockeyed caravan." But Sturges himself occasionally made pictures with social significance. And so did other producers.

The earliest American movies contained considerable social commentary. Not only did they picture the everyday life of working-class movie audiences with sympathy and understanding; they also reflected the concerns of Progressive reformers in the early years of the twentieth century. There were films dealing with the plight of the poor and unemployed, with the greed and heartlessness of rich bankers and industrialists, and with graft and corruption in politics. There were also films about specific issues: child labor, prostitution, alcoholism, crime, prison conditions, women's suffrage, and capital-labor strife. "Some of the best film makers of our country," noted the *Moving Picture World* approvingly in April 1912, "have given us pictures dealing with social evils and making a strong appeal for redress and reform."[1] But World War I killed the Progressive movement and the social-issues films that went with it. After the war, in the Roaring Twenties, sexual liberation, on-screen and off, not social reform, was the main interest of America's moviegoers.

But the Great Depression of the thirties soon roused Hollywood's social conscience. The social-problem film, in fact, took shape as an important movie genre during the early Depression years. First came the prison film, exposing the wretched conditions in the nation's penitentiaries; then came the "shyster" movies, in which crooked politicians, cynical newspapermen, and corrupt lawyers were busily at work bamboozling and exploiting the masses. The endings, though, were usually happy: prisons cleaned up, cynics converted to reform, and the wicked men corrupting America defeated in the last reel. But the best of these films—Warners' *I Am a Fugitive from a Chain Gang* (1932)—ended tragically, not triumphantly. In it, Paul Muni is unjustly sentenced to a long prison term and subjected to cruel exploitation on a chain gang in Georgia. When he escapes and finds refuge in another state, prison officials offer to clear up his record if he agrees to return and serve a token ninety-day sentence. But when he does so, they renege on their promise and subject him again to the brutality of the chain gang. "Why, their crimes are worse than mine," he cries at the betrayal. "Worse than anybody's. They're the ones who should be in chains, not we!" He escapes a second time and becomes a permanent fugitive from the law, living as a petty criminal in Depression America. In the final scene in the picture he visits his wife briefly, and, as he slinks away, she cries, "How do you live?" "I steal," he mutters. Despite the downbeat ending, the Muni film was a smash hit at the box office and touched off cries for reform. It also made Warner Bros. known as the studio with a social conscience.

Warners' subsequent message films were all upbeat. They mirrored the revival of the nation's morale with the coming of Franklin D. Roosevelt to the White House in 1933 and the launching of the New Deal. They also reflected Jack Warner's personal friendship with and admiration for FDR and his conviction that New Deal programs provided solutions for the nation's ills. From Warners came films about slums, sharecroppers, juvenile delinquents, reform schools, and ex-cons, all of which came to hopeful conclusions in the final reel. There were also films about lynchings and right-wing terrorism that electrified audiences. There was a series of films, too, about working men—electric linemen, fishermen, cabbies, truckers—who by their devotion to their jobs and willingness to take risks contributed enormously to the building of a strong democratic nation on this continent. Before long Warners was being called "the working-class studio."

But Warners didn't produce the only problem films during the New Deal years; nor did it produce the best of them. Fritz Lang's *Fury* (1936), a searing drama about lynching, was made at MGM and was far superior in subtlety to Warners' *They Won't Forget* (1937), a horrendous picture of a mob gone mad. Lang's *You Only Live Once* (1937), a melancholy story of fugitives from the law, starring Henry Fonda and Sylvia Sidney, was, if anything, even better. Lang's films were not unrelievedly pessimistic (the way *I Am a Fugitive from a Chain Gang* had been five years earlier), but they did shun the easy last-reel solutions that the Warners people came to love. Samuel Goldwyn's *Dead End* (1937) was also far more realistic than the Warners' topical films: the slums more depressing, the ghetto lives bleaker, and the ambiguity of the ending more convincing than any of the finales delivered by Warner Bros.

But the best of all the social films came from Twentieth Century-Fox: *The Grapes of Wrath* (1940). Based on John Steinbeck's novel of the previous year, *The Grapes of Wrath* pictured the plight of the "Okies" during the "dust-bowl" years in the Midwest and the trek of the Joad family, thrown off the land, to California in search of jobs in the citrus-fruit valleys there. Producer Darryl Zanuck and director John Ford muted Steinbeck's radicalism and centered the film on family solidarity rather than class consciousness. But though this disappointed left-wing critics at the time, it broadened the film's appeal, saved it from tendentiousness, and made it eminently viewable long after the specific conditions it portrayed had passed into history. But the film was not without a message. For the picture's final scene producer Zanuck provided a passionate populistic pronouncement for Ma Joad (Jane Darwell) to make: "Rich fellas come up an' they die, an' their kids ain't no good, an' they die out. But we keep a'comin'. We're the people that live. Can't nobody wipe us out. Can't nobody lick us. We'll go on forever."[2]

Zanuck's paean to the people was unexceptionable. Populism was Hollywood's favorite ideology in the thirties and forties. Film after film revealed a passionate (not to say sentimental) faith in the people that goes back at least as far as Abraham Lincoln in the American tradition. The populist films liked to pit the People against the Powerful, personalize the conflict, and come up with melodramas in which the heroes (representing the People) were idealistic and un-sophisticated small-town lads, while the villains (representing the predatory forces trying to take over the country) were corrupt big-city politicians, greedy bankers, and power-mad industrialists. Films like this were neither radical in intent nor profound in insight, and their values were almost wholly individualistic. But in a Time of Troubles—economic doldrums at home, Fascist aggression abroad—their ringing assertion of traditional democratic values was enormously heartening to millions of moviegoers in the United States and elsewhere. Director Frank Capra was perhaps Hollywood's most eloquent champion of the "little fellow" at this time. In a trilogy of films—*Mr. Deeds Goes to Town* (1936), *Mr. Smith Goes to Washington* (1939), *Meet John Doe* (1941)—he put forth the populist message with fervor and imagination. "I have a definite feeling that the people are right," he told an interviewer. "People's instincts are good, never bad. They're right as the soil, right as the clouds, right as rain."[3] Capra's films were strewn with clichés, sentimentalities, and simplicisms; but they were also filled with warmth, charm, grace, ingenuity, and good humor. Reviewing movies for the The *Spectator*, Graham Greene rated them as among the best films of the day.[4]

World War II killed the problem film for the duration and turned Hollywood's attention to movies about the terrible conflict raging around the world and America's role in it. There were anti-Fascist films, too, at long last, and also films expressing goodwill toward America's wartime allies: Britain, China, and even Russia. After the war came films about the returning serviceman ("nervous from the service") and the difficulties he encountered in adjusting to civilian life again after his traumatic war experiences.

The most striking postwar films, however, took up problems Hollywood had once shunned: anti-Semitism, alcoholism, and mental illness. And in a remarkable new departure the studios began making films about the plight of America's black people in a society that regarded them at best as second-class citizens. Hollywood had once mostly relegated blacks to bit parts in its movies, or if it did more than that, it tended to present them as happy-go-lucky, inarticulate, and comic figures bound to amuse white audiences. The postwar films about blacks broke sharply with these stereotypes, and while they never went as far as black militants demanded, they did attempt to cope courageously and compassionately with the prejudice and bigotry permeating the nation. There were friendly films, too, after World War II, about Chicanos, Indians, and Japanese-Americans, which discarded the old conventionalities. Like the New Deal problem pictures, the new message movies undoubtedly both reflected and shaped the postwar generation's thinking. Movies, producer Dore Schary once pointed out, "seldom lead opinion; they merely reflect public opinion and perhaps occasionally accelerate it. . . . No motion picture ever started a trend of public opinion or thinking. Pictures merely dramatize these trends and keep them going."[5]

In recent years the message film has largely disappeared as a distinct entity. With the breakup of the big studios and the decline of censorship, American filmmakers since the late 1960s have been able to explore a whole new range of human experience previously denied them: drug addiction, homosexuality, rape, prostitution, adultery, abortion, sexual promiscuity, suicide, cowardice, coprolalia, anomie, and nihilism. There has been plenty of social criticism in the new films (especially in those made during the Vietnam years), but it is implied, not articulated, and at times the message seems to be that American society is hopelessly corrupt and that little or nothing can be done about it. The new, young, worldly-wise, and seemingly cynical audiences in the multitheatered showplaces of the late twentieth century snicker at any obvious do-goodism they see on the silver screen. And yet at film revivals they seem to enjoy the old populistic Capra films of the New Deal era almost as much as their parents had. It is one of their few concessions to the past.

Touchy Subject

Not long after Hitler came into power in Germany and launched his brutal persecution of Jews, Darryl Zanuck (a Gentile, though taken for a Jew by many of his associates) decided to do a movie about the Rothschilds, the famous Jewish banking family. He assigned Nunnally Johnson to do the script and assembled an impressive cast: George Arliss as Lionel Nathan Rothschild, who settled in London and developed close relations with British prime minister Benjamin Disraeli; C. Aubrey Smith as the Duke of Wellington; Alan Mowbray as Count Metternich; and Loretta Young as Julie Rothschild. Boris Karloff played Ledrantz, an anti-Semitic rabble-rouser, and for him Johnson wrote a savage anti-Semitic speech to which Arliss makes an eloquent reply in one scene.

When Joseph Schenck, Zanuck's associate at Twentieth Century-Fox, read the script, he was upset. "Look, that anti-Semitic speech that Karloff delivers," he said, "I'm a little worried about that." "What are you worried about?" asked Zanuck. "People are not going to complain about its nastiness once they hear what Arliss says in reply." "That's not what I'm worried about," said Schenck. "What I'm afraid of is that when Karloff finishes saying what he thinks about the Jews, a lot of people are going to get up and cheer." "It will be interesting if they do, won't it?" returned Zanuck. But they never did. When *House of Rothschild* was released in 1934, audiences listened to Ledrantz's speech in silence and frequently applauded when they heard Arliss's reply.

Zanuck and Johnson were proud of the blow their film had struck against prejudice. For once, Johnson said years later, "the movies were not shying away but dealing with a real touchy subject right up there on the screen." After *Rothschild*, Zanuck continued to sponsor movies dealing with controversial subjects. "People will accept enlightenment," he insisted, "if it is skillfully served to them. They will not go to the theater for enlightenment alone."[6]

Extra-ordinary Slum

When William Wyler was shooting *Dead End* (1937), Sidney Kingsley's play about New York slums, Samuel Goldwyn was continually dropping by to see how things were going and looking with distaste at the filth and squalor of the tenement-street set. "Why is everything so dirty here?" he asked one day in his high-pitched voice. "Because it's supposed to be a slum area, Sam," explained Wyler. "Well," grumbled Goldwyn, "this slum cost a lot of money. It should look better than any ordinary slum."[7]

Mr. Capra Goes to Washington

October 16, 1939, was declared "Mr. Smith" day in Washington. That evening, Frank Capra's *Mr. Smith Goes to Washington,* a film about an idealistic young senator's struggle against corruption in the nation's capital, had its premiere in Constitution Hall. For the occasion a dazzling array of dignitaries—Supreme Court justices, cabinet members, senators, congressmen, generals, admirals, Washington socialites—assembled to see the celebrated director's latest film. Since the film's Mr. Smith was a Montanan, Capra invited Montana senator Burton K. Wheeler and his family to sit in the official box with him. At 8 P.M., the lights went down, a spotlight sought out Capra, and the audience gave him a big ovation. The show began.

About twenty minutes into the picture, the film jumped a sprocket and the soundtrack began burbling. Capra jumped up, headed for the projection booth, banged his head on a steel pipe en route, and found the operator had put the film on track again by the time he got there. He returned to his seat, head throbbing, only to see a couple of people get up and leave the theater, making thumbs-down gestures. Several other people also got up and left. And by the time Jimmy Stewart began his dramatic filibuster in the Senate to block the machinations of a corrupt colleague, Capra realized that much of the audience had turned hostile. When the picture ended there was little applause. The Wheelers took a frosty leave.

In the Press Club bar afterward, newsmen descended on Capra. They criticized him for showing graft in the nation's capital in a picture to be shown around the world; they also denounced him for portraying the reporter in the film as a near-alcoholic. Only when the reviews began coming in, most of them friendly, was Capra reassured. But he was bothered by the editorials and columns calling his film a disservice to democracy. And he was upset by the harsh words uttered about him in the U.S. Senate. South Carolina's James F. Byrnes called the picture "outrageous" and said it was "exactly the kind of picture that dictators of totalitarian governments would like their subjects to believe exists in a democracy. . . ." Majority leader Alben W. Barkley of Kentucky called the film "silly and stupid," and said it "makes the Senate look like a bunch of crooks." "I did not hear a single Senator praise it," he told a reporter. "I speak for the whole body." Senator Wheeler, he added, shared his views.

Columbia Pictures's Harry Cohn, who had backed the film, was extremely upset. He showed Capra a long cablegram, marked URGENT AND CONFIDENTIAL, from Joseph P. Kennedy, U.S. ambassador in London, saying that Mr. Smith ridiculed democracy, struck a blow at the morale of America's allies, might be construed as pro-Axis propaganda, and should be withdrawn from distribution in Europe. "Harry," Capra told Cohn, "no Ambassador has the right to censor films. Besides, he's mistaken. I *know* he is. Even if the Pope sent that cable I'd still say that we are what we are, and Mr. Smith is what he is—a shot in the arm for all the Joes in the world who resent being bought and sold and pushed around by all the Hitlers in the world." And he added: "Let public opinion answer. Let the voice of the people tell the Ambassador he's mistaken. . . ."

In a day or two Capra assembled a collection of reviews, editorials, and columns, some from Britain and Canada, and mailed them to Kennedy. They were overwhelmingly favorable to the picture and, in fact, thought it represented democracy in action at its best. When Capra learned later that Mr. Smith was particularly popular with anti-Nazis in Europe, he felt vindicated.[8]

Cream Puff

After he agreed to direct the film version of John Van Druten's play *Old Acquaintance* in 1942, Edmund Goulding had second thoughts about it. "Alas, when you come down to it," he wrote associate producer Henry Blanke, "it is a very light cream puff with no cream. And in the light of the furious things that are going on in the world, the petty quarrels of a couple of bitches seem fragile and inconsequential." When Jack Warner saw the letter, he told Blanke, "The only cream puff in this matter is Eddie Goulding. Tell him to get back to the pastry kitchen and produce something that will keep the public's mind off this goddamn war." In the end the picture was made with Bette Davis and Miriam Hopkins, directed by Vincent Sherman, and released in 1943.[9]

Sunday on Third Avenue

In *The Lost Weekend* (1945) there is a dramatic sequence in which Ray Milland, playing the part of an alcoholic writer, walks along Third Avenue in New York City carrying his typewriter and looking desperately for a pawnshop. The scene was filmed on location one quiet Sunday morning; Milland walked uptown, looking sick, dirty, and unkempt, while a camera, concealed in a bakery truck, followed him. None of the people he passed seemed to realize what was going on, but when he reached the eighties and started banging at the gates of a pawnshop, a young woman came up to him and cried: "Mr. Milland, may I have your autograph?" "I'm not Mr. Milland," said the actor impishly, knowing the take had been ruined. "I'm just a guy who needs a drink bad and trying to pawn my typewriter." "Who do you think you're kiddin', wise guy?" snorted the woman. "I been a fan of yours from away back. Why'n't you come over to my place—I got a quart of Seagram's Seven—which is looking for a guy like you. The bars don't open till one." Milland then realized the woman thought he really was an alcoholic and began wondering how he was going to get off the hook. At this point Billy Wilder, the director of the film, came up, told the woman they were making a movie, and showed her the camera in the truck to prove it. But she remained a skeptical New Yorker until he finally took her name and address and promised her a screen test.[10]

Never Again
Shortly after *The Lost Weekend*, a searing drama, opened in New York, comedian Joe E. Lewis mentioned it in his show at the Copacabana. "Anybody except me see that picture, that picture *The Lost Weekend*?" he cried. "I want to tell you something, ladies and gentlemen, it sure got to me, that picture. And I want to tell you, after seeing that picture, I have sworn off. I am *through*!" Then, after a dramatic pause, he added: "I will never go see another picture again as long as I live!"[11]

Crossfire
When *Crossfire* (1947), a film about anti-Semitism, was completed and a rough cut shown the sound and music department, one of the young sound cutters, an Argentine, praised director Edward Dmytryk highly. "It's such a fine suspense story"; he then went on to say, "Why did you have to bring in that stuff about anti-Semitism?" "That was our chief reason for making the film," Dmytryk exclaimed. "But there is no anti-Semitism in the United States," protested the cutter. "If there were," he added, "why is all the money in America controlled by Jewish bankers?" Dmytryk looked at him in astonishment and then commented: "That's why we made the film."[12]

State of the Union

Frank Capra's *State of the Union* (1948) appeared in an election year—the year that Harry Truman and Thomas E. Dewey battled for the presidency. The film, which starred Katharine Hepburn and Spencer Tracy, seemed timely; it dealt with the influence of machine politics on presidential elections. *The New Republic's* Robert Hatch, in fact, said the Capra film "will not be popular with the current presidential candidates or their campaign managers, for it states explicitly that almost all aspirants to public office are the willing dupes of machine politicians and vested interests." But President Truman loved the film. He didn't mind the little cracks at him in the picture; he insisted on having it run off for him several times on his presidential yacht. One of his campaign workers, Charles Alldredge, in fact, thought the film helped shape Truman's campaign. "The most important film of 1948—if importance lies in influencing people and events—was Frank Capra's *State of the Union*," he wrote in *Variety* after the election. "In that film, a presidential candidate beats the political bosses by going over their heads with a dramatic appeal to the public." According to Alldredge, Truman surprised all the experts by beating Dewey because he did exactly what Spencer Tracy, the movie candidate, did—took his case straight to the people.

Not everyone liked Capra's film about public virtue. The film critic for the ultra-rightist *New York Daily Mirror* charged that Capra was using the film "to peddle some peculiar 'advanced' thinking" and hawking un-American propaganda to audiences "through two wonderful and irresistible salespersons," Hepburn and Tracy. "This stuff," said the critic, "slipped through the customers by one of the oldest dodges in the game, 'Sure I'm against communism, but—' . . . The indictment against this country, its customs, manners, morals, economic and political systems, as put in the mouths of Tracy and Miss Hepburn, would not seem out of place in *Izvestia*. . . ." Capra exploded when he saw the review. "Your review of *State of the Union* knocked me into a tailspin. . . ," he announced angrily. "If you've come to the conclusion I am a Communist manipulator or a Communist stooge, you are completely off your nut."

The charges were of course preposterous. Few people took them seriously. Shortly afterward, the Truman administration persuaded Capra to represent the United States at a film festival in India and praised him for doing "one helluva job" when he returned from his mission. But Capra always felt that the right-wing attacks on him at the time damaged his career and that he was never "quite as 'on top' again after that."[13]

Passing

When Otto Preminger read *Quality*, a novel about a young black woman who "passed for white," he thought Darryl Zanuck might be interested. "Dayrell," he said in his heavy Austrian accent, "do you know what means pessing?" "What are you talking about?" cried Zanuck. "Pissing. Yes, I know what pissing means. It's when you've had fourteen beers and all you can think of is where's the nearest urinal." But Preminger finally got through to him, and Zanuck bought the movie rights to the book, renamed it *Pinky*, after the heroine, and picked John Ford to direct it. "What would a Kraut know about such things anyway?" he laughed, when Preminger grumbled about not being selected as director. But Zanuck discovered that Ford was trying to get Ethel Waters (who played Pinky's grandmother) to act "like Aunt Jemima," and decided to replace him with Elia Kazan. "Some directors are great in one field," he explained, "and totally helpless in another."

This change of directors was not unusual for Zanuck. On other occasions he had swapped horses in midstream when he thought one director could handle the demands of a script better than another one. Zanuck insisted on having a script completed to his satisfaction before he assigned a director. In that way he was able to keep complete control over a picture. At 20th Century-Fox, according to Philip Dunne, who with Dudley Nichols wrote the screenplay for *Pinky*, "Movies were made on what amounted to an assembly line: writers wrote, directors directed, cutters cut, and Zanuck himself supervised every detail of each stage of production."

Pinky (1949) was the first major motion picture to deal with race, and it remains the most controversial, largely because Zanuck cast a white actress, Jeanne Crain, as Pinky, the black nurse who can pass for white. But Zanuck and his associates gave careful thought to the casting. When the picture was in its planning stages, there was much speculation about the possibility that a distinguished black actress, like Dorothy Dandridge or Lena Horne, might be picked for the part. As a result, when Zanuck decided on Jeanne Crain, who was not only lily-white, but also usually cast in films as America's favorite Girl Next Door, there was an indignant outcry from people who had not thought the problem through, from some black leaders, and from what Dunne called "the usual gaggle of avant-garde critics."

Dunne himself participated in the casting process. So did Jane White, daughter of NAACP founder Walter White; a black actress herself, she served as adviser on race-related problems during the production of *Pinky*. With her firm support, Zanuck decided on Crain, not because he was reluctant to cast a black actress as Pinky, but because he knew that no black performer could possibly satisfy the basic criterion the Pinky part demanded: that the actress be able to pass for white. The actress had to be lily-white for the simple reason that Pinky herself was lily-white. The casting of Crain doubled the impact of the movie as an indictment of racism. Pinky is physically "white" and only technically "black." Yet she is the victim of prejudice even though she is as "white" as the racists who persecute her. The film underscores the senselessness as well as the viciousness of racial prejudice.[14]

Storm Center

In August 1955, Bette Davis began shooting a movie called *Storm Center*. It had been written in 1951, when Wisconsin senator Joseph R. McCarthy was riding high, and its story about a librarian accused of being a left-winger was strongly reminiscent of the kind of reckless charges that McCarthy became famous for. When the crew went to the little town of Santa Rosa, California, to do some scenes, Davis received letters from local women's club leaders calling the film subversive and urging her to cease work on it. But Davis ignored them; she was thoroughly sympathetic to the film's theme.

One day, when Davis had no scenes to do, director Daniel Taradash was shooting a sequence in which some of the kids in the film discuss communism as they walk along a street lined with small residential houses. Suddenly a hostile-looking old woman with wild hair came running out of one of the houses and started screaming: "I told you motion-picture people I didn't want you around! Now you get the hell out of here or I will call the police!" Taradash was extremely upset. "Didn't you get permission from all these residents?" he asked the assistant director. "You should have given them fifty dollars apiece." "Fifty dollars!" shrieked the old lady. "You're out of your ever-loving mind! Think that would buy me off? You're crazy, the whole lot of you! I'm calling the police right now." But just as Taradash and the crew were about to retreat, the old lady pulled off her wig. It was Bette Davis and she was highly amused at the way she had tricked them.[15]

CHAPTER 25

B Pictures

B pictures appeared in direct response to the decline of audiences during the early Depression years. Between 1930 and 1933 weekly movie attendance dropped from 110 million to 60 million. In an effort to lure the public back into the theaters, Hollywood introduced the double bill, with one of the features a low-budget supporting picture. From 1935 until the late 1940s the studios ground out thousands of seventy-minute B movies and by 1936 75 percent of the nation's theaters were offering double features.[1] While the double bill was adopted by some principal urban chains, neighborhood and small-town theaters were especially dependent on double features to attract working-class audiences. Most towns with a population of over ten thousand had at least two movie houses, and both usually changed their bill three times a week.[2] "Our real job was not making our films," said one Poverty Row alumnus, "it was the task of getting our pictures into all the side street theaters of the nation."[3]

But B-movie makers developed a special expertise of their own. Every major studio had a B unit that served a vital role in absorbing overhead. At Warner Bros. Bryan Foy, an ex-vaudevillian and one of the "seven little Foys," headed B production. He was noted for his speed, his assembly-line mentality, and his ability to stretch a four-line news clipping into five or six reels. During his thirty-six years at Warners, Foy made so many quickies he became known as the

Keeper of the Bees.[4] Sol Siegel headed the B unit at Paramount, Irving Briskin at Columbia, Lucien Hubbard and Michael Fessier at Metro, Sol Wurtzel at Twentieth Century-Fox. Each of them knew all the angles of the low-budget business, although Wurtzel's name prompted the inevitable quip, "from bad to Wurtzel."[5]

Studio heads knew that if a picture cost less than $100,000 it would make a profit. Warners owned 1,600 theaters, and Paramount owned 2,500 in this country alone. Budget pictures were simply booked into these theaters as part of a package. Since "block booking" was then the standard arrangement, theater owners were forced to take bad pictures along with the good. Although major studios hoped that at least ten films a year would be big money-makers, they needed many others to supply their theaters, hoping that with them, they would at least break even. All of the studios had contracts with stars, directors, writers, producers, and top crew members, so assignments had to be found to justify keeping each of them on the payroll. "At the end of the year," Paramount executive Eugene Zukor explained, "you had to total up all the unused time of these people and account for it somewhere on your balance sheet."[6] B pictures became a mechanism for utilizing studio space and talent between major projects, thereby absorbing costs without undue financial risk at the box office.

The average B picture was filmed in twelve to eighteen days. Most actors and directors considered them excellent training for the big break they hoped would come soon. Young stars, backed by established character people, often played leads in B pictures, while they were still restricted to secondary roles in A pictures. On the other hand, making too many B's could jeopardize a career by limiting a performer's marquee value. But Brian Donlevy and Claire Trevor starred almost exclusively in B pictures, and both played strong supporting roles in better films; Trevor even won an Academy Award for her performance in Key Largo (1948).

In order to reduce story costs, writers on B movies frequently found themselves reworking A pictures the studio had made a few years earlier. Previous hits were given new settings, in what became known as "switches." Westerns sometimes were switched to South Sea islands, horse races became automobile races, while classics were turned into melodramas. Bryan Foy kept a stack of scripts on his desk at Warners. Whenever he was stuck for an idea, he'd pull a script off the bottom of the pile and instruct his writers to change it into a new concept.[7] Writer-director Charles Marquis Warren made a

Western at Fox called *Copper Sky* (1957). "It was a damn good picture," Warren declared, "simply because I stole it from a helluva script—*African Queen!*"[8]

While some viewed B assignments as slumming, others saw them as an opportunity to demonstrate resourcefulness by making an inexpensive picture appear important. Often the technicians used were among the best on the lot, individuals who didn't have a major assignment at the moment. Val Lewton, who headed a B unit at RKO, produced a series of high-class psychological horror pictures during the early 1940s that were acclaimed by serious critics: *Cat People* (1942), *I Walked with a Zombie* (1943), and *The Body Snatchers* (1945), all now minor classics. Lewton became known for giving young directors their first chance, among them Jacques Tourneur, Mark Robson, and Robert Wise, all of whom moved on to A productions.[9] Edward Dmytryk directed over a dozen movies at RKO before *Hitler's Children* (1943) lifted him out of the B's. The film cost $100,000 and made $7.5 million, propelling Dmytryk into a top category. "It was a learning ground," the director said of his B experience. "Most of it was crap, but I tried to make it good crap. B's were a good exercise, because I had to take what was crap and make it believable."[10]

Cutting corners was a way of life in budget-film making. Whereas thousands of extras might be used in the big A productions, a full stadium would probably be suggested by no more than three hundred people on a B assignment. Two or three tables often served in restaurant scenes, while sets had likely been used time and again in previous productions. Liberal use of stock footage was characteristic of B movies, especially for large action sequences, which would have been out of the question on a B budget. Since "pace" was the watchword, most B pictures were edited to the bone. Warners' formula for success was "make 'em fast, make 'em loud, make 'em fun."[11]

Metro's B movies were more lavish than most, bolstered by the studio's impressive contract-player roster, and polished to look like A's elsewhere. Series remained one of the great staples of the B's, and Metro relied heavily on profits from the *Andy Hardy* series, *Maisie*, and *Dr. Kildare* to pay for more expensive productions. Twentieth Century-Fox had the *Cisco Kid* series, whereas Universal would later earn millions with its *Ma and Pa Kettle* pictures and those featuring Francis, the talking mule. The *Blondie* series did much to put Columbia on a sound financial footing, as did *Nancy Drew, Mr.*

Moto, Hopalong Cassidy, Red Ryder, Tarzan, and Charlie Chan for their studios. The B's always relied heavily on stereotypes, and constant repetition caused actors to view featured roles as professionally limiting. Once established in a series, furthermore, there was always the problem of getting out of it. When Laraine Day, who played Mary Lamont, left the Kildare pictures, it was necessary to have her killed by a truck, but audiences were devastated.[12]

Universal, Columbia, and Republic made a number of B musicals, although the preparation time required for dance numbers was reduced from weeks to days. Republic went in for the bucolic musical, featuring country types like Judy Canova and the Hoosier Hot Shots, whereas Columbia leaned more toward swing and the contemporary big-band sounds. Donald O'Connor, Peggy Ryan, and Jack Oakie teamed for The Merry Monahans (1944) at Universal, while the Andrews Sisters made thirteen low-budget musicals there during the war years, as one of them said, looking "like the Ritz brothers in drag."[13] The war also produced a spate of combat films, especially submarine movies, which offered action plus the economic advantage of extended use of a single set, the sub's interior.

At most of the lesser studios, Westerns—sixty-minute "oaters"— were the mainstay of B production. Republic, Monogram, and Producers Releasing Corporation depended almost entirely on budget Westerns that emphasized rapid movement and plenty of outdoor action. Costs rarely exceeded $70,000 a picture. If the writing was weak, Republic at least had efficient technicians—good sound and adequate photography. Although schedules were tight and directors were more concerned with pace than any subtleties of motivation, Republic did have John English. Unlike most directors of "oaters," English found or introduced nuances in scripts that would have driven A directors mad. Ironically, he hated the outdoors, turned his nose up at the sweat and horse manure, and was known by his crew as a "boudoir man," who preferred working amid sophisticated surroundings.[14]

To the B thrillers and horror pictures, in the 1950s Hollywood added science fiction, raw material for which lay all around: nuclear testing, the flying-saucer craze, and eventually Sputnik and the burgeoning space program. Invasion of the Body Snatchers (1956), The Incredible Shrinking Man (1957), and I Married a Monster from Outer Space (1958) all did a lively business, especially among teenagers, at a time when television was cutting deeply into theater attendance. The B picture in particular suffered, since television built much of its programming on entertainment modeled after or similar to the old budget movies. Cheaply made exploitation films and variations on the youth-runs-wild theme proved exceptions. Often shown at drive-in theaters, they consistently attracted audiences.

Keep 'em Busy

Warner Bros. had over twenty stages and hundreds of people on the payroll. Whenever a stage was unoccupied and actors were idle, Jack Warner was upset because he knew he was losing money. Whether good, bad, or mediocre, he wanted to keep cranking out pictures. Even a poor movie that broke even was better than nothing, for it paid salaries. Warner called Vincent Sherman one time about a picture the director didn't want to make. "Listen," Warner told him, "I've got eight actors sitting on their asses doing nothing, getting paid. I want to put them to work. Now take this script and do the best you can with it and give me twelve reels of film." That's the way Jack worked. "So under pressure," said Sherman, "you did the best you could with the material."[15]

Top Bananas

Although cheaply made, some B's were enormously profitable. *Buck Privates* (1941) was the first of five inexpensive comedies director Arthur Lubin made with the comedy team Bud Abbott and Lou Costello at Universal. The picture used sets that had appeared in several earlier films, but was so successful the studio repeated the formula for more than a decade. Abbott and Costello had been burlesque comedians whose crude humor was based on original gags they had worked out over the years. They did routines like "Spin the Dragon" and "Slowly I Turn," which they had to act out so Lubin would know what they were talking about. The boys had perfected their comedy to such a degree it all seemed spontaneous and uproariously funny. In private they approached humor in much the same way. On Lubin's birthday one year, they were in the middle of a scene when suddenly Lou yelled, "Hold it, hold it." The boys threw a suitcase to their director that turned out to be full of condoms! Clearly the prank smacked of the old burlesque wheels.[16]

Thursday

Theater director Michael Gordon made four pictures for Columbia early in his film career, all low-budget. Suddenly he glimpsed his chance to make a marvelous little picture he thought would be a critical triumph. All went well until he fell a half day behind the shooting schedule and was called in to see Irving Briskin, the studio's head of B pictures. Like Harry Cohn, Briskin knew the movie business inside out. He explained to the idealistic young director the financial facts of life—they were making a picture for $90,000. "If it's a good picture, it's going to gross a hundred and fifty thousand dollars. If it's a bad picture, it's going to gross a hundred and fifty thousand dollars." Then Briskin added his definitive line: "I don't want it good—I want it Thursday!"[17]

Durango

Making B films had many of the same problems and tensions as making A's. Between more dramatic assignments, Ann Doran played in a number of B Westerns at Columbia. She enjoyed the congeniality of the wranglers, but never considered herself much of a horsewoman. She appeared in one of the *Durango Kid* pictures with Charles Starrett, a Dartmouth graduate who disliked making Westerns despite having been featured in dozens of successful B "oaters." In the movie Doran made with Starrett they were to come out of a bank, jump over the rumps of their horses, and take off at a full gallop. Ann doubted that she could do it, but the wranglers showed her how and, throwing caution to the wind, she somehow made it. As the horses raced down the studio street, Ann sensed something was wrong. She looked around to see Starrett still on the ground. The Durango Kid hadn't made the leap onto his horse.[18]

Same Names

In one of John Wayne's B Westerns, Noah Beery was playing the villain and the legendary stunt man Yakima Canutt was doubling for Wayne in a fight sequence between the two actors, while Duke was shooting an interior scene to save time. Beery had gotten into a hot argument with the producer, during which he cursed him loudly enough for the crew to hear. Taking Canutt aside, the producer said, "Yak, you could do me a big favor. In this fight you and Beery are shooting I'd like you to *really* rough him up—just beat the hell out of him, will you?" Canutt replied, "Sure, I'd be happy to beat the living daylights out of him on one condition." The producer wanted to know what the condition was. "That you get Noah to call me the same names he's been calling you," explained Canutt.[19]

The Andrews Sisters

The Andrews Sisters found making B musicals at Universal in the 1940s exhausting. Shooting schedules were seldom more than ten days, and the women had to devise most of their own choreography, making it up as they went along. Not only were things done fast, but everything seemed secondhand. For one picture, the trio had recorded a song called "Pennsylvania Polka" and were shooting the number, trying to stay in sync with the soundtrack. Several extras were on the set that morning, making every minute count from a cost standpoint. Maxene Andrews was concentrating on the physical movements of the number and made a mistake in the lyrics. Realizing the error would be evident to anyone watching closely, she stopped. "Why did you stop?" the director asked. "It was going along beautifully." "Because I made a mistake in the lyrics and was out of sync," Maxene explained. There was a young man standing nearby who was supposed to catch such errors, but he hadn't said anything. So the sisters started again. They got past that point where the physical routine changed, when Maxene stopped again. Patty looked at her sister and asked, "What are you doing?" Maxene confessed she had made another mistake in the lyrics. "Well, he didn't stop you," said Patty. "How did you know you made a mistake?" So Maxene walked over to the fellow and inquired, "Young man, why didn't you stop me?" The fellow looked at her and said something. Maxene suddenly realized he couldn't speak a word of English! He'd escaped from Nazi Germany and been given a job in Universal's music department.[20]

Give Up

On *Give Out Sisters* (1942), again with the Andrews trio, there were so many problems during the shooting that the cast started calling it *Give Up Sisters*. Patty was to do a dance with an elderly extra during an interlude in one of their numbers. The man was a handsome gentleman with a distinguished goatee and formal clothes, and he was to take Patty in his arms and pull her around in a simple polka. The three sisters were costumed in long skirts, made up to look like old ladies. During the dance the director yelled, "Stop!" He told the extra, "I don't want to see your face. I want to see Miss Andrews's face." Three different times the director stopped them with the same complaint. They began again, and this time the old gentleman stepped on Patty's dress, and she fell and broke her ankle. The singer sat on the floor in pain until one of the grips picked her up and carried her into her portable dressing room. Maxene thought, "Oh, great! She can't work. We still have work to do on this picture. While she's recuperating, we'll get paid, and Laverne and I can just vacation." But that's not the way things were done at Universal on B pictures. The producer figured out the women could end that sequence by hopping out of the scene on one foot. And that's what they did![21]

A Horse

In 1945 William Faulkner and Stephen Longstreet were supposedly standing outside Warner Bros. studio waiting for their car, both a little glum since they'd been working on the screenplay for *Stallion Road,* a B picture a cut above average. "Who's going to star in this?" Faulkner asked. "A horse," said Longstreet. "I mean human," said Faulkner. "Ronald Reagan," Longstreet told him. Faulkner thought awhile, puffed on his Dunhill, and then said, "I don't know. Back home we'd run him for public office." "Why?" asked Longstreet. Faulkner thought some more and then said, "An actor now has to be the part he's playing, but this boy is too much of everything, and none of it settles down. You can't go too wrong in politics going from no place to nothing." Later, when the film, starring Reagan, was released, Faulkner sent Longstreet a note: "If you're a horse, you'll like the picture."[22]

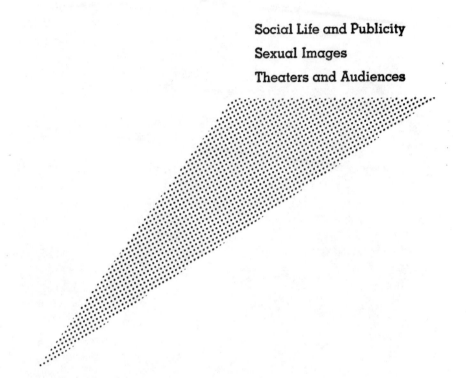

IV. HOLLYWOOD
AND ITS
PUBLIC

CHAPTER 26

Social
Life and
Publicity

In the beginning Hollywood was a sleepy little village of white-frame houses and dirt roads cut through orange groves. Vine Street was half paved, with pepper trees on both sides, while Sunset Boulevard was lined with palms and rosebushes. Wild holly grew in the hills above Franklin Canyon and some say that's why the town got its name.[1] There was nothing worldly about the community, but it quickly became eager for social status. As in most small towns, rumors carried more weight than fact, although as the movie colony grew, Hollywood gossip received national attention.

Before long this rural village had been transformed into Tinsel Town, Lotus Land, a mythical kingdom of sunshine and flowers and endless mansions, where parties were the grandest, people the most beautiful, and clothes the most elegant. Thousands poured into the mushrooming community each week to gawk and stare, many of them eager to join this world of glamour and excitement. Youngsters climbed over studio fences night after night to wander awestruck among the sets and backlots, imagining what working in the movies must be like. For better or worse, Hollywood was painting a dream for the American people that would soon spread around the world.

By the 1920s stories of movieland's hedonism became part of the publicity torrent. Tales about dope, booze, and unbridled sex all reached scandalous proportions. Clara Bow was said to have taken on the entire University of Southern California football team,[2] while Fatty Arbuckle's supposed rape, resulting in the death of model Virginia Rappe during a Labor Day party, produced a wave of protest that destroyed Arbuckle's career.

Glamour gradually replaced scandal as Hollywood's symbol. When actress Jayne Meadows arrived at MGM in the mid-1940s, she was agog at the conspicuous frills. "Everybody had on false eyelashes," Meadows remembered. "Everybody wore dark glasses. Everybody had dyed hair. Everybody wore slacks. Everybody went around in fancy cars, and everything was show-off."[3] Yet Budd Schulberg maintained that Hollywood represented a picture of America itself run through the projector at triple speed. "If the Hollywood party was excessive," observed Schulberg, "it was only because Hollywood had always been an excessive, speeded-up, larger-than-life reflection of the American Way."[4]

While Hollywood's casual marriages received national publicity through the years, records indicate that the divorce rate in the movie capital was no higher than that in New York, Chicago, or Detroit. But Warren Beatty once joked, "The best time to get married is noon. That way if things don't work out, you haven't blown the whole day."[5] On the other hand, Henry Koster insisted he loved Peggy Moran, his wife of many years, so much that if he were married to someone else he'd cheat on his wife to be with Peggy.[6] Samuel Goldwyn so admired his wife Frances that he once said, as only Sam could, that he'd like "to have a bust made of her beautiful hands."[7] Edward Dmytryk, who taught at two major universities following his career as a director, remarked that he found far more graduate students than Hollywood actresses breaking up marriages. After nearly fifty years in the film colony, Margaret Tallichet Wyler claimed she was still looking for the orgies she had heard so much about. Most of their friends, the wife of director William Wyler maintained, were happily married couples who had been together as long as the Wylers had. Many of the young girls coming to Hollywood under contract lived at the sedate Studio Club, while Jayne Meadows taught a Sunday-school class the whole time she was at Metro.

New Yorkers in particular found Hollywood a cultural wasteland, rushing back east for stimulation whenever possible. "I thought Hollywood was a horrible place," songwriter Harry Warren confessed. "God, I hated it. It was like being in Iowa or someplace."[8] Helen Gahagan Douglas recalled standing on Hollywood Boulevard and looking up and down the dreary street. "Frances Starr hadn't exaggerated," Douglas wrote, "when she said that Hollywood Boulevard resembled a movie set built to collapse the moment the stage manager cried, 'Strike it!'"[9] Wilson Mizner, part-owner of the Brown Derby, remarked that Hollywood "was like a play with a bad cast."[10] Jack Warner, Douglas Fairbanks, and Sid Grauman were sitting in the Derby one evening at a table that rocked. When Fairbanks complained, Mizner responded, "How can you expect anything in Hollywood to be on the level?"[11] But it was Tallulah Bankhead who leveled perhaps the most damning charge at Hollywood. "Dahling," drawled Tallulah upon meeting Irving Thalberg, "how does one get laid in this dreadful place?"[12]

Outsiders tended to find Hollywood self-consumed. Social gatherings more often than not involved watching other people's pictures. "You only talked about films, you only read about films," remembered comedienne Nancy Walker. "It was the most insulated kind of existence."[13] As in any small town, life in Hollywood was lived in a fishbowl; privacy didn't exist. Those who were working found themselves besieged with social obligations; those who weren't sensed that their pool of friends was drying up. Character actor Arnold Moss frequently worked in Hollywood but refused to live there. Some acquaintances assumed the actor preferred New York because of his children. "No," Moss told them, "I think Hollywood's fine for children. I'm not sure it's so good for adults."[14]

Initially Mack Sennett, ensconced in his huge Mexican house, was more or less the social leader. "He'd give a dinner party," producer Walter Wanger recalled, "and if you didn't take the young lady on your right upstairs between the soup and the entrée, you were considered a homosexual."[15] Later, the first organized social system came with Mary Pickford and Douglas Fairbanks. Their mansion, Pickfair, became the Buckingham Palace of Hollywood, the most impregnable social fortress of the West. Dinners there were strictly formal, with butlers in pantaloons waiting behind each guest.[16] In their travels all over the world, Mary and Doug had acquired an international set of friends, seldom missing anyone with a title. One day they supposedly received a message that the Princess Vera Romanoff was in town. The couple sent a car to the Biltmore Hotel and brought "the princess" to Pickfair for a wonderful weekend, with parties in her honor. She was actually a little secretary from San Francisco who went back to work on Monday morning, having thanked her hosts effusively.[17]

William Randolph Hearst and Marion Davies were the next to

take over as arbiters of the Hollywood social scene, jealously guarding their position. Nearly every weekend forty or fifty select guests were invited to San Simeon, the Hearst castle on the coast north of Santa Barbara. Special railroad cars took the guests to San Luis Obispo, where they were met by a cavalcade of limousines. Still later, David and Irene Selznick reigned over Hollywood until the breakup of their marriage.

Within this stratosphere were enclaves unique unto themselves. C. Aubrey Smith and Basil Rathbone presided over a British colony that included Ronald Colman, David Niven, screenwriter Charles Bennett, Anna Lee, and Charles Boyer, whose wife was English. For years Salka Viertel was a beacon for the growing European colony, while Charles Laughton became the center of an intellectual and literary assemblage concerned with quality drama. L. B. Mayer was famous for Sunday brunches at his home, where the President or a cardinal might appear. During Sunday afternoons another clique gathered at Gene Kelly's house for volleyball, a casual supper, and maybe charades: Frank Sinatra, Judy Garland, Jule Styne, Betty Comden and Adolph Green, Stanley Donen, Nancy Walker, Keenan Wynn, and Leonard Bernstein if he was in town. The Holmby Hills residents had their neighborhood gatherings, which included Joan Bennett and Walter Wanger, Humphrey Bogart and Lauren Bacall, director Alan Crosland, and Bing Crosby, whose sons frequently came along to play with Joan Bennett's daughters. Agnes Moorehead always gave a smashing Christmas party that guests really enjoyed instead of standing around bored with drinks in their hands. "Aggie's parties went on all night," actress Jean Porter remembered, "and there was entertainment and great food and warmth."[18]

At Hillcrest Country Club a gin-rummy group regularly met, consisting of Jack Benny, George Burns, and Edward G. Robinson and their cronies. Betty Grable, Harry James, director Eddie Goulding, and actress Binnie Barnes played poker together, and there was a similar game at Metro. Ernst Lubitsch, Pandro Berman, and Marlene Dietrich rode horses at stables in Bel Air, while Clark Gable, Gary Cooper, Robert Taylor, Fredric March, Robert Stack, and Fred MacMurray knew each other through shooting sports. James Cagney, Pat O'Brien, Spencer Tracy, Jimmy Gleason, Ralph Bellamy, Frank McHugh, and Lynne Overman, all of whom had been acquainted on Broadway, formed a group sometimes referred to as "the Irish Mafia." They met for dinner every week at one of their homes or at Dave Chasen's or Mike Romanoff's restaurant.

The Hollywood social hierarchy, unlike that associated with the New York stage, was extremely rigid. Visitors from Broadway were often amazed to discover that cameramen and technicians weren't invited to parties with stars and studio executives, even when they were working on the same project. Outsiders claimed that "big stars" seemed reluctant to spend much time at parties with "middling stars," although at the studio social barriers appeared less formidable. Even insiders admitted that arrogance paid off in Hollywood. "If you walk around pretending you're the tops," veteran screenwriter Charles Bennett commented, "you are the tops."[19]

Clearly Hollywood was not one community but several, its denizens meeting under different circumstances and on various levels. Conflicting values either strained relationships or resulted in quiet acceptance when opposites were thrust together. Dan Dailey was under contract to Metro when singer John Raitt, later a success in Carousel and The Pajama Game on Broadway, showed up for a screen test. Since Raitt was fresh out of college and had no immediate job prospects, Dailey offered to let him share his own quarters. Raitt at the time was making $40 a month singing at a church and earlier had considered going into the ministry. Dailey, on the other hand, ran with a fast crowd, drank a great deal, and knew his way around the local night spots. While Johnny Raitt read the Bible in the living room, Dan might be entertaining a girl in the bedroom. "I had to sort of shift gears a little bit," Raitt confessed.[20]

For most stars the loss of anonymity caused a serious adjustment. Not to be able to stop by a drugstore without being recognized and possibly mobbed was a definite inconvenience and potentially dangerous to personal development. "There's a euphoria that comes along with it," singer Rosemary Clooney confided, "where you're not prepared for that kind of life-style, the unending escalation or earnings—people that you meet that you had no idea in the world you would ever associate with at all. And you're really not prepared for all of it happening so quickly. It's hard, very hard."[21] Gregory Peck recognized the danger, but denied that his star status caused him to lose perspective. "I think because of my stage training and my years in New York," Peck said, "I had a respect for the craft of acting and a fascination with it, so that the intent to do work of top quality was always of more interest to me than being a movie star. I can honestly say I never went off the rails on becoming a celebrity."[22] Still, those with well-grounded values often found the veneer and ballyhoo of Hollywood distasteful. When Arnold Moss left John

Houseman's production of *King Lear* in New York to make a picture with Bob Hope and Hedy Lamarr, he sighed to friends, "From *Lear* to Lamarr in twenty-four hours!"[23]

Studios employed staffs of publicists whose job was to see that the film colony's every move was covered in newspapers and fan magazines. A number of actors were assigned to each publicist, and the staff worked constantly to keep its stars in the limelight. Actors and actresses not involved with a picture were expected to participate in newsworthy activities that fed a press hungry for details, whether it be attending the opening of a supermarket or a premiere, or dancing the night away at the Mocambo or Cocoanut Grove. Los Angeles alone had five newspapers during Hollywood's Golden Era, and no shred of gossip was too insignificant for them or fan magazines to report. Studio publicists were responsible for turning young stars into known commodities, so they fed the media with romanticized stories that seemed more personal than they actually were until fans felt they knew their favorites intimately. When a dam was constructed at Richland, Washington, Janis Paige was named Miss Dam Site. When the baseball season opened, Alexis Smith was shown throwing out the first ball. Fan-mail departments sent out hundreds of photographs each week in response to letters that poured in daily.

Reporters by the hundreds praised Hollywood films and film-makers, while even the six-day quickies had a unit man to circulate day-to-day happenings on the set. Studios hired a field man for each principal city, and billboards advertised their latest releases. Paramount had 360 twenty-four-sheet billboard locations in New York City alone, generally depicting the studio's current movies in the most lurid images conceivable. "It was always a challenge to come up with something that was new, striking, and different," Warner Bros. publicist Bill Hendricks explained.[24]

The major forces studio publicists reckoned with, of course, were gossip columnists Louella Parsons and Hedda Hopper, whose combined readership at their height totaled an estimated 75 million. Parsons had the power of the Hearst press behind her and enjoyed the largest circulation, yet both women were feared and courted even by Hollywood giants. Hopper occasionally pointed to her home in Beverly Hills and boasted, "That's the house that fear built."[25] If a star stormed off a set, Hedda or Louella likely knew within the hour. If one got a scoop before the other, someone was in trouble. "You'd better make peace with that old broad," Jack Warner told Bill Hendricks when the publicist got crossways with Parsons. Hendricks hurriedly sent Louella flowers and arranged to eat breakfast with her. "We can get along," she told him. "All you have to do is just give me all the stories."[26]

During Christmas season Parsons made her rounds of the studios in a chauffeur-driven station wagon, imbibing a glass of holiday cheer as she collected presents. Once, she emerged from her last stop to find the station wagon had been robbed of thousands of dollars' worth of perfumes, expensive wines, and monogrammed lingerie. Parsons's secretary was instructed to inform the various studios that her driver would be calling for replacements, which she received without protest.[27] When Hedda Hopper printed unkind remarks about Joan Bennett, the actress sent her a live skunk in a hatbox. Hedda thanked the actress the next day in her column, announcing that she had named the varmint "Joan."[28] Another time Merle Oberon demanded to know why Hedda had written such vicious things about her. Hedda leaned over and patted the star's arm: "Bitchery, dear. Sheer bitchery."[29]

Swimming Pools and Religion

One day Mary Pickford and Douglas Fairbanks were sitting around the pool at Pickfair with their friend Charlie Chaplin. Somehow the conversation turned to religion, a matter on which they sharply disagreed. Chaplin, fully clothed, jumped into the swimming pool shouting, "I'm an atheist. If there's a God, let Him save me." The actor was gasping and going down for the third time when Fairbanks, also completely dressed, dived in to save him. Meanwhile Mary was racing around the pool yelling, "Let the heathen drown!"[30]

Glorious Technicolor

During the early 1940s there was a fashionable whorehouse in the Hollywood Hills called Mae's, where the girls looked, dressed, and talked amazingly like current movie stars. The madam of the establishment was "Miss Mae West," a close facsimile of the Paramount star. Mae's also had a "Barbara Stanwyck," a "Marlene Dietrich," a "Joan Crawford," a "Claudette Colbert" (who spoke perfect French), a "Myrna Loy," a "Ginger Rogers," and so on. Clothes were frequently bought from the studios and remade to fit the girls at Mae's, so it was possible to see a dress on Myrna Loy in a *Thin Man* picture and later the same night find it on "Myrna Loy" at Mae's. When a star went on location, her Mae's counterpart was likewise absent.

The girls read *Variety* and *The Hollywood Reporter* regularly in order to converse knowledgeably with clients. There were four maids, excellent food prepared by a French chef, and old films projected upon request—all for a price.

Garson Kanin, then a young Hollywood bachelor, was directing *They Knew What They Wanted* (1940) with Charles Laughton and Carole Lombard. Like many who came in contact with Lombard, he fell for her instantly, finding her the warmest, most beautiful, talented, funny, on-the-level woman he'd ever encountered. The fact that she was married to Clark Gable failed to restrain his fantasies. He became absolutely bedazzled. When Kanin's brother married, a group of friends gave him the customary stag party, which ended at Mae's. In due course, in walked "Carole." The smitten Garson Kanin took her aside, and they talked for some time, discussing what they had shot that day and what they would be doing tomorrow. "Carole" loved his ideas and shared his opinion of Laughton. She told him she was considering a divorce from Clark, since their careers often conflicted. Kanin agreed she was doing the sensible thing. "Carole" finally suggested they have supper in her suite, and Kanin readily agreed. "The rest is a Glorious Technicolor, out-of-focus, slow-motion dream," he later reported.

On the set the next morning Carole Lombard and Frank Fay joined the director for coffee in his trailer after the first shot. Soon they fell to discussing what each had done the night before, and Kanin told of his visit to Mae's and about meeting "Carole," sparing them none of the details. His account was punctuated by the real Carole screaming with laughter. "I'll die! I'll die!" she kept repeating. "Wait till I tell Clark! Jesus, no, I better not. He'll *go* there!"[31]

Norma's Party

The Thalbergs and the Fairbankses were next-door neighbors in Santa Monica and in and out of each other's houses at all hours. MGM star Norma Shearer (Mrs. Thalberg) and Douglas Fairbanks's third wife, Sylvia, were best friends. One day in December 1939 Norma decided to give Doug and Sylvia a party and invited their closest friends to it, but during the afternoon Fairbanks was taken ill. No one thought it was serious until seven that evening, when Sylvia phoned Norma. "I'm terribly sorry," she said, "but we can't come. Douglas is much worse." Their place cards were removed from the table and the other guests sat down to dine at nine o'clock. During the first course, Norma's butler gave her a whispered message. One or two people noticed she turned pale, but the dinner went on without a ripple. Afterward they danced, played cards, and had a gay old time until the party broke up at three in the morning. As one of the guests got into her car to leave, her chauffeur said, "Did you know that Mr. Fairbanks died?" "Good Lord!" she exclaimed. "When?" "Nine-thirty, madam," he said. Later, gossip columnist Hedda Hopper asked Norma how she could have gone on with her party after hearing about her friend Doug's death. "What else could I do?" she wailed. "I couldn't say anything—it would have spoiled my party."[32]

Flynn, Walsh, and Barrymore

The day John Barrymore died director Raoul Walsh was at Errol Flynn's house drinking heavily. Flynn had idolized Barrymore and was deeply saddened by his death. "Uncle," he told Walsh, "I can see the old fellow sitting there now telling us his most marvelous tales. How I miss him." The phone rang, and Flynn returned to say that he had to see his lawyer but would be back shortly, and asked Walsh to stay for dinner.

Walsh poured himself another drink and got into his station wagon, having found out from a friend that Barrymore's body had been taken to Malloy Brothers on Temple Street. One of the Malloy brothers had been a character actor who'd worked in Walsh's pictures. "I'd like to borrow Barrymore's body for about two hours," the director told him upon arriving at the mortuary. "I want to take him somewhere to surprise somebody." The former actor drank a great deal and, as usual, was loaded. "All right, for you I'll do it," he said. They got hold of Barrymore's stiff body and put him in the back of Walsh's station wagon. The director drove carefully to Flynn's house, not wanting the police to stop him. He pulled into the driveway and told Errol's servant, "Alex, Mr. Barrymore didn't die, he's drunk. Help me carry him in the house." The servant helped carry Barrymore in, agreeing he'd never seen a man so drunk. They propped the dead actor up on a couch, and before long Flynn walked in. He saw Barrymore's body sitting there and dashed from the house. "You missed the old boy and I brought him up here," Walsh shouted out the door. "At least come in and say hello to him." Flynn wanted no part of it. "All right, Alex," Walsh said, "let's get him back before he falls asleep." They loaded Barrymore into the station wagon again, and Walsh drove down to Malloy Brothers, where the former actor was waiting. "Where the hell did you take him, Mr. Walsh?" the drunken brother wanted to know. "I took him up to Errol Flynn's," explained the director. "Why the hell didn't you tell me?" Malloy exclaimed. "I'd have put a better suit on him."[33] It's an amazing story, although some authorities claim it never happened.

Sure Thing

Many Hollywood personalities—among them Bing Crosby and Betty Grable—loved to play the horses. One weekend Jack Warner made the mistake of going to the races at Hollywood Park with director Mervyn LeRoy. LeRoy had all sorts of connections with jockeys and trainers and knew all the inside information on winning horses. "Jack," he said, "I know a horse in the last race that looks good." Warner asked the name. "Sh-h-h-h," LeRoy answered. "Don't ask me now." Jack kept trying to pry the red-hot tip from the director, but without success. "Now, Jack," LeRoy said, "it's absolutely vital to say absolutely nothing. Even after the race, don't give away his name. Just follow me to the ticket window. Buy what I buy." As the last race neared, Warner tiptoed after LeRoy to the window and put his money down on number 8 to win, glancing over his shoulder to make sure no one was watching. "Remember now," LeRoy said as they returned to the clubhouse, "not a word!" The race was run, and number 8 came in a poor last. When Jack got home, he sent Mervyn LeRoy a wire: NOW CAN I TELL?[34]

My Type of Woman

Producer Frederick Brisson left London in December 1939 on a ship that took two weeks to cross the Atlantic because of the zigzagging to avoid German submarines. The ship had eight bunks in each stateroom, and people were sitting on top of one another on the decks. On this trip the crew had only one movie aboard, The Women. Brisson's deck chair was right outside the main salon, and day after day he heard a lot of screaming women and the audience laughing. Finally on the tenth day he went in to see the picture himself. He immediately became fascinated with Rosalind Russell, who played the energetic woman in the film. "I've just got to meet this girl and marry her," he thought. "She's my type of woman. She's beautiful, she's funny, she has energy." He knew nothing about her other than what he had seen in the film.

He arrived in California a few days before Christmas. Cary Grant had invited him to stay in the house he shared with Randolph Scott in Santa Monica. Cary's secretary, Frank Horn, met Brisson at the station, and on the drive to Santa Monica Freddie asked, "Frank, what's Cary doing now?" Horn explained that Grant was shooting a picture called *His Girl Friday*, which was a remake of *The Front Page* with one of the leads changed to a woman. "Rosalind Russell is playing the part opposite Cary." Brisson's ears perked up. "Rosalind Russell?" he said. "Is that the girl I saw in *The Women*?" Horn confirmed that she was the one: "She's terrific. Believe me, Cary's having to fight all the way; she's stealing scene after scene."

After exchanging greetings, Brisson remarked to his host, "I understand you're making a film called *His Girl Friday*. How is Rosalind Russell?" "Terrific," Grant answered. "I've got to watch every step. Obviously she knows what she's doing." Brisson said he'd love to meet her. "Easy," Cary replied, "why don't we invite her for New Year's Eve?" Brisson thought that was a wonderful idea and kept asking Cary, "Have you invited Rosalind Russell for New Year's yet?" Grant assured him all was well. But New Year's Eve came and went and no Rosalind Russell. "Don't worry," Grant consoled him. "She really didn't know whether she could get out of a long-standing engagement that evening."

A few days later Grant asked Freddie what he was doing for dinner that night. "Nothing," replied Brisson. "Then join me at Chasen's at eight-thirty." Freddie entered to discover Cary had invited Roz to dinner directly from the studio. They were in the middle of the first course when Brisson walked in. "You know Freddie Brisson, don't you?" Cary said to Roz. "No, I don't," she replied. "Well, I just thought you two ought to meet, and I've been telling him I could get him a date with you. So here we are." Russell and Brisson started dating and were married for twenty-five years.[35]

Bring on the Girls

A story, probably apocryphal, concerns the Earl of Warwick's trip to Hollywood. The distinguished visitor had heard of a famous whorehouse run by a Madam Francis, and he sought its location. By mistake he was given the address of Warner Bros. star Kay Francis. The night the earl rang the wrong doorbell happened to be Kay's wedding night. She had just married producer Kenneth MacKenna, and she was upstairs in a negligee sipping champagne with her groom when the earl appeared at her door. Francis's maid answered the ring and, flustered by the title, showed his lordship into the drawing room. When Francis learned who was waiting downstairs she was touched that so regal a guest would call on this special occasion. She kissed her new husband on the forehead and promised to hurry back to him as quickly as possible.

Kay was graciousness itself when she entered the drawing room. The earl gallantly admired her gown, inquired about the paintings on the walls, but soon tired of this meaningless chatter. "You're delightful, Madam Francis," he said, slightly impatient, "but would you mind bringing in the girls?"[36]

False Alarm

Ida Lupino and Howard Duff had been happily married for several years, and so had David and Hjördis Niven. But for some reason both couples were subjected to a spate of rumors, and they decided to have a little fun with gossip columnists Hedda Hopper and Louella Parsons. They chose Ciro's for the scene of action. After making reservations for two in a dark corner of the place, Niven and Lupino arrived there around midnight and the headwaiter's eyebrows soared. Vibrating with excitement he led the two into a dark corner in the far end of the room and stood with eyes wide as Ida started nibbling Niven's ear. Somebody got to the phone quickly; by the time Niven and Lupino had finished their second drink a battery of photographers was massing in the bar. About this time Howard Duff arrived with Hjördis, and the entire restaurant watched spellbound as a jittery headwaiter led them to a table as far away as possible from Niven and Lupino. Out of the corner of his eye Niven could see Howard draping himself over Hjördis like a tent. After a few minutes, Duff, who had quite a reputation as a brawler, suddenly pushed the table over with a crash, rose to his feet, and pointed his finger accusingly at Niven across the room. Hjördis tried to restrain him, as did Ida when Niven got to his feet. "No, no! Darling!" cried Ida. "You must flee. . . . He'll kill you!" Shrugging off their partners, Niven and Duff advanced on each other, while the place went deathly quiet and the photographers moved expectantly in for a scoop. Niven and Duff removed their jackets and rolled up their sleeves and began circling each other. By this time people were standing on their chairs. Suddenly, the two men sprang, grabbed each other around the waist, kissed each other, and began waltzing slowly around the floor. A disappointed headwaiter set up a new table for four and the ensuing revelry was recorded by the more sporting among the photographers. But Hopper and Parsons were not amused. The next day both called to tell Niven they would not tolerate being awakened in the middle of the night for a false alarm.[37]

Memorable

Among the notables at the Academy Awards dinner in 1942 was the Chinese ambassador to the United States, Dr. Hu Shih, whose country was at the time fighting Japanese invaders. In his introduction of Hu Shih, Cecil B. De Mille referred to him as "the Japanese Ambassador." He quickly corrected the error, but returned to his seat amid oppressive silence. Smiling, Mrs. De Mille leaned toward her husband and whispered, "Cecil, at last you have done something that Hollywood will remember you for."[38]

Teacher

Sam Goldwyn and Chico Marx were once engaged in a backgammon encounter, with Chico proving himself a far better player. Three times Goldwyn's son Sam junior knocked over the board, so they had to keep starting the game over. Finally Chico told Sam to get rid of his son. Goldwyn did, but Sammy kept returning. Fed up, Chico escorted the boy from the room and came back five minutes later, alone. The game was played with no more interference. Amazed at Chico's ability with children, Goldwyn asked, "How'd you do it?" "I taught him to masturbate," Chico answered proudly.[39]

Merely Excellent

Hollywood hyperbolizes. A director or producer or screenwriter isn't merely a "genius," he's a "very great genius." Once two producers met on the street. "How's your picture doing?" asked the first. "Excellent," said the second. "Only excellent?" cried the first. "That's too bad!"[40]

Not an Actress

The cast of Citizen Kane (1941) enjoyed close esprit, with the exception of Dorothy Comingore, who kept her distance. She played the would-be singer Kane befriended and later married, only to have her leave him and wind up a booze-sodden nightclub entertainer. Orson Welles treated Comingore with contempt on the set, while he was courteous to Ruth Warrick, who played the first Mrs. Kane. When Warrick objected, Welles shook his head. "You just don't understand," he said. "I treat her that way because she has got to hate my guts when we get to the later scenes. When she yells and screams and finally walks out on me, I want her to feel every bit of it in her bones." Warrick insisted an actress doesn't have to experience abuse to show pain. "That's just the point," said Welles. "She is *not* an actress. She *is* Susan Alexander, and she'll probably end up just like the woman she's playing. I'm not mistreating her. I treat her exactly as she *expects* to be treated. She wouldn't respect anything else."

Comingore's subsequent life bore out Welles's prediction. Her next picture was not a success, and after that parts were few. Several years later her marriage failed and her husband received custody of their children. She started to drink heavily, bending any available ear in Musso & Frank's Grill night after night with tales of suffering. Eventually she was arrested for soliciting from a car off Hollywood Boulevard, and the newspaper photograph captured how hard her life had been. Her haggard face resembled that of Susan Alexander in the final scenes of *Citizen Kane*. A few years later she died tragically.[41]

Professional
At a party once, John Huston and Errol Flynn supposedly had a fight that proved no contest. After two punches John was flat on the ground. Errol helped him up, and a splash of cold water and a shot of bourbon revived him. Huston again started throwing punches at Flynn, and back he went to the ground. Errol helped revive him, but John was soon slugging him again, only to hit the ground once more. Errol emptied a bucket of water on him, and when Huston came around, whispered kindly, "John, you have no chance. I was a professional fighter. Please don't be a fool." Huston remained undaunted. "When Errol said that to me," he claimed, "I knew I had him!"[42]

Names
In 1946 World War II British military leader Field Marshal Montgomery appeared in Hollywood, and Samuel Goldwyn gave a dinner for him attended by many Hollywood celebrities. When the time came, Goldwyn rose from his table, tapped a knife on his wineglass for silence, and cleared his throat. "It gives me great pleasure tonight to welcome to Hollywood a very distinguished soldier . . .," he said.

"Ladies and gentlemen, I propose a toast to Marshall Field Montgomery." There was a stunned silence and then Jack Warner exclaimed: "Montgomery Ward, you mean."[43]

A Ride Home

When Lauren Bacall first arrived in Hollywood, she didn't feel comfortable at parties, partly because she had no stature among the celebrities there and partly because she didn't drink and everybody else did. After a party at his house, Howard Hawks, who was sponsoring her, found that he had to drive her home afterward. "What's the matter?" he asked her testily. "Couldn't you get someone to offer you a ride?" "I don't get along too well with these people," Bacall said. Hawks wanted to know if she was nice to them. "I try to be," she answered. Hawks thought for a moment. Finally he said, "Don't be nice the next time. Try insulting them and see whether maybe you do a little better." The following Saturday night Bacall was a guest at another party at Hawks's house. When the party ended, she told him with a smile, "I've got a ride home." "Good for you," Hawks said. "What did you do?" Bacall reported that she had done what he'd suggested: "I insulted a man. I asked him where he got his tie. He said, 'Why do you want to know?' I said, 'So I can tell other people not to go there.'" Hawks was delighted. "Who was the man?" he asked. "Clark Gable," she said, smiling broadly.[44]

Nunnally

Actress Dorris Bowdon met screenwriter Nunnally Johnson during the shooting of The Grapes of Wrath (1940) and their mutual attraction was instantaneous. The witty Johnson spoiled her for all other men, although Dorris and her roommate Mary Healy had plenty of dates. Once they double-dated, Mary with Franchot Tone, Dorris with Burgess Meredith. All evening Dorris talked incessantly about Johnson. When Meredith took her home, instead of kissing her, he said, "Get thee to a Nunnally."[45]

Glass Animals

Interviewers always asked young Lizabeth Scott what her hobby was. She grew annoyed at the question, since at that point she was totally devoted to her career and had no hobby. Shortly after her second film, The Strange Love of Martha Ivers (1946), she was at Schwab's Drugstore one evening and noticed a whole counter full of glass animals. As she looked at them, she said to herself, "That's my hobby." She asked Mr. Schwab how much he wanted for every animal in the counter. He told her $75. "I'll take the whole lot of them," she said. During her next interview Scott sat back securely. "And what is your hobby?" the interviewer asked in due course. Lizabeth looked him squarely in the eye and answered, "I collect glass animals." Before long people all over the United States were sending her glass animals.[46]

Guest List

Virginia Zanuck, the great mogul Darryl's wife, was skilled at handling Hollywood's sometimes complex sexual pairings and enjoyed keeping tabs on who was sleeping with whom. When Tyrone Power showed up one weekend with his French wife, Annabella, and returned the next with Linda Christian, subsequently wife number two, Virginia took it in stride. She had heard that Lilli Palmer and her husband Rex Harrison had separated but were possibly on the brink of reconciliation, so when they visited her, she deftly assigned them separate but adjoining rooms. She didn't even bear grudges against women she suspected of having slept with her own husband, provided the affair had been carried out discreetly and was in the past, nor did she bar them from enjoying a weekend at the Zanucks' house. "After all," she once explained, "that could cut down the available guest list considerably."[47]

Making Friends

Henry Koster and his wife, Peggy, invited a young Dutch girl to live with them for a while. The girl, a rather dour-faced, shy child, attended Beverly Hills High School. Peggy grew concerned about her social development and kept asking, "Did you sit with anybody for lunch?" The girl always said no, and Peggy continued to worry, realizing that the girl was afraid to talk to others. When the youngster broke her leg, Peggy suspected that it was partly to avoid the pain of going to school.

One evening, after she had given up her career and had moved to France, Deanna Durbin came to visit. At the time Koster was directing Desiree (1954) with Marlon Brando, and Brando called the same day and said he wanted to drop in. "Deanna Durbin is going to be here tonight," the Kosters informed him. "Oh," said Brando, "I'd love to meet her." So he came that evening. Durbin's pictures had been popular in Europe after World War II, and when Peggy Koster told the Dutch girl Deanna Durbin was coming, she asked, "Could I meet her?" After both Durbin and Brando arrived, Peggy turned to Deanna. "Would you go upstairs and say hello to this little Dutch girl who's living with us? She wants to meet you and she's a fan of yours." Deanna agreed, and Brando accompanied her. Together they went up and talked to the girl, and both signed her cast.

The next morning the girl was thrilled at having met Deanna Durbin, but asked, "Who was that man?" "You don't know who Marlon Brando is?" Peggy exclaimed. The girl confessed she'd never heard of him. "Well, when you go back to school," Peggy told her, "you tell your classmates that Marlon Brando came up to your bedroom, and he signed your cast. Now don't forget." Suddenly the girl became extremely popular. She made many friends, and the Kosters had teenage girls running in and out of their house at all hours, perhaps hoping to meet Brando.[48]

Exact Change

At Thanksgiving one year Dorothy Lamour and husband William Howard went east to Baltimore to visit Bill's family. They all went to dinner at the Belvedere Hotel, where a young sailor came over to their table and said, "Miss Lamour, I saw your last four pictures. They were terrible, and I want my dollar and sixty cents back." Too stunned to say anything, Lamour reached into her purse and handed him two dollars. Then recovering a bit, she said, "I'd like my forty cents change, please."[49]

Soul Mates

British director Ronald Neame, who later achieved great success with *The Poseidon Adventure* (1972), was eager to come to Hollywood. When he was offered *The Seventh Sin* (1957), based on a Somerset Maugham story, he readily accepted, even though he knew the script wasn't the best. After serious rewrites, the cast and crew went to Hong Kong for location shooting, then returned to MGM. Neame's British approach was a bit reserved for Hollywood at the time, and there was criticism that he wasn't getting the maximum drama out of the script. He sensed that Metro executives didn't like him, and with that he began losing confidence. He'd been on the picture about six weeks, with things going from bad to worse, when his agents called and said, "Look, Ronnie, we think you should resign from this picture. We think it's too much of a strain for you, and it's not worth it." Neame realized they were being kind, knowing that if he didn't resign he'd be fired. So he resigned.

He went home that night convinced his career as a director was finished; maybe he could go back to being a cameraman. He and his wife had just sat down to dinner when the telephone rang. His wife answered it and said, "There's a Mr. George Cukor on the phone." Neame had never met Cukor, but knew he was currently making a film called Les Girls at Metro. "Is that Ronald Neame?" Cukor asked when Ronnie picked up the receiver. "This is George Cukor." Neame said, "How are you, Mr. Cukor?" "Well, I'm fine, but I suppose you're feeling pretty miserable this evening," Cukor replied. Neame agreed he was feeling very miserable. "Well, that's why I'm phoning," said Cukor. "I'm phoning to tell you not to worry. It's not going to make the slightest difference to your career. And I should know, because I was the man that was taken off Gone With the Wind."[50]

Our S.O.B.

Publicity head Howard Strickling was a devoted company man who found it difficult to speak disparagingly of any Metro employee. He did, however, admit to having differences with Wallace Beery, who refused to cooperate and even ridiculed studio publicists. Nearly every other department had similar complaints, and eventually Strickling felt the need to go to L. B. Mayer about what he'd heard. "Beery is stealing the props off the set, and he won't cooperate," said Strickling, whose list of affronts went on and on. Finally Mayer broke in: "Yes, Howard, Beery's a son-of-a-bitch. But he's our son-of-a-bitch."[51]

Bear on Top

Before Mary Martin went to Hollywood to make The Great Victor Herbert (1939), she had been warned by a friend in New York: "Now, Mary, they're going to ask you to do every crazy thing on earth. Crazy pictures, all kinds of silly stunts. Don't do anything foolish, because you don't want to start off that way." Mary arrived at the studio with a full entourage that had met her plane. A car drove her to a patch of grass where cameramen stood waiting. "This is going to be your first photographic session for Paramount," someone told her. Mary got ready to be photographed, then noticed a big brown bear standing near the cameras. "Is he going to be in the picture too?" she asked innocently. "Yes," she was told. "For the first photograph we want you to shake hands with him." Remembering her friend's advice, Mary said, "Well, I really don't think I should do that." The publicist in charge whispered to her, "Miss Martin, you can't start off like this or you'll have trouble through the entire picture. Are you afraid?" Mary answered, "Of course I'm not afraid. But I just don't think it suits the character I'm playing." Still, the publicist insisted. "This will make every paper in the United States," he told her. "Now, the trainer will hold the bear until it's time to take the picture, and then the bear will put out his paw and you shake hands."

Mary finally agreed and took off her coat for the picture. Instead of shaking hands, however, the bear grabbed her all the way around, and down they both went, the bear on top. Mary was squealing and everybody else, including the trainer, was trying to pull the bear off. At exactly that moment Paramount story editor Richard Halliday came out of his office. "What on earth is happening?" Halliday asked. "Oh, there's a new girl who's just arrived here," someone said. "What's her name?" inquired Halliday, who had seen Mary singing "My Heart Belongs to Daddy" on Broadway and hadn't liked her. "Mary Martin," he was told. "With that bear on top?" Halliday snorted. "There's nothing that girl won't do! Absolutely nothing."

Mary was rescued. The bear hadn't hurt her, and she and Richard Halliday were later married for over thirty years.[52].

Pipits
For a time Universal had a tie with the Rank Organisation in England and imported a Rank film called *Tawny Pipit* (1944). A group of Universal writers and directors were sitting around one day complaining about how ridiculous it was. With the current retrenchment, they grumbled, they couldn't get what they needed for their own pictures, and the studio had brought in an idiotic English film about bird watchers. Clearly the sales department and the front office had miscalculated. But Nunnally Johnson spoke up: "Boys, you're wrong. *Tawny Pipit* is going to go out there and make a bundle of money. Every lover of pipits will see it."[53] As Johnson suspected, the film did not do well in the United States.

Sea Monster
Like all major studios, Warner Bros. had an exploitation man whose job it was to come up with stories to publicize current pictures. Just

before *The Beast from 20,000 Fathoms* (1953) was released, the Warners publicity office sent a man to check on rumors about a sea beast in Catalina Channel. The publicist located the crew of a fishing boat in San Pedro who claimed to have encountered an ocean monster a week or two before, and he immediately called out Warners Pathé newsreel photographers and the Los Angeles press to interview the crew. The witnesses described how the beast had reared its head up out of the sea, its eyes as big as tubs, and hair all over it. It made an exciting story, and since news was scarce that summer, the newspapers began digging in their archives and found recurring reports of a monster in Catalina Channel. The item ran for several weeks and stirred up a lot of interest. Then someone discovered that *The Beast from 20,000 Fathoms* was about to hit the theaters and that the whole thing had been a publicity stunt.[54]

Facts

The Goldwyn publicity office always made sure crowds were on hand whenever the boss arrived in New York or Los Angeles, and hired extras to supplement press conferences. Sam's advertising head once put a poster on the chief's desk advertising his forthcoming production of *We Live Again* (1934) that featured Goldwyn's recent European discovery Anna Sten. The poster read: THE DIRECTORIAL GENIUS OF MAMOULIAN, THE BEAUTY OF STEN, AND THE PRODUCING GENIUS OF GOLDWYN HAVE BEEN COMBINED TO MAKE THE WORLD'S GREATEST ENTERTAINMENT. Goldwyn looked it over solemnly and said, "That's the kind of ad I like. Facts. No exaggeration."[55] But the film turned out to be what Hollywood called a "stinkeroo."

Titles

Movie titles often posed problems for studios and distributors. James Barrie's *Half an Hour* (1913) was changed to *The Doctor's Secret* because the producers feared the public would dismiss it as a short. De Mille changed Barrie's *The Admirable Crichton* (1919), about a butler named Crichton, to *Male and Female*, because he thought people would think it about an admiral. Small-town exhibitors sometimes changed titles to enhance the local box office. One altered *The Asphalt Jungle* (1950) to *Babes and Bullets*, while *A Ticket to Tomahawk* (also 1950) became *The Sheriff's Daughter*. Bob Condon, a well-known ribster, once posted a notice on the bulletin board at Eagle-Lion Studio: THE PICTURE *THE NOOSE HANGS HIGH* WILL BE RE-

TITLED *LAUGHTER ON THE GALLOWS. THE NOOSE HANGS HIGH* WAS FOR-
MERLY TITLED *THE TIGHT NECKTIE* AND WAS ADAPTED FROM THE NOVEL
GIVE HIM SOME ROPE. IN ALL COMMUNICATIONS PLEASE REFER TO THE PIC-
TURE AS *LAUGHTER ON THE GALLOWS.* A ROUGH PRINT, UNSCORED, NOW
HAS THE WORKING TITLE *LAUGH TILL YOU CHOKE.* THE FINISHED PRINT WILL
CARRY THE FINAL TITLE. IF FURTHER CHANGES COME THROUGH, YOU WILL
BE NOTIFIED.[56]

Gable's Back

Metro's New York publicity head, Howard Dietz, offered $250 to
any MGM publicist who came up with a usable marketing slogan.
With *Adventure* (1945), Clark Gable's first picture since his release
from the army, approaching completion, Emily Torchia in the Culver
City office suggested the slogan "Gable's Back and Garson's Got
Him." Emily collected her $250, although not everyone thought the
marketing line appropriate. After the picture proved a bomb someone
suggested that "Gable Puts the Arson in Garson" would have been
better.

A couple of years later Torchia was working with Ethel Barrymore
on a picture called *The Great Sinner.* Barrymore was living near
Laguna at the time, and Emily went there one afternoon with an interviewer. "Well, I'm glad, Emily, we're working together," Miss
Barrymore exuded. "You never did anything cheap in your advertising." The publicist was pleased the great lady had such confidence
in her. "I shall never forget," Barrymore went on, "I was doing a
play in New York, and there blazing on a marquee was this awful,
vulgar thing: 'Gable's Back and Garson's Got Him.' Isn't that horrid?" Emily swallowed hard but said, "Dreadful, Miss Barrymore, just
dreadful."[57]

Pinocchios

For the opening of *Pinocchio* (1940) Walt Disney's publicity department decided to hire eleven midgets, dress them in Pinocchio outfits,
and have them frisk about on top of the theater marquee on opening
day. At lunchtime, food and refreshments were passed up to the marquee, including a couple of quarts of liquor. By three o'clock that
afternoon things had gotten out of hand and an amused crowd in
Times Square was regaled by the spectacle of eleven stark-naked
midgets belching noisily and enjoying a crap game atop the Broadway marquee. Police with ladders removed the gamblers in pil-
lowcases.[58]

Lolly's Pop

Movie gossip columnist Louella Parsons was married to Dr. Harry Watson Martin, whom she called Docky. To others he was known as Lolly's Pop. Docky's special field was venereal disease and urology, and he served as head of the Twentieth Century-Fox medical department. Through Docky's office Louella had a private line to testing laboratories, particularly those making rabbit tests for pregnancy. Many times Louella had heard that an actress was pregnant before the girl herself knew.

Both Lolly and Docky tossed down the booze well beyond moderation. One evening at a party Dr. Martin drank so excessively he fell on the floor and lay there in a stupor while guests stepped over him. When a friend tried to help him up, Louella, with a thick tongue, said, "Leave Docky alone. He has to operate in the morning."[59]

Snow Job

During the shooting of one of Gary Cooper's films in the fall of 1930, the young star made headlines when there was a report that he and the cast were trapped by a snowstorm in the Sierras. "Two state highway department snowplow tractors," newspapers reported, "nosed their way up the steep automobile road, clearing the snow, which was reported to be eighteen inches deep. The flock of sheep, also marooned at Dardanelle, was first to plod down the mountain road after the tractors had opened the way. This, highway experts said, hardened the remaining snow and made the road smoother for the automobiles and trucks of the motion picture company. The company was on location at Dardanelle, a tiny summer resort, filming a Western picture. Several thousand dollars worth of motion picture equipment was reported buried in three feet of snow on the summit of the Sierra Nevada 5,700 feet about sea level. . . ." Cooper's fans waited anxiously for more news about his plight. None ever came. For the report was a fake. It was the work of a publicity man assigned to the picture.[60]

What Happened?

During World War II stars were expected to work at the Hollywood Canteen periodically, serving coffee and doughnuts to soldiers and sailors passing through Los Angeles or stationed at a nearby base. One night in the smoky canteen, a young sailor was jitterbugging with a glamorous lady, chewing his gum in time to "Cow Cow Boogie." Glancing up at his elegant partner, the gumchewer exclaimed, "Say, you look just like Joan Crawford. Whatever happened to her?" The star smiled and answered, "I *am* Joan Crawford." "Yeah?" replied the sailor without missing a beat. "Whatever happened to ya?"[61]

Question
In the days of the Production Code, Hollywood stars were expected to behave decorously off-screen as well as on. The Sunday after the news broke that Ingrid Bergman, who had gone to Italy to make *Stromboli* (1949), was expecting a child out of wedlock by her director, Roberto Rossellini, gossip columnist Louella Parsons wailed on the radio: "Ingrid, Ingrid! Whatever got into you?"[62]

making on bearskin rugs. Born Theodosia Goodman in Cincinnati, Ohio, the Jewish Theda Bara represented for young Americans of the Roaring Twenties the emancipation from sexual taboos that they sought.

In addition there was the sultry Polish beauty Pola Negri, who appeared to be seething with passion, and Barbara La Marr, "the girl too beautiful to live," whose life was cut short in 1926 by a combination of drugs, alcohol, and tuberculosis. Clara Bow more than anyone symbolized the flaming youth of the jazz decade, as fresh as yesterday's bathtub gin—effervescent, giddy, almost boyish in appearance. Called the "It" girl, Bow wore her hose rolled down to show her bee's knees, strummed a ukulele, and ran with the college crowd who drove fast cars, chewed gum, and played kazoos. Worse still, she drank, smoked, and made love in the rumble seat—all to the delight of liberated movie audiences.

Among the men, Douglas Fairbanks cast a potent sexual shadow with his muscular physique and dashing antics. But the 1920s also saw the emergence of Latin lovers Ramon Novarro, Ricardo Cortez, and the greatest silent lover of them all, Rudolph Valentino. Born in Taranto, Italy, Valentino made his first major film appearance as Julio in Metro's *The Four Horsemen of the Apocalypse* (1921). Within a year he had played a young Arab chieftain in *The Sheik*, boosted the sale of Vaseline for hair grooming, introduced bellbottom trousers to male fashion, and revolutionized the techniques of movie lovemaking. With his reputation as the great lover soaring, a condom was named "Sheik," and the tango, which Valentino handled with aplomb, became the newest dance craze. By 1922 the star's influence on American popular culture had registered with such impact that Senator Henry L. Meyers listed "the sheik" among the major reasons why movie censorship should be immediately endorsed.[2] A gymnast and horseman, Valentino was in private a shy man, uncertain of his virility. Perhaps because of this he loved to display his physique, and dressing scenes became one of his hallmarks. With *Blood and Sand* (1922) he added a menacing element to his sexual image, yet there remained an inherently feminine quality as the great lover sought his own narcissistic reflection in his beloved's eyes. "Valentino's great talent," according to one biographer, "lay in the completely natural way he was able to humanize this mythical figure in terms of his own sexuality—and if the latter quality contains a strong element of sexual ambiguity, this is not something that should entirely surprise us."[3] While women found Valentino's Latin approach to courtship intriguing, he made lovemaking too time-consuming a process for the impatient American male to emulate.[4]

When macho Clark Gable came along during the Depression era, men could identify with him easily. American males were unwilling for their wives to fall in love with a foreigner, particularly a "dago gigolo" like Valentino, but they were perfectly happy to have them fall for Gable, who was essentially what they themselves wanted to be—powerful, earthy, a man's man who was irresistible to women.[5] Similarly, Jean Harlow was the kind of girl one might encounter in commonplace settings, behind a Woolworth store counter or seated across the aisle on a bus. A man didn't have to worry about money when he fantasized about Harlow, for she appeared to be as available and willing as she was desirable. Her platinum-blond hair, her moist lips, and her obvious disregard for wearing brassieres made it clear that she was no ordinary woman.[6] The "Blonde Bombshell" was also a tough gal who knew the score and could talk a man's language, but she displayed enough vulnerability to reinforce the masculinity of the opposite sex.

Foreign imports, like Hedy Lamarr and Marlene Dietrich, continued to quicken the pulse of male moviegoers as well as influence feminine fashion. Because Dietrich wore slacks that style swept the country, although many found it shocking. Still, no one scandalized the way Mae West, "the Queen of Sex," did nearly every time she opened her mouth. Mae flaunted sex, knew her way around a commercial boudoir, and frankly enjoyed it all. "You know," a typical West line declared shamelessly, "it was a toss-up whether I went in for diamonds or sang in the choir. The choir lost." Mae took an ax to the dying vestiges of American puritanism and made herself a household word. In the process she, along with Bing Crosby musicals, saved Paramount from financial disaster during the early 1930s, while she taught a repressed nation to laugh at its own stodginess. Not that Depression audiences felt movies had much to do with real life. Mae West, a working girl whose sexual favors kept her off the streets, was gowned in velvet, festooned with rhinestones, and smothered in furs. With all her boasting, however, it was difficult to take Mae seriously. Censors might condemn her bragging about her sinful ways, but the public knew she was putting them on. Mae once claimed she had mirrors in her bedroom because she liked to see how she was doing. "When I'm good, I'm very good," she insisted. "But when I'm bad, I'm better." And she was—better box office than practically anyone else in the business.

Errol Flynn didn't use mirrors but he did collect scads of sexual toys and his appetites ran the gamut. While he was the bare-chested swashbuckler in films, his sexual prowess in private gave rise to the expression "in like Flynn," after highly publicized statutory-rape charges.[7] According to Clara Bow, at least, Gary Cooper was heroically endowed, and the young actor's reputation as an offscreen lover certainly matched anything seen on celluloid. Robert Taylor and Tyrone Power, while delicately masculine on-screen, were prettier than many of their leading ladies; it would not be made public until years later that both Power and Flynn led actively bisexual lives, and the two of them engaged in a secret dalliance.[8]

Warner Bros. announced in 1940 that twenty-five noted men had selected Texas-born Ann Sheridan as America's "Oomph Girl," while Lana Turner shortly became the "Sweater Girl." Veronica Lake was known for the "peek-a-boo look" until government officials urged her to cut her blond, over-the-eye tresses during World War II because long hair was proving hazardous among female factory workers. Tough gals returned to the screen with Lauren Bacall and Lizabeth Scott, but servicemen seemed to prefer pinup beauties like Betty Grable and Rita Hayworth. Exotic types such as Maria Montez and Yvonne De Carlo remained popular and specialized in what the industry called "Tits and Sand" pictures, concentrating on Arabian nights, harem frolics, and Technicolor adventure. Shortly after the war Ava Gardner rose in popularity; her classy sex appeal was not what such girl-next-door types as June Allyson, Laraine Day, Donna Reed, and Jeanne Crain had to offer.

The postwar trend in sexuality was launched with the long-awaited release of Howard Hughes's The Outlaw (1947), featuring the ample chest of Jane Russell. Censor Joseph Breen saw the Western and immediately wrote his boss, Will Hays: "I have never seen anything quite so unacceptable as the shots of the breasts of the character of Rio. . . . Throughout almost half the picture the girl's breasts, which are quite large and prominent, are shockingly uncovered." Hughes himself designed a special bra to give Russell's bosom the boost needed. "This is really just a very simple engineering problem," said Hughes, as he retired to his drawing board. He understood exactly what the film's appeal would be and devoted take after take to Russell leaning over the wounded Billy the Kid. Censorship problems held up the release of The Outlaw for years, but its impact proved indelible. At the movie's premiere, when Russell first leaned forward, a member of the audience yelled, "Bombs away!"[9]

Catching the spirit, producer Hunt Stromberg reputedly said during a discussion of a projected South Seas picture at Metro: "Boys, I've got an idea. Let's fill the screen with tits."[10] During the 1950s, with the emergence of Jayne Mansfield, Mamie Van Doren, Sophia Loren, and Kim Novak, his suggestion came close to realization. As director Joshua Logan once commented about Novak, "Trying to hide what she's got is like trying to hide an elephant in a phone booth."[11]

But the greatest sex symbol of the decade undoubtedly was Marilyn Monroe, who quickly entered the realm of legend. A canny person whose talent was largely instinctive, Marilyn possessed a face and body that cameramen loved. Publicists overnight projected her image so much bigger than life that her insecurities were magnified to the breaking point. She grew frightened, forgetful, petulant. Colleagues found her exasperating to work with. Billy Wilder, who directed Monroe in *The Seven Year Itch* (1955) and *Some Like it Hot* (1959), said: "The question is whether Marilyn is a person at all or one of the greatest DuPont products ever invented. She has breasts like granite and a brain like Swiss cheese, full of holes." She repeatedly arrived on the set late, telling Wilder she couldn't find the studio when she'd worked there for years. The director would shoot forty-two takes of a single scene, call her aside, and to calm her down say, "Don't worry, Marilyn." She'd look at him with an innocent expression and ask, "Don't worry about what?"[12]

During the war, male sex symbols on the screen were in short supply because of the draft. Afterward, hunks like Victor Mature and elegant types like Gregory Peck were popular with movie audiences, and such newcomers as Tony Curtis, Rock Hudson, Tab Hunter, Marlon Brando, and Paul Newman soon appeared. Latin lovers returned with the arrival of Ricardo Montalban and Fernando Lamas. Like other highly publicized sex symbols, Lamas recalled strangers knocking on his door in hotels, expecting him to prove his reputation as the "last of the red-hot Lamas." Fans, generally of the opposite sex, approached him in bars and restaurants, as if he might demonstrate his manliness then and there. "It wasn't me," said Lamas, "it's what they thought I was. I always knew that and thought it was funny."[13]

In the 1960s Warren Beatty, Robert Redford, and Sean Connery became sexual images, as did Raquel Welch, Julie Christie, and Claudia Cardinale. By the 1970s screen sex symbols, like many film personalities, frequently came from television: Burt Reynolds, Ryan

O'Neal, Farrah Fawcett, John Travolta, Morgan Fairchild, and eventually Tom Selleck. Nudity became acceptable on the screen, along with increasing doses of deviant behavior. Bo Derek, Hollywood's much heralded *Ten* on a one-to-ten rating scale, emerged as a sex object of the late 1970s without achieving major stardom, whereas Brooke Shields joined Rob Lowe and Tom Cruise as popular teenage idols. In recent years actors such as Richard Gere, Robert De Niro, and Christopher Reeve have shuttled back and forth between Broadway and Hollywood, holding their own as sexual heroes, while Sylvester Stallone has concentrated the bulk of his energy on films (and most of those films have concentrated on his bulk).

Adoration for Valentino

When Rudolph Valentino died in 1926, over 100,000 people filed past the catafalque at Campbell's funeral parlor in New York. Italian dictator Benito Mussolini sent a wreath of flowers and screen star Pola Negri a blanket of red roses. A thousand policemen were summoned to enforce order, but they were helpless against the hysterical mob. Finally a system was devised whereby mourners moved in single file past Valentino's bier for three days.[14] His body was then taken to its final resting place in the mausoleum of Hollywood Cemetery. On August 23, 1928, the "lady in black" first knelt before Valentino's marble crypt and left flowers. Every year thereafter, on the anniversary of Rudy's death, a mysterious lady dressed in black arrived promptly at noon bearing thirteen roses—a dozen red and one white.[15]

One day a dark-eyed girl named Marie came to the cemetery from New York. She knelt at Valentino's crypt and said a prayer before kissing the dank marble. When custodian Roger Peterson approached her, he saw tears streaming down her cheeks. "I have come a long way to be near him," she told Peterson. "I saw him in his casket in New York. They had to take me away, for I became hysterical. I wanted to come to California when they brought his body here, but my husband wouldn't let me." Marie had saved her money, then hitchhiked and worked her way across the country. She remained at Valentino's tomb until the custodian locked the mausoleum for the night. Each day for weeks afterward, Marie returned, bringing flowers and saying prayers.

After closing time one night Peterson happened to go back to the mausoleum for something he had left. He found Marie trying to enter through a small window. A man was with her, so the custodian hurried over to ask what they were doing. In a frightened voice, Marie explained, "This is my husband. He has followed me out here to take me home. I didn't want to leave without saying goodbye to Rudy. We are starting back to New York tonight." Peterson told them to come around to the door and he'd let them in. He left the two alone by Valentino's crypt. After a while he went to see why they were taking so long. He found the husband trying to drag Marie away as she sobbed, "Rudy! Rudy!" Peterson insisted she must go, since it was getting late. Marie made her way into the night, still crying Valentino's name. It was the last he saw of her.[16]

No Dirty Words

Publicist Arthur Mayer drew the task of planning Paramount's initial advertising campaign for Mae West. Mae had once gone to jail because of a stage production in New York, and it was clear her pictures were going to be extremely sexy. There was no strict enforcement of the censorship code in 1932, but Mayer knew that handling her publicity required discretion. He prepared a big still for his campaign, a simple sketch of a huge bust, under which he wrote one line that he felt was safe copy: HITTING THE HIGH SPOTS OF LUSTY ENTERTAINMENT. The advertising was sent out, and for a while nothing happened. Then Adolph Zukor called Mayer into his office. "Mr. Mayer, I'm shocked and surprised," said Zukor sternly. "I thought you were such a gentleman and you use a dirty word." Mayer didn't understand. "*Lusty*," answered Zukor. "What a word to use." Mayer explained that *lusty* came from the German word *lustig*, meaning life, energy, vigor. "There's nothing dirty about the use of that word," the publicist insisted. "Look, Mr. Mayer," said the exasperated Zukor, "I don't need your Harvard education. When I look at that dame's tits, I know what *lusty* means."[17]

Sacred Cows

Although in MGM pictures all mothers were portrayed as saintly and all men as true to their wives, the studio's films were full of young cuties, and studio executives themselves tended to have roving eyes. There were always plenty of pretty girls around willing to surrender to the men who held the keys to filmdom. Metro writers called these girls "Moos" when they became the bosses' "sacred cows." Frequently the writers would tip one another off: "It might be smart to

write in a juicy part for So-and-So. She's L.B.'s latest Moo." A male
scenario writer, after a few drinks, once walked up to a dazzling
redhead who had just received a diamond bracelet and a studio contract. "Whose Moo is oo?" he asked. The girl snapped back, "Don't
get fresh with me or I'll tell Sam Katz on you!"[18]

Gary and His Countess

On a trip to Europe during the early 1930s, Hollywood heartthrob
Gary Cooper showed up in Rome and promptly had an affair with
Countess Dorothy Di Frasso, the American-born daughter of New
Jersey multimillionaire Betrand Taylor. When Cooper returned to
Hollywood to begin a new picture, the countess followed. The actor
spent several weeks playing around with di Frasso and her fast
crowd, setting Hollywood gossips buzzing. Friends soon noticed that
Coop was losing weight and looked more than a bit wilted. As work
on his picture progressed, Cooper's condition grew steadily worse,
and he finally consulted a doctor, who prescribed rest. A short time
later Tallulah Bankhead attended a party in Santa Barbara and was
asked why she thought Coop hadn't arrived yet. "He's probably
worn to a frasso," Tallulah responded.[19]

Slendang-Sarong Girl

After Dorothy Lamour was assigned to her first picture, The Jungle
Princess (1936), Paramount's Edith Head went to work on her costume. When Head draped some beautiful cotton print material
around the young actress, the latter asked how many dresses she
would wear in the film. "Dresses?" exclaimed Head. "Young lady,
this is going to be a sarong." Lamour was astonished to learn she was
going to wear only a little piece of cloth in the film; she was embarrassed, too, for, unlike the Paramount people and, later, millions of
fans, she wasn't sure her figure was all that good. But after appearing
in several South Sea Island pictures, she became famous as the
"sarong girl," and during World War II became one of the servicemen's favorite pinups. But a Bali-Javanese dancer once insisted
that "Dorothy Lamour is not wearing a sarong," and a Los Angeles
newspaper consulted an East Indies expert to settle the ensuing con-
troversy. Lamour "does, indeed, wear a sarong," announced the expert, "but if she had stopped at that, the Hays office would need a
double sedative to quiet their nerves. The garment that clings cozily
below her waist is a sarong. But the cloth wound around her upper

part is called a 'slendang.' So Dorothy Lamour is really a 'slendang-sarong' girl."[20]

Thunderstorm

During Howard Hughes's censorship battles over The Outlaw, a Maryland judge upheld his state's ban on the film with the remark that Jane Russell's breasts "hung over the picture like a summer thunderstorm spread out over a landscape."[21] As if to prove the point, when the movie was released, publicity genius Russell Birdwell hired skywriters to decorate the southern California skies with a pair of enormous circles with dots in their centers.[22]

Marilyn's Reading

Robert Mitchum became curious about what Marilyn Monroe was reading during the making of River of No Return (1954). He checked into the matter and found the sex symbol poring over a dictionary of Freudian terms. When Mitchum asked why she was reading it, Marilyn answered, "I feel one should know how to discuss oneself." The actor inquired what chapter she was reading. "Anal Eroticism," Marilyn told him. "That's charming," commented Mitchum, "and do you think that will come up in a discussion?" Monroe returned to her reading, but after a while looked up and said, "What's eroticism?" Mitchum explained. A minute or so later she again looked up from the book and asked, "What's anal?"[23]

Missed One

Richard Burton, although a serious actor, also had the reputation of being a womanizer. After his highly publicized romance with Elizabeth Taylor during the filming of Cleopatra (1963), Burton suddenly became an international sex symbol. Character actor Raymond Massey was once asked by a fellow actor if there was any woman Burton hadn't managed to seduce. Massey thought it over and said, "Yes. Marie Dressler." "But she's dead!" the other actor replied. "Yes, I know," said Massey.[24]

Freudian Slip

During the making of Bus Stop (1956) Don Murray was supposed to come into Marilyn Monroe's room and say, "Wake up, Cherie. It's nine o'clock—the sun's out. No wonder you're so pale and white." But somehow the actor muffed the line, saying, "No wonder you're so pale and scaly." Director Joshua Logan called, "Cut," and while they waited for the cameras to reload, Monroe said, "Don, do you realize what you did? You just made a Freudian slip." She raised up from the bed to explain. "You see, you must be in the proper emotional mood for this scene because it's a sexual scene, and you made a Freudian slip about a phallic symbol. You see, you were thinking unconsciously of a snake. That's why you said 'scaly.' A snake is a phallic symbol. Do you know what a phallic symbol is, Don?" The actor replied, "Know what it is? I've got one!"[25]

Standing

For *The Adventures of Don Juan* (1949), Errol Flynn made sure his jerkins were cut high enough to display an abundant crotch. After the first costume test, cameraman Woody Bredell complained to director Vincent Sherman, "For God's sake, Vince, I can't photograph that. Especially if he stands sideways. The Breen office would never stand for it." Flynn overheard the remark and said, "I'm the one who'll be doing the standing."[26]

Art's Not Enough

Luchino Visconti's *The Leopard* (1963), shot in Italy and featuring Claudia Cardinale, was more beautiful visually than most of Burt Lancaster's pictures. Proud of the achievement, Burt went to enjoy Visconti's film in a public theater. His smile faded when he heard the man behind him impatiently ask his wife, "When's Lancaster going to screw Cardinale?"[27]

CHAPTER 28

Theaters and
Audiences

The earliest movie houses were sleazy places: dank, dark, dirty, crowded, smelly. The nickelodeons were nicer than the little-store shows, but many of them were almost as dingy. Patrons sat on hard chairs and benches, booed when the flickering film broke, purchased snacks from kids running up and down the aisles during the show, and shouted and whistled as slides periodically interrupted the program: ONE MINUTE PLEASE WHILE THE OPERATOR REPAIRS THE BROKEN FILM; DO NOT SPIT, REMEMBER THE JOHNSTOWN FLOOD; PLEASE DO NOT STAMP, THE FLOOR MAY CAVE IN; KEEP YOUR CHILD FROM CRYING; LADY, THERE'S SOMEONE BEHIND YOU, WILL YOU KINDLY REMOVE YOUR HAT. To quiet audiences managers began hiring young ladies to pound tinny pianos during the show. Sometimes it only added to the commotion.[1]

The noisy nickelodeons were no place for the fastidious. The white-bread crowd scornfully dismissed them as "cheap places for cheap people."[2] But working-class families in the cities flocked to see the movies they showed; it was about the only entertainment they could afford. And after a while the nickelodeons became cleaner and more comfortable, and middle-class people began sneaking off to see a show now and then. But it took the development of feature pictures to bring about real improvements in movie theaters.

Features meant longer programs. But longer programs meant that exhibitors could no longer depend on a rapid turnover of audiences for their profits. To keep the money rolling in they decided to raise prices and build larger theaters that would accommodate more people. In the spring of 1914, Mitchell L. Mark, veteran theater owner, opened the Strand theater in New York City with a huge auditorium holding almost three thousand people and offering five shows a day and a weekly change of programs. The Strand packed them in from the outset, and its success touched off a frenzy of theater building elsewhere. During the next two years thousands of fine new movie houses sprang up in cities and towns all across the country, and the humble little nickelodeon gradually disappeared from the scene. Movies were no longer a diversion of the working-class poor; they had become a major middle-class preoccupation.

The Strand's owners called their place "the model of Moving Picture Palaces." It featured crystal chandeliers, plush carpeting, upholstered seats, artwork on the walls, a thirty-piece orchestra, and a Mighty Wurlitzer.[3] But its preeminence as a palace was short-lived. In 1916 came the elegant Rialto, in 1917 the luxurious Rivoli, and in 1919 the mammoth Capitol theater, with 5,300 seats and a mezzanine that, said *Photoplay*, "looks as if it has been designed for eight-day bicycle races."[4] The Capitol had a glorious opening and then went into the doldrums. In a panic, the owners hired S. L. ("Roxy") Rothafel, theater expert, to redo the place and liven up its offerings. In June 1920 came the proud announcement: TRIUMPHAL RE-OPENING—THE CAPITOL—THE WORLD'S LARGEST, COOLEST, MOST BEAUTIFUL THEATRE. NEWEST, LATEST ROTHAFEL MOTION PICTURE AND MUSIC ENTERTAINMENT.[5] The refurbished Capitol, which presented concerts and stage shows as well as movies, was packed to the gills for every performance after its second opening.

But the Capitol was by no means the last word in New York's movie theaters. In 1926 came the Paramount, in 1927 the Roxy (Rothafel's own special baby), and in 1932 Radio City Music Hall, the last of the movie palaces and the largest and most lavish of all. But New York was not the only city with mighty movie houses. San Francisco, Los Angeles, Chicago, Detroit, Tampa, Dallas, Houston, Seattle—every city, in fact, with any pride and self-respect—came up with movie theaters during the twenties that were just as lush, if not quite as large, as New York City's finest showplaces. Sid Grauman's Chinese Theatre in Hollywood, which opened in 1927, was not only breathtakingly sumptuous, it also boasted something no other theater in the country possessed: the handprints and footprints of the movie stars in the concrete forecourt. It began as an accident—Grauman stepped by mistake into the wet concrete blocks as the theater was being constructed—and ended as an added attraction.

Grauman's Chinese Theatre soon became a mecca for starry-eyed tourists from all over the country—and the world. But every movie palace, even those in Peoria, Podunk, and Pocatello, had something special to offer: marble staircases, immense chandeliers, arcades of mirrors, classical columns, Persian mosaics, rare antiques, towering electric signs, galleries of oil paintings, lush lobbies, lavish lounges, posh promenades, gargantuan grand foyers, and magnificent auditoriums modeled after the royal palaces, cathedrals, and temples of Europe, the Orient, and the Middle East. Even the second-run neighborhood houses were nicely designed and the third-run theaters far pleasanter than the old nickelodeons had been. Marcus Loew, who built a chain of fine theaters across the country, put it simply: "We sell tickets to theaters, not movies."[6] And so it seemed. "In our big modern movie palaces there are collected the most gorgeous rugs, furniture and fixtures that money can produce," theater decorator Harold Rambusch noted in 1929. "No kings or emperors have wandered through more luxurious surroundings."[7]

Why the pentagonish extravagance? Acerbic economist Thorstein Veblen (who lived until 1929) thought that in America's pecuniary culture the ostentatious display of wealth was a key to social standing and that the "canons of conspicuous waste" (if you're wasteful you must be well-off and thus worthy of respect) governed architecture as it did other aspects of American life and thought. But the nation's best architects were revolted both by the flamboyance of the movie palaces and by the way they shamelessly copied the great art, sculpture, and architecture of bygone ages. "So this is the Taj Mahal," one critic imagined an American tourist in India remarking. "Pshaw! The Oriental Theatre at home is twice as big and has electric lights besides."[8] But despite the strictures of architectural critics, the moviegoing public loved the Xanadus and Angkor Wats and Petit Trianons that theater owners erected for their pleasure. Curiosity about the rich (which the movies themselves encouraged) had something to do with it; the passion for the exotic (stimulated by the travel books of Richard Halliburton and the travelogues of Burton Holmes) also played a part. There was nothing "isolationist" about American moviegoers in the 1920s; they loved the foreign flavor of their favorite movie houses. Perhaps World War I had internationalized their tastes.

The theater architects themselves came up with democratic reasons for their lavishness. Entering a movie palace, they said, meant that the ordinary American could live like royalty for a time. COME! BE KING FOR A DAY! went advertisements for the new Fox theater in San Francisco in 1929.[9] "Watch the eyes of a child as it enters the portals of our great theaters and treads the pathway into fairyland," wrote theater architect George Rapp in 1925. "Watch the bright light in the eyes of the tired shopgirl who hurries noiselessly over carpets and sighs with satisfaction as she walks amid furnishings that once delighted the hearts of queens. See the toil-worn father whose dreams have never come true, and look inside his heart as he finds strength and rest within the theatre. There you have the answer to why motion pictures are so palatial." The movie palace, Rapp insisted, was "a shrine to democracy where there are no privileged patrons. The wealthy rub elbows with the poor—and are better for this contact. Do not wonder, then, at the touches of Italian Renaissance, executed in glazed polychrome terra-cotta, or at the lobbies and foyers adorned with replicas of precious masterpieces of another world, or at the imported marble wainscoting or the richly ornamented ceilings with motifs copied from master touches of Germany, France, and Italy, or at the carved niches, the cloistered arcades, the depthless mirrors, and the great sweeping staircases. These are not impractical attempts at showing off. These are part of a celestial city—a cavern of many-colored jewels, where iridescent lights and luxurious fittings heighten the expectations of a pleasure. It is richness unabashed, but richness with a reason."[10]

The richness was short-lived. The Great Crash of 1929 and the Great Depression it touched off put an end to the boom in movie palaces. The downtick in the economy also killed the lavish kind of stage show that the big theaters had gotten in the habit of presenting along with their feature pictures. To keep people coming to the movies in the 1930s, theater managers were forced to lower prices, present double features, give away china and silverware, and offer their customers games like Bingo, Screeno, and Banko, with cash prizes for the lucky ticket holders. World War II revived movie attendance for a time, but after the war people began staying away from the movie houses in droves. Many moviegoers preferred the drive-ins (begun in Camden, New Jersey, in the early 1930s) that sprouted everywhere; still more preferred sit-ins: watching television in the living room. Fewer and fewer adults were taking in the movies, so movie audiences were increasingly becoming youthful.

By the 1960s the number of people going to the movies regularly had declined so drastically that one movie palace after another was forced to close its doors. Some of the once-proud showplaces became bowling alleys, garages, and supermarkets; others (including New York City's Capitol, Paramount, and Roxy) were razed to make way for office buildings, hotels, and parking lots. A few, though, were divided into several small theaters—sometimes, as many as six—with plain little screens, seats, and surroundings (and plenty of pop and popcorn), making moviegoing much like it had been just before the age of the movie palaces. But some of the old palaces became symphony halls or survived as national historic landmarks; and a few were even converted into churches. In 1977, the Loew's Corporation donated its finest movie palace in Queens to a Pentecostal church, which arranged to redo the interior. "We covered the naked ladies up there," the minister told a reporter. "We put wings on them and they are angels." Then he added thoughtfully: "That one on the left, though, she has a miniskirt."[11]

Vibes
Audiences laughed so hard at Chaplin comedies, according to *Photoplay* on March 3, 1917, that the vibrations loosened the bolts on seats in the theaters and managers had to have them tightened up periodically.[12]

Tinkle
Shortly after the Avalon theater, designed as a Persian palace by John Eberson, opened its doors in Chicago, the manager phoned the architect and asked him to come by as soon as he could. When Eberson reached the theater, the manager took him to a seat in the balcony overlooking the auditorium and asked him to sit there and watch what was going on below. During the movie, Eberson noticed, people on the right side of the auditorium had their eyes glued to the screen, but on the left side, they were continually getting up, going down the aisle, leaving, and then returning a few minutes later. Puzzled by the traffic in the aisle, Eberson went downstairs to see what was going on. Before long he found out: the "bridal fountain" (located in a mosaic niche beneath the minarets housing the organ

pipes) was continually tinkling, and the sound was producing an overpowering desire in the people sitting near it to head for the rest room. Eberson saw to it that the plumber eliminated the tinkle as soon as he could.[13]

Too Much Money

One morning Douglas Fairbanks arrived at the studio full of excitement over the enormous success of The Black Pirate (1926) at the box office. An hour later, however, Joseph Schenck, United Artists head, encountered him staggering across the lot with a dazed look in his eyes. "My God, Doug, what's the matter?" exclaimed Schenck. "Has anything happened to Mary? Speak, man, speak!" Fairbanks handed him a letter. It was from an exhibitor, enclosing a check, explaining he had made so much money on a week's engagement of The Black Pirate that his conscience bothered him and he was sending some of it to Fairbanks.[14]

Preview

When City Lights (1931) was finished, Charlie Chaplin wasn't sure the public would accept a silent film (with only music on the soundtrack) in the Sound Era. The preview in a downtown theater in Los Angeles was not encouraging. The house was half empty, and the audience, who had come to see a drama, not a comedy, didn't catch on until halfway through the picture, and the result was there were only a few laughs and some people even walked out on it. So with mounting apprehension Chaplin arranged an opening in the George M. Cohan theater in New York, with a seating capacity of 1,150, and in a large new theater in Los Angeles. In both places, City Lights went over big; the crowds were large and enthusiastic.

There was a momentary crisis, though, at the Los Angeles opening, which Chaplin attended with Albert Einstein and his wife. Things went well for three reels and then suddenly in the middle of the laughter the picture stopped, the house lights went up, and a loudspeaker announced: "Before continuing further with this wonderful comedy, we would like to take five minutes of your time and point out the merits of this beautiful new theater." Chaplin was furious. "Where's that stupid son of a bitch manager?" he raged, leaping from his seat and racing up the aisle. "I'll kill him!" The audience was mad too; people began stamping their feet and yelling and booing. Finally the manager stopped talking and let the picture resume. It took a reel before the laughter got back into its stride. But when the picture was over Chaplin realized he had another winner.[15]

Threat

Sometimes audiences like films better than the stars appearing in them. When Helen Hayes and her husband attended the premiere of *The Sin of Madelon Claudet* (1931), in which she starred, they were so disappointed in her performance (though it won her an Oscar) that they emitted one groan after another as the picture proceeded. Finally someone sitting behind them leaned forward and threatened to have them thrown out of the place if they didn't shut up.[16]

Fan Mail

In *Elmer the Great* (1933), comedian Joe E. Brown had to drink a cup of coffee, and, to show how uncouth Elmer was, he left the spoon in the cup when he drank it. Every time he tried to drink, the handle of the spoon would come around and hit him in the eye. After five or six times, he bent the spoon and put it back in the cup and then drank the coffee successfully. Brown thought it a good gag, but a few weeks after the picture was released he began receiving hundreds of letters from angry parents complaining they didn't have a straight spoon in the house after their kids saw Brown's movie.

But Brown's fan mail was usually favorable. One woman wrote to tell him that she and her six-year-old daughter had just seen one of his movies and after the show the little girl asked, "Mommy, when Joe E. Brown dies, will he go to heaven?" "Why of course darling," replied the mother. "Golly, Mommy," said the child, "won't God laugh?"

Brown was puzzled by another letter. "The other day me and another fellow had an argument," it ran. "He said Joe Cook was the world's greatest comedian and I said you was. We finally came to blows . . . and I socked him one and broke his arm. It cost him $12 to get the arm fixed and he's going to make me pay for it. Could you please send me the $12 to pay the expenses on account of I was fighting for you?"[17]

Killed Her

At a sneak preview of *Sylvia Scarlett* (1936), which Katharine Hepburn herself attended, it quickly became clear that Hepburn's latest was a disaster. Halfway through the picture, people began leaving in droves; some of them even ran out. Hepburn escaped to the ladies' room, where she found a woman lying in a dead faint. "My God," gasped Hepburn, "the picture's killed her!"[18]

Don't Care to Know
Neither Katharine Hepburn nor Cary Grant liked to give autographs. Once, when Hepburn refused to sign her name, one of her fans yelled: "How dare you refuse? We made you what you are today!" Shot back Hepburn: "Like hell you did!" As for Grant, when one disappointed autograph seeker cried, "Who the hell do you think you are?" the debonair actor said coolly, "I know who I am, but I haven't the vaguest idea who you are, and furthermore I don't care to know."[19]

Bad Influence
One day, as Edward G. Robinson, star of several gangster pictures, came out of a movie theater, an elderly woman holding a little boy by the hand, came up to him, asked if he was the actor who "played 'Little Caesar' and so many other bad men," and when he said he was, exclaimed: "Well, I'm glad I have this opportunity of telling you to your face what a bad influence your pictures have had on our young people." "What makes you think so?" asked Robinson. "I ought to know," she said firmly. "I've taken my grandchild to see *Little Caesar* eight times."[20]

Opens in New York
One day Sam Goldwyn stopped every man he met on the Goldwyn lot and asked: "Do you think it is going to rain tonight?" Several said, "No," and one man said, "Of course not. There's not a cloud in the sky." Goldwyn withered him with a look. "I mean in New York," he said impatiently. "Our picture opens tonight in New York."[21]

Won the War
At the Atlanta premiere of *Gone With the Wind* in the summer of 1939, Margaret Mitchell was impressed by the scene in which Scarlett O'Hara is nursing wounded soldiers and the camera draws back to reveal thousands of Confederate troops in the area. "Mah Gawd,"

she whispered to Clark Gable, "if we'd-ah had as many soldiers as that, we'd-ha wan the woah!"[22]

Double Features and Dishes

As radio programs improved in quality in the 1930s, movie attendance began declining and exhibitors used all kinds of inducements to lure people back into their theaters: reduced their prices, held lotteries, gave away dishes and other prizes, and began presenting two pictures for the price of one.

For a time sets of dishes, one piece each week, helped fill the movie houses. The "dish houses," as they were called, booked their pictures according to dish; with a big showy dish they could get away with a grade F film, but if the dish was a "cheater" (a little piece) they had to book a better picture. In Chicago, an exhibitor ran into the film exchange holding a big teapot in his hand. "What picture have you got to go with this?" he wanted to know.

Plates, not pictures, became the main attraction. In one city a woman called a theater and asked, "What you got tonight?" When the exhibitor began telling her about the picture he was showing, she interrupted him. "Nuts to the picture!" she cried impatiently. "I want to know what dish you got!" In Los Angeles a Hollywood executive dropped by to see how a new film of his was going and was pleased to see a large crowd at the theater. But as he was leaving he was startled to see a woman rush up to the box office, shove some bills under the window, and cry: "Give me all the dishes since January, when you had the creamer. I've been on a long vacation." Then she grabbed her dishes and clanked off with them.

Some theaters stressed double (and even triple) features. A theater in Kansas City went so far as to offer three features and lunch, all for a dime. "I'm surprised they don't offer a free breakfast instead," sighed Samuel Goldwyn, "because it must be breakfast time when such programs are finished. Breakfast," he added disconsolately, "is about all they haven't offered yet. The list of giveaways already includes linen, cutlery, tea, encyclopedias, costume jewelry, doughnuts, ice cream, compacts, dictionaries, coffee, candy, razors, silverware, silk stockings, and the Harvard classics. If you want to furnish your home, go to a movie!"

Goldwyn agreed with Spyros Skouras: "Double bills are a cancer which will devour the industry." To satisfy the demands of the double-feature houses, he noted, Hollywood was turning out six hundred pictures a year, only a small number of which could be called excellent. In an article attacking the double-feature craze in 1940, he told the story of the man whose wife had nagged him into a nervous breakdown. "What you need," the doctor told him, "is a good, long rest." The man thought for a moment, according to Goldwyn, and then said: "I can't afford it, doctor. Would it be all right if I sent my wife to see a double feature?"

What was needed, Goldwyn insisted, was quality, not quantity. If Hollywood made fewer, but better, pictures, he thought, people would start coming back to the movie houses and exhibitors could abandon both dishes and double features.[23]

No Feathers

Not everyone liked costume dramas. To MGM came a letter from a movie-theater owner in a small town in Iowa: "Dear Sir: Please don't send me any more pictures where they write with feathers." MGM officials had the letter framed and placed on an office wall to remind producers of the public for which they were making pictures.[24]

Too Many Z's

Right after a film entitled *Razzamatazz* was completed at Columbia, studio boss Harry Cohn angrily summoned the producers to his office. "Now, which one of you smart college guys," he roared, "figured there was a theater owner in the country that had eight Z's [yes, eight!] in his marquee letters?" There was a quick title change.[25]

Wartime Audience

During World War II, when pictures were sent overseas to be shown American servicemen, they were usually run off three days in a row and then sent on to the next base. But if the new film failed to arrive on time, the current film was held over and the G.I.'s, thirsting for entertainment, saw it over again. In the Marianas, one army unit watched Bing Crosby's *Going My Way* (1944) for seven nights in a row, and the soldiers came to hate it. One night they captured eleven Japanese soldiers who had sneaked in from their nearby hideouts to see the picture. When someone suggested letting them stay to see the end of the picture before being taken off to the prisoner-of-war camp, the Japanese politely declined. They, too, had seen it several nights in a row and were also heartily sick of it.[26]

Cheering

After making a trip to Korea to entertain American troops, Marilyn Monroe told Joe DiMaggio: "Joe, you've never heard such cheering!" "Yes, I have," said the baseball hero quietly.[27]

Fitted In

Charlton Heston, who played the circus manager in Cecil B. De Mille's *The Greatest Show on Earth* (1952), thought the greatest compliment he ever received was from a woman who wrote to say she thought the picture had captured the feeling of a circus beautifully, liked the way Betty Hutton, Cornel Wilde, and Jimmy Stewart had played their parts, and then added: "I also was amazed at how well the circus manager fitted in with the real actors."[28]

Smellies

One promoter tried to interest the Rialto theater in New York City in an invention he called the greatest advance in movie technique since the arrival of sound. It was an odor track, attached to the film. As it passed through the projector, it emitted appropriate odors for various scenes at exactly the right time. The promoter brought a sample of film to demonstrate to the manager. The first scene took place in an apple orchard, where a young couple had built a fire and were cooking lunch. The odors: burning leaves, ripe apples, and bacon. The next scene was in church, where the couple was being married in front of an altar smelling of roses and honeysuckle. The last scene was in a hospital (where the new father was getting the happy news it was a boy) reeking of ether and disinfectant.

But there was one problem with the new invention. The blowers that wafted all the odors out into the theater with such precision were supposed to take them back in as well, but, sad to say, this part of the invention didn't work. The result: Soon the theater was so full of ripe apples, bacon, roses, ether, and Lysol that it took over an hour to clear the air. The apple smell, in fact, persisted for days, and some people thought the manager was secretly manufacturing applejack in the theater.[29]

Little Squirt

In *Kiss of Death* (1947), Richard Widmark played the part of a psychopathic killer with a sinister laugh and for a while was typecast as a tough, mean guy. "It's weird, the effect actors have on an audience," he said in an interview in 1987. "With the roles I played in those early movies, I found that quite a few people wanted to have a go at me." Once, he recalled, he was walking down the street in a small town and a lady came up, slapped him in the face, and cried, "Here, take that, you little squirt!"[30]

Sideways

To lure people away from television and back into movie houses in the early 1950s, the big studios began experimenting with wide screens. For *The Robe* (1953), Twentieth Century-Fox introduced CinemaScope; its image on the screen was two and a half times as wide as it was high and required new ways of arranging performers on the set. When critics said it was wrong to change the shape of the screen, Darryl Zanuck growled: "But who ordained that a movie screen has got to be *square*?" And when someone asked screenwriter Nunnally Johnson how he was going to handle the new demands of CinemaScope, he said: "Easy. What I'm going to do from now on is put the paper in my typewriter sideways!"[31]

In Depth

While technicians worked hard to perfect movies in the third dimension during the 1950s, comedians busily produced 3-D jokes. One was about the man watching a 3-D movie who asked the lady in front of him to take off her hat and she said she couldn't because she was in the picture. Another was about the man watching a 3-D picture who asked the lady *behind* him to take off her hat.[32]

Your Side

After seeing a picture on one of the new panoramic screens, one moviegoer said to a friend, "There was quite a lot of action at my end—what happened over on your side?"[33]

Would Have Too

In 1960, Bette Davis and her husband Gary Merrill toured the country doing readings of Carl Sandburg poems. In one small town where they performed, two elderly sisters who had been Davis fans for years arrived in the theater in high excitement over the prospect of seeing their favorite star in person. As the show began and Davis appeared on the stage, the women were spellbound. They followed every movement she made and drank in every word she uttered. But sud-

denly one of the women put her hand to her chest, fell back uncon-
scious, and died of a heart attack. As she was being taken out of the
theater, her sister refused to go with her. Instead, she stood up and
begged the Merrills to continue the performance. When the show
ended, there was a big ovation, and Davis invited the old woman to
come up on the stage. "I adored the performance," the woman said
as she took her place beside Davis. "And my sister would have too if
she hadn't died two hours ago!"[34]

Suggestion

Shortly after the release of *Psycho* (1960), Alfred Hitchcock's famous
thriller in which Janet Leigh is murdered in the shower, a man wrote
the director to say that ever since seeing the movie his wife had been
afraid to bathe or shower and he wanted suggestions as to what he
should do. "Sir," Hitchcock wrote back, "have you ever considered
sending your wife to the dry cleaner?"[35]

Keep On Living

Once Groucho Marx was walking down State Street in Chicago and a
middle-aged couple came up and began circling him. They went
around him two or three times, inspecting him carefully, and then
the wife said hesitantly, "You're him, aren't you? You're Groucho?"
Groucho nodded. Then she touched him shyly on the arm and said,
"Please don't die. Just keep on living."[36]

Print It

One day when actress Carol Burnett was having lunch with a friend
in the Beverly Hills Hotel a slightly tipsy woman came up to her table
and handed her a piece of paper. "Hey," she said, "you're
Car'burnett, aren't ya?" Burnett nodded and the woman said,
"Wouldja sign your name . . . please? Jus' make it out to Pat."
Burnett obligingly wrote, "To Pat, Best Wishes, Carol Burnett," and
the woman thanked her and returned to her table. But a few minutes
later she came back. "Hey, Car' Burnett," she screamed. "This is no
good." "What's the matter, Pat?" asked Burnett. "I can't for the life
of me read your name," said the woman, handing her another piece
of paper. "Gimme another autograph, will ya? Only this time, for
heaven's sake, PRINT IT!"[37]

Lulu's Debut

The Leopard (1963), starring Burt Lancaster, was on the screen, but a street cat named Lulu stole the show at the Carnegie Hall Cinema in New York one September night in 1985. Lulu, the adopted mascot at the little revival theater, usually greeted patrons affectionately as they arrived and then retired to the back of the auditorium when the house lights went down. But when a cat appeared in the closing moments of Luchino Visconti's film, Lulu ran up the stairs to the stage and sat there transfixed, her ears throwing a pointed shadow on the screen. The highbrow audience who had been watching the Visconti epic quietly for more than three hours burst into sudden laughter at the sight of Lulu. "She decided that this would be her debut," said one of the theater's managers later. "It's strange, in a sense. But that's Lulu."[38]

"Movies Are Better Than Ever"

The Sexual and Social Revolution

Movies in the Age of Reagan

V. AFTER THE GOLDEN ERA

"Movies Are Better
Than Ever"

By 1950 movie attendance had declined more than 25 percent from its postwar height. Wags insisted the picture business hadn't kept pace with the times, smirking at "Sixteenth Century-Fox" and the rest. "The old gray Mayer," a Hollywood saying held, "he ain't what he used to be."[1] Cutbacks were soon rife throughout the industry. Not only were production budgets sharply reduced, but within the next few years studios began letting their contract players go, even the great stars. In March 1954 MGM dropped both Clark Gable and Greer Garson, part of a retrenchment that reached even file clerks and janitors. When Paramount had neglected to pick up Carolyn Jones's option three years earlier, the actress realized she was part of the new economic wave that was sweeping over the film industry. "I was one of the cuts," Jones said philosophically. "Me and sixteen secretaries!"[2]

Shooting schedules were faster, pictures fewer. More and more films were made overseas, so that the studios appeared empty. By 1957 only a third of Metro's stages were in use at any given time, while the studio was renting out half of its facilities to independent producers. Suddenly the studio orchestras were gone and music departments dissolved. Symbolic of the drastic change was the fact that limousines once used to pick up Metro stars and drive them to the soundstages had been replaced by bicycles.[3] Before long the commissaries either closed or were reduced to fast-food operations. With box-office returns dropping steadily and production costs soaring, it was obvious the Golden Age of Hollywood was over. "The gravy train has gone round the bend," someone told character actress Mildred Natwick,[4] as nervousness gave way to panic and finally to a melancholy acceptance of the situation. Looking back over the halcyon days, Sam Goldwyn summed it up in his own inimitable way: "We have passed a lot of water since then."[5]

At the same time glamour was being superseded by realism. The old vehicles, tailor-made for specific stars, gave way to gargantuan productions that backers hoped would attract an indifferent public but that frequently resulted in financial disaster. Gone were the beautiful faces, costumes, sets, and jewelry that Golden Age audiences had equated with glamorous Hollywood. "It ended in the late 1940s with the unexplained but seemingly premeditated murder of glamour," Robert Taylor observed later. "Television, taxes, actors pricing themselves to the skies are all part-causes, but not the definite ones . . . I can't explain the demise."[6]

Television, of course, was the immediate culprit, but Hollywood had suffered a number of blows in the postwar decade that made it an easy prey. The death knell sounded in 1948, when by government decree the studios were divorced from their theaters on the assumption that antitrust laws had been violated. This meant that the major studios no longer had an assured market for their products. Exhibitors lacked the resources to promote pictures with the elaborate advertising they formerly received. Whereas four-column or half-page ads were customary earlier, now a single column often had to suffice. "When it's your own baby," Eugene Zukor observed after the loss of the theater chains, "you really go much further than if someone else is the custodian."[7] The big studios had depended on the steady income from picture after picture, B's as well as A's. Without it, they were in trouble. "So the studios declined, and the stars all left," commented dancer Dan Dailey. "And the grass grew in the streets."[8]

One by one the old movie palaces disappeared. The first to go were the neighborhood theaters that a decade before families had attended two or three times a week. Then the lesser downtown theaters closed their doors, and eventually the major exhibition houses followed. In New York City the Roxy was torn down, as were hundreds of imitations throughout the country. Some survived for a time on exploitation films, and ultimately the historic preservationists saved the few that remained by converting them into opera houses or legitimate theaters.

Not only did stars no longer enjoy the security of a studio home, Hollywood would soon be devastated by a political purge. Conservatives back in the 1930s had become alarmed by the growing unionization of the movie industry, and strikes occurring shortly after the war convinced many that radicals had taken over. In 1946 a Hollywood strike involving craft unions had grown so ugly that armed men stood outside the gates of Warner Bros. Before long right-wingers like Hedda Hopper were referring to "Metro-Goldwyn-Moscow," convinced that Communists were in control. In January 1947 the House Un-American Activities Committee was made a permanent congressional body. Soon publicity-hungry congressmen began looking to Hollywood for opportunities. In September 1947 the first subpoenas were delivered, ordering nineteen "unfriendly" witnesses to appear before the committee for questioning.

While there were actually relatively few Communists in Hollywood, mainly in the Writers Guild, with perhaps seven or eight in the Directors Guild, the ensuing discord injured the whole industry. When the "unfriendly" witnesses returned from Washington, they were confronted with the ultimatum that they either purge themselves of Communist association or be fired by their respective studios. At a Screen Directors Guild meeting, the question whether that organization should back its members or the congressional committee resulted in a heated battle. "This is war!" extreme right-winger Cecil B. De Mille shouted, and the guild even split over the issue of a secret ballot.

In November 1947 motion-picture producers and studio heads, fearing reprisals at the box office, met at the Waldorf-Astoria Hotel in New York to decide what steps to take. They released a statement pledging that they would not knowingly hire anyone who was a member of the Communist party or of any group advocating the overthrow of the United States government by force. After the Waldorf-Astoria decree was released, blacklisting went into effect. The Hollywood Ten, who refused to answer questions before the House committee, were subsequently sentenced to prison terms for contempt of Congress. "The ten of us that went to jail knew what we were doing," Edward Dmytryk later said. "We knew what we were being punished for. We had asked for it. But there were hundreds and hundreds of people who had done nothing that were blacklisted."[9] The committee forced others to list names, thereby turning friend against friend.

Careers were eventually ruined or interrupted, lives destroyed or damaged beyond repair. When Larry Parks, who had recently scored great successes with *The Jolson Story* and *Jolson Sings Again*, was called before the committee, he admitted his former Communist affiliations and suffered terribly for it. Columbia immediately dropped his contract, and his wife, Betty Garrett, was dropped by MGM even though she had never been a Communist. "Suddenly we had to make our own jobs," Garrett remembered with emotion years later. "My God, we could have been the most popular kids around. And that was cut off."[10]

Anne Revere, who had won an Academy Award for her supporting role in *National Velvet* two years earlier, was blacklisted and couldn't work in Hollywood for many years. The same was true of Will Geer, Howard Da Silva, Gale Sondergaard, and Marsha Hunt, even though the latter had merely taken a stand in favor of freedom of political belief. Film composer David Raksin was unemployable in Hollywood for a number of years because he had belonged to the China Aid Council, an organization that simply opposed Japanese involvement in China. Before long, on every producer's desk was a copy of *Red Channels*, listing names of the hundreds who were blacklisted. Many of them had never been Communists, yet they suffered a stigma they couldn't erase. Writers, most notably Dalton Trumbo, continued to sell scripts under assumed names for reduced fees, but actors and directors who were blacklisted generally worked in New York or spent time in Europe. It was a shabby period in Hollywood's history, and the pain has not yet subsided. "To have been in the middle of that was to be in the middle of hell," recalled David Raksin decades later.[11]

Badgered and bruised, Hollywood was in no condition to meet the challenge of television, which invaded the area of mass entertainment around 1948. Seven and a half million television sets were sold in 1950, whereas two years before sales had been less than a million.[12] Even then backward-looking movie moguls failed to realize the growing threat to the movie industry. "Television doesn't mean a damn thing," Darryl Zanuck insisted. "It's just a passing fad."[13] Unwilling to admit that their tastes no longer represented what the younger generation wanted, the moguls persisted in the self-satisfied delusion that "movies are better than ever." When Hollywood producers even mentioned television, their attitude was one of condescension and scorn. When Marilyn Monroe, as a would-be actress in *All About Eve* (1950), asked if they had auditions for television, her critic-sponsor coolly replied, "Auditions, my dear, are *all* they have on television."

By 1952 studio heads were at least willing to consider alternative ways to attract declining audiences. *Bwana Devil* and *House of Wax* ushered in 3-D, filmed with two cameras and requiring audiences to wear Polaroid glasses. During 3-D shooting actors had to move slowly and avoid getting too close to the camera. "Otherwise," jested *Bwana Devil*'s star Robert Stack, "a woman's left breast might be hanging over the first three rows of the theater."[14] Next came Cinerama, utilizing three projectors to fill a gigantic curved screen. Less cumbersome was CinemaScope, which produced a huge mural-like image, yet with little depth to the focus. Twentieth Century-Fox based its whole future on CinemaScope, beginning with *The Robe* (1953). While the period 1954–56 is sometimes called the "CinemaScope rebound," it proved temporary, and by 1958 the downward spiral had resumed.

In hope of restoring its days of glory, Paramount developed VistaVision, which the studio called motion-picture high fidelity because the foreground and background were both in focus at the same time. Stereophonic sound was installed in all the larger theaters, while any number of gimmicks were tried briefly, then abandoned. Smell-O-Vision proved a fleeting experiment; its products were called "smellies" for short, and most people agreed the name was appropriate. Desperate though many of its efforts were, the industry wishfully proclaimed at every opportunity, even on the sides of popcorn boxes, that "Movies Are Better Than Ever!" The sale of popcorn and candy actually kept most theaters operating, prompting one moviegoer to suggest a more accurate slogan: "Movies Are Butter Than Ever."[15]

While independent production companies were already eroding the solidarity of the big-studio system, Mike Todd gave Hollywood a new transfusion of showmanship when he filmed *Around the World in Eighty Days* (1956), sweeping the Academy Awards that year. Mike shot the movie in his new Todd-AO process, filled the screen with stars in cameo roles, and turned the Jules Verne yarn into a cinematic romp. "It's fun working for Todd," said Marlene Dietrich, who played a Barbary Coast saloon proprietress in the picture. "He still has the enthusiasm that has gone out of Hollywood. The atmosphere here has become like a factory, General Motors."[16] Soon the factories were taken over by vast conglomerates, and businessmen and agents became the new rulers of Hollywood.

No Television

In Warner Bros. films, living rooms had no television sets. Jack Warner had banned them, for television was to Jack a dirty word. Sammy Fain and Paul Francis Webster were writing songs for some Warners musicals at the time and asked scriptwriter Mel Shavelson to stop by their bungalow to hear a tune they had just composed. Shavelson listened but immediately said, "It'll never be in the picture." "What do you mean?" the songwriters asked. "We just played the first eight bars." Shavelson repeated, "It'll never be in the picture." They each reached for their wallets and bet $10 that it would. The next day, after the songwriters had played their number for Jack Warner, Webster and Fain ran into Shavelson again and paid off the bet. "How did you know?" they asked. The reason was obvious, for the first line of the chorus was "I'm in love with the girl on Channel Nine."[17]

Held Up

In 1948 comedienne Kathleen Freeman was just beginning her career when Larry Parks and Elizabeth Taylor made *Love Is Better Than Ever* at MGM. It was Freeman's best part so far, and she was counting heavily on the picture to land her a Metro contract. But toward the end of shooting, Parks called Kathleen into his dressing room. "I know how much this film means to you," he told her. "But you're not going to get a contract." Freeman immediately concluded that he hadn't liked her work, but that was not the reason. "I've been called to testify in Washington," Parks explained, "and this picture is going to be held up for a long time." He was right. After Parks admitted past membership in the American Communist party before the House Un-American Activities Committee, Columbia terminated his contract and he found it hard to get work after that. The picture he made with Freeman wasn't released until 1952.[18]

War!

During the House Un-American Activities Committee's purge of Hollywood, liberal members of the Screen Directors Guild called on the guild to take a stand protesting the Waldorf-Astoria decree that brought about the notorious blacklisting. A meeting of the guild was held, with everyone, including right-wingers Cecil B. De Mille and Michael Curtiz, in attendance. The room was filled with tension. Early in the session one of the liberals moved that all votes be cast by secret ballot. As those in favor lifted their hands, Curtiz rose to his feet, shouting, "Take their names! Take their names!" In the midst of the uproar that followed De Mille jumped up and screamed: "This is war!"

De Mille and his supporters wanted each director to sign a loyalty oath and supply information on the political views of all actors and technicians employed on their sets. Both liberals and reactionaries struggled to seize control of the guild, and a storm of protests broke out on both sides. William Wyler threatened to punch the next person who suggested he was a Communist because he disagreed with De Mille. For four hours John Ford sat silent, although it was assumed he supported the right wing. Finally Ford rose. "My name's John Ford," he said. "I make Westerns. I don't think there is anyone in the room who knows more about what the American public wants than Cecil B. De Mille. In that respect I admire him." Then, staring at De Mille, he added, "But I don't like you, C.B. I don't like what you stand for and I don't like what you've been saying here tonight." He moved that De Mille resign from the board of directors and that Joseph Mankiewicz, the guild's president, be given a vote of confidence. Both measures carried, and the meeting was over.[19]

Wide Screen

Previews of *The Robe* (1953) in CinemaScope brought enthusiastic if sometimes puzzled responses. When one exhibitor returned to his home territory, he was asked what the movie was about. "I don't know," he claimed. Then remembering a huge close-up of Victor Mature, he added, "I think it's about a guy with thirteen-foot lips."[20]

Two Dimensional 3-D

When his studio made *House of Wax* (1953), Jack Warner was convinced that 3-D glasses would soon be in every man's pocket and every woman's purse, like fountain pens. The film's director, André de Toth, didn't seem like the most logical choice for this particular picture. He was an excellent director, but he had only one eye and therefore wasn't able to see the third dimension. Instead of going to watch the rushes, he'd sit on the soundstage and collar people as they came out. "How was it?" he'd ask. "Did it come off?" Poor de Toth never fully understood what all the commotion was about.[21]

Movies Smell
If perfumed movies had any future, the speculation favored Mike Todd, Jr.'s Smell-O-Vision. Young Todd spent two million dollars on his picture *Scent of Mystery* (1960). When the film was released, Henny Youngman gave it a two-line review: "I didn't understand the picture," he said. "I had a cold."[22]

Television
In August 1958 Hedda Hopper happened to turn onto Gower Street and into an unexpected traffic jam. Suddenly she noticed that the famous RKO symbol with its jagged streaks of lightning was no longer on the studio's water tower. Instead the lone word *Desilu* was stenciled on the tank. Realizing the finality of the situation, Hedda muttered to herself, "That bastard, television."[23]

CHAPTER 30

The Sexual and
Social Revolution

In the 1960s American movies experienced a thoroughgoing transvaluation of all values. The old Production Code, with its long list of prohibitions, wasn't simply thrust aside; it was, in effect, turned upside down. What the Hays Office had once proscribed the new movies virtually prescribed. What Hays had censured the new films commended. What Hays had hated the new pictures hailed. Where Hays had drawn a circle to shut things out, the new filmmakers drew a circle to take them in. Just about all of Hays's abominations—profanity, obscenity, nudity, explicit sex, drugs, excessive violence, homosexuality—became commonplace on American screens during the sixties.

The change was breathtaking. "Did you know," Claudette Colbert exclaimed to an interviewer in 1985, "that when Clark Gable and I made It Happened One Night in 1934, there was never a clinch?" She smiled and added: "Much to my sorrow!"[1] By the time she spoke such forbearance had long been abandoned. Thirty years after Colbert and Gable had traipsed chastely around the country in Frank Capra's famous comedy classic, lovemaking on the screen—in bed, on the floor, in hallways, cars, alleys, even on kitchen tables—had become open, undisguised, and unrestrained. Cameras no longer shifted as of old to the fireplace at climactic moments; nor did they zoom discreetly to the window and to the shining moon outside and the starry heavens above. Instead they remained riveted on the busy performers. And the missionary position, it was strongly suggested, was out, and fellatio, cunnilingus, and even sodomy, in. Premarital sex, adultery, and masturbation (once considered a deadly vice) were taken for granted. Monogamy, not homosexuality, it seemed, was now the "love that dare not speak its name."[2] While working on one of his last musical scores for Warners in the early sixties, Max Steiner complained that young Troy Donahue got to "screw" three girls in the movie and that meant he had to write three separate themes for the picture.[3]

There was music for scenes of unprecedented violence in the sixties as well as for increasingly steamy lovemaking sequences. The old Production Code prohibitions soon seemed quaint and quirky: "Action suggestive of wholesale slaughter of human beings, either by criminals, in conflict with the police, or as between warring factions of criminals, or in public disorder of any kind, will not be allowed"; "There must be no display, at any time, of machine guns, sub-machine guns or other weapons generally classified as illegal weapons in the hands of gangsters, or other criminals, and there are to be no off-stage sounds of the repercussions of these guns."[4] The new violence and brutality unfolding on the nation's screens shocked some reviewers at first, but before long they, and movie audiences generally, came to endure, and then to enjoy it all.

When *Newsweek*'s Joseph Morgenstern first reviewed *Bonnie and Clyde* (1967), he was revolted by the picture's gruesome carnage and called it "a squalid shoot-'em-up for the moron trade." A week later he backtracked. His rationale: The director was presenting a faithful representation of the violence inherent in American life, not an endorsement of it; the mayhem, in short, was moral. Renata Adler, who reviewed films for *The New York Times* for a time, took a different view of what movies do. Whatever directors say about their intentions, she once observed, "movies always say yes."[5] But hers remained a minority position. And the violence appearing in *Bonnie and Clyde* came to seem mild compared to that featured in *The Wild Bunch* (1969) and subsequent films. There was a tendency, too, to glamorize outlaws like Bonnie Parker and Clyde Barrow despite their murderous careers. Slaughter almost came to seem stylish in the new movies.

Some people were bothered by the language as well as by the graphic sex and inordinate violence occurring in American movies after the death of the Production Code. "Pointed profanity," the

Code had declared, "and every other profane or vulgar expression, however used, is forbidden."⁶ But by the mid-sixties, profane and vulgar expressions were not only common in movies; they were also practically *de rigueur*. Screen people began taking the name of the good Lord in vain so casually when they communicated with each other that He probably wished He could change it. It was the day of the Saxon too; the contempt-and-violence-laden quadriliterals became standard. In the old days, scriptwriters racked their brains for strong but permissible epithets: *billygoat, scum, bum, fourflusher, deadbeat, crackpot, lying, white-livered skunk, lardhead, filth, moron.* (W. C. Fields's favorite ejaculation: "Godfrey Daniel!") After the new day dawned there was no problem: simply cast doubts on someone's ancestry or resort to the all-purpose Anglo-Saxonisms. It was hard to believe that back in 1939 David Selznick had to seek special permission for Clark Gable to say at the end of *Gone With the Wind:* "Frankly, I don't give a damn!" Or that in 1944's filming of the play *Arsenic and Old Lace,* Cary Grant could not utter the play's punch line when he learns he is illegitimate (and thus mercifully unrelated to the family of kookaboos featured in the play): "Thank God I'm a bastard!" Instead, he had to say, "Thank God I'm the son of a sea cook!"

New themes, as well as new approaches to old themes, opened to filmmakers in the sixties. *The Trip* (1967) dealt with the heady experiences of Peter Fonda after taking a dose of LSD on top of a marijuana high. In *Midnight Cowboy* (1969), the protagonist is a male whore trying to make out in Manhattan, who gradually develops a deep friendship with a crippled young thief and pimp from the Bronx. *Bob & Carol & Ted & Alice* (1969) was about two California couples who experiment with adultery and mate swapping in an effort to be open and honest about sex. *The Boys in the Band* (1970) centered on a birthday party celebrated by a group of homosexuals in New York City. *Carnal Knowledge* (1971) examined the sexual attitudes and adventures of two men from their college days until they reach middle age. *Last Tango in Paris* (1972) chronicled the relations between a middle-aged American and a young French girl and contained some of the most graphic sexual encounters, including sodomy, ever to appear in a major movie. There were films, too, after the sixties about prostitution, rape, seduction, adultery, lesbianism, transvestism, and even incest.

Not all the post-Hays films concentrated on sex. Some of them dealt with the "identity crisis" of young Americans and with the alienation they felt in what was seen as America's increasingly corrupt, hypocritical, uptight, and materialistic society. *The Graduate* (1967) was about a young college graduate who rejects the plastic world of his elders. *Alice's Restaurant* (1969) pictured a group of misfits who try to find peace with themselves and the world by means of drugs, music, and communal living and loving. In *Easy Rider* (1969), two young men (Peter Fonda and Dennis Hopper) make money smuggling cocaine into the country and then take off on a motorcycle (and drug) trip across the country from California to Florida, hoping to see what America is like en route. They find out all right; the countryside is beautiful but the people they encounter are mostly narrow-minded, mean-spirited, and hostile to their freewheeling ways. In the end the two hippies meet violent death at the hands of some vicious rednecks. *They Shoot Horses, Don't They?* (1969) focused on a marathon dance contest held during the Great Depression; but the degrading struggle for survival on the dance floor is presented as an allegory for America as a whole and the film ends with one of the losers (Jane Fonda) having her partner shoot her. *Five Easy Pieces* (1970), a study of a talented but aimless young drifter, played by Jack Nicholson, does not end in death but it is equally depressing. Unhappy endings became almost as common in the sixties as happy endings had been in the thirties. Some films came close to suggesting that life itself (though not moviemaking) was essentially pointless.

Political as well as social protest turned up on the screen in the sixties and seventies. "You know, this used to be a hell of a good country," says Jack Nicholson (playing an alcoholic civil rights lawyer in *Easy Rider*). "I can't understand what's wrong with it." Some filmmakers doubted that the country had ever amounted to much. Their pictures dwelt on America's shortcomings: greed, racism, repression, corruption, widespread poverty and squalor, imperialism, militarism. In *Medium Cool* (1969), a TV news cameraman becomes radicalized when he hears about the oppression of blacks and the depths of poverty in the Appalachians; he is horrified, too, by police brutality at the time of the Democratic convention in Chicago in 1968. In *Little Big Man* (1970), the whites slaughter the Indians with murderous delight; in *Sweet Sweetback's Baadasssss Song* (1971), the blacks defy the white establishment and warn: "A BAADASSSSS NIGGER IS COMING BACK TO COLLECT SOME DUES"; in films like *Mean Streets* (1973) and *Chinatown* (1974), American society appears riddled with corruption and evil. There were antiwar movies, too, some of them, like *Coming Home* (1978), directed against the Vietnam War, and others, like *M*A*S*H* (1970) and *Catch-22* (1970), satirizing war and militarism in general. The best of the anti-war films, *Dr. Strangelove* (1964), was a black comedy about the accidental eruption of nuclear war.

Films about student-protest movements in the sixties and seventies also became popular for a time. Movies like *The Strawberry Statement* (1970) and *Getting Straight* (1970) focused on the student revolts against authoritarianism on the campus and the evils (racism, poverty, militarism) of American society at large. In the latter film, a clean-cut young college boy becomes an outspoken radical after learning how bad it is on and off campus. "Haven't you heard?" graduate student Elliott Gould exclaims to the college president after the campus uprising begins. "Repression breeds revolution. See that kid? A week ago all he wanted to do was get laid, and now he's ready to tear the place apart. You should have let him get laid!" The film climaxes in a student sit-in and a police bust. So does *The Strawberry Statement*. But neither film can be regarded as seriously radical or revolutionary in purpose.

Only one film, Michelangelo Antonioni's American-made *Zabriskie Point* (1970), toyed with the idea of revolution. While it was being shot, the FBI launched an investigation of several members of the company producing it. In the end, though, MGM executives saw to it that all the controversial material—including the skywritten obscenity, "F--k you, America," with which the picture was to end—was deleted. On its release the film was a dud with both critics and audiences. For all the hyperbolic talk, in short, the revolution called for by a minority of American leftists in the sixties never got very far, on-screen or off. Even the radical rhetoric was short-lived. As U.S. forces began withdrawing from Vietnam under the Nixon administration, the antiestablishment crusade soon petered out everywhere.

Still, something of a revolution did take place in movies during the stormy sixties. The ending of movie censorship (in a series of Supreme Court decisions) and the movement of producers to stories and themes previously off limits represented a major turning point in the history of American films. But this big change in movies did not take place in a vacuum. Movies in the sixties, as in all decades, responded to the trends of the times, and reflected as well as helped shape the nation's culture. The sixties was a decade of protest, and most filmmakers cheerfully joined the protest. In taking an antiestablishment stance, they were reacting to the agitations of the

Johnson-Nixon years: the civil rights movement, the war against poverty, the rise of feminism, the outburst of black militancy, and, above all, the development of a powerful antiwar movement, especially among college students, directed against American involvement in the Vietnam War thousands of miles away. And in dealing more frankly with sexual behavior than their predecessors in the big studios had, they were responding to the transformation of manners and morals in America's increasingly sizable youth population. During these stormy sixties, large numbers of young people were defying middle-class conventions, dropping out of the system, and developing a "counterculture" of their own, based on drugs, rock music, long hair, informal garb, and carefree attitudes toward sex.

Filmmakers didn't always treat the new youth culture with respect. Their audiences were mainly youthful and they tended to cater to the passing fads and fancies of the younger generation rather than probe their aspirations and discontents with sensitivity and imagination. "Some movies are creating the myths of the young," complained director Arthur Penn in 1970. "They promote the notion that freedom from all authority is an unqualified good, that mobility as a life-style is superior to permanence, that the older generation is totally corrupt, that cool is the only legitimate emotional response. And what's worse about these films is that they patronize young people. They reduce them to their accouterments—their grass, their bikes, their music—all their labels." But, as Penn well knew, there was nothing new about audience exploitation in the film industry.[7]

In 1974 came the end of the Vietnam War and the end of an era. Social protest dwindled and so did films about social injustice. The counterculture began shucking its excesses and moving into the mainstream, and movies became less iconoclastic. Still, the agitations of the sixties left a permanent imprint on American society and culture. There was no return to reticence about sex when the tumult and shouting died. Permissiveness, at least for large numbers of Americans, appeared to be here to stay, and it continued to shape filmmaking.

Back in the old Hays days, writers, producers, and directors had managed to summon up enough imagination, ingenuity, and creative energy to produce first-rate movies from time to time despite the heavy-handed censorship. After the sixties there was a new challenge: to muster enough sense and sensibility to produce films of stature despite the absence of guidelines and restraints.

Personal Question

When Rock Hudson died of acquired immune deficiency syndrome (AIDS) in the fall of 1985 and his homosexuality became public knowledge, few people were shocked by the revelation. Before the sexual revolution of the late sixties, though, studios had always carefully concealed the popular romantic star's sexual preferences from the public, although movie journalists knew about it and kept it off the record.

In 1962, Hudson was in Dallas to promote his latest film, *The Spiral Road*, and agreed to an interview with Dallas and Fort Worth reporters at lunch. "Mr. Hudson," said one young reporter who was not acquainted with the film world, "I've got a very personal question for you. I hope it's not too embarrassing, and you may not want to answer it." There was an uncomfortable silence; the movie reporters stared into their salads. "I've heard this rumored for years," the woman continued, "but there's no way to know for sure unless I ask you." Hudson looked impassively at the woman and waited. And then she said: "Is it true that your teeth are capped?"[8]

At Last Free

After Jack Valenti became president of the Motion Picture Association of America in 1966 and began relaxing Production Code rules, *Variety* published a poem entitled "Ode to Revised Motion Picture Code":

> In urban nabes and drive-in glades,
> The screen at last is free.
> Four-letter words, explicit verbs
> Titillate tots of three.
> With derrieres and pubic hairs
> Blithely exposed today,
> When they say "he went thataway,"
> Means the hero turned gay.[9]

Doesn't Make It Right

In 1968, when Paul Newman was campaigning for antiwar candidate Senator Eugene McCarthy in the New Hampshire presidential primary, one of the officers in the police escort pointed to his partner and said the latter had received word the night before that his son had been killed in Vietnam. Saddened by the news, Newman offered the policeman his sympathy and then said thoughtfully, "What do you think about some creep, some Hollywood peacenik . . . coming in here and telling you about the war?" The policeman assured Newman he didn't resent what the actor was doing. "Even if a war takes your boy," he said, "that doesn't make it right."[10]

Substitute
When *Medium Cool* (1969) was completed, it was withheld from release for several months. Its assault on the establishment offended some members of the conglomerate owning the studio that produced it; the obscenities in the dialogue also displeased Jack Valenti and other members of the Motion Picture Association of America. Valenti and his associates put heavy pressure on Haskell Wexler, writer and director of the film, to tone down the strong talk in the picture. "I wrote them," Wexler said later, "and said I'd be glad to fix it up. Only I said every time someone said a 'dirty' word I would substitute the word, kill. That way we'd have things like 'kill you' and 'Put me down, you killer!' I haven't heard any complaints from them since."[11]

Good Taste
In 1968 the Motion Picture Association of America established the Code and Rating Administration Board to classify movies according to the kind of material they contained and their suitability for young people. A couple of years later, when the rating board was evaluating *Myra Breckinridge* (1970), the movie version of Gore Vidal's satirical novel, most members of the board were offended by the scene in which Raquel Welch turns to the camera and says, "All right, you mother-f-----s!" One of the raters put it this way: "Now, when we have a picture about Negroes in the ghetto, and some of the characters use the word, 'mother-f----r,' that is valid. But to hear Raquel Welch say it—there's no excuse for *that!*" When someone pointed out that Welch seemed to have her own code of good taste because she never appeared nude in her films, another board member exclaimed: "I'd rather see her take her clothes off than hear her use language like 'mother-f----r'!"[12]

Union Rules
Former Code administrator Will Hays would have gone haywire had he visited the set of *Five Easy Pieces* (1970) during the heyday of the

sexual revolution. In one scene, four people, including Jack Nicholson and Sally Struthers, are sitting around quietly in their underwear having some drinks, and just before the take Nicholson decided to do the scene with only a cigar in his mouth and boots on his feet. Before taking off his undershorts, however, he insisted that the crew disrobe too. "Hey, now, listen," he cried. "If actors have to work nude, and they're embarrassed about it, it should be union rules that the crew be nude, too, and then nobody will be staring at anybody." But as people in the crew, who adored Nicholson, started ripping off their clothes, director Bob Rafelson hastily intervened. "Hey, wait a minute," he exclaimed. "We can't do this here." In the end there was no nude scene after all.[13]

Great Deal to Say

When it looked as if antiwar activist Jane Fonda would win an Academy Award for her portrayal of a call girl in *Klute* (1971), some people were afraid she might use the occasion to give a strident speech against the Vietnam War. "I implore you not to," pleaded her father, and she thought long and hard about what she should do if an Oscar came her way. When her name was announced the night of the Academy Awards dinner in April 1972, she went up to the platform, and, as millions of people watched on television to see what she would do, she started speaking quietly. "There is a great deal to say," she declared, "and—I'm not going to say it tonight."[14]

Con Kid

After winning an Oscar for playing a tough-talking, cigarette-smoking girl in *Paper Moon* (1973), the ten-year-old Tatum O'Neal was called the greatest child star since Shirley Temple. But tastes in film kids had changed since Shirley's day. "I was a con artist," Tatum told an interviewer after the film was released, "and she was a dainty little lollipop." Tatum's father, Ryan, who appeared with her in the film, hastily explained that his daughter admired Shirley. "Shirley may have been coy," he said, "but she sure could sing and dance." "Yeah," added Tatum, "but I'd rather learn karate!"[15]

CHAPTER 31

Movies in the
Age of Reagan

In the late seventies came the Big Chill. The country took a sharp turn to the right—liberalism foundered and conservatism became the rage. By the eighties the youthful iconoclasts of the sixties had grown into respectable citizens and once-impassioned demonstrators had turned into loyal champions of the established order. Yippies became Yuppies; knocking yielded to boosting. The crusading fervor of the Johnson years gave way to the complacent impulses of the Reagan era. "Who'd've thought we'd both make so much money?" exclaims Tom Berenger to Kevin Kline in Lawrence Kasdan's *The Big Chill* (1983). "Two revolutionaries!"

In Kasdan's film, Berenger is a former student protester of the 1960s, who is now, in the 1980s, a successful TV actor. And Kline, also once a critic of the system, is now a prosperous businessman. The picture brings the two of them (and several other friends) together for the funeral of a classmate—and for rap sessions about the old days and new. They have all cooled off and calmed down; their idealistic days as college kids seem a dim memory. "You Can't Always Get What You Want," booms the soundtrack with a song from the sixties. But the people in *The Big Chill* no longer want what they once wanted. They have made their peace (if an uneasy one) with the world.

The country's change in mood, which *The Big Chill* reported, has been pervasive; it has affected popular culture as well as politics. And with the change in mood has come a change in movies. The movie industry, following trends, as always, began heading away from controversial subjects during the 1970s. By the 1980s protest films were out; so were films about alienation and disenchantment with the nation's social arrangements. There have been, to be sure, occasional message movies: *Nine to Five* (1980) and *Tootsie* (1982), about sexism; *Missing* (1982), about American complicity in a military takeover of a Latin American country; *Silkwood* (1983), about the efforts of a big corporation to suppress information about contamination by plutonium; and *WarGames* (1983), a cautionary story about a nuclear scare produced by computers. But the latter-day films with a social theme have had none of the shrillness of the didactic movies of the sixties.

What has been called "faywraying"—screaming all the time, as Fay Wray did in *King Kong* (1933), about what was going on—now seems a thing of the past. Even the satirical comedies of the eighties have been quieter; talented young black comedian Eddie Murphy teases the country in his enormously popular films, but he does not rage against it. In the new comedies, there are no hoots and hollers at the system. Making a stridently satirical picture like *M*A*S*H* (1970), with its frenetic nose-thumbing at middle-class mores, seemed unthinkable ten years later. Agitprop is now out, while entertainment (but not black comedy) is in. And entertainment in the eighties means science-fiction spectaculars, teenage teasers, law-and-order (even vigilante) melodramas, and macho movies about the Vietnam War. Like President Ronald Reagan, a former movie actor, filmmakers are now anxious to make Americans feel good about themselves. "We're getting back into the Frank Capra era of happier movies," observed Louis Gossett, Jr., star of *Iron Eagle* (1986). "This sort of movie lets us know that there can be a happy ending, the good guys can win out, there's probably going to be a brighter tomorrow." In the films he was making, said director Ivan Reitman, he was trying to "recreate the sensibility where people stood up for what was right, where people trusted each other, where there was an order to life."[1]

Judging from box-office returns, movie audiences apparently got their best "vibes" from watching the new lavish space odysseys that began appearing in the late 1970s. At any rate, science-fiction films (sometimes called "sci-fi" or simply "sf") suddenly became top grossers in movie theaters across the land, and, later on, in videotape rentals. *Star Wars* led the way in 1977. Planned as a "real gee-whiz movie for youthful audiences," George Lucas's film, taking place "a long, long time ago, in a galaxy far, far away" took off with adults as well as children and soon broke all box-office records.[2] Sequels were inevitable: *The Empire Strikes Back* (1980) and *Return of the Jedi* (1983). There was even talk of a cycle of nine *Star Wars* films in all— three separate trilogies. And soon people were calling the Reagan administration's proposal for space-based defense against missiles "Star Wars." Another sci-fi picture, *Superman* (1978), based on the popular comic strip, also did enormously well, and, like *Star Wars*, has had its follow-ups in the 1980s. And *Star Trek—The Motion Picture* (1979), taken from the TV series of the late sixties, was another successful space opera that pleased general audiences as well as "Trekkies" and became a popular film series too.

Time was when a thoughtful science-fiction film (like 1936's *Things to Come,* 1956's *Forbidden Planet,* and 1968's *2001: A Space Odyssey*) stimulated the imagination, encouraged audiences to think of the world in a new way, raised questions, and produced speculations about the future. The new sci-fi movies did little of this. They provided escape, not mind stretching: stunning special effects (visual, mechanical, audio) and exciting melodramas in which Good (humans) just about always triumphed over Evil (aliens). For many critics such films were tolerable only when they did not take themselves seriously. Stanley Kauffmann liked *Superman III* (1983) because he thought it was "one exciting, gigantic wink." But Pauline Kael found all the space-adventure movies "faintly dumb."[3]

More to Pauline Kael's liking were director Steven Spielberg's sci-fi fantasies: *Close Encounters of the Third Kind* (1977) and *E.T.—The Extra-Terrestrial* (1982). *Close Encounters* or *CE3K* (as it is sometimes designated), a film about some friendly aliens who land on Earth and begin to communicate with humans, appeared about the same time as *Star Wars* and did almost as well as the latter with audiences. Unlike *Star Wars*, though, *CE3K* contained a real human dimension; in it, Richard Dreyfuss plays the part of an ordinary adult who has retained his childlike sense of wonder about things and in the end is vindicated (and thus becomes out-of-the-ordinary) when a real spaceship is discovered. Kael found *CE3K* "the best-humored of all the technological-marvel fantasies" and praised its "visionary magic" and "childlike comic spirit." She also thought well of *E.T.*, a picture about a young alien who is accidentally left on Earth by a visiting spaceship and becomes the friend of a lonely ten-year-old boy and his friends.[4]

Spielberg has done ghostly chillers as well as sci-fi fantasies in the eighties. *Poltergeist* (1982) dealt with a family besieged by mischievous (and mean) spirits; and *Gremlins* (1984) showed what happens when some impish little creatures begin multiplying furiously and running riot in Kingston Falls, U.S.A. Both Spielberg films contained smiles as well as shivers and succeeded in charming adults (and critics) as well as children. Not so charming, though, were the low-budget "teen screamers" (or "slice 'em and dice 'em movies") that began appearing in the late seventies: films about high school kids being picked off one by one on Friday the thirteenth or on Halloween by a mad killer who seems to take umbrage at their smooching around so much. *Halloween* (1978), featuring a batty bogeyman, was so popular with teenage moviegoers that it was followed by several sequels. *Friday the 13th* (1980) was also turned into a series by popular demand. The third *Friday* thriller was presented in 3-D, and *Time's* film critic reported that the way "the eyeball of one of Jason's victims pops out of his skull and seems to sail out over the audience's head is alone worth buying a ticket [for] and putting on funny glasses."[5]

Not all the youth-oriented movies have been scare flicks. Equally popular have been the high-school and college-kid farces, featuring toga parties, beer busts, food riots, sexual hanky-panky, panty raids, fraternity pranks, and general hell-raising. *National Lampoon's Animal House* (1978), starring John Belushi, set the pattern. A runaway hit, it spawned a flock of riotous roughhousers filled with the kind of sleazy gags, dirty jokes, and raunchy dialogue that have kept grammar and high school kids (and even some adults) in stitches for decades. *Porky's* (1981), a cheaply made film centering on a bawdy house where six Florida boys seek their first sexual experiences, was so astonishingly successful at the box office that it soon had followups: *Porky's II: The Next Day* (1983) and *Porky's Revenge* (1985). Other low-budget teen pleasers: *Hardbodies, Weekend Pass, Joysticks, Private Lessons, Zapped!, My Tutor, Goin' All the Way, Bachelor Party, The Last American Virgin, Hollywood Hot Tubs.* "They're basically about guys trying to get laid," acknowledged one director. There were, of course, a few films—like *Diner* (1982), *Tex* (1982), and *The Sure Thing* (1985)—that took adolescents seriously and examined their youthful *angst* with sympathy and perception.

Most of the teenage movies, though, were based on Hollywood's belief that, as one producer put it, "Children love dirty and they love the silliness of this kind of comedy."[6] Some adults even got a kick out of the high-school soft porn. "A lot of this," according to P. J. O'Rourke, editor of National Lampoon, "is a backlash against the enormous seriousness of the 1960s. . . ."[7]

There was another backlash: against the alleged permissiveness of the sixties toward lawbreakers, which, conservatives claimed, encouraged crime. In the film industry the call for a crackdown appeared in the law-and-order movies that began attracting huge crowds in the seventies. Charles Bronson's Death Wish (1974) was the prototype; it was a real vigilante film. In it, the pacifistic Bronson's wife is murdered by muggers and his daughter raped and driven insane, and as a result he takes the law into his own hands and goes around New York City at night, shooting and killing thieves, punks, hoodlums, and muggers wherever he finds them at work, and soon becomes the city's hero. In the end, the New York City Police Department deports him and he resumes his work in Chicago. Most critics shared Richard Schickel's view: "a meretricious film—in its curious lack of feeling even for innocent victims of crime, in its hysterical exaggerations of an undeniable problem, and especially in its brazen endorsement of violence as a solution to violence."[8] But the movie drew large audiences the first time around and also on reruns. Death Wish II did not appear until 1982, and Death Wish 3 (using 3,500 rounds of machine-gun and small-gun ammunition) until 1985, but a dozen other vigilante films made the rounds in the meantime. Perhaps the most irresponsible was The Star Chamber (1983), a film about a secret organization of judges that assigns hit men to take care of vicious criminals who have escaped conviction because of legal technicalities. The picture eventually acknowledges the dangers of lynch law, but not before building up considerable sympathy for it among viewers.

Clint Eastwood was filmdom's most famous crook chaser. He emphasized lowering the boom on lawbreakers in his tremendously popular Dirty Harry films—Dirty Harry (1971), Magnum Force (1973), The Enforcer (1976), and Sudden Impact (1983)—and these films helped make him the nation's most popular movie star. As Dirty Harry Callahan, Eastwood plays the part of a tough, street-smart, nononsense San Francisco cop who chafes at the constitutional restraints on police activity and knocks off slimy criminals with zest and joy and without any misgivings about his methods. In a famous scene at the beginning of Sudden Impact, Dirty Harry interrupts a stickup in a restaurant, quickly disposes of two of the thugs, and then forces the third (who is holding a waitress as hostage) to surrender by raising his .44 Magnum and saying with icy disdain: "Go ahead. Make my day." The make-my-day remark soon became a catch phrase around the land, and President Reagan himself quoted it humorously when assailing congressional critics of his plans for tax revision.

President Reagan seems to have liked Sylvester Stallone's Rambo (1985) as much as he did Eastwood's Sudden Impact. In June 1985, shortly after the release of thirty-nine Americans who had been taken hostage by some Lebanese terrorists, he remarked: "Boy, I saw Rambo last night. I know what to do the next time this happens!"[9] It was easy to understand the President's enthusiasm. Stallone's film is thoroughly Reaganite; in telling the story of a dangerous mission undertaken by Stallone to rescue American soldiers missing in action during the Vietnam War, it not only displays the kind of macho derring-do that the President admires (and personally displayed in World War II's Desperate Journey, appearing in 1942), it also defends American military intervention in Vietnam in the 1960s and takes the view that the United States could have won the war had not the military been hamstrung by timorous leaders in Washington. Reagan was by no means alone in liking Rambo. The film broke all first-week box office records when it opened and continued to attract huge audiences for months afterward. "With Rambo," observed Marvin Antonowsky, who marketed the picture for Universal, "you're dealing with the emotional climate in this country. Audiences cheer when Stallone says that this time he hopes we'll win the Vietnam War." But he added thoughtfully: "If the picture had come out two years ago, nothing like this would have happened."[10]

Antonowsky was right about the timing. For years Hollywood had been skittish about treating the Vietnam War in films because of the deep division of opinion about it during the Johnson-Nixon years. Until 1974, when the United States withdrew its last forces from Vietnam, producers mainly avoided the issue or dealt with it obliquely. It wasn't, in fact, until 1978 that a movie appeared dealing directly with Vietnam—Coming Home with Jane Fonda—and it took a critical view of American intervention there. The Deer Hunter (1978) was similarly critical, and Apocalypse Now (1979), though more ambiguous, was certainly no paean to the Vietnam War. But with Reagan in the White House, hawkish conservatives began trumpeting their opinions with increasing confidence, and their views soon began appearing in films about Vietnam: *Uncommon Valor* (1983), *Missing in Action* (1984), and *Missing in Action 2—The Beginning* (1985). Like *Rambo*, the new Vietnam movies dealt with the rescue of American prisoners of war, officially listed as missing in action; like *Rambo*, they also took the new upbeat view of the once unpopular war. "People have been waiting for a chance to express their patriotism," said Stallone, as the *Rambo* fever spread. "*Rambo* triggered long-suppressed emotions that had been out of vogue."[11]

Richard Grenier, film critic for the ultraconservative *Commentary*, could barely conceal his joy at the turn of events. He had chafed at the antiestablishment films of the sixties; he adored the patriotic movies of the eighties. For Grenier, the contrast between *M*A*S*H* (1970) and *Stripes* (1981) was instructive. Both were army comedies, but the first maliciously damned the system and the second good-naturedly supported it. Grenier especially liked the funny speech that Bill Murray, the comic star of *Stripes,* makes to the sloppy platoon he is trying to whip into shape for the graduation parade the following day. "We're going to do this," cries Murray, "because we're Americans! And what does it mean to be an American? It means our forefathers were kicked out of every decent country in the world. We're mutts! Feel his nose! [And he feels the nose of one of the soldiers.] It's cold. You see? But there's nothing more lovable than a mutt! And we're American soldiers! Now, make me proud!" And his platoon makes a proud appearance the next day.[12]

There is certainly nothing lasting about the country's Reaganite mood. The country will change again—it has always oscillated between liberal and conservative impulses—and then the vast majority of the films of the Reagan Era will come to seem hopelessly dated, like most films of earlier eras. But the very best films of the eighties— films like *Amadeus* and *A Passage to India* (both 1984)—will doubtless continue to delight future generations of movie-lovers. The finest in films, as in other arts, has a long life.

Visual

Director Stanley Kubrick thought the average viewer was oriented more to words than to images. This accounted for the cool reception, he thought, that *2001: A Space Odyssey* (1968) received at the hands of the New York critics. Most of the critics conceded that the special effects in the picture were impressive, but looked in vain for "content," meaning characters, drama, and dialogue. It was young people, Kubrick observed, who assured his film's success. "At one point in the film," he said, "Dr. Floyd is asked where he is going. And he says, 'I'm going to Clavius,' which is a lunar crater. Then there are about fifteen shots of the moon following this statement, and we see Floyd going to the moon. But one critic was confused, because he thought Floyd was going to some planet named Clavius. I've asked a lot of kids: 'Do you know where this man went?' And they all replied: 'He went to the moon.' And when I asked, 'How did you know that,' they all said: 'Because we saw it.' Those who 'don't believe their eyes' are incapable of appreciating the film."[13]

Next Year
Once a man came up to Woody Allen and started exclaiming ecstatically, "You're a star, you're a star!" "This year I'm a star," sighed Allen afterward, "but what will I be next year—a black hole?"[14]

Immortality
"I don't want to achieve immortality through my work," Woody Allen once exclaimed. "I want to achieve it through not dying!"[15]

Cheaper
In *The Electric Horseman* (1979), Jane Fonda plays a TV reporter who gets to know an ex-rodeo star (Robert Redford) who travels around on horseback as a pitchman for a cereal. To get them to kiss the way he liked, director Sydney Pollack did forty-eight takes, between 9 A.M. Tuesday and 6 P.M. Wednesday, at a cost of $280,000. "It would have been cheaper," muttered the film's cost accountant, "if Redford had kissed the horse!"[16]

Eastwood Picture
While he was in New York on location for *Bronco Billy* (1980), Clint Eastwood agreed to a television interview. His host, somewhat hostile, began by defining a Clint Eastwood picture as a violent, ruthless, lawless, and bloody piece of mayhem, and then asked Eastwood himself to define a Clint Eastwood picture. "To me," said Eastwood calmly, "what a Clint Eastwood picture is, is one that I'm in."[17]

Heart

Since many movie studios are presently run by former agents, a recent Hollywood story had a patient going to see a surgeon about a heart transplant. "I'll give you a choice," the surgeon reportedly said. "You can either have the heart of a twenty-five-year-old marathon runner or a sixty-year-old agent. Which do you want?" "Easy," the patient answered, "let me have the agent's." The surgeon looked dumbfounded. "Why would you pick the heart of a sixty-year-old agent over a twenty-five-year-old marathon runner?" he asked. "I want one that's never been used," the patient replied.[18]

Totally Different

When Dustin Hoffman was playing the lead in Tootsie (1982), a film in which his character disguises himself as a woman in order to get a job, he went to the Russian Tea Room one day in costume to see how his makeup was working. There he ran into Jon Voight, his old co-star from Midnight Cowboy (1969). "I went up to him," Hoffman said later, "and told him how much I liked his work. We talked for twenty minutes. I finally had to tell him who I was."

Hoffman had a similar experience when he visited his daughter's school and palmed himself off as her Aunt Dorothy from Little Rock. The teacher had met Hoffman before, but this time she thought he really was the girl's aunt and started talking to him, he noticed, "as if she was talking to another woman. Which is much more open than when I was a man." When Hoffman got home he told his wife he had learned that "it is a totally different life being a woman. Life is different for a woman. I'm convinced of that."[19]

Topping It

When Dustin Hoffman's fans tell him they love the way he played a woman in Tootsie and ask him to do a sequel, he says it's a real possibility. "But," he adds, "I wouldn't want to do it unless I could top it. . . ." Then he brightens and says, "If I could give birth. . . ."[20]

Something for the Nerds

In the original version of Risky Business (1983), the high school boy (Tom Cruise) who turns his parents' home into a brothel for a night, loses his girl at the end of the picture and fails to get into college. At the preview, though, only 38 percent of the audience indicated they "would recommend" the picture. Faced with such a lukewarm reception, producer David Geffen decided that the "nerds in the audience needed to win something," and instructed director Paul Brickman to shoot a two-minute scene for the end of the film in which the boy learns that he did get into college. At the next preview 70 percent of the audience checked "would recommend" on their rating cards, and the picture went on to great success. Happy endings were popular with moviegoers again.[21]

Acne
"If Hollywood keeps gearing movie after movie to teen-agers," sighed comedian-director Mel Brooks in the mid-eighties, "next year's Oscar will develop acne."[22]

Totally Irrelevant
In the 1980s, Jack Nicholson, once the hero of young moviegoers because of the antiestablishment roles he played, was beginning to feel out of it. When he saw *Ferris Bueller's Day Off* (1986), a film about a high school kid (Matthew Broderick) who cuts school to go on the town with his pals, he could hardly sit through it. "That movie made me feel totally irrelevant to anything that any audience could want and [made me feel] 119 years old," he told an interviewer. "Believe me, everyone else watching it liked it. And, you know, I literally walked out of there thinking my days are numbered in the Hollywood film industry!"[23]

Save It
In *Stand by Me* (1986), Richard Dreyfuss plays the part of an author who is writing about his childhood, and since this is the 1980s he uses a word processor instead of a typewriter. At the end of the movie he types his last few words, reads them over, and then reaches over to turn off his machine before going out to play with his children. But in one New York theater, as he seemed for a moment about to turn his machine off before pressing the button to store what he had recorded on the disc, some of the people in the audience began shouting nervously, "Save it! Save it!"[24]

Shuffling
One day in the fall of 1986, Paul Newman, popular star of *The Hustler* (1961), *Hud* (1963), *The Sting* (1973), and *The Color of Money*

(1986), was strolling down New York's Fifth Avenue when he saw a woman in a white dress attracting a lot of attention. "A real stunner," he recalled. "Man, drivers were jumping the curb to get a better look." As he passed her, their eyes met, and a minute or two later, when he stopped to look in a shop window, he felt a tap on his shoulder. It was the woman in white; she explained that she was a call girl, but that for him she would skip the usual fee. Newman, known for his "cool" among countless fans, found himself blushing. "You think about how you would play a moment like that," he told an interviewer afterward. "You want to send her off with something classy and stylish, the way Cary Grant would, or Clint Eastwood. You think, how would Hombre handle this?" But Newman failed to rise to the occasion. "And when this woman came up to me—the guy who played Hud—what comes through?" he cried. "Laurel and Hardy. Both of them. All I could manage was this massive foot shuffling and dancing around, like a worm on the end of a hook." He jumped up to show his interviewer the Laurel-and-Hardy bit. "I was still shuffling," he added with a grin, "eight blocks later."[25]

Wicked Things
In the top-grossing *Back to the Future* (1985), the pint-size Michael J. Fox did so well in his role as a young man who travels back to 1955 that he became a superstar overnight. But he was bothered by the fact that his image was a bit too goody-goody and began looking for grittier roles. "I've been fortunate that up until this point I've been able to play nice guys," he told an interviewer in 1987. "But if a script popped across my desk that had an interesting character who happened to be a raving sex maniac, I'd consider playing him too." What "true-life experiences," asked the interviewer, would he have to fall back on? "I've done wicked things," Fox insisted. "What things?" "Well," he said, "if I wake up in the morning and my hair is messed up and pointing in nine million directions—almost to the point where I can pick up satellite transmissions—and I don't feel like combing it, then I won't."[26]

A Future in Politics
Ronald Reagan wasn't the only Hollywood actor to co-star with a monkey (*Bedtime for Bonzo*, 1951). Clint Eastwood appeared in two pictures (*Every Which Way but Loose*, 1978, and *Any Which Way You Can*, 1980) in which an orangutan named Clyde was his con-

stant companion. In April 1986, when Eastwood was elected mayor of California's Carmel-by-the-Sea, President Reagan exclaimed: "Can you imagine that? What makes him think a middle-aged movie actor who's played with a chimp could have a future in politics?"[27]

One of Us

In February 1987 actor Gene Hackman flew to Washington to promote his new film, *Hoosiers*, and officials of the Motion Picture Association of America arranged for him to go to the White House to meet President Ronald Reagan. To their surprise, Hackman showed signs of stage fright, so they reminded him that the President was "one of us, an actor." "I don't care if he came from Hollywood," said Hackman afterward. "When he's behind the desk in that room, he's the President of the United States. I haven't been that nervous in twenty years!"[28]

Real Person

One day, while shooting a scene, Jack Nicholson was thrown from a horse, landed on his face in the dirt, broke his wrist, and cut his lip. But he picked himself up, climbed back on the horse, and did the scene again. "I was scared," he admitted later. "I wouldn't have gotten back on the horse if I were a real person."[29]

Macho Image

In the spring of 1987, when Interior Secretary Donald P. Hodel sought a dramatic way to protect the nation's parks against vandals, he decided to turn for help to three of Hollywood's most popular tough guys: Charles Bronson *(Death Wish)*, Clint Eastwood *(Dirty Harry)*, and Lou Gossett, Jr. *(An Officer and a Gentleman)*. All three volunteered their services and were soon making sixty-second, thirty-second, and ten-second TV spots warning punks against trashing the public lands.

"Charles Bronson Isn't Happy," began one spot, and then Bronson appeared, looked disgusted, and announced: "Sure takes guts to vandalize public parks or beat up on trees. But that's what some jerks are doing to our public lands." Then he added grimly: "Only the land can't fight back. But we can—you and me. Let's face it, someone who gets his kicks punching out flowers shouldn't be too much of a match for us." The Eastwood spot began as the Bronson spot did: "Clint Eastwood Is a Little Upset." Then Eastwood entered and said firmly: "These people who are abusing our public lands can either clean up their act or get out of town." Lou Gossett, moviedom's toughest top kick, echoed the other two toughies. "Y'know," he declared on his spot, "we've got some real bad guys in this country—abusing public lands, defacing parks, robbing historic sites." Then he asked televiewers: "Are you going to let a bunch of bad guys run us off our public lands? Or are you going to help us save the lands?"

When the interior secretary sponsored the tough-guy spots, he hoped the "macho image" these performers projected on the screen would "put a negative social stigma" on people who might abuse public lands. If it did, it would undoubtedly "make his day."[30]

CHAPTER

Notes

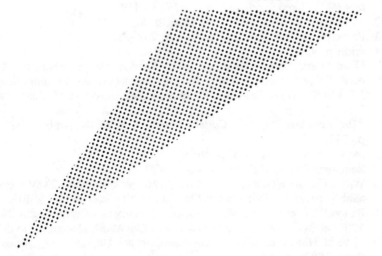

Preface

1. David Niven, *Bring on the Empty Horses* (N.Y.: Putnam, 1975), p. 297; Bill Davidson, "The Mutiny of Marlon Brando," *The Saturday Evening Post,* CCXXXV (June 16, 1962), p. 18.
2. *The New York Review of Books,* November 7, 1985, p. 26.
3. Mashey M. Bernstein, "The Birth of an American," *Newsweek,* CV (July 15, 1985), p. 12.
4. Quoted, *The New York Times Book Review,* August 4, 1985, p. 1.
5. Arthur M. Schlesinger, Jr., "The Duplicitous Art," *Saturday Review,* V (October 29, 1977), p. 46.
6. Leo C. Rosten, *Hollywood: The Movie Colony* (N.Y.: Harcourt, Brace, 1941), p. 51.
7. Rex Reed, "And They Lived Happily . . . etc.," *The New York Times,* January 18, 1970, p. D13.
8. Ibid.
9. Bosley Crowther, *Hollywood Rajah: The Life and Times of Louis B. Mayer* (N.Y.: Holt, 1960), pp. 277–78.
10. Samuel Marx, *Mayer and Thalberg: The Make-Believe Saints* (N.Y.: Random House, 1975), p. 167.
11. Jack Severson, "Actor Marvin Is All He Seems to Be," *Fort Worth Star-Telegram,* April 22, 1979, p. 12a; Dan Wakefield, "Dan Wakefield's Guilty Pleasures," *Film Comment,* XXI (July–August 1985), p. 28.

I. The Beginning

Chapter 1. *Penny Arcades and Nickelodeons*

1. Terry Ramsaye, *A Million and One Nights: A History of the Motion Picture* (N.Y.: Simon and Schuster, 1926), p. 119.
2. *The New York Times*, April 24, 1896, p. 5.
3. Ramsaye, *Million and One Nights*, pp. 232–33.
4. Ibid., p. 425.
5. Lloyd Morris, *Not So Long Ago* (N.Y.: Random House, 1949), p. 34.
6. A. R. Fulton, *Motion Pictures: The Development of an Art from Silent Films to the Age of Television* (Norman, Okla.: University of Oklahoma Press, 1960), p. 54.
7. "The Actorless Theatre," *Current Literature*, XLVII (November 1909), p. 555.
8. Morris, *Not So Long Ago*, p. 46.
9. Ramsaye, *Million and One Nights*, p. 473.
10. William Dean Howells, "Easy Chair," *Harper's Monthly*, CXXV (September 1912), p. 635; *Current Opinion*, LVII (August 1914), p. 105.
11. Barton W. Currie, "The Nickel Madness," *Harper's Weekly*, August 24, 1907, in Gerald Mast, ed., *The Movies in Our Midst: Documents in the Cultural History of Film in America* (Chicago: University of Chicago Press, 1982), p. 49.
12. Ramsaye, *Million and One Nights*, pp. 257–60, 270–71.
13. Ibid., p. 397.
14. Arthur Mayer, *Merely Colossal* (N.Y.: Simon and Schuster, 1953), pp. 23–24.
15. *Moving Picture World*, I (June 29, 1907), p. 270.
16. Ibid., II (February 22, 1908), p. 270.
17. Ibid., II (April 4, 1908), p. 291.
18. Ibid., II (May 23, 1908), p. 458.
19. Ibid., XII (May 11, 1912), p. 518.

Chapter 2. *Silent Features*

1. Louis Reeves Harrison, *Moving Picture World*, XII (April 6, 1912), p. 23.
2. Arthur Knight, *The Liveliest Art* (N.Y.: Macmillan, 1957), p. 37.
3. Lloyd Morris, *Not So Long Ago* (N.Y.: Random House, 1949), p. 60.
4. Ibid., p. 71; Laurence Kardish, *Reel Plastic Magic* (Boston: Little, Brown, 1972), p. 71.
5. Knight, *Liveliest Art*, p. 35.
6. Morris, *Not So Long Ago*, p. 199.
7. Ibid., p. 76.
8. Gilbert Seldes, *The 7 Lively Arts* (N.Y.: Harper, 1924), p. 20.
9. Knight, *Liveliest Art*, p. 41.
10. Adolph Zukor, *The Public Is Never Wrong* (N.Y.: Putnam, 1953), p.

154; Charles Chaplin, *My Autobiography* (N.Y.: Simon and Schuster, 1964), pp. 144–46.

11. Lionel Barrymore, *We Barrymores* (N.Y.: Appleton-Century-Crofts, 1951), p. 149.
12. Karl Brown, *Adventures with D. W. Griffith* (N.Y.: Farrar, Straus and Giroux, 1973), p. 167.
13. Josef von Sternberg, *Fun in a Chinese Laundry* (N.Y.: Macmillan, 1965), p. 31.
14. Lillian Gish, *Lillian Gish: The Movies, Mr. Griffith, and Me* (Englewood Cliffs, N.J.: Prentice-Hall, 1969), p. 76; James Kotsilibas-Davis, *The Barrymores* (N.Y.: Crown Publishers, 1981), p. 9.
15. Terry Ramsaye, *A Million and One Nights* (N.Y.: Simon and Schuster, 1926), p. 766; Bob Thomas, *Selznick* (Garden City, N.Y.: Doubleday, 1969), p. 16.
16. Michael Wood, "A Traveling Man," *The New York Review of Books*, December 6, 1984, p. 10; Arthur Mayer, *Merely Colossal* (N.Y.: Simon and Schuster, 1953), p. 26; Mervyn LeRoy, interview taped in Los Angeles, May 16, 1977, Southern Methodist University Oral History Collection.
17. A. B. Paine, *Life and Lillian Gish* (N.Y.: Macmillan, 1932), pp. 99, 115, 147–48, 158–59, 200, 208, 231, 235, 273; Gish, *Lillian Gish*, pp. 232–34; Michael Wood, *The New York Review of Books*, December 6, 1984, p. 10.
18. Richard Griffith and Arthur Mayer, *The Movies* (N.Y.: Bonanza Books, 1957), p. 151.
19. Paine, *Life and Lillian Gish*, pp. 218–19; King Vidor, in Richard Schickel, *Men Who Made the Movies* (N.Y.: Atheneum, 1975), p. 139.
20. Ralph Hancock, *Douglas Fairbanks: The Fourth Musketeer* (N.Y.: Holt, 1953), pp. 136–37.
21. Ibid., p. 168.
22. "Cal York's Monthly Broadcast from Hollywood," *Photoplay*, XLI (September 1932), p. 94; Samuel Marx, *Mayer and Thalberg: The Make-Believe Saints* (N.Y.: Random House, 1975), p. 101.
23. Gish, *Lillian Gish*, p. 295; Frances Marion, *Off with Their Heads!* (N.Y.: Macmillan, 1972), p. 150.
24. Zukor, *Public Never Wrong*, p. 210; Robert Oberfirst, *Rudolph Valentino: The Man Behind the Myth* (N.Y.: Citadel, 1962), pp. 298–309; see also Irving Schulman, *Valentino* (N.Y.: Trident Press, 1968), pp. 259–63.
25. Cecil B. De Mille, *Autobiography* (Englewood Cliffs, N.J.: Prentice-Hall, 1959), p. 216.
26. Phil A. Koury, *Yes, Mr. De Mille* (N.Y.: Putnam, 1959), p. 87; Norman Zierold, *The Moguls* (N.Y.: Coward-McCann, 1969), p. 132; Frank Manchel, *Cameras West* (Englewood Cliffs, N.J.: Prentice-Hall, 1971), p. 34; Arthur Mayer, *Merely Colossal* (N.Y.: Simon and Schuster, 1953), p. 33.
27. De Mille, *Autobiography*, pp. 215–16; William C. De Mille, *Hollywood Saga* (N.Y.: Dutton, 1939), pp. 140–44.

28. De Mille, *Autobiography*, pp. 157–58.
29. Ibid., p. 263.

Chapter 3. *The Coming of Sound*

1. *Photoplay*, XXXVIII (September 1930), p. 28, a reprint of an editorial first appearing in May 1921, p. 19.
2. "Let's Drop in and Gossip with Old Cal York," *Photoplay*, XXXVIII (October 1930), p. 128.
3. Kevin Brownlow, *The Parade's Gone By* (N.Y.: Knopf, 1968), p. 566.
4. Benjamin Hampton, *History of the American Film Industry* (N.Y.: Covici, 1931), p. 566.
5. Brownlow, *Parade's Gone By*, p. 566.
6. Stark Young, "A Terrible Thing," *The New Republic*, LII (September 14, 1927), pp. 98–99.
7. Leonard Mosley, *Zanuck: The Rise and Fall of Hollywood's Last Tycoon* (Boston: Little, Brown, 1984), pp. 100–103.
8. *The New York Times*, October 7, 1927, p. 24.
9. "Al Jolson with Vitaphone Noises," *Photoplay*, XXXIII (March 1927), p. 144.
10. Cal York, "Gossip of All the Studios," *Photoplay*, XXXIV (November 1928), p. 101; "The Talkies," *Time*, XII (July 9, 1928), p. 39.
11. Lloyd Morris, *Not So Long Ago* (N.Y.: Random House, 1949), p. 193; Richard Griffith and Arthur Mayer, *The Movies* (N.Y.: Bonanza Books, 1957), p. 246; Brownlow, *Parade's Gone By*, p. 575; Adolph Zukor, *The Public Is Never Wrong* (N.Y.: Putnam, 1953), pp. 254–55.
12. Brownlow, *Parade's Gone By*, p. 576; Zukor, *Public Never Wrong*, p. 255; Cal York, "Through the Studios with Pen and Camera," *Photoplay*, XXXVII (January 1930), p. 42; Katherine Albert, "Is Jack Gilbert Through?" *Photoplay*, XXXVII (February 1930), pp. 128–29; Hedda Hopper, *From Under My Hat* (Garden City, N.Y.: Doubleday, 1952), pp. 200–201.
13. Cal York, "Gossip of All the Studios," *Photoplay*, XXXV (January 1929), p. 47.
14. Morris, *Not So Long Ago*, p. 193; Griffith and Mayer, *The Movies*, pp. 249–53.
15. Louella Parsons, *The Gay Illiterate* (Garden City, N.Y.: Doubleday, 1944), p. 117.
16. Gilbert Seldes, "The Movies Commit Suicide," *Harper's*, CLVII (November 1928), p. 711.
17. Ibid., p. 706.
18. Bob Thomas, *Thalberg: Life and Legend* (Garden City, N.Y.: Doubleday, 1969), p. 146; James R. Quirk, "Close-Ups and Long Shots," *Photoplay*, XXXVII (May 1930), p. 30; James Kotsilibas-Davis, *The Barrymores: The Royal Family in Hollywood* (Englewood Cliffs, N.J.: Crown, 1981), p. 78; Pat O'Brien, *The Wind at My Back: The Life and Times of Pat*

O'Brien (Garden City, N.Y.: Doubleday, 1965), p. 197; "Talking Art into the Talkies," *Literary Digest*, CI (April 20, 1929), p. 27.

19. *Photoplay*, XXXV (January 1929), p. 93; Cal York, "Gossip of All the Studios," Ibid. (April 1929), p. 48; Ibid., XXXIV (November 1928), p. 48; "Talking of Talkies," Ibid., XXXVII (May 1930), p. 150; Bosley Crowther, *Hollywood Rajah: The Life and Times of Louis B. Mayer* (N.Y.: Holt, 1960), p. 134.

20. Crowther, *Hollywood Rajah*, p. 134; James R. Quirk, "Close-Ups and Long Shots," *Photoplay*, XXXVII (February 1930), p. 28; "Wanted—A New Name for Talkies," Ibid., XXXV (March 1929), p. 29.

21. Tom Dardis, *Keaton: The Man Who Wouldn't Lie Down* (N.Y.: Scribner, 1979), p. 184.

22. Cal York, "Gossip of All the Studios," *Photoplay*, XXXVI (November 1928), p. 48; Ibid. (March 1929), p. 96; Ibid., XXXVII (December 1929), p. 30.

23. Gary Cooper, "Well, It Was This Way," *The Saturday Evening Post*, CCXXVIII (March 24, 1956), p. 139.

24. Stuart M. Kaminsky, *Coop: The Life and Legend of Gary Cooper* (N.Y.: St. Martin's, 1980), pp. 44–45.

25. Brownlow, *Parade's Gone By*, p. 574; William C. De Mille, *Hollywood Saga* (N.Y.: Dutton, 1939), p. 292.

26. Griffith and Mayer, *The Movies*, p. 247.

27. "Let's Drop in and Gossip with Old Cal York," *Photoplay*, XXXVIII (October 1930), p. 128.

28. Cal York, "Through the Studios with Pen and Camera," *Photoplay*, XXX-VII (January 1930), p. 114.

29. Ibid., p. 113.

30. Ibid., p. 42.

31. "Let's Drop in and Gossip with Old Cal York," *Photoplay*, XXXIX (September 1930), p. 47.

II. Production

Chapter 4. *Moguls*

1. Douglas Gomery, *The Hollywood Studio System* (N.Y.: St. Martin's, 1986), p. 6.

2. Gregory Peck, interview taped in Los Angeles, August 22, 1980, Southern Methodist University Oral History Collection.

3. Arthur Mayer, in Bernard Rosenberg and Harry Silverstein, *The Real Tinsel* (N.Y.: Macmillan, 1970), p. 168.

4. LeRoy Prinz, interview taped in Los Angeles, July 16, 1975, SMUOHC.

5. Eugene Zukor, interview taped in Los Angeles, July 31, 1975, SMUOHC.

6. Ibid.

7. Gary Carey, *All the Stars in Heaven* (N.Y.: Dutton, 1981), p. 181.

8. Marshall Thompson, interview taped in Los Angeles, August 22, 1980, SMUOHC.

9. Ezra Goodman, *The Fifty-Year Decline and Fall of Hollywood* (N.Y.: Simon and Schuster, 1961), p. 173.

10. Melville Shavelson, in Michael Freedland, *The Warner Brothers* (N.Y.: St. Martin's, 1983), p. 3.

11. Freedland, *Warner Brothers*, p. 173; Norman Zierold, *The Moguls* (N.Y.: Coward-McCann, 1969), p. 236.

12. Freedland, *Warner Brothers*, p. 222.

13. Ibid., p. 1.

14. Ibid., p. 107.

15. Zierold, *Moguls*, p. 195.

16. Bob Thomas, *King Cohn* (N.Y.: Putnam, 1967), p. 142; Charles Bennett, interview taped in Los Angeles, August 14, 1980, SMUOHC.

17. Thomas, *King Cohn*, p. v.

18. Ibid., p. 6.

19. Zierold, *Moguls*, p. 200.

20. Mala Powers, interview taped in Los Angeles, July 26, 1984, SMUOHC; Jean Negulesco, *Things I Did and Things I Think I Did* (N.Y.: Simon and Schuster, 1984), pp. 171–73.

21. Vincent Sherman, interview taped in Los Angeles, August 5, 1981, SMUOHC.

22. Zierold, *Moguls*, p. 261.

23. William Tuttle, interview taped by Ann Burk in Los Angeles, August 12, 1976, SMUOHC; Bosley Crowther, *Hollywood Rajah: The Life and Times of Louis B. Mayer* (N.Y.: Holt, 1960), pp. 7–8; Zierold, *Moguls*, p. 290.

24. Jack Warner, *My First Hundred Years in Hollywood* (N.Y.: Random House, 1964), p. 201; Mervyn LeRoy, interview taped in Los Angeles, May 16, 1977, SMUOHC.

25. Thomas, *King Cohn*, pp. 244–45.

26. Ralph Bellamy, interview taped in Los Angeles, May 18, 1977, SMUOHC; Bellamy, *When the Smoke Hit the Fan* (Garden City, N.Y.: Doubleday, 1979), pp. 122–24.

27. Warner, *My First Hundred Years*, pp. 22–23.

28. Samuel Marx, *Mayer and Thalberg* (N.Y.: Random House, 1975), p. 201.

29. Warner, *My First Hundred Years*, p. 9; Freedland, *Warner Brothers*, pp. 136–37; Zierold, *Moguls*, p. 235.

30. Dolly Haas, interview taped in New York City, October 6, 1986, SMUOHC.

31. Dickie Moore, *Twinkle, Twinkle, Little Star* (N.Y.: Harper and Row, 1984), pp. 178–79; Walter Wagner, *You Must Remember This* (N.Y.: Putnam, 1975), p. 114.

Chapter 5. *Studio Life*

1. Janet Leigh, interview taped in Los Angeles, July 25, 1984, Southern Methodist University Oral History Collection.
2. Harry Warren, interview taped in Los Angeles, October 24, 1977, SMUOHC.
3. Lizabeth Scott, interview taped in Los Angeles, July 27, 1984, SMUOHC.
4. Pat O'Brien, interview taped in Dallas, February 4, 1975, SMUOHC.
5. Irving Rapper, interview taped in Los Angeles, August 13, 1980, SMUOHC.
6. Charles Walters, interview taped in Los Angeles, August 21, 1980, SMUOHC.
7. Gene Autry, interview taped in Los Angeles, July 24, 1984, SMUOHC.
8. Helen Hayes, interview taped in Nyack, N.Y., October 19, 1979, SMUOHC.
9. Ralph Bellamy, interview taped in Los Angeles, May 18, 1977, SMUOHC.
10. Fernando Lamas, interview taped in Los Angeles, August 6 and 14, 1981, SMUOHC.
11. Carolyn Jones, interview taped in Los Angeles, August 3, 1976, SMUOHC.
12. Jayne Meadows, interview taped in Dallas, November 11, 1975, SMUOHC.
13. Arlene Dahl, interview taped in Dallas, September 24, 1975, SMUOHC.
14. Joan Lorring, interview taped in New York City, January 7 and 11, 1985, SMUOHC.
15. Meadows interview.
16. Pauline Kessinger, interview taped in Los Angeles, July 29, 1976, SMUOHC; Norman Zierold, *The Moguls* (N.Y.: Coward-McCann, 1969), p. 179.
17. Keenan Wynn, interview taped in Los Angeles, July 18, 1984, SMUOHC.
18. Tay Garnett, *Light Your Torches and Pull Up Your Tights* (New Rochelle, N.Y.: Arlington House, 1973), pp. 259–60.
19. Jack Warner, *My First Hundred Years in Hollywood* (N.Y.: Random House, 1964), p. 282.
20. Colleen Moore, *Silent Star* (Garden City, N.Y.: Doubleday, 1968), p. 100.
21. Ann Doran, interview taped in Los Angeles, August 10 and 15, 1983, SMUOHC.

Chapter 6. *Producers*

1. Harry Carey, Jr., interview taped in Los Angeles, July 23, 1984, Southern Methodist University Oral History Collection.

2. Andrew Sinclair, *John Ford* (N.Y.: Dial, 1979), p. 52.
3. Joseph Ruttenberg, interview taped in Los Angeles, August 18 and 24, 1978, SMUOHC.
4. Arthur Mayer, in Bernard Rosenberg and Harry Silverstein, *The Real Tinsel* (N.Y.: Macmillan, 1970), p. 158.
5. Willi Frischauer, *Behind the Scenes of Otto Preminger* (N.Y.: Morrow, 1974), p. 138.
6. Norman Zierold, *The Moguls* (N.Y.: Coward-McCann, 1969), p. 120.
7. Walter Wagner, *You Must Remember This* (N.Y.: Putnam, 1975), pp. 106–7.
8. Zierold, *Moguls*, p. 119.
9. Arthur Marx, *Goldwyn* (N.Y.: Norton, 1976), p. 119.
10. Joan Fontaine, interview taped in Dallas, April 12, 1979, SMUOHC.
11. Charles Bennett, interview taped in Los Angeles, August 14, 1980, SMUOHC.
12. Irving Rapper, interview taped in Los Angeles, August 13, 1980, SMUOHC.
13. Lizabeth Scott, interview taped in Los Angeles, July 27, 1984, SMUOHC.
14. Pandro S. Berman, interview taped in Los Angeles, August 21, 1978, SMUOHC.
15. Joseph and Juanita Walker, *The Light on Her Face* (Hollywood, Calif.: ASC, 1984), p. 256.
16. William Wyler, interview taped in Los Angeles, July 19, 1979, SMUOHC.
17. Zierold, *Moguls*, p. 65.
18. Albin Krebs, "Sam Spiegel, Film Maker Is Dead at 84," *The New York Times*, January 1, 1986, p. 20.
19. Carol Easton, *The Search for Sam Goldwyn* (N.Y.: Morrow, 1976), p. 150; Alva Johnston, "The Great Goldwyn," *The Saturday Evening Post*, CCIX (May 8, 1937), p. 82.
20. Stephen Farber and Marc Green, *Hollywood Dynasties* (N.Y.: Delilah, 1984), p. 31.
21. Easton, *Search for Sam Goldwyn*, pp. 246–47.
22. Michael Freedland, *The Warner Brothers* (N.Y.: St. Martin's, 1983), p. 161.
23. Alva Johnston, "The Great Goldwyn," *The Saturday Evening Post,* CCIX (May 22, 1937), p. 24.
24 Leo C. Rosten, *Hollywood: The Movie Colony* (N.Y.: Harcourt, Brace, 1941), p. 35.
25. Arthur Mayer, *Merely Colossal* (N.Y.: Simon and Schuster, 1953), p. 49.

Chapter 7. *Directors*

1. Fritz Lang, in Bernard Rosenberg and Harry Silverstein, *The Real Tinsel* (N.Y.: Macmillan, 1970), p. 347.
2. Edward Dmytryk, *On Screen Directing* (Boston: Focal, 1984), p. viii.

3. Dmytryk, interview taped in Austin, Tex., December 2, 1979, Southern Methodist University Oral History Collection.
4. Vincent Sherman, interview taped in Los Angeles, August 5, 1981, SMUOHC.
5. Signe Hasso, interview taped in Los Angeles, August 16, 1980, SMUOHC.
6. Sherman interview.
7. Eugene Zukor, interview taped in Los Angeles, July 31, 1975, SMUOHC.
8. LeRoy Prinz, interview taped in Los Angeles, July 16, 1975, SMUOHC.
9. Yul Brynner, interview taped in Los Angeles, August 1, 1975, SMUOHC.
10. Robert Stack with Mark Evans, *Straight Shooting* (N.Y.: Macmillan, 1980), p. 117.
11. Rise Stevens, interview taped in New York City, January 8, 1982, SMUOHC.
12. Walter Wanger, *You Must Remember This* (N.Y.: Putnam, 1975), p. 55.
13. Harry Carey, Jr., interview taped in Los Angeles, July 23, 1984, SMUOHC.
14. George Cukor, interview taped in Los Angeles, May 27, 1977, SMUOHC.
15. Rouben Mamoulian, interview taped in Los Angeles, August 19, 1980, SMUOHC.
16. Walter Abel, interview taped in New York City, January 5, 1979, SMUOHC; Jean Negulesco, *Things I Did and Things I Think I Did* (N.Y.: Simon and Schuster, 1984), p. 106.
17. Abel interview.
18. Ring Lardner, Jr., interview taped in New York City, January 11, 1985, SMUOHC.
19. Bob Thomas, *Marlon* (N.Y.: Random House, 1973), p. 168.
20. Hal Wallis and Charles Higham, *Starmaker* (N.Y.: Macmillan, 1980), p. 24.
21. Jack Warner, *My First Hundred Years in Hollywood* (N.Y.: Random House, 1964), pp. 9–10.
22. Hal Wallis, interview taped in Los Angeles, July 20, 1982, SMUOHC.
23. Charles Bennett, interview taped in Los Angeles, August 14, 1980, SMUOHC.
24. Tippi Hedren, interview taped in Acton, Calif., July 24, 1982, SMUOHC.
25. William Wyler, interview taped in Los Angeles, July 19, 1979, SMUOHC.
26. Gregory Peck, interview taped in Los Angeles, August 21, 1978, SMUOHC.
27. Ralph Blane, interview taped in Tulsa, Okla., March 12, 1979, SMUOHC.
28. James Cagney, *Cagney by Cagney* (Garden City, N.Y.: Doubleday, 1976), p. 151.
29. Dmytryk, *On Screen Directing*, p. 31.

30. Michael Sragow, "A conversation with Steven Spielberg," *Rolling Stone* (July 22, 1982), p. 28.

31. "I Dream for a Living," *Time* CXXV (July 15, 1985), p. 54.

32. Prinz interview; Henry Wilcoxon, interview taped in Los Angeles, August 25, 1983, SMUOHC; Norman Zierold, *The Moguls* (N.Y.: Coward-McCann, 1969), pp. 175–76; Phil A. Koury, *Yes, Mr. De Mille* (N.Y.: Putnam, 1959), pp. 158–59; *Time*, XX (December 5, 1932), p. 32.

33. Keenan Wynn, interview taped in Los Angeles, July 18, 1984, SMUOHC.

34. Barbara Leming, *Orson Welles* (N.Y.: Viking, 1985), pp. 194–95.

35. Jesse L. Lasky, Jr., *Whatever Happened to Hollywood?* (N.Y.: W. H. Allen, 1973), pp. 132–33.

36. Marshall Thompson, interview taped in Los Angeles, August 22, 1980, SMUOHC.

37. Kevin Brownlow, *The War, The West, and The Wilderness* (N.Y.: Knopf, 1979), p. 391.

38. Dick Sheppard, *Elizabeth: The Life and Career of Elizabeth Taylor* (Garden City, N.Y.: Doubleday, 1974).

39. Gerd Oswald, interview taped in Los Angeles, July 20, 1979, SMUOHC.

40. Koury, *Yes, Mr. De Mille*, pp. 140–41.

41. Pat O'Brien, interview taped in Dallas, February 4, 1975, SMUOHC.

42. Donald Spoto, *The Dark Side of Genius* (Boston: Little, Brown, 1983), p. 269.

43. Carol Easton, *The Search for Sam Goldwyn* (N.Y.: Morrow, 1976), p. 219.

44. Samuel Marx, *Mayer and Thalberg* (N.Y.: Random House, 1975), p. 34.

45. Wyler interview.

46. Joseph Henry Steele, *Ingrid Bergman: An Intimate Portrait* (N.Y.: McKay, 1959), p. 27.

47. Easton, *Search for Sam Goldwyn*, pp. 162–63.

Chapter 8. *Writers*

1. Mervyn LeRoy, interview taped in Los Angeles, May 16, 1977, Southern Methodist University Oral History Collection.

2. Edward Buzzell, interview taped in Los Angeles, July 17, 1982, SMUOHC.

3. Gregory Peck, interview taped in Los Angeles, August 22, 1980, SMUOHC.

4. Charles Marquis Warren, interview taped in Los Angeles, August 14 and 20, 1980, SMUOHC.

5. Walter Wanger, in Bernard Rosenberg and Harry Silverstein, *The Real Tinsel* (N.Y.: Macmillan, 1970), pp. 85–86.

6. Edward Dmytryk, interview taped in Austin, Tex., December 2, 1979, SMUOHC.

7. Ibid.

8. Robert Nathan, interview taped in Los Angeles, August 12, 1981, SMUOHC.

9. Melville Shavelson, interview taped in Los Angeles, August 8, 1981, SMUOHC.

10. Dorris Bowdon Johnson, interview taped in Los Angeles, August 11, 1981, SMUOHC.

11. Jean Negulesco, *Things I Did and Things I Think I Did* (N.Y.: Simon and Schuster, 1984), p. 140.

12. Dorris Johnson and Ellen Leventhal, *The Letters of Nunnally Johnson* (N.Y.: Knopf, 1981), p. 233.

13. John H. Lenihan, *Showdown* (Urbana, Ill.: University of Illinois Press, 1980), pp. 119–20.

14. Charles Bennett, interview taped in Los Angeles, August 14, 1980, SMUOHC.

15. Adolphe Menjou, *It Took Nine Tailors* (N.Y.: McGraw, 1948), pp. 103–4.

16. Sheilah Graham, *Beloved Infidel* (N.Y.: Holt, 1958), p. 214.

17. John Gregory Dunne, "So You Want to Write a Movie," *Atlantic Monthly*, CCXXXIV (July 1974), p. 42.

18. W. R. Robinson, ed., *Man and the Movies* (Baton Rouge, La.: Louisiana State University, 1967), p. 268.

19. Michael Freedland, *The Warner Brothers* (N.Y.: St. Martin's, 1983), p. 172. Screenwriter Curt Siodmak tells a similar story about one of the Epstein twins.

20. Carol Easton, *The Search for Sam Goldwyn* (N.Y.: Morrow, 1976), p. 187.

21. Shavelson interview.

22. Marjorie Johnson Fowler, interview taped in Los Angeles, July 20, 1985, SMUOHC.

23. William F. Nolan, *John Huston, King Rebel* (Los Angeles: Sherbourne, 1965), pp. 63–67; John Huston, *An Open Book* (N.Y.: Knopf, 1980), pp. 138–45; Stuart Kaminsky, *John Huston, Maker of Magic* (Boston: Houghton Mifflin, 1978), pp. 49–50.

24. Arthur Marx, *Goldwyn* (N.Y.: Norton, 1976), pp. 310–11; Axel Madsen, *William Wyler* (N.Y.: Crowell, 1973), pp 126–27.

25. Jack Warner, *My First Hundred Years in Hollywood* (N.Y.: Random House, 1964), pp. 309–10; Freedland, *Warner Brothers*, pp. 171–72.

26. Ben Hecht, *A Child of the Century* (N.Y.: Simon and Schuster, 1954), pp. 486–87.

27. Garson Kanin, *Hollywood* (N.Y.: Viking, 1974), p. 244.

28. Kenneth Barrow, *Helen Hayes* (Garden City, N.Y.: Doubleday, 1985), pp. 132–33.

29. Carolyn Jones, interview taped in Los Angeles, August 3, 1976, SMUOHC.

Chapter 9. *Discovery and Casting*

1. Robert Sklar, *Movie-Made America* (N.Y.: Vintage, 1976), p. 228.
2. Jayne Meadows, interview taped in Dallas, November 11, 1975, Southern Methodist University Oral History Collection.
3. Arlene Dahl, interview taped in Dallas, September 24, 1975, SMUOHC.
4. Ezra Goodman, *The Fifty-Year Decline and Fall of Hollywood* (N.Y.: Simon and Schuster, 1961), p. 243.
5. Allan Jones, interview taped in New York City, January 9, 1985, SMUOHC.
6. Martha Hyer, interview taped in Los Angeles, July 30, 1982, SMUOHC.
7. Edward Dmytryk, *On Screen Directing* (Boston: Focal, 1984), p. 29.
8. Harry Lang, "Einstein in Hollywood," *Photoplay*, XXXIX (April 1931), p. 36.
9. David Niven, *The Moon's a Balloon* (N.Y.: Putnam, 1972), pp. 197–98.
10. LeRoy Prinz, interview taped in Los Angeles, July 16, 1975, SMUOHC.
11. Leonard Mosley, *Zanuck: The Rise and Fall of Hollywood's Last Tycoon* (Boston: Little, Brown, 1984), p. 114.
12. Henry Wilcoxon, interview taped in Los Angeles, August 25, 1983, SMUOHC.
13. Mary Martin, interview taped in Dallas, June 11, 1984, SMUOHC.
14. Larry Swindell, *Body and Soul* (N.Y.: Morrow, 1975), p. 111.
15. Iron Eyes Cody and Collin Perry, *Iron Eyes* (N.Y.: Everest House, 1982), p. 86.
16. Lucille Ball, interview taped in Los Angeles, August 21, 1980, SMUOHC; Bob Thomas, *King Cohn* (N.Y.: Putnam, 1967), pp. 246–48; Desi Arnaz, *A Book* (N.Y.: Morrow, 1976), pp. 234–35.
17. Sherryl Connelly, "Who're You Calling a Bimbo?" New York *Daily News*, August 17, 1986, p. 14.
18. Dina Merrill, interview taped in New York City, January 8, 1985, SMUOHC.
19. Yul Brynner, interview taped in Los Angeles, August 1, 1975, SMUOHC.

Chapter 10. *Actors and Actresses*

1. Louella O. Parsons, *The Gay Illiterate* (Garden City, N.Y.: Doubleday, 1944), p. 42.
2. Norman Zierold, *The Moguls* (N.Y.: Coward-McCann, 1969), p. 93; Kevin Brownlow, *Hollywood: The Pioneers* (N.Y.: Knopf, 1979), p. 156.
3. Jesse L. Lasky, Jr., *Whatever Happened to Hollywood?* (N.Y.: W. H. Allen, 1975), p. 188.
4. Cal York, "The Monthly Broadcast of Hollywood Goings-On!" *Photoplay*, XXXIX (February 9, 1931), p. 48; Leatrice Gilbert Fountain, *Dark Star* (N.Y.: St. Martin's, 1985), p. 171.

5. Walter Abel, interview taped in New York City, January 5, 1979, Southern Methodist University Oral History Collection.

6. Gregory Peck, interview taped in Dallas, November 3, 1974, SMUOHC.

7. Mervyn LeRoy, interview taped in Los Angeles, May 16 1977, SMUOHC.

8. Allen Eyles, *James Stewart* (N.Y.: Stein and Day, 1984), p. 14.

9. George Cukor, interview taped in Los Angeles, May 27, 1977, SMUOHC.

10. Lloyd Nolan, interview taped in Los Angeles, July 28, 1976, SMUOHC.

11. King Vidor, interview taped in Los Angeles, August 4, 1975, SMUOHC.

12. Ezra Goodman, *The Fifty-Year Decline and Fall of Hollywood* (N.Y.: Simon and Schuster, 1961), p. 257.

13. Lizabeth Scott, interview taped in Los Angeles, July 27, 1984, SMUOHC.

14. Bob Thomas, *Joan Crawford* (N.Y.: Simon and Schuster, 1978), p. 57.

15. Irving Rapper, interview taped in Los Angeles, August 13, 1980, SMUOHC.

16. Gary Carey, *Katharine Hepburn* (N.Y.: St. Martin's, 1983), p. 180.

17. Rosemary DeCamp, interview taped in Los Angeles, July 13, 1982, SMUOHC.

18. Helen Hayes, interview taped in Nyack, N.Y., October 19, 1979, SMUOHC.

19. Gordon MacRae, interview taped in Dallas, October 25, 1979, SMUOHC.

20. Gregory Peck, interview taped in Los Angeles, August 21, 1978, SMUOHC.

21. Abel interview; Edward Buzzell, interview taped in Los Angeles, July 17, 1982, SMUOHC.

22. Pandro Berman, interview taped in Los Angeles, August 21, 1978, SMUOHC.

23. Benay Venuta, interview taped in New York City, January 5, 1979, SMUOHC.

24. Vincent Sherman, interview taped in Los Angeles, August 5, 1981, SMUOHC.

25. Fernando Lamas, interview taped in Los Angeles, August 6 and 14, 1981, SMUOHC.

26. Florence Henderson, interview taped in Los Angeles, August 18, 1983, SMUOHC.

27. Tichi Wilkerson and Marcia Borie, *The Hollywood Reporter* (N.Y.: Coward-McCann, 1984), p. 60.

28. Fountain, *Dark Star*, p. 230.

29. Cesar Romero, interview taped in Dallas, February 26, 1979, SMUOHC.

30. Keenan Wynn, interview taped in Los Angeles, July 18, 1984, SMUOHC.

31. *Time*, CXXVIII (October 27, 1986), p. 103.

32. Ralph Bellamy, interview taped in Los Angeles, May 18, 1977, SMUOHC; Bellamy, *When the Smoke Hit the Fan* (Garden City, N.Y.: Doubleday, 1979), pp. 111–12.
33. Marshall Thompson, interview taped in Los Angeles, August 22, 1980, SMUOHC.
34. Elston Brooks, "But He Came Back to Haunt the Living," *Fort Worth Star-Telegram*, September 28, 1986, p. 4D.
35. Jean Negulesco, *Things I Did and Things I Think I Did* (N.Y.: Simon and Schuster, 1984), p. 137.
36. *Newsweek*, CVI (September 8, 1986), p. 56.
37. Brooks, "But He Came Back," *Fort Worth Star-Telegram*, September 28, 1986, p. 4D.
38. Rosalind Russell, *Life Is a Banquet* (N.Y.: Random House, 1977), p. 198.
39. Jerome Lawrence, *Actor: The Life and Times of Paul Muni* (N.Y.: Putnam, 1974), p. 176.
40. Garson Kanin, *Tracy and Hepburn* (N.Y.: Viking, 1971), p. 218; Charles Higham, *Kate* (N.Y.: Norton, 1975), p. 186; Carey, *Katharine Hepburn*, p. 193; Patricia Bosworth, *Montgomery Clift* (N.Y.: Harcourt Brace Jovanovich, 1978), p. 307.
41. "Party Chatter," *Reader's Digest*, XL (April 1942), p. 50.
42. James Kotsilibas-Davis, *The Barrymores* (N.Y.: Crown, 1981), pp. 4–7.
43. "Big Deal," *Time*, LIV (August 22, 1949), p. 52n.
44. Charles Higham, *Marlene* (N.Y.: Norton, 1977), p. 197.
45. Colleen Moore, *Silent Star* (Garden City, N.Y.: Doubleday, 1968), pp. 164–65.
46. Norman Zierold, *Child Stars* (N.Y.: Coward-McCann, 1965), p.165.
47. Geoffrey Wansell, *Haunted Idol: The Story of the Real Cary Grant* (N.Y.: Morrow, 1984), pp. 266–67.
48. Norman Zierold, *Garbo* (N.Y.: Stein and Day, 1969), p. 105.
49. Leslie Frewin, *Dietrich* (N.Y.: Stein and Day, 1967), p. 154.
50. David Niven, *Bring On the Empty Horses* (N.Y.: Putnam, 1975), pp. 460–61.
51. Robert Atwan and Bruce Forer, *Bedside Hollywood: Great Scenes from Movie Memoirs* (N.Y.: Moyer Bell, 1985), p. 76.
52. Dimitri Tiomkin, *Please Don't Hate Me* (Garden City, N.Y.: Doubleday, 1959), p. 227.
53. Hedda Hopper, *The Whole Truth and Nothing But* (Garden City, N.Y.: Doubleday, 1963), p. 109.
54. Beverly Linet, *Susan Hayward* (N.Y.: Atheneum, 1980), pp. 295–98; Christopher P. Anderson, *A Star, Is a Star, Is a Star!* (Garden City, N.Y.: Doubleday, 1980), pp. 251–53; Robert La Guardia and Gene Arceri, *Red* (N.Y.: Macmillan, 1985), pp. 224–25; Frank Westmore and Muriel Davidson, *The Westmores of Hollywood* (Philadelphia: Lippincott, 1976), pp. 239, 242.
55. Larry Swindell, *Spencer Tracy* (N.Y.: World, 1969), pp. 265–76; Carey, *Katharine Hepburn*, pp. 220–21.

Chapter 11. *Child Stars*

1. Norman J. Zierold, *The Child Stars* (N.Y.: Coward-McCann, 1965), pp. 51–52.
2. Diana Serra Cary, *Hollywood's Children: An Inside Account of the Child Star Era* (Boston: Houghton Mifflin, 1979), p. 204.
3. Leonard Maltin and Richard W. Bann, *Our Gang: The Life and Times of the Little Rascals* (N.Y.: Crown, 1977), p. 18.
4. Ibid., p. 26.
5. Norman J. Zierold, *The Moguls* (N.Y.: Coward-McCann, 1969), p. 263.
6. Mel Gussow, *Don't Say Yes Until I Finish Talking: A Biography of Darryl F. Zanuck* (Garden City, N.Y.: Doubleday, 1971), pp. 84–85.
7. Zierold, *Child Stars*, pp. 19, 220; Andrew Sinclair, *John Ford* (N.Y.: Dial, 1979), p. 95; James Brough, *The Fabulous Fondas* (N.Y.: McKay, 1973), p. 93.
8. Leo C. Rosten, *Hollywood: The Movie Colony* (N.Y.: Harcourt, Brace, 1941), p. 48n; Mickey Rooney, *I.E., An Autobiography* (N.Y.: Putnam, 1965), p. 18.
9. William K. Everson, "The Career of Deanna Durbin," *Films in Review*, XXVII (November 1976), pp. 513–29.
10. Cary, *Hollywood's Children*, p. 91.
11. Zierold, *Child Stars*, p. 69.
12. Stanley Kauffmann, "High on High School," *The New Republic*, CXCII (April 8, 1985), pp. 24–25.
13. Russell Baker, "Longing for an Oater," *The New York Times Magazine*, March 24, 1985, p. 18.
14. Adolphe Menjou, *It Took Nine Tailors* (N.Y.: McGraw, 1948), p. 220.
15. Zierold, *Child Stars*, p. 22.
16. James R. Quirk, "Close-Ups and Long Shots," *Photoplay*, XLI (January 1932), p. 25; Jackie Cooper and Richard Dix, "Unfortunately I Was Rich," *The Saturday Evening Post*, CCXXXIV (March 25, 1961), p. 96; Jackie Cooper, *Please Don't Shoot My Dog: The Autobiography of Jackie Cooper* (N.Y.: Morrow, 1981), pp. 35–38.
17. Cal York, "Monthly Broadcast from Hollywood," *Photoplay*, XLI (February 1932), p. 98; Ibid., (March 1932), p. 78.
18. Leonard Mosley, *Zanuck: The Rise and Fall of Hollywood's Last Tycoon* (Boston: Little, Brown, 1984), p. 163; J. P. McEvoy, "Little Miss Miracles," *The Saturday Evening Post*, CCX (July 9, 1938), p. 11.
19. Mosley, *Zanuck*, pp. 162–63.
20. Lester David and Irene David, *The Shirley Temple Story* (N.Y.: Putnam, 1983), p. 20.
21. Ibid., p. 70.
22. Ibid., p. 73; Zierold, *Child Stars*, p. 80.
23. David, *Shirley Temple*, pp. 93–94.
24. Ibid., p. 70; "Peewee's Progress," *Time*, XXVII (April 27, 1936), p. 44.
25. Zierold, *Child Stars*, pp. 221–22.
26. Frederick Van Ryn, "Alias Andy Hardy," *Reader's Digest*, XL (April 1942), p. 50.

27. Jerome Lawrence, *Actor: The Life and Times of Paul Muni* (N.Y.: Putnam, 1974), p. 216.
28. Arthur Marx, "Ambitious Mothers: Hollywood's Headache," *Collier's,* CXXX (August 2, 1952), p. 24.
29. Ibid., pp. 24–25.
30. Zierold, *Child Stars,* p. 127.
31. Dick Sheppard, *Elizabeth: The Life and Career of Elizabeth Taylor* (Garden City, N.Y.: Doubleday, 1974), pp. 26–27; Kitty Kelley, *Elizabeth Taylor: The Last Star* (N.Y.: Simon and Schuster, 1981), pp. 20–21.
32. Elizabeth Taylor, *An Informal Memoir by Elizabeth Taylor* (N.Y.: Harper and Row, 1964), p. 163.
33. Ronald Reagan, *Where's the Rest of Me?* (N.Y.: Duell, 1965), p. 194.
34. Max Wilk, *The Wit and Wisdom of Hollywood* (N.Y.: Atheneum, 1971), p. 231.

Chapter 12. *On the Set*

1. Mervyn LeRoy, interview taped in Los Angeles, May 16, 1977, Southern Methodist University Oral History Collection.
2. Tom Ewell, interview taped in Dallas, January 24, 1974, SMUOHC.
3. Signe Hasso, interview taped in Los Angeles, August 16, 1980, SMUOHC.
4. Mel Tormé, interview taped in Dallas, February 9, 1976, SMUOHC.
5. Ann B. Davis, interview taped in Dallas, April 2, 1975, SMUOHC.
6. Cornel Wilde, interview taped in Los Angeles, August 12, 15, and 20, 1980, SMUOHC.
7. Rosemary DeCamp, interview taped in Los Angeles, July 13, 1982, SMUOHC.
8. Jayne Meadows, interview taped in Dallas, November 11, 1975, SMUOHC.
9. Lizabeth Scott, interview taped in Los Angeles, July 27, 1984, SMUOHC.
10. Robert Stack, interview taped in Los Angeles, August 12, 1975, SMUOHC.
11. Lucille Ball, interview taped in Los Angeles, August 21, 1980, SMUOHC.
12. Gregory Peck, interview taped in Los Angeles, May 27, 1977, SMUOHC.
13. Norman Zierold, *The Moguls,* (N.Y.: Coward-McCann, 1969), p. 13.
14. Joan Fontaine, interview taped in Dallas, April 12, 1979, SMUOHC.
15. Alma Power-Waters, *John Barrymore: The Legend and the Man* (N.Y.: Messner, 1941), p. 182; Gary Carey, *Katharine Hepburn* (N.Y.: St. Martin's, 1983), p. 42; Charles Higham, *Kate* (N.Y.: Norton, 1975), p. 29.
16. David Chierichetti, *Hollywood Director* (N.Y.: Curtis, 1973), pp. 130–31.

17. Nathaniel Benchley, *Humphrey Bogart* (Boston: Little, Brown, 1975), p. 105.
18. Mike Sten, *Hollywood Speaks! An Oral History* (N.Y.: Putnam, 1974), p. 31.
19. Walter Abel, interview taped in New York City, January 5, 1979, SMUOHC.
20. Bob Thomas, *Golden Boy* (N.Y.: St. Martin's, 1983), pp. 51–52.
21. Charles Higham, *Bette* (N.Y.: Macmillan, 1981), p. 126.
22. James Kotsilibas-Davis, *The Barrymores* (N.Y.: Crown, 1981), pp. 128–30.
23. Patricia Morison, interview taped in Los Angeles, August 25, 1983, SMUOHC.
24. Jerome Lawrence, *Actor: The Life and Times of Paul Muni* (N.Y.: Putnam, 1974), p. 296.
25. Harold Russell with Dan Ferullo, *The Best Years of My Life* (Middlebury, Vt.: Eriksson, 1981), p. 43.
26. Aljean Harmetz, *The Making of The Wizard of Oz* (N.Y.: Knopf, 1977), p. 163.
27. Leonard Mosley, *Zanuck* (Boston: Little, Brown, 1984), pp. 269–70.
28. Charles Higham, *Marlene* (N.Y.: Norton, 1977), p. 108.
29. Tichi Wilkerson and Marcia Borie, *The Hollywood Reporter* (N.Y.: Coward-McCann, 1984), pp. 85–86.
30. Dick Sheppard, *Elizabeth* (Garden City, N.Y.: Doubleday, 1974), pp. 53–54.
31. Joan Fontaine, *No Bed of Roses* (N.Y.: Morrow, 1978), p. 67.
32. Joan Leslie, interview taped in Los Angeles, August 13, 1981, SMUOHC; DeCamp interview.
33. Kotsilibas-Davis, *Barrymores*, pp. 269–70.
34. Bob Thomas, *King Cohn* (N.Y.: Putnam, 1967), p. 222.
35. LeRoy Prinz, interview taped in Los Angeles, July 16, 1975, SMUOHC.
36. Kotsilibas-Davis, *Barrymores*, p. 181.
37. Carolyn Jones, interview taped in Los Angeles, August 3, 1976, SMUOHC.
38. Errol Flynn, *My Wicked, Wicked Ways* (N.Y.: Putnam, 1959), pp. 224–30.
39. Rock Hudson, interview taped in Los Angeles, August 24, 1983, SMUOHC.
40. Doug McClelland, *Hollywood on Ronald Reagan* (Winchester, Mass.: Faber and Faber, 1983), p. 229.

Chapter 13. The Crew

1. Gerd Oswald, interview taped in Los Angeles, July 20, 1979, Southern Methodist University Oral History Collection.
2. Otto Lang, interview taped in Los Angeles, August 7, 1981, SMUOHC.
3. Joseph Ruttenberg, interview taped in Los Angeles, August 18 and 24, 1978, SMUOHC.

4. Donald Spoto, *Dark Side of Genius* (Boston: Little, Brown, 1983), p. 352.
5. Mervyn LeRoy, interview taped in Los Angeles, May 16, 1977, SMUOHC.
6. William Wyler, interview taped in Los Angeles, July 19, 1979, SMUOHC.
7. Edith Head, interview taped in Los Angeles by Ann Burk, July 29, 1975, SMUOHC.
8. Henry Koster, interview taped in Los Angeles, August 13, 1980, SMUOHC.
9. Melville Shavelson, interview taped in Los Angeles, August 8, 1981, SMUOHC.
10. Spoto, *Dark Side of Genius*, pp. 281–82.
11. Gregory Peck, interview taped in Los Angeles, May 27, 1977, SMUOHC.
12. Armand Deutsch, interview taped in Los Angeles, July 28, 1982, SMUOHC.
13. Michael Gordon, interview taped in Los Angeles, August 7 and 12, 1981, SMUOHC.
14. Andrew Stone, interview taped in Los Angeles, July 15, 1985, SMUOHC.
15. Edmund North, interview taped in Los Angeles, August 15, 1986, SMUOHC.
16. Charles Higham, *Kate* (N.Y.: Norton, 1975), pp. 84–85.
17. Ezra Goodman, *The Fifty-Year Decline and Fall of Hollywood* (N.Y.: Simon and Schuster, 1961), p. 202.
18. Andrew Sinclair, *John Ford* (N.Y.: Dial, 1979), p. 67.
19. Rosalind Russell, *Life Is a Banquet* (N.Y.: Random House, 1977), pp. 185–86.
20. Tay Garnett, *Light Your Torches and Pull Up Your Tights* (New Rochelle, N.Y.: Arlington House, 1973), pp. 297–98.

Chapter 14. *On Location*

1. Jesse L. Lasky, Jr., *Whatever Happened to Hollywood?* (N.Y.: W. H. Allen, 1975), p. 272.
2. William Le Massena, interview taped in New York City, January 11 and 12, 1979, Southern Methodist University Oral History Collection.
3. Gregory Peck, interview taped in Los Angeles, August 21, 1978, SMUOHC.
4. Virginia Mayo, interview taped in Dallas, November 30, 1973, SMUOHC.
5. Pandro S. Berman, interview taped in Los Angeles, August 21, 1978, SMUOHC.
6. Margaret Tallichet Wyler, interview taped in Los Angeles, July 19, 1982, SMUOHC.
7. Gerd Oswald, interview taped in Los Angeles, July 20, 1979, SMUOHC.

8. Delbert Mann, interview taped in Los Angeles, July 21, 1984, SMUOHC.
9. Ralph Hancock and Letitia Fairbanks, *Douglas Fairbanks: The Fourth Musketeer* (N.Y.: Holt, 1953), pp. 134–36.
10. Bob Thomas, *King Cohn* (N.Y.: Putnam, 1967), pp. 100–101; Norman Zierold, *The Moguls* (N.Y.: Coward-McCann, 1969), p. 201.
11. Pat O'Brien, interview taped in Dallas, February 4, 1975, SMUOHC.
12. Anna Lee, interview taped in Los Angeles, August 13, 1981, SMUOHC.
13. John Mills, *Up in the Clouds, Gentlemen Please* (New Haven, Conn.: Ticknor and Fields, 1981), p. 241.
14. Jan Clayton, interview taped in Los Angeles, August 19, 1980, SMUOHC.
15. Ralph Bellamy, interview taped in Los Angeles, May 18, 1977, SMUOHC.
16. Nanette Fabray, interview taped in Los Angeles, August 5 and 12, 1975, SMUOHC.
17. Norman Lloyd, interview taped in Los Angeles, July 23 and 24, 1979, SMUOHC.
18. Mildred Natwick, interview taped in New York City, January 4, 1979, SMUOHC.
19. Charles Higham, *Kate* (N.Y.: Norton, 1975), pp. 139–40.
20. Gregory Peck, interview taped in Los Angeles, July 28, 1979, SMUOHC.
21. Henry Wilcoxon, interview taped in Los Angeles, August 25, 1983, SMUOHC.
22. Frank Westmore and Muriel Davidson, *The Westmores of Hollywood* (Philadelphia: Lippincott, 1976), pp. 216–17.
23. Shirley Jones, interview taped in Los Angeles, July 27, 1984, SMUOHC.
24. Mike Munn, *The Stories Behind the Scenes of the Great Film Epics* (London: Illustrated Publications, 1982), p. 110.
25. Delbert Mann, interview taped in Los Angeles, July 21, 1984, SMUOHC.

Chapter 15. *Editing and Scoring*

1. Edward Dmytryk, *On Film Editing* (Boston: Focal, 1984), p. vii.
2. "The Progress of the Motion Picture," *The Independent* (New York), LXXII (April 15, 1915), p. 21.
3. Leonard Mosley, *Zanuck: The Rise and Fall of Hollywood's Last Tycoon* (Boston: Little, Brown, 1984), p. 75.
4. Edward Dmytryk, *On Screen Directing* (Boston: Focal, 1984), pp. 116–17; Dmytryk, *Film Editing*, pp. 131–32n.
5. Max Wilk, *The Wit and Wisdom of Hollywood* (N.Y.: Atheneum, 1971), p. 3.
6. Paul F. Boller, Jr., "The Sound of Silents," *American Heritage*, XXXVI (August/September 1985), pp. 98–107.

7. Paul F. Boller, Jr., "Music by Max Steiner," *Southwest Review,* LI (Summer 1966), pp. 256–71.

8. "On the Hollywood Front," *Modern Music,* XVI (November–December 1938), p. 62.

9. Ralph Rosenblum and Robert Karen, *When the Shooting Stops . . . the Cutting Begins: A Film Editor's Story* (N.Y.: Viking, 1980), p. 296.

10. Janet Maslin, "The Pollack Touch," *The New York Times Magazine,* December 15, 1985, p. 106.

11. Lillian Gish, *Lillian Gish: The Movies, Mr. Griffith, and Me* (Englewood Cliffs, N.J.: Prentice-Hall, 1969), pp. 60–61.

12. Ezra Goodman, *The Fifty-Year Decline and Fall of Hollywood* (N.Y.: Simon and Schuster, 1961), p. 170.

13. Budd Schulberg, *Moving Pictures: Memories of a Hollywood Prince* (N.Y.: Stein and Day, 1981), pp. 242–44.

14. Cal York, "Monthly Broadcast from Hollywood," *Photoplay,* XXXVIII (July 1930), p. 114.

15. David Zinman, *50 from the 50s: Vintage Films from America's Mid-Century* (New Rochelle, N.Y.: Arlington House, 1979), p. 309n.

16. Joe Adamson, *Groucho, Harpo, Chico and Sometimes Zeppo* (N.Y.: Pocket Books, 1976), pp. 85–86.

17. Mel Gussow, *Don't Say Yes Until I Finish Talking: A Biography of Darryl Zanuck* (Garden City, N.Y.: Doubleday, 1971), pp. 14–15; Mosley, *Zanuck,* pp. 160–61.

18. Gussow, *Don't Say Yes,* p. 82.

19. Oscar Levant, *A Smattering of Ignorance* (Garden City, N.Y.: Doubleday, 1940), pp. 116, 127–28; Dimitri Tiomkin, *Please Don't Hate Me* (Garden City, N.Y.: Doubleday, 1959), p. 229.

20. Levant, *A Smattering of Ignorance,* p. 99.

21. Ibid., pp. 33–34.

22. Ibid., pp. 115–16.

23. Frank Capra, *The Name Above the Title: An Autobiography* (N.Y.: Macmillan, 1971), pp. 199–201; Bob Thomas, *King Cohn* (N.Y.: Putnam, 1967), pp. 122–23; William H. Rosar, "Lost Horizon: An Account of the Composition of the Score," *Filmmusic Notebook,* IV (1978), pp. 45–46.

24. Alva Johnston, "The Great Goldwyn," *The Saturday Evening Post,* CCIX (June 19, 1937), p. 98.

25. Bronislaw Kaper interview, *Filmmusic Notebook,* IV (1978), p. 21.

26. "Father Goose," *Time,* LXIV (December 27, 1954), p. 43.

27. Max Wilk, *The Wit and Wisdom of Hollywood* (N.Y.: Atheneum, 1971), pp. 212–13; Albert K. Bender, "Max Steiner," *Filmmusic Notebook,* I (Autumn 1974), pp. 6–7.

28. Elston Brooks, "Here's Z Reel Story on 'Razzamatazz,'" *Fort Worth Star-Telegram,* September 14, 1986, p. 2D.

29. Brooks, "But He Came Back to Haunt the Living," *Fort Worth Star-Telegram,* September 28, 1986, p. 4D.

30. Tiomkin, *Please Don't Hate Me,* p. 171.

31. Mosley, *Zanuck,* pp. 222–24.

32. David Raksin, "Whatever Became of Movie Music?" *Filmmusic Notebook*, I (Autumn 1974), p. 22.

33. Bob Thomas, *Selznick* (Garden City, N.Y.: Doubleday, 1970), pp. 232–35; Tiomkin, *Please Don't Hate Me*, pp. 220–22.

34. Charles Higham, *Kate: The Life of Katharine Hepburn* (N.Y.: Norton, 1975), p. 124.

35. Elmer Bernstein, "The Aesthetics of Film Scoring: A Highly Personal View," *Filmmusic Notebook*, IV (1978), p. 25.

Chapter 16. Censorship

1. *Moving Picture World*, I (April 27, 1907), p. 127.

2. Ruth Inglis, *Freedom of Movies* (Chicago: University of Chicago Press, 1947), pp. 63–64.

3. *Congressional Record*, Vol. 62, 67th Congress, June 29, 1922, p. 9657.

4. Inglis, *Freedom of Movies*, p. 99.

5. Raymond Moley, *The Hays Office* (Indianapolis: Bobbs, 1945), p. 35; Norman Hapgood, "Will Hays," *Atlantic*, CLI (January 1933), p. 77; William S. Hart, *My Life East and West* (N.Y.: Houghton, 1929), pp. 313–14; Will H. Hays, *The Memoirs of Will H. Hays* (Garden City, N.Y.: Doubleday, 1955), pp. 325–26.

6. Morris L. Ernst and Pare Lorentz, *Censored: The Private Life of the Movies* (N.Y.: Cape, 1930), pp. 129–130.

7. *Photoplay*, XXXVII (July 1930), p. 29.

8. Ben Hecht, *A Child of the Century* (N.Y.: Simon and Schuster, 1954), p. 479.

9. Ibid., pp. 86–87.

10. J. P. McEvoy, "The Back of Me Hand to You," *The Saturday Evening Post*, CCXI (December 24, 1938), p. 8.

11. Lester Velie, "You Can't See That Movie," *Collier's*, CXXV (May 6, 1950), pp. 11–12.

12. Ben Ray Redman, "Pictures and Censorship," *Saturday Review of Literature*, XIX (December 31, 1938), p. 13.

13. Murray Schumach, *The Face on the Cutting Room Floor* (N.Y.: Morrow, 1964), p. 164.

14. Vincent Canby, "Freedom from Code Shackles, Movies Still Limp Along," *The New York Times*, March 9, 1986, "Arts and Leisure," p. 20.

15. Lillian Gish, *Lillian Gish: The Movies, Mr. Griffith, and Me* (Englewood Cliffs, N.J.: Prentice-Hall, 1969), p. 235.

16. Phil A. Koury, *Yes, Mr. De Mille* (N.Y.: Putnam, 1959), pp. 280–81.

17. Gloria Swanson, *Swanson on Swanson* (N.Y.: Random House, 1980), pp. 173–74.

18. Arthur Mayer, *Merely Colossal* (N.Y.: Simon and Schuster, 1953), p. 123.

19. Pat O'Brien, interview taped in Dallas, February 4, 1975, Southern Methodist University Oral History Collection; Lewis Milestone, interview taped in Los Angeles, July 23, 1979, SMUOHC.

20. Joe Adamson, *Groucho, Harpo, Chico and Sometimes Zeppo* (N.Y.: Pocket Books, 1976), p. 229.
21. Jesse L. Lasky, Jr., *Whatever Happened to Hollywood?* (N.Y.: W. H. Allen, 1973), p. 43.
22. John Harrington, *Films And/As Literature* (Englewood Cliffs, N.J.: Prentice-Hall, 1977), p. 109.
23. Hecht, *A Child of the Century*, pp. 495–97.
24. Ronald Haver, *David O. Selznick's Hollywood* (N.Y.: Knopf, 1980), p. 299.
25. Jack Vizzard, *See No Evil: Life Inside a Hollywood Censor* (N.Y.: Simon and Schuster, 1970), pp. 118–19.
26. Charles Higham, *Charles Laughton: An Intimate Biography* (Garden City, N.Y.: Doubleday, 1976), pp. 103–4.
27. Gary Carey, *Katharine Hepburn: A Hollywood Yankee* (N.Y.: St. Martin's, 1984), p. 148.
28. Charles Higham, *Bette: The Life of Bette Davis* (N.Y.: Dell, 1982), p. 251.
29. Ingrid Bergman, *Ingrid Bergman: My Story* (N.Y.: Dell, 1980), pp. 199–200.
30. Lilli Palmer, *Change Lobsters and Dance: An Autobiography* (N.Y.: Dell, 1975), pp. 165–66.
31. Kitty Kelley, *Elizabeth Taylor: The Last Star* (N.Y.: Simon and Schuster, 1982), p. 105.
32. Schumach, *Face on Cutting Room Floor*, pp. 214–15.

III. The Playbill

Chapter 17. *Drama*

1. Lewis Jacobs, *The Movies as Medium* (N.Y.: Farrar, Straus and Giroux, 1973), pp. 16, 76.
2. Pauline Kael, *Reeling* (Boston: Little, Brown, 1976), p. xi.
3. Kael, *5001 Nights at the Movies* (N.Y.: Holt, Rinehart and Winston, 1982), p. 456.
4. Roger Manvell, *Theater and Film* (Rutherford, N.J.: Fairleigh Dickinson University, 1979), pp. 126–33.
5. Welford Beaton, in Stanley Kauffmann, ed., *American Film Criticism* (Westport, Conn.: Greenwood Press, 1979), p. 355.
6. Theodore Dreiser, in Harry M. Geduld, *Authors on Film* (Bloomington, Ill.: Illinois University, 1972), p. 206.
7. William Faulkner, in ibid., p. 199.
8. Vincente Minnelli, interview taped in Los Angeles, August 14, 1980, Southern Methodist University Oral History Collection.
9. Pauline Kael, *I Lost It at the Movies* (Boston: Little, Brown, 1965), pp. 234–35.
10. James Agee, *Agee on Film* (N.Y.: McDowell, Obolensky, 1958), p. 353.
11. Kael, *5001 Nights*, p. 165.

12. Geoffrey Wagner, *The Novel and the Cinema* (Rutherford, N.J.: Fairleigh Dickinson University, 1975), pp. 296–97.
13. Stanley Kauffmann, *Before My Eyes* (N.Y.: Harper and Row, 1980), p. 183.
14. Gabriel Miller, *Screening the Novel* (N.Y.: Ungar, 1980), pp. 46–47.
15. Ross Hunter, interview taped in Los Angeles, July 17, 1984, SMUOHC.
16. Kael, *5001 Nights*, p. 220.
17. Lewis Milestone, interview taped in Los Angeles, July 23, 1979, SMUOHC; Dimitri Tiomkin, *Please Don't Hate Me* (Garden City, N.Y.: Doubleday, 1959), pp. 170–71.
18. Michael Freedland, *The Warner Brothers* (N.Y.: St. Martin's, 1983), pp. 55–56.
19. Edward Buzzell, interview taped in Los Angeles, July 17, 1982, SMUOHC.
20. William Wyler, interview taped in Los Angeles, July 19, 1979, SMUOHC.
21. Frank Capra, *The Name Above the Title* (N.Y.: Macmillan, 1971), pp. 153–54.
22. Arthur Marx, *Goldwyn* (N.Y.: Norton, 1976), p. 210; Jesse L. Lasky, Jr., *Whatever Happened to Hollywood?* (N.Y.: W. H. Allen, 1973), p. 118.
23. Charles Higham, *Marlene* (N.Y.: Norton, 1977), pp. 90–91.
24. *The Washington Post*, June 1, 1986; David Bird, "'The Mankiewicz Story,' at Columbia," *The New York Times*, November 16, 1986, p. 21.
25. Bob Thomas, *King Cohn* (N.Y.: Putnam, 1967), p. 281.
26. Robert Wise, interview taped in Los Angeles, July 26, 1979, SMUOHC.

Chapter 18. *Comedy*

1. Robert Giroux, "Mack Sennett," *Films in Review*, XIX (December 1968), p. 594.
2. "Mack Sennett's At It," *Newsweek*, LII (October 6, 1958), p. 90.
3. James Agee, "Comedy's Greatest Era," *Life*, XXVII (September 5, 1949), p. 76.
4. John McCabe, *Mr. Laurel and Mr. Hardy* (N.Y.: Grosset, 1961, 1966), p. 86.
5. John Russell Taylor, ed., *Graham Greene on Film* (N.Y.: Simon and Schuster, 1972), p. 273.
6. Frank Manchel, *The Talking Clowns: From Laurel and Hardy to the Marx Brothers* (N.Y.: Watts, 1976), p. 100.
7. Steven V. Roberts, "76—And Still Diamond Lil," *The New York Times Magazine*, November 2, 1969, p. 72.
8. Manchel, *Talking Clowns*, pp. 55, 56, 60; George Eells and Stanley Musgrove, *Mae West: A Biography* (N.Y.: Morrow, 1982), pp. 12, 47; Mark Rego, *The Best of Modern Screen* (N.Y.: St. Martin's, 1986), p. 125.
9. Roberts, "76—And Still Diamond Lil," p. 72.
10. Manchel, *Talking Clowns*, p. 54.

11. "King of Comedy," *Newsweek*, CVI (July 7, 1986), p. 58.
12. William M. Gibson, ed., *The Mysterious Stranger* (Berkeley, Calif.: University of California, 1969), pp. 164–66.
13. Adolph Zukor, *The Public Is Never Wrong* (N.Y.: Putnam, 1953), pp. 150–51; Ezra Goodman, *The Fifty-Year Decline and Fall of Hollywood* (N.Y.: Simon and Schuster, 1961), p. 347; William Cahn, *Harold Lloyd's World of Comedy* (N.Y.: Duell, 1964), pp. 42–43; Betty Harper Fussell, *Mabel* (New Haven, Conn. and N.Y.: Ticknor and Fields, 1982), p. 67.
14. Rudi Blesh, *Keaton* (N.Y.: Macmillan, 1966), pp. 140–42.
15. Tom Dardis, *Keaton: The Man Who Wouldn't Lie Down* (N.Y.: Scribner, 1979), pp. 127–28.
16. *Parade*, April 13, 1986, p. 6.
17. Gene Fowler, *Father Goose: The Story of Mack Sennett* (N.Y.: McLeod, 1934), pp. 314–15; David Niven, *Bring On the Empty Horses* (N.Y.: Putnam, 1975), pp. 488–89.
18. Garson Kanin, *Hollywood* (N.Y.: Viking, 1974), pp. 154–55.
19. Leonard Martin, ed., *The Laurel & Hardy Book* (N.Y.: Curtis, 1973), pp. 57–58.
20. Arthur Mayer, *Merely Colossal* (N.Y.: Simon and Schuster, 1953), p. 35.
21. Manchel, *Talking Clowns*, p. 98; Maxine Marx, *Growing Up with Chico* (Englewood Cliffs, N.J.: Prentice-Hall, 1980), p. 45; Scott Meredith, *George S. Kaufman and His Friends* (Garden City, N.Y.: Doubleday, 1974), p. 267.
22. Meredith, *George S. Kaufman*, p. 276.
23. Marx, *Growing Up with Chico*, pp. 112–13.
24. Joe Adamson, *Groucho, Harpo, Chico and Sometimes Zeppo* (N.Y.: Simon and Schuster, 1973), p. 223.
25. Niven, *Bring on the Empty Horses*, p. 453.
26. Ruth Gordon, "Returning to a Beloved Island," *The New York Times*, July 22, 1984, "Arts and Leisure," p. 14.
27. Leonard Hall in *Photoplay*, XXXIV (May 1930), p. 78.
28. Bob Thomas, *Thalberg* (Garden City, N.Y.: Doubleday, 1969), pp. 281–82; Groucho Marx, *Groucho and Me* (N.Y.: Random House, 1959), p. 236.
29. Marx, *Growing Up with Chico*, pp. 19–20.
30. Ibid., p. 116.
31. Adamson, *Groucho, Harpo, Chico*, p. 224.
32. Marx, *Groucho and Me*, pp. 243–47; Adamson, *Groucho, Harpo, Chico*, pp. 417–18.
33. Groucho Marx, *The Secret Word Is Groucho* (N.Y.: Putnam, 1976), p. 84; Adamson, *Groucho, Harpo, Chico*, p. 28.
34. Adamson, *Groucho, Harpo, Chico*, p. 227.
35. Ibid., p. 23.
36. Frank Condon, "Come Up and Meet Mae West," *Collier's*, XCIII (June 16, 1934), p. 42.
37. Hedda Hopper, *From Under My Hat* (Garden City, N.Y.: Doubleday, 1952), p. 304; Eells and Musgrove, *Mae West*, p. 106.

38. Eells and Musgrove, *Mae West*, p. 304.
39. Ibid., p. 16.
40. Ibid., p. 150.
41. Ibid., p. 284.
42. Alva Johnston, "Who Knows What Is Funny?," *The Saturday Evening Post*, CCXI (August 6, 1938), p. 45.
43. Ibid., p. 46; Cal York, "Gossip of All the Studios," *Photoplay*, XXXIII (February 1928), p. 86.
44. Jonathan Hicks, "As Tax Increase Nears," *The New York Times*, September 16, 1985, p. 33.
45. Marx, *Growing Up with Chico*, p. 97.
46. Johnston, "Who Knows What Is Funny?," p. 43.
47. Phil A. Koury, *Yes, Mr. De Mille* (N.Y.: Putnam, 1959), pp. 14–15.
48. Wallace Markfield, "The Dark Geography of W. C. Fields," *The New York Times Magazine*, April 24, 1966, p. 12.
49. Frank Capra, *The Name Above the Title: An Autobiography* (N.Y.: Macmillan, 1971), pp. 161–72; Bob Thomas, *King Cohn* (N.Y.: Putnam, 1967), pp. 90–93.
50. Adolphe Menjou, *It Took Nine Tailors* (N.Y.: McGraw, 1948), pp. 232–33.
51. Charles Higham, *Kate: The Life of Katharine Hepburn* (N.Y.: Norton, 1975), p. 86.
52. Richard Schickel, *The Disney Version: The Life, Times, Art and Commerce of Walt Disney* (N.Y.: Simon and Schuster, 1968), p. 33.
53. Leonard Mosley, *Disney's World* (N.Y.: Stein and Day, 1985), pp. 137–40, 149.
54. Ibid., pp. 174–75.
55. Mary Livingston Benny and Hilliard Marks, *Jack Benny* (Garden City, N.Y.: Doubleday, 1978), pp. 134–35.
56. Doug Warren, *Cagney: The Authorized Biography* (N.Y.: St. Martin's, 1983), p. 174.
57. Stephen Birmingham, *The Rest of Us* (Boston: Little, Brown, 1984), pp. 259–60.
58. Gregory Peck, interview taped in Los Angeles, August 22, 1980, Southern Methodist University Oral History Collection; Marvyn Rothstein, "A Bouquet of Laurel & Hardy," *The New York Times*, December 11, 1984, p. 14.
59. Elston Brooks, "But He Came Back to Haunt the Living," *Fort Worth Star-Telegram*, September 28, 1986, p. 4D.
60. Sheliah Graham, *Hollywood Revisited* (N.Y.: St. Martin's Press, 1985), pp. 126–27.

Chapter 19. *Musicals*

1. Ted Sennett, *Hollywood Musicals* (N.Y.: Abrams, 1981), pp. 67–68.
2. Henry Koster, interview taped in Los Angeles, August 13, 1980, Southern Methodist University Oral History Collection.

3. Ray Bolger, interview taped in Los Angeles, August 5, 1976, SMUOHC.
4. Gene Kelly, interview taped in Dallas, June 20, 21, and 25, 1974, SMUOHC.
5. Vincente Minnelli, interview taped in Los Angeles, August 14, 1980, SMUOHC.
6. Kelly interview.
7. Fred Astaire, interview taped in Los Angeles, July 31, 1976, SMUOHC.
8. Harry Warren, interview taped in Los Angeles, October 24, 1977, SMUOHC.
9. Julie Newmar, interview taped in Dallas, November 3, 1977, SMUOHC.
10. Warren interview.
11. Dan Dailey, interview taped in Dallas by Sally Cullum, July 13 and 25, 1974, SMUOHC.
12. Gene Nelson, interview taped in Los Angeles, August 15, 1980, SMUOHC.
13. Leo Robin, interview taped in Los Angeles, July 24, 1979, SMUOHC; Michael Freedland, *Maurice Chevalier* (N.Y.: Morrow, 1981), pp. 106–8.
14. Michael Freedland, *The Warner Brothers* (N.Y.: St. Martin's, 1983), p. 70.
15. Ralph Bellamy, interview taped in Los Angeles, May 18, 1977, SMUOHC; Ralph Bellamy, *When the Smoke Hit the Fan* (Garden City, N.Y.: Doubleday, 1979), p. 157.
16. Hermes Pan, interview taped in Los Angeles, January 12, 1983, SMUOHC.
17. Adolphe Menjou, *It Took Nine Tailors* (N.Y.: McGraw, 1948), p. 234.
18. Arthur Marx, *Goldwyn* (N.Y.: Norton, 1976), p. 233.
19. Ralph Blane, interview taped in Tulsa, Okla., March 12, 1979, SMUOHC.
20. Ronald Reagan, *Where's the Rest of Me?* (N.Y.: Duell, 1965), pp. 121–22.
21. Dailey interview.
22. Aljean Harmetz, *The Making of the Wizard of Oz* (N.Y.: Knopf, 1977), pp. 62–63.
23. Blane interview.
24. Anna Lee, interview taped in Los Angeles, August 13, 1981, SMUOHC.
25. Rosemary Clooney, interview taped in Dallas, January 25, 1975, SMUOHC.
26. Bob Thomas, *Astaire: The Man, the Dancer* (N.Y.: St. Martin's, 1984), pp. 129–31.

Chapter 20. *Westerns*

1. Ralph Willett, "The American Western: Myth and Anti-Myth," *Journal of Popular Culture*, IV (Fall 1970), p. 455; Walter C. Clapham, *Western Movies: The Story of the West on the Screen* (N.Y.: Octopus Books,

1974), p. 7; George N. Fenin and William K. Everson, *The Western: From Silents to the Seventies* (N.Y.: Grossman, 1973), p. xix.

2. Jay Hyams, *The Life and Times of the Western Movie* (N.Y.: Gallery Books, 1983), p. 34.

3. Richard A. Maynard, *The American West on Film* (Rochelle Park, N.J.: Hayden, 1974), p. 62; Jenni Calder, *There Must Be a Lone Ranger* (N.Y.: Hamilton, 1975), p. 185; David Rothel, *The Singing Cowboys* (Cranbury, N.J.: A. S. Barnes, 1978), p. 17.

4. "Westerns," *Time*, LXXIII (March 30, 1959), p. 52.

5. Rita Parks, *The Western Hero in Film and Television* (Ann Arbor, Mich.: UMI Research, 1982), p. 28.

6. Elizabeth Hartman, "Cowboys Wore White Hats in Hollywood Westerns," *Fort Worth Star-Telegram*, September 9, 1986, p. 6C.

7. Tony Thomas, *The Great Adventure Films* (Secaucus, N.J.: Citadel, 1976), p. 1.

8. "Westerns," *Time*, p. 53.

9. Hyams, *Life and Times of Western Movie*, p. 192; James Robert Parish and Michael R. Pitts, *The Great Western Pictures* (Metuchen, N.J.: Scarecrow Press, 1976), p. 263.

10. Pitts, *Great Western Pictures*, p. 400; Arthur Knight, "SR Goes to the Movies," *Saturday Review*, LII (September 27, 1969), p. 39.

11. Knight, *Saturday Review*, LII (July 5, 1969), p. 21.

12. James Horwitz, *They Went Thataway* (N.Y.: Dutton, 1976), p. 275.

13. Pauline Kael, "The Street Western," *The New Yorker*, L (February 25, 1974), p. 100.

14. Kevin Brownlow, *The War, the West, and the Wilderness* (N.Y.: Knopf, 1979), p. 301.

15. Cecil B. De Mille, *Autobiography* (Englewood Cliffs, N.J.: Prentice-Hall, 1959), pp. 103–4.

16. William S. Hart, *My Life East and West* (N.Y.: Houghton, 1929), pp. 287–88.

17. Ibid., pp. 259–63.

18. Olive Stokes Mix, *The Fabulous Tom Mix* (Englewood Cliffs, N.J.: Prentice-Hall, 1957), pp. 118–20.

19. Diana Serra Cary, *Hollywood Posse* (Boston: Houghton Mifflin, 1974), p. 48.

20. Hedda Hopper, *From Under My Hat* (N.Y.: Doubleday, 1952), pp. 176–77; Frances Marion, *Off with Their Heads!* (N.Y.: Macmillan, 1972), pp. 126–27; *Time*, XXVII (March 3, 1941), p. 80.

21. Paul O'Neill, "Rawboned, Soft-Spoken, but Casting a Shadow Taller Than Life," *Life*, L (May 26, 1961), p. 30.

22. Mike Tomkies, *Duke: The Story of John Wayne* (Chicago: Regnery, 1971), pp. 26–29.

23. J. B. Griswold, "King of the Giddyaps," *American Magazine*, CXXV (January 1938), p. 74.

24. Walter C. Clapham, *Western Movies: The Story of the West on the Screen* (London: Octopus Books, 1974), p. 33; Richard J. Anobile, *John*

Ford's Stagecoach (N.Y.: Universe Books, 1975), p. 7; Andrew Sinclair, *John Ford* (N.Y.: Dial, 1979), p. 85.

25. Alva Johnston, "Tenor on Horseback," *The Saturday Evening Post,* CCXII (September 2, 1939), p. 18; "Double Mint Ranch," *Time,* XXXV (January 15, 1940), p. 48.
26. H. F. Hinz, *Horses in the Movies* (Cranbury, N.J.: A. S. Barnes, 1979), p. 23.
27. John Reese, "Movie Horses Are Real Hams!" *The Saturday Evening Post,* CCXXVIII (June 30, 1956), p. 42.
28. "John Wayne as the Last Hero," *Time,* XCIV (August 8, 1969), p. 53.
29. Paul Seydor, *Peckinpah: The Western Films* (Urbana, Ill.: University of Illinois, 1980), p. 267; John Gregory Dunne, "So You Want to Write a Movie," *Atlantic Monthly,* CCXXXIV (July 1974), p. 44.

Chapter 21. *Spectacles*

1. Arthur Mayer, *Merely Colossal* (N.Y.: Simon and Schuster, 1963), p. 76; Frank Manchel, *Cameras West* (Englewood Cliffs, N.J.: Prentice-Hall, 1971), p. 67.
2. Paul O'Dell, *Griffith and the Rise of Hollywood* (N.Y.: A. S. Barnes, 1970), p. 38.
3. Frederick James Smith, *"Intolerance* in Review," *New York Dramatic Mirror,* LXXVI (September 16, 1916), p. 22.
4. "Second Thoughts on First Nights," *The New York Times,* September 10, 1916, sec. 2, p. 5.
5. Pauline Kael, *Going Steady* (Boston: Little, Brown, 1970), p. 44.
6. Gabe Essoe and Raymond Lee, *De Mille: The Man and His Pictures* (N.Y.: A. S. Barnes, 1970), p. 48.
7. *Time,* XXVI (September 2, 1935), p. 38.
8. Phil A. Koury, *Yes, Mr. De Mille* (N.Y.: Putnam, 1959), p. 200; "New Picture," *Time,* L (October 27, 1947), p. 99.
9. Bosley Crowther, *The Great Films: Fifty Golden Years of Motion Pictures* (N.Y.: Putnam, 1967), p. 136.
10. Koury, *Yes, Mr. De Mille,* p. 256.
11. Essoe and Lee, *De Mille,* p. 195.
12. *Time,* LIV (December 26, 1949), p. 53; *The New Yorker,* XXVI (April 1, 1950), p. 59.
13. Jon Solomon, *The Ancient World in the Cinema* (N.Y.: A. S. Barnes, 1978), p. 43; *Time,* LXIV (July 5, 1954), p. 77; Foster Hirsch, *The Hollywood Epic* (N.Y.: A. S. Barnes, 1978), p. 45.
14. Ralph Hancock, *Douglas Fairbanks: The Fourth Musketeer* (N.Y.: Holt, 1953), pp. 190–95.
15. Ibid., pp. 198–99.
16. Cecil B. De Mille, *Autobiography* (Englewood Cliffs, N.J.: Putnam, 1959), pp. 249–50; Koury, *Yes, Mr. De Mille,* pp. 88–89, 106; Mervyn LeRoy, *Mervyn LeRoy: Take One* (N.Y.: Hawthorn, 1974), pp. 58–59.
17. LeRoy, *Mervyn LeRoy,* p. 59.

18. Arthur Mayer, *Merely Colossal*, p. 161; Koury, *Yes, Mr. De Mille*, p. 92; William C. De Mille, *Hollywood Saga* (N.Y.: Dutton, 1939), p. 241.
19. Gary Carey, *All the Stars in Heaven: Louis B. Mayer's MGM* (N.Y.: Elsevier-Dutton, 1981), p. 84.
20. Koury, *Yes, Mr. De Mille*, pp. 120–24; De Mille, *Hollywood Saga*, p. 248; Richard Griffith and Arthur Mayer, *The Movies* (N.Y.: Bonanza Books, 1957), p. 188; Jesse L. Lasky, Jr., *Whatever Happened to Hollywood?* (N.Y.: W. H. Allen, 1972), p. 117.
21. Cal York, "Gossip of All the Studios," *Photoplay*, XXXIII (February 1928), p. 96.
22. Ibid., XXXIV (June 1928), p. 44.
23. James R. Quirk, "Close-Ups and Long Shots," *Photoplay*, XLI (December 1931), p. 26.
24. Cal York, "Gossip of All the Studios," *Photoplay*, XXXIV (August 1928), p. 51.
25. Lasky, *Whatever Happened to Hollywood?*, p. 190; Edward Dmytryk, *It's a Hell of a Life But Not a Bad Living* (N.Y.: Times Books, 1978), pp. 7–8.
26. Charles Higham, *Charles Laughton: An Intimate Biography* (Garden City, N.Y.: Doubleday, 1976), p. 36.
27. De Mille, *Autobiography*, pp. 322–23.
28. Koury, *Yes, Mr. De Mille*, pp. 23–25.
29. Lasky, *Whatever Happened to Hollywood?*, p. 72.
30. Ibid., pp. 202–3; Charles Higham, *Cecil B. De Mille* (N.Y.: Scribner's, 1980), p. 235.
31. Budd Schulberg, *Moving Pictures: Memories of a Hollywood Prince* (N.Y.: Stein and Day, 1981), p. 301.
32. Bob Thomas, *Thalberg* (Garden City, N.Y.: Doubleday, 1969), pp. 315–16.
33. Bob Thomas, *Selznick* (Garden City, N.Y.: Doubleday, 1972), p. 135.
34. Ibid., pp. 134–47; Gary Carey, *Katharine Hepburn: A Hollywood Yankee* (N.Y.: St. Martin's, 1984), p. 103; Charles Higham, *Kate: The Life of Katharine Hepburn* (N.Y.: Norton, 1975), pp. 89–90; Ronald Haver, *David O. Selznick's Hollywood* (N.Y.: Knopf, 1980), pp. 236–311; Lloyd Shearer, "GWTW: Supercolossal Saga of an Epic," *The New York Times Magazine*, October 26, 1947, pp. 53, 55; *Time*, XXXIV (December 25, 1939), p. 31.
35. Thomas, *Selznick*, p. 164n.
36. Koury, *Yes, Mr. De Mille*, pp. 206, 286–87; De Mille, *Autobiography*, p. 402.
37. Koury, *Yes, Mr. De Mille*, p. 160.
38. Shelley Winters, *Shelley* (N.Y.: Ballantine, 1980), p. 101.
39. De Mille, *Autobiography*, pp. 254–55; Koury, *Yes, Mr. De Mille*, p. 103.
40. LeRoy Prinz, interview taped in Los Angeles, July 16, 1975, Southern Methodist University Oral History Collection.
41. Mike Munn, *The Stories Behind the Scenes of the Great Film Epics* (London: Illustrated Publications, 1982), p. 29.

42. Ibid., p. 27; Lasky, *Whatever Happened to Hollywood?*, p. 132.
43. "New Picture," *Time*, L (October 27, 1947), p. 100n.
44. Munn, *Stories Behind Scenes of Great Film Epics*, p. 85.
45. Ibid., p. 47.
46. Donald Shepherd and Robert Slatzer, *Duke: The Life and Times of John Wayne* (Garden City, N.Y.: Doubleday, 1985), p. 259.
47. John Huston, *Open Book* (N.Y.: Knopf, 1980), p. 320.
48. Ibid., p. 360.

Chapter 22. *Horror and Suspense*

1. Robert Louis Stevenson, *The Works of Robert Louis Stevenson*, Vol. VII (26 vols., N.Y.: AMS Press, 1922), p. 340.
2. Drake Douglas, *Horror!* (N.Y.: Macmillan, 1966), pp. 206–7.
3. Carlos Clarens, *An Illustrated History of the Horror Film* (N.Y.: Putnam, 1967), p. 60.
4. Daniel Cohen, *Horror in the Movies* (N.Y.: Clarion Books, 1982), p. 48.
5. Maurice Richardson, "The Psychoanalysis of Ghost Stories," *Twentieth Century*, 166 (December 1959), pp. 427, 429.
6. Roul Tunley, "TV's Midnight Madness," *The Saturday Evening Post*, CCXXI (August 16, 1958), p. 85.
7. Ibid.
8. Peter Underwood, *Karloff* (N.Y.: Frewin, 1972), p. 72.
9. Seth Cagin and Philip Dray, *Hollywood Films of the Seventies* (N.Y.: Harper and Row, 1984), p. 200.
10. Lawrence Hammond, *Thriller Movies* (London: Octopus Books, 1974), p. 20.
11. Cal York, "Monthly Broadcast from Hollywood," *Photoplay*, XLI (January 1932), p. 84; Underwood, *Karloff*, p. 68.
12. Charles Starrett, conversation in Laguna Beach, Calif., August 13, 1983.
13. Underwood, *Karloff*, p. 60.
14. Arthur Mayer, *Merely Colossal* (N.Y.: Simon and Schuster, 1953), pp. 170, 175–76.
15. Underwood, *Karloff*, p. 96.
16. Ronald Haver, *David O. Selznick's Hollywood* (N.Y.: Knopf, 1980), pp. 77, 86, 113.
17. R. G. Hubler, "Scare 'Em to Death," *The Saturday Evening Post*, CCXIV (May 23, 1942), p. 76.
18. Dimitri Tiomkin, *Please Don't Hate Me* (Garden City, N.Y.: Doubleday, 1959), pp. 224–26.
19. Hubler, "Scare 'Em to Death," p. 76.
20. Pete Martin, "I Call on Alfred Hitchcock," *The Saturday Evening Post*, CCXXX (July 27, 1957), p. 73; Donald Spoto, *The Dark Side of Genius: The Life of Alfred Hitchcock* (Boston: Little, Brown, 1983), p. 300.
21. John Kobler, "Master of Horror Movie," *The Saturday Evening Post*, CCXXXII (March 19, 1960), pp. 31, 97.

22. Elston Brooks, "But He Came Back to Haunt the Living," *Fort Worth Star-Telegram*, September 28, 1986, p. 4D.
23. James Robert Parish and Steven Whitney, *Vincent Price Unmasked* (N.Y.: Drake, 1974), p. 110.
24. Lena Tabori, "Mia Farrow Talks," *Ladies' Home Journal*, LXXXV (August 1968), p. 94.

Chapter 23. *Classics and Biopics*

1. Arthur Marx, *Goldwyn: A Biography of the Men Behind the Myth* (N.Y.: Norton, 1976), p. 98; Philip French, *The Movie Moguls* (Chicago: Weidenfeld, 1969), pp. 47, 48; "One-Man Studio," *Time*, LV (June 12, 1950), p. 65.
2. French, *Movie Moguls*, p. 2.
3. Marx, *Goldwyn*, p. 102; French, *Movie Moguls*, p. 47; Alva Johnston, "The Great Goldwyn," *The Saturday Evening Post*, CCIX (June 5, 1937), p. 20.
4. Robert Richardson, *Literature and the Film* (Bloomington, Ind.: Indiana University, 1969), pp. 37–40; John Harrington, *Film And/As Literature* (Englewood Cliffs, N.J.: Prentice-Hall, 1977), p. 124.
5. Robert Hamilton Bell, *Shakespeare on Silent Film* (London: Allen and Unwin, 1968), p. 52.
6. Ibid., p. 39.
7. Ibid., p. 271.
8. *Time*, XIV (December 9, 1929), p. 38.
9. *New Republic*, LXXXIV (October 16, 1935), p. 272.
10. Ibid., LXXXVIII (September 2, 1936), p. 104.
11. Charles W. Eckert, *Focus on Shakespearean Films* (Englewood Cliffs, N.J.: Prentice-Hall, 1972), p. 13.
12. Bob Thomas, *Selznick* (Garden City, N.Y.: Doubleday, 1972), pp. 86–87; *Time*, XXV (January 28, 1935), p. 32.
13. Robert M. Miller, *Star Myths: Show Business Biographies* (Metuchen, N.J.: Scarecrow, 1983), p. viii.
14. *New Republic*, LXXXV (February 5, 1936), p. 369.
15. Will H. Hays, *The Memoirs of Will H. Hays* (Garden City, N.Y.: Doubleday, 1955), pp. 359–60; Jesse Lasky, Jr., *Whatever Happened to Hollywood?* (N.Y.: W. H. Allen, 1973), pp. 58–60.
16. Johnston, "The Great Goldwyn," pp. 21, 74; Marx, *Goldwyn*, pp. 105–6; French, *Movie Moguls*, p. 47.
17. Cal York, "Gossip of All the Studios," *Photoplay*, XXXIII (April 1928), p. 46.
18. Cal York, "Through the Studios with Pen and Camera," *Photoplay*, XXXVII (February 1930), p. 49.
19. George Arliss, *My Ten Years in the Studios* (Boston: Little, Brown, 1940), p. 66.
20. Alva Johnston, "Hollywood's Ten Per Centers," *The Saturday Evening Post*, CCXV (August 8, 1942), p. 38.

21. Marx, *Goldwyn*, p. 195; Carol Easton, *The Search for Sam Goldwyn: A Biography* (N.Y.: Morrow, 1976), p. 110.
22. Johnston, "Hollywood's Ten Per Centers," p. 9; Joe E. Brown, *Laughter Is a Wonderful Thing* (N.Y.: A. S. Barnes, 1956), pp. 207–9.
23. Alva Johnston, "Shakespeare in Hollywood," *Woman's Home Companion*, LXIII (April 1936), p. 17.
24. Jerome Lawrence, *Actor: The Life and Times of Paul Muni* (N.Y.: Putnam, 1974), p. 218.
25. Bob Thomas, *Selznick* (Garden City, N.Y.: Doubleday, 1972), pp. 81–87; Ronald Haver, *David O. Selznick's Hollywood* (N.Y.: Knopf, 1980), pp. 156–61; *Time*, XXV (January 28, 1935), p. 32.
26. Haver, *Selznick*, p. 175.
27. Johnston, "Shakespeare in Hollywood," p. 16.
28. Lawrence, *Muni*, p. 209.
29. David Niven, *Bring on the Empty Horses* (N.Y.: Putnam, 1975), p. 425.
30. Aljean Harmetz, *The Making of the Wizard of Oz* (N.Y.: Knopf, 1977), pp. 241–42.
31. David Niven, *The Moon's a Balloon* (N.Y.: Putnam, 1972), pp. 175–76; Easton, *Search for Sam Goldwyn*, pp. 182–83.
32. Bob Thomas, *Astaire: The Man, the Dancer* (N.Y.: St. Martin's, 1984), pp. 170–71.
33. Mel Gussow, *Don't Say Yes Until I Finish Talking: A Biography of Darryl Zanuck* (Garden City, N.Y.: Doubleday, 1971), p. 111.
34. "Laurence Olivier's Creative Side," *The New York Times*, September 13, 1986, p. 13.
35. Mike Munn, *The Stories Behind the Scenes of the Great Epic Films* (London: Illustrated Publications, 1982), p. 112.
36. Ibid., p. 113.

Chapter 24. *Message Movies*

1. *Moving Picture World*, XII (April 27, 1912), p. 305.
2. John Baxter, *The Cinema of John Ford* (N.Y.: A. S. Barnes, 1971), p. 88.
3. "Thinker in Hollywood," *The New Yorker*, XVI (February 24, 1940), pp. 23–24.
4. Victor Scherle and William Turner Levy, *The Films of Frank Capra* (Secaucus, N.J.: Citadel, 1977), pp. 139, 171.
5. Richard D. MacCann, *Film and Society* (N.Y.: Scribner, 1964), p. 54.
6. Leonard Mosley, *Zanuck: The Rise and Fall of Hollywood's Last Tycoon* (Boston: Little, Brown, 1984), pp. 140–42; "One Man Studio," *Time*, LV (June 12, 1950), p. 72.
7. Arthur Marx, *Goldwyn: A Biography of the Man Behind the Myth* (N.Y.: Norton, 1976), p. 250.
8. Frank Capra, *The Name Above the Title: An Autobiography* (N.Y.: Macmillan, 1971), pp. 280–93; "Mr. Smith Riles Washington," *Time*, XXXIV (October 30, 1939), p. 49; "Barkley Assails Film," *The New York Times*, (October 24, 1939), p. 19.

9. Charles Higham, *Bette: The Life of Bette Davis* (N.Y.: Dell, 1982), p. 202.
10. Maurice Zolotow, *Billy Wilder in Hollywood* (N.Y.: Putnam, 1977), pp. 131–32.
11. Garson Kanin, *Hollywood* (N.Y.: Viking, 1974), p. 166.
12. Edward Dmytryk, *It's a Hell of a Life But Not a Bad Living* (N.Y.: Time Books, 1978), p. 92.
13. Capra, *Name Above Title*, pp. 398, 426, 428–29, 437; Charles Higham, *Kate: The Life of Katharine Hepburn* (N.Y.: Norton, 1975), p. 127; Robert Hatch, *The New Republic*, CXVIII (May 10, 1948), p. 30.
14. Mosley, *Zanuck*, pp. 237–40; Philip Dunne to Ronald L. Davis, Malibu, California, May 19 and 24, 1987 on the making of *Pinky*.
15. Higham, *Bette*, pp. 281–82.

Chapter 25. *B Pictures*

1. Robin Cross, *The Big Book of B Movies* (N.Y.: St. Martin's, 1981), pp. 6–7.
2. Don Miller, *"B" Movies* (N.Y.: Curtis, 1973), p. 35.
3. Gene Fernett, *Poverty Row* (Satellite Beach, Fla.: Coral Reef Publications, 1973), p. 9.
4. Jack Warner, *My First Hundred Years in Hollywood* (N.Y.: Random House, 1964), pp. 185, 259.
5. Cross, *Big Book of B Movies*, p. 7.
6. Eugene Zukor, interview taped in Los Angeles, July 31, 1975, Southern Methodist University Oral History Collection.
7. Ring Lardner, Jr., interview taped in New York City, January 11, 1985, SMUOHC.
8. Charles Marquis Warren, interview taped in Los Angeles, August 14 and 20, 1980, SMUOHC.
9. Robert Wise, interview taped in Los Angeles, July 26, 1979, SMUOHC.
10. Edward Dmytryk, interview taped in Austin, Tex., December 2, 1979, SMUOHC.
11. Miller, *"B" Movies*, p. 11.
12. Laraine Day, interview taped in Los Angeles, July 17, 1979, SMUOHC.
13. Cross, *Big Book of B Movies*, p. 150.
14. Peggy Stewart, interview taped in Los Angeles, July 19, 1985, SMUOHC.
15. Vincent Sherman, interview taped in Los Angeles, August 5, 1981, SMUOHC.
16. Arthur Lubin, interview taped in Los Angeles, July 15, 1985, SMUOHC.
17. Michael Gordon, interview taped in Los Angeles, August 7 and 12, 1981, SMUOHC.
18. Ann Doran, conversation in Los Angeles, August 15, 1983.
19. Maurice Zolotow, *Shooting Star* (N.Y.: Simon and Schuster, 1974), p. 107.

20. Maxene Andrews, interview taped in Los Angeles, July 21, 1984, SMUOHC.
21. Ibid.
22. "Don't Go Near the Horses," *Time*, LXXXVIII (November 4, 1966), p. 19.

IV. Hollywood and Its Public

Chapter 26. *Social Life and Publicity*

1. Joseph Newman, interview taped in Los Angeles, July 23, 1984, Southern Methodist University Oral History Collection.
2. Joe Morella and Edward Z. Epstein, *The "It" Girl* (N.Y.: Delacorte, 1976), pp. 134–40.
3. Jayne Meadows, interview taped in Dallas, November 11, 1975, SMUOHC.
4. Budd Schulberg, *Moving Pictures* (N.Y.: Stein and Day, 1981), p. 155.
5. Suzanne Munshower, *Warren Beatty* (N.Y.: St. Martin's, 1983), p. 111.
6. Henry Koster, interview taped in Los Angeles, August 13, 1980, SMUOHC.
7. Frances Marion, *Off with Their Heads!* (N.Y.: Macmillan, 1972), p. 122.
8. Harry Warren, interview taped in Los Angeles, October 24, 1977, SMUOHC.
9. Helen Gahagan Douglas, *A Full Life* (Garden City, N.Y.: Doubleday, 1982), p. 94.
10. Tichi Wilkerson and Marcia Borie, *The Hollywood Reporter* (N.Y.: Coward-McCann, 1984), p. 10.
11. Jack Warner, *My First Hundred Years in Hollywood* (N.Y.: Random House, 1964), p. 159.
12. Samuel Marx, *Mayer and Thalberg* (N.Y.: Random House, 1975), p. 119.
13. Nancy Walker, interview taped in Los Angeles, August 18, 1978, SMUOHC.
14. Arnold Moss, interview taped in New York City, January 9, 1985, SMUOHC.
15. Walter Wanger, in Bernard Rosenberg and Harry Silverstein, *The Real Tinsel* (N.Y.: Macmillan, 1970), p. 91.
16. Wini Shaw, in ibid., p. 267.
17. Wanger, in ibid., p. 91.
18. Jean Porter, interview taped in Dallas, April 18, 1980, SMUOHC.
19. Charles Bennett, interview taped in Los Angeles, August 14, 1980, SMUOHC.
20. John Raitt, interview taped in Dallas, October 22, 1976, SMUOHC.
21. Rosemary Clooney, interview taped in Dallas, January 25, 1975, SMUOHC.

22. Gregory Peck, interview taped in Los Angeles, May 27, 1977, SMUOHC.
23. Moss interview.
24. Bill Hendricks, interview taped in Los Angeles, July 26, 1979, SMUOHC.
25. George Eells, *Hedda and Louella* (N.Y.: Putnam, 1972), p. 15.
26. Hendricks interview.
27. Joan Fontaine, *No Bed of Roses* (N.Y.: Morrow, 1978), p. 155.
28. Ibid., p. 165.
29. Eells, *Hedda and Louella*, p. 209.
30. Robert Windeler, *Sweetheart: The Story of Mary Pickford* (N.Y.: Praeger, 1974), p. 137.
31. Garson Kanin, *Hollywood* (N.Y.: Viking, 1974), pp. 358–66.
32. Hedda Hopper, *From Under My Hat* (Garden City, N.Y.: Doubleday, 1952), pp. 80–81.
33. Raoul Walsh, in Richard Shickel, *The Men Who Made the Movies* (N.Y.: Atheneum, 1975), pp. 50–51; Walsh, *Each Man in His Time* (N.Y.: Farrar, Straus and Giroux, 1974), pp. 328–33.
34. Warner, *My First Hundred Years in Hollywood*, 313–14.
35. Frederick Brisson, interview taped in Los Angeles, August 11, 1981, SMUOHC; Rosalind Russell, *Life Is a Banquet* (N.Y.: Random House, 1977), pp. 85, 91.
36. Fontaine, *No Bed of Roses*, pp. 152–53.
37. David Niven, *Bring on the Empty Horses* (N.Y.: Putnam, 1975), pp. 372–77.
38. Phil A. Koury, *Yes, Mr. De Mille* (N.Y.: Putnam, 1959), p. 319.
39. Arthur Marx, *Goldwyn* (N.Y.: Norton, 1976), p. 247.
40. Leo C. Rosten, *Hollywood: The Movie Colony* (N.Y.: Harcourt, Brace, 1941), p. 48.
41. Ruth Warrick, *The Confessions of Phoebe Taylor* (Englewood Cliffs, N.J.: Prentice-Hall, 1980), pp. 59–60.
42. Jean Negulesco, *Things I Did and Things I Think I Did* (N.Y.: Simon and Schuster, 1984), pp. 198–99; John Huston, *An Open Book* (N.Y.: Knopf, 1980), pp. 96–98.
43. Niven, *Bring on the Empty Horses*, p. 418.
44. Joe Hyams, *Bogart and Bacall* (N.Y.: McKay, 1975), pp. 66–67.
45. Nora Johnson, *Flashback* (Garden City, N.Y.: Doubleday, 1979), p. 86.
46. Lizabeth Scott, interview taped in Los Angeles, July 27, 1984, SMUOHC.
47. Leonard Mosley, *Zanuck: The Rise and Fall of Hollywood's Last Tycoon* (Boston: Little, Brown, 1984), p. 231.
48. Peggy Moran Koster, interview taped in Camarillo, Calif., July 21, 1982, SMUOHC.
49. Dorothy Lamour, *My Side of the Road* (Englewood Cliffs, N.J.: Prentice-Hall, 1980), p. 145.
50. Ronald Neame, interview taped in Los Angeles, July 18, 1985, SMUOHC.
51. Gary Carey, *All the Stars in Heaven* (N.Y.: Dutton, 1981), pp. 108–9.

52. Mary Martin, interview taped in Dallas, June 11, 1984, SMUOHC.
53. Michael Gordon, interview taped in Los Angeles, August 7 and 12, 1981, SMUOHC.
54. Hendricks interview.
55. Alva Johnston, "The Great Goldwyn," *The Saturday Evening Post*, CCIX (June 19, 1937), p. 102; Carol Easton, *The Search for Sam Goldwyn* (N.Y.: Morrow, 1976), p. 110.
56. Arthur Mayer, *Merely Colossal* (N.Y.: Simon and Schuster, 1953), pp. 134–35; *Variety*, July 30, 1951.
57. Emily Torchia, interview taped in Los Angeles, July 16, 1984, SMUOHC.
58. Niven, *Bring on the Empty Horses*, p. 27.
59. Hedda Hopper, *The Whole Truth and Nothing But* (Garden City, N.Y.: Doubleday, 1963), p. 65; Eells, *Hedda and Louella*, p. 147; Jesse Lasky, Jr., *Whatever Happened to Hollywood?* (N.Y.: W. H. Allen, 1975), pp. 124–25.
60. Stuart M. Kaminsky, *Coop: The Life and Legend of Gary Cooper* (N.Y.: St. Martin's, 1980), pp. 48–49.
61. Fontaine, *No Bed of Roses*, p. 138.
62. Lili Palmer, *Change Lobsters and Dance: An Autobiography* (N.Y.: Macmillan, 1975), p. 184.

Chapter 27. Sexual Images

1. Phil A. Koury, *Yes, Mr. De Mille* (N.Y.: Putnam, 1959), p. 191.
2. Brad Steiger and Chaw Mank, *Valentino* (N.Y.: MacFadden-Bartell, 1966), pp. 111–12.
3. Alexander Walker, *Rudolph Valentino* (N.Y.: Hamilton, 1976), p. 119.
4. Ibid., p. 69.
5. Kevin Brownlow, *Hollywood: The Pioneers* (N.Y.: Knopf, 1979), p. 185.
6. Irving Shulman, *Harlow* (N.Y.: Random House, 1964), pp. 349–50.
7. Norman Zierold, *The Moguls* (N.Y.: Coward-McCann, 1969), p. 250.
8. Charles Higham, *Errol Flynn: The Untold Story* (Garden City, N.Y.: Doubleday, 1980), pp. 119–21. Also see Hector Arce, *The Secret Life of Tyrone Power* (N.Y.: Morrow, 1979).
9. Jeremy Pascall and Clyde Jeavons, *A Pictorial History of Sex in the Movies* (London: Hamlyn, 1975), p. 93.
10. Philip French, *The Movie Moguls* (Chicago: Weidenfeld, 1969), p. 52.
11. Willi Frischauer, *Behind the Scenes of Otto Preminger* (N.Y.: Morrow, 1973), p. 142.
12. Ezra Goodman, *The Fifty-Year Decline and Fall of Hollywood* (N.Y.: Simon and Schuster, 1961), pp. 231–32.
13. Fernando Lamas, interview taped in Los Angeles, August 6 and 14, 1981, Southern Methodist University Oral History Collection.
14. Alan Arnold, *Valentino* (London: Hutchinson, 1952), p. 161.
15. Steiger and Mank, *Valentino*, pp. 189–90.

16. Roger C. Peterson, *Valentino the Unforgotten* (Los Angeles: Wetzel, 1937), pp. 150–52.
17. Arthur Mayer, in Bernard Rosenberg and Harry Silverstein, *The Real Tinsel* (N.Y.: Macmillan, 1970), p. 168.
18. Frances Marion, *Off with Their Heads!* (N.Y.: Macmillan, 1972), p. 164.
19. Stuart Kaminsky, *Coop* (N.Y.: St. Martin's, 1980), p. 56; George Carpozi, Jr., *The Gary Cooper Story* (New Rochelle, N.Y.: Arlington House, 1970), p. 116; Adela Rogers St. Johns, *Love, Laughter and Tears* (Garden City, N.Y.: Doubleday, 1978), p. 263.
20. Dorothy Lamour, *My Side of the Road* (Englewood Cliffs, N.J.: Prentice-Hall, 1980), pp. 48–49, 84–85.
21. Betty Lasky, *RKO: The Biggest Little Major of Them All* (Englewood Cliffs, N.J.: Prentice-Hall, 1984), p. 205.
22. James Mason, *Before I Forget* (London: Hamilton, 1981), p. 294.
23. Goodman, *Fifty-Year Decline,* p. 223.
24. Jeff Rovin, *Joan Collins: The Unauthorized Biography* (N.Y.: Bantam, 1984), p. 70.
25. Joshua Logan, *Movie Stars, Real People, and Me* (N.Y.: Dell, 1978), pp. 64–65.
26. Charles Higham, *Errol Flynn,* p. 259.
27. Minty Clinch, *Burt Lancaster* (N.Y.: Stein and Day, 1984), p. 120.

Chapter 28. *Theaters and Audiences*

1. Lewis Jacobs, *The Rise of the American Film* (N.Y.: Harcourt, Brace, 1939, 1967), p. 56.
2. Benjamin B. Hampton, *A History of Movies* (N.Y.: Covici, 1931, 1970), p. 61.
3. Ben M. Hall, *The Best Remaining Seats: The Story of the Golden Age of the Movie Palaces* (N.Y.: Potter, 1961), p. 39.
4. Hampton, *History of Movies,* p. 292.
5. Hall, *Best Remaining Seats,* p. 66.
6. David Naylor, *American Picture Palaces: The Architecture of Fantasy* (N.Y.: Van Nostrand Reinhold, 1981), p. 11.
7. Hall, *Best Remaining Seats,* p. 93.
8. Ibid., p. 94.
9. Preston J. Kaufmann, *Fox, the Last Word: Story of the World's Finest Theatre* (Pasadena, Calif.: Showcase Publications, 1979), p. 111.
10. Hall, *Best Remaining Seats,* p. 136.
11. Naylor, *American Picture Palaces,* p. 201.
12. David Robinson, *Chaplin: His Life and Art* (N.Y.: McGraw, 1985), p. 215.
13. Hall, *Best Remaining Seats,* pp. 99–100.
14. Ralph Hancock, *Douglas Fairbanks: The Fourth Musketeer* (N.Y.: Holt, 1953), p. 210.
15. Charles Chaplin, Jr., *My Father: Charles Chaplin* (N.Y.: Random House, 1960), pp. 128–29.

16. Kenneth Barrow, *Helen Hayes: First Lady of the American Theatre* (Garden City, N.Y.: Doubleday, 1985), p. 105.

17. Joe E. Brown, *Laughter Is a Wonderfull Thing* (N.Y.: A. S. Barnes, 1956), pp. 214–16.

18. Charles Higham, *Kate: The Life of Katharine Hepburn* (N.Y.: Norton, 1975), p. 74; Gary Carey, *Katharine Hepburn: A Hollywood Yankee* (N.Y.: St. Martin's, 1984), p. 82.

19. Higham, *Kate*, p. 116; Geoffrey Wansell, *Haunted Idol: The Story of the Real Cary Grant* (N.Y.: Morrow, 1984), p. 266.

20. Edward G. Robinson, "The Movies, the Actor, and the Public Morals," in William Perlman, ed., *The Movies on Trial* (N.Y.: Macmillan, 1936), p. 30.

21. Alva Johnston, "The Great Goldwyn," *The Saturday Evening Post*, CCIX (May 8, 1937), p. 6.

22. Warren G. Harris, *Gable and Lombard* (N.Y.: Simon and Schuster, 1974), pp. 117–18.

23. Earl Wilson, "Dorothy Lamour: Big Pie Plate," *The Saturday Evening Post*, CCXIV (June 10, 1942), pp. 19, 68; Samuel Goldwyn, "Hollywood Is Sick," Ibid., CCXIII (July 13, 1940), p. 44.

24. Elston Brooks, "Here's Z Reel Story on 'Razzamatazz,'" *Fort Worth Star-Telegram*, September 14, 1986, p. 2D.

25. Ibid.

26. Arthur Mayer, *Merely Colossal* (N.Y.: Simon and Schuster, 1953), pp. 202–3.

27. Roger Ebert, *A Kiss Is Still a Kiss* (Kansas City, Kan.: Andrews, McMeel and Parker, 1984), p. 12; Groucho Marx and Richard J. Anobile, *The Marx Bros. Scrapbook* (N.Y.: Darien House, 1974), p. 251.

28. Robert Atwan and Bruce Forer, eds., *Bedside Hollywood: Great Scenes from Movie Memoirs* (N.Y.: Moyer Bell, 1985), p. 165.

29. Mayer, *Merely Colossal*, pp. 189–90.

30. "Actor's No Tough Guy," *Fort Worth Star-Telegram*, February 20, 1987, p. A3.

31. Leonard Mosley, *Zanuck: The Rise and Fall of Hollywood's Last Tycoon* (Boston: Little, Brown, 1984), p. 256.

32. Chester Morrison, "3-D; High, Wide, and Handsome," *Look*, June 30, 1953, in Gerald Mast, ed., *The Movies in Our Midst: Documents in the Cultural History of Film in America* (Chicago: University of Chicago, 1982), p. 653.

33. Ezra Goodman, *The Fifty-Year Decline and Fall of Hollywood* (N.Y.: Simon and Schuster, 1961), p. 435.

34. Charles Higham, *Bette: The Life of Bette Davis* (N.Y.: Macmillan, 1981), pp. 295–96.

35. Bill Davidson, "Alfred Hitchcock Resents," *The Saturday Evening Post*, CCXXXV (December 15, 1962), p. 62.

36. Groucho Marx, *Groucho and Me* (N.Y.: Random House, 1959), p. 344.

37. Carol Burnett, "Hurray for Fans!" *Parade*, October 12, 1986, p. 5.

38. "New York, Day by Day," *The New York Times*, September 3, 1985, p. B20.

V. After the Golden Era

Chapter 29. "Movies Are Better Than Ever"

1. Ezra Goodman, The Fifty-Year Decline and Fall of Hollywood (N.Y.: Simon and Schuster, 1961), p. 452.
2. Carolyn Jones, interview taped in Los Angeles, August 3, 1976, Southern Methodist University Oral History Collection.
3. Arlene Dahl, interview taped in Dallas, September 24, 1975, SMUOHC.
4. Mildred Natwick, interview taped in New York City, January 4, 1979, SMUOHC.
5. Goodman, Fifty-Year Decline, p. 178.
6. Jane Ellen Wayne, Robert Taylor (N.Y.: Warner Paperback Library, 1973), pp. 245–46.
7. Eugene Zukor, 'interview taped in Los Angeles, July 31, 1975, SMUOHC.
8. Dan Dailey, interview taped in Dallas by Sally Cullom, July 13 and 25, 1974, SMUOHC.
9. Edward Dmytryk, interview taped in Austin, Tex., December 2, 1979, SMUOHC.
10. Betty Garrett, interview taped in Los Angeles, August 23, 1978, SMUOHC.
11. David Raksin, interview taped in Los Angeles by Ann Burk, August 2, 1976, SMUOHC.
12. Andrew Dowdy, "Movies Are Better Than Ever" (N.Y.: Morrow, 1973), p. 5.
13. Cesar Romero, interview taped in Dallas, February 26, 1979, SMUOHC.
14. Robert Stack, interview taped in Los Angeles, August 12, 1975, SMUOHC.
15. Goodman, Fifty-Year Decline, p. 434.
16. Ibid., p. 197.
17. Melville Shavelson, interview taped in Los Angeles, August 8, 1981, SMUOHC.
18. Kathleen Freeman, conversation in Los Angeles, July 24, 1984.
19. Edward Dmytryk, It's a Hell of a Life But Not a Bad Living (N.Y.: Times Books, 1978), p. 103; Andrew Sinclair, John Ford (N.Y.: Dial, 1979), pp. 157–58.
20. Dowdy, "Movies Are Better Than Ever," p. 53.
21. Jones interview; Stack interview.
22. Dowdy, "Movies Are Better Than Ever," pp. 58–59.
23. Betty Lasky, RKO: The Biggest Little Major of Them All (Englewood Cliffs, N.J.: Prentice-Hall, 1984), p. 1.

Chapter 30. *The Sexual and Social Revolution*

1. Enid Nemy, "Broadway," *The New York Times,* June 28, 1985, p. 17.
2. Barbara Grizzutti Harrison, *The New Republic,* 182 (May 3, 1980), p. 34.
3. Harry Haun, New York *Daily News* staff writer, to authors.
4. "The Production Code," Appendix, Ruth A. Inglis, *Freedom of the Movies* (Chicago: University of Chicago, 1947), pp. 209–10.
5. Joseph Morgenstern, "Two for a Tommy Gun," *Newsweek,* LXX (August 21, 1967), p. 65; "The Thin Red Line," Ibid. (August 28, 1967), pp. 82–83.
6. Inglis, *Freedom of Movies,* p. 207.
7. "The New Movies," *Newsweek,* LXXVI (December 7, 1970), p. 72.
8. Elston Brooks, "'Giant' of a Man Remembered," *Fort Worth Star-Telegram,* October 13, 1985, p. 4D.
9. Jack Vizzard, *Life Inside a Hollywood Censor* (N.Y.: Simon and Schuster, 1970), p. 340.
10. J. C. Landry, *Paul Newman* (N.Y.: McGraw-Hill, 1983), p. 106.
11. *Time,* XCIV (August 22, 1969), p. 65.
12. Gerald Mast, ed., *The Movies in Our Midst: Documents in the History of Film in America* (Chicago: University of Chicago, 1982), pp. 710–11.
13. Robert David Crane and Christopher Fryer, *Jack Nicholson, Face to Face* (N.Y.: Evans, 1975), p. 68.
14. James Spada, *Fonda: Her Life in Pictures* (Garden City, N.Y.: Doubleday, 1985), p. 126; Thomas Kiernan, *Jane Fonda: Heroine for Our Time* (N.Y.: Delilah Books, Putnam, 1982), p. 281.
15. Geraldine Carro, "Tatum: The New Scene-Stealer," *Ladies' Home Journal,* XC (August 1973), p. 84.

Chapter 31. *Return to Entertainment*

1. Michael Price, "Veteran, Novice Show Compatibility in Movie," *Fort Worth Star-Telegram,* January 28, 1986, p. 4B; Joy Horowitz, "From Slapstick to Fantasy," *The New York Times Magazine,* June 15, 1986, p. 32.
2. Phil Hardy, ed., *Science Fiction* (N.Y.: Morrow, 1984), p. 337.
3. Stanley Kaufmann, "New Twists, Old Troubles," *The New Republic,* CLXXXIX (July 18 and 25, 1983), p. 22.
4. Pauline Kael, "The Greening of the Solar System," *When the Lights Go Down* (N.Y.: Holt, Rinehart and Winston, 1980), pp. 348–54.
5. *Time,* CXX (August 30, 1982), p. 89.
6. "And Animal House Begat. . . ," *Time,* CXXV (April 5, 1985), p. 103.
7. Tony Schwartz, "College Humor Comes Back," *Newsweek,* XCII (October 23, 1978), p. 91.
8. *Time,* CIV (August 19, 1974), p. 73.
9. *The New York Times,* July 5, 1985, p. 6.

10. "Industry Fears a Summer Film Glut," *The New York Times,* July 11, 1985, p. 24.
11. "An Outbreak of Rambomania," *Time,* CXXV (June 24, 1985), p. 72.
12. Richard Grenier, "Arms & the Movies," *Commentary,* LXXII (October 1981), p. 72.
13. Michel Ciment, "The Odyssey of Stanley Kubrick," in William Johnson, ed., *Focus on the Science Fiction Film* (Englewood Cliffs, N.J.: Prentice-Hall, 1972), p. 150.
14. Gary Herman, compiler, *The Book of Hollywood Quotes* (London: Omnibus, 1979), p. 38.
15. Ibid., p. 115.
16. James Spada, *Fonda: Her Life in Pictures* (Garden City, N.Y.: Doubleday, 1985), p. 191.
17. Iain Johnstone, *The Man with No Name: The Biography of Clint Eastwood* (London: Plexus Publishing, 1981), p. 138.
18. William Goldman, *Adventures in the Screen Trade* (N.Y.: Warner Books, 1985), p. 42.
19. *Dallas Times-Herald,* February 18, 1982.
20. Leslie Bennett, "Tootsie Taught Dustin About the Sexes," *The New York Times,* December 21, 1982.
21. Don Shewey, "On the Go with David Geffen," *The New York Times Magazine,* July 21, 1985, p. 49.
22. Noel Carroll, "Back to Basics," *Wilson Quarterly,* X (Summer 1986), p. 65.
23. *Dallas Times-Herald,* July 22, 1986.
24. Nina Darnton, "At the Movies," *The New York Times,* December 12, 1986, p. 26.
25. Maureen Dowd, "Testing Himself," *The New York Times Magazine,* September 28, 1986, p. 93.
26. "Michael J. Fox," *Ladies' Home Journal,* CIX (April 1987), p. 181.
27. New York *Daily News,* April 10, 1986.
28. "Oval Office Fright," *The New York Times,* February 11, 1987, p. 10.
29. Betty Ford, *The Times of My Life* (N.Y. Ballantine Books, 1978), p. 290.
30. "New Ad Drive," *The New York Times,* April 10, 1987, p. 10.

INDEX

About the Authors

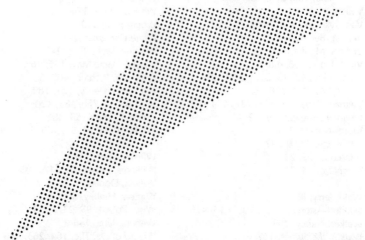

Paul F. Boller, Jr., Ph.D., author of *Presidential Anecdotes, Presidential Campaigns,* and other books, has been a film buff all his life. In addition to teaching American intellectual and cultural history at Texas Christian University and elsewhere, he enjoys playing the piano for revivals of old films from the Silent Era.

Ronald L. Davis, Ph.D., author of a three-volume history of American music, heads the Oral History Program on the Performing Arts at Southern Methodist University. He has taped more than 450 interviews with film, stage, and concert performers, all of which provide the basis for much of this book.

"It was totally absorbing, exciting, entertaining, fascinating, entrancing and amusing. Each anecdote is a delicious morsel to be savored and relished."

—LIZABETH SCOTT

"I found the book provides not only entertainment and anecdotal nuggets but a comprehensive look at Hollywood history and a treasure trove of information—Bravo!"

—CAROL BRUCE

"*Unbelievably interesting!* We found it to be so informative about people and things in show business and stories we never heard about. Terrific!!"

—BEBE AND PINKY LEE

"A potpourri of delectable, inside, very funny stories, plus, importantly, an authentic history of the world's most fascinating workplace, and the 'cast of characters' which it engendered"

—BETTY GARDE

"Very, very good...I enjoyed every page."

—ELLA RAINES

"Entertaining and illuminating!"

—JULIE ADAMS